China's development, at least in part, is driven by patriotism and pride:...The Chinese people have made great contributions to world civilization... Our commitment and determination is rooted in our historic and national pride... It's fair to say that we have achieved some successes, [nevertheless] we should have a cautious appraisal of our accomplishments. We should never overestimate our accomplishments or indulge ourselves in our achievements... We need to assess ourselves objectively... [and aspire to] our next higher goal... [which is] a persistent and unremitting process.

Xi Jinping
Politburo Standing Committee member

In the face of complex and ever-changing international and domestic environments, the Chinese Government promptly and decisively adjusted our macroeconomic policies and launched a comprehensive stimulus package to ensure stable and rapid economic growth. We increased government spending and public investments and implemented structural tax reductions. Balancing short-term and long-term strategic perspectives, we are promoting industrial restructuring and technological innovation, and using principles of reform to solve problems of development.

Li Keqiang
Politburo Standing Committee member

I am now serving my second term in the Politburo... President Hu Jintao's character is modest and low profile... we all have the highest respect and admiration for him—for his leadership, perspicacity and moral convictions... Under his leadership, complex problems can all get resolved... It takes vision to avoid major conflicts in society. Income disparities, unemployment, bureaucracy and corruption could cause instability...This is the Party's most severe test. In seven years under President Hu, the CPC has successfully maintained stability while pushing forward with reform and opening-up.

Liu Yunshan
Politburo member; Head, CPC Publicity Department

D1016679

China's democratic development should cater to its own conditions... the American political system should not be used to judge the Chinese political system... We have our own models and goals for political reform... We will do what is in the best interests of our people—which surely includes the development of democracy and the rule of law... China's political and legal system is certainly not perfect, and we are certainly not satisfied. This is why President Hu stresses advancing intra-Party democracy and democracy of society... Reformers must take risks... The people must decide.

Li Yuanchao
Politburo member; Head, CPC Organization Department

Our growth model of 30 years, which enriched us rapidly, has come to the end of its cycle.... During the economic downturn, we've reached consensus on the need to transform our developmental model... We are determined to develop Guangdong's capability for independent innovation.... We're not interested in 'facelifts'.

Wang Yang
Politburo member; Party Secretary, Guangdong Province

How China should develop is a hard issue. China has achieved great economic success, but with many severe problems arising as a result—such as widening income gaps and increasingly strained human relationships. So, regarding urban development, the issues awaiting solution are how to produce a harmonious environment between human beings and nature, and among human beings themselves.

Yu Zhengsheng
Politburo member; Party Secretary, Shanghai Municipality

We must have passion for our work, enthusiasm for our career, and care for our people... We stress dedicated work, honest performance, innovation, and unity among our officials. We will go nowhere if we ignore reality or fear innovation... I'm not interested in 'reports', only results.

Zhang Gaoli
Politburo member; Party Secretary, Tianjin Municipality

How China's Leaders Think

The Inside Story of
China's Past, Current and
Future Leaders

Revised Edition

Robert Lawrence Kuhn

WILEY
John Wiley & Sons (Asia) Pte Ltd

Copyright © 2011 by Robert Lawrence Kuhn.
Published in 2011 by John Wiley & Sons (Asia) Pte. Ltd.
1 Fusionopolis Walk, #07-01 Solaris, South Tower, Singapore 138628

Other Wiley Editorial Offices

John Wiley & Sons, Inc., 111 River Street, Hoboken, NJ 07030, USA
John Wiley & Sons Ltd., The Atrium, Southern Gate, Chichester PO19 BSQ, England
John Wiley & Sons (Canada) Ltd., 5353 Dundas Street West, Suite 400, Toronto, Ontario M9B 6H8, Canada
John Wiley & Sons Australia Ltd., 42 McDougall Street, Milton, Queensland 4064, Australia
Wiley-VCH, Boschstrasse 12, D-69469 Weinheim, Germany

Library of Congress Cataloging-in-Publication Data:

ISBN 978-111-808590-5 (paperback)
ISBN 978-111-810427-9 (e-pdf)
ISBN 978-111-810426-2 (e-mobi)
ISBN 978-111-810425-5 (e-pub)

Printed in Singapore by Toppan Security Printing Pte. Ltd.
Typeset in Plantin, 10 point, by MPS Limited, a Macmillan Company
10 9 8 7 6 5 4 3 2 1

Contents

About the Author

Dr. Robert Lawrence Kuhn is an international investment banker, corporate strategist, China expert, and public intellectual. Since 1989[1], he has worked with China's leaders and advised the Chinese government (economic policy, industrial policy, mergers and acquisitions, science and technology, media and culture, Sino-U.S. relations, international affairs, and international communications). He has visited more than 50 cities in over 20 provinces and regions in China, working with leaders in government and business.

Dr. Kuhn advises leading multinational companies, CEOs and C-Suite executives, on formulating and implementing China strategies (sectors include financial services, technology, energy/resources, industrial, media and entertainment, and consulting), and he works with major Chinese companies on structuring their capital markets financings and M&A activities. Specializing in M&A for over 30 years, Dr. Kuhn was president and co-owner of the largest M&A firm in the U.S. representing middle-market companies (which he sold to Citigroup in 2000).

Dr. Kuhn advises and works with China senior leaders on special projects. He is recognized as the author of *The Man Who Changed China: The Life and Legacy of Jiang Zemin*, a precedent-setting biography—the first of a living Chinese leader published in China—which was China's best-selling book of 2005. He is the author of two event-marking books: *China 30 Years: A Great Transformation Of Society* (2008, in Chinese), which commemorates China's 30th anniversary of reform and opening up and emphasizes President Hu Jintao's political philosophy and policies; and *How China's Leaders Think* (this book, first published in October 2009), which commemorates China's 60th anniversary and focuses on China's new ("Fifth") generation of leaders (conversations with ~100 leaders), including Vice President Xi Jinping. Dr. Kuhn advised then Zhejiang Party Secretary (now Vice President) Xi Jinping on his U.S. visit (2006); he wrote exclusive articles with Politburo Member Li Yuanchao on China's political reform (*Business Week*, 2008) and the Party's commitment to learning (*Forbes*, 2010), and with Politburo Member Wang Yang on transforming Guangdong Province (*Business Week*, 2009).

Dr. Kuhn is the author or editor of 25 books on business strategy, finance and investment banking, including Dow-Jones Irwin's seven-volume

(5,500-page) *Library of Investment Banking* and *China's Banking and Financial Markets: The Internal Research Report of the Chinese Government.* Five of his books have been published in China, including the first on investment banking (Mainland China).

Dr. Kuhn is often in the international and Chinese media. He appears on CNBC, BBC, Euronews, Bloomberg and China Central Television (CCTV); he writes for *Bloomberg Business Week, Forbes, People's Daily* and *Xinhua News Agency*; and he is quoted in numerous publications, including *The Wall Street Journal, The New York Times, USA Today,* and *The Los Angeles Times.* He is featured essayist in *Chief Executive* magazine and senior international advisor of *Global People* magazine (published by *People's Daily*).

Dr. Kuhn appears regularly as the senior China commentator on Euronews, the largest television and new media news network in Europe (also prominent in Russia, Africa and the Middle East), and as the senior international commentator on CCTV News, which is broadcast internationally in over 100 countries as well as throughout China. Dr. Kuhn created, co-produced, wrote and presented CCTV News' official six-part television series on Expo 2010 Shanghai and the future of Shanghai (*"Expo's Meaning, Shanghai's Mission"*).

Dr. Kuhn was profiled in *Barron's* (2010) and on CCTV Channel 1's "Focus Talk" (2009), and he is one of the "China Visionaries" in the ten-episode television series produced by Shanghai Media Group (Dr. Henry Kissinger and Dr. Kuhn are the only Americans). Dr. Kuhn is senior advisor to CCTV and Xinhua News Agency.

Dr. Kuhn is chairman of The Kuhn Foundation, which produces *Closer To Truth*, the PBS / public television series (which Dr. Kuhn hosts) on the meaning of state-of-the-art science and the relationship between science and philosophy/theology (www.closertotruth.com). The Kuhn Foundation also sponsors projects facilitating communications between China and the world.

Dr. Kuhn has a B.A. (Phi Beta Kappa) in Human Biology from Johns Hopkins University; a Ph.D. in Anatomy and Brain Research from the University of California at Los Angeles (UCLA), and an S.M. in Management (Sloan Fellow) from the Massachusetts Institute of Technology (MIT).

Endnote

1   Personal Note: After the Tiananmen crackdown on June 4, 1989, I determined not to return to China. Over a year later, during the summer of 1990, I co-chaired a conference at UCLA on "Generating Creativity and Innovation in Large Bureaucracies" and invited Professor Kong Deyong of the State Science and Technology Commission, whom I had met in early 1989 on my first visit to China. It was Professor Kong, who later became Science and Technology Counselor at China's Mission to United Nations, who convinced me to come back to China to support those, particularly in the science communities, who sought reform and opening-up. I returned in the fall of 1990.

Acknowledgments

When China celebrated the 30th anniversary of reform and opening-up in December 2008, I was about to celebrate the 20th anniversary of my first coming to China in January 1989. The invitation had come from Dr. Song Jian, state councilor and chairman of the State Science and Technology Commission, who asked a small group of American investment bankers to advise Chinese research institutes in their first, fledgling efforts to adapt to the market economy. A scientist and a gentleman, as well as a senior leader, Dr. Song is an inspiration to all who know him and it is my honor to acknowledge him first.

I was hooked from the moment I arrived. The Chinese had a fresh, if naïve, enthusiasm; they were eager to learn, and ready to improve their civic and material lives. I knew then that China's culture, history, politics and economics would soon come to matter a great deal to the world. What I didn't know then was how much China would come to matter to me.

In recent years, especially since the financial crisis of 2008–2009, I have been commenting on China—appearing on CNBC, BBC, Bloomberg, others; writing for *Business Week, Forbes, Chief Executive, Xinhua News Agency,* others. Beginning in 2010, I am appearing regularly on China Central Television (*CCTV News*), where I often explain Western or American views, and on *Euronews,* where in the context of current or breaking news, I describe and analyze Chinese perspectives—often, extending the theme of this book, explaining "how China's leaders think." I am privileged to facilitate communications between China and the world. The need has never been greater.

There are many people to whom I give credit for this book, but one stands above all, my long-time friend and partner, Adam Zhu. I met Adam on my first trip to China when Adam was assigned by the State Science and Technology Commission to be my guide. It has been Adam's vision, acumen, creativity, intensity, perseverance, commitment, dedication, and all manner of innovative ideas that has made my work in China and this book possible. His understanding, insight and special sensitivities are appreciated at the highest levels in China. His political knowledge and savvy instincts make things happen, even "impossible" things. If books like films, had "producers," Adam Zhu would be credited as this book's "producer."

To describe all the challenges that Adam and I have faced since 1989, and all the adventures we've shared, would require another book. We are committed to China and its future—to help in our small way China's historic reform and development; to tell the true story of China to the world.

I am appreciative of the advice and counsel of Minister Liu Yunshan, head of the CPC Publicity Department, and Minister Li Yuanchao, head of the CPC Organization Department; and Minister Wang Chen, head of the State Council Information Office; Minister Leng Rong, head of the CPC Party Literature Research Center; Minister Cai Wu of the Ministry of Culture; Zhao Qizheng, chairman of the Foreign Affairs Committee, Chinese People's Political Consultative Conference (and former minister of the State Council Information Office); and Yang Yang, head of the International Cooperation Bureau, Chinese Academy of Social Sciences. I appreciate the research of Yang Mingwei of the CPC Party Literature Research Center.

I am in debt to all those whom I interviewed for this book. I have learned a great deal from them and I have tried to represent their views faithfully and fully. I am honored to be in trust of their memories.

I appreciate the wise advice and insightful (and sometimes critical) suggestions of Shanghai-based writer Duncan Hewitt. I appreciate the steadfast, all-around help of David Cao, my assistant in Beijing, who somehow, single-handedly at night, did most of the translations.

I thank the team at John Wiley & Sons, particularly C.J. Hwu, for their content commitment and publishing excellence.

Finally, the encouragement and love of my family—Dora, Aaron, Adam, Daniella, and Mother Lee—mean a great deal.

Though I have received a good deal of advice, I take full responsibility for all ideas, opinions, errors and mistakes. The book is anchored by exclusive interviews and special (though limited) access in China, which I appreciate but for which I made no concessions. I received many suggestions—some helpful, some contradictory—but always with unambiguous agreement that all editorial decisions would be mine and mine alone.

I am proud to be considered an old friend (*lao pengyou*) of China, a high compliment indeed, achieved after these two decades of learning and living. I dedicate this book to those good people, particularly my friends and colleagues, whose commitment, foresight, persistence, and courage are helping to strengthen economic, social and political reform in China and to help China understand the world and the world understand China.

Those who have taught me to understand and appreciate China come from all walks of life. They include farmers, soldiers, policemen, drivers, waiters, janitors, students, graduate students, factory workers, office workers, migrant workers, retired workers, laid-off workers, children, teenagers and grandmothers, as well as leaders, ministers, officials, executives, managers, scientists, professors and scholars. I have had the privilege of visiting more than 40 cities in China, from Guangzhou to Harbin, Shanghai to Lanzhou, Qingdao to Kunming, Tianjin to Chengdu. My activities in China have been an overwhelming life experience.

Some years ago, after finishing a late-night meeting in Beijing, I was asked when do I take vacations, since my Chinese friends knew that I had intense business and media lives in the U.S. "This is my vacation!" I said.

I wasn't kidding. To me, working in China, is energizing and exhilarating, even when frustrating and challenging. There is an infectious enthusiasm among the Chinese that is refreshing. Some may call my zest naïve, but I am invigorated by the Chinese spirit. The fact that personal relationships, not just business competitiveness, still play a role in commerce I find satisfying—and I hope that these Chinese ways will not fall fast victim to the market economy. Perhaps those special "Chinese characteristics" can continue to embed respect for traditional values such as honoring old friends.

To conclude, I would like to express my appreciation to some of these who, over the years, have helped me to learn and love China and to understand the Chinese people. They are friends, colleagues, and associates; some I have interviewed formally, others informally. Others I have appreciated their insights, whether in person or in writing. Still others have facilitated and supported my work, which was not always simple or risk free. Although the list is long—and I fear I am forgetting some people—I am pleased to thank all who have assisted Adam and me, in our limited way, to communicate the real China to the world: Xi Jinping; Li Keqiang; Liu Yunshan; Li Yuanchao; Wang Yang, Yu Zhengsheng; Bo Xilai; Zhang Gaoli; Wang Huning; Meng Jianzhu; Zeng Peiyan; Sun Jiazheng; Sheng Huaren; Song Jian; Chen Jinhua; Yan Mingfu; Wang Chen; Leng Rong; Wang Guangya; Cai Wu; Liu Binjie; Zhao Qizheng; Cai Fuchao; Wang Zhongwei; Teng Wensheng; Zheng Bijian; Liu Mingkang; Li Zhaoxing; Quan Zhezhu; Zhou Qiang; Wu Jichuan; Tie Ning; Huang Jiefu; Li Bing; Lu Zhangong; Zhao Hongzhu; Yuan Chunqing; Lu Hao; Xu Guangchun; Han Zheng; Tu Guangshao; Ai Baojun; Hu Wei; Feng Guoqin; Li Hongzhong; Wu Xinxiong; Wang Yongsheng; Ma Xuming; Wang Weiguang; Li Yining; Wu Jinglian; Lu Baifu; Wang Huijiong; Gao Shangquan; Xing Bensi; Chen Yuan; Sun Zhijun; Jiao Li; Wei Dichun; Zheng Hongfan; Wang Yibiao; Shi Rende; Zhao Xuewei; Ye Xiaowen; Cai Mingzhao; Lu Wei; Wu Jincai; Mi Ligong; Zhao Peng; Wang Guoqing; Qian Xiaoqian; Jiang Weiqiang; Zhang Yanbin; Liu Zhengrong; Li Xiangping; Xu Ying; Wu Jianmin; Zhang Yesui; Zhou Wenzhong; Zhang Yan; Lan Lijun; Wang Baodong; Xiao Tian; Cai Zhenhua; Cong Jun; An Wenbin; Xu Lin; Zhang Jingan; Jin Xiaoming; Zhao Shaohua; Ding Wei; Dong Junxin; Jia Tingan; Liu Yongzhi; Xiong Guangkai; Li Zhen; Yang Guhua; Bao Guojun; Guo Zhigang; Bao Bing; Wen Bing; Wu Xiaoling; Zhao Shi; Zhang Haitao; Tian Jin; Zhang Pimin; Zhu Hong; Shao Ning; Ni Di; Du Daozheng; Zhao Huayong; Zhang Changming; Hu En; Li Xiaoming; Gao Feng; Sun Yusheng; Li Ting; Li Jian; Zhu Tong; Jiang Heping; Wang Wenbin; Guo Zhenxi; Zhang Haichao; Jiang Mianheng; Fang Xinghai; Wang Luolin; Yang Yang; Cheng

Enfu; Wu Enyuan; Lu Xueyi; Zhang Xiaoshan; Li Yang; Wang Tongsan; Zhuo Xinping; Jin Chongji; He Chongyuan; Liu Aichen; Qin Zhigang; Gu Xia; Jiang Zehui; Shen Yongyan; Tong Zonghai; Song Ning; Yin Yicui; Wang Jianjun; Song Chao; Jiao Yang; Xue Peijian; Li Ruigang; Hu Jinjun; Ren Zhonglun; Sun Wei; He Lifeng; Qi Huaiyuan; Gou Lijun; Duan Chunhua; Ren Xuefeng; Wang Hua; Chen Miner; Bayin Chaolu; Li Qiang; Huang Kunming; Ding Minzhe; Zhang Baogui; Qiu He; Huang Yunbo; Xie Xinsong; Zhu Qing; Wang Min; Sun Yongchun; Liu Baoju; Zhang Xinqi; Liu Changyun; Zhu Xiaodan; Gan Lin; Ge Changwei; Li Shoujin; Wang Jingsheng; Mo Gaoyi; Liu Geli; Huang Xiaodong; Yang Xingfeng; Li Weiwei; Liu Lianyu; Mo Dewang; Ouyang Changlin; Huang Qifan; Li Xiaojie; Jiang Jianqing; Yang Chao; Wang Jianzhou; Xu Lejiang; Zhang Jianguo; Gao Xiqing; Fu Chengyu; Ren Jianxin; Liu Chuanzhi; Zhang Ruimin; Yang Mianmian; Zong Qinghou; Zhu Jianghong; Li Rucheng; Liu Lefei; Liu Leting; Xiao Qingping; Fan Yifei; Pan Gongsheng; Tian Guoli; Li Xiaowei; Hu Wenming; Wang Guoliang; Pu Jian; Pan Gang; Niu Gensheng; Wang Hai; Zhou Houjian; Mao Xiaofeng; Simon Chen; Miao Jianmin; Yu Yibo; Margaret Ren; Jiao Zhen; Zhang Weihua; James Liao; Wang Xianshu; Qiu Zhizhong; Eugene Qian; Zhao Jing; Wei Christiansen; Francis Leung; Zhang Yu; Li Nan; Wang Jianqi; Yu Long; Chen Zuohuang; Wang Liguang; Chen Xieyang; Ann Hu; Li Qiankuan; Xiao Guiyun; Molly Gong Zhongxin; Fan Yun; Wang Feizhou; Pang Xinhua; Chen Bing; Zhu Gongshan; Hunter Jiang; Pan Shiwei; Tong Shijun; Su Yunsheng; Wang Lifen; Lu Dongfu; Bi Dachuan; Zeng Jinsong; Guan Runlin; Ren Yinong; Jesse Chang; Cui Jin; Tan Xiangjiang; Ruan Wei; Li Qiang (CCTV); Xu Changdong; Annie Zhang; Chen Yaoyao and Jin Qingzhong. A special thanks to Shi Zhihong and Zhang Jianmin.

To all I say, *Xie Xie*.

Robert Lawrence Kuhn
Beijing, People's Republic of China
New York, New York
Los Angeles, California

August 20, 2009
February 18, 2011 (second printing)

Overview

How China's Leaders Think

On January 18, 2011, just as China's President Hu Jintao was arriving in Washington, D.C. on a four-day state visit to the United States, I was standing on the historic Bund along the Shanghai riverfront during a rare Shanghai snowfall, about to be interviewed by CNBC on the significance of President Hu's visit. I had been prepped to comment on the consequences of 2010, the year in which China had become the world's second largest economy but also the year in which a cascade of China-related confrontations and controversies had led some to call 2010 China's worst diplomatic year since 1989.

But this was not what CNBC decided to ask me. Live on camera, and without notice, the astute CNBC hosts questioned me about China's next leader, Xi Jinping, who is in line to become general secretary of the Communist Party of China and president of the country, in 2012 and 2013, respectively. I was surprised by what they said.[1]

The first CNBC host, Martin Soong, began appropriately by asking, "How much do we know about Xi Jinping?"

"We know a good deal," I said. "He comes from a distinguished family. His father (Xi Zhongxun) was one of the founders of New China and a true reformer under Deng Xiaoping. His father was also imprisoned by Mao Zedong for many years and suffered during the Cultural Revolution (1966-1976). And Xi Jinping, as his son, in his early life, also suffered during the Cultural Revolution. But Xi Jinping's experiences in remote mountainous areas (of Shaanxi Province) put him in touch with the people."

Speaking on CNBC, I explained that during his career, Xi made steady advances at all levels of government—beginning at the county level, rising through municipality administration, and then serving as Party secretary running Zhejiang Province, which with 50 million people is one of China's wealthiest and most balanced provinces. Zhejiang's key characteristic, I said, is that the province is considered the center of entrepreneurship in China, and Xi's success in managing it was studied by central authorities (Chinese Academy of Social Sciences), which labeled the province's economic structure as the "Zhejiang Model"—and scholars published six volumes on it, describing how entrepreneurship works in the real world and on a large-scale as a prototype for other regions of China to consider. I concluded my opening statement on CNBC by making a forecast: "I expect Xi Jinping to be a leader who is business-oriented, rooted in patriotism for his country, and perhaps, more of a personality."

Then came the unexpected. "He's also known to be, or thought to be, *pro-Soviet*," CNBC host Soong said to me pointedly, "How's that going to play out?"[2]

"No, that's not the case," I responded. "Xi is very sophisticated. He understands the way the world works. In his early career, he served for two years in the military (in an administrative capacity), which differentiates Xi from (former) President Jiang Zemin and President Hu Jintao, neither of whom had military experience (prior to assuming the presidency). Because of Xi's background (which includes the Zhejiang Model of entrepreneurship) he has had broad experiences. He has friendships with many Westerners, so I think that we're going to find an urbane, sophisticated leader."

Then the second CNBC host, Oriel Morrison, hit me with "a sense of opinion . . . from analysts" that Xi Jinping "could well be the *weakest* leader of the Communist era."

"It's a mistake to say that Xi Jinping will be the weakest leader," I answered. "That misunderstands everything that's been happening in China—frames it negatively—when in reality it is quite a positive development that China has been maturing into a substantial and normal country. . . . Xi Jinping's accession (to China's top posts), assuming that happens, will be part of China's maturation process. The so-called 'weakness' is a misnomer, because it mischaracterizes China's administrative and governmental reform. . . . (Under Xi's leadership,) I look for a strong patriotic country, a China that will stand up on many issues, particularly on economic issues—but above all, a China that must focus on serving its own people. That's leadership's primary objective. China is still, on a per capita basis, one of the poorest countries in the world, and therefore China's leaders must continue to focus domestically."

Off camera, I noted the irony in foreign forecasts that Xi Jinping will be a weak leader. China critics, who often over simplify and underrate China's political system, on the one hand complain that China is a dictatorship, and on the other hand complain that Xi Jinping will be a weak leader. "Which way do we want it?" I asked, half in jest.

I also said that at the highest echelon of state power, the Standing Committee of the Political Bureau of the Central Committee of the Communist Party of China, all the likely members of the next generation of senior leaders, who will assume their positions immediately following the 18th National Party Congress in late 2012, will be strong personalities. All the candidates are well educated and highly experienced (having run large provinces, municipalities, institutions), and, knowing them, I can say that they will have individual identities and independent ideas. Working with China's collective leadership will not, I predict, diminish Xi Jinping and make him a "weak leader" in governance. Rather, appreciating China's system of leadership and understanding all the candidates for top posts, I expect that China's capacity for controlled innovation will be enhanced and the country's decision-making prowess strengthened. This bodes well, I think.

"The West is quite ignorant about Xi Jinping," J. Stapleton Roy, former U.S. Ambassador to China (1991–1995), told me in early 2011, "and this is not good for China or for the world."

A primary purpose of this book is to introduce the new generation of China's leaders to the world. For our collective future, how China's leaders think matters.

★ ★ ★

What then of 2010, that backsliding year in Sino-U.S. relations? Discord erupted just prior, in December 2009, when China bore the brunt of blame, perhaps unfairly, for the poor progress made on global warming at the Climate Conference in Copenhagen, and throughout the year, heated and parochial disputations over China's undervalued currency, massive trade surplus and swelling foreign reserves dominated economic debate. Contentious events escalated in early 2010 with U.S. arms sales to Taiwan and President Barack Obama meeting the Dalai Lama, both of which infuriated China (more so, tellingly, than in prior years). China's intensified territorial claims, featuring a sea clash between a Chinese fishing boat and a Japanese patrol vessel near disputed islands in the East China Sea, ignited nationalistic emotions on both sides, and China's assertion that the South China Sea was a "core interest" frightened and galvanized China's neighbors, particularly Vietnam, into seeking closer relations with the U.S. North Korea's outrageous torpedoing of a South Korean navy ship, killing 46 sailors, and its wanton shelling of a South Korean island, isolated China, which maintained an awkward, outward neutrality while being widely perceived to be protecting Kim Jung-il, the maniacal dictator of North Korea, who seemed obsessed with bequeathing his tyrannical power, emperor-like, to his young, unknown son.

Then, as if piling on, came the award of the Nobel Peace Prize to Liu Xiaobo, a literary critic whom China had imprisoned for promoting democracy. China's reaction seemed pre-modern, knee-jerk reflex as it mobilized a ham-handed campaign to bully countries into boycotting the Nobel ceremonies (e.g., calling Liu's backers "clowns")—a self-defeating effort that only amplified the public relations agony—which anyway netted only 18 absentee nations (and largely a rogue's list at that), not the "more than 100 countries and international organizations opposed to awarding the prize to Liu," as claimed by China's foreign ministry spokesperson. Adding to China's chagrin was a hastily erected and risibly competitive "Confucius Peace Prize," allegedly organized by private individuals, which degenerated into farce when the winning recipient never showed up.

Finally, with 2011 having barely begun, and right before President Hu's trip to the U.S., China's military conducted the first test flight of its J-20 stealth fighter jet, the People's Liberation Army's most advanced warplane. It was an inopportune moment, apparently even for President Hu, at the precise time when U.S Secretary of Defense Robert Gates was in Beijing seeking more mutual transparency and better military-to-military communications. As one China critic put it, "What if you could prepare for a state visit in Washington that boosts your public image while at the same time humiliating your rival and intimidating your neighbors? . . . They tested the J-20 during Gates' visit because they knew they could get away with it: . . . embarrass the secretary of defense, show allies America's impotence, and still have a summit that makes your president look good."[3] Although in my opinion this calculating scenario overthought the event and overestimated its significance, among many foreign policy analysts it did represent common conclusion.

Considering China's spectacular success in just over three decades of reform, not only becoming the world's second-largest economy and lifting hundreds of millions of its citizens out of poverty, but also emerging as one of the world's most admired countries, China's diplomatic trajectory needed course correction and President Hu's state visit to Washington did just that. In my commentary on *Euronews*, I reiterated the metaphor of the moment— pushing the "reset button," as it were, in Sino-U.S. bilateral relations. Even if the January 2011 summit's success was more form than substance, in a media-intense world, form is substance.

China's Ambassador to the United States, Zhang Yesui, uses his sophisticated understanding of international affairs and nuanced appreciation of American politics to build good relations between the U.S. and China. "I explain the real China to Capitol Hill," he told me in early 2011, less than a month after President Hu's state visit. "I encourage senators and congressmen to visit China." Unruffled by China's difficult diplomatic year in 2010, Ambassador Zhang was rightly proud that President Hu's visit was viewed so positively by President Obama's administration.

At about the same time, across town in Washington at The Jamestown Foundation, a symposium was held on "China Defense & Security 2011." The overflowing crowd of U.S. government, military and think tank professionals heard America's best analysts of China's armed forces voice almost unanimous concern that China's military might was growing beyond that which would be needed solely for the country's defense, that China's overarching strategic intent was becoming increasingly assertive (or even aggressive), and that greater, not fewer, confrontations between China and its neighbors, and thus between China and the U.S., were looming on the horizon.

What seem to be hardening attitudes of military leaders and security experts in both China and the U.S., irrespective of civilian oversight, could turn my prognostications pessimistic. Many Chinese and American defense professionals truly and firmly believe that the other side harbors malicious intent—the U.S. side suspecting that China seeks untoward expansion and the Chinese side suspecting that the U.S. seeks to surround and contain China. These disconnected perceptions, amplified by the fact that the technological gap between the American and Chinese armed forces is narrowing, suggest that dangerous times lie ahead. (Addressing the problem head on, Chinese Ambassador Zhang Yesui asserts that pragmatic solutions must involve regular military-to-military visits, talks and communications.)

There were other indications that a change in relative power between China and the U.S. had taken place, an increasingly common occurrence after the financial crisis of 2008-2009. Exemplifying this subtle shift in preparation for President Hu's state visit, it was the U.S. side that sought to sign substantial business deals at the summit, chasing and beseeching the Chinese side to make it happen. This was in stark contrast to previous state visits to the U.S. by Chinese leaders when China sought business deals while the U.S. resisted "mixing politics and business." The world had turned, irreversibly (or so it seemed), as China continues its long march towards the center of the world. (The Chinese name for China, *Zhongguo*, means center country).

In 2010, China's GDP rose to $5.75 trillion, still well behind the U.S.'s $14.6 trillion, but catching up fast. China's GDP grew 10.3 percent year-on-year, whereas the U.S. GDP, still weighted by the financial crisis and depressed by unemployment, only grew 2.9 percent, thus enabling China to keep closing the gap. Experts forecast that China's economy will surpass that of the U.S. between 2020 and 2030. (In terms of Purchasing Power Parity, China's 2010 GDP was already about $10 trillion.) China's total foreign trade in 2010 was almost $3 trillion, with $1.6 trillion of exports (up 31 percent) and $1.4 trillion of imports (up 39 percent). China's sustained growth through the financial crisis, attributed in part to its strong, authoritative government taking rapid, decision action (i.e., a massive stimulus and a flood of new bank loans), helped prevent the world from sinking deeper into recession, perhaps even avoiding a worldwide depression—a generally acknowledged if inconvenient truth that triggers mixed emotions in many Westerners.

Yet for all its economic triumphs China has vast arrays of domestic problems, mainly severe imbalances among social classes, lack of adequate social services (especially healthcare), energy and water shortages, severe pollution and environmental degradation, and endemic corruption. Internationally, too, China is increasingly challenged: Diverse countries, especially China's Asian neighbors, now find common interest in resisting what they perceive to be China's expansionist imperatives even as they are more dependent on what they know to be China's economic might.

The challenges and opportunities for President-in-Waiting Xi Jinping and the new generation of China's leaders will be formidable. I want a ringside seat.

★ ★ ★

October 1, 2009—the 60th anniversary of the People's Republic of China. Surprising itself as well as the world, China had transformed itself into an economic superpower involved with every major issue in foreign affairs and competing in every important area of human endeavor. From trade, business and finance to diplomacy, defense and security; from science, technology and innovation to culture, media and sports—China's growing strengths have global implications.

Two statistics, telephones and Internet users, say it all. In 1980, there were barely two million phones in China, all fixed line of course. In 2009, less than 30 years later, China had over one *billion* phones, about two-thirds of them mobile. During 2010, the number of mobile phones exceeded 850 million and the number of short messages sent via mobile phones was approaching one trillion. Moreover, the number of Internet users in China exceeded 500 million, well overtaking America as the world's largest Internet-user market.

The creation of new wealth has been astonishing. In 2010, the number of billionaires on *Forbes* China Rich List ballooned to 128 (from 79 in 2009), second only to the 400 billionaires in the U.S., and the gap was closing fast. (In 2004, China had one billionaire; in 2005, two.) Of the 20 richest self-made women in the world, 11 were from China, including the top three.

The first edition of this book marked New China's 60 years by focusing on China's past and current leaders during three decades of reform and opening-up, and on China's future leaders for the coming decades of great opportunity and high uncertainty. I highlight President Hu Jintao's philosophies and policies, and look to the next generation of China's leaders. Who are China's future leaders? What are they doing today? What's their way of thinking about China's place in the world? How about prospects for political reform and democracy?

"The change China has undergone is the greatest China and the Chinese people have experienced in thousands of years," Li Yuanchao told me, soon after his 2007 elevation to the Politburo and appointment as head of the powerful Organization Department of the Communist Party of China ("CPC" or "Party"). "It may also be the greatest sustained change in human history."

It was an extraordinary period that radically changed the mission of the Communist Party, from ideological purity and class struggle to political pragmatism and economic growth. It ushered in not only national development, but ultimately a greater change: the transformation of the spirit of the Chinese people and the increasing scope and depth of their personal freedoms.

It was evening, and Minister Li and I were sitting, with only Adam Zhu, my long-time partner, as translator, in Li's office building just off Chang'an Avenue, the main East-West thoroughfare in Beijing that unevenly bisects Tiananmen Square, closer to Mao Zedong's portrait on the rostrum to the north than to Mao's Mausoleum farther to the south. Surrounded by a Beijing skyline festooned with cranes and new construction, his assessment seemed apt.

As Li put it, "the tremendous progress in the freeing and emancipation of the minds of the Chinese people" has been central to China's transformation.

"The very first step was to eliminate the obstacles of 'leftist' ideas which had constrained people's thinking," he explained. "We call this the 'liberalization of thinking', which took place in all areas, including education and culture as well as economics and politics. This was the starting point of China's reform."

Above all, China is a story of challenge and exploration, risk-taking and caution, a spirit which has informed three generations of China's leaders. The career of Li Yuanchao, a "rising star" in Chinese politics and a long-time colleague and confidante of President Hu Jintao, China's most senior leader, epitomizes this transformation and presages deepening reform to come. "To be honest," Minister Li told me, "if I hadn't carried out such risky reform experiments, I wouldn't be sitting here today. But I was reflecting the policies of the central government's spirit."

Li was referring to his five years as Communist Party secretary, the highest official, of Jiangsu Province, one of the most advanced in China with about 75 million people and a GDP (2010) of about 4 trillion RMB ($612 billion), larger than Switzerland, Poland or Saudi Arabia. As Jiangsu Party secretary, Li introduced a procedure for soliciting public opinion (*gong shi*) of candidates who were selected for official positions, a procedure which made appointments less opaque to the public.

Li and his team developed what for China was such startlingly fresh transparency in close coordination with CPC General Secretary Hu Jintao who, in his report to the 17th National Party Congress in 2007, alluded to this "oversight role of public opinion" as a model that should be applied to the entire country. But when Jiangsu's initiatives in political reform were first introduced they were experimental, daring, and controversial.

I told Li that at the time when he introduced these political reforms some Party insiders thought they could damage his political career and they "worried" about his personal future.

Li responded with a laugh. "Worry," he said, "may be considered as an expression of acceptance or the highest level of sympathy or empathy." But, Li stressed, "Reformers must take risks."

About two years later, in late 2009, Li told me (in a discussion which I later summarized in *Forbes*) that China's leaders had determined to build a "learning-minded party," emphasizing "the Party's long-held devotion to learning." To construct a learning-oriented Party, Li said, "we need to learn both theoretical knowledge, such as Marxist classics and the theory of socialism with Chinese characteristics, and all the advanced human scientific knowledge and advanced experience. In addition to learning, we must also apply leading-edge science and technology. The Internet was invented in America," he added, "but has found its largest number of users in China."

"We ask our officials to cultivate a reading habit and encourage them to read more books, and more importantly, good books," Li continued. "The Chinese have a habit of reading. Many families regard books as the most valuable family asset. They can do without cars, but there would be cases of books in the house. Recently we recommended a whole set of books in various genres to officials of the CPC Organization Department. This may sound hard to believe, but we also included *A Brief History of Time*, a classic by Stephen Hawking. Not only do we want our officials to learn latest knowledge of physics and cosmology but also to develop a way of scientific thinking."

"Every year all ministerial-level officials in the Organization Department will take time out for intensive study and discussions together," said Li. "This year's topic was how to expand democracy in our work. We read books by Marxist classic writers, expositions on democracy by Deng Xiaoping, Jiang Zemin and Hu Jintao, even *The Theory of Democracy Revisited* by Giovanni Sartori. All of us read together. After we finished, we had comparative discussions, taking into account China's special reality."

"We believe that a ruling party only remains viable and vibrant when it masters state-of-the-art knowledge," Li said.

Li calls talent "the primary resource of scientific development," and has established "democratic, open, competitive, merit-based" principles in selecting, training and promoting future leaders. In response to the financial crisis, and in order to achieve the "goal of making China an innovation-oriented nation," Li instituted a "Thousand People Plan" to attract high-level personnel to China from overseas, such as scientists, financial experts, entrepreneurs and senior managers. Li's plan promises high salaries and attractive government funding to elite Chinese professionals, especially top science and technology researchers, who are working abroad and willing to return home. (Many whom China hopes to repatriate have been pursuing careers in the U.S.) Recognizing China's new place in the world, Li wants leaders with transnational knowledge and global perspective—the "internationalization of the mind," he said, is a needed new way to "emancipate the mind."

As a senior leader focused on upgrading officials and on political reform, Li Yuanchao has the vision, experience and can-do charisma that characterize China's future leaders (Chapter 39).

★ ★ ★

The best way to know China—the best way to do business with China—is to know what motivates China's leaders and what drives their policies. This book is founded on my discussions with China's leaders. I speak with them about economic development, political reform, domestic difficulties and international conflicts. I engage them in private companies, state-owned enterprises, banking, foreign affairs, military, science and technology, law, agriculture, healthcare, religion, education, culture, media, press, Internet, film, literature, ideology and more. I invite readers to question the validity of the so-called "China threat" and to consider the relevance of an emerging "China model."

I do not shirk from confronting China's leaders with China's problems. I target economic imbalances, environmental pollution, unsustainable development, human rights, democracy, rule of law, media censorship, corruption, crime, unemployment, migrant workers, minorities, ethnic conflicts, religious tension, social instability, protests and demonstrations, ideological shake-up, shifting moral and family values, death penalty, organs from executed prisoners, global confrontations, resource competition, military expansion, and the impact of the worldwide financial crisis. I find frank acknowledgement of the long road that China must still travel in order to realize President Hu Jintao's vision of a Harmonious Society. There is a deep conviction that China must never repeat its errors of the past and a fervent expectation that the country's long future is bright and ascendant.

★ ★ ★

For three decades, from Mao Zedong's founding of the People's Republic in 1949 to the beginning of Deng Xiaoping's reforms in 1978, China's economy had largely stagnated: the state owned all the means of production and people had to live and work where they were assigned. Citizens had virtually no rights, civil or human, and even expressions of personal beliefs were restricted. In today's market economy, people live as they want and work as they please. On the crowded shopping streets of China's cities, there is movement and choice—expressed by the brisk pace of pedestrians, dazzling arrays of products, latest fashions, and ubiquitous mobile phones ringing constantly. People pursue personal goals and satisfy personal wants. They own private property and start private businesses. And they think what they like—even criticize the government—with the single caveat that they do not threaten the leadership of the Communist Party.

Little wonder then that, for many, the 30th anniversary of reform and opening-up was the most meaningful event of 2008, even more than the Beijing Olympics.

Yet the astonishing pace of reform, which generated growth rates that averaged almost 10% per year for three decades, has naturally also brought with it challenges and contradictions. For all its spectacular development, today's China has accumulated a host of seemingly intractable problems which would have been unthinkable in the perennial poverty of its past, including severe income disparity, endemic corruption, and widespread industrial pollution.

Furthermore, the global financial crisis, with its sudden onset and severe impact, threatened China's stability. "Of course, the world keeps changing," Li Yuanchao noted. "We have a metaphor in Chinese that the world is like the clouds in the sky, always changing. In some places, the sky turns from menacing with thick black clouds to sunny with no clouds in sight, while in other places it's the opposite. On Chinese soil, 1.3 billion people are progressing with confidence to a better and brighter tomorrow under the leadership of the Party."

★ ★ ★

New China's 60th anniversary in 2009 provides my organizing framework for understanding *How China's Leaders Think* with three periods of (roughly) 30 years each:

- The first, from the founding of the People's Republic in 1949 to the death of Mao Zedong in 1976, embedding the early idealism followed by two decades of political extremism, mass movements and ideological oppression that culminated in the horrific, decade-long Cultural Revolution (1966–1976).
- The second, from Deng Xiaoping's seminal "Emancipate the Mind" speech at the 3rd Plenary Session of the 11th CPC National Congress on December 18, 1978 to President Hu Jintao's "Scientific Perspective on Development" at the 17th CPC National Congress in 2007 and the international financial crisis of 2008.
- The third, beginning in 2009, after all the struggles and accomplishments and with all the problems and challenges, going out into the middle decades of the 21st century.

Each period should be understood in light of its predecessor period: the first in terms of ancient and modern Chinese history; the second in reaction to the traumas and tragedies of the first; and the third in response to the complications, opportunities and responsibilities generated by the second.

The thrust of this book is the future, the third 30 years, the period in which China plays an increasingly central role in world affairs, the period commencing right now. In forecasting this future, understanding *How China's Leaders Think* is central.

★ ★ ★

This book is not a comprehensive description of China, nor a history of the past three decades. It is more an exploration of the present and a forecast of the future in light of the inside story of the past. As the title declares, China's leaders are my focus, and I seek to examine how they think as well as what they say and do.

Since 2005, when my biography of former President Jiang Zemin, *The Man Who Changed China: The Life and Legacy of Jiang Zemin* was published in China, the first biography of a living Chinese leader on the mainland, I am asked why did I, a scientist by training and an investment banker by profession, write such a book. Similarly, when my interviews and articles about President Hu Jintao's philosophy and policies appear in the American and international media, often in opposition to the views of China experts, I am asked why do I, with a doctorate in brain science and expertise in mergers and acquisitions, allocate such time and effort to explain a Chinese leader's political vision?

The answer to both questions is the same. The reason why I wrote former President Jiang's biography, and the reason why I explain President Hu's policies, is because I feel it essential for international readers to understand the true story of China.

Many Western media have a certain slant in their coverage of China and a built-in assumption about the motivation of China's leaders. It's not so much that such coverage is overtly or demonstrably wrong, it's that Western media largely stress the real problems but ignore the real successes; for example, emphasizing the continuing limitations on certain freedoms in China (i.e., no competing political parties, no public political dissent, no free media) while downplaying the enormous advances in personal and social freedoms (i.e., where to live, work, travel; what to study, believe, say; diversity of entertainment, and the like).

I do not believe that, overall, Western media are malicious or deliberately distort the truth (as some in China suppose). There is a common assumption in the West that unless a nation's political system has multiple political parties that compete legitimately in free elections, a one-person-one-vote democracy, and a free media, that nation is a dictatorship. Furthermore, giving apparent credence to the assumption, there was a time, when Mao still ruled and before the 30 years of reform began, when China was indeed such a dictatorship—a chaotic, self-destructive one at that—and the consequences to the Chinese people were devastating. Thus the common perception in the West is that China's leaders are authoritarians—not as brutal as was Mao, of course, but coercive nonetheless—and that their primary, if not their sole interest is perpetuating their own power. China's leaders, it's assumed, are dictators.

This common perception is untrue. I know some of these leaders personally and they are not dictators. This parody of reality is detrimental to China's development and corrosive to world stability, because it enables attributions of dire and dastardly motivations to Chinese leaders, and a twisting of the meaning of Chinese pride and patriotism, which, when combined with China's growing economic and military strength, can give rise to the so-called "China threat" syndrome.

A case in point occurred in 1999, when an American aircraft accidentally bombed the Chinese Embassy in Belgrade during the NATO military campaign against ethnic cleansing in Yugoslavia. When the Chinese government organized buses to transport students from college campuses across Beijing to the U.S. Embassy, for the specific purpose of protesting, the American media assumed that China's leaders had orchestrated the demonstrations to whip up nationalistic fervor in order to divert attention from domestic problems. Chinese leaders, however, say they felt that the students could not be stopped, and they were worried that if marauding students were allowed to march across the city their ranks would swell with workers and citizens, creating an even larger, less manageable problem. So busing the students *contained,* rather than exacerbated, the volatile situation (Chapter 32).

The bombing revealed another dichotomy: More than 90% of Chinese, including highly educated professionals often critical of their own government, saw the American bombing of their Belgrade embassy as deliberate and provocative. The vast majority of Americans, on the other hand, believed that the bombing had been, as U.S. officials maintained, an accident due to "old maps." Why such disparity? The Chinese have an idealized picture of America as so technologically advanced that it would have been seemingly impossible to have made such a stupid mistake. Americans are quite used to their government making stupid mistakes.

Such gulfs in perception run deep: Many Chinese believe that America seeks to "contain China" and thwart its historic resurgence as a great nation. This is the real reason, many Chinese imagine, why America supports Taiwan—not as a worthy democracy, but as an "unsinkable aircraft carrier" by which the U.S. can assert its dominance over China and keep the "motherland" divided. These Chinese people see America encircling them through military alliances with Japan, Taiwan, and perhaps India; forcing open their markets to control China's industries and exploit Chinese consumers; fomenting "extremism, separatism and terrorism" in the violent riots or "mass incidents" (or uprisings) in Tibet and Xinjiang (Uyghur Muslims); and introducing Western culture to overwhelm Chinese culture, thereby eroding China's independence and sovereignty.[4]

Many Americans, meanwhile, believe that China is not only a voracious economic competitor but also a looming political and military challenger, an emergent superpower whose opaque intentions grow threatening. The perception is that China acts solely in its own interests, even to the detriment of the international order (e.g., selling weapons to Iran and supporting rogue states like North Korea). China is seen as a mercantile predator which keeps its currency artificially low to boost exports and steal jobs; as a repressed society that tramples human rights to maintain Communist control; and as a potential military force that harbors expansionist ambitions.

China's leaders, of course, do not deny that their policies benefit their own people. But they assert that, in an integrated global economy, China's stability and development is essential for world peace and prosperity. Disturb the former, they warn, and you disrupt the latter. One-party rule, they insist, is essential to maintaining such stability and development.

One way to mitigate misunderstandings and reduce distortion is for foreigners to appreciate how China's leaders think. This is my purpose. In this book, I focus not only on the country's most senior leaders, but also on officials and intellectuals who form the foundation of thinking in China today. I do not claim to represent the views of every sector of society, but I would suggest that in today's China—unlike in pre-reform China—what the nation's leaders think is well aligned with the reality of the country and the needs of the people. (As for the conspiratorial charge that what China's leaders tell me is *not* what they really think and believe, but rather what they want me, a naïve foreigner intoxicated by China's allure, to hear and repeat, I can only plead my case: 20 years back-and-forth to China, thousands of conversations, a fascination with belief systems, and a not wholly dull sense of human cognition. Anyway, I'd argue, the charge is moot: First-hand, content-specific talk from dozens of China's leaders—too varied to be rehearsed and even if subliminally modulated—can be used to triangulate ways of thinking valuable for assessing this now-critical country.)

I therefore seek to make China's leaders more transparent, their ideas and attitudes more accessible, and to help foreign readers understand the challenges they face and the decisions they make. President Hu Jintao would be frustrated by the assumption that he is an authoritarian dictator controlling a totalitarian state: Hu is recognized in China as an intelligent, decent man of humility and high integrity who is fundamentally committed to maintaining stability, continuing reform and building China.

Indeed, one objective of the book is to describe how President Hu thinks—specifically by introducing his Scientific Perspective on Development a modern, sophisticated way of thinking that optimizes social, environmental and political concerns along with continuing economic growth. Since my personal perspective is scientific—I created and host a public television series on new knowledge in science, *Closer To Truth* (www.closertotruth.com)[5]—I was intrigued when Hu, who studied technology at Tsinghua University, China's finest science school, first articulated this theory. After studying its foundations and witnessing its real-world applications (particularly in different provinces with different challenges), I began to use it as a conceptual lens through which to view contemporary China, its remarkable development and current challenges.

The book also highlights political reform, notably the theory of "intra-Party democracy," which is not only vital for understanding China's continuing reforms but also provides insight into the current thinking and future direction of senior leaders. Political reform is the aspect of China most criticized by foreigners, and, not surprisingly, one of the least understood. But it is a critical component of President Hu's core political philosophy—which also includes the concepts of Harmonious Society and Putting People First.

This is not to say that China's political system is free in the Western sense. Obviously it is not. Political parties do not compete and there are no national elections. But the transformation of Chinese society and the change in how the Chinese people think is, as we shall see, the biggest and best part of this epic story. That is why this book explores the impact of reform on diverse sectors of society, including, as noted, culture, media, science, education, healthcare and religion, as well as on state-owned enterprises, private business, and banking.

★ ★ ★

This book also reflects my own engagement with China. I first came to China in early 1989, at the invitation of Dr. Song Jian, chairman of the State

Science and Technology Commission (under the auspices of former CPC General Secretary Zhao Ziyang), to advise Chinese research institutes on their early efforts of reform, especially how to adapt to the incipient market economy. As an investment banker trained as a scientist, not as a lawyer, I've joked that perhaps at the time I seemed less threatening.

Over the years, I've advised on economics, finance, M&A, media, culture, international communications, Sino-American relations, science, and religion (never for payment).[6] Yet, although for 20 years I have spent a good deal of time in China, I am neither a China scholar by training nor a China hand by profession. I speak only rudimentary Chinese and recognize only a few characters. In 2005, when I was starting work on a new book, friends advised me to make a series of trips around China, saying that while I knew much about the country, my Beijing-centric focus limited my vision.

In particular, Minister Leng Rong, then vice president of the Chinese Academy of Social Sciences[7] (now head of the CPC Party Literature Research Center) recommended an ambitious itinerary targeting special situations in each of China's primary regions—northeast, central, southern, western, border areas. Leng, who first helped me plumb the depths of Chinese political theory, stressed that one cannot understand China, or appreciate the significance of the Scientific Perspective on Development, without seeing the diversity and challenges of all China. In addition, Leng called my attention to the "Zhejiang model," which stressed private business and entrepreneurship: he and then Zhejiang Provincial Party Secretary Xi Jinping, now China's vice president, and their teams were then collaborating on a multi-volume analysis of Zhejiang's astonishing success.

As a result, in 2005 and 2006, I had the privilege of visiting some 35 cities (22 provinces, regions, and major municipalities) in China, meeting local leaders (Party, government, business, academic) and ordinary people (farmers, students, soldiers, workers, migrant workers, laid-off workers, retirees, reporters, police). These travels, often driving five to six hours between cities, provided me with first-hand experience of what was happening on the ground and what the people, leaders and common folk, were saying. I learned how different provinces had and handled different problems. The complexities of the real China undercut the generally simplistic view of China held by many abroad.

My journeys, taken with my partner Adam Zhu, revealed both the commonality and the cacophony that compose the real China. I witnessed China's multifaceted struggle with serious, systemic problems—including, as listed earlier, increasing economic disparity, widespread unemployment, endemic corruption, fragile financial systems, energy limitations, unsustainable development, environmental pollution, and more. Some problems resulted from dramatic economic growth; some from rapid transition to a market economy; and some from the need for deepening economic, social and political reforms. ("Deepen" is a Chinese way to express progress toward a market economy.)

In March 2006, I met with then Zhejiang Party Secretary Xi Jinping, who, although we had arrived unexpectedly, graciously offered advice on how to communicate China to the world. Xi said that it was natural foreigners would seek to characterize China in a single sentence, or to encapsulate the country with a single methodology, but the nation was far too complex to do so. He used the classic story of blind men touching different parts of an elephant: "The blind man who felt the leg believed it was a pillar, the blind man who felt the back believed it was a wall," he said. "None reached the truth because all of them failed to feel the whole elephant and get the whole picture."

It was an analogy, he explained, which was appropriate to China, a nation of 56 ethnic groups with great disparities between wealthy coastal and poorer inland areas. "China is a diverse country," he went on. "Those who only stay in eastern regions are like the blind man who felt the leg of the elephant, while those who only stay in western regions are like the blind man who felt the back of the elephant. Xi recommended that I study China both "horizontally" across diverse regions and "vertically" through the history of its development. I couldn't know it at the time, but this book would become the expression of both: following the horizontal approach (across sectors as well as geographies) and embedding the vertical approach, over the decades, as I sought to discern how China's leaders think. (In October 2010, Vice President Xi Jinping was appointed vice chairman of the Central Military Commission of the CPC, reconfirming expectations that he would become general secretary of the CPC in 2012 and president of China in 2013—the country's most senior leader.)

My dual objective is to trace China's monumental story of trauma and transformation and to understand the motivations and mechanisms underlying the decisions and policies of China's leaders, individually and in their sequential generations. I am honored by the trust of those whom I interviewed, some of whom had not spoken publicly of these matters before, not even to the Chinese media. After my interview with one high-ranking person, he said to me anxiously: "You now have my head on your chopping block."

In writing this book, I have held as model the incisive and far-sighted spirit of "Huang Fuping," the pseudonymic author representing several Party theorists who, in 1991, a difficult year for reform, pioneered new thinking about reform—and were penalized on account of it. (Two decades later, one of the courageous authors, Shi Zhihong, is deputy minister of the Policy Research Office of the CPC Central Committee and a special aide to Vice President Xi Jinping.)

★ ★ ★

I planned, wrote and financed this book myself. Never did anyone assume that I must write what I was told. I was offered advice, but never did anyone even attempt to coerce or control me or monitor or check my words. I had special access but made no concession in terms of independence. I selected what I liked, rejected what I did not. I've made mistakes, no doubt, but they are all my own.

I checked facts and ideas with others, including some in China—various experts, Party historians, friends (many of whom work in government). But at all times I maintained absolute editorial control, and no one in China ever thought otherwise. In fact, prior to publication, no one in China—no government official, no interviewee, no intermediary—ever even asked to see the English manuscript. (Several interviewees wanted to edit their own quotes but never beyond.)

I learned from reactions to the Chinese edition of this book, which was published and publicized prior to the English, and I have incorporated these ideas here.8 Although I delivered the manuscript to English and Chinese publishers at the same time, the Chinese published faster, even with the added burden of translation and multiple layers of editing and censorship— primarily because the launch date of the Chinese-language book was to coincide with the 30th anniversary of reform and opening-up in mid December 2008. In addition to restoring wholly in the English edition material censored in the Chinese edition, I have had further conversations with China's leaders and incorporate here those of their ideas or ways of thinking which I deem revelatory, insightful or suggestive.

I'm often asked how I react when my published works are censored in China. My flip answer is that if 15% is removed, that means 85% remains, which enables Chinese readers to access what are often perspectives that differ from the official "Party line."

More seriously, here's the deal for my Chinese-language versions: I can be cut but not altered. It is never the case of changing what I write (unless I make errors of fact). I do suppose that more is excised than "has to be"— that's simple sociology with multiple censors—but the excisers aren't joyous in their excising and most wish it were otherwise.

Even so, considering this book's political sensitivity, the Chinese publisher felt compelled to insert a disclaimer upfront, something to the effect that although "the author has rather good understanding of China's history, national conditions, and social conditions, as a Westerner, his understanding has certain differences from ours. We believe our readers would understand and grasp this." That this English edition differs from the Chinese edition is known widely in China, and some Chinese look forward to reading it. This, I submit, is a real step in the right direction. History is history and all should be told. Diverse interpretations exist and all should be heard.

There were three probative reactions to this book's Chinese edition from Chinese media and bloggers: wondering how I'd arranged so many high-level interviews; weighing how I deal with China's widespread and virulent problems; and assessing (or questioning) my motives. Each of the three had an investigative edge, scratching (and occasionally digging) beneath the surface. Good progress for China, I thought! (I face such inquiries often and enjoy engaging my interlocutors.)

I repeat in public what Politburo member Liu Yunshan, the head of the CPC Publicity (Propaganda) Department, told me in private: "Pure facts tell China's story. The truth about China is best told in an honest, matter-of-fact way. Painting rosy pictures doesn't work; beautifying us isn't helpful. Real-life stories and cases are what counts. Convey the interviewees' own words; dig out their life experiences; reveal their innermost thoughts. That will capture the real China."[9]

One of my interviewees, Du Daozheng, the 85-year-old Party intellectual who facilitated deposed Party chief Zhao Ziyang's memoirs,[10] made the point memorably: "I'm a Communist Party insider," he said. "I used to be a 'leftist' [i.e., Communist ideologue, conservative[11]], and I attacked others for what they believed. After many rounds of attacking and being attacked, I gradually woke up, gained some independent thinking, and became a little bit more objective. Therefore [he told me] my advice for you is to interview and listen to people from all sides. They all have their own opinions. Listen first; judge later. There have been intense conflicts and historic struggles. We have a great many stories of China's leaders."

I try to tell these stories as truthfully as I can. In general, this book is about what China's leaders think, not about what I think. (When my opinion intrudes, I try to make it obvious.) What follows, I proffer, is *How China's Leaders Think.*

★ ★ ★

On November 10, 2010, in Palm Spring, California, I moderated the China session at Ernst & Young's Strategic Growth Forum; with over 1,700 business leaders attending, it is the largest gathering of successful entrepreneurs in the United States (and features the prestigious "Entrepreneur of the Year" award). It was the first time in the event's 24 years that China was a major topic on its agenda, underscoring the fact that companies in the U.S. and worldwide—companies of all sizes—recognize the reality of China as a central force in international commerce.

Ernst & Young Global Chairman and CEO James Turley stated, "China's economy is vibrant, vigorous, complex and challenging, unique in many ways, and we are pleased to participate in its global emergence. The rapidly developing industrial strength of China's state-owned enterprises and the fast-growing market power of its entrepreneurial firms combine to make the country's economic landscape especially dynamic."

Personifying the importance of China for business leaders, I had on my China panel Cerberus Operations CEO Bob Nardelli (former CEO of Home Depot and Chrysler); GE Vice Chairman John Rice, who leads GE's global operations; and Manpower CEO Jeff Joerres. "Every company has a China strategy," I said. "If you think you don't have a China strategy, you have one by default—and that's not good enough."

Nardelli reflected on how doing business in China has changed radically over the span of his career and pointed out that China's advantage lies in its capacity to leapfrog over Western countries. To do business in China today, he said, new ways of thinking are required. "To be relevant in China, you need to be there," Nardelli advised. "That means a car ride across the city, not a plane ride across the ocean."

Rice said that GE has joint ventures with more than 20 state-owned enterprises—including one proposed to support China's dramatic entry into the production of large-scale commercial aircraft. "Twenty years ago we would have never thought about such structures," he added. Rice noted that while big companies might enjoy an advantage due to their size and brand, "in the end, the company that gets the deal is the one that brings the most value. You'd better be prepared to really create win-win, or your venture is not going to work."

Joerres reported that the "talent wars" in China were increasingly fierce as companies struggle to recruit and maintain employees. He quoted Manpower surveys showing that increasing numbers of Chinese workers want to work for Chinese companies, and so while the majority of Chinese workers would still rather work for foreign firms, this attractiveness gap favoring foreign firms is shrinking. China, Joerres predicted, would become Manpower's top market worldwide—the company already has over 20 wholly owned offices across the country.

I said that there is no doubt that China is an increasingly vast and attractive market for foreign companies—China is currently the world's second largest economy, having surpassed Japan, and in 15 to 25 years it will likely be the largest, surpassing the United States. Yet I cautioned that in its commercial policies the Chinese government has become more selective, and perhaps more restrictive. No longer is any firm with capital and an assembly operation in need of cheap labor easily able to set up shop in prime coastal regions, especially if their processes are polluting or their wages and working conditions are below a rapidly rising standard.

By early 2011 China's foreign reserves were approaching $3 trillion, and China's leaders were enacting regulations, which were often complex and unstable, to favor foreign companies that would bring advanced technologies and managerial skills, and/or had the willingness to venture inland to Western and rural areas where standards of living were lower and where government policy encouraged investment.

In addition, to protect "national security," China established a state-level investment review body to evaluate merger and acquisition deals by non-Chinese firms or investors of Chinese enterprises in China. Guidelines were very broad, encompassing areas pertaining to national defense, agriculture, energy, resources, infrastructure, transport, technology and equipment manufacturing. The new regulations enabled wide government discretion in blocking deals, though officials promised that reviews would be fair, transparent and swift.

In addition, China's leaders sought to support the historic emergence of Chinese companies as strong market competitors, so that in the not-so-distant future, in every industry of any economic importance, Chinese firms would be among the world leaders. Indeed, in every arena of human endeavor— from trade, business and finance to diplomacy, defense and security; from science, technology and innovation to culture, media and sports—China will compete with all other world powers. Though such international competition should boost global standards of living, and should not be a zero-sum game, over time, many believe, China will be second to none.

But between now and then China faces major obstacles and must avoid potential pitfalls. China is in the midst of a vast industrial transformation, critical for the country's continuing tectonic shift from an agrarian to an urban society and for its increasingly serious need to raise the living standards of all Chinese people by redressing the economic imbalances that threaten social stability. China must wean itself away from its three-decade-long reliance on low-cost assemblers that export cheap products and require a low value of the Chinese currency—this is a domestic necessity as well as the hot focus of intense, broad-based international pressure. China's economic transformation must be built on two pillars: substantial and sustained increases in domestic demand and consumer consumption, and a radically new industrial structure led by high-capability companies that manufacture high-value-add products.

In times of such upheavals and growth, there are special opportunities for foreign companies willing to invest the time and resources, particularly those companies with targeted competitive advantages, because the huge size of China's expanding markets, and their growing worldwide impact, can make participation extraordinarily valuable. Alternatively, not to participate, not to take the risk of doing business in China, carries its own risk. Not doing business in China could prove to be, in hindsight, the riskiest decision of all.

Meeting with CEOs at Ernst & Young's Strategic Growth Forum, I was pleasantly surprised by the outpouring of interest in China from all sectors and sizes of American companies. Every executive, it seemed, had a particular perspective, concern or question, evincing that each of them had been thinking hard about China. In offering prescriptions for how to do business in China, I explained how business is conducted at central, provincial and local levels; I noted the importance of being important to one's Chinese counterparts; and I stressed that aligning with government policies, by designing complementary strategies and structures, is almost always optimum positioning (if not always an absolute necessity). Though government policies can be a moving target, maintaining such alignment is the guiding mechanism for achieving commercial success in China.

★ ★ ★

Four days earlier, on November 6, 2010, my birthday, in Shanghai, I had given a keynote address to the 4th World Forum of China Studies (along with Shanghai Mayor Han Zheng, State Council Information Office Minister Wang Chen, and former vice president of the CPC Party School

Zheng Bijian). I spoke about how China scholars, domestic and foreign, play a unique role in facilitating China's integration into the global community of nations, which is one of humanity's great goals of the early 21st century.

Scholars are essential for the flourishing of all influential or consequential civilizations, and scholars have been especially respected and honored throughout China's long history (except for brief periods, such as during the Cultural Revolution, 1966–1976). Scholars seek truth, and because truth is elusive and often disputed, it is incumbent on scholars to present their views without fear or favor. Scholars also have a corollary responsibility: they should not distort or mislead—but an absolute standard of what is, or is not, distortion or misdirection can be challenging to set. Scholars ideally should be individuals, more loyal to their own intellectual integrity than to this or that group of which they may happen to be members.

What role do China scholars play in China's development? Although I have come to spend a good deal of my time in China, immersed in China-related activities, and communicating about China in the international media, I am not, as I have said, a China scholar.

Whether through the benevolent vicissitudes of life, or by the mysterious wisdom of fate, for over two decades I have been coming to China, now more than 100 times. For fifteen years I have been writing books and articles about China, and producing television programs on China—all based on my first-hand interviews, intimate discussions and personal observations, especially with Chinese leaders (in all sectors). Professor Tong Shijun, Director of the Institute of Philosophy of the Shanghai Academy of Social Sciences, uses critical theory to describe my work as "participatory scholarship."

I have learned to appreciate the significance of Chinese political philosophy, including the semiotics of slogans, such as President Jiang Zemin's "Three Represents" (*San Ge Daibiao*) and President Hu Jintao's Scientific Perspective on Development (*Kexue Fazhan Guan*). Such slogans can be deep probes of social context, economic conditions, and political development—and occasionally also of political conflict. Such slogans can reveal the dominant thinking of preeminent leadership, direct real-world policies, and drive the practical behaviors of leaders and officials. (A few years ago, I found myself in a stiff, lackluster meeting with a provincial leader. I decided to shake things up by asking how he was applying the Scientific Perspective on Development in his province—and I did so with a slightly threatening air of confidence such that the provincial leader could be forgiven for inferring that I might be reporting what I would then hear back to Beijing. How quickly that meeting brightened! How energetic that leader became!)

Foreigners, especially those who set opinions or make decisions about China (in business or government), should understand the way of thinking of China's leaders—how they think, not only what they say and what they do. For example, a senior leader was explaining to me a portion of leadership's framework for the 5th Plenary of the 17th CPC Congress (held in October 2010)—which stressed boosting domestic demand and increasing the living standards of all citizens—and he did so by categorizing three kinds of "change": things that have changed; things that have not changed; and things that will never change.

- *Things that have Changed*: Reform and opening up; the dramatic improvement in the standard of living of people's lives; the increasing personal and social freedoms in society; China's international stance of cooperation and engagement; and more.
- *Things that have Not Changed*: 1) China is still in the "primary stage of socialism" (with a very low GDP per capita, China is still very far from idealistic "pure communism"). 2) China still has conflicts and contradictions, such as those between the legitimate demands of the people and the insufficient productive capacity of the country, and those between different and diverging strata of society. 3) China still belongs to the developing world; even though China has experienced enormous development, China as a whole is not a developed country. 4) China's economy still has great opportunities to grow; even with all the crises in domestic and international affairs, China's economy can continue to expand at high current rates for ten to twenty more years (generated by the continuing urbanization of the country as hundreds of millions of rural peasants migrate to cities and suburbs and enter the middle class).
- Things that will Never Change: 1) China will continue to follow its own model, walking the "Socialist Road with Chinese Characteristics" (China will learn from other countries but will never copy other countries). 2) China will continue to promote new ways of thinking as expressed by the well-known slogans—"Seek truth from facts," "Emancipate our minds," and "Keep up with the times." 3) Economic development will remain China's primary goal, because economic development is the engine that drives the achievement of all other goals; this means that even while vital, countervailing goals are added—particularly inclusive development that must rebalance a dangerously imbalanced society, sustainable development, and environmental protection—economic development must still predominate. 4) China's continuing high goals are national prosperity, social democracy, a civilized country, and a harmonious society.

In the collegial atmosphere of Chinese and foreign scholars attending the World Forum of China Studies, I sought to clear the air for honest, candid discussions by articulating "common assumptions" that, perhaps, may not sound so polite.

The common assumption in the West is that domestic China scholars are not free. This is not correct, in that such a simplistic and anachronistic accusation undervalues the great progress that has been made. Although there are indeed still deep pockets of unpleasant restrictions, the off-limits areas have shrunk significantly, and over time continue to shrink (although they do not shrink continuously). What is without controversy is that scholars in today's

China have vastly more freedoms today than their predecessors had four and five decades ago, including freedoms to criticize aspects of government.

The common assumption in China is that many Western China scholars, just like much of the Western media, are biased about China and conspire against China. This is not correct, I told the largely Chinese audience of about 300 China scholars. Scholars, like the media, often focus more on what's wrong than on what's right, I said, and they derive intellectual satisfaction from finding faults and digging out problems. This is the nature of scholars and critics, and society can benefit from it. It is not easy or fun to learn from those who criticize you, I stressed, but this is precisely what great societies do (or learn to do).

The problem with many foreign critics of China is often not so much that what they state is wrong—the problems they pound are usually real and present—but rather that they may give the impression that these problems compose the whole of the picture of China, when in reality these problems, the real and present problems, compose just part of the picture.

Constructive critics of China, those who root for China's success but are concerned enough to point out China's problems, are China's best friends and closest allies. Constructive critics of China, both domestic and foreign, should be praised not scorned, I said.

China scholars have multiple functions. Here are five:

1) Pure scholarship: the discovery or creation of truth, whether historical or contemporary, exemplifies the pinnacle of the human spirit and enriches China.
2) Generating intellectual energy and expressing scholarly passion: the special intensity of scholarly heat can focus broad attention on critical issues and thus can enable China to address such critical issues.
3) Articulating critical issues (irrespective of opinions about those issues): this is scholarly analysis and it functions by breaking down critical issues into their constituent elements and thus facilitates the formulation of targeted sets of solutions.
4) Creating a market place of ideas: even if fractious and competitive, ideas astir in the bright light of public scrutiny bring out the best minds, thinkers who can address complex issues and solve multifaceted problems.
5) Distinguishing between fact and opinion: this is the scholarly ideal that we prize (but scholars often conflate fact and opinion, taking themslves so seriously that they come to believe that their personal opinions are truly independent facts).

The degree of scholarly openness at the World Forum—primarily in private, frank conversations between Western and Chinese scholars—was encouraging. Speaking publicly on international security, David Shambaugh, professor and director of the China Policy Program at George Washington

University, said that while "China's global security involvement has grown in some (non-traditional) areas [e.g., disaster relief, poverty alleviation, public health, counter-terrorism, monitoring financial institutions for money laundering, strengthening controls against human and drug trafficking, and cracking down on organized international crime networks], and has been very positive," but "in other areas, China's participation remains quite limited." Shambaugh called for China to "help its own case for global multilateral security cooperation through continually enhancing its military transparency, acting in non-provocative ways towards its neighbors (including Taiwan), and through continually expanded participation in multilateral and bilateral peacekeeping activities and security forums."

★ ★ ★

I was proud to participate in Expo 2010 Shanghai by creating, co-producing, writing and presenting China Central Television's (CCTV News) series on Expo and the future of Shanghai, called "Expo's Meaning, Shanghai's Mission." I would like to report publicly that in producing this six-part CCTV series I had total editorial freedom, and I can *almost* affirm that this was the case—CCTV and I had only two points of minor disagreement (i.e., CCTV cut two small segments in the final edit—one an allusion by a mainstream Chinese sculptor to abortion as a metaphor for the destruction of a historic factory to make way for Expo's modernity; the other a comment by a sophisticated Shanghai entertainer that the revolutionary songs he had sung as a child, under Mao Zedong, seemed contradictory in their admonitions).

Such is the nature of creative collaboration in China and all were well pleased with the production. An abridged version of our Expo-Shanghai series was broadcast by Euronews, the largest television and new media news network in Europe, Russia, Africa and the Middle East. Featured were my interviews of Shanghai Party Secretary Yu Zhengsheng and former senior Chinese diplomat Wu Jianmin.

There was great international interest in our CCTV Expo series because there is great hunger in the world for information about China. Globally, people want to understand China. This heightens the responsibility of those who really know China. As China scholars—into whose camp I now squeeze myself (I hope they won't mind)—we should make sure our information is accurate, even if our understandings differ.

I am often in the Western media, and because I describe the ideas and policies of China's leaders, I am asked whether I try to be "balanced" about China. I say, "No. I do *not* try to be balanced about China. I try to tell the truth about China." (If I were commentating during the Cultural Revolution, I would not want to be "balanced.")

Now, maybe I differ with some over what is truth about China, maybe I do not have all the facts about China, but I really do try to tell the truth.

Endnotes

1 CNBC - Xi Jinping vs. Hu Jintao, January 17, 2011 - http://classic.cnbc.com/id/15840232?
video=1749050647&play=1

2 This may have been a further distortion of the comment in the Wikileaks disclosures, attributed to a source in the U.S embassy, that Vice President Xi is "redder than red"—a typical foreign confusion in erroneously transforming personal patriotism into leftist ideology.

3 Dan Blumenthal, "China Humiliates Gates, Obama," The Weekly Standard, January 12, 2011.

4 American insensitivity and egocentric naïveté do not help. Ambassador James Sasser relates an incident from a 1997 congressional visit to Beijing. After a senior Chinese official briefed the delegation, he invited questions. "I just want to know," a Congressman inquired, "if you've accepted Jesus Christ as your personal savior." The Chinese official, Sasser recalls, looked stunned. (Robert M. Hathaway, "The Lingering Legacy of Tiananmen," *Foreign Affairs*, September/October 2003.)

5 *Closer To Truth: Cosmos, Consciousness, God*—www.closertotruth.com. Prior season, *Closer To Truth: Science, Meaning and the Future*—www.pbs.org/closertotruth. I have argued how a scientific way of thinking can influence global society and bring together people with disparate ethnicities, religions or politics ("Science as Democratizer," *American Scientist* magazine, September-October 2003).

6 I've lectured on mergers and acquisitions for the State Economic and Trade Commission, on political philosophy and the American experience at the China Executive Leadership [Party] Academy Pudong, and on Western religion at the State Administration of Religious Affairs. I created a China-U.S. workshop on "Scientists' Social and Ethical Responsibilities" between the American Association for the Advancement of Science and the China Association for Science and Technology. I've spoken at a conference on Taoism (*Daodejing*) focusing on science and religion. I've had several co-productions with China Central Television (CCTV) and five of my books have been published in China (*Investment Banking Study*, published in 1996, was said to be the first of its kind published on the Chinese mainland).

7 The Chinese Academy of Social Sciences is the leading national think tank housing more than 3,000 scholars and researchers.

8 Robert Lawrence Kuhn, *Zhongguo 30 Nian: Renlei Shehui De Yici Weida Bian Qian* (China 30 Years: A Great Transformation of Human Society), Horizon Media/Shanghai Century Publishing Group, 2008.

9 Author's meeting with Liu Yunshan, Beijing, December 2007, June 2008.

10 Zhao Ziyang, *Prisoner of the State: The Secret Journal of Premier Zhao Ziyang* (Simon & Schuster, 2009). There were reports that Du withdrew his support for the book, claiming that both the title and the preface of the English book lack objectivity and misrepresented Zhao's original intention.

11 In China, the political labels "left" and "right" mean the reverse of what they do in America with respect to "conservative" or "liberal" views. In America, "left" is liberal and "right" is conservative. In China, "leftists" are "conservatives," whose political views skew towards traditional socialist or Communist ways along with the political controls to keep them such. On the other hand, "rightists" are "liberals," more inclined to the principles and policies of the free-market economies and open democratic governments of the West. If one doesn't know the linguistic landscape, one can be facing the wrong direction and not even realize it.

Part I

Guiding Principles

Pride

Observing New China's 60th anniversary in 2009, Westerners marveled at the country's momentous changes. The obvious improvement in the standard of living of most Chinese, and the economic strength of the country, is evidenced in virtually every city and town. The diversity in dress and entertainment, the new flexibility in sexual behaviors—even the increase in divorce and legions of lawyers—all speak to the uncontestable fact that China is no longer the drab, monolithic society so ingrained in Western consciousness.

But even more fundamental is the change in outlook and spirit. One need only speak with Chinese people in the major cities to sense their newfound self-confidence and enthusiasm. They tell you plainly what they think—whether how to make money, or their dislike of government bureaucracy, or of the omnipresent air pollution. They give you their opinions bluntly—you don't have to ask twice—and they don't look over their shoulder before they speak out.

The change in the economic lives of the Chinese people has been staggering: Since 1978, China's GDP per capita has increased more than 40 fold. Arguably, the Chinese economy is now the second largest in the world,[1] and in another 30 years it may well be the largest. Average salaries are low by Western standards, but prices are also low, so that most people, even rural farmers, are living far better than the income statistics indicate. Over a billion people have access to television; three decades ago only 10 million did. In 1978 there were 200 foreign companies doing business in China; today there are hundreds of thousands. In fact, China absorbs more foreign investment than any country in the world except the United States. Chinese corporations are selling internet routers and refrigerators competitively around the world and Chinese entrepreneurs are building strong private businesses on the Internet. The old communist ideal of the glorious masses in class struggle is dead and buried. It has been replaced by something new and dynamic, an economic engine fueled by personal dreams and national pride.

Although economic improvement—higher standard of living, financial success, luxuries of life—are goals in every country, there is extra energy to achieve these goals in China. The motivation goes beyond material benefits: the Chinese want to show the world that they are in every way a modern nation and in every sense a great power. If this demonstration requires material wealth, technological prowess, military strength, a world-class aerospace program, then these are what they must and will achieve. In every sphere of human endeavor, from business to culture, Olympic athletes to space *taikonauts*, music and art to modern science and ancient philosophy, China seeks its fair share of world leaders. For example, in every industry of importance, China's leaders expect its corporations to become among the largest and most successful in the world. When Zhang Ruimin, CEO of household electronics giant Haier, stated in the middle 1990s that Haier's goal was to become a leading global company, foreign analysts yawned or smirked. Today, Haier is the world's second largest manufacturer of refrigerators (after Whirlpool), among the top 1000 manufacturers in the world, and its brand name has joined the prestigious list of the World's 100 Most Recognizable Brands. China is proud that the stock market capitalizations of its companies in energy, telecommunications and banking are among the largest in the world.

The roots of this pride go deep, to the visceral feelings of a people whose civilization of culture and technology led the world for centuries, only to be humiliated and oppressed by foreign invaders and then stymied and scourged by domestic tyrants.

"To understand our dedication to revitalize the country, one has to appreciate the pride that Chinese people take in our glorious ancient civilization," says China Vice President Xi Jinping. "This is the historical driving force inspiring people today to build the nation. The Chinese people made great contributions to world civilization and enjoyed long-term prosperity," he explains. "Then we suffered over a century of national weakness, oppression and humiliation. So we have a deep self-motivation to build our country. Our commitment and determination is rooted in our historic and national pride."[2]

Xi is at pains to stress that pride in China's recent achievements should not engender complacency: "Compared with our long history, our speed of development is not so impressive, because it took thousands of years for us to reach where we are now. We need to assess ourselves objectively," he emphasizes. "But no matter what, China's development, at least in part, is driven by patriotism and pride."

Li Yuanchao, head of the Party Organization Department, which is responsible for all high-level personnel appointments in the Party, government and large state-owned enterprises, emphasizes that it's China's national spirit that has motivated people to keep looking ahead and seeking further progress.

"Although the Chinese people are not as wealthy as Westerners, and China lags behind developed countries in many areas such as technology, social systems, and environmental protection," Li says, "I am confident that the Chinese people as a whole are very positive about their country's development and have confidence in their future. We have a sense of adventure and pride and we are ambitious to build our society."[3]

★ ★ ★

My first lesson in how deep such pride runs came in 1992. I had arrived in China for the first time three years earlier, in February of 1989, about six weeks before students began gathering in Tiananmen Square, but it would be years before I would begin to understand what was really going on here. After the tragic events of June 4, I determined not to return to China. About 15 months later, however, my mind was changed by appeals for support from reform-minded friends. When I did come back, I came to know Professor Bi Dachuan, an academic (mathematician) and defense analyst with quick wit and trenchant criticism. It was a time of repressed freedoms: the post-Tiananmen conservatism was in its ascendancy; if anyone in Beijing wanted to talk politics—when confiding to foreign friends, for example—they would insist on leaving their offices or homes and walk around in the open air or drive around in moving cars.

That's what made Bi stand out. Even then, he remained cavalier in his criticism of the government, the planned economy, classical communism. His comments were slyly comical, delivered with a mischievous glint of impolitic cynicism. Bi was certainly not alone among the Chinese intelligentsia in disparaging the government, but I was nonplussed when he offered these barbed witticisms in much-too-public situations, such as when addressing a dozen of his professional colleagues. How could he get away with such an unbridled tongue, I wondered?

Although I didn't at the time know him well, I couldn't recall Bi having said anything complimentary about China's political or economic system—and so, one fine day on a remote hilltop outside Beijing, I felt secure in applauding the American action in preventing the 2000 Olympics from being held in Beijing. This was how the U.S. government intended to punish the Chinese government for its armed response in Tiananmen Square. Bi and I were alone, and I was fully expecting his hearty support of America's blackball.

His response left me speechless.

"You stupid Americans," he scolded me sharply. "You insult China and you offend me!" He continued, unsmiling. "How stupid and insulting," he said again, glaring at me as though I myself had cast the blackballing vote. "How stupid of your country and how insulting to mine!"

It was a verbal stinging I shall not forget, and a searing tutorial of what really counts in China. Don't allow the internal disputes to cloud your vision. Don't assume that derogations of the government, or of communist ideology, indicate a diminished patriotism. The pride of the Chinese people—pride in their country, heritage, history; pride in their economic power, personal freedoms, and international importance; and, yes, pride in their growing military strength—is a fundamental characteristic that one encounters over and over and over again. As I see it, Pride is the first of the guiding principles that energizes a great deal of what is happening in China today.

★ ★ ★

Chinese pride invites itself into diverse policy debates. Rarely does it determine decisions, but often it influences them. "It involves the pride of the nation," is how former Information Minister Zhao Qizheng characterizes Chinese advances in science and technology. Consider China's spaceflight programs, including the *Shenzhou* manned spacecraft and lunar missions, an apparent luxury in a country still grappling with widespread poverty, but enthusiastically supported by an overwhelming majority of the people. Why? Pride.

Although President Hu Jintao stresses how science and technology drives China's development, he also radiates pride in China's renewed contributions to humanity. Speaking just after the successful return of China's first manned space voyage, *Shenzhou* V, in 2003, Hu said, "Our science-based civilization is due to the efforts of all nations and is a sterling demonstration of human creativity . . . spurred by the interaction and integration of the world's diverse wisdom and cultures." Hu asserted that, over time, each great civilization has contributed to the global advancement of science and technology, and that history shows that the active, free-flowing exchange of information among civilizations promotes such advancement.[4] Hu attends ceremonies for each of China's manned space flights.

Zhao Qizheng also points with pride to the fact that, during World War II, China was the only country in the world that gave shelter for Jews seeking to escape the Nazi Holocaust in Europe. While even America and Britain refused entry for Jewish refugees, China, though enduring severe tribulation at the hands of the Japanese, opened its doors so that more than 20,000 Jews could come to safety in Shanghai, where they became known to history as the "Shanghai Jews."

Moreover, consider the long-standing internal debate over whether China should enter the World Trade Organization (WTO). Although the contesting views pitted the economic benefits of foreign investment against the heightened competitive pressure from foreign companies, an underlying motivation was that China belongs in the WTO because China is a great nation and must be counted as such.

This quest for pride is woven into the fabric of much of China's modern history. In the West, for example, the Korean War is remembered as a wretched, miserable conflict, which epitomized the bleak years of the Cold War. For many in China, however, the same conflict is viewed as a crucible of national resuscitation and revival. After three years of hurling wave after wave of human sacrifices, China managed to end the war in a stalemate. It was an exceptional achievement. The United States, the greatest military

President Hu Jintao presents medals to Chinese *taikonauts* after the successful completion of the Shenzhou VII manned space mission (which included China's first extra-vehicle activity) at the Great Hall of the People in Beijing (November 7, 2008; Xinhua News Agency, Ma Zhancheng).

power in the world, which less than ten years earlier had vanquished both Germany and Japan, was battled to a draw – grit and determination, in the Chinese view, having thwarted far superior military technology.

Though "victory" came at a tremendous cost—700,000 to one million Chinese lives were lost,[5] including that of Mao Zedong's own son—for many Chinese citizens, the war seemed a turning point. The war was all about national sovereignty and national pride. The treaty ending the Korean War was the first in over a century which was not "unequal." Chinese credited the Communists, particularly Mao, with the country's reemergence as a world power. After interminable years of subjugation and humiliation, China finally had a unified and independent government, not beholden to foreigners. Though Sino-American relations had hit an all-time low, China had stood up with pride.

Such pride was in evidence again 45 years later, as China celebrated the end of British rule in Hong Kong, and its return to Chinese sovereignty. For 925 days before July 1, 1997, a huge "countdown board" in Tiananmen Square ticked off the seconds to the historic event. As the Chinese flag reached the top of the flagpole eight seconds after midnight, the precise time determined in painstaking negotiations, joyous pandemonium broke out across China as huge crowds screamed, jumped and

President Jiang Zemin with Prince Charles at the ceremony of Hong Kong's repatriation to China, with UK Prime Minister Tony Blair (right) and Chinese Premier Li Peng (left) (July 1, 1997; Xinhua News Agency).

danced, waving Chinese and Hong Kong flags. Colonial humiliation of 155 years had come to an end.

In 2006, Hong Kong's stock market surpassed New York as the world's second most active board (after London) to float initial public offerings. The largest new stock listings were companies from China.

If the stock exchange in Hong Kong, with its legions of investment bankers wearing elegant tailored suits, seem from a different planet than the killing fields of Korea, with its legions of exhausted soldiers wearing filthy military fatigues, they draw together under the rubric of Chinese pride.

★ ★ ★

Sovereignty exemplifies Chinese pride. Even the Soviet Union, China's fraternal-socialist-communist big brother, found out the hard way that if China's pride as an independent nation was at stake, there was no compromise. In 1958, the Soviets proposed building a long-wave transceiver station in China and establishing a joint fleet. Mao rejected both.

China's fractious relationship with Moscow—in part because of a common and disputed border running for thousands of miles—exploded in the 1960s. One of the untold stories of this under-reported hot war was how Soviet tanks were unstoppable in their advance into Chinese territory until

Israel, in highly secret arrangements while China still refused to recognize the fledgling Jewish state, provided the Chinese with special weaponry to destroy those Soviet tanks and defend their own tanks.[6]

In 1963, when the United States, the Soviet Union and Britain signed the Partial Test Ban Treaty, China denounced the "act of hegemony," and took action to break the tripartite nuclear monopoly. The mushroom cloud rising into the desert sky in northwest China in October 1964 startled the world, revealing the rapid progress of China's nuclear technology and affirming the country's determination to safeguard its sovereignty and independence.

China's pride in its nuclear achievements, like the pride in its aerospace enterprises, made American accusations of Chinese nuclear spying, particularly in 1999,[7] all the more galling. The underlying affront was not so much the spying charge itself but the implication that China was incapable of developing advanced technology on its own. To the Chinese, an independent nuclear and aerospace capability makes the unmistakable assertion that China will never again be humiliated by foreigners, that China will control its own destiny, and that if there is to be peace in the world, an independent China must help guarantee it.

★ ★ ★

China did of course eventually win the right to stage the Olympics. On July 13, 2001, when the International Olympic Committee would announce the name of the host city of the 2008 Summer Games, an estimated 400,000 expectant Beijingers gathered in Tiananmen Square, hoping to celebrate victory. As China Central Television flashed the message "We Have Won" in triumphant red characters across the screen, a roar of excitement rumbled through the square and from there across the city. People of all walks of life celebrated by throwing flowers, waving flags, and banging on drums and gongs, while cars zoomed along Beijing's main thoroughfares honking incessantly.

Six-and-a-half years later, in early 2008, Chinese pride assumed a different form, one born of nationalism and anger, as the Olympic Torch began its traditional journey from the birthplace of the games in Olympia, Greece, and, carried by 22,000 torch bearers, traveled in a worldwide relay some 137,000 kilometers (85,000 miles) on its way to Beijing. After riots erupted in Tibet in March, and the Chinese government sent in troops, highly visible protests dogged the Olympic Torch in cities along its route, changing the character of the relay from celebratory to confrontational.

The backlash was sharp and swift. Chinese citizens throughout society were infuriated by what they deemed to be the hijacking of their Olympics for political purposes, and, significantly, by what they saw as intent to embarrass China. Chinese chat rooms were set aglow with fiery indignation. Counter-protests by overseas Chinese and Chinese nationals, largely students, ignited spontaneously, heated by the incandescent fury of national pride.

One of the torchbearers in the Paris stage of the relay, a 27-year-old amputee and Paralympics fencer named Jin Jing, became a national hero when she was assaulted by supporters of Tibetan independence. Defending the Olympic flame from her wheelchair—she determined to hold it herself – she was bruised and scraped when protesters tried to extinguish the torch.

"I felt no pain from the scratches and injury on my right leg, I would die to protect the torch," Jin Jing said, adding, "I was moved to tears seeing so many Chinese students waving national flags and singing the national anthem along the route."[8]

Hailed by the Chinese media as the "Smiling Angel in Wheelchair," images of Jin Jing protecting the torch and smiling in her wheelchair were splashed across front pages all over China; when she returned to Beijing, she was treated to a hero's welcome.

Some Chinese reacted to the events in Paris by organizing a boycott of Carrefour, the large French retailer. Any foreigner imagining the boycott to have been instigated by the Chinese government could not have spoken with ordinary, normally nonpoliticized people (including my young assistant, who never before had protested anything but who was determined to protest against France).

Jin Jing herself remained calm, saying she didn't want her compatriots to boycott Carrefour. She called on the Chinese people to "handle the situation rationally," adding that "most French people are very friendly."

That national pride can turn ugly was confirmed when Jin Jing's desire to defuse the crisis drew sharp rebuke from Chinese radicals on the Internet, some of whom even branded her a "traitor," perhaps the ugliest accusation in China. Nonetheless, because she had burnished the pride of China, she remained a national icon.

* * *

At 8 minutes after 8:00 pm on the 8th day of the 8th month in the 8th year of the new millennium – the number "8" being a propitious number in Chinese (it sounds similar to the word meaning "prosper" or "wealth")—the Beijing Olympics, the most anticipated in history, opened in spectacular fashion.[9] With dramatic displays of breathtaking pyrotechniques and elaborate traditional performances involving 15,000 performers and 29,000 fireworks, China showcased for the world its vision and its artistry, rooted in its 5,000-year civilization and symbolizing its contemporary re-emergence.

Accompanying President Hu Jintao, who rose from his seat to wave to the cheering crowds, was a star-studded audience, including U.S. President George W. Bush, who had resisted political pressure to boycott the opening ceremony. "It would be an affront to the Chinese people," said Bush, who became the first U.S. president to attend an Olympics abroad.

More than 80 foreign heads of state or governments attended the games, a new Olympic record. Prior to the opening ceremony, President Hu held

President Hu Jintao announces the opening of the 29th Summer Olympic Games in Beijing (August 8, 2008; Xinhua News Agency, Lan Hongguang).

separate meetings with 11 foreign leaders, each for about 20 minutes. Calling for "the building of a harmonious world featuring lasting peace and common prosperity," Hu said "The world has never needed mutual understanding, mutual toleration and mutual cooperation as much as it does today."

The ceremony was presided over by acclaimed film director Zhang Yimou. With his early, gritty films *Red Sorghum*, *To Live*, and *Raise the Red Lantern*, Zhang portrayed the resilience of the Chinese people in the face of want and suffering and in enduring all manner of adversities. His later, lavishly photographed films *Hero* and *House of Flying Daggers*, set new standards in cinematography.

Critics accused Zhang of "selling out" by supporting the Chinese government in its Olympic efforts. Others, though, believed it was not Zhang who had changed, but China itself, in that reform and opening-up had transformed the country. For Zhang, the Olympics were all about patriotism and pride—pride in Chinese civilization and artistry, pride in China.

★ ★ ★

When the Chinese edition of this book was published, the concept of Pride as a guiding principle struck a resonant chord and this surprised me. Several Chinese political leaders and theorists considered my four guiding principles—Pride, Stability, Responsibility, Vision—a helpful framework for seeing themselves in a fresh light. One minister said that although China's leaders do not think in these terms themselves it was useful to see how a foreigner would try to plumb the depths of their motivations and behaviors.

Another minister, Party theorist Leng Rong, was intrigued that Pride was my first guiding principle, a word that in translation connotes dignity and patriotism. He noted that while other countries, such as India, could achieve industrialization by being colonized by Western powers, China could not. The only time China could industrialize was, first, after it had achieved political independence, and second, when the country itself determined to take aggressive, pro-active steps to reform and open-up. He attributed this failure of forced, colonized industrialization, and this success of voluntary self-modernization, to the pride or dignity of the Chinese people, especially in light of their 5,000-year civilization.

★ ★ ★

It was coincidence that the year of the Olympics in Beijing, 2008, also marked the 30th anniversary of the beginning of reform and opening-up in China. Well, perhaps not complete coincidence, because the two historic events were not unrelated. Were it not for reform, with all its challenges and frustrations, triumphs and tragedies, these Olympics would not have been possible and likely none at all.

But to the Chinese people, thrilled by the stirring victories of their athletes and beaming at the artistic magnificence of the ceremonies, history was hardly on anyone's mind. And that would have been just fine with Deng Xiaoping, who had initiated reform so that China could once again become a great nation, with its people increasingly enjoying life and the country increasingly respected in the world, a renewed China in which all the Chinese people could take pride.

Endnotes

1 Based on a calculation using Purchasing Power Parity (PPP), a system that normalizes prices of goods and services relative to income or gross domestic product. PPP helps explain how such significant improvements in Chinese standards of living are supported by such seemingly low per capita incomes.
2 Author's meeting with Xi Jinping, Hangzhou, March 2006.
3 Author's meeting with Li Yuanchao, Beijing, December 2007.

4 *China Daily*, April 19, 2006. President Hu Jintao's opening address of the Third World Academy of Sciences, Beijing, October 16, 2003 - http://beijingtwas.sdb.ac.cn/meeting/20anniversary/200409030011.html

5 According to official sources in China, 170,000 lives were lost.

6 Author's communication in Beijing.

7 Accusations against China's nuclear spying were epitomized by the so-called Cox Report. It was released in declassified, redacted version in May 1999, engendering much disputation between China and America.

8 "Handicapped Jin receives hero's welcome for protecting Olympic torch in Paris." Xinhua, April 10, 2008.

9 *People's Daily*, August 8, 2008.

2

Stability

To understand how China's leaders think, if Pride is the first guiding principle, Stability comes a close second. Together they underlie much of what happens in China. If one appreciates just these two overarching themes, and can recognize their variations and expressions, one already knows a good deal about what drives this nation and informs its leaders.

If stability is the watchword, a good part of the reason can be traced back to the Cultural Revolution, that devastating decade (1966–1976) when political madness created social turmoil and personal torment, when self-inflicted national mutilation turned the entire country inward against itself, pitting students against teachers, children against parents and friend against friend.

Initiated by Mao Zedong in the twilight of his mercurial career, the Cultural Revolution was his sad and vainglorious attempt to re-revolutionize China and reaffirm his own potency and preeminence. Begun as an effort to ferret out elitist elements from society and expunge alleged capitalists from the Communist Party, it was quickly usurped by radicals and self-aggrandizers, and dissolved into colossal chaos which nearly destroyed the country. Ultra-leftists concocted a Mao-centered personality cult in order to assert their political dominance. Universities were closed; intellectuals and professionals were exiled to farms; children were urged to denounce their parents; and young Red Guards, waving their little red books of Mao's quotations, stood in judgment over everyone in authority.

A frenzy of terror and anarchy paralyzed the country. The human toll was horrific; torture was rampant; hundreds of thousands died violently. Almost everyone of accomplishment in China suffered. Liu Shaoqi, the president of China, and Deng Xiaoping, the general secretary of the Party, were both purged. Accused of advocating capitalism and opposing Mao's policies—the famine-causing Great Leap Forward in particular—their "crime" was supposedly that they gave individual farmers some freedom to own land. In truth, Mao feared that they, along with other high-level Party leaders, no longer supported him, and he wanted an excuse to be rid of them.

It is impossible to overstate the searing memory of the Cultural Revolution—the accusations, denunciations, castigations, humiliations. I have not met a single educated person over 50 years old in China who was not emotionally scarred by the experience. That all of China, the entire country, was caught in chaotic thrall to Mao's political extremism remains an ever-present symbol of what China's leaders are determined to never let happen again. To understand China, one must understand the Cultural Revolution.

★ ★ ★

Professor Bi Dachuan, from whom I first began to appreciate the deep meaning of Chinese pride, is a case in point. Puzzled as to how, in those cautious, conservative months after June 4, 1989, he could remain so outspoken, I asked him about the Cultural Revolution. Bi said that when the ideological madness began he had been a graduate student. Like all his colleagues, he was forced to abandon his studies as Mao sought to purify communism.

"What happened to you?" I asked. "They put me into a room with other scholars and we were forced to criticize each other," he replied dryly.

"For how long?" I enquired. "Sixteen hours a day." "For how many days?" "Seven years."

I fell silent, stunned. Bi continued. "My suffering wasn't special. There were millions like me. Many endured worse; some didn't survive. But I wouldn't let them imprison my soul, steal my life. With great difficulty I continued my studies at night. Every night, all night, I would study, mostly mathematics. During the days, of course, I would fall asleep in the endless self-criticism sessions, and they would beat me up—with glee. But I was determined not to let them stop my learning. After all that they did to me then, what more can anyone do to me now?"

That's how I came to realize why Professor Bi was so seemingly nonchalant in his outspokenness. He had survived hell, and what hadn't killed him had made him stronger. And he was no renegade: Bi had contributed to China's national defense, and was no proponent of Western-style democracy for China.

It seems a paradox. Most Westerners assume that if one rejects communist-style central planning then one must espouse Western-style democracy. In China that is not the case. Indeed, such reasoning seems one-dimensional and untextured to many Chinese, even to those who seek fundamental change in the political system. Many Chinese intellectuals believe, in accord with China's leaders, that collective rights trump individual rights, and that improving standards of living for all citizens is a higher good to allowing greater freedom of speech for some citizens.

This is the legacy of the Cultural Revolution: a desire, in fact an obsession, with stability—a deep-seated need for social order and an almost paranoid fear of turmoil and chaos. The nightmare memories are seared in the collective national soul and cannot be eradicated. A recurrence in any form must be prevented. Nothing good can happen without stability—no economic growth, no social progress. This is what one hears over and over again in China; it is hard to overstate the importance of this concern.

Ironically, the obsession with stability has led to the return of the term "class struggle"—the classic epitome of Marxist ideology and frenzied goal of Mao Zedong's politics—as a core concern of China's leaders, though neither Marx nor Mao would recognize current incarnations of the emotionally burdened term.

Today China's leaders recognize that different classes are an undeniable fact. Thus the first new use of "class struggle" is as part of a subtle domestic campaign to recognize the existence and persistence of classes as an inextinguishable reality (at least for the foreseeable future). The second use of "class struggle" deals with how to handle the severe inequalities in China, which is broadly recognized as China's most vexing problem. Thirty years ago, when Mao's death mercifully ended the Cultural Revolution and China's ten-year descent into self-immolating political turmoil finally finished, there were no classes in China—everyone was equal, equally poor. Even a decade ago, classes, the natural and inevitable result of reform anywhere, were so sensitive a subject in China that senior leaders, even among themselves, felt uncomfortable discussing this taboo.

Not so today. Although standards of living have risen dramatically, the rise has been a sharply uneven one. Deng Xiaoping recognized that some people would have to get rich first, though he couldn't have imagined the extent of today's disparities. Some areas and sectors, largely coastal and urban, have become highly developed and relatively rich; others, mostly inland and rural, have experienced slower development and become relatively poor.

Even though China's rural population, which is about 60% of the entire population, is substantially better off in absolute terms, in relative terms, compared to the urban population, it is not. And human beings are wont to judge their circumstances not in comparison to what they had in the past but in comparison to what others have in the present. As China's economy continues to grow, and economic imbalances continue to escalate, social unrest continues to increase. If instability would ever again visit its chaotic opprobrium on China it would come at the hands of those who desire better standards of living, not of those who seek Western-style democracy.

Thus the primary goal of China's leaders, over the next few decades, is to enhance standards of living of all Chinese to decent levels. Building a "moderately well-off society" is President Hu Jintao's grand goal, which is expressed by his guiding philosophical slogan of "Harmonious Society." Harmony is needed *because* there are now classes, caused by endemic disparities, which naturally generate resentment.

To achieve such harmony, China must continue its economic growth, which, China's leaders know, cannot happen without the wealth-creating vision and energy of risk-taking entrepreneurs. This is another reason why confrontational "class struggle," Communism's traditional tenet, is recognized as archaic and counterproductive.

At the same time China's leaders earnestly believe that due to China's huge population, which is still largely rural and poor, and also for historical and cultural reasons, the Communist Party—which is increasingly referred to simply as the "Ruling Party"—must maintain its monopoly on power, in order to guide such a vast and disparate people to material well being and personal freedoms.

Yet these days China's leaders also go out of their way to emphasize the kind of political reform that, while not Western-style democracy, does provide for increasing transparency in government; collective decision-making (making dictatorship and irrational leadership impossible); more representative selection (if not election) of CPC officials; and increasing the powers of people's congresses, national and local. These political reforms, which are also designed to ensure social stability, will, they say, lead to "China's own kind of democracy consistent with the historical, cultural, economic, and social needs of 1.3 billion Chinese people."

★ ★ ★

When ethnic violence flared in West China's Xinjiang Uyghur Autonomous Region (2009) between Uyghur Turkic Muslims and Han Chinese, President Hu interrupted his participation in the high-profile G8 economic summit in Italy and returned home to deal personally with the problem. Though the world economic crisis was severe, China's leaders considered the social turmoil to be the higher priority. Ethnic conflict was obviously inimical to national harmony, but the more worrying threat was that, with information impossible to control and reports of the violence gripping the nation's consciousness, the social virus of mob action could spread to other disaffected groups and classes, such as unemployed migrant workers, and catalyze national chaos. Overwhelming force was brought to bear—upwards of 20,000 armed police saturated Urumqi, Xinjiang's capital and the epicenter of the clashes—restoring stability, if not harmony.

Internationally, China's leaders see another kind of "class struggle" which could undermine the nation's stability—a determined "class" of foreign-based anti-China foes made up of those in politics, academia and the media who, they believe, wish China ill and "struggle" for the country's instability and collapse. (A prime example were the riots, or uprisings, by the Uyghur Muslims and the Tibetans, both of which were characterized by Chinese leaders as "violent crime instigated and organized by the three forces of terrorism, separatism and extremism at home and abroad.")

Thus China's leaders feel forced, as a countermeasure, to become more defensive, resulting in more human rights restrictions, media control and military development—which, of course, only serve to reinforce the charges of anti-China factions.

A senior Chinese leader told me that George W. Bush's absolute belief in imposing American-style democracy on other nations was analogous to Mao Zedong's absolute belief in fomenting Marxist-style revolutions in other nations. The world today, China's leaders believe, is more complicated, which is why President Hu calls for a "Harmonious World," which recognizes that differences in local conditions and governance not only exist but cannot be eliminated. Now it's China not America, this leader emphasized (while Bush was president), which has the more flexible, rational, realistic vision of the world.

For President Hu, as for all of China's leaders since the Cultural Revolution, stability is a recurrent theme. Whether in stressing political stability as a key factor for driving China's economic growth, or price stability as essential for world energy markets, Hu is consistently on message. China is now tied tightly to the global economy, and international instability—such as the global financial crisis—could cause domestic disruptions. "The past 30 years of reform and opening-up have told us that China cannot develop itself in isolation from the world," Hu said in 2008. "And it is equally true that the world cannot enjoy prosperity or stability without China. . . . China's future is more closely linked with the future of the world than ever before."

For international leaders—in particular America's—it's important to appreciate the thought patterns and motivations of China's leaders, who see the inequality in the world, both within national borders and across them, as the single most important problem to be solved. The stability of the world, and hence its peace and prosperity, depends on it.

It may seem simplistic to reduce one's analysis of an entire nation—an entire people—to two basic themes. Nonetheless, if one characterizes contemporary China by the twin themes of Pride and Stability, the first two of our four guiding principles, one can explain a great deal. But to know how China's leaders think, we must add two more guiding principles: Vision and Responsibility.

Responsibility

Responding to the tragic 2008 earthquake, President Hu Jintao made five trips – two to Sichuan, one each to Gansu, Shaanxi, Zhejiang and Hebei.

"Why did President Hu go to Zhejiang and Hebei," Politburo member Liu Yunshan asked rhetorically? "Those provinces weren't affected by the earthquake. He went to inspect the companies manufacturing tents and temporary housing for the tens of thousands of citizens who were made homeless. This exemplifies President Hu's sense of responsibility."

Later in 2008, facing the gravest global financial crisis since the Great Depression, President Hu was realistic, determined and confident. "The global financial crisis has noticeably increased the uncertainties and factors for instability in China's economic development," he said, stressing that China "must first and foremost run its own affairs well." China's best contribution to world stability was to keep itself stable.

In November 2008, China announced a huge economic package of looser credit, tax cuts and a massive economic stimulus of RMB four trillion ($586 billion) to be spent over a two-year period to boost domestic demand.[1] Its size was unprecedented—equivalent to one-third of China's total fixed-asset investment in 2007 and about equal to *all* central and local government spending in 2006. The stimulus package—which would be spent on roads, railways, subways, airports (largely in less-developed provinces), subsidized housing, and communities destroyed in the Sichuan earthquake—was intended to catch attention and boost confidence.

And in March 2009, with the financial crisis exacting an increasingly harsh toll on China's economy and employment, President Hu and Premier Wen Jiabao, along with other senior leaders, spoke virtually in unison of "ensuring economic growth, people's well-being and social stability."[2]

Hu speaks often of the Party's responsibilities to the people. Reporting to the 17th Party Congress (2007), he catalogued areas for improvement: balanced development; socialist democracy, people's rights, social equity and justice; cultural development and ethical quality; social programs (particularly education); and a culture of conservation.

Fulfilling these responsibilities require that China's economy continues to grow, and Hu laid out the Party's strategy: make China an innovative country; accelerate economic transformation through science and technology; boost consumer demand; build a "new socialist countryside;" improve conservation of energy, resources, ecology and environment, and enhance sustainable development; improve the modern market system and its legal safeguards; increase the opening of China's economy, including taking further steps to go global.

★ ★ ★

Western criticism of President Hu, particularly regarding human rights, often misses his commitment to addressing China's multifaceted problems. Hu's pragmatic, non-ideological agenda has three core values—maintaining social stability to further economic development; instituting social fairness and rectifying imbalances; and sustaining Chinese culture in order to secure national sovereignty and enrich people's lives.

China's leaders' sense of responsibility is heightened by the stark facts of an increasingly bimodal society—the poorest 10% of China's citizens earn

President Hu Jintao and former President Jiang Zemin at the 4th Plenary Session of the 16th CPC Central Committee, when Jiang Zemin retired as chairman of the CPC Central Military Commission and Hu Jintao became chairman, thus completing the transition of power from Jiang Zemin to Hu Jintao (September 19, 2004; Xinhua News Agency, Li Xueren).

only 1.4% of total income, whereas the wealthiest 10% control 45% of total assets.[3] In theory, China's rural population is about 800–900 million, though estimates of China's "floating population" of migrant workers are about 150–200 million or more—no one knows for sure—with about two-thirds working within their home provinces and about one-third moving to other provinces (mostly eastern-coastal).

In 1997 CNN reporter Andrea Koppel asked then President Jiang Zemin, "When you wake up in the morning, what weighs heaviest on your mind?"

"I usually go to bed quite late," Jiang replied, "and the biggest question of domestic affairs is how to provide enough food and clothing to the 1.2 billion Chinese people. How can we improve their lives? Regarding human rights, that is their right to subsistence. It would be difficult for a country which does not face the same kinds of conditions that we do to imagine . . . I am always thinking how to finally achieve the objective of common prosperity. This is always the most important task for us. Although I once studied higher mathematics, I still find it quite difficult to solve this equation."[4]

★ ★ ★

Leadership in China is bifurcated between the government and the Communist Party of China (CPC), though the Party controls the government. This is true at every level—national, provincial, municipality, county, towns and villages—and in large industrial enterprises too. The CPC operates, in essence, a parallel and controlling governance structure. It is headed by a general secretary (Hu Jintao), who is China's most senior leader; the National Party Congress, which convenes every five years, is the highest Party organ. The Central Committee (204 full members and 167 alternative members), elected by the National Party Congress, makes key decisions, such as electing the Politburo, the Standing Committee of the Politburo and the general secretary. Ultimate control over Party machinery resides with the Politburo Standing Committee, which currently consists of nine members, all with an equal vote, and is the highest authority in China. Day-to-day Party operations are managed by the six-person Secretariat, led by Vice President Xi Jinping.

A largely ceremonial but prestigious president is head of state (also Hu Jintao); predetermined by the Party, the candidate is formally elected to a five-year term by the National People's Congress, China's legislature. Government power resides with the State Council, which is comprised of a premier (Wen Jiabao), four vice premiers (of whom one, Li Keqiang, is executive Vice Premier), and five State councilors. All commissions and ministries of the central government, all 22 provinces, five autonomous regions, the Hong Kong and Macao Special Autonomous Regions, and four large municipalities—Beijing, Shanghai, Tianjin and Chongqing—report directly to the State Council.

In addition, China has another and unique representative body, the Chinese People's Political Consultative Conference (CPPCC), a legislative-type assembly that draws on diverse segments of Chinese society to advise the Communist Party in a "united front." Included are eight, small (so-called) "democratic" parties.

China's military forces, the People's Liberation Army (PLA), is commanded by the Central Military Commission (CMC), of which Hu Jintao is the chairman, thereby affirming civilian control of the military. (The precedent was set by a far-sighted Deng Xiaoping, when in 1989 he selected the newly appointed CPC General Secretary Jiang Zemin as CMC chairman, even though Jiang had had no prior military experience; Hu Jintao, similarly, had no prior military experience.)

Thus in China's governance structure, the most senior leader in the country is the general secretary of the CPC Central Committee (Hu Jintao)—and because the Party exercises monopoly control of national policy and of its implementation by the government, the general secretary has final authority for all matters of Party, State, government and military.

This structure undoubtedly gives cohesion to China's leadership, but it meant that, in the past, all real decision-making was carried out by the Party, with the government implementing the directives. (Even this process was more form than substance since leaders occupied parallel positions in both the Party and the government.) In recent years, however, there have been moves to limit the unconstrained exercise of power, such as by institutionalizing regular meetings of Party and government bodies. Although top leaders continue to hold dual positions, the government has assumed greater responsibility for true decision making. This trend, of greater separation between the Party and State, is expected to continue.

★ ★ ★

Westerners assume that although China has enjoyed substantial economic reform, it has undergone no political reform. This is not the case. China's leaders today feel responsible for making China's system more accountable to the people. Certainly, economic reform has been the priority, but political reform has been real and continuous, if cautious and methodical. Consider the beginning of relatively free direct elections in rural areas, the increasing (non-rubber stamp) power of the National People's Congress (NPC, the legislative assembly)[5] and provincial people's congresses, the enhanced role of the Chinese People's Political Consultative Conference (CPPCC, the advisory assembly)[6], mandatory retirement ages, and term limits (two five-year terms) for senior leaders. Political reform has occurred—though it's surely correct to say that much more is needed.

One leader argued that while permitting political freedoms prematurely led to the tragedy in Tiananmen Square in 1989, suppressing the will of the people today could lead to another tragedy. He noted that some Western pressure on China has been helpful, making leaders more aware of foreign social and political norms—China's integration into the world economic system has made its leaders more sensitive to world opinion—but he cautioned that China still needed to progress at its own pace on the road to democracy in order to avoid social disruption. Still, he cited as evidence of China's increasing democracy the now regular solicitation of public opinion during the legislative decision-making process.[7]

For example, the NPC held open hearings and requested public letters on two controversial proposed laws: protecting private property, and the appropriate threshold of income for taxation. (On the private property law alone, the government received over 20,000 letters.) Soliciting public opinion may be adapted from Western models, the official said, but it is configured to fit into the Chinese system.

★ ★ ★

Reflecting on China's leaders' sense of responsibility in 2006, then Zhejiang Party Secretary Xi Jinping said that even though after almost 30 years of reform and opening-up, "it's fair to say that we have achieved

Xi Jinping, Party secretary of Zhejiang Province (later Politburo Standing Member, vice president of China, secretary of the Secretariat, and president of the Central Party School), with Robert Lawrence Kuhn (Hangzhou, March 2006).

some successes," nevertheless "we should have a cautious appraisal of our accomplishments."[8] Xi told me that China's leadership cannot be satisfied with the status quo: "We should never overestimate our accomplishments or indulge ourselves in our achievements," he said. He called for China to aspire to "our next higher goal," and to appreciate "the gap between where we are and where we have to go." He described this as "a persistent and unremitting process."

The man who in less than two years would become China's vice president gave his analysis of how four generations of China's leaders had fulfilled their responsibilities. "As the founding father of the People's Republic, Chairman Mao Zedong led the Chinese people to overthrow the 'three big mountains' [imperialism, feudalism and bureaucratic-capitalism] and enabled them to stand on their own two feet," Xi said. "Mao aimed to build a strong socialist country through a new democratic and socialist revolution."

"Under Deng Xiaoping's leadership," Xi continued, "the new era of reform and opening-up was ushered in, and the 'three-step' strategy was put forward: One: solve the problems of food and clothing shortages [by doubling the 1980 GDP]; two: realize a comfortable life for the people [by quadrupling the 1980 GDP by 2000, a goal achieved by 1995]; three, complete the nation's modernization [raising per-capita GDP to the level of an intermediate developed country, and achieving a fairly well-off life for the people]."

"Under President Jiang Zemin's leadership," said Xi, "the important theory of the 'Three Represents' articulated the CPC's historic and modernized mission. And under President Hu Jintao's leadership," he concluded, "the CPC is promoting the significant strategy of the 'Scientific Perspective on Development'."

Xi emphasized that the path of "socialism with Chinese characteristics" was the only way for China to achieve ultimate prosperity. But he insisted that the necessary emphasis on economic growth "must not overshadow the importance of all-round development. We must maintain the scientific development of the nation."

Xi explained that this meant pursuing growth based on actual conditions and coexisting with nature. "We should always go back to local realities and be responsive to local conditions by seeking truth from facts," he said. "Local realities are different realities. Before we implement new policies broadly, we always test them thoroughly at the grassroots level, gain experience and subject them to analysis."

He stressed that "people, not material, are what we focus on," and that the driving force of China's development is science and technology ("we attach great importance to innovation"). And he emphasized that "in order to realize a well-off society, the biggest challenge is rural development."

China's leaders "constantly draw theoretical lessons from our work," Xi said, "and use them to guide our practice." These are not "long-winded theoretical exercises," he added with a smile. "We don't discuss these matters all day long without making any decisions. Leaders are responsible to be decisive and action oriented, to make good things happen."

★ ★ ★

And there is evidence that China's citizens appreciate their leaders' emphasis on social responsibility. An extensive survey of the Chinese people conducted by the *Pew Global Attitudes Project* during spring 2008 reported that an astonishing 86% said they were "satisfied" with their country's direction, almost double the percentage who felt the same way in 2002. Of all the countries in which Pew conducted similar surveys, China had, by far, the largest percentage of satisfied citizens. (Australia was second at 61%; Britain was at 30%; America and Japan languished in the lowest quartile at 23%.) To many outside China, particularly in the media, who assume that the Chinese people are oppressed by an authoritarian state, these numbers were disconcerting.

Summarizing the report, Pew stated: "The Chinese people express extraordinary levels of satisfaction with the way things are going in their country and with their nation's economy. With more than eight-in-ten having a positive view of both, China ranks number one among 24 countries on both measures in the 2008 survey … Most Chinese citizens polled rate many aspects of their own lives favorably, including their family life, their incomes and their jobs."

At the same time, China's leaders are aware of the widening scope of their responsibility in an increasingly complex society. One put it this way: "We used to think that if we could build our economy and lift our people's standard of living, we would have fulfilled our responsibility. Today we realize while economic achievements are necessary they are not sufficient. Our responsibility goes further: we must provide our people with opportunities to develop culturally and spiritually, to participate in the political process in accord with China's maturing democracy, and to enjoy life in diverse ways befitting such a huge and variegated country. We are also responsible to work actively with other nations to construct a peaceful, prosperous, and harmonious world."[9]

Endnotes

1 Xinhua, November 9, 2008.
2 "Chinese leaders: Crisis also means opportunity," Xinhua, March 4–8, 2009.
3 "Inequality's Specter Haunts China," *Far Eastern Economic Review*, June 2008, pp. 19–22. In 2008, the government raised the poverty line so that those living under jumped from 25 million to 43 million. A 2005 report had 200 million poor people.
4 CNN, May 9, 1997.
5 The Constitution of the People's Republic of China established two national legislative bodies, the National People's Congress (NPC) and the Chinese People's Political Consultative Conference (CPPCC). The NPC "is the highest organ of state power" and it exercises the

legislative power of the state. The NPC is "elected [selected] from the provinces, autonomous regions and municipalities directly under the Central Government and of deputies elected from the armed forces. All minority nationalities are entitled to appropriate representation."

6 The CPPCC is a congress-like organization of diverse elements of Chinese society that "advises" the Communist Party in a "united front." Although the Communist Party dominates, included are eight, small (so-called) "democratic" parties; representatives of Hong Kong, Macau and Taiwan; leaders from culture, academics, science, industry, minorities, military, etc.

7 Author's communication in Beijing.

8 Author's meeting with Xi Jinping, Hangzhou, March 2006.

9 Author's communication with a senior leader, Beijing 2007.

Vision

Speaking to foreign journalists prior to the 2008 Beijing Olympics, President Hu summarized his vision: "The current dream of the Chinese people is to accelerate building a modern country, realize the great renaissance of the Chinese nation and, with the peoples of the world, seek peaceful progress, amicable co-existence and harmonious development."

Nevertheless, Hu acknowledged that "the problems and contradictions China will face in the next decades may be even more complicated and thorny than others . . . with its social structure and ideological setup also in major shake-up." Furthermore, he said, "the independent thinking of the general public, their newly developed penchant for independent choices and thus the widening gap of ideas among different social strata will pose further challenges to China's policy makers."[1]

Having traveled extensively in China, I came to appreciate why China's leaders speak, among themselves, of "twin nightmares." One is an economic nightmare of slowing growth (caused by international crises), exacerbated by energy shortfalls, unsustainable development and growing pollution. The other is a political nightmare of envy, tensions and fissures resulting from social disparities made blatant by the uncontrollable flow of information through media, mobile phones and internet.

China's fundamental problem is an addiction to growth perilously combined with a widening gap between rich and poor, imbalances that the Communist Party calls China's "most serious social problem." China *must* grow because, with hundreds of millions of rural residents needing to be brought into urban areas, along with millions of laid-off workers and young people entering the workforce, unemployment could threaten social stability. Optimum growth comes most efficiently from areas that are the most developed, and while such growth increases the vibrancy of the economy overall, it exacerbates the imbalances in society, which leads to social unrest.

Decades ago, when Chinese leaders ruled by edict, they could solve problems by fiat and force—peremptorily. Classic Communist techniques included commanding the centralized economy, instituting political mass movements, and whipping up emotional, xenophobic nationalism. But past patterns of dictatorial state behavior are no longer viable. Since China's economy is integrated into the world economy, and the private sector generates much of the country's growth, the government cannot wield arbitrary power without unacceptable disruptions. China is no longer exempt from the norms and practices of mature nations.

China's leaders now face the natural consequences of the country's prodigious economic transformation, which, along with China's historic success, have spawned complicated and interwoven issues—issues that are more complex than those faced by predecessors. China's leaders know that they must be flexible, innovate, consider diverse opinions, and make measured decisions. In a word, to navigate the uncertain waters of New China's third 30-year period, China's leaders must have Vision.

★ ★ ★

President Hu Jintao's overarching vision is summarized by three slogans relating to domestic issues—Harmonious Society, Scientific Perspective on Development and Putting People First—and by two slogans related to international issues—Peaceful Development and Harmonious World. To appreciate the power of Party slogans, which are designed to drive Party coherence under the senior leader, is to understand how Chinese leaders think in formulating and implementing policy.

A Harmonious Society is the goal, stressing social and political reform and seeking fairness and equity (if not equality) across China's diverse populations and geographies. Hu describes a Harmonious Society as one that "should feature democracy, the rule of law, equity, justice, sincerity, amity and vitality. . . . It will give full scope to people's talent and creativity, enable all the people to share the wealth brought by reform and development, and forge an ever closer bond between the people and government."

The Scientific Perspective on Development is the strategy for achieving this goal of a Harmonious Society; it calls for integrated sets of solutions to arrays of economic, social, political, and cultural problems—while always retaining economic development as the primary driver; it seeks the rectification of economic imbalances (rural-urban, coastal-inland), and includes sustainable development and environmental protection as requirements. It's a strategy of optimizing multiple objectives, as opposed to maximizing the single objective of economic growth to the detriment of other social goods.

Putting People First is the reason for setting the goal, the underlying motivation for creating a Harmonious Society. In this sense, Putting People First is the fundamental principle and on this foundation all else is built.

Peaceful Development signifies that no matter how strong China may become, it has learned the lessons of world history: it will remain a bulwark of stability in international affairs and will never threaten its neighbors.

A Harmonious World expresses Chinese leaders' view that the world is "multi-polar," its diversity should be appreciated, and the right of nations to choose their own systems is sacrosanct.

The political philosophy of China's leaders, generally expressed by such slogans, is frequently dismissed by foreigners, even by China scholars, as just so much empty rhetoric or mass manipulation. This is a mistake. Much can be learned from understanding and analyzing the slogans of China's leaders, which characterize the issues and attitudes of the times.

Chinese political slogans highlight those aspects of society which are deemed most problematic and sensitive, and which need change or improvement. Setting a Harmonious Society as China's goal recognizes that such is not the situation today – that disharmony, generated by disparities in standards of living, between urban and rural areas, coastal and inland, is China's most serious and pressing problem. Hu's approach to a Harmonious Society stresses economic metrics such as balancing disparities between regions, and includes social welfare, such as improved medical care, and political reform.

Hu's Scientific Perspective on Development is his primary policy-directing slogan. It embeds multiple social, political, and environmental objectives, while maintaining economic growth as the primary objective. Added to the CPC Constitution in October 2007—a major milestone for Hu—the Scientific Perspective on Development is the guiding principle for building a Harmonious Society. It is thereby a benchmark against which senior officials are judged.

When one speaks to such officials, particularly in the provinces, it's abundantly clear that they take these slogans seriously (even if foreign China experts don't). I remember a lackluster meeting with a leader of a western province, which instantly livened up when I inquired, "How are you applying President Hu's Scientific Perspective on Development?" Local leaders know their careers will depend on how well they implement these policies (not just talk about them). For example, the Scientific Perspective on Development sets sustainable development as a critical objective and thus senior administrators are evaluated based on measures of efficiency, such as increasing provincial gross domestic product (GDP) per unit of energy utilization. If Chinese officials take these slogans seriously in implementing policies, so should we in understanding them.[2]

★ ★ ★

How then does President Hu integrate these various concepts and principles which define how to build China? China's leaders recognize the impossibility of dictating a Harmonious Society from the top down with idealistic political principles, without also implementing it from the bottom up by integrating diverse segments of society.

The foundation is people: Putting People First is the characterizing core of the social contract between leaders and people. All is driven by what works for the Chinese people; all else serves to actualize and support this goal. (The Three Closenesses, another of Hu's policy-directing slogans, affirms the focus on people—Close to Reality, Close to Life, and Close to the People.)

Thus, economic growth is no longer an end in itself but is now rather the mechanism for Putting People First. Still, economic development must remain primary, with increased need for economic productivity, because only by means of efficient economic growth can all the social goals and programs be funded and facilitated. In keeping economic development foremost, Hu Jintao follows Deng Xiaoping and Jiang Zemin.

What's been added at this new stage of China's development is a host of other objectives for constructing a Harmonious Society, including: rebalancing wealth and standards of living among sectors and classes; an environment that minimizes pollution and allows people clean air to breathe and pure water to drink; access to quality medical treatment and care for the elderly; human rights, including the complete range of personal and social freedoms, such as freedom of personal speech (but not the complete range of political freedoms, such as freedom of speech or assembly); the rule of law; greater democratic participation in the process of governance; and equality for all citizens, rural and urban, in areas such as quality education and cultural activities (if not yet in the possession of material things).

Certainly, Deng Xiaoping and Jiang Zemin were equally intent on achieving these objectives, but China's backward condition in those days meant that they had to follow economic development, rather than be co-equal and co-temporal with it. Now, after three decades of economic development, all of these other objectives can be elevated in importance. But how best to achieve them at the same time? How best to integrate the process? That's the theoretical essence of the Scientific Perspective on Development, Hu's broad strategy of transformation.

The Scientific Perspective on Development is, in effect, an "optimizing mechanism" which handles multiple objectives simultaneously and seeks to generate the highest aggregate benefit of all objectives combined. If used properly, it will yield the greatest benefit of all objectives collectively, but is unlikely to yield the greatest benefit of any single objective individually. Its key components—economic development, cultural advancement, social fairness, sustainable development, environmental protection, reducing income disparity—must all work together. The reliance on science and technology, and on education, is crucial.[3] (Specific applications include a coastal county rejecting a battery factory because of pollution and the Tianjin Municipality's large investment in a world-class hospital with a Health Management Center to promote healthy lifestyles and prevent illness.)

China's leaders should be applauded for their new commitment to harmonize and democratize the country's diverse society. But no one should underestimate the complexity and difficulty of this next large leap in China's transformation. It behooves the international community to encourage China's leaders in their vision.

★ ★ ★

Yet in the international media, CPC Publicity head Liu Yunshan tells me, there is distortion. "We notice what is written in the foreign press about China," he says, "including 'biographies' of China's leaders published in Hong Kong, Taiwan and other countries. Most have slanted viewpoints and taken-out-of-context approaches; some show hostile partisanships that serve their own ideologies. Putting aside editorial opinion, the facts themselves are often fabricated."[4]

Minister Liu uses President Hu as a paragon of a visionary leader with an unpretentious style. "I am now serving my second term in the Politburo," Liu relates. "President Hu Jintao's character is modest and low key. I've always said that he was born with these traits." Many close associates admire Hu's management and control skills, personal rectitude, and clear vision for China—and that as a human being he is personally humble and always approachable.

Foreigners may not appreciate how the Politburo works. "Of course, we are a 'collective leadership' and practice 'democratic centralism'," Liu says of China's senior leadership, referencing the shared and common powers of Politburo members. But, he adds, "the role of the main leader is significant. And I can tell you," Liu continues, "that we all have the highest respect and admiration for President Hu—for his leadership, perspicacity and moral convictions—and so do 1.3 billion Chinese people."

According to Liu Yunshan, Hu Jintao has a "unique style" and "special way of thinking," which are "naturally expressed through his personal philosophies, ideas and policies—People-oriented [Putting People First],

Liu Yunshan, Politburo member and head of the CPC Publicity Department (Beijing, May 2009).

Scientific Perspective on Development, Harmonious Society, Harmonious World, and Coordinated Development—and which are essential to the overall development and progress of the nation." Many times, Liu says, "I've seen complex problems move toward solutions through application of President Hu's principles," which, Liu says, have "profound richness and depth." Although decision-making deals with specific matters, he states, "there are usually guiding principles behind the decision-making process. For example, 'People-oriented' has become governing philosophy for the Party and the government, affecting how we deal with economic, social, political and cultural issues. Under his leadership, complex problems can all get resolved."

China is in transition, Liu explains, and "it takes vision to avoid major conflicts in society. Income disparities and sharp 'contradictions' between people—as exacerbated by unemployment, bureaucracy and corruption—could cause instability, if not handled properly." Tellingly, he says, "this is the Party's most severe test. In seven years under President Hu, the CPC has successfully maintained stability while pushing forward with reform and opening-up. Even our breakthroughs with Taiwan are rooted in Hu's personality."

Liu stresses that "balancing reform, development and stability" is the CPC's biggest challenge and this exemplifies President Hu's vision. "Few foreigners can appreciate the multifaceted, interconnected issues involved," Liu says. "Some foreigners don't understand the nature of our political reform: they urge us to expedite political system reform, including democratic elections, constitutional government, and separation of powers. In actuality, copying the American system could be disastrous for China—balancing reform, development and stability being but one of the subtleties. Some foreigners don't appreciate that if we get even one of these three wrong, it could jeopardize China's accomplishments and be catastrophic for our vast population—we might have to start our 30-year reform all over again."

Comparing China's stability with the instability of neighboring countries, Liu Yunshan says, "I cannot imagine what tragedies might have befallen the Chinese people had such political instability descended upon us. President Hu has been stressing, as had Deng Xiaoping and Jiang Zemin before him, that China should choose its own path—the road of 'socialism with Chinese characteristics'. It's a path unique to China; we don't think there's a one-size-fits-all national model. As an ordinary Party member—as an ordinary Chinese citizen—I have the highest respect for President Hu, for his leadership, character and vision."

★ ★ ★

China makes news. Stories about trade disputes, currency exchange rates, human rights, financial reserves, natural resource competition, diplomatic rivalries, military tensions, and even corporate takeovers fill the American media, and in some quarters scare screeds about "Communist China" that sound like Cold War satire are taken seriously. In my opinion, good bilateral relations between America and China are essential for the peace and prosperity of the 21st century. If there is no strategic partnership, we risk worse than strategic rivalry. This is why all should appreciate the inner attitudes and primary concerns of China's leaders.

Here then are key elements of the grand vision that China's leaders have for their country's next 30 years:

- A China which is economically prosperous and whose national wealth is shared, if not equally, at least not terribly unequally, among all its citizens.
- A China of culture and civility, where the rule of law governs and high-minded endeavors of "spiritual civilization" are appreciated.
- A China which is increasingly transparent in its governance and democratic in its political structure.
- A China that protects the human rights of all its people in their personal lives and social activities.
- A China of advanced science and technology, which empowers economic development, strengthens national defense, and contributes to human knowledge.
- A China that is creative and innovative, whose products and services are knowledge-based and have high incremental value.
- A China that is self-sufficient and develops sustainably.
- A China that is environmentally friendly and enables its citizens to enjoy a high quality of life.
- A China that internationally is a bulwark of peace and a catalyst of prosperity.
- A China that is respected by, and respectful of, the grand community of nations.
- A China that has regained its rightful role as a great and responsible nation of the world.

Endnotes

1 "Building harmonious society crucial for China's progress: Hu," Xinhua, June 26, 2005.
2 I was told that I was one of the first foreigners to lecture on the Scientific Perspective on Development in China. My observations were published in *People's Daily* (March 21, 2005).
3 This collective maximization can be called a "frontier," and the aim is to come as close as possible to "reaching the frontier." In a sense, the Scientific Perspective on Development for the real world of people, institutions and society is like linear programming in mathematics, where given a certain number of unknowns and constraints, the unknowns can be collectively maximized or minimized—i.e., "optimized"—which usually means that no single unknown is maximized or minimized. The real world, with innumerable variables, is exceedingly more complicated.
4 Author's meeting with Liu Yunshan, Beijng, May and August 2009.

Part II

Thinking Reform

Subjugation, Humiliation, Oppression

There are few countries where history and tradition remain as relevant today as they do in China. They influenced those who fought to make China free from foreign influence in the 20th century—and they affect China's leaders today as they seek to redefine their country's place in the new world order. To appreciate the grandeurs of China's civilization, and then the horrors of China's humiliations, is to discern the deep, dual emotions that empower China's leaders.

China's pride in itself is emphasized in the nation's name: *ZhongGuo*, in Chinese, literally means the Middle or Center *(zhong)* Kingdom or Country *(guo)*—the kingdom, as it were, at the middle of the world or the center of civilization. China has one of the oldest continuous civilizations, and for a millennium or more, as late as the fifteenth century, Chinese science and technology were supreme. At its peak, China's GDP was about one-third of the entire world's GDP, coincidentally about the same proportion as America's at its peak.

The Chinese were the originators of much that underlies modern civilization. No matter how embattled their circumstances, no matter how poor their condition, the Chinese have always considered their culture as being of the highest order. Foreigners were traditionally characterized as barbarians—"long-nosed devils." There is great pride in China about Chinese civilization and achievements, and great bitterness over the long years of foreign subjugation.

★ ★ ★

One cannot understand China today without appreciating its long, tragic legacy of foreign domination. The great pride that Chinese people take in their country's growing economic strength and increasing recognition as a world power has its roots in this history of humiliation. After centuries of domination and subjugation at the hands of foreign conquerors, they are united in their pleasure at seeing China taking its long overdue place at the center of power in international commerce and diplomacy.

It is difficult for non-Chinese to imagine the depth of the bitterness that Chinese people harbor toward their historic oppressors, even though China's decline came about as much from the neglect and complacency of its feudal rulers as from the rapacious greed of foreign powers.

In the 13th and 14th centuries, the Chinese were ruled by the Mongols. In the mid-19th century, China was defeated in the Opium Wars, the result of British smuggling opium from India into China and the Chinese government's hapless efforts to enforce its drug laws. Not only was China compelled to accept the debilitating drug trafficking, it also was forced to sign the Treaty of Nanking and the Treaty of Tianjin, thereafter known as the Unequal Treaties, which forced open additional Chinese ports to foreign trade, ceded Hong Kong to Britain (a national abasement only recently redressed), and granted various degrading extraterritorial rights. Other countries, including Russia, Japan, Korea, Germany, and France, pressured China into similar agreements, tempted by the easy pickings of "gunboat diplomacy." During the Boxer Rebellion in 1900, an Eight-Nation Alliance (consisting of British, Japanese, Russian, Italian, German, French, American and Austrian troops) invaded China, burned, ransacked and looted its capital, stole priceless works of art, and slaughtered thousands of citizens.

In suing for peace, having lost battle after battle, China was forced to give "concessions:" territories in China, generally enclaves within major cities, which were occupied and governed by various foreign powers. Shanghai, famously, had its French concession and its International Settlement (merging the U.S. and U.K. concessions.) The Germans had Qingdao (its zone of influence covered Shandong Province); the Russians had Harbin. At its peak, Tianjin had nine concessions, which seems something of a world record of shame.

Exacerbating the indignity, Chinese citizens were originally not even permitted to live inside the concessions. When they were permitted, they were largely consigned to provide menial services for foreigners— the Chinese were literally second class citizens in their own country. A wealthy Chinese businessman in Hong Kong once told me of his continuing bitterness toward the British. No matter their office or station, he said, any Englishman, as a matter of course, would cut ahead of any Chinese standing in any line, "as if the Chinese person waiting patiently ahead of them in the bus queue or at the bank did not even exist—as if it were ordained that the British be the rulers and the Chinese the ruled." The fact that China had regained sovereignty over Hong Kong, and that this Chinese tycoon now had more financial clout than virtually any Englishman left in the former colony, had done little to dull his resentment.

★ ★ ★

Worse was to come. Nothing could compare with the vast and unspeakable horrors visited on the Chinese people from Japan. The Japanese occupation of China during World War II was brutal and sadistic and deliberately so; millions were terrorized, tortured, murdered.

Japan invaded Manchuria in 1931, but full-scale war did not break out until 1937 when the Japanese army seized most of Manchuria, conquered Shanghai and took the Yangtze River valley all the way to Nanjing. Former President Jiang Zemin was 13 years old when his school in Yangzhou, Jiangsu Province, was requisitioned by Japanese troops, who converted the gymnasium into a stable for their horses. Books were torched; teachers and students dismissed.

Still, the city could consider itself lucky. Only 50 miles away the citizens of Nanjing faced devastation. The Japanese slaughtered an estimated 40,000 to 60,000 people in a city of one million.[1] Bodies lined the streets, as burning, looting, and torture became the order of the day, the Japanese army treating the Chinese as little more than rodents as they implemented their infamous Three Alls Policy—Burn All, Kill All, Take All. The appalling events would later come to be called the Rape of Nanking, in large part because of the atrocities that were committed there against women.

As many as 20,000 Chinese females of all ages—from seven-year-old girls to 70-year-old grandmothers—were raped, many gang-raped by groups of soldiers. The crimes were often committed in front of husbands and children. The usual practice, condoned by the Japanese army, was to murder the women afterward. Sometimes the procedure involved cutting off their breasts or disemboweling them with bayonets. Every rank, from foot soldiers to senior officers, participated. One group of Japanese soldiers raped a pregnant woman, then ripped out her fetus and stuck it on a bayonet. When they presented the trophy to their commanding officer, he laughed.

Japanese atrocities were gruesome and legion. In what the Chinese call the Anti-Japanese War or the War of Resistance Against Japan—they do not refer to it as World War II—the Chinese citizenry endured wanton slaughter, including fiendish medical experiments (biological weapons were tested on civilians) and sexual enslavement. Only in recent years has the revolting abomination of the "comfort women" come fully to light. Young girls were abducted and forced to service Japanese soldiers—dozens of harsh sexual acts every day—and most were then tortured and killed when they could no longer perform their horrific assignments.

Coming four years before Japanese bombers attacked Pearl Harbor, commencing the war in the Pacific, the enormity of the Nanjing Massacre went largely unnoticed in the West. When other Chinese cities fell, the treatment by the Japanese and the response from overseas were similar. Rape, pillage, and murder marked the fall of Beijing, Shanghai, Hankow (Wuhan), and Canton (Guangzhou). Before the bloodletting was over, more than 2.5 million people would lie dead.

All these horrors are stamped indelibly on the collective Chinese consciousness. A 30-something Chinese-American entrepreneur in my office noticed some mementos I had brought back from China. He ignored the elegant water-colors and the carvings of ancient warriors; the only thing he could see, lying among a small collection of much older and more valuable Chinese swords, was one rusted Japanese sword. The young-entrepreneurial glow faded, his visage grew dark. "I can still smell Chinese blood on it," he muttered.

The lesson, for many Chinese, is clear: If China is to survive, the Chinese people must take charge of their own destiny.

★ ★ ★

To appreciate New China's 60 years, one must understand not only what China accomplished during its second 30 years of reform, but also all that happened during its first 30 years. "Reform" implies a substantial difference from the methods, systems and ways of thinking of previous times.

Throughout the Anti-Japanese War, resentment against the Nationalist (Kuomintang) government had been growing. After Japan's surrender in 1945, China soon fell into all-out civil war. By mid-1947, Nationalist forces were losing battle after battle. Near the Anhui-Jiangsu border, a 43-year-old officer named Deng Xiaoping led 200,000 troops to a major victory. In fall 1948 in Manchuria, the Nationalists lost nearly half a million soldiers. In January 1949, the Communists took Beijing.

When peace talks collapsed, Mao Zedong issued the order "Marching Toward the Whole Country!" which aimed at "steadfastly and completely killing off all reactionary Nationalist forces that were resisting." More than a million PLA soldiers crossed the Yangtze River and marched south and inland. As Communist forces overwhelmed the Nationalist capital of Nanjing, a tide of refugees flowed to Taiwan.

On October 1, 1949, from the Gate of Heavenly Peace (Tiananmen), the front entrance of the Imperial City high above Tiananmen Square in central Beijing, Mao Zedong proclaimed the founding of the People's Republic of China. He promised the masses a "New China" without foreign occupation or civil war.

In fact, peace would not come easily, and prosperity would take decades to achieve. Nevertheless, it would be a mistake to think that because classical Communism failed China as an economic system, it also failed to build a reservoir of goodwill towards the Party among the Chinese people. For restoring their national dignity and bringing international respect to their ancient civilization, most Chinese still look with pride on Communism's nationalistic accomplishments—though the subsequent political campaigns, the Cultural Revolution in particular, eroded much of this goodwill, especially that relating to Mao himself.

★ ★ ★

In 1949 when the People's Republic was founded, the economy of China had been decimated by the wars—the eight-year war of resistance against

Japan and the subsequent three-year civil war (which had actually been fought, in one form or another, for more than 20 years). China's large cities were on the brink of collapse. Thus when the Communists took over, their urgent task was to restore basic necessities. Mao announced: "The goal of the first five-year plan is to build an industrialized, highly modernized, culturally developed country."

A planned economy, it was thought, was the swiftest way to build the economy, a fact that was conveniently consistent with Communist ideology. Mao adopted the Soviet Union's economic model. Extreme measures to control resources, enterprises, and land were put in place, establishing a command economy that was born as much out of necessity as out of a desire to conform to Marxist-Leninist ideology. The state would own all the means of production and determine in advance how much each factory would produce.

China had entered its Soviet period. Central planners in Beijing, copying their counterparts in Moscow, pushed the collectivization of agriculture, the development of heavy industry, and the setting of production targets for each factory. From 1949 to 1960, more than 20,000 Soviet specialists streamed into China to supervise the installation and operation of factories, and tens of thousands of Chinese were sent to Russia to study their methods. In retrospect, it may seem odd that a newly liberated China, so despising of foreign domination, would allow itself to become so heavily dependent on the Soviet Union, but Mao and his senior colleagues were ideologues who believed ardently in the unifying elixir of socialism; moreover, their practical options were limited.

China had been influenced by Marxism-Leninism since the 1920s, and it was widely believed that under a cooperative socialist system all work and rewards would be shared, as Marx had imagined, and the country would grow rapidly. But the planned economy did not work in China, most Westerners believe, just as it did not work anywhere and it made China extremely poor.

Many Chinese leaders and scholars disagree with this blanket generalization. They argue that the planned economy did play an important role in developing China's economy in the early days (early to mid 1950s) and it did improve people's standard of living. For jump-starting a moribund economy, they say, a command structure works well—but they do admit that it didn't fundamentally lift China out of poverty. (Like it or not, most people work harder when they work for their own benefit. Here's an analogy. A planned economy is when the government requires, say, fishermen to produce an inviolate quota of 200 pounds per day, but comes not to care whether the catch is composed of fish, shells, mud, or rocks, just so long as those 200 pounds are delivered, weighed, documented, and reported to superiors.)

There was something utopian, though, about the early 1950s in China, notwithstanding the poverty, conflicts at home and abroad, and myriad difficulties. National pride at having achieved revolution and independence was palpable, and there was an uplifting, expectant feeling that China was taking charge of its own destiny, and that the people were united and making common cause in building their country. Chairman Mao was greatly admired, respected and honored; economic improvement was real, if not entirely tangible; and the future, it seemed, would be better than the past.

The idyll was not to last. To Mao, whose ideological fervor eclipsed all economic sense, China's level of communism did not meet his standard of orthodoxy. In 1956 Mao launched the Hundred Flowers Campaign, a call for intellectuals to voice their true feelings. "Let a hundred flowers bloom," he proclaimed, quoting a Chinese poem; "let a hundred schools of thought contend." By reaching out to intellectuals, Mao hoped to promote new forms of art and cultural institutions, his lifelong passion. Premier Zhou Enlai appealed for constructive criticism.

What followed was tragedy: the momentary flash of freedom metamorphosed into a means for flushing out, and then eliminating, all opposition. At first, suspicious "intellectuals"—people with university education—figured that Mao's appeal was a ruse and few spoke out. But when Mao began reprimanding those who did not offer "healthy criticism," many succumbed to their pent-up yearnings and presented what they thought were honest, helpful ideas for improving governance.

But when the proffered advice began including democracy, human rights, and suggestions that the Party should "open up," and when the number of critical letters reached avalanche proportions, Mao took it personally and badly. Not without reason, the Great Helmsman saw the criticism as a blatant attack on his own leadership and became resentful and enraged. Mao labeled the opposition "Rightists" and accelerated his nascent Anti-Rightist Campaign.

Sweeping accusations were initiated against these so-called Rightists. Blaming intellectuals for all manner of ills, Mao ordered the letter writers, who were now branded "counterrevolutionaries"—the worst of all sins—to be arrested, purged and punished. At its onset, only a few thousand people were purged, but the Anti-Rightist Campaign fed on its own vitriol and soon the condemned swelled to more than half a million. The best a Rightist could expect was demotion and "reeducation through labor." Some were beaten and imprisoned, others maimed and even killed.

★ ★ ★

Not satiated by the Anti-Rightist Campaign, Mao's next ideological assault on the Chinese people came quickly in the form of the Great Leap Forward, his disastrous campaign to enlist China's vast population—mainly via rural communes—in a fanciful, harebrained attempt to accelerate China's industrial and agricultural production in a ludicrously short period of time (he imagined China could overtake England within 15 years[2]).

Begun in 1958, Mao's plan, rooted in Communist theory, had a lofty goal, bizarre economics, and horrendous results. The idea he proclaimed was that labor-intensive methods of production, which stressed manpower over machines, could be as effective as expensive technology. He aggregated vast masses of peasants into large-scale rural communes for collective farming. Small backyard steel furnaces dotted every village; according to the delusion of the Great Leap Forward, they would eliminate the need to build large factories.

A once-great leader, revered for founding New China and enabling the Chinese people to "stand up" in the world, Mao was now setting a trajectory of ideological fanaticism, inspired by personal (and perhaps age-induced) megalomania, which would soon shatter millions of lives.

Under the commune system, ideological purity was valued far more than technical expertise. The peasants were organized into brigade teams, military style, and communal kitchens were established so that women could be freed for work.

Initially, there was passionate support for Mao's Great Leap Forward, which was expected to transform China into a superpower almost overnight. Motivated largely by repressed pride, the Chinese masses felt with legitimacy that China had suffered at the hands of imperialist powers because of its primitive economy. They intended to right this wrong with a vengeance, a concerted will. But the Great Leap was overseen and spurred on by fanatical "cadres" (Party officials); the Chinese people were gathered and managed in a military style, and in such haste and with such lack of foresight that unmitigated disaster soon descended.

In 1959 the Party convened a meeting to review the Great Leap Forward. The Minister of Defense, Marshal Peng Dehuai, the hero of the Korean War, attacked the radicalism and ineffectiveness of the Great Leap. Mao was not amused: he took this, perhaps rightly, as a personal attack on his authority, and he responded by condemning Peng viciously and stripping him of all his military positions. Unstoppable, Mao then commenced a general purge.

Any reform of the destructive Great Leap policies was now impossible. China's downhill cascade accelerated for another year or more, so that by 1960 virtually the entire country was consumed by famine. Over the three years (1958–1961), as a direct result of gross mismanagement of agriculture, wildly unrealistic quotas and forced labor—all exacerbated by drought—a pandemic of malnutrition, starvation, and associated diseases swept China. No one really knows how many people died in the world-record famine. The unprecedented number of "excess deaths" is at least 15 million, likely more than 20 million, and possibly as high as 50 million.

Mao never would admit the enormity of his mistake. Indeed he was eventually to respond by calling for more revolution, leading to even more chaos. The so-called continuous revolution, back-to-back political movements and class struggle, destroyed China's economy and social fabric, and led to continuing loss of life. Mao once said, "You must struggle with heaven, you must struggle with earth, then you will find your happiness. And if you struggle with people, you will be much happier." This theory, based on the

Marxist model that "struggle" was a "weapon" of human advancement, was Mao's motto.

By 1961, some of China's leaders, including Deng Xiaoping and Chen Yun, a long-time Party stalwart, tried to reverse some of the damage. A limited, rural-based, free-market system, which included private vegetable gardens and a merit-based pay structure, was permitted. At the same time, factory managers were chastised or even fired for submitting false production reports, which they had generated under pressure of Beijing's ideologically inspired and wildly unreasonable production quotas.

Optimism was in the air; it seemed that the political movements were finally receding. Pragmatic Party officials, led by Liu Shaoqi, who had succeeded Mao as head of state in 1959, and Deng Xiaoping, became increasingly bold in confronting the radical Leftists. In 1962, President Liu told a meeting of 7,000 Party officials that only 30% of the country's abysmal condition could be blamed on poor weather ("visitations of providence"). The other 70%, he said, had been caused by human error ("our wrong policies"). Many senior leaders, including Mao and Liu, made self-criticisms. Deng blamed lack of experience and said all should share responsibility. Mao, who continued to be revered as the founder of New China, was uncharacteristically and unnervingly docile at the meeting, but the critique must have rankled him deeply.

Mao came to believe that the emergency measures taken to save the country from the disastrous consequences of the Great Leap Forward, such as decentralizing the communes, gravely betrayed his inviolable image of pure socialism. It would take him four years to exact his revenge on Liu and Deng, but when he did, he would take the entire country down with them. In 1966, yearning to purify the Party and re-stamp his megalomaniacal imprint on the Communist revolution, Mao launched the Cultural Revolution.

★ ★ ★

The first hint of impending doom came in November 1965, when a Shanghai newspaper published a caustic review of a play, written by a vice mayor of Beijing, titled "Hai Rui Dismissed from Office." The reviewer, a literary critic named Yao Wenyuan, claimed that the work was a veiled attack on Chairman Mao and suggested darkly that certain senior Party officials were behind it. As it turned out, Yao himself was a puppet of others, particularly Mao's wife, Jiang Qing, and a Shanghai propagandist named Zhang Chunqiao. The three, along with a once-obscure factory security guard named Wang Hongwen, would come to be known, infamously, as the Gang of Four.

By early 1966, their efforts to manipulate Mao in his dotage were succeeding. "Your orders are being ignored," he was warned, "and your authority is being usurped." Mao thought he could hasten China's development by re-revolutionizing China—and to do so, he had to reaffirm his potency and assert his preeminence. This meant, for starters, that Liu Shaoqi and Deng Xiaoping had to go.

As he had done in the past, Mao turned to the masses, urging them to denounce their leaders and the Party's Central Committee, which he termed "the palace of hell." President Liu Shaoqi and CPC General Secretary Deng Xiaoping were labeled, respectively, "the biggest capitalist" and "the second biggest capitalist," and accused of opposing Mao. Their supposed "crime" was giving individual farmers some freedom to own land. In truth, Mao feared that Liu and Deng, along with other high-level Party leaders, no longer followed him, and he wanted an excuse to get rid of them. Both were purged. Liu and his wife endured protracted physical and mental torment, and after three years, when jailers refused to give him medicine for his diabetes, Liu Shaoqi died. Deng Xiaoping would find a better fate, though not without enduring long hardships.

Similar punishment was meted out to intellectuals and professionals throughout the country. At first many refused to believe that such madness could last, but the Cultural Revolution quickly spiraled out of control, having been taken over by radicals and opportunists, with a fundamentalist fervor which fanatical religions would envy. Mao-worship terrorized the nation. Young Red Guards, most with scant education, condemned anyone they deemed counterrevolutionary, screaming divisive slogans: "Better poor under Communism than rich

Artwork being smashed at the China Central Academy of Fine Arts at the beginning of the Cultural Revolution (Beijing, August 1966).

Huge parade in Harbin "Showing Loyalty to Chairman Mao." (August 14, 1968).

under capitalism;" "Always loyal to Chairman Mao", and "Destroy the 'Four Olds'!" (i.e., expunge old customs, old culture, old habits, and old ideas).

Following the latter prescript, Red Guards ransacked Chinese architecture, smashed Chinese antiquities, tore up Chinese paintings, and burned Chinese books. Anything classical, anything representative of Chinese civilization, was suspect and often destroyed. Anyone owning these things—intellectuals—were mocked, ridiculed, beaten, tortured, imprisoned, maimed and/or murdered.

Universities and colleges were shut down; professors were exiled to farms to clean pigpens and work in rice paddies. Virtually every student was "sent down" to rural areas. Fanatic "revolutionary committees" took over the few institutions that remained open; admissions were based on political qualifications.

Begun as an effort to prevent China from going down the "revisionist road" of Khrushchev's Soviet Union, the Cultural Revolution dissolved into a decade of colossal chaos and decimated the country. Those whom Mao hoped to help—workers, farmers, peasants—became all the more destitute.

Zhang Xiaoshan, a rural expert, spent more than nine years in the communes of Inner Mongolia. "In our village we grew a kind of herb called 'Chinese wolfberry'," Zhang recalls. "It produces small red fruits, which have a medicinal use, and can also be used to brew wine. People planted wolfberry trees in their courtyards so that they could exchange the fruits for cash. However, this was criticized as 'spontaneous capitalist intention' and military militias were ordered to chop down and dig up all the trees, which reduced the old women who desperately needed the pitifully small amount of money to tears."

Zhang's own experiences were similar. "Once we grew watermelon and certain roots for cash. But our bosses ordered us to destroy them. At that time, China had a slogan warning against capitalist tendencies: 'If you are not on guard, a mighty wind will come through the eye of a needle.' Political commands affected even ordinary farming households."

The Cultural Revolution visited protracted hardships upon the Chinese people—but the worst offense of all was against their hearts and minds and spirits. People were made to turn on one another—worker against worker, friend against friend, spouse against spouse, child against parent. An entire generation was traumatized as millions were purged and civilization was trashed. "People's natures were distorted," says Zhang Xiaoshan. "Not only those who were criticized suffered, but also those who did the criticizing—their hearts and minds became warped. They were no longer normal human beings. All the political movements inflicted deep psychological trauma. Can you imagine members of the same family afraid of one another? It wasn't their fault. It was the fault of the system."

★ ★ ★

When the Cultural Revolution began, President Hu Jintao was 23 years old and working on his postgraduate studies and as a political instructor in the Water Conservancy Engineering Department of Tsinghua University. He had graduated two years earlier, in 1964, and had joined the Communist Party in that same year. While his research continued to 1968, his work as a political instructor did not. One can only imagine what difficulties a "political instructor" might have faced in those traumatic, feverish years. One uncorroborated report says that Hu was caught up in the "struggle" campaigns of the time and was "one of the few student Party members to be criticized and denounced," after which he "went scot-free."[3] What is for certain is the tragedy which befell Hu's father.

Hu Jintao was born on December 21, 1942. His official biography states that he is a native of Jixi in southern Anhui Province, the hometown of several famous figures in Chinese history.[4] But this is taken to mean that Hu's ancestors, his grandfather's generation, came from this region, because in the late Qing Dynasty, they migrated to Jiangyan, a county-level city with a long and storied history[5] in Taizhou prefecture in central Jiangsu Province.[6] Hu's father, Hu Jingzhi, was born nearby, and his mother, Li Wenrui, came from a local village. Hu's father's family were educated tea merchants and they did business in Shanghai, which was where Hu Jintao was apparently born, though the family's official residency registration remained in Taizhou in Jiangsu Province.[7] As the Japanese occupation of Shanghai intensified, the family likely moved back to Jiangyan.

Tragedy struck early in Hu's life. He was only seven years old when his mother died, following which he and his two younger sisters moved in with their grandparents. Hu was raised by an aunt and grew up in a traditional grey brick courtyard home in Taizhou. The home can still be seen, tucked away in an old back alley in the shadow of nearby modern buildings, including a high-rise branch of a major Chinese bank. The house itself is unremarkable and, indeed, it's unmarked, not at all special and not a local attraction.[8]

"He's not interested in adulation," Hu Juncai, a former childhood friend of Hu's told a visiting reporter.[9] "His family was very poor, so his uncle looked after him. His life was very simple; even when he was a kid he wasn't vain. He was a mild boy, very calm, not naughty. He kept his promises – when he said something he meant it."

Hu is said to have been a talented student in high school, excelling both in his academic studies and in singing, dancing, and table tennis. (He is rumored to have a photographic memory.) His abilities and diligence were recognized when, despite the fact that his background was humble and he had no special connections, he won admission to Beijing's prestigious Tsinghua University. The youngest student in the class, he earned almost straight As in his courses and had a reputation as a handsome and personable young man.[10]

At Tsinghua, Hu not only earned a degree but also found a wife, a fellow student named Liu Yongqing. They later had two children, a son and daughter. (While Hu was vice president, his wife worked in the Beijing Municipal Construction Committee.)

President Hu's father, Hu Jingzhi, owned and managed a small tea shop in Taizhou. After the Communist revolution, this "ownership" put the family in the "petit bourgeois" class. In the ideological zealotry of the Cultural Revolution, this could only mean trouble. The family remained relatively poor, but predictably, tragically, in 1968 Hu Jingzhi was denounced and arrested, falsely accused of "capitalist transgressions," including embezzling public funds. He was publicly humiliated, dragged on a stage for open denunciations and "struggle sessions." He was then imprisoned and perhaps tortured, enduring such harsh treatment in jail that his body withered and he never recovered.[11] Hu Jingzhi died ten years later. He was only 50 years old.

His father's trials and tribulations, deeply unfair and traumatic to the family, had a profound effect on Hu Jintao. After his father's death, Hu tried valiantly to clear his father's name, though he had no power to do so. In the late 1970s, he reportedly went back to Taizhou and tried to convince officials of the local revolutionary committee to help. A story circulates that the young Hu was told to arrange a banquet for these Communist Party officials, but when no one turned up, Hu invited the kitchen staff to partake of the lavish dishes. The officials ignored him, the exoneration of his father remained ambiguous, and Hu, apparently, never forgot it.[12]

In 1968, the same year his father was arrested, the People's Liberation Army established some order in Beijing by shipping most of the students off to the countryside. Hu Jintao was likely no exception, though he is said to have volunteered for service in Gansu, a poor province in China's northwest where he sought work on a hydropower project, reflecting his academic study. He did manual labor on a housing construction team for about a year, and then from 1969 to 1974 he served successively as technician, office secretary and Deputy Communist Party Secretary in the Sinohydro Engineering Bureau No. 4, a hydro-power station under China's Ministry of Water Resources and Electric Power, thus beginning his career in Party affairs work.

In 1974, Hu Jintao became Secretary of the Gansu Provincial Construction Committee. Gansu Governor Song Ping, who would later become a Politburo member and head of the CPC Organization Department, took the young engineer under his wing, and Hu rose to vice director in just one year. One report has it that Song praised young Jintao as a "walking map of Gansu" because he had visited every part of the province and reputedly knew the counties and their problems intimately.[13] Later, Hu became Secretary of the Gansu branch of the Communist Youth League of China, an organization which would become his springboard into national prominence.

Hu's experience in Gansu was formative. To be effective, a political leader's philosophy must be founded on long-standing beliefs or intrinsic personality. When President Hu was a young official in Gansu in the 1970s, he was close to the people, much as his philosophy, more than three decades later, would prescribe. Yan Feng, a former Gansu subordinate of Hu's, told me he had once accidentally burst into his boss's office. Hu, though at first startled, invited Yan to sit down, and they talked for an hour. Hu is "a people person", Yan said. "He turns crisis into opportunity."[14]

★ ★ ★

To many Chinese, 1976 was a year when the heavens sparkled and the earth groaned. In March, a huge meteor exploded over Jilin Province, enveloping 500-square miles with streams of lights and showers of rocks. In July the deadliest earthquake of the 20th century obliterated the city of Tangshan, near Tianjin, killing 240,000 people.

Cataclysmic developments also occurred politically. Eight months after Zhou Enlai died, on September 9, 1976, Mao Zedong, the Great Helmsman, expired at the age of 83. His death marked the end of an era. Across the country people wore black ribbons and white flowers. They wept tears of heartfelt grief but also waited anxiously for what would follow. It did not take long.

Endnotes

1 Nicholas Kristof, *The New York Times*, December 20, 2003. Chinese sources put the deaths in Nanjing at 300,000. No matter the number, the horrors were unspeakable.

2 The Great Leap Forward was so believed by the Chinese people that some even named their babies after slogans of the time. The renowned investment banker Margaret Ren, born in 1958, has, considering her capital markets achievements, an ironic Chinese name – "Ke Ying," meaning "Exceed England." (Full disclosure: Margaret Ren is a friend and colleague.)

3 John Tkacic, "A Biographical Look at Vice President Hu Jintao," quoting Xu Zhenxing, "A Cross Century CCP Leader: Hu Jintao," *Guangjiao Jing* (Wide Angle), No. 242, November 16, 1992, pp. 20–23.

4 Juxi (Anhui Province) luminaries included Hu Fu, Hu Zongxian, and Hu Shi (none related to Hu Jintao). Hu Fu was minister of revenue, and Hu Zongxian was minister of war, during the Ming Dynasty (1368–1644). Hu Shi (1891–1962), a pragmatic philosopher, was ambassador to the US, chancellor of Peking University, and later president of the Academia Sinica in Taiwan. His *Free China Journal* was shut down for criticizing Chiang Kai-shek. Hu Shih's work fell into disrepute in China until a 1986 article, "A Few Words for Hu Shi." Wikipedia: http://en.wikipedia.org/wiki/Hu_Shih.

5 Jiangyan has relics from the Zhou Dynasty (~770 BCE – 221 BCE) and a Buddha statue from the Tang Dynasty (618 – 907). During the civil war in the 1940s, General Chen Yi commanded the Battle of Huangqiao from here. There have been many well-known people from Jiangyan, including generals, painters, philosophers, poets, even a Go chess master. The city is crisscrossed by canals and rivers. The Chinese navy was born in Jiangyan's Baima Temple.

6 Xia Xiangren, "Hu Jintao and his bitter banquet of injustice," Asia Times Online http://www.atimes.com/atimes/China/FH27Ad02.html, August 27, 2004. If Hu Jintao was born with Taizhou residency, why does his official biography state he is a native of Jixi in Anhui Province? There is speculation that when Hu was elevated to the Politburo Standing Committee in 1992, concern was expressed that Taizhou was too close to Yangzhou, which is the hometown of then President Jiang Zemin. It might have seemed politically incorrect in China for two successive senior leaders to come from the same place—Taizhou and Yangzhou are only about 25 miles apart in Jiangsu Province and at the time had not yet been separated into different jurisdictions. In Chinese politics, the traditional ideal is diversity: leaders should hail from "the five lakes and four seas."

7 John Tkacik, "A Biographical Look at Vice President Hu Jintao. Andrew J. Nathan and Bruce Gilley (March 2003). *China's New Rulers: The Secret Files*. Second, Revised Edition, New York: *The New York Review of Books*. pp. 78.

8 Joe Havely "Getting to know Hu", Al Jazeera.net. October 19, 2007 -- http://english.aljazeera.net/news/asia-pacific/2007/10/2008525172536374792.html

9 Ibid.

10 Tkacik, op.cit.

11 Xia Xiangren, "Hu Jintao and his bitter banquet of injustice," ' "Biography of Hu Jintao," About.com: Asian History — http://asianhistory.about.com/od/profilesofasianleaders/p/HuJinTaoProfile.htm

12 Xia Xiangren, "Hu Jintao and his bitter banquet of injustice;" Joe Havely, Al Jazerra.net, op.cit.

13 Tkacik, op.cit.

14 Author's meeting with Yan Feng, Lanzhou, 2006.

Reform's Epic Struggle

Within hours of Mao's demise, China's leaders were meeting in various combinations, seeking alliances and planning strategies. Although Mao had named Hua Guofeng as his successor, the Gang of Four, led by Jiang Qing (Mao's widow), attempted to maintain power by discrediting him. In response, Hua Guofeng joined with moderate Party and army leaders to bring down the Gang of Four and restore normalcy to China. The tyranny of ultra-Leftism, which had tormented China and ruined millions of lives, was over.

★ ★ ★

In February 1977, about five months after Mao's death, *People's Daily*, the "mouthpiece" of the Party, published an editorial which inadvertently triggered a national debate about the standard for examining and ascertaining truth. The debate would change China.[1] The editorial called for all Party members to learn and live by the Two Whatevers, a phrase coined by Hua Guofeng to perpetuate Maoism, which stated: "We will resolutely uphold *whatever* policy decisions Chairman Mao made, and we will unswervingly follow *whatever* instructions Chairman Mao gave." In other words: "Whatever Mao said we should believe, we believe; whatever Mao said we should do, we do."[2]

Fortunately, change was coming. In March 1977, at the first Central Committee meeting after the Gang of Four was crushed, Chen Yun proposed that Deng Xiaoping rejoin the leadership.[3] After the meeting, Deng wrote to the Central Committee, saying, "Generations of the Party must use the accurate, complete Mao Zedong Thought. . . ." Deng's audience understood the implicit meaning of his words.

In May, Deng noted that the Two Whatevers was not Marxism, had no historical basis, and did not work. He pointed out that Marx and Engels

Mao Zedong meets with Deng Xiaoping in Mao's study (Beijing, 1975).

had never used such words, nor had Lenin and Stalin; even Mao Zedong had never said "whatever"! Moreover, Deng said that the Two Whatevers negated Mao Zedong's Thought on the critical role of "practice" and on his foundational principle of "seeking truth from facts." It was a masterful interpretation of Mao's original idea, which had lain dormant during two decades of raging ideological fever.[4] It is not correct, Deng asserted, that we should be prohibited from remedying anything erroneous that Mao said or did. The quintessence of Mao Zedong Thought, Deng stressed, was seeking truth from facts.

And so it came to pass that Deng Xiaoping, a diminutive man in his 70s re-emerging from his second purge, came to change the course and history of China. Deng's powerful aphorisms challenged Mao's insistence that rigid Communist ideology was the supreme arbiter for all decision-making in China, and everyone understood that new thinking was afoot. The Chinese people were ready for renewal.

In changing China, nothing was more important than the "truth debate," which became the ideological foundation on which the new policy of reform and opening-up could be built. The conclusion was that the sole criterion for testing truth, the only standard, was "practice"—in other words, real results not idealized theory is what counts.

According to Xing Bensi, former vice president of the Central Party School, the "truth debate" became more important as it evolved. "We didn't know it at the time," he said, "but it would become the turning-point in the history of China's reform. Because if we had stuck to the 'Two Whatevers', it would have been impossible to correct our past mistakes, impossible to 'seek truth from facts', and impossible to shift the Party's work from class struggle to economic development."

According to Wang Chen, now China's Information Minister, "A few months later in 1978, Deng remarked that the "truth debate" was very good for China. He said, "If a party or nation does everything based on dogmatism, if it's rigid in thinking and obsessed by personality cult, then it cannot advance and its vitality withers. In the end, such a party or nation will collapse."

Once Deng Xiaoping had prevailed, a nationwide initiative to redefine "truth" was begun. The campaign was conducted at every level of Chinese society, from grade schools to universities, from countryside to cities, and featured official study documents from Beijing and open discussions among the people.

It was a not-so-subtle effort to wean the Chinese people away from blind obedience to the Great Helmsman, to re-evaluate the infallibility of Mao's utterances, and to commence a gradual but fundamental change in sanctioning Chinese individuality. This debate changed Chinese history. Deng's more pragmatic policy, amplified by his more dynamic personality, enabled him to win the power struggle: In 1980, Deng deposed Hua as Party leader, redefined Mao's role in Chinese history, and set China on the long road to reform.

★ ★ ★

Deng Xiaoping's speech at the 3rd Plenary Session of the 11th CPC Central Committee, on December 18, 1978, is recognized as the singular milestone that marked the beginning of reform and opening-up in China. Entitled "Emancipate the Mind, Seek Truth from Facts, and Unite as One in Looking to the Future," the speech made powerful points, including stay away from old doctrines and let some people get rich first—breaking the sacred dogma of total equality for all classes. "This is very courageous," Teng Wensheng, one of its drafters, remembered thinking at the time.[5]

Deng's speech became the Party's new manifesto as its mission changed virtually overnight from class struggle to economic growth, setting the agenda for decades to come. Deng's aphorisms challenged Mao's godlike stature, and refuted his erroneous policies. The government also adopted an "opening-up" or open-door policy, welcoming the participation of foreign interests (trade and investment) in the modernization process. It also began the process of gradually loosening controls on Chinese society, allowing the slow flowering of personal freedoms.

The Four Modernizations—agriculture, industry, national defense, science and technology—became the cornerstone of Deng's program. From here on, the achievement of economic goals would be the measure of success or the mark of failure. Policies and careers would rise or fall on the quantifiable test of growth and development. "If we do not start reform," Deng said, "then our goal to modernize socialism will be buried."

Deng said on many occasions, "No longer mention struggles in the ideological sphere" – a reflection of his view that 19th-century Marxism could not be transplanted wholesale into 20th-century China. Deng, who had lost most of his hearing in one ear, even joked about his deviation from rigid Marxism: "Marx sits up in heaven, and he is very powerful," he said. "He sees what we are doing, and he doesn't like it. So he has punished me by making me deaf."[6]

★ ★ ★

Collective farming had failed. Not enough food was being produced to feed China's people; an air of desperation hung over the country. A severe drought had turned many people, already very poor, into outright beggars. In October 1978, two months before the official beginning of reform, deep in the countryside in the village of Xiaogang, Anhui Province, 18 impoverished farmers held a secret meeting. With their families near starvation, they agreed that they could not survive under the collectivist system of common ownership, and they decided to split the commune's crop land into individual plots and allocate them among its member households. This became known as the "household contract responsibility system," but these farmers could not have cared less about economic theory or ideological purity. This was a matter of pure survival.

★ ★ ★

Zhao Ziyang was a long-time reformer. He served in the Communist underground during both the Anti-Japanese War and the Civil War. After the founding of the People's Republic, he was transferred to Guangdong Province where, early on, he pioneered agriculture reform by experimenting with private plots and production contracts for households, and even some incipient market activities which permitted peasants to engage in light industry.

In 1965 Zhao was made Party secretary of Guangdong, but because he was an overt supporter of President Liu Shaoqi, in 1967, when the Cultural Revolution reached its height, he was denounced, purged and humiliated – paraded around in a dunce's cap and labeled as "a stinking remnant of the landlord class." (His father had been a wealthy landowner in Henan Province). Zhao spent four years consigned to manual labor in a factory. He was partially rehabilitated in 1971 and sent to Inner Mongolia, and in 1972 he was sent back to Guangdong.

It was Zhou Enlai who fully rehabilitated Zhao Ziyang in 1973, appointing him to the Central Committee, and in 1975 appointing him Party secretary of Sichuan, China's most populous province. Zhao's seemingly impossible task was to revitalize Sichuan, which had been devastated by the Great Leap Forward and Cultural Revolution. He did so, remarkably, by introducing what were at the time radical market-related reforms, such as compensating workers on the basis of performance rather than need, and using material incentives rather than government-set quotas to encourage individual initiative. The results were startling. In three years, industrial production increased by about 80% and agricultural output by about 25%.

At this time, even before the household contract responsibility system officially commenced rural reform, some leaders were quietly beginning to plan how to pilot the much more challenging reform of state-owned enterprises (SOEs). Sichuan Province in central China, an unlikely place, was the earliest to experiment.

To reform SOEs, the critical success factor would be to mobilize the enthusiasm of managers by expanding corporate autonomy. The tight controls of the planned economic system had stifled the vitality and dynamism of enterprises. The corporate culture had to change and this meant relaxing the strict controls of government by transferring some decision-making authority to the enterprise and by limiting or foregoing residual claims to their profits.

To Deng Xiaoping, the Sichuan Experience became the model for national reform and he promoted Zhao into the Politburo—as an alternate member in 1977, a full member in 1979 and, in 1982, to the all-powerful Standing Committee. In 1980, Zhao Ziyang became vice premier and a few months later premier. Later, after a series of modest student protests in 1986, Zhao replaced Hu Yaobang as CPC general secretary in early 1987. At the 13th Party Congress (1987), Zhao presented the coastal development strategy that would come to power China's economic boom. He envisioned the Pearl River Delta in Guangdong Province, and the Yangtze River Delta

Politburo Standing Committee members (left to right): Chen Yun, Zhao Ziyang, Deng Xiaoping, Ye Jianying, Hu Yaobang, and Li Xiannian (Beijing, October 1983).

Premier Zhao Ziyang and UK Prime Minister Madame Thatcher sign the joint statement for the repatriation of Hong Kong to China. Deng Xiaoping is the middle of the first row (December 19, 1984).

CPC General Secretary Zhao Ziyang delivers his report "Advance along the Road of Socialism with Chinese characteristics" at the 13th CPC National Congress (Beijing, October 1987).

around Shanghai, as the two "dragon heads" which would drive development of China's southern and eastern coasts. Partially conceived as a way of catching up with booming Taiwan, Zhao's policy was summarized by the phrase "Two heads facing abroad; big imports, big exports."

Reflecting back years later, with the special insights that only lifetime house arrest can provide, Zhao Ziyang discussed reform. "In hindsight," he said, "it was not easy for China to carry out the Reform and Open-Door Policy. Whenever there were issues involving relationships with foreigners, people were fearful, and there were many accusations made against reformers: people were afraid of being exploited, having our sovereignty undermined, or suffering an insult to our nation."[7]

Zhao explained that the reason he "had such a deep interest in economic reform" was that "I was determined to eradicate the malady of China's economic system at its roots," adding, "Without an understanding of the deficiencies of China's economic system, I could not possibly have had such a strong urge for reform."[8] His most profound realization, he stated, "was that the system had to be transformed into a market economy, and that the problem of property rights had to be resolved"—conclusions, he said, he had arrived at "through practical experience, only after a long series of back-and-forths."

★ ★ ★

In 1980, as he sought to deepen reform, Deng Xiaoping initiated the Four Transformations program, the objective of which was to develop Party leaders who were "more revolutionary, younger, more knowledgeable, and more specialized." In response to this nationwide search for future leaders, Song Ping, Gansu's governor and Hu Jintao's mentor, promoted Hu several ranks to the position of vice chairman of the Gansu Provincial Construction Committee.[9]

That same year Song recommended his protégé to the Central Party School's "middle-and-young cadre training class" in Beijing, an essential program for future Party leaders.[10] Coincidentally, the school's vice president at the time was Jiang Nanxiang, who had been Tsinghua's president and had recognized Hu for his academic and social achievements. Jiang mentored his former student, facilitating his entry into Central Party echelons in Beijing.

As fate would have it, Deng Xiaoping's second daughter, Deng Nan, who would later become vice minister of science and technology, and Hu Yaobang's son, Hu Deping (no relation to Hu Jintao), were also attending the Central Party School at the same time. It is said that Hu Jintao made a favorable impression on Deng Nan, who happened to mention it to her father. Hu Deping, meanwhile, invited Hu Jintao to his home, where he met Hu Yaobang, a Politburo Standing Committee member. Hu Yaobang is said to have appreciated Hu Jintao's modesty. Now, with the support of Deng Xiaoping and Hu Yaobang, both of whom knew Hu Jintao and recognized his potential, Song Ping could position Hu for significant advancement, and while Hu was still attending the Party school, Song appointed him deputy secretary of the Gansu Communist Youth League.

In 1981, Song Ping was transferred to Beijing, as vice chairman and then chairman of the Central Planning Commission, and in September 1982, Song arranged for Hu to become secretary of the Gansu Communist Youth League. More importantly, at about the same time, Song's position and growing political clout enabled him to recommend Hu Jintao as an alternate member of the 12th CPC Central Committee, the ultimate source of power in China. At 39, Hu was the youngest member of the Central Committee and one of the few whose position was only that of a provincial commission head. It was no surprise then, that in December 1982 Hu was brought to Beijing and appointed to the Secretariat of the (national) Communist Youth League and chairman of the All-China Youth Federation. This was a national office and a major promotion. (Another protégé of Song Ping, Premier Wen Jiabao, also came to prominence at about this time.)

In 1984, Hu Jintao was promoted to First Secretary of the Communist Youth League of China, becoming its chief executive officer. From this point forward, for the entirety of Hu Jintao's ascending political career, the Youth League would remain the core of his political base.

Running the Party Youth League, with its vast networks and programs, demands political savvy as well as organizational intelligence. During his term, Hu is said to have resisted a conservative campaign that denounced Western ideas as "spiritual pollution," and in the process alienated two "princelings" whose fathers were powerful generals.

A more pleasurable part of Hu Jintao's tenure as Youth League chief was escorting Hu Yaobang, then CPC general secretary, on his travels around the country. Despite the 27-year age gap, the two Hu's got along well. Hu Yaobang himself had come to prominence in the Youth League: perhaps he could see something of his own youth in Hu Jintao.

The bond between the younger and older Hu would lead, many years later, to Hu Jintao's insistence that Hu Yaobang, who would be demoted from his leadership post in 1987, should be posthumously rehabilitated. An early indication came in 1998, when then Vice President Hu marked the 20th anniversary of reform by noting pointedly, in a keynote speech at a celebratory forum, that the famous article "Practice Is the Sole Criterion of Truth" was published by the order of "Comrade Hu Yaobang." It was the only time during the forum that anyone recognized Hu Yaobang's substantial contribution to the "truth debates."

Another echo of Hu's links with Hu Yaobang, and their shared values, came in March 2004, when Hu Jintao, now CPC general secretary, attended a meeting of delegates from Hubei Province at China's National People's Congress (NPC). Zhou Xianwang, the governor of the Enshi Tujia and Miao Autonomous prefecture, produced a 20-year-old dinner receipt signed by Hu. Later, Zhou told reporters the story. In April 1984, Hu Yaobang and

Qiao Shi, accompanied by Hu Jintao and their teams, visited Enshi Prefecture on an inspection tour. After lunch in a local commune, their staff asked for the bill. The manager refused, telling the three leaders that they would not be charged. According to Zhou, Hu Jintao responded: "CPC leaders who come down to study [in the countryside] must pay for their expenses. And since this is a poverty-stricken mountainous region . . . there's all the more reason we should do so."[11] The quick-thinking manager, seeing an opportunity to get the signatures of these important visitors, filled in all the details on the receipts, except for the names of the customers. Hu had smiled and filled in the names: Hu Yaobang, Qiao Shi, and Hu Jintao. The amount filled out was 0.2 yuan per person.

During his meeting with the Hubei NPC delegation, Hu Jintao empha-sized that he still believed China's leaders "should go down to the grassroots to investigate and study, especially to those areas where there are many con-tradictions, great difficulties and poor conditions, to understand what the masses are thinking about and longing for." Senior officials, he said, "should stick to ascertaining the actual situation, telling the truth, doing solid work, and seeking practical results." He warned against "demanding unrealisti-cally high targets, shouting empty slogans, or promoting costly and wasteful projects." And he stressed that officials should not preen themselves, nor should they "cover up contradictions or evade problems." These, Hu said, were "expectations which I myself should take the lead in trying to realize, and which all of us should try to do."

★ ★ ★

In the late 1970s, 20 years had passed since the People's Republic had been founded, and when the Chinese began looking beyond their borders and across the seas, they found an embarrassing truth: the capitalist countries which they had despised as relics of the old order were developing rapidly, while socialist China, which they had acclaimed as the harbinger of the new order, was backward and stagnant. Faced with this grim reality, people expected China's leaders to make changes.

In 1979, Deng Xiaoping suggested selecting some places in the south where foreign investors would be encouraged to build factories to manufac-ture and export consumer goods. The first such Special Economic Zones (SEZs), located in Shenzhen, Zhuhai, and Shantou in Guangdong Province, and Xiamen in Fujian Province, begun about a year later, would become prototypes and symbols of reform.

Guangdong Province, contiguous to Hong Kong in the south, was the ideal spot to locate and isolate—quarantine really—most of the experi-mental SEZs. At the time (1978-1980), Xi Zhongxun, who had been vice premier under Premier Zhou Enlai for ten years, and had suffered terribly during the Cultural Revolution, was first Party secretary of Guangdong.[12] Yang Shangkun, who would later become president of China (1988–1993),

Xi Zhongxun (right), Party secretary of Guangdong Province, meets Hu Yaobang, Party general secretary, at Guangzhou Airport, Guangdong Province (Spring 1980).

was second Party secretary.[13] Xi Zhongxun was the first to propose that Guangdong should lead other provinces in reform and opening-up by leveraging its cultural and geographic advantages. Together, Xi Zhongxun and Yang Shangkun urged China's leaders to "take the first steps" to build Guangdong into a "battlefront" and "demonstration zone" for national reform and opening-up.[14] Xi told Deng Xiaoping, "We need to reform China and implement these economic zones even if it means that we have to travel a bloody road ahead, and I am responsible for it."[15]

Xi Zhongxun, open-minded and pragmatic, played a central role in Guangdong's historic transformation. A revolutionary hero, Xi joined the Communist Youth League in 1926, at age 13, and following his arrest for taking part in a patriotic student movement in 1928, he became a Party member while detained in a Kuomintang prison. He was a founder of the rugged Shaanxi-Gansu Revolutionary Base area in the 1930s, and is said to have welcomed Mao Zedong at the end of the Long March in 1935.[16] Later, following the revolution in 1949, Xi Zhongxun held various senior posts, including minister of Propaganda and secretary of the Secretariat as well as vice premier.

For 58 years, Xi was happily married to Qi Xin, who was first impressed by his "affable attitude, approachable manner, and unique charm."[17] Even when Xi was deputy prime minister, his wife recalled, he spared time to take care of their four children—bathing them and washing their clothes. Playing with his children was always his most enjoyable activity.

Yet the path of Xi Zhongxun's life was not straight. Three times he was purged by Mao, and imprisoned for a total of 16 years, before and during the Cultural Revolution. For nearly eight years, he was held in a single cell. ("I admire Xi's unfailing perseverance," his wife said.)

On one occasion, in 1962, after 36 years of "putting the Party's interests first," Xi was accused of being disloyal to Mao—on a trumped-up charge involving his support for, of all things, a particular novel. "Disloyalty to the Chairman" was a serious offence, and Xi was stripped of all positions. He was consigned to menial work in a factory in central China, later tortured during the Cultural Revolution, and held under house arrest in Beijing for years.[18]

When Xi was taken back to his hometown in Shaanxi Province for further public humiliation, local people came—not to criticize him, but to express their support. They remembered how Xi had sustained them during the three-year famine by providing food. And they even cooked a hometown meal for him.

Despite the "unredressed injustice" his wife recalled, and her own distraught emotions, Xi comforted and calmed her, though he himself was "pained to the heart." For many years, Qi Xin later wrote, "I did not see my husband and our children did not see their father," stressing "this period was a severe test for us—it's fortunate that we are a strong family." Near the end of the Cultural Revolution, when Xi was allowed to see his family for the first time in years, he "flowed with tears and said repeatedly, 'this is happiness.'"

In early 1978, about a year and a half after Mao's death, Xi Zhongxun was exonerated and reinstated in the Party, facilitated by Hu Yaobang. One month later, in April, Xi took the helm of Guangdong Province, "to guard the southern gate." Speaking at the Guangdong People's Congress, he impressed deputies with a simple remark: "In the first half of my life I was raised by the water and soil of the North. Now that I'm in Guangdong, I will dedicate the second half of my life to the water and soil of the South." Immediately after his arrival, he embarked on a month-long inspection tour, visiting more than 20 counties, including Bao'an County, an undistinguished fishing village which in March 1979 would be renamed Shenzhen.

Xi summed up Guangdong in a short, well-known sentence: "Good situation, many problems." By "good situation," he meant multiple advantages: good harvests provided stability; proximity to Hong Kong and Macao facilitated foreign trade; forestry, animal husbandry and fisheries had potential; and, most importantly, the Pearl River Delta region had a foundation for economic reform because its people had experience of a market economy.

The "many problems" included Guangdong's low amount of arable land per capita and severe grain shortages due to rampant natural disasters, and deficiencies in infrastructure, particularly energy and transportation. In addition, the Cultural Revolution had wrought immense damage. Many people who had been purged on false charges needed to be rehabilitated.

Solving these problems "left over from history" was one of Xi's most urgent and tortuous tasks.

Xi Zhongxun was obsessed, thinking constantly about Guangdong's economic direction, about how to utilize the province's unique advantages and overcome its shortcomings. He worked day and night, often until 2:00 A.M., as if, in his wife's words, "he were trying to recapture those lost 16 years."

He would often contemplate Hong Kong, a thriving city close by in distance but far away in terms of vitality, activity, confidence and achievement, and reflect on the farmers of Shenzhen, many of whom tried to enter Hong Kong illegally, some repeatedly. Why, he wondered, since over 80% of Hong Kong's population was from Guangdong, was Hong Kong so developed and Guangdong so backward? What was the difference?

Xi would lie awake at night, mulling these questions. His eldest daughter, Xi Qiaoqiao, who was with him in Guangdong, begged him to rest more and take better care of himself. Xi's health was poor: he had never fully recovered from the Cultural Revolution. However, Xi had a mission, and was determined to succeed.

Xi came to realize what now seems obvious but at the time was not: if the difference between Hong Kong and Guangdong was not geography or people, it must be the system. He concluded that the key to Guangdong's development was policy. If Beijing could give Guangdong preferential policies and certain flexibilities, the province should be able to revive its own economy.

Even before the reform-setting plenary in December 1978, Xi Zhongxun implored the central government to allow Guangdong "to absorb capital from Hong Kong and Macau, so that we could import advanced equipment, technologies, power, and feed. We would then use these advanced farms as models to train capable personnel and gain experience."

After the plenary, Xi rushed back to Guangdong, where he set the goal of implementing "socialist modernization." Xi's directive was the turning point for Guangdong and, in retrospect, for all China. It resolved that Guangdong could now take full advantage of its special characteristics, and utilize foreign capital. Areas of focus would be trade, processing, assembly, and agriculture; joint ventures were encouraged. Xi said: "Now that the Central Committee supports Guangdong, if Guangdong still stagnates or develops very slowly, we would feel guilty."

When in 1979 Bao'an County (Shenzhen) first proposed inviting foreign capital to help develop processing industries and small-volume foreign trade, Xi Zhongxun immediately approved: "Just do it. Don't wait!" he said. "As long as you can boost the economy so that the people can enjoy a better life, just go ahead and make it happen. Don't fret about the '-ism' problem [i.e., socialism vs. capitalism]; there are good things we can learn from capitalism too."

Xi was not timid: he suggested reforming "not only the economic system, but also the whole administrative system." He said: "China is a large country.

Every province has its own characteristics. Some issues should be dealt with according to the special nature of each province." Xi cited a comment of Chairman Mao's, about "centralizing big power, and delegating small powers" to justify this theory. He asked the Central Committee to "give us some freedom." When asked what freedoms Guangdong wanted, he stressed: "Guangdong is a province, but it's the same size as a country, or even several countries, in other parts of the world. However," he said, "our local power is too limited and the central government's power is too great. This is not conducive to economic development. Our request is that central government control over Guangdong be relaxed a little, and more flexibility given. It would be beneficial to the nation as well as the province. It's highly possible that in just a few years we could make great economic progress."

Deng Xiaoping concurred. "Set up a special zone," Deng said to Xi. "However, the central Government doesn't have money; you'll have to finance it yourself. You may have to shed blood to explore the new road."

When in July 1979 the Central Committee authorized the Special Economic Zones—in which special policies and flexible methods could be used—to be piloted first in Shenzhen and Zhuhai, Xi said, "Now I am feeling rather happy and somewhat scared. 'Happy' because we are now able to take the first step in the 'Four Modernizations' cause. 'Scared' because I know that this task is a huge burden and we haven't any experience."

But Guangdong's reform was inevitable, Xi continued. "If we don't do it today or tomorrow, we have to do it the day after tomorrow. To develop, we have to change. We have to do it even if we have to lose our lives . . . Comrades, let us work hard for the pilot."

If China's reform first began in the countryside, then China's opening-up first began in Guangdong. In November 1980, Xi Zhongxun was promoted to the central government. In his later years, Xi would become a strong pro-market reformer, and a mentor of future leaders Hu Jintao and Wen Jiabao. True to his principles, Xi would be one of the few Party leaders to defend Hu Yaobang when, after student protests in 1986, Hu was removed as general secretary—and it would be said that Xi criticized the 1989 crackdown in Tiananmen Square.

In 2002, Xi Zhongxun died at the age of 89 and would be remembered for his integrity, kindness and friendship. Given his life-long commitment, no matter the personal hardships, to the betterment of China, including the rights of minorities and religions, he would have been pleased that one of his four children, Xi Jinping, would become the country's vice president in 2007 and possibly its president in 2012.

★ ★ ★

As reform moved into the cities during the mid 1980s, discontent began brewing. Whether because reform was happening too quickly, or not quickly enough, frustrations were on the rise. While some people got rich, others were suffering; prices were unstable; corruption increased; wages were not related to performance. "Surgeons are no richer than barbers," went one popular saying. Increasingly, such anger was directed towards the government: in September 1985 Peking University students protested: "Down with corrupt officials!"

The demonstration took China's leadership by surprise. General Secretary Hu Yaobang, who had led the campaign to rehabilitate those who had been persecuted during the Cultural Revolution, and known for his Theory of the Three Tolerances (leniency, generosity and tolerance), sought to address the problems. Rather than punishing the demonstrators, he championed the need to fight corruption, promote younger leaders, and initiate modest political reform. Initially, Deng Xiaoping gave Hu moderate support, though he stressed that "decision-making must be cautious to avoid disorder" and "the Party must retain ultimate leadership."

Resurgent conservatives, uncomfortable with reform's rapid pace, were on watch for an occasion to line up against Hu. At the Party plenum in September 1986, they added the words "strongly oppose bourgeois liberalization" to a document that Hu Yaobang had submitted. ("Bourgeois liberalization" was a catch phrase which stood for certain perceived "negative tendencies," and the worrying slide toward them: Western-style, multiparty democracy, which threatened the Communist Party's ruling monopoly; Western-style popular culture, which threatened traditional Chinese culture; and Western-style economic capitalism, which would undermine socialism.) However vague the phrase, it was contentious and disparaging to Hu and, as it was intended, it stoked the political furnace.

Deng made what some saw as an about-face. "Opposing bourgeois liberalization, I am the one who speaks the most and I am the one who most perseveres," he said. "What is liberalization? In fact, it's something that will lead our policies to capitalism, which they call 'modernization.'. . . If we don't stop liberalism, this and other rotten thinking that develop in the course of opening-up would form a powerful force to destroy socialism."

Others, however, said Deng's stance showed both the clarity of his political commitment and the subtlety of his political sense: with a dual agenda of promoting reform but not weakening socialism, Deng accomplished both by taking up the Leftist-conservatives' own complaint. His strategy relieved pressures against reform (by depriving Leftists of a hot-button issue) while bolstering socialism to withstand opposing pressures from the Rightist—liberals.

The main victim of the protests was Hu Yaobang. On December 30, Deng Xiaoping convened an emergency meeting, which was critical of Hu. Deng supported "dialogue and persuasion" in dealing with students, but warned that if they destabilized the social order, action would have to be taken. "It is said in Shanghai," Deng observed, "that the central government has two conflicting opinions on anti–bourgeois liberalization. They are waiting to see what will come out of this."[19] Senior leaders, including Zhao Ziyang, met at Deng's home and decided to relieve Hu Yaobang of his position.

A week later, at what seemed to be a standard Politburo meeting, the decision was formalized. Hu was accused of failing to submit to the Party's collective decisions, particularly the struggle against "bourgeois liberalization." Zhao Ziyang was appointed general secretary in Hu's place, and Li Peng was chosen to replace Zhao as premier.

After an obligatory self-criticism, Hu went into seclusion. Although he remained a member of the Politburo, he was a beaten man. On April 15, 1989—little more than two years after his ouster—Hu Yaobang would be dead. But not, as he had expected, forgotten. The day he died, in commemoration, students began gathering spontaneously in Tiananmen Square. Thereafter, for more than 15 years, Hu's name and his contributions were rarely mentioned in the Chinese media. But that too would change. In private, the respect in which Hu was held by many senior officials was undimmed.

Endnotes

1 Author's meeting with Xing Bensi, Beijing, April 2008.
2 The Two Whatevers dictum was part of a formal policy directive of Chairman Hua Guofeng and China's post-Mao senior leadership formalized in joint, simultaneous editorials, entitled *"Study the Documents Well and Grasp the Key Link"*, published on February 7, 1977, in *People's Daily, Liberation Army Daily*, and *Red Flag* magazine.
3 CPC Party Literature Research Center; whole section.
4 In 1958, at the beginning of the Great Leap Forward, Mao noted in a speech how the slogan "Seek the truth from facts" had been put forward once again, which he said meant that it was necessary to both "have lofty aspirations and yet at the same time carry out considerable scientific analysis." (Stuart R. Schram, *The Thought of Mao Tse-Tung*, Cambridge University Press, 1989).
5 Author's meeting with Teng Wensheng, Beijing, 2004.
6 George J. Church, "Deng Xiaoping" *Time* magazine, January 6, 1986.
7 Zhao Ziyang, *Prisoner of the State*, p. 107.
8 Ibid, p. 112–113.
9 Personal communications in Beijing; Nathan and Gilley, p. 42; "Hu Jintao," Wikipedia.org; whole section.
10 Tkacik, op.cit., entire section.
11 CPC Party Literature Research Center.
12 CPC Party Literature Research Center; whole section.
13 Yang Shangkun, an early backer of Mao, had been purged during the Cultural Revolution for supporting Liu Shaoqi and Deng Xiaoping. (Yang was accused of planting listening devices to spy on Mao.) After being reinstated in November 1978, Yang Shangkun was appointed second provincial party secretary of Guangdong. In 1981, he was appointed to the Central Military Commission, and in 1988 president of China.
14 Author's communication in Beijing.
15 CPC Party Literature Research Center.
16 Bill Savadove, *South China Morning Post*, October 23, 2007.
17 Ni Hong, *Earth Biweekly*, 7th Issue, 2009; whole section.
18 Nathan and Gilley, op.cit.
19 Yang Zhongmei, *Jiang Zemin Zhuan* (Biography of Jiang Zemin) (Taipei: China Times Publishing, 1996).Xi Zhongxun and his wife, Qi Xin, at Huashibian, Yan'an, Shaanxi Province (Spring 1947).

Tiananmen and Thereafter

For all the sharp political differences among China's senior leaders in the late 1980s, no one of importance disagreed fundamentally with the necessity of reform to spur economic development. The fault line between the so-called "liberals" and "conservatives" was the speed and style of the reforms. Still, the division was seismic, and the epicenter would be Tiananmen Square.

The tectonic shift began with tragedy. On April 8, 1989, at the regular Friday meeting of the Politburo chaired by General Secretary Zhao Ziyang, the man he had replaced, Hu Yaobang, fell ill.[1] Since 1987, when he had been removed from his position, Hu almost never spoke at Politburo meetings. One of his greatest regrets, he told a former aide, was that after his forced resignation, he had engaged in ritual self-criticism, thus disappointing his intellectual supporters. Hu doubted that people would ever miss him.

For the next week he appeared to be doing better, but on April 15 he suffered a massive myocardial infarction. Within ten minutes Hu Yaobang was dead.

That evening China Central Television broadcast the news. Within hours students began milling around on campuses across Beijing, wondering how to honor the one man who had stood up for their rights. The next day students from Peking University entered Tiananmen Square. What began as a memorial to the late leader soon transformed itself into a demonstration supporting the liberal values that Hu Yaobang had espoused. Students slapped together posters and banners that called for ending corruption, promoting democracy, and allowing greater freedom of the press. They also demanded that Hu Yaobang's record be reexamined and that he be posthumously exonerated.[2]

Senior leaders grew anxious, fearing violence. Some ten thousand military personnel were brought in for crowd control. A worried Deng Xiaoping remarked that the student movement did not seem to be of the ordinary kind.

On April 24, 60,000 students from 38 universities and colleges in Beijing began a strike, stating that they would boycott their classes indefinitely to press their demands. Student leaders also said that they would be sending delegations to factories to solicit support from workers.

The next morning after listening to Li Peng's report, Deng made his defining statement about the nature of the student movement, branding it "turmoil," a word associated with the Cultural Revolution. (By contrast, the 1986 student protests had been designated as "disturbances.")

"This is a well-planned plot," Deng said, "whose real aim is to reject the Chinese Communist Party and the socialist system at its most fundamental level. . . . We've got to be explicit and clear in opposing this turmoil."

On May 17, the axial meeting took place at Deng Xiaoping's home. Zhao Ziyang made an impassioned case for "dialogue" over martial law, imploring his colleagues that they should seek ways to ease tension rather than make harsh threats. In response, two conservative leaders criticized Zhao personally, essentially blaming him for the surging, out-of-control masses.[3] The internal struggle was over: Zhao was out.

After the meeting, Zhao told his wife and children, "If the conflicts intensify, it would not be acceptable to history. Since I am sitting in this position, I will not agree [to military action]. But I may be jailed because of that and you may be implicated. You will have to be psychologically prepared."[4]

Deng himself voiced the military option. "We old comrades . . . have no choice," he said, with seven elders, Party leaders, and senior army officers present.[5] "At bottom they [our opponents] want to overthrow our state and our Party—that's what's really going on here. If you don't see this point, you can't be clear about what's going on. If you do see it, then you'll know why we need martial law in Beijing." Still haunted by the chaos of the Cultural Revolution, Deng added, "Some people object to the word [turmoil], but it hits the nail on the head." Martial law gave the government a legal basis for moving the army into the capital.

Zhao Ziyang, looking back, disagrees. He argues that the meeting at which martial law was declared was illegal because it violated the Party charter stipulating that the general secretary must chair the meeting—and he, still the general secretary, wasn't even notified of it.[6] Furthermore, there was no Politburo vote.

Zhao's primary nemesis was Premier Li Peng, whom he accuses of having "hidden ill intentions" to crush the student protestors by armed violence. Deng Xiaoping, meanwhile, appears manipulable if not cunning in Zhao's view. "Deng had always stood out among the party elders as the one who emphasized the means of dictatorship," Zhao wrote. "He often reminded people about its usefulness."

As for Zhao himself, "I refused to become the General Secretary who mobilized the military to crack down on students," he said.

On May 19 Zhao Ziyang entered Tiananmen Square. With tears in his eyes, he begged the students to end their hunger strike, saying, "We have come too late, and we are sorry."[7]

"I was trying to persuade them to end the hunger strike," Zhao later wrote. "I felt it was a waste for these young students to end their lives like this. [The students could not] imagine the treatment in store for them."

Throughout the day, tension mounted as news of the government's intentions reached student leaders. At 7:00 P.M. they decided to end the hunger strike but remain where they were. At 10:00 P.M. Premier Li Peng called for "serious measures to end the riot." Two hours later, at midnight, a loudspeaker in Tiananmen announced the imposition of martial law.

More than 100,000 troops had been activated in an overwhelming show of force. Before morning on May 20 they were in position to enter the city and clear the square. That was when Li Peng and Beijing Mayor Chen Xitong issued decrees imposing martial law. Included were strict prohibitions of any type of demonstration, a media clampdown, and authorization for the armed police and military to "use all necessary means, including force, to deal with prohibited activities."[8]

In response, some students raised the stakes; they began using obstructionist measures such as blocking transportation, accosting police and soldiers, and sabotaging public facilities. A few now believed that violence and bloodshed would help their cause.

According to senior Party officials, it was on May 20 that the decision was made to nominate Jiang Zemin to become the new general secretary of the Communist Party.[9] The officials say this was "suggested by Deng Xiaoping," at a meeting at his residence.[10]

"After long and careful consideration," Deng told his inner group, "the Shanghai Party secretary, Comrade Jiang Zemin, does indeed seem a proper choice. I think he's up to the task. Comrades Chen Yun, Xiannian, and I all lean toward Comrade Jiang Zemin for general secretary. What do the rest of you think?" After two elders agreed—based more on their trust of Deng than on their familiarity with Jiang—Li Xiannian said "It's true that Jiang Zemin lacks experience at the center. But this man has a political mind, is in the prime of life, and can be trusted." Sources say Li Xiannian and Bo Yibo were instrumental in Deng's decision to appoint Jiang.[11]

Yang Shangkun concurred, emphasizing that "the new leadership team [must] maintain the image of reform and opening and win the trust of the people," adding that if it were "stodgy, rigid or mediocre," the people wouldn't trust it, Party members wouldn't respect it, there would be constant disturbances, and "we can forget about economic growth." For China to seal itself off again, he said, would be "frightening." Deng himself would later reportedly use similar words to explain the choice: "If the leadership we present seems rigid, conservative, or mediocre," he said, "there will be more trouble in the future. . . . We will never have peace . . . We must establish credibility among the people."[12]

Elder Bo Yibo also endorsed the new generation. "As long as we stay out of the way and let them go," he said, "I think they'll do well." Deng then called a formal vote on appointing the new Politburo Standing Committee with Jiang Zemin as general secretary. Agreement was unanimous.

On May 22 troops tried to enter the capital but were forced back when large numbers of residents and students blocked the streets with hastily erected barricades. That evening in Beijing senior leaders gathered to effect the ouster of Zhao Ziyang.[13] At the same time, the central government brought the Party secretaries of every province, and other senior leaders to Beijing, where they were briefed on the coming change of leadership.[14]

On June 1 the Politburo received a lengthy report from the Beijing Party Committee. Entitled "On the True Nature of the Turmoil," it placed the blame for the protests on putative plotters backed by "foreign and domestic hostile forces," including Taiwan and America.[15] Seizing the moment, Premier Li Peng urged that "we move immediately to clear Tiananmen Square, and that we resolutely put an end to the turmoil and the ever-expanding trouble." Deng Xiaoping agreed. "Martial law troops," he suggested, should "begin tonight to carry out the clearing plan and finish it within two days."[16]

President Yang Shangkun tried to rein in emotions. "The Martial Law Command must make it quite clear to all units that they are to open fire only as a last resort," he said. "And let me repeat: No bloodshed within Tiananmen Square, period."

For several days Chinese armed forces from provinces outside Beijing had been arriving at staging camps on the outskirts of the city. China's leadership was taking no chances that local troops might sympathize with the students. Small groups of soldiers, disguised in plain clothes, had begun slipping into the city, and on the evening of June 3, 1989, the army received word to enter the city en masse. Their explicit order: "Clear Tiananmen Square." As they had before, crowds of angry residents blocked the tanks and heavy transports and alternately taunted and pleaded with the troops.

This time, the soldiers did not turn back. Late that night, tanks and armored vehicles, followed by troops, forced their way into the center of Beijing and the first casualties were reported. The army came from several directions to avoid bottlenecks and assure penetration. In accord with President Yang's directive, the troops generally held their fire in Tiananmen Square, but in other parts of the city hundreds, at least, were killed and thousands injured as fighting raged for about 12 hours.

On the afternoon of June 4, rain began to fall. A few bodies could be seen on roadsides. Tanks rumbled through the streets. CCTV announced the enforcement of martial law. TV anchors dressed in dark colors and spoke with weak voices.

On June 5, a young man in a white shirt, armed with nothing but a large shopping bag, as if he had just loaded up at a discount store, stood defiantly before a long line of tanks, stopping 17 of them in their tracks. When the lead tank tried to maneuver around the lone, unknown hero, he side-stepped right back into its path, and standing defiantly erect, blocked its advance. Captured by photojournalists and flashed around the world, the picture made the front page of almost every major news publication and helped galvanize Western opinion.

Protests against the military action were heard across China and around the world, but Beijing itself was quiet. After months of agitation and euphoria, an eerie silence descended on the city.

The mortality count varied wildly—a reliable number has never been established, but it's likely in the hundreds not thousands. In addition to those killed, thousands were injured or arrested. Student leaders received up to 13 years in prison. Statistics aside, the nation remained traumatized well after the violence subsidized.

★ ★ ★

Four or five days after the announcement on June 24, 1989 that the new CPC general secretary would be Jiang Zemin—surprising everyone including Jiang's family—Jiang called Shen Yongyan, his close friend from their days together working at the First Automotive Works in Changchun.

"Congratulations," Shen said, surprised to hear his old friend's voice. "We're so proud of you." He felt awkward and uncertain about how to address the new leader of the country.

"Don't be so fast to congratulate me," Jiang said. "*Yuntou zhuanxiang.*"[17] This self-deprecating expression means something like "My head is spinning—I'm confused, disoriented, dizzy."

In the wake of June 4, economic reforms were largely deferred, and political reform was shut down altogether. In a throwback to the past, new policies, programs, and ventures now had to be categorized as either

Following the military action in Tiananmen Square, an expanded Politburo meeting builds consensus for Jiang Zemin's elevation to CPC general secretary. Jiang is seated right center (sitting straight up); Deng Xiaoping is back center (short); Li Peng is left of Deng (Beijing, June 19–21, 1989; Xinhua News Agency).

"socialist" or "capitalist," and those with the latter label were rejected. Foreign investment all but dried up. China had started to stagnate.

$$\star \ \star \ \star$$

In November 1990, on the tenth anniversary of the establishment of the Special Economic Zones, Jiang Zemin attended celebrations in Shenzhen and Zhuhai. On the three-hour flight back to Beijing, accompanied by senior officials including Wen Jiabao, Jiang was eager to discuss China's early, limited experiments with the stock market. In Shenzhen, five companies had publicly issued stock and the stock exchange was about to be established; in the same period, the Shanghai Stock Exchange, which had a storied history going back to the 19th century, was about to re-open. Selling stock was controversial—some called it "bourgeois liberalism."

"General Secretary Jiang asked me many questions," recalled Liu Hongru, who would later become the first chairman of the China Securities Regulatory Commission, "and he took many notes."

"Where does the stock market's money come from?" Jiang inquired.

"Ninety-five percent of the money comes from individual investors," Liu stated, hastening to add that the fundamental ownership of the companies did not change "since over 60% of the equity would still be owned by the State or collective organizations."

"When stock prices go up," Jiang continued, "who makes money, and who suffers losses?"

Liu explained that the pricing of stocks was determined by the market theory of supply and demand. Since only five companies had been selected for the experiment, too much money was chasing too few stocks. "The demand is very strong, and that's why prices are continuing to go up," Liu said, adding, "This is not realistic."

Jiang also asked about supervision and regulation, specifically what to do when government officials bought stocks.

At the end of the flight, Liu told Jiang, "No matter what, we should continue our stock market experiment—our reform must not go backward. Please trust me, as an old Party member, I would not carelessly push for privatization. But since mistakes are unavoidable, I hope that we don't punish people or affix political labels. If that happens, no one would be willing to take responsibility."

Jiang agreed to continue the stock market experiment but cautioned that it be carefully studied and not expanded further until China gained more experience.

As of mid 2008, the New York Stock Exchange (NYSE) listed 57 companies from Greater China, including 41 from the mainland. The total market capitalization was over $1.2 trillion. The five largest global IPOs by NYSE-listed Chinese companies had raised a total of approximately $16 billion. "The entrance of China-based corporations into the world's capital markets exemplifies China's reform and opening-up," said Margaret Ren, a prominent investment banker who arranged several of the historic offerings, "This reciprocal relationship benefits both China and the world." Margaret Ren is the daughter-in-law of former Party General Secretary Zhao Ziyang.

In 2009, almost precisely 20 years after Zhao Ziyang was deposed and weeks before the 20th anniversary of the Tiananmen crackdown, Zhao's secret memoirs were published worldwide.[18] Although Zhao died in 2005, and had been under house arrest for over 15 years, he would chronicle for history his view of reform and the inner-Party struggles that yielded the tragic events of 1989.

Endnotes

1 Author's interview with first-hand witness to Hu Yaobang's heart attack at the Politburo meeting.

2 This section on Tiananmen Square is derived from various sources, including: Zhang Liang (complier, pseudonym), Andrew J. Nathan and Perry Link (editors), *The Tiananmen Papers: The Chinese Leadership's Decision to Use Force Against Their Own People - In Their Own Words* (New York: Public Affairs), 2001; Yang, *Biography*, Chapter 7; Gilley, *Tiger*, 114–148; *NYT*; AP; Shanghai City Service (BBC). China News Service (Beijing, BBC); Xinhua (English and Chinese [BBC]); UPI; WP; LAT; JEN; *Christian Science Monitor*; *Ming Pao* (Hong Kong, BBC); TKP (BBC); *Financial Times*; *Newsday*; author's meeting with Wang Daohan, Jiang Zehui and Ye Gongqi; and author's communication in Beijing.

3 Zhao Ziyang, *Prisoner of the State*; whole section.

4 Josephine Ma, "Zhao wrote book as a 'historic gift' to China's future generation." *South China Morning Post*, May 22, 2009, quoting Du Daozheng.

5 Liang, Nathan and Link, *The Tiananmen Papers*, 204–205.

6 Perry Link, "From the Inside, Out: Zhao Ziyang Continues His Fight Postmortem" *Washington Post*, May 17, 2009.

7 Liang, Nathan and Link, *The Tiananmen Papers*, 217.

8 Ibid., 233–234.

9 Author's communication with historians, Beijing.

10 Attending were Li Xiannian, Chen Yun, Peng Zhen, Yang Shangkun, Wang Zhen, Li Peng, Qiao Shi, Yao Yilin, and Song Ping. This assertion and the timeline do not seem consistent with the sequence of events as described in *The Tiananmen Papers*, a book purporting to reveal secret Party records, which puts the meeting that selected Jiang Zemin on May 22 (which is the date subsequently followed in the text.)

11 Author's communication in Beijing.

12 Gilley, *Tiger*, 131; Robert L. Suettinger, *Beyond Tiananmen: The Politics of U.S.-China Relations 1989–2000* (Washington, D.C.: Brookings Institution Press), 2003, 76.

13 Liang, Nathan and Link, *The Tiananmen Papers*, 268–272.

14 Ibid., 278–279. The briefing was conducted by Yang Shangkun, Li Peng, Qiao Shi, and Yao Yilin. Government sources claim this never happened.

15 *The Tiananmen Papers*, 330-338. A similar report by the State Security Ministry (338–348), also prepared on instructions from Li Peng, also alleged "ideological and political infiltration" by clandestine Western sources, including George Soros.

16 Ibid., 362.

17 Shen Yongyan.

18 Christopher Bodeen, AP, May 21, 2009; Kristine Kwok and Minnie Chan, and Josephine Ma, *South China Morning* Post, May 22, 2009; Adi Ignatious, "The Secret Memoir of a Fallen Chinese Leader" *Time* magazine, May 14, 2009.

What's a "Socialist Market Economy?"

After June 4, Party conservatives used their resurgent power to rein in the speed of Deng's reforms, which they felt were distorting the economy and undermining the ideological purity of Chinese communism. Party elder Chen Yun believed that the "planned economy is primary, the market economy supplementary" and that deviations in recent years had caused a "mortal wound" to the economy. At the Party plenum in November 1989, such conservative views were restored as the Party line and explicitly laid out in a thorough, systematic critique of the pace and process of reform.

During 1990 and 1991, Leftists launched waves of criticism against market economics. They demanded China oppose "peaceful evolution" (code for a supposed plot by the West, particularly America, to overthrow China's socialist system by subtle social transformation rather than overt military action), and claimed that the CPC now had a "dual mission: class struggle and massive construction."

Deng Xiaoping however quickly grew unhappy with the now glacial pace of reform. In 1991 he arranged for the enterprising and aggressive Zhu Rongji, then Shanghai Party secretary, to become vice premier. Zhu's portfolio was industry, agriculture, and finance. An ardent reformer and brilliant economic thinker, Zhu would become a counterweight to Premier Li Peng and other conservatives.

Yet on August 19, 1991 came a shock from afar. Hard-line politicians in the Kremlin, desperate to maintain Party supremacy, took Soviet Union leader Mikhail Gorbachev captive in an ill-fated coup attempt. The next day, Deng Xiaoping called a meeting to assess the still-murky situation in Moscow. Some Chinese leaders praised the conservative resurgence, even hailing the coup as a "good deed." But they were left aghast just two days later when Boris Yeltsin, backed by overwhelming mass support, defeated the coup plotters – and effectively broke the back of the Soviet Communist Party. Although Gorbachev was reinstated, the Soviet Union never recovered: the Soviet Party was declared illegal and the Soviet Union collapsed, a 70-year experiment in communism failed and finished.

The lesson was not lost on China's leaders. As if by reflex, reformist moves were slowed. Even though Deng suggested that Chinese leaders might be overreacting, a new level of caution was indicated. Arguments raged over whether Deng's reforms were leading the country, via "peaceful evolution," to capitalism.

For his part, General Secretary Jiang Zemin took a reflective approach, seeking underlying reasons for the Soviet demise. Socialism, he concluded, was not one of them. Instead, he attributed the collapse to mishandling the diverse nationalities and ethnic groups within the vast union, and to placing too much emphasis on political reform and not enough on economic reform—too much *glasnost* (openness) and not enough *perestroika* (restructuring). In China the priorities were reversed. "We must gradually aim at separating the functions of government and enterprise," Jiang said in a speech supporting Deng's reforms. "We must cut down on unnecessary administrative interference in enterprises, so that they can have autonomy in management and be financially self-sufficient." Even conservatives agreed that only a thriving economy could keep the Party in power.

★ ★ ★

Since 1979, Deng Xiaoping had been leading largely from "behind the curtain"—he held no formal titles but had enormous influence on those who did. He would give his grand thinking and others would do the implementation. Now at 87, Deng was no longer much involved—he was more than a figurehead but less of a factor. Though he continued to be revered as an icon in China, his actual power and influence had diminished. Also, he was enjoying retirement: dining with his large family and playing bridge, a game at which he excelled.

Nonetheless, China's Paramount Leader remained deeply dissatisfied with the pace of development. Before he died, he yearned to see his country irreversibly on the road to greatness. For this to happen, things had to change.

And so, as 1992 began, Deng Xiaoping decided to go it alone. With failing senses, but with a will of steel, this diminutive old man emerged from his life of leisure to do political battle one last time.

To breathe new life into the economy, Deng told confidants, he needed to leave Beijing. And so he did, barnstorming around southern China stumping for reform—a passionate, personal journey to force matters open and revitalize the nation. Deng's journey would later become known as *Nanxun*, or Southern Tour, a phrase which harkens back to the days when China's emperors would make inspection tours of far-flung provinces – and which also suggests the significance of a journey now recognized as a defining event in making China what it is today.

At his first stop in Wuhan, Deng got straight to the point. "Here's what our problem is right now: it's called 'formalism', which is a kind of excessive bureaucracy," he told Hubei provincial leaders who met him in his private rail carriage at the train station. "Our leaders look like they're doing something, but they're not doing anything really worthwhile," he went on. "When I watch television, all I see are meetings and ceremonies—our leaders must think they're television stars. The meetings are excessive and the speeches have repetitious content and no new ideas. We should give priority to deeds not to words."[1]

Deng then drew a line in the sand. "Anyone who is against reform," he warned, "will be put out of office."[2] Deng was contesting for the soul of the Party; this time he was not turning back. It was a stark message and Deng told the Hubei Party leaders to send it, in full, to Beijing.

Deng's next stop was Guangdong.[3] Touring downtown Shenzhen, with its broad, bustling streets, landscaped green areas and rows of high-rise buildings, Deng marveled at the drastic transformation since his last visit in 1984. He said: "After eight years of such fast development, Shenzhen has changed a great deal. It is beyond my expectations. On seeing it, I feel even more assured."

Deng was in high spirits. He discussed differences of opinion within the Party over the Special Economic Zones, noting that "Some worried that SEZs would give rise to capitalism. However," Deng said, "Shenzhen's achievements put a halt to such worries. SEZs are established under the

Deng Xiaoping (first row, center) inspects Huanggang Port, Shenzhen, Guangdong Province during his Southern Tour (Nanxun) (January 19, 1992).

socialist system, not the capitalist one." Indeed, he insisted, "There was no need to worry whether we are following 'socialism' or 'capitalism.'"[4]

Deng stressed that "We can benefit much from foreign-invested enterprises. We should be bold," he said, noting that "Some maintain that foreign investment enhances capitalism. In my opinion, these people do not even have fundamental economic knowledge." In fact, Deng said, China "should increase foreign investment, form more joint ventures, and take advantage of Western technology and management."[5] In a rebuke to his critics, he asserted that "These foreign joint-venture firms make profits under our law, pay taxes, and provide our workers with jobs and pay. What's wrong with that?" And he insisted: "If we don't continue to improve people's living standard, if we don't continue to build the economy, there will only be a dead-end road for our Party."

Deng was exasperated, indignant, at the criticism. Driving back to the guesthouse, Deng erupted again, "They just speak nonsense!" he said of his conservative critics.

The next day, from the revolving restaurant at the top of the 50-story Shenzhen International Trade Center, Deng overlooked the city's panorama. He was delighted. "Most important is Shenzhen's pioneering courage," Deng said. "Without such courage, we wouldn't be able to forge a new road and create new deeds. It's impossible to achieve success without taking risks. There is no such thing as 100% correct judgment at the beginning of any project. . . . We must be fearless and daring, willing to experiment without restriction. Once the way is determined, we should move ahead boldly."

Looking out of the window, Deng continued: 'We dare not shrink back in the process of opening-up because we are afraid of capitalist things or of taking the wrong way. The criteria for judging activities should be based on whether they facilitate socialist productivity, whether they enhance the comprehensive strength of our socialist country, and whether they improve the living standard of people." It was a defining directive: ever since the beginning of opening-up, there had been competing viewpoints for judging the merit of new guidelines and policies. Deng's criteria, set forth here and later known as the Three Favorables, provided an objective standard – and would eventually become an important aspect of Deng Xiaoping Theory.

Deng's impromptu speech was the most important of his *Nanxun*. He stressed the anti-corruption campaigns, and using legal measures to enforce clean and honest administration. "We should implement two parallel tactics: promoting opening-up on the one hand and attacking criminal activities on the other," Deng said, adding that there was a need for "powerful measures to eliminate all sorts of social evils."

Deng also emphasized that China should cultivate leadership successors who were "revolutionary, young, educated and professional," so as to select talented people of political integrity and professional competence for senior posts in the future.

Before Deng left Shenzhen, he defended the socialist market economy, emphasizing that "a planned economy is not equivalent to socialism, because there is planning under capitalism too," while "a market economy is not capitalism, because there are markets under socialism too."

As he embarked on a ship for the journey to Zhuhai, Deng suddenly turned back and told the Shenzhen Party secretary, "You should speed up economic reform." It was an astonishing statement. Nowhere else in China was reform moving as fast as in Shenzhen – indeed critics in Beijing often pointed to the city as a case study of what happens when reform moves *too* fast. Now Deng, in a resounding rebuke to his conservative opponents, was telling Shenzhen leaders to move even faster. He took up a metaphor used by Mao: "We must not act like women with bound feet," he said.[6]

Deng reserved most of his criticism for "ultra-Leftist" thinking. The allegation that "reform and the opening-up policy are a means of introducing capitalism, and that there is real danger of 'peaceful evolution' towards capitalism," was, he said, "a charge coming chiefly from the Left." Deng said that China was currently "affected by both Right and Left tendencies," and acknowledged that "Rightist tendencies can destroy socialism." But, he said, "so can Leftist ones." And he noted that, "It is the Leftist tendencies that have the deepest roots. Some theorists and politicians try to intimidate people by pinning political labels on them. That is not a Rightist tactic but a Leftist one . . . In Party history, those tendencies have led to dire consequences—fine things were destroyed overnight. China should maintain vigilance against the Right but primarily against the Left. . . Throughout the 70-year history of our Party, the most serious problems were 'ultra-Leftist'."[7]

"From Deng's tone, I felt that he hated the 'ultra-Left' bitterly," said Chen Kaizhi, a local official who had organized Deng's trip. "His assertions were powerful enough to shake the whole Pacific Ocean."

★ ★ ★

As Deng traveled across southern China and continued to speak out bluntly, the mainland media's silence was becoming problematic. Hong Kong reporters were capturing every comment, but not a single notice appeared in any mainland paper. A decision had apparently been made to suppress the news.

Uncertain of where Deng's Southern Tour would lead, no one in Beijing wanted to get trapped in a definitive position. Rumors questioned Deng's status; after all, it was whispered, Deng was retired, had no real power, and was almost 88-years-old. Some said that he was in no position to talk about strategic issues; others even accused him of violating the Party Constitution. Yet word of Deng's travels and incisive comments was becoming widespread, and the absence of official reports was undermining leadership credibility.

On February 12th, the Politburo agreed to allow a limited dissemination of Deng's remarks to senior officials—perhaps hoping that Deng would be satisfied and his ideas contained. But the wily patriarch used local papers in Shanghai and Shenzhen to give his views first exposure in the mainland media. Deng Xiaoping was on a crusade, and many now knew it.

Party Chief Jiang Zemin was concerned. He knew that Deng's *Nanxun* comments were being interpreted as critical of him. He realized that his skewing to the more conservative views of Party elders and Politburo colleagues was, in the light of Deng's onslaught, becoming progressively less viable. His leadership was at stake. Furthermore, deep down, Jiang was an economic reformer, even if he did not share Deng's missionary zeal.

Jiang decided to take action. He reached agreement with Premier Li Peng, an erstwhile rival but now equally vulnerable, to accelerate reform. Over the next few months, they would authorize a slew of papers promoting Deng's speeches, perhaps 20 or more. Once he made the decision to back Deng, Jiang would not be half-hearted about putting it into practice. (To his credit, Jiang has been candid, admitting openly that he made mistakes in his early years – when he made conservative assertions such as "I hate private enterprises and would like to destroy them." Before Jiang stepped down in 2002, he told friends: "Yes, I confess that many of my early speeches were not so right. We wade across the river by feeling for stones [i.e., take a trial-and-error approach], because truth is a long road; nobody knows exactly what truth is."[8])

On February 28, a paper summarizing Deng's main ideas was circulated to Party branches throughout the country. The Central Party School, the citadel of Communist thought, distributed written copies of Deng's talks to its 2,000 students and faculty. With its national network of alumni in key positions, the Party school was an ideal vehicle to propagate the new policy.

The final breakthrough came in early March. In a two-day Politburo meeting, Deng's *Nanxun* speeches were studied carefully, and in one of its most important decisions ever, the Politburo agreed to endorse his words and ideas.[9] President Yang Shangkun, Deng's longtime friend, began by advocating that the Party's highest body ratify Deng's reforms. Jiang immediately supported Yang and, in a candid admission, said that he himself had been lax in promoting reform. The more conservative members of the Politburo, realizing that they were now outmaneuvered, sought to limit the damage by arguing that Deng's admonition to "guard against Leftism" applied only to economics.

On March 11, six weeks after Deng Xiaoping's Southern Tour finished, the official Xinhua News Agency finally reported its occurrence. "We must be more daring in opening-up and reform," read the article. Deng's *Nanxun* was now Party policy; his *Nanxun* commentaries would become the "great guidelines" of China's reform and development, the essence of socialist modernization, and the theme of the forthcoming 14th Party Congress.

Encouraged by the new thinking, intellectuals and army leaders mounted their own campaigns to combat Leftist dogma. Deng and Jiang loyalists formed investigative "work groups" to root out Leftist influence in major newspapers such as *People's Daily*.[10]

Once the Chinese media were permitted to report on Deng's *Nanxun*, his every step became a political earthquake, his every word a revealed truth. Virtually every report about public affairs now contained references to Deng's *Nanxun*. Mainland writers gushed over Deng, describing the new round of reform as "a warm spring wave that spread over all China, clearing away people's hesitation, anxiety, and doubt."[11]

Provinces across China suddenly sought new ways to reform. The entire nation was upshifting into the fast lane. From here on, China's growth rates would lead the world. In 1992 China's GDP grew an unprecedented 12.8%, far exceeding earlier estimates of 6%. Though such white-hot growth would cause serious side effects, particularly inflation and increased corruption, it would turn China into an economic superpower whose modernization and prosperity would astound the world. Had it not been for Deng Xiaoping's *Nanxun*, such development might not have happened for years—if at all.

When Deng told audiences to "watch out for the Right, but mainly defend against the Left," he was making an explicit, final break with the Party's rigid, doctrinaire past. Though Deng was rejecting Maoist mass movements with all their ideological strictures, he believed he was enhancing—not rejecting—the original essence of Mao Zedong Thought. From the beginning of Deng's reforms in 1978, until his Southern Tour, China had continuously debated political ideology. After 1992 the debate was over: the path was clear and the pace was swift. Deng Xiaoping, the man who had instituted reform and opening-up, had now resuscitated it, changing China for good. "I can't imagine what China would be like today," one senior leader told me, "had not Deng Xiaoping made his *Nanxun*."

★ ★ ★

Today, Deng Xiaoping Theory is recognized as the foundation of reform in China, the political rock on which all subsequent political theories have been built. It wasn't always that way, especially not to Deng himself, who was simply saying and doing what he thought best for China in response to specific situations.

Leng Rong is one of China's leading experts on Deng Xiaoping Theory. Now minister of the CPC Party Literature Research Center, which is responsible for the thoughts and works of senior leaders, Leng has been one of my primary teachers in China, particularly on political theory.

"I started to work at the Institute of Deng Xiaoping in the 1980s," recalled Leng Rong. "Many of the theories that Deng formed were based on circumstances at that time. Through speeches at Party meetings and discussions with foreign friends, he kept exploring, spelling out and developing his thoughts. They began as independent sparkles of ideas and in the end they would form a systematic theory."

Leng asserted that Deng's thinking was best manifested in one speech and two articles. The speech was his pathbreaking 1978 "Emancipating the

Leng Rong, executive vice minister (later minister) of the CPC Party Literature Research Center, explains Chinese political theory to Robert Lawrence Kuhn (Beijing, September 2002).

Mind" address, which is regarded as the commencement of reform and opening-up.

One article was "Building Socialism with Chinese Characteristics" (1984), which answered China's then most fundamental questions. "It was a milestone in the formation of Deng Xiaoping Theory," said Leng. "The notions of well-off society, reform and opening-up, democracy, rule of law, spiritual civilization, one-country-two-systems, and also various foreign policies, many of which came to prominence later, all were stipulated and streamlined by Deng himself."

The second article was "Deng's Talk in the South in 1992," a collection of his *Nanxun* speeches and talks in Wuhan, Guangdong, and Shanghai. "This article was prepared by Deng himself, and he purposefully summarized his overall thoughts," Leng said. "He was 88 at that time and edited it personally. He made a thorough analysis of all the major disputes since reform began and drew conclusions about them. He stressed that such should be the Party's basic line, and that it shouldn't waver for the next 100 years. This article laid the foundation for our future development and success."

Deng's era was unique, Leng Rong said. "Remember, we were starting to set up and try out a new system. We encountered many challenges, but we made it through. Our subsequent leaders, Jiang Zemin and Hu Jintao, are different from Deng. They not only have to put forward a grand vision, but they also have to do practical work. They must strike a balance between theory and practice. However, this also depends on Deng's achievements. He came up with the overarching vision. When he was in power, there were intense debates within the Party. But in the end all debates died down."

★ ★ ★

With Deng Xiaoping's *Nanxun* now holding sway, Jiang Zemin proclaimed the new vision with zeal, lacing his speeches with quotes from Deng and calling for rapid reform virtually every time he spoke. In May 1992, he asked the Politburo to be more enthusiastic about Deng's talks and ideas, and in June he gave a path-breaking speech to a graduating class of fast-rising cadres at the Central Party School. In this intensely scrutinized address, Jiang declared that any Party official who criticized or altered Deng's policies "could be sacked at any time." Although he castigated decadent Western values, Jiang rebuked Leftism for equating reform with "going down the capitalistic road" and for arguing that the Party's central task was not economic development but "class struggle."

Jiang stressed that the key for establishing a new economic system was to understand how the market allocates resources. He said that at the 14th Party Congress the current official terminology, "socialist commodity economy," would be replaced by the explicitly reformist "socialist market economy." In a culture attuned to slight shifts in wording, the new phrase, putting the "market" overtly up front, was an ideological bombshell.[12]

"Jiang's Party school speech was extremely sensitive," recalls Teng Wensheng, his chief speechwriter. "It came just after Deng's *Nanxun* and had to reflect his reformist ideas, but the Party and the country were not prepared for such new thinking. There was resistance; many different constituencies had to be considered. As such, Jiang took the tone of a discussant, not a directive giver. He had to build consensus."

According to Teng, Jiang chose the phrase "socialist market economy." He had concluded that a fresh label was needed for China's new system, and, after considering many options, he decided that this was the one he liked best. It placed prominent emphasis on the word "market" while making it clear that such a market must be consistent with socialism.[13]

Jiang Zemin had not consulted Deng Xiaoping in advance of the speech. Since Deng's Southern Tour, Jiang had been figuring things out for himself. In this sense, Deng's *Nanxun* was a test for Jiang, and his Party school speech was his final exam. Three days later, Jiang went to Deng's home to request the Paramount Leader's agreement to use "socialist market economy" as the new banner of reform.[14] Deng gave his endorsement: "In fact," he said, "we are already practicing such a system, as the economy in Shenzhen is a socialist market economy. Without the market economy, there will be no competition, no comparison, even no science and technology. Therefore, the quality of our products will always fall behind others."[15]

The phrase "socialist market economy" was a natural for Deng. For years, he had been saying that capitalist systems have planning and socialist systems have markets. Deng concluded, "If everyone agrees, we have a theme [for the 14th Party Congress]. We don't want to waste time with further debate."[16]

Jiang had set a precedent. In preparing Party leaders for new policy at a Party Congress every five years, the CPC general secretary would first float the ideas in a speech at the Central Party School in the spring, allowing it to be discussed widely so that when the new policy was formally presented at the Party Congress in the fall, it would already be accepted.

★ ★ ★

The 14th National Party Congress, held in October 1992, made three related decisions with far-reaching implications. First, it established the guiding principle that the country should "build socialism with Chinese characteristics." Second, it specified that the goal of reform was to build a "socialist market economy." Third, it asserted that the Party must focus on developing the economy.

Deng Xiaoping (center) and Jiang Zemin (left), with Deng's daughter, Deng Rong (right), at the 14th CPC National Congress in Beijing (October 1992).

The Congress also saw a meaningful change to the structure of governance. A more reform-minded Politburo Standing Committee was installed: Vice Premier Zhu Rongji and the 49-year-old Hu Jintao replaced two conservatives. Furthermore, the Central Advisory Commission, whose members were Party elders with at least 40 years of Party service, was abolished—a move which confirmed the emergence of China's third generation of leaders, centered on Jiang Zemin, from the shadow of the elders. Deng Xiaoping had set the road to reform in cement.

Hu Jintao was by far the youngest member of the Politburo Standing Committee. In an unambiguous nod towards the future, Deng thus made Hu his personal choice—and odds-on favorite—to become China's top leader ten years hence, after Jiang Zemin would complete two terms in office.

Prior to the Congress, Deng had proposed that in addition to confirming China's third-generation leaders, Party elders should also look ahead to the fourth generation. Song Ping, who had promoted Hu Jintao's career from their days together in Gansu Province, played the central role in recommending Hu. Song was in the perfect position to make such a recommendation; he was head of the CPC Organization Department, which was responsible for appointments and promotions, and he was an established elder who himself would be retiring from the Standing Committee.

Hu Jintao was acceptable to broad sections of the Party: Jiang Zemin was pleased to work with him, and he had good relations with the liberal followers of Hu Yaobang, who had championed his promotion from the Communist Youth League to Party secretary of Guizhou in 1985—making, him, at 42, the youngest of his rank in the country.

Hu Jintao's move to Guizhou was critical for his career and two reasons seem to have motivated it.[17] First, Hu Yaobang, who genuinely liked Hu Jintao, and Song Ping, Hu Jintao's mentor, recognized that for Hu to move up into highest echelons of Party power, he should have the experience of running a province. Second, Hu's apparent conflict with powerful conservative forces at the Youth League called for protective political action. Reportedly, Qiao Shi, then Organization Department head, advised Hu to "go find a safe haven that is also a training base."[18]

Guizhou was a poor rural province in south-central China, where more than one-third of citizens were non-Han ethnic minorities. Hu proved his mettle by working to improve people's lives, and by his careful handling of the 1986 student protests. Even today, he remains proud that during his tenure in Guizhou, he visited 86 counties, cities and prefectures, studying local situations, inspecting border regions, mountain villages, troubled factories, working mines—often taking notes of issues, achievements and complaints. For example, in comparing the failure of a state-owned tea plantation with the success of a semi-private tea plantation in the same county—tea being his family's traditional business—Hu concluded that the critical difference was that the state-owned farm lacked a "contract system or leased management."[19]

Hu also took strong interest in education, rebuilding antiquated or inadequate facilities and waiving tuition for students unable to afford the fees. He is said to have audited classes at Guizhou University. Summarizing his Guizhou experiences, Hu said that the development of poverty-stricken areas requires the effort of one full generation of dedicated people.

In 1987, Song Ping was appointed head of the CPC Organization Department, and in late 1988 he recommended Hu to become Party secretary of the sensitive Tibet Autonomous Region, a move likely supported by General Secretary Zhao Ziyang based on Hu's work in high-minority Guizhou.

His appointment, however, was motivated by what was deemed best for Tibet's development, rather than for Hu's career—he was the first Tibet Party secretary without military experience and running Tibet was not normally on the path for attaining high office in China.

Not only was Tibet a difficult region with a restive indigenous population, but Hu's appointment came at an especially problematic time, and immediately there was trouble. Even before Hu came to the region, a large demonstration was held in the capital Lhasa on International Human Rights Day and it resulted in violence.[20]

When Hu arrived, one of his first meetings was with a Tibetan Buddhist leader, signaling that he would be respectful of Tibetan religious beliefs and cultural traditions. On January 23, 1989, he traveled to Shigatse, to visit the Panchen Lama, the second highest figure in Tibetan Buddhism. Sitting next to the Panchen Lama, Hu said that he "considered himself a member of the Tibetan people," and "would share a common fate with the Tibetan people and work wholeheartedly for their benefit."

There are conflicting views about what the Panchen Lama said to Hu regarding Chinese rule, but tragically, a few days after meeting Hu, the Panchen Lama died unexpectedly—triggering fanciful conspiracy theories. Less than two months later, in March 1989, thousands of Tibetans took to the streets, barricading Tibetan sections of Lhasa and looting Chinese shops. Several dozen people were killed as the People's Armed Police battled demonstrators. Hu Jintao was required to restore order by imposing the first declaration of martial law in Lhasa, a decision taken not by Hu himself but by China's leaders in Beijing, and implemented by the People's Liberation Army. By dealing directly with the Chengdu Military Region Command in moving troops into Tibet, Hu impressed Deng Xiaoping.

There are those who believe that Hu Jintao's intimate understanding of Tibet, its people and its culture has led to a more nuanced Chinese approach to the region over the past 15 years. The claim is that although China has taken a tough line on Tibet, it would have been tougher still if not for Hu. Certainly during annual meetings of the National People's Congress, Hu regularly represented central leadership in meeting Tibetan delegates. His call was for improving people's living standards as the central task for Tibet and the basis for solving problems there.

In September 1989, Hu became excessively fatigued due to difficulties adapting to the high altitude (shortage of oxygen), and he began spending more time in Beijing. In addition to maintaining his role as Tibet Party chief, he became involved in high-level Party doings, providing support to senior leaders during the post-Tiananmen malaise. He worked under Song Ping, his mentor, in the Organization Department, where he handled sensitive, high-level negotiations between competing factions in the allocation of appointments. Some speculate that Hu helped facilitate the alleged arrangement by which Jiang Zemin pledged to enshrine Deng Xiaoping Theory as the core ideology of the Communist Party, while Deng Xiaoping authorized Jiang to be designated the Core of the Third Generation of Leaders.

In any event, it was certainly Deng Xiaoping who determined that Hu Jintao should succeed Jiang Zemin as CPC general secretary and president of China. Confirming Hu's position as heir apparent, in addition to joining the Politburo Standing Committee, he became head of the CPC Secretariat with responsibility for managing Party affairs and personnel. In March 1993, Hu became president of the Central Party School, the Party's leadership academy.

Hu's contributions would include tougher rules banning nepotism and establishing training and performance standards for promotions. Under Hu's leadership, the Party school began to teach finance, Western economics, and management, along with modernized Marxist theory, as it sought to explore China's new frontier in integrating market economics, foreign investment, and increasing privatization with the continuing requirements of state control. He also encouraged new thinking on how the Party should handle social dissatisfaction and the new personal freedoms of the information age, maintaining one-party rule without relying on repressive measures favored by conservative factions.

On foreign policy, Hu was more conservative, warning against American hegemonism, power politics and the pursuit of an aggressive anti-China strategy. Taken together, Hu Jintao was increasingly recognized as a thought leader and Party loyalist upon whom the future of the Party, and the country, would depend.

★ ★ ★

It wasn't long before the business world, and the international community, began to take note of China's surging growth. But by late 1992, China's economy was overheating, and inflation was spiraling out of control. The cost-of-living index climbed 15% for the year, fueled by a 46% increase in fixed-asset investments. Jiang Zemin called for full-blown measures to prevent "major upheavals and major losses," adding that "small-scale shocks are inevitable."[21]

In June 1993, Jiang visited Deng Xiaoping at his home and received his support for instituting an austerity plan. Stressing "financial work," Deng told him, "no matter what, the government should have complete control of the financial system and of prices in the market; inflation would bring major losses to the people."[22]

Galloping inflation, spurred on by consumer fears and worker unrest, continued into 1994. Rumors of grain shortages led to panic buying and food-hoarding frenzies, spiking prices by as much as 50%. The national inflation rate, fueled by explosive growth, was 22%, the worst since the People's Republic was founded; urban inflation, driven by quick-profit real-estate construction, was higher still. Desperate workers demanded living wages, compelling state banks to transfer money to hopeless state-run factories through "stability and unity loans" that had no chance of being paid back.

"The frightening specter of runaway inflation was a major challenge," recalls Wu Xiaoling, then vice governor of the People's Bank of China. "How could we cool the economy and still maintain the momentum of reform?" The answer, according to Wu, was to tackle the root causes of the problem, "such as unauthorized fund-raising and too much credit." In July 1993, Jiang Zemin dispatched Executive Vice Premier Zhu Rongji to serve as governor of the People's Bank of China, the nation's central bank. According to Wu, "both Jiang and Zhu agreed that local investments had to be curtailed."

"Zhu Rongji's role in curbing serious inflation was crucial," says Song Ning, former director general in the State Council Research Office (the think tank supporting central leaders). Zhu led the search for a "soft-landing." His focal point was financial system reform and when the Central Committee issued "16 Points for Macro-Controls," 13 were financial, including severe restrictions on bank credit and fixed-asset investments.

The austerity measures were unpopular; Zhu became the bête noir of free-wheeling provinces accustomed to acting as if they were independent countries with unlimited budgets. Famously, Zhu threatened to "chop off the heads" of bank officials who defied his edicts. It exemplified his legendary management style: despite his calm and unhurried manner, he was renowned for rapid action and swift decision making, and he never hesitated to humiliate incompetent officials in public or sack corrupt ones on the spot. (He once summarily fired a senior administrator who displayed a cigarette lighter that he could not possibly have afforded on his salary.)

"My criticism is sometimes too severe and that is not good," Zhu once acknowledged. "But why do you have to wait until your leader flies into a rage before starting to do your work? It's not that you can't do it, rather that you won't do it."[23]

In spring 1994, Jiang Zemin traveled the country, reinforcing Zhu's message by warning regional officials that they must put the "overall situation of the country" ahead of local interests. The State Planning Commission had recommended holding a major conference to promote the "16 Points" But, Jiang wisely decided to hold successive individual colloquia with local leaders.

"If a large-scale meeting had been held, it would have been impossible to reach consensus," says Chen Jinhua, then head of the State Restructuring

Commission. "At smaller, regional meetings, the leaders could exert their influence. What a hard task Jiang Zemin had had during that period!" he adds. "On the one hand we needed to implement macro-economic austerity, and on the other hand we needed to maintain Party unity. In order to achieve both, we needed special methods and skills."

According to Chen, "it was because of Jiang's cool thinking and timely measures—warning, discussing and studying – that various localities and departments gradually realized that the economy was seriously distorted and overheating due to large fixed-assets investments, disorderly inter-bank loans and funding, real-estate fever, development zones fever, and especially inflation – and that the matter was indeed very serious."

Chen recalls that he later visited Britain and France where he explained how China had achieved its soft landing through "control of credit, taxation, and other economic means, supported by legal and administrative means," adding "I told them that the CPC general secretary directly got provincial Party secretaries to exert their influence. My foreign hosts appreciated what we did but said that they would be unable to do the same thing in their countries. Such influence, they said, was an advantage of the Chinese system."

In the view of Minister Leng Rong, cooling the economy was a test for Jiang Zemin. "The overheated economy was a major threat, not only to reform but to social stability," he says, "and President Jiang had to guide China through its first experience with macroeconomic controls of a market economy. In a planned economy," he notes, "there is no need for such tools. If the economy is overheating, if there's inflation, you just shut down the factories or change their output. Now China had a new system. It was," Leng says, "experimental and risky."

Ultimately, China not only tamed price increases, but also maintained rapid economic growth, making the soft landing successful. In 1995, consumer price increases were modulated to 17.1%, then tamed to 8.3% in 1996 and 2.8% in 1997. Since that time, China has maintained high growth and low inflation. According to Leng Rong, "When the soft landing was achieved, it demonstrated the superiority of the new system, which was reinforced by the springing up of new products, goods, and services, many of them available to almost everyone by the middle 1990s. This was a major breakthrough."

Yet while the fix began to work, financially strapped enterprises suffered. Nevertheless, Jiang and Zhu were convinced that Deng was right: the way to improve China's economy was not to back away from reform but to pursue it more aggressively. They advocated further freeing pricing controls, eliminating command quotas, and imposing new policies on taxation and banking. The goal was finally to tip the balance from a planned economy to a market economy. Any prescription for the economy had to answer the critical questions: How fast can we grow? Can we afford (or tolerate) the consequences? Will it benefit the masses?

According to economist Song Ning, who worked directly with Zhu Rongji, "Zhu was the most powerful promoter and implementer of market reforms. Without his organization and execution," Song says, "the reforms would not have been such a success."[24]

Beginning in 1993, Vice Premier Zhu led four major systems reforms: fiscal and taxation, financial, foreign exchange, and foreign trade. These were instituted in parallel on January 1, 1994, and all had fundamental significance.

First, fiscal and tax reform converted chaotic and arbitrary taxation into a unified value-added tax (VAT) system for the whole country. Previously, the government had individual tax "contracts" with each state-owned enterprise (SOE), making competition not only unfair for non-SOEs but also confused for SOEs themselves. Furthering the confusion, national companies paid their taxes to the central government, while provincial and municipal companies paid their taxes to the local government. The implementation of a unified turnover (VAT) tax made the playing field level for all enterprises.

Moreover, before Zhu's reforms, China had no standard for allocating tax income between central and provincial governments. Provincial governments were only required to submit a "guaranteed number" to the central government—a fixed amount of tax revenue, not a percentage of provincial income—which the central government negotiated separately and often arbitrarily with each province. "It was known as 'separate kitchens, separate eating,'" says Song. As a result Beijing was under great financial pressure: it had almost no money and had no capacity to exercise macroeconomic controls – a situation which exacerbated the weakness of the central government relative to China's more developed provinces.

But after the tax reform, with the uniform VAT income, the central government could now determine how to divide taxation income between itself and local governments. The central government kept 75% of taxes and allocated 25% to provincial governments, which these then divided up among provincial, municipal and county bodies.

Vice Premier Zhu and his working group met with officials from every province to explain and implement the new policy. "We met great resistance from certain provinces," Song Ning recalls. The toughest came from Guangdong—not surprisingly since it was the wealthiest. "Through hard work we convinced Guangdong to accept the division of tax income," says Song. "We recognized the coastal regions' vested interests and worked out a compromise.[25] Following this breakthrough, the policy was then rolled out across the country. Thus Beijing was able to strengthen its capacity for macroeconomic control and administrative leadership, and could better support the development of backward areas in central and western regions.

Zhu Rongji's reform of the financial system was equally significant. In the past, the People's Bank of China (PBOC) had not been a real central bank. As Song Ning puts it, "It was just a cashier. When SOEs ran out of money, they would turn to PBOC for an overdraft and PBOC would print more money," leading both to inefficient SOEs and rampant inflation.

Zhu Rongji transformed PBOC into a genuine central bank. Henceforth PBOC could only issue currency and effect macroeconomic controls. Fiscal deficits could only be erased through issuance of national debt—putting an end to the over-issuance of banknotes. Moreover, no SOE could come to PBOC for an overdraft; PBOC could no longer issue loans. Instead, new commercial banks were set up, separate from the central bank (Chapter 23).

Under Zhu Rongji's leadership, the central government also established regulatory bodies to supervise the various financial sectors – including the China Securities Regulatory Commission and the China Banking Regulatory Commission. Furthermore, he rationalized China's foreign exchange regulations, abolishing the prior dual-track system (with separate fixed and market-adjusted rates.)

According to Song Ning, Zhu Rongji's hands-on role was vital. "A good many of the effective reform measures and programs, including the ideas behind them, were Zhu's. He was personally and directly involved—doing research, visiting regions and companies, and working on the documents himself, discussing and revising them before submitting them to the Central Committee for approval." Song highlights the fact that Zhu's reforms "were carried out during the period of China's severest inflation, conditions that were least conducive to reform."

Zhu's other critical demonstration of leadership came, according to Song, in stabilizing the Asian Financial Crisis, which began in Thailand in 1997 and spread across the region, triggering widespread currency devaluations. China was put under enormous pressure. If it did not similarly devalue, its products would become less competitive in international markets and exports would fall. Yet if China did devalue, other countries might devalue further, unleashing a damaging downward spiral. To make matters worse, Hong Kong had just been returned to Chinese sovereignty and its dollar was under attack.

Under Jiang Zemin's guidance, Zhu Rongji decided to resist domestic pressure and not devalue China's currency—and to support Hong Kong's exchange rate. Predictably, China's commodity exports fell and its economy was hurt. In 1998 export growth was zero and in 1999 it went negative. China faced its first-ever deflation, with economic growth sliding, exports stagnating, prices dropping, workers being laid off, and social instability increasing (a situation not unlike the financial crisis of 2008-2009). In response, states Song Ning, "we initiated a proactive fiscal policy by expanding domestic demand and building major infrastructure, funded by issuing national debt. We weathered the financial storm without depreciating the RMB. China's stabilizing contribution was appreciated throughout the world."

Liu Mingkang, who was then PBOC vice governor, recalls accompanying Zhu Rongji to meetings with foreign visitors. "They all held the same view: 'Why not depreciate your currency? If not, you'll be punishing yourself.' Finally, we said, 'No. We will not devalue our currency. We want a stable currency. Devaluation could boost our exports, but it would hurt our neighbors and other economies and trigger off another round of panic devaluations.'" Furthermore, Liu notes, "devaluation would raise the prices of imports. China needed to open its door wider to the world: we needed more equipment to build our infrastructure and upgrade our industrial and technical capacities. So Zhu Rongji said, 'We have been fighting inflation for five years now. Devaluation does us no good in any sense.'" According to Liu, "the rapid recovery of the Asian economy was attributed rightly to China's policy."

China's strategy of boosting domestic demand by investing in infrastructure was modeled on President Roosevelt's policy during the Great Depression, Liu explains. "We kept the GDP growing and our heads above water. Because China had huge domestic infrastructure needs, we were luckier than other Asian countries." By increasing its national debt for five consecutive years, starting in 1998, China did many things that it had neglected to do previously, all of which improved national productivity. It constructed airports, railways, highways, bridges, and hydroelectric projects such as the Three Gorges Dam (Yangtze River). This new infrastructure provided a solid foundation for further economic development in the new century. In Song Ning's view, "Zhu Rongji's successful management of both the inflation and deflation crises proved his leadership, ability, courage and determination."

Zhu Rongji was also committed to protecting China's environment. From 1998, following serious floods, China stopped the felling of natural forests. Large-scale ecological construction was begun—hillsides were closed to facilitate reforestation, cultivated land returned to forests and grasslands (to compensate for the huge swaths of trees cut down during the Cultural Revolution), reclaimed fields in lakeside areas were allowed to return to the lakes. Once, when asked what he would do when he retired, Zhu joked that he would go West and plant trees.

★ ★ ★

As reform flourished in the 1990s, outpourings of appreciation for Deng Xiaoping increased. But as such recognition grew, Deng himself began to voice distaste for what he deemed to be a "cult of personality" being raised up around him. He was unhappy with the veneration of his ideas, now officially tagged Deng Xiaoping Theory, uneasy about exhibitions that eulogized him, and uncomfortable with plans to erect statues of his likeness.[26]

"There is no need to say that Deng Xiaoping Theory is particularly great, completely correct, or exceptionally thorough," Deng said. "It is neither penetrating nor perfect; in future practice, it will have to be enriched, improved, and revised." He added, "I am not being humble, just practical."

In August 1994, when Jiang Zemin went to Deng's home to celebrate the Paramount Leader's 90th birthday, Deng complained that many organizations were honoring him with activities. "We should not do that," Deng ordered sharply. "They should not be allowed to do that."

Deng Xiaoping died on February 19, 1997 at the age of 92. It may be said that if his greatest contribution to China was reform, his second greatest was his self-imposed limits. For one thing, he retired. Prior to Deng, which Chinese leader had ever given up so much power, other than by dying or by force? Certainly not Mao. By stopping cold the pernicious cult of personality, with which Mao had brought China almost to ruin, Deng set a critical precedent for his beloved country's emergence into a great and responsible nation. For his role in changing China, Deng Xiaoping was one of the 20th century's great figures.

Endnotes

1 Author's communication, Beijing; Chen Kaizhi; Gilley, *Tiger*, 184;
2 Zong, Nathan (editor), *Zhu Rongji in 1999* (I), 52
3 Source for the entire section: Chen Kaizhi, who later served as vice-mayor of Guangzhou.
4 Author's communication, Beijing.
5 Gilley, *Tiger*, 184.
6 Selected Works of Deng Xiaoping (Volume III), CPC Party Literature Research Center.
7 Selected Works of Deng Xiaoping, Volume III (1982-1992) - http://english.peopledaily. com.cn/dengxp/vol3/text/d1200.html
8 Author's communication with central leader in Beijing.
9 Author's communication with historians in Beijing. The meeting was March 9–10, 1992.
10 Willy Wo-Lap Lam, *South China Morning Post*, April 8, 1992.
11 Author's communication, Beijing.
12 The subtlety of politically tinged descriptions in China is fascinating. For example, "private" business was often called "non-public;" and the "unemployment rate" used to be known as the "waiting to be employed rate," since a core tenet of the Communist system was to guarantee lifetime employment and Communist propaganda had disparaged capitalism for its unemployed workers and business cycles.
13 Author's meeting with Teng Wensheng, 2004. Other options, all longer and more awkward, were wisely rejected; they included: "planned and socialist market economy," "market combined with planned economy," "market economy with planning," "planning economy with market adjustments," "commodity economy with planning," and the ultra-awkward "planned economy as the main and market economy as the minor."
14 Author's communication with historians in Beijing. Jiang's speech was on June 9; his talk with Deng was on June 12.
15 Source: Chen Jinhua
16 Teng Wensheng.
17 Tkacik, op.cit.
18 Tkacik, op.cit., referencing Yi Ming, "The Logical General Secretary Designate; Among the Seven CPC Politburo Standing Committee Members, Hu Jintao Ranks Fifth and Is the Youngest, At 54," *Chiu-shih Nien-tai* (The Nineties), Hong Kong in Chinese, January 1, 1998, No. 1, pp. 50–52.
19 Tkacik, op.cit., referencing "The Nation's Youngest Vice President Hu Jintao," *Ming Pao*, March 17, 1998.
20 Tkacik, op.cit., whole section.
21 Willy Wo-Lap Lam, "President in bid to slow down growth," *South China Morning Post*, June 1, 1993.

22 Author's communications with historians in Beijing.

23 http://english.peopledaily.com.cn/leaders/Zhurongji.htm.

24 Author's meeting with Song Ning, November 2008.

25 The province would keep the same absolute amount of income as it had in the past. But for any new taxation, particularly the new VAT, the central government took 75% and the provincial government 25%. As China continued to grow at 10% or more per year, the central government received progressively more funds, both in absolute amounts and in its percentage of total revenues (since the base amount the province kept was low and fixed).

26 Willy Wo-Lap Lam, "Deng warns against old mentality." South China Morning Post, July 3, 1993 (quoting the pro-Beijing journal *The Mirror*); *Ching Pao*, July 5, 1993.

How Communism Adopted Capital and Ownership

By early 1997, the urgent need to restructure China's deteriorating state-owned enterprises (SOEs) had become the hot topic in the run-up to the 15th Party Congress. The debate centered on the issue of ownership, and whether the Party should endorse the controversial idea of converting SOEs into shareholding companies—in other words, allowing institutions and individuals, rather than just the state, to own the means of production. To some conservatives, the move seemed uncomfortably close to privatization, the opposite of communism.

Party Chief Jiang Zemin floated the ideas that he intended to present at the upcoming Congress in a highly anticipated address at the Central Party School (May 1997), which turned out to be a milestone in the history of reform.[1] The speech focused on how to revitalize China's moribund SOEs, which employed more than 100 million urban workers and, aggregated together, were losing money. Many SOEs were clamoring for permission to declare bankruptcy, because that was the only way to get government aid for their workers.[2]

But Jiang worried that too many bankruptcies, in the absence of an effective social security system, could swell unemployment and threaten stability. He preferred a strategy, championed by Zhu Rongji, in which healthy enterprises acquired sick ones, with the government offering almost $25 billion in incentives.[3] In many cases, a successful company would be forced to absorb a failing one in a desperate effort to protect jobs. (Coercing such anti-market interventions, of course, often meant that the sick firm would infect the healthy one.)

Speaking at the Party school, Jiang explained that the socialist principle of "public ownership" did not necessarily mean "state ownership."[4] Socialism could be maintained, Jiang argued, through a broad range of diverse "owners," such as cooperatives, collectives, worker groups, local and regional governments, other SOEs, and to a lesser degree, private firms and individuals, and foreign capital. He also backed such financial market ideas as company mergers and stock exchange listings to help revitalize state industries. Ultimately, Jiang claimed, better management and more efficient allocations of capital would produce more goods and services for the overall benefit of the masses, thus achieving the ultimate ends of socialism, even if through nontraditional means.

To outside observers, the debate over ownership may seem odd, arcane, or even frivolous. But in China, the question of who should own what was central, prominent, and very serious. Political ideology is like religious conviction in that both are belief systems and can generate uncompromising dogmas and white-hot emotions. To some true believers, the Communist Party broadening its position on the ownership of enterprises would be like the Catholic Church loosening its doctrine on the virginity of Mary.

Leftists charged that the reforms would be leading China "down the capitalist road." Nor did hardliners spare the recently deceased Deng Xiaoping in their assault, blaming the epidemic of corruption—which they said was "at least several times worse than in the days of the Kuomintang"—on market reforms.

★ ★ ★

The radical shift in the idea of ownership was a defining moment in China's two-decades-long reform. It came about after a long and intricate process of inner-Party machinations involving study and analysis, argument and debate, maneuvering and frustration, and on occasion personal accusations and animus.

New and diverse forms of ownership had begun to sprout in China in the late 1980s. By the mid-1990s private business was the fastest-growing sector. Many economists believed that conversion into shareholding companies offered the only hope for China's SOEs. But such a solution required a change in Party theory, not just policy.

In fall 1996, a team of 40 experts set to work under Wen Jiabao, along with Zeng Qinghong (director of the CPC General Office and Jiang Zemin's closest adviser), to draft Jiang's report for the 15th Party Congress. State Council researcher Lu Baifu, one of the drafters, recalls the period of preparation for the 15th Congress as one of "three difficult periods in the modern history of reform"—the others being the early years 1978–1980, and the period from June 4, 1989 until 1992.[5]

"I lived the history; I was there for all the breakthroughs," Lu says. "China's reform is a story without precedent." After five years of growth, by 1997 the country had come to a crossroads. "The collective process of drafting and editing the report," Lu says, "was intense."

"There were two basic questions," he explains. "First, should ownership of Chinese enterprises be restricted to the state? Or could there be multiple kinds of owners, representing various social sectors? More controversially, should China permit privatization, as Eastern Europe did? The second question," Lu notes, "was whether the strategy of an enterprise would change if the state was the sole owner, a majority owner, or a minority owner. All of this may sound theoretical," he adds, "but please understand, in China, theory meant ideology, which was the foundation on which our social and political system had been built. This is why arguments over ownership were so passionate. The whole system was at stake."

"Jiang Zemin focused on this ownership controversy with utmost seriousness," recalls Lu Baifu. During the sensitive period—late 1996 to early 1997—Jiang met with scholars and officials, read magazines and letters, heard oral testimony, and received summaries of technical documents. He re-read some of the classic works of Marx and Lenin and reviewed the history of Chinese reform since 1978.

Jiang came to conclude that reform was best implemented gradually. "He used a clever psychological approach to win over some of the opposition," Lu adds. "I was in a meeting where Jiang noted that in one of Lenin's works—it happened to be on grain taxes—the Communist icon said that policy had to be formulated according to the real situation. Lenin said, 'Marxists believe that revolutionaries should not bind their hands and feet by theory.' Elaborating on Lenin, Jiang said, 'Reality should dictate; dogma has no place.' Jiang wanted to find in the Communist classics—the works of Marx, Engels, and Lenin—antecedents for China's reforms," says Lu. "In this way, he could move the country forward and still keep the Party united."

Before 1997 the governing principle of China's economy was that the private sector would "supplement" the state sector. Jiang now recommended that the private sector be classified as an "important component" of the economy, along with the state. The state should withdraw from certain sectors, such as retail and light manufacturing, while retaining control of key industries, such as natural resources and infrastructure. Like many of China's economists, Jiang had come to believe that shareholding was the best hope for SOEs.

★ ★ ★

Just prior to the 15th Party Congress, according to custom, the last plenum of the 14th Party Congress was held. It recommended that Deng Xiaoping Theory be inscribed in the Party Constitution, and thus elevated to the same status as Mao Zedong Thought—even though, as many recognized, parts of Deng Theory contradicted parts of Mao Thought.

On September 12, Jiang Zemin delivered his political report in Beijing's Great Hall of the People. Broadcast live on CCTV, at two-and-a-half hours long it was the most far-reaching speech of Jiang's career: it called for reform and restructuring while reaffirming the country's core values and mores. With this report Jiang set the agenda for Chinese policy into the 21st century.

Under the umbrella of Deng Xiaoping Theory, Jiang articulated an ardently reformist position. China should judge every policy, he stated, "by the fundamental criteria of whether it is favorable for promoting the growth of the productive forces in a socialist society, for increasing the overall strength of the socialist state, and for raising the people's living standards." These were the Three Favorables, which Deng Xiaoping had coined during his *Nanxun* in 1992. "Any form of ownership that meets the criteria of the Three Favorables," Jiang said, "can and should be utilized to serve socialism."

Jiang took care to highlight the continuing importance of orthodoxy. "We must never discard Marxism-Leninism and Mao Zedong Thought," he reassured his audience. "If we did, we would lose our foundation." At the same time he asserted that Marxism, like any science, needed to change as time and circumstances advanced. He explained that China was in "the primary stage of socialism," a period in which it would remain for a long time to come. (The common estimate was a comfortable 100 years, at least.) During this stage, Jiang said, the country had to use market forces to develop and industrialize. "This is a historical stage over which we cannot jump."

Jiang reiterated his call for steadiness in the face of change. "It is of the utmost importance to balance reform, development, and stability," he said, "and to maintain a stable political environment and public order." Without stability, he added, "nothing could be achieved."

The newly elected Politburo Standing Committee elected at the 15th CPC Central Committee. Left to right: General Secretary Jiang Zemin, Li Peng, Zhu Rongji, Li Ruihuan, Hu Jintao, Wei Jianxing, Li Lianqing (Beijing, September 1997).

In terms of specific reforms, Jiang focused on restructuring SOEs—estimated to number about 370,000—into shareholding companies. He then called for "removing the fetters of the irrational ownership structure on the productive forces and bringing about a situation featuring multiple forms" of ownership. Although he said that "public ownership" should always dominate China's economy, he enlarged the meaning of the term to include many different forms, including collectives and even shareholding companies. This expanded definition alone was an ideological breakthrough. He also recognized the importance of capital and financial market tools such as mergers and acquisitions.

Jiang separated government and business, enabling SOEs to become viable marketplace competitors. "The government should not directly interfere in the operation of enterprises," he cautioned. "And enterprises have to be restrained by the owner and should not harm the owner's equity." From now on, market forces would dominate.

"President Jiang rid the Party of the ideological obstacles to different kinds of ownership," says Party theorist Leng Rong. "He did not give up Marxism or socialism. He strengthened the Party by providing a modern understanding of Marxism and socialism—which is why we talk about a 'socialist market economy' with Chinese characteristics.'"

★ ★ ★

Li Yining, professor of economics and president of the Guanghua Management College at Peking University, has been, over the years, one of China's most influential proponents of the market economy in general and shareholding in particular. When I met him in 1998, Professor Li emphasized how deeply engrained the planned economy had been in China's society. He said this was based on two mistaken assumptions: first, people thought a planned economy facilitated productive forces; second, they thought that only in a planned economy could the government guarantee that citizens would get equal salaries and equal rights—in other words, fairness.

"But they were proved wrong on both counts," Li Yining said. "After several decades under the planned economy, the facts tell us that enterprises and people are not motivated—and without motivation, productive forces cannot develop. Under the planned economy, there is no competition, no equal opportunities, and no freedom to relocate. Hence, fairness cannot be realized. After the Cultural Revolution, China's economy was on the brink of destruction. At that point, the Chinese people had to choose a new system. And they chose the market economy."

Professor Li, like many Chinese economists of his generation, had trained under the influence of Soviet scholars. "My intellectual conversion occurred during the 1960s when I began wondering why we Chinese were so poor while other countries were so developed," he explained. "I realized that our problems could only be blamed on our system. That was when I surreptitiously started to desert the planned economy and accept the market economy."

During the Cultural Revolution, Li endured hardships. "I suffered a great deal," he said. "I did forced labor; my house was searched, my head shaved" – though, he added, with a hint of pride: "you can't imagine how good a manual laborer I was!" After the Cultural Revolution, when he suggested market reforms ideas, he faced three criticisms. The first was that a market economy and stock system would mean that China was going over to the capitalist side. The second was that the Chinese economy needed to be well regulated, and that a market economy would dissolve into a mess. And the third criticism was that since at that time the prices for various commodities were stable, if prices were allowed to fluctuate according to market conditions, prices would become chaotic."

"I answered these criticisms in this way," Li asserted: "The market economy and stock system could be used both in a capitalist society and in a socialist society. If it helps develop the economy, then it could be used. And since all those countries that have a planned economy are poor, maintaining the old system would push the Chinese people to a dead end." As for the need for regulation, Li stressed that a market economy could increase people's standard of living and keep society stable. "I turned the criticism around and argued that if a market economy isn't used and some crisis arises, then society will really be in a mess," he said.

Regarding the role of a planned economy in keeping prices stable, Li countered that under such a system, "in fact people can't buy the commodities they want, because those commodities aren't available!" And he emphasized that "When the government artificially controls prices, it's actually a kind of inflation. If those price controls are released, the prices immediately go up. It's like pushing a ball into water; if you release your hand the ball will immediately pop back up. This practice, too, has been proved wrong."

Now, Li said, China was undergoing a unique "dual transition," moving from a planned economy to a market economy and from a traditional agricultural society to a modern industrial society at the same time.

Asked about the differences between a "socialist market economy" and capitalism, Li was unequivocal. "In my personal opinion, there is no real difference," he said. "The only apparent difference is that the environments are different. By tradition, one is capitalist and the other socialist."

Lest there should be any misunderstanding, Li stressed that "the market economy and the planned economy cannot coexist and cannot be merged." There can be only one major factor governing an economy, he said: in the market economy, the market is the major factor; and in the planned economy, government control is the major factor. "I should be clear here: China is not merging the two systems," Li insisted. "China is deleting the planned economy and enabling the market economy."

But, he said, regulatory methods can coexist—financial, tax, monetary, and other policies. And he stressed that there was still a role for government in a market economy. "Remember," Li said, "that there have been significant historical modifications in how, over time, the market economy has operated in the U.S. In the 19th century, the market economy was completely free—not controlled by the government at all. But problems and crises arose [such as rapacious monopolies, robber barons, stock manipulations, and the Great Depression], so that in the 20th century the government had to step in and regulate some aspects of the market."

Thus, Li added, the key difference was between "the old market economy and the modern market economy." In the modern system, he explained, "all the problems that can be solved by the market should be solved by the market. If there are some problems that can't be solved by the market," he said, "they should be solved by the government. So the market is the first way to regulate, and government policies are the second way to regulate."

Li said he did not fear reversals in China's reforms, "because it has been thoroughly demonstrated that the market economy is the best way to develop China." He did however suggest that "a three-way split is optimum for China —state ownership, collective ownership, and private ownership." (Many economists believe that a key to reform is lowering state ownership of virtually all SOEs to less than 50%.)

It's a not-insignificant fact about China's current leaders that two Politburo "rising stars" took economic degrees under Li Yining, this distinguished and demanding reformist economist: Li Keqiang, executive vice premier of the State Council (doctoral degree) and Li Yuanchao, head of the CPC Organization Department (master's degree). Both Li Keqiang and Li Yuanchao are widely expected to be among China's top leaders of the next generation in 2012.

★ ★ ★

By 1998, about one-third of China's SOEs were losing money—some put the figure at one-half. Rooted in the old planned economy—where the government decided factories' inputs and outputs—they were plagued by overstaffing, inefficient use of assets, little concern for customers, and low productivity. Few had a chance of being competitive in a market economy.

After 1997, economic reform focused on large SOEs—those that played a strategic role in the national economy or defense. Every effort was made to improve their productivity. The new guiding principle for SOE reform was known as "Control the large ones, and free the small ones." Small and mid-sized firms were deregulated and allowed to seek alternative ownerships. It was an historic decision, and it would change dramatically how business would henceforth be done in China. It signaled that mergers and acquisitions (M&A), heretofore considered a tool of capitalism and not relevant for socialism (other than to save failing enterprises), were now acceptable.

For seven years prior to these changes, I had been speaking and writing about how instituting an M&A market in China would improve efficiencies.[6] I was told that although my ideas were interesting, they did not apply to China.

At the time, many people felt that because state-owned property was being "looted" by what appeared to be M&A, therefore M&A itself must be the problem—the epitome of rapacious capitalism. I argued that, on the contrary, the problem was not too much M&A but too little—that hole-and-corner deals encouraged corruption where well-connected people, often from Taiwan or Hong Kong, could take advantage of special relationships, whereas the creation of a broad and open M&A market in China would establish standardized valuations and protect state-owned assets. The more M&A transactions, the more buyers and sellers in the market, the more efficient the market becomes.

As soon as policy permitted, M&A was accepted with a sudden intensity and a naïve enthusiasm. It was as if a dam had burst. Chinese entrepreneurial spirit was set free, but because the Chinese had had no M&A experience and were now exercising little restraint in its pursuit, problems surfaced. Almost overnight, M&A had become an imagined panacea, and many companies propelled themselves headlong into the M&A market. As in many areas of reform, China was experiencing in a few years the same stages, complete with the same problems, which occurred over roughly a 100-year period in America.[7]

★ ★ ★

In 1998, at the 9th National People's Congress, Zhu Rongji was elected premier and pledged to make SOEs profitable in three years. It was a startling goal, and although seemingly unattainable, Zhu's vision set a new agenda. It was just one of a range of bold initiatives which Zhu, who was concurrently dean of Tsinghua University's School of Economics and Management (a title of which he was most proud), set for his administration: these included Guarantees (growth, control inflation, no devaluation); Repositionings (SOEs, financial and banking systems, streamline government); and Reforms (food, investments, housing, medical care, taxes).

The tough-minded Zhu was unconcerned with personal tenure and permanent power. He knew what to do and he was ready to sacrifice anything, including himself, in order to get it done. A staunchly pro-market reformer with an "iron face" and fierce temper, Zhu would need both to restructure China's bureaucracy and enhance SOEs' efficiency. Certainly on shrinking the government, Zhu delivered: through sheer intelligence, and shielded by a mighty thick skin, he eliminated ministries and cut bureaucracies—notwithstanding the hoots and howls of high-level bureaucrats whose enmity he earned by abolishing their jobs. (Since Zhu, along with President Jiang and other senior leaders, came from Shanghai, there was extra sensitivity when Beijingers lost their positions, given the perennial competition between the two cities.)

Significantly, China's Constitution was also revised in 1998 to legalize private enterprises.[8] Although they had been allowed, and indeed encouraged, to operate for years, this formal legalization of private businesses was significant. Chinese banks could now provide loans and stock exchanges could list them. It was recognition of how much private businesses were contributing to the country's economic reform and growth: even by 1998, outputs from "non-state-owned" enterprises—private companies owned solely by Chinese citizens, foreign or joint ventures, and collectively owned firms—accounted for about 55-60% of China's GDP.

Making SOEs profitable would be more messy. Many ridiculed Premier Zhu's "boast" to make China's large SOEs profitable within three years, but Zhu professed himself unconcerned with the political fallout of failure. "No matter whether there is a minefield ahead of me," he announced, "or whether there is a deep ravine in front of me, I will bravely forge ahead, will not turn back, and will do my best until my last breath."

The structure of SOEs embedded certain distortions, such as executives not allowed to own stock in their own companies. They were also prohibited from raising their salaries or gaining other monetary rewards. The idea was that stringent limitations on executive compensation prevent corruption (these restrictions also precluded a large salary disparity between SOE executives and their putative government bosses). Yet in practice these created inappropriate behavioral incentives and hence economic inefficiencies: without ownership or high salaries, SOE managers would find other avenues of compensation, such as lavish expense accounts. Worse, they might make reckless decisions to increase their power, oblivious to risks which imperiled corporate value.

Turning SOEs into shareholding companies was the key reform, with some shares held by management and workers providing incentives aligned with the majority owners (government). As SOE reform deepened over the years, more appropriate compensation and control mechanisms were instituted.

SOEs were restricted in other ways. They were not completely free to run their operations; managers could not fire employees. Streamlining staff, critical to SOE success, required the government to set up a social security system to protect laid-off workers. A legacy of the planned economy, SOEs traditionally provided for all the needs of employees and their families: housing, food, education, healthcare, pensions, and the like. How to provide these services when SOEs were restructured was a central problem of China's transition to a market economy.

Traditionally, an enterprise's Communist Party branch secretary was often more powerful than its president. Over time, however, this has been changing so that large Chinese companies today are looking increasingly like their peers in developed countries.

★ ★ ★

In 1998, as Zhu Rongji initiated SOE reforms, I visited Yili Group, makers of milk and milk-related products, for a documentary co-production between PBS and China Central Television.[9] Now a flagship enterprise in China's dairy industry, Yili exemplified the potential—and complexity—of SOE reform.

Based in Inner Mongolia, Yili was once a typical SOE: unburdened by the need to compete, Yili simply churned out its allotted quota of ice cream, then its primary product, irrespective of demand. The ice cream didn't taste very good either. When Beijing determined it could no longer afford to prop up non-essential industries, Yili had to fend for itself. Yili's management restructured company operations and business practices—and transformed a lagging, bankruptcy-bound business into a market leader, its ice cream China's most popular brand. Senior executives characterized market share as "a life-and-death struggle."

And as is often the case in China's transition to a market economy, the company adopted some unique strategies not to be found in western management manuals. Yili's executives wore military-style uniforms at meetings. Employees took two weeks of compulsory basic training, as if they were army inductees, before starting their jobs. Yili's then president, Zheng Junhuai, told me proudly: "We made the decision to model Yili after the Chinese military." The idea was to strengthen employees' discipline and sense of responsibility. "Chinese are familiar with the military model," Zheng said, "because China used to be like one huge military camp."

"I've seen the movie *Patton* many times, and I've studied the ancient Chinese generals," added Yili's then vice president, Niu Gensheng. "A disciplined army is the most powerful force. The only thing in our hearts," he said, "is the field of battle of the marketplace. Our minds are consumed by the fire of competition and the smell of the battle is very strong."

Vice President Niu argued that such an approach helped create market sensitivity from scratch. "All these workers were farmers," said Niu. "So our greatest task was to make them feel the pressure and anxiety of being replaced."

At the time, many companies were laying off workers. Yili was paying the highest wage in the area, and there was no shortage of applicants. "Our workers are constantly reminded of the crowd waiting outside ready to take over their spots," Niu continued. "And our managers are constantly aware of those who have more knowledge and better skill and who are lusting for their positions."

A huge banner hanging in the factory reiterated the point: "If you don't work hard at your job today, you'll have to look hard for a job tomorrow."

Nevertheless, President Zheng stressed that the company also had to offer its staff opportunities for career development, to prevent them being poached by competitors. "Whether it's for honor or whether it's for money," he said, "we must have an ambitious culture."

But Yili stressed adaptation. "Our company will eventually change from labor intensive to machine automated," Zheng said. "We won't need thousands of workers. We'll come up with new management methods to replace old ones."

Another huge banner sought to provide inspiration: "The Chinese are not inferior to the West," it said. "We can do it ourselves."

In 2007, Yili's revenues reached about $3 billion. Yet the diverting fates of Yili's president and vice president offer a kind of moral microcosm of the vicissitudes of China's market transformation.

Soon after my 1998 visit, Vice President Niu Gensheng resigned, apparently because of differences with President Zheng. Niu immediately founded Mengniu Group, which he transformed, remarkably, within eight years from the 1116th dairy producer in China to the number one.[10] By 2007, with revenues slightly higher than Yili's, Mengniu was the country's leading liquid milk producer – and is considered one of China's great entrepreneurial success stories. In 2004, meanwhile, President Zheng Junhuai was arrested, accused of embezzling funds to support a management buyout of Yili, and sentenced to six years in prison.[11]

Nonetheless, and despite the severe scandals which shook China's milk industry in 2008, Yili remains intent on becoming one of the leading milk industry companies worldwide.

★ ★ ★

In March 1998, also at the 9th National People's Congress, Hu Jintao was elected state vice president. It was another sign that Hu was being groomed to succeed Jiang Zemin.

Working in Hu's favor, as Jiang told the CPC Central Committee, were his "lofty morality and high prestige." Hu enjoyed strong support from Party members, Jiang said, and had the backing of non-Communists and ethnic minorities as well. Jiang emphasized that the new vice president "must not be a controversial figure, and he must not be tinged with factionalism."[12]

Recounting his numerous trips abroad, Jiang observed that he had often felt that he was of a different generation than most Western leaders. The leaders of those nations were young, he said, attuned to new knowledge, and physically vigorous. Jiang admitted that his own stamina occasionally failed him in their presence. It would soon be time for a change. Jiang thus sought to expand the powers of Hu's office, making him the country's first active vice president. Having come to know U.S. Vice President Al Gore, Jiang wanted China's vice president to play a similar role. Chinese diplomats subtly explained to foreign governments about the special status of Hu.

Jiang also proposed that at some point Hu should become a vice chairman of the Central Military Commission (CMC). For his entire political career, Hu had worked in the Party apparatus, where he had built a solid reputation, but he had no army experience, a handicap with which Jiang could empathize. With this appointment, Hu would have time and opportunity to learn about the military. Jiang insisted that such an appointment, at the right time, would ensure "the Party's absolute leadership over the Army." (Despite resistance from some senior PLA officers to appointing civilians to the CMC, Hu's appointment would come in 1999.)

At a national publicity (i.e., propaganda) conference, Vice President Hu noted that the Party would face challenges of changing times. Strengthening ideological foundations, according to Hu, would encourage all citizens to "advocate patriotism, collectivism, socialism, and hard work." The core of ideological work, Hu said, is to help the people cultivate lofty ideals and correct convictions. As vice president, Hu Jintao himself embodied a dignified combination of continuity and progressiveness—stability and pride.

Endnotes

1 *Ming Pao* (Hong Kong), September 19, 1997 (BBC).
2 Ian Johnson, *Asian Wall Street Journal*, May 19, 1997. In 1996, 6,000 enterprises had been closed down. In 1997, the bankruptcy program was expanded from 58 to 110 cities.
3 Willy Wo-Lap Lam, *The Era of Jiang Zemin* (New York: Prentice Hall, 1999), 62.
4 Jasper Becker, "Jiang's state sector reform strategy revealed," *South China Morning Post*, July 29, 1997.
5 Author's meeting with Lu Baifu, April 2002.
6 My thesis was that M&A would bring numerous benefits to China's emerging market economy: (i) M&A aligns owners and managers for optimum productivity; (ii) M&A replaces inefficient management; (iii) M&A re-sizes enterprises for optimum effectiveness (ideal sizes differ by industry); (iv) M&A provides sources of liquidity for investors (critical for companies that cannot be listed), thus encouraging initial investments.
7 Suddenly, I found myself on the opposite side of the M&A barricades, now urging great care and caution in its use. I likened M&A to an "amplifier" or "accelerator," so that if a company's strategic direction was poor or misguided, and if that company acquired another company, the result would amplify or accelerate that initial poor strategy, making the combined companies much worse much faster. Only if a company's strategy was good and its management sound would its M&A prove successful. I cautioned against shoddy financial analysis, overeager decision making, overoptimistic financial forecasts, a lack of planning for post-acquisition integration and the risks of diversification outside of corporate competence.
8 Definitions differ. In China, "public companies" are owned by the state, whereas in America "public companies" are listed on stock exchanges. "Private companies" in China are not owned by the state, whereas in America private companies are not listed. In China, most listed companies are also "public" in that they are controlled by the state.
9 "In Search of China" was the "Pick of the Week" by the *Washington Post* (September 3, 2000). This was the first time that a CCTV co-production was featured on PBS. I was creator and executive producer; Adam Zhu, producer; Li Qiang, China / CCTV director; Emma Joan Morris and Rob Fruchtman, U.S. directors; Aaron Kuhn, editor.
10 *China Daily*, November 9, 2007.
11 www.CRIENGLISH.com, January 5, 2006.
12 Willy Lam, "Jiang moves to block Qiao bid" South China Morning Post, February 28, 1998.

The Hidden Power of Jiang Zemin's "Three Represents"

President Jiang Zemin believed that economic practice and political theory were partners, and that China's development needed both policy and ideology to be enabling, efficient and effective. As such, in February 2000, he was ready to float a new idea.[1]

On an inspection tour of Guangdong Province, Jiang spoke in Gaozhou, a small, underdeveloped city where he focused on the complaints of peasants, assuring them of Party support.[2] "As long as our Party always remains the loyal representative of the development needs of China's advanced productive forces, the forward direction of China's advanced culture, and the fundamental interests of the large majority of the Chinese people," he told 600 village and township officials, "it will stand invincible forever . . . and lead the people onward."

It was a threefold dictum—advanced productive forces, advanced culture, fundamental interests of the people—and this was Jiang's first expression of it. It had no name, did not make the headlines, seemed simple and casually mentioned. Jiang's words were few, but their impact would be profound.

In March, *People's Daily* published a high-profile commentary, which marked the first national exposure of Jiang's campaign to modernize the Party through what the article labeled, for the first time, the Three Represents.[3] "All the struggles carried out by our Party are, in the final analysis, aimed at liberating and developing productive forces," *People's Daily* declared, adding that "any move to surpass the present historical development stage by indiscriminately copying and applying to today's practice a number of characteristics and practices of socialism at its mature stage will all the same hinder the development of productive forces."

Turgid and mind-numbing as this may seem to Westerners, for many Chinese, this was riveting stuff. What the Party's mouthpiece was saying, in essence, was that it was permissible to abandon, for the foreseeable future, any idealistic principles of socialism which did not work in today's world. Moreover, it was warning that some aspects of "mature-stage" socialism might actually "hinder" progress!

According to Li Changchun, then the Guangdong Party secretary (who would, within three years, come to run ideology and media in China), "President Jiang's Three Represents speech in 2000 was just like Deng Xiaoping's *Nanxun* speeches in 1992 – a tremendous driving force."[4]

★ ★ ★

"Wang Huning and I wrote the Gaozhou speech," said Party researcher Teng Wensheng, describing the origin of Three Represents.[5] "Just before President Jiang's trip to the south, he called me to his office. He had obviously given the concept serious thought," Teng recalled. "'Marxism has so many theories out there,' Jiang said, 'Marxism, Leninism, dialectical materialism, historical materialism—we need something applicable to the realities of contemporary China that makes sense and is easy to remember.' " Jiang told Teng that his new theory "didn't have to explain everything."

"In Jiang's first presentations, the theory was very preliminary," explained Teng. "Over time it would mature."

Jiang knew that to develop China's global, knowledge-based economy, he had to modernize the Party's ideology, and the Three Represents was the mechanism by which he would do it. Developed in concert with his chief adviser Zeng Qinghong (who in three years would become China's vice president) and Wang Huning (a law professor and strategic theorist who would become a Secretariat member and director of the CPC Policy Research Office), the Three Represents enabled the Party to "advance with the times."

It was during this period that President Jiang made clear his support for Hu Jintao as his successor. In a high-level Party meeting, Jiang lauded Hu for his "ideological resoluteness," particularly with respect to Hu's leadership of the not-so-memorable Three Stresses campaign ("stress study, stress politics, and stress healthy trends) in 1999."

★ ★ ★

In English, the Three Represents sounds syntactically strange – apparently just another dense thicket of Communist rhetoric. Yet the Chinese phrase, *san ge daibiao*, has coherence and subtlety. Jiang's point was that although Communism, in its industrial age formulation, might not be viable as a contemporary economic system, the Communist Party, by "representing" these three powerful principles, would be modernizing Marxism, advancing with the times, and securing its place at the vanguard of society. "Success in running things well in China," Jiang said in 2000, "hinges on our Party."

Still, the Three Represents had its opponents, and the battle over its significance would have long-range consequences. Critics charged that the Three Represents contained "six kinds of errors,"[6] and that Jiang's intention was to substitute his own Three Represents for Deng Xiaoping Theory as the Party's guiding ideology. The charge was misleading, perhaps deliberately so, since Jiang actually planned to extend Deng Theory, not replace it. What was truly being replaced, though no one would come out and say it, was 19th-century Marxism and Maoist class struggle.

In response to the resistance, the Party began to promote the theory more aggressively. At Party meetings, Vice President Hu Jintao defended the idea, stressing that "Comrade Jiang Zemin's theory of Three Represents is a development of Comrade Deng Xiaoping's theory on building a socialist road with Chinese characteristics."

Allying with Deng meant that Jiang could safely pronounce that the Communists of today are not the Communists of yesteryear, just as the "socialist market economy" was not the kind of straitjacket socialism the world used to know. About this there was no dissension among China's active senior leaders, all of whom followed Deng more closely than they did Marx or Mao. "old wine in new bottles" was not what was happening here; it was more like "new wine in old bottles"—the label on the bottles did not change, but the wine inside tasted very different.

In June 2001, a foreign reporter, perhaps tracking rumors, asked senior Party intellectual Xing Bensi if capitalists could join the Party. "I answered the question in a very diplomatic way," recalled Xing. "First, I told him that the definition of capitalists needed updating. We used to think that because they were exploiting others, they shouldn't be allowed to join the Party. Current private entrepreneurs aren't equivalent to old-time capitalists. Second, I said that if capitalists would be eligible to join the Party, they would do so only as long as they were different from those of the past, they made their fortune through lawful means, and they did not exploit their employees. But," Xing added, "the reporter misinterpreted my answer and proclaimed to the world that the CPC was going to admit capitalists as members. Many friends called me, asking, 'How could you say that?'"

Xing may have been misquoted, but the report was to prove prescient.

★ ★ ★

July 1, 2001 marked the 80th anniversary of the founding of the Communist Party of China, an event celebrated across the country with cultural events, concerts and exhibitions. The anniversary was also commemorated with an 18-hour television marathon, which featured a major address by General Secretary Jiang Zemin. Speaking before a live audience of 10,000 in the Great Hall of the People and hundreds of millions on television, Jiang praised the Party for China's resurgence after a century of decline, hailed the past two decades of social and economic reform, gently criticized dogmatic attitudes, and pointed to his new theory of Three Represents, which adapted Marxist principles to current conditions, as key to the Party's future. But hidden in the otherwise unsurprising speech were a few electrifying sentences.

Telling Party officials to give up "outdated notions" about communism, Jiang declared that reform had created "new social strata" of entrepreneurs, technical personnel, managerial staff, freelance professionals, and the self-employed in the "nonpublic sector." And he said that most people in the private sector were engaged in "honest labor and work," obeyed the law, and contributed to society. Such people, he asserted, "are also working to build socialism with Chinese characteristics."

Then he dropped his bombshell: in order to maintain the momentum of reform, Jiang argued, these new social strata should be welcomed as members of the Communist Party. "It is also necessary," he said, "to accept those outstanding elements from other sectors of society who have subscribed to the Party's program and Constitution, worked for the Party's line and program wholeheartedly, and proved to meet the requirements for Party membership through a long period of tests."

Though he had maneuvered around the historically loaded term by referring to such people as the "new social strata" and by packaging the startling new policy, as it were, in what seemed to be a traditional political box, Jiang's message was clear: under certain conditions, capitalists would now be allowed to join the Chinese Communist Party.

Jiang explained that entrepreneurs and technical personnel were the driving force behind China's "advanced productive forces," the first of his Three Represents. If such people continued to be banned from Party membership, he said, the Party could not truly claim to be leading the nation.

"It is not advisable to judge a person's political orientation simply by whether he or she owns property or how much property he or she owns," he added. "Rather, we should judge him or her mainly by his or her political awareness, moral integrity and performance, by how he or she has acquired the property, how it has been disposed of and used, and by his or her actual contribution to the cause of building socialism with Chinese characteristics."

Later that day Jiang called Shen Yongyan, his old friend. "What did you think of my speech?" he asked, after some family small talk.

"You gave a good speech," said Shen. "I didn't see any problem with it."

"Then you didn't listen too carefully," said Jiang. "Many people are against it."

"Why?" asked Shen. "The controversy centers on whether we should allow private business owners to join the Party," Jiang replied.

★ ★ ★

It was the first practical application of Jiang's Three Represents, and it was a stunning blow to Party conservatives. Realizing that Jiang's speech spelled fundamental change in the essence of the Communist Party, Leftists erupted. One of the first public objections came from Ma Bin, a high-level researcher and Party member since 1935. Agitated by Jiang's speech, Ma, who had studied metallurgy in the Soviet Union, prepared a principled refutation and sought sympathetic former officials to join with him. Recruiting 13 supporters, including prototypical hardliner Deng Liqun—who was in the process of drafting his own letter—Ma Bin published the "Letter of Fourteen." It was distributed samizdat-fashion in Beijing and circulated on the Internet.

Ma Bin's short letter struck to the heart of the issue. Writing in the name of "a group of old Communist Party members," he said: "We hereby solemnly declare that we firmly and without reservation oppose the proposition that private business owners be allowed to join the Party. We believe that Comrade Jiang Zemin's position in this regard is entirely wrong." The letter argued that the "admission of capitalists to membership in a Communist Party is unheard of in Marxist theory or practice that has emerged since the Communist Manifesto was first published. This in no way constitutes a 'creative renewal' of Marxism," Ma stated, "but rather, an outright negation of its basic principles." He then put the rhetorical question "How could a capitalist, as a member of the exploiting class, be expected to devote his or her whole lifetime to struggling for the realization of Communism? Comrade Jiang Zemin's views," he added, "do not make any sense in this respect." And he ended with a stark accusation: "This constitutes political misconduct unprecedented in the history of our Party."

But Ma's attempts to recruit fellow travelers to cosign his open letter proved frustrating. One of those he approached was his old friend Professor Bi Dachuan, the outspoken mathematician (Chapters 1 and 2). "Look what's happening to China under current policies," said Ma. "Workers no longer have a right to a job as they once did under traditional socialism."

"Burdening and bankrupting companies with overstaffed workers just sets China further and further behind the West," said Bi. "The only products China could sell on world markets 'under traditional socialism' were bamboo baskets and poor shoes. Now we sell computers and launch satellites."

The exchange exemplified just how strongly China's science community supported Jiang's Three Represents. According to Bi, "Jiang's Three Represents are liberation for China's development. That's why our entire scientific community backs him. This is the first time that scientists and engineers—the 'vanguard' of 'advanced productive forces'—are recognized for our enormous contribution to China."

Now that Ma Bin had gone public criticizing Jiang, and had done it so vehemently, his colleagues were worried about him, according to Wang Huijiong, Jiang's longtime friend who worked in the same think tank. "They asked me, 'Will President Jiang take action against Ma Bin?' But I told them no, he would not," Wang said.[7]

"Whatever happened to Ma Bin?" Jiang Zemin asked Wang Huijiong. "He may be a little conservative, but he's not thinking right about this issue. Ma Bin is a good person; some people must have influenced him."

In Wang's view, "Jiang respected Ma Bin because of his dedication to the Party and the country, and for his knowledge and rectitude. The president went out of his way to protect Ma Bin, who is still active." And Wang added: "Foreigners don't appreciate how democratic China has become."

The most dangerous Leftist challenge to Jiang Zemin's modernizing vision for the Party came a few days later, in the form of a public petition spearheaded by Deng Liqun, the 86-year-old Marxist ideologue and former propaganda chief. Since 1997 he had become increasingly militant in challenging Jiang's leadership. With true-believer fervor, Deng Liqun denounced the general secretary's plan in a 10,000-character letter. Distributed widely on the Internet, Deng's manifesto galvanized old-line Communists, incensed progressive Party members, and generally provided grist for political mills of all colors.

"Whom does he represent?" asked Deng Liqun, referring to Jiang Zemin. "Jiang's speech represents the 0.3% of the population who are private business people. According to the definition of Mao Zedong, our Party should represent the 95% of the people who are the masses and revolutionary cadres. So Jiang has become an 'enemy of the people,'" Deng wrote, "and should be condemned and punished by the Party and the people."

Deng's petition, which was also signed by 16 other hardcore Marxists, characterized Jiang's move as an "extremely serious political mistake." Deng accused Jiang of currying favor with Western media by presenting China as an increasingly capitalistic country. He then quoted Jiang's own words against him, referring to a 1989 Party ruling forbidding private businessmen from joining the Party. "Entrepreneurs of privately owned business cannot join the Party," Jiang had said at the time. "I agree with this position. Our Party is the pioneer of the proletarian class. If we allow persons who do not want to give up exploitation and live by exploitation to join the Party, what kind of Party on earth would we want to construct?"[8]

Deng Liqun's letter also attacked the entrepreneurs themselves, calling them "tax dodgers and tax evaders who paid barely 10% of what they really owed," who promoted "many non-regulated and illegal business behaviors," and who were a "hotbed" of corruption. "They send officials one chicken in order to get back one cow," he charged, in a memorable metaphor. Business owners, Deng Liqun wrote, were increasing the "wealth gap" in China, since "the great disparity between the poor and the rich is primarily embodied in the ownership of property."

Teng Wensheng, who drafted the speech for Jiang, had a different view. "President Jiang's 80th anniversary speech offers a fully mature and complete understanding of Three Represents," Teng commented. "Chinese experience has proved that having only a state-owned sector doesn't work, can't work. We should encourage other sectors to coexist."

On the controversial decision to allow business owners to join the Party, Teng noted "We have Party members 'jumping into the sea' [the metaphor for going into business, capturing the excitement and uncertainty of the market economy.] They are upright citizens, earn their money lawfully, pay their taxes, and accept the Party Constitution. Why not let similar people join the Party? If it works in one direction, why not the other?" As for Deng Liqun, his old boss with whom he had shared a small room when they were both banished during the Cultural Revolution, Teng added: "I can't convince him. Let him take time to figure it all out."

Though most Party officials applauded Jiang's reforms, traditional Leftists enjoyed support in certain circles. Some mid- and lower-level Party officials, who felt threatened by social change or unhappy about erosion of personal power, backed Deng Liqun, albeit often in secret.

But Jiang Zemin argued that unless changes were made, and the system "modernized," the Party would wither. That would mean no socialism in any form. A *China Daily* editorial suggested that by modernizing the Party, Jiang was enabling it to avoid the terminal fate of its sister parties in the former Soviet Union and Eastern Europe, adding, "To imagine a China without the Communist Party is nightmarish."

In the days following, every member of the Politburo endorsed Jiang's speech. Heir apparent Hu Jintao noted that Jiang had thought about the speech for a long time. Jiang's conclusions, Hu said, were based on both China's domestic conditions and the "historical lessons concerning the rise and fall, successes and failures of some political parties in the world."

Jiang Zemin had always been a true believer in socialism. As a student protester, he had marched under the Communist banner, confronting foreign domination and decrying domestic decrepitude; as an adult, he had helped drive out the corrupt Kuomintang regime, restore Chinese dignity, and build the New China.

Indeed so committed was Jiang to the core tenets of Communism that, very early in his tenure as general secretary, he had informed a group of senior leaders, "I don't like private businessmen."[9] Jiang was responding to an upbeat report about a middle-aged manager who had been laid off from an ailing state-owned enterprise, and had begun hawking cheap knickknacks on the street to support his family. He had become so successful so quickly—hiring other laid-off workers and expanding to several locations—that he threw a big party in celebration, and invited his former colleagues who were barely hanging on at the ever-declining government factory. "If we don't stop these business owners," Jiang had warned, "they will put an end to socialism."

Years later, at an informal get-together of state leaders, Jiang walked over to an attendee of that decade-old meeting and admitted that he had been wrong: "What I said back then about private business was not correct. Experience has proven that China needs entrepreneurs and business owners; they are part of our socialist system for building our economy and society."

"At heart, I'm an engineer, not an ideologue," Jiang said, by way of explanation. "Systems work or they don't work. If they don't, you fix them; if they do, you keep them. Private business works. All that matters is what's good for China."[10]

★ ★ ★

Following Jiang's speech, the Party dispatched lecture teams to spread the new Party line. The one question that kept coming up was why allow capitalists to join the Party?

"Today's capitalists should be classified as entrepreneurs," responded Xing Bensi, a team member. "They are a different kind from their old-time namesakes who accumulated their wealth through generations of exploitation. They are a diverse group of previous government officials and ordinary citizens who are business-savvy, facilitate China's reform and opening-up, and help develop socialism with Chinese characteristics."

The lecture teams prepared for their presentations. "Before we departed," Xing recalls, "we had a sort of huddle to construct ready and consistent answers. But first we had to buy it ourselves. I had bought it earlier," he adds, "but I dared not say so before the official line came out. With such a sensitive and political issue, you don't want to be the first to utter it!"

★ ★ ★

Preparations for the 16th CPC National Congress, due to be held in November 2002, were separated into various areas: political report; Constitutional amendments; and personnel. Each area was handled by a different group, with no knowledge of the others' activities; each group reported to Hu Jintao, who was in charge of the preparatory committee and reported to Jiang Zemin. Hu also coordinated the drafting of the political report, a long and elaborate process that took over a year and involved a team of 30 drafters, and which was designed to engage the Party's collective leadership and produce an authoritative consensus document.[11]

Despite their often turgid language, CPC political documents facilitate understanding of current conditions, leadership policy, and future trends. This is especially true for the general secretary's "work report" (or "political report") to National Party Congresses, held every five years—not least because of the immense collective effort that always goes into its drafting.

Jiang was involved throughout. In September he devoted eight full days to scrutinizing and finalizing the political report, says Jin Chongji, the official biographer of Mao Zedong and Zhou Enlai. Jin, who was on the Drafting Committee, recalls an "intense, highly detailed" working meeting, at which Jiang added eight points to the text.[12]

Significantly, Jiang said that he wanted to communicate a "sense of insecurity" in the document, which he said reflected the real world. "Don't think the good times will last forever," he said. "China is facing great challenges, including torrid foreign competition. We have to maintain a strategic focus and treasure unity." Jiang modified the report's second-to-last paragraph to emphasize this insecurity.

The political report was entitled "Build a Well-Off Society in an All—Round Way and Create a New Situation in Building Socialism with Chinese Characteristics."

To no one's surprise, Jiang highlighted the Three Represents as the operating mandate to renew the Party and set the future course for China. Calling the new theory "crucial for advancing with the times," he said the Three Represents was a "powerful theoretical weapon" for strengthening the Party and developing socialism, adding that it would be "the guiding principle that the Party must uphold for a long period of time."

Jiang called the Three Represents "the crystallization of the collective wisdom of the Party." And almost every time the Three Represents was mentioned, the phrase "the important thought of," rather than Jiang's name, was used to introduce it. That was the trade-off. By abandoning the notion that it was his own personal theory, Jiang was raising the philosophy to the highest level of importance.

In promoting his theory, Jiang stressed that Party leaders had to "consciously free our thinking and understanding from the shackles of outdated concepts, practice, and systems, and from our erroneous understanding of Marxist dogmatist theories." At the same time he rooted the Three Represents in Marxism by stating that it was derived from Marxist methodology, and fulfilled the Marxist imperative of "liberating and developing productive forces."

With this line of reasoning, Jiang was leading up to his most controversial initiative—the admission of entrepreneurs and private business owners into the Communist Party. He reaffirmed the importance of the working class and then implied that businessmen constituted a new stratum of this class. They were, in short, "all builders of the cause of socialism with Chinese characteristics."

Jiang believed that the core of Marxism was less about the differences between owners and workers than about an ultimate goal and a defining methodology. That ultimate goal was still an idyllic Communism, but for society to reach it, the methodology would have to "advance with the times."

Entrepreneurs and private business owners, Jiang said, should be "encouraged," "protected," and "commended." To those who understood the subtleties of the wording, it was an outright endorsement and groundbreaking reform. China's prosperity was now increasingly dependent on private enterprise.

Jiang was making the Party more pluralistic, and as such more modern and energetic. Only through "the spirit of reform" and by injecting "new vitality" into its organization, he believed, could the Party retain its "vanguard" position in leading the country.

Jiang's report then looked to the future and set China's overall goal for the next 20 years as the creation of a "well-off society" for its 1.3 billion citizens. The Chinese word was *xiaokang*, which literally means "small well-being" and connotes less affluent than "well off" but better than "free from want." Echoing Deng Xiaoping, Jiang expressed the desire that all China should become a "midlevel developed nation," on a level with a country like, say, Portugal, by the year 2050 and, as part of this plan, to quadruple its 2000 GDP by 2020.

To accomplish this, Jiang said, "We must give full scope to the important role of the non-public sector of self-employed, private, and other forms of ownership of the economy in stimulating economic growth, creating more jobs, and activating the market."

"Private" had now been used openly. Though buried in the sentence, the formerly scorned word was nonetheless present, positive and official. Furthermore, Jiang asserted that privately owned firms should not be at a disadvantage with respect to financing, investment, taxation, land use, market access, and foreign trade, and he pledged more legal protection for private property.

As long as public ownership still had the dominant role, Jiang said, the government could increase its support for the "non-public" sector, which would keep the economy growing at its high rate. Wisely, Jiang did not define "public ownership" or "dominant role," two terms with increasingly loose definitions in Chinese political life.

Jiang then confirmed what had already happened and virtually everyone accepted: the abandoning of the utopian Communist principle "to each according to his needs." China, he said, "should establish the principle that labor, capital, technology, managerial expertise, and other productivity elements participate in the distribution of income in accordance with their contributions." At the same time Jiang sought a new balance of fairness in income levels, opposing both extreme differences and forced equality – or as he put it, "guarding against an excessive disparity in income while opposing egalitarianism."

The final section of Jiang's report was devoted to "Party construction"—strengthening the Party. Key was "intra-Party democracy," which he described as "the life of the Party." Jiang called for "regular annual congresses" (as opposed to every five years) and congresses in more cities and counties, and for entrusting these congresses with oversight of leading officials. His purpose was to break the unchallengeable, monopolistic power of local Party secretaries and oligarchic standing committees by subjecting Party leaders to the permanent, decentralized supervision of Party congresses.

Jiang hoped that these structural changes would reduce corruption. "If we do not resolutely crack down on corruption," he warned, "the flesh-and-blood ties between the Party and the people will suffer a great deal, the Party will be in danger of losing its ruling position, and it is possible the Party could be headed for self-destruction."

In laying out requirements for building a well-off society, Jiang also stressed social harmony—a "harmonious and stable social climate" where all the people could use their abilities and receive what they deserve. In fact, Jiang used the word "harmony" or harmonious seven times in his report, a point of interest since some foreign commentators would later speculate that Hu Jintao's promotion of a Harmonious Society somehow contradicted or usurped Jiang's thinking.

The 16th Party Congress ratified Jiang's far-reaching changes by amending the Party Constitution. The opening sentence of the Party's statement of beliefs was changed, expanding the mission of the Party from being "the vanguard of the working class" to being "the vanguard both of the Chinese working class and the Chinese people and the Chinese nation." This codified what had been an accepted truism for some time: The Communist Party had been transformed from a "revolutionary party" engaged in "class struggle" into a ruling party whose primary role was national development.

In the second paragraph, the Three Represents was inserted in the same sentence as its well-known predecessors. "The Communist Party of China," the line read, "takes Marxism-Leninism, Mao Zedong Thought, Deng Xiaoping Theory, and the important thought of Three Represents as its guide to action." Jiang's Zemin's path-changing theory was now enshrined, albeit without his name attached, in the Party Constitution.

★ ★ ★

Jiang Zemin's sister Jiang Zehui has said that Jiang sees his most important accomplishments as: revitalizing China through science and education; sustainable development; the Go West policy; and the Three Represents.[13]

"When Jiang Zemin became general secretary in 1989, China was still largely a planned economy," says Minister Leng Rong. "The transition to the market was all new, and no one knew what to expect. People were still asking how to do this or that in a socialist market economy: enterprise ownership, enterprise management, macroeconomic controls, legal system, government structure, value systems and moral norms—in ways consistent with socialism. This was uncharted territory," Leng stresses, "and as China underwent tremendous changes in the years after 1989, so did Jiang's ideas." And he notes that to Deng Xiaoping's maxim that the true spirit of Marxism is "seeking truth from facts," Jiang added "advancing with the times."

Jiang had three interrelated objectives—material civilization, spiritual civilization, and political civilization—and one unifying mechanism, the Three Represents. Material civilization referred to economic wealth—products and services of all kinds. Spiritual civilization involved culture, morality, ethics, philosophy, literature, art, natural and social sciences, and even religion. Political civilization stood for governmental, social and legal systems which would bring about decency, consistency, and ultimately some kind of democratic society.

Jiang believed that in order to develop the three civilizations, he had to strengthen and modernize the Party by aligning its ideology with current realities. That was what the Three Represents set out to achieve. The result, in Jiang's vision, would transform China into a "well-off society in an all-around way."

At first blush the Three Represents may have seemed bland and harmless, but to orthodox Communists they were disruptive and disturbing.

The first "represent," "advanced productive forces," developed the Marxist phrase "productive forces" in a clever way, in order to elevate the status of, and bring into the Party, the most dynamic strata of society—managers, entrepreneurs, and private business owners. The first represent, the Party's primary goal in rejuvenating China, promoted the construction of "material civilization." For Jiang, it was epitomized by innovation in science and technology. The Party would now be representing intellectuals, and in the process the Party itself would be intellectualized. Those who had suffered grievously during Mao's Cultural Revolution were now, three decades later, in the vanguard of China's new society.

The second represent, "advanced culture," encompassed morality, civil behavior, high-minded personal traits, progressive social attitudes, shared beliefs, and the arts. This was the Party's complementary goal as it sought to rejuvenate China. It signified the building of "spiritual civilization"—in Jiang's words, "lofty ideals, moral integrity, better education, and a good sense of discipline." And "advanced culture" symbolized a renewed pride in the glories of Chinese civilization, after their rejection during the early Communist era (when the teachings of Confucius, for example, were denounced as "feudal"). Jiang Zemin, with his strong cultural roots, sought to restore such traditional values and virtues, and integrate them with Marxism.

The third represent, "the fundamental interests of the overwhelming majority of the people," reached out to all Chinese society, extending the Party's reach beyond its traditional proletarian base of workers and farmers to include those who create knowledge (e.g., scientists), and more controversially, those who create wealth (e.g. entrepreneurs). Leftists attacked the third represent for replacing key elements of the Party's founding theories—class struggle, vanguard of the working class, and dictatorship of the proletariat—with a concept of an all-encompassing Party which embraced advanced or elite members from all sectors of society. Yet while Jiang was criticized for making the Party more inclusive and less class-obsessed, he felt sure that having knowledge and wealth creators within the Party was the only way to ensure it would continue to exercise leadership.

Du Daozheng, the intellectual Party veteran and close associate of Zhao Ziyang, describes the Three Represents as Jiang's "legacy." He acknowledges that some intellectuals see it as nothing new, and even "shake their heads every time they hear the term," yet he insists that "scientifically speaking it's a good theory which denies the completely false theories of 'class struggle as the center' and 'continuing the revolution under dictatorship of the proletariat'." In Du's opinion, "although Jiang Zemin's appointment was an historical accident, given the reality and difficulties he faced, he did a rather good job during his tenure."

To Leng Rong, the erudite Party theoretician, the Three Represents is a methodology. "It doesn't solve specific problems," he explains, "but it's a way of categorizing and analyzing problems so that they can be solved. It is consistent with Marxism and extends it by linking traditional theory with current reality." Thus it's a guiding principle for adapting the Party to a high-tech, information-dense world. "Innovation, innovation, and more innovation!" adds Leng.

★ ★ ★

In accordance with Party custom, right after the Party Congress came the formal announcement that Hu Jintao was succeeding Jiang Zemin as CPC general secretary and, as expected, in March 2003 as state president. Three years younger than Jiang had been on assuming China's highest offices, Hu was perceptive: his long-term success would require inner harmony as well as outer unity.

Hu found a near-perfect opening balance. He told the Central Committee that he would "seek instruction and listen to the views" of Jiang. The words were a mark of respect, not of subservience. "Seeking instruction isn't the same as seeking orders; it suggests respectfully seeking out a teacher," noted one Party official. A stable working relationship between Hu and Jiang would virtually assure amity, if not always unity, on the Politburo Standing Committee.

Newly elected General Secretary Hu Jintao (far left) and Politburo Standing Committee members Wu Bangguo, Wen Jiaobao, Jia Qinglin, Zeng Qinghong, Huang Ju, Wu Guanzheng, Li Changchun, and Luo Gan meeting with journalists after the 16th CPC Congress (Beijing, November 15, 2002; Xinhua News Agency, Yao Dawei).

Just under two years later, in September 2004, Jiang Zemin retired as chairman of the CPC Central Military Commission, and Hu Jintao was elected to take his place. CCTV dedicated its evening newscast to the transition, showing the 78-year-old Jiang and the 61-year-old Hu walking together in the Great Hall of the People, shaking hands warmly, and being applauded loudly by members of the Central Committee. "Today we are all very happy," said Hu. In a short but emotional farewell speech, Jiang thanked the Central Committee for accepting his resignation, expressed "heartfelt gratitude" to his comrades for their longtime help and support, and called on everyone to work hard under Hu's leadership. "I'm convinced that our Party's cause will witness more and bigger victories!" he concluded.

About a year later Jiang stressed that "I am very pleased that Hu Jintao has taken over responsibilities. He has worked on the Politburo Standing Committee for over ten years, and to some extent, I may say that it was ten years ago that I set my eyes on him [*kanzhong;* literally, targeted, settled on him]."[14]

Jiang Zemin had taken China through a remarkable metamorphosis—from a fretful country traumatized by the turmoil and crackdown in Tiananmen Square into a vibrant and socially open (albeit still politically restrained) nation which had become a primary engine of global economic growth and had emerged as a center of commerce. In a little over a decade, China had gone from international pariah to diplomatic power. One measure of Jiang's contribution is that he made governance more normal for all who would follow him.

Hu was now the undisputed leader of China, in command of the Party, state, and armed forces. His appointment reaffirmed the sacrosanct principle of the leadership of the Party over the military, and was greeted by virtually unanimous approval. (Since his appointment as CMC vice chairman in 1999 Hu had worked unobtrusively but conscientiously to win the army's respect.) All in all, it was the only orderly and peaceful transition of power since the founding of the People's Republic in 1949. A permanent precedent had been set.

Endnotes

1 Robert Lawrence Kuhn, *The Man Who Changed China: The Life and Legacy of Jiang Zemin* (Crown Publishing, 2004).
2 Xinhua, February 20, 2000.
3 Xinhua, March 5, 2000.
4 Josephine Ma, "President's trip to boost south, says party boss." *South China Morning Post,* April 2, 2000.
5 Teng Wensheng.
6 First, critics said that the Three Represents presented neither new thoughts nor new themes. Second, since the ideology of Three Represents had been proposed without practice and testing, it might cause ideological confusion. Third, opponents suggested that its

ideological and political development was weak. Fourth, critics doubted whether a new ideological theory was even necessary. Fifth was the charge that Three Represents were aimed at developing a cult of personality around Jiang Zemin. Finally, there were those who wondered, in light of the Three Represents, whether Marxism and Deng Xiaoping Theory were still relevant. (*Cheng Ming* [Hong Kong], July 1, 2000, 14–16 [BBC].)

7   Wang Huijiong.
8   "The Public Letter to Jiang Zemin from Deng Liqun et. al." referencing The Important Literature Since the 13th Central Committee, 584.
9   Author's communication in Beijing. During 1989–1990, Jiang, influenced by others, had sought to limit the growth of private business, some of which had bankrolled the student protests. (Ching Cheong, ST Asia News Network, *The Korea Herald*, March 5, 2003.)
10 Personal communication with senior leader in Beijing.
11 Kuhn, *The Man Who Changed China*.
12 Author's meeting with Jin Congji, 2003.
13 Kuhn, *The Man Who Changed China*.
14 Author's communication in Beijing in late 2003.

11

The Driving Relevance of Hu Jintao's "Scientific Perspective on Development"

It is natural for a new leader to characterize his new era with the stamp of a new slogan: U.S. President John F. Kennedy had The New Frontier; President Lyndon Johnson followed with The Great Society. Since taking over as China's top leader in 2002, President Hu Jintao has espoused a series of philosophies and policies, summed up by the slogans of Harmonious Society, Putting People First, and, most relevant for directing policy, the Scientific Perspective on Development.[1]

President Hu's political philosophy stresses the following ideas: putting people first and staying close to the people; transparency in government; progressive democracy in society (where propitious); increasing democracy and openness in the Party; and an all-round pragmatism. Hu's commitment to promoting democracy, which people close to him claim he takes very seriously, is tempered by the higher good of social stability, which precludes instituting Western-style democracy at this stage in China, with its huge and diverse population and manifold problems.

Some foreign observers have suggested that President Hu's philosophies and policies mark a break with those of former President Jiang Zemin, and even represent a downgrading of Deng Xiaoping Theory, because both Jiang and Deng stressed economic growth. Such interpretations, however, reflect a tendency to overstress or exaggerate political struggles among China's senior leaders, and miss the basic point that, as China undergoes extraordinarily rapid development, it has different needs at different stages.

Because ideological genetics is the Party's political science, the official view is that its "four generations of collective leadership" have operated at "four historical junctures," thus resulting in "four exhortations:" Mao Zedong made "China stand on its own feet" as an independent country; Deng Xiaoping "liberated and unleashed the productivity of Chinese society"; Jiang Zemin "modernized, rejuvenated and developed the Communist Party and the Chinese nation"; while Hu Jintao is now "reorganizing, reprioritizing and re-energizing China in a more complex domestic and international environment."

Such a view, Party theorists argue, follows "a continuous line of inheritance" between Mao Zedong Thought, Deng Xiaoping Theory, Jiang Zemin's Three Represents and Hu Jintao's Scientific Perspective on Development—even though, in practice, parts of subsequent theories negate parts of previous ones, especially in rejecting Mao's extremism. Thus Deng Xiaoping had to initiate reform and opening to the world, and so his theory had to free the Party from Mao's ideological strictures (i.e., class struggle as the Party's purpose). As Hu Jintao put it, China's second generation leadership, dominated by Deng, focused on "emancipating the mind and seeking truth from facts, and, displaying immense political and theoretical courage, made a scientific appraisal of Comrade Mao Zedong and Mao Zedong's erroneous theory and practice of "taking class struggle as the key link," and made the historic policy decision to shift the focus of the work of the Party and the state onto economic development and introduce reform and opening-up."[2]

Then, as China's economy began growing, Jiang Zemin sought to institutionalize this pragmatism by "advancing with the times"—modernizing the Party and transforming it from a revolutionary party to a ruling party, enlarging it to include leaders from all walks of contemporary life, and promoting economic and intellectual productivity. Jiang too needed to secure his theoretical linkage to Mao and Deng in order to protect his practical ideas.

Hu Jintao's Harmonious Society and Scientific Perspective on Development, meanwhile, build on Deng Xiaoping Theory and Jiang's Three Represents, and address the amalgam of economic, social and political issues that have emerged in recent years. It would have been impossible for Deng or Jiang, contending with the debilitating combination of economic weakness, ideological battles, and social confusion, to be able to do before what Hu is able to do now: for either of them to have delayed economic development in pursuit of social fairness or "harmony" would not have served people's interests in the short term, and would have damaged China's strength in the long term. Furthermore, it was precisely the economic successes of Deng and Jiang that caused disparities in China.

But without having changed the Party's mission from class struggle to economic development, China today would still look more like North Korea than it does like South Korea. China's society might have remained "harmonious" in that everyone might have continued to be equal, but everyone would have continued to be equally destitute, miserable and hopeless, and their once-proud nation weak, helpless and inconsequential. Before Deng, everyone was relatively equal and thoroughly poor; after Deng, as he prescribed and predicted, while all people prospered, some people got rich first.

One senior leader drew an analogy between China's development and constructing roads. Before Deng Xiaoping, there were no roads; in fact, people didn't think they needed roads. Deng changed people's thinking about roads; he struggled to build some dirt roads. Then Jiang Zemin converted the dirt roads into paved highways, even though when he began some people still did not believe that roads were the right things to have. Now Hu Jintao is enlarging the highways into expressways and reducing the pollution of the vehicles that travel them.

Surely Hu was younger, more pragmatic, less flamboyant, more in tune with contemporary times, closer in sense and style to the new generation of international leaders like British Prime Minister Tony Blair. Hu liked getting out among the people, hearing and helping them. After all, Hu had spent the majority of his career outside the major centers—more than 20 years in the less-developed provinces of Gansu, Guizhou and Tibet.

President Hu developed his Scientific Perspective on Development in order to modify excessive reliance on economic expansion, and to seek, as a national goal, a "people-centered," "all-round" approach which, he argues, "strives to take a civilized development path characterized by the development of production, a well-off life, and a good ecological environment."[3]

★ ★ ★

To understand the motivation for Hu's philosophy, one has to appreciate the scope and depth of China's problems, particularly income imbalances, environmental pollution, sustainable development and political reform. Mostly the unavoidable consequences of rapid industrialization, they are extremely serious and getting worse.

Top of the list is economic disparities between sectors of society—urban vs. rural, coastal vs. inland. Though many urban Chinese have become middle class, the majority of China's population is still rural with standards of living significantly below their urban counterparts. In 2007, the average urban resident had more than three times the disposable income of the average farmer.

And the imbalance between the wealthy few and the rural masses has only been growing. One reason is that, for the whole country to maintain the necessary growth rate, the major engines of growth, the developed areas such as Guangdong, Jiangsu, Shandong and Zhejiang provinces, along with Beijing, Shanghai and Tianjin, *must* contribute an outsized proportion. This keeps China as a country on target—but exacerbates income disparity. Furthermore, restructuring SOEs have thrown many people out of work, and because China's farms cannot support all of its rural population, peasants have flooded to the cities looking for jobs.

Hence, income imbalance has become China's most serious problem, a challenge to stability—and nothing gets leadership attention faster than instability: "China's economic reform must not turn shared poverty into uneven wealth," stressed President Hu. "All Chinese citizens should benefit from the reform."[4]

Environmental pollution, a consequence of rapid industrialization, is another terribly serious problem. China's urban air and water supply are among the dirtiest and most dangerous in the world, causing 400,000-750,000 premature deaths per year. Fumes and residues from coal-fired power plants, which account for about two-thirds of China's energy production, fill the skies with millions of tons of pollutants per year (China has become the world's largest source of sulfur dioxide emissions). Of the world's 20 most polluted cities, more than half are now in China.

Industrial and chemical factories spill their toxic effluent into rivers and lakes, 70% of which are contaminated; more than half of China's seven main rivers contain water deemed unsafe to drink, and half of China's population cannot drink unpolluted water. Some scholars believe that losses caused by environmental damage in China each year are about equal to its GDP growth—essentially keeping the country at a net zero in terms of overall quality of life. And China's poor are disproportionately affected by environmental health burdens.[5]

Concerns about such issues, combined with rising costs of raw materials and energy (before the fall in commodity prices during the worldwide financial crisis) have led to "sustainable development" becoming a key watchword in China: officials in provinces and municipalities are now judged not only by the amount of economic growth their areas generate but also by the efficiency of that growth. The central government set a goal to reduce the energy intensity index—energy consumption per GDP unit—by 20%, and major pollutant discharges, by 10% during 2006-2010.[6]

"We must make conserving energy, decreasing energy consumption, protecting the environment and using land intensively the breakthrough point and main fulcrum for changing the pattern of economic growth," Premier Wen Jiabao told legislators in 2007.

The issue of political reform is also looming. As China's economic reforms deepen, its middle class grows more plentiful and powerful—and its members are likely to want to express their views, and to seek all kinds of personal and collective freedoms. The government's hope is that political freedom will never outrun broad economic development, as it believes happened in Russia, to the great detriment of the Russian people. Moreover, China has experienced rising social unrest, including protests, demonstrations, picketing, and group petitioning. Official sources say "public order disturbances" or "mass group incidents" have been growing dramatically—tens of thousands per year. Although the vast majority are local in nature—often complaints over land appropriation or an incident of some kind amplified by instant messaging through ubiquitous mobile phones—these disturbances reflect a society in flux.

All this and more gives background to Hu Jintao's Scientific Perspective on Development. His commitment to environment protection is no recent awakening. A water conservation engineer, Hu is technically expert as well as socially conscious. In fact, because many Chinese leaders were trained as engineers, they treat pollution as an engineering problem as well as a social issue—the nation is now putting enormous emphasis on solving the problem.

However, there is a tension here: China has no choice but to retain economic growth as its top priority—in order to provide employment, particularly for surplus farmers and laid-off workers; if the country cannot sustain employment, social disintegration looms. And economic growth means increased energy consumption, which generates greater pollution.

While national policy maintains economic development as its primary objective, it must now integrate other, potentially diverging or even contradictory, concerns—particularly the rectification of economic imbalances, the institutionalization of sustainable development, and the protection of the environment. Thus economic growth, social equity, cultural development, educational excellence, scientific and technological advancement, environmental protection, sustainable development, and political progress compose the coordinated goals which Hu seeks to achieve through the Scientific Perspective on Development, which has become China's overarching guiding principle.

★ ★ ★

The Scientific Perspective on Development was the centerpiece of Hu Jintao's 20,000-word report to the 17th National Party Congress in October 2007. Its aim was "to continue to build a moderately prosperous society in all respects and develop socialism with Chinese characteristics at the new stage of development."[7]

Hu was candid in his assessment of China's situation: "The economic strength has increased markedly, but the overall productivity remains low, the capacity for independent innovation is weak, and the longstanding structural and mode-of-growth problems are yet to be fundamentally addressed." He stressed that "further reform in difficult areas is confronted with deep-seated problems," and while "A relatively comfortable standard of living has been achieved for the people as a whole, the trend of a growing gap in income distribution has not been thoroughly reversed, there are still a considerable number of impoverished and low-income people in both urban and rural areas, and it has become more difficult to accommodate the interests of all sides . . . " As a result, Hu said, "we face an arduous task to narrow the urban-rural and interregional gaps in development, and promote balanced economic and social development."

On political and social development, Hu was blunt in acknowledging that his administration's "efforts to improve democracy and the legal system fall somewhat short of the need to expand people's democracy," adding: "political restructuring has to be deepened." And Hu noted that, while "socialist culture is thriving as never before . . . the people have growing cultural needs and have become more independent, selective, changeable and diverse in thinking, setting higher requirements for the development of an advanced socialist culture."

Hu then set out the Scientific Perspective on Development, stressing that it "takes development as its essence, putting people first as its core, comprehensive, balanced and sustainable development as its basic requirement, and overall consideration as its fundamental approach." And he spelled out what this meant in practice:

- "We must regard development as the top priority . . . releasing and developing the productive forces. . .rejuvenating the country through science and education . . . We must strive for harmonious development . . . and we must strive for peaceful development, in the course of which China develops itself by safeguarding world peace and contributes to world peace by developing itself.
- We must always put people first . . . realize, safeguard and expand the fundamental interests of the overwhelming majority of the people. We must respect the principal position of the people in the country's political life, give play to their creativity, protect their rights and interests . . . to ensure that development is for the people, by the people and with the people sharing in its fruits.
- We must pursue comprehensive, balanced and sustainable development . . . adopt an enlightened approach to development that results in expanded production, a better life and sound ecological and environmental conditions, and build a resource-conserving and environmentally-friendly society.
- We must balance urban and rural development, development among regions, economic and social development, relations between man and nature, and domestic development and opening to the outside world . . . We must develop a global and strategic perspective, be good at seizing opportunities for development and coping with risks and challenges in a changing world, and work for a favorable international environment.

Summing up, Hu said that applying the Scientific Perspective on Development meant always taking economic development as the central task; building a harmonious socialist society; continuing to deepen reform and opening-up; and strengthening efforts to build the Party in earnest. Hu claimed that his theory was "a concentrated expression of the Marxist world outlook and methodology with regard to development." How is the Scientific Perspective on Development Marxist? Party theorists point to two core reasons: First, its methodology is "scientific" and based on real-world historical conditions in "the primary stage of socialism;" and second, its ultimate goal is still communism, an affluent, classless and perhaps stateless society sometime in the (far) future.

The Scientific Perspective on Development was inscribed in the CPC Constitution at the 17th Party Congress. It was a culminating moment. The message was clear: Hu Jintao was now among the paramount leaders of New China.

★ ★ ★

The practical impact of Hu's theories can be appreciated when one speaks with local leaders. In the past, provincial Party secretaries and governors would tout high GDP growth and perhaps low inflation rates. Today, they still talk about GDP growth, of course, but they add statistics for energy efficiency, pollution, and rebalancing incomes.

When I met Shaanxi Governor Yuan Chunqing in early 2008, for example, he told me from memory the province's 2007 growth rates by sector—energy and chemicals up 22%, food up 3%, and the like—and then, barely pausing for breath (and still from memory), added that energy consumption was down 4.5% and pollution emissions decreased by 3.9%. Improved air quality, he said, meant that Xi'an, Shaanxi's capital, had had 294 "good air days." He knew precisely how many of Shaanxi's roughly 40 million citizens had to drink "bitter water": 2.9 million. He added that polluted water largely affected rural citizens, and that he was determined to alleviate this problem ahead of the national standard.

Governor Yuan spoke too about implementing a Harmonious Society through education and health care. He said that his goal for poorer towns was to make "the best building a school and the second best a hospital."

Jiangsu is among China's leading provinces in almost every important statistic: GDP (#3); GDP per capita (#2); growth (double digits for 15 consecutive years); most privately owned companies (663,500 in 2006); and most foreign direct investment. When I met Jiangsu Party Secretary Li Yuanchao in September 2007, he explained how the Scientific Perspective on Development drove policy.

Secretary Li stressed Jiangsu's non-economic achievements: the province ranked No. 1 by the number of ecological cities, environmental protection model cities, clean cities, and forestation in cities; by number of universities and number of enrolled college students; and by the rate of satisfaction with the security of its society. (Citizen satisfaction with law enforcement had risen to 97% in 2006. The number of murder cases per 100,000 persons in Jiangsu was 1.02, compared to 1.63 nationally and 5.61 in the U.S. And 94% of Jiangsu's murder cases were solved, compared to 88% in China and 62% in the U.S.)

But Li noted that there was still a significant difference between urban and rural areas in Jiangsu, and a wealth divide between the highly developed areas in the south (cities such as Suzhou and Wuxi near Shanghai) and the much less-developed areas further north. In this sense, Jiangsu was like a microcosm of all China, Li said, though the income gap between rural and urban residents remained the smallest in the country.

Acknowledging problems, Li Yuanchao listed "four difficulties for scientific development in Jiangsu": upgrading poor quality township enterprises; increasing average income of wage earners; reconciling the long-standing gap between north and south; and repairing the damaged ecological system.

In the spirit of "putting people first," the provincial government promised its citizens Three Haves and Four Ensures. These were:

- Let every urban resident of Jiangsu *have* food to eat, clothes to wear, and a home to live in.
- *Ensure* that all children receive public education; no qualified student drops out due to poverty; all people receive timely medical assistance when ill; and people facing legal difficulties receive legal assistance.

Jiangsu's environmental problems, meanwhile, had erupted a few months earlier: in May 2007 a severe outbreak of algae in Taihu Lake—China's third largest freshwater lake, and the source of drinking water for about 30 million people—had rendered tap water undrinkable for half of the 2.3 million residents of nearby Wuxi city.[8] High levels of nitrogen and phosphorus, generated by industrial pollution and sewage, caused the algae.

Jiangsu officials, led by Secretary Li, pledged to clean up Taihu, in part by closing small, non-environmentally friendly manufacturing plants, including 2,130 small chemical firms. They also committed to improve sewage treatment; to ensure safe drinking water; and to revive the lake by 2010. Jiangsu now has implemented the most rigorous environmental assessment standards; the strictest monitoring procedures; and the most severe punishments.

★ ★ ★

According to Minister of Culture Cai Wu, Hu Jintao's vision of a Harmonious Society seeks to improve the way individuals behave toward one another and how social groups get along together. Cai noted the debilitating interpersonal problems of the past, when accusations and denunciations were a hovering presence and constant fear: "Our past political system made people afraid of saying wrong words or not being politically dedicated," he explained; "people were scared of being accused or denounced for some infraction." Now, he said, "Chinese society is more tolerant. We should communicate with one another in a more relaxed, light-hearted manner, and work in a harmonious human environment."[9]

"The core building blocks of a harmonious society are strong, uplifting human relationships," Cai added. "A harmonious society is one of democracy and rule of law, fairness and justice, integrity, fraternity, vitality, stability, order, and harmony between man and nature. We are encouraging a brand new style of interpersonal relationships."

★ ★ ★

Considering his critical importance to China, relatively little is known about Hu Jintao as an individual. The 2007 Party Congress described his domestic vision, and the 2008 Beijing Olympics reflected his international vision, yet his public persona remains reserved, cautious. This undersells the man: those who know him say he is a warm and compassionate person.

As vice president of the Central Party School, Xing Bensi had frequent contact with Hu Jintao, who for many years was the school's president. Xing recalls a seemingly small incident, which he says exemplifies Hu.[10] In 1994, a senior foreign media official visited China, and Xing was in charge of organizing his schedule. When all appropriate officials were unable to meet the visitor, Xing, in desperation, asked Hu, his boss at the Party school, to receive the guest. Hu was properly hesitant: media was not his area of responsibility and according to Politburo protocol he should not intervene. (Territorial matters are sensitive in any government system, particularly so in China.) But after Xing implored him to help out, Hu met the foreign visitor and all went well.

"Frankly, helping me was a testament to the kind of person Hu Jintao is," says Xing Bensi. "It would have been very convenient for him to turn down my request since it was not his job. But he took a risk to do me a favor."

In 1999, shortly before his retirement, Xing Bensi met Hu, who wanted to discuss how best to develop the Party school. "Hu suggested that future Party school leaders should not just come from within the school itself, because he was worried that 'there might be too much inbred thinking,'" Xing recalls. "Hu wanted to recruit some officials and scholars from outside the school to encourage different perspectives and intellectual diversity."

Xing gives this comparison of his two former bosses at the Party school, Hu and Qiao Shi (former Politburo Standing Committee member): "Qiao Shi came across as a very sophisticated politician," Xing remembers. "He didn't talk much, but when he spoke, people listened. He was somewhat reserved, sometimes even a bit distant. In contrast," he says, "Hu Jintao is much younger, more energetic, and more passionate. He reaches out to people and treats his subordinates warmly. He is approachable and empathetic."

It's a view echoed by Professor Huang Jiefu, a leading surgeon and China's vice minister of health, who, among other duties, is responsible for the medical care of China's senior officials, including President Hu.[11] "When we are alone together, I do not feel he is the president of China," says Professor Huang. "He is very engaging and very friendly, not just like some bureaucrat. When he meets me," he adds, "he just calls me 'Jiefu', not 'Minister Huang'. He treats his colleagues with a natural closeness; you can feel the intimacy . . . Every time I see him, it's just like meeting a friend. I can talk to him, just like that."

In Huang's view, Hu is "always approachable and open-minded. He respects intellectuals, because he himself is an intellectual. He has vision. He is very sincere and pragmatic. He knows how to handle complicated situations." Of Hu's vision for the future, Huang adds: "President Hu thinks strategically. He wants to change things gradually, enable transitions to be calm. He doesn't want to institute change overnight—in order to avoid potential disruption."

"President Hu Jintao and I joined the central government at about the same time and I know him well," comments Dr. Song Jian, former state councilor and chairman of the State Science and Technology Commission. "Hu is extremely smart and very patient—an unusual combination." Song, who is now retired and focused on science and writing, says that President Hu "is concerned about China's elders and seeks advice from many of us. Speaking personally," Song adds, "Hu wants to be sure that I have proper working conditions." (To be characterized as "extremely smart" by Dr. Song—always a first-rate scientist, never a patronizing politician—is praise indeed.)[12]

Former colleagues say Hu is a persuasive person who is "very good at coping with complex situations" and combines "firm principles and flexible tactics." Hu's ability to win over colleagues was emphasized by one high-ranking Chinese official—who significantly came from a different wing of the Party—who told me "Hu Jintao is a very decent and humble man," which was not how this official characterized certain other leaders.

Hu himself has said that "a good leader must have firm beliefs and lofty goals, do solid work, seek no fame or gain, avoid bureaucratic airs, and share the feeling of the masses of people." He has also noted that "a good leader should encourage democracy and also be capable of taking resolute actions at critical moments—and must love life."[13]

Indeed, Hu loves literature and art, with interests in movies, operas and novels, and still plays table tennis fairly well. He once said that it was not his original intention to go into politics.

Hu's previous experience running the Communist Youth League has led him to focus on issues relating to the country's younger generation. He has emphasized that China's young people should have not only a sense of urgency and mission, but also a good understanding of the hardships and complicated nature of reform, advising them: "do not cherish excessively high expectations if your psychological capacity to bear [rejection or loss or lack of success] is low."

There's no doubt that Hu's working experience has shaped his principles. Before joining the central government in 1992 he spent virtually his entire career among China's less advantaged peoples in three inland provinces (Gansu, Guizhou and Tibet). His political philosophy of rebalancing growth and redressing income and lifestyle disparities, by striving to develop China's underdeveloped provinces and sectors, is thus not a recent reaction to social inequality but rather the product of deep experience, which has fostered a long-standing commitment to improving the lives of China's masses.

All this, plus his education at China's leading science and technology university and ten years experience in the Politburo Standing Committee—including five years as president of the Central Party School and vice president of the country—have prepared Hu Jintao to be China's leader during these complex times.

★ ★ ★

In 1978, Deng Xiaoping initiated China's reform and opening-up by calling for the Chinese people to "emancipate the mind." Now President Hu calls anew for further reform, which must be empowered by a new kind of mental emancipation. Circumstances have changed; the world is more complicated and variegated. Life, society, business, environment, communications and international relations all have more moving parts, more considerations to address. In today's hyper-complex world, Hu Jintao's vision of the Scientific Perspective on Development as the strategy for creating a Harmonious Society creates requirements for new kinds of thinking. This is why Hu stresses creativity and innovation in all areas: science and technology, industry and commerce, global partnerships, political transparency and participation, and cultural and spiritual life in all their diverse expressions. Without a further emancipation of the mind, Hu says, China's development will face obstacles and difficulties.

"Jiang Zemin and Hu Jintao had to be different from Deng Xiaoping," said Party theorist Leng Rong. "They not only had to put forward a grand vision, but they also had to do practical work, striking a balance between theory and practice. We've encountered many challenges during 30 years of reform and opening, but we've made it through and achieved a great deal."

Endnotes

1   The Chinese phrase *Kexue Fazhan Guan* was originally translated by the government as Scientific Development Concept; more recently, the official translation has been the improved Scientific Outlook on Development. I prefer Scientific Perspective on Development, which to me feels more active and engaged, conveying efficacious action and the policy-directing power of an idea which seeks integrated sets of solutions to multiple, complex economic, social and environmental problems.
2   President Hu Jintao's work report to the 17th CPC National Congress.
3   "Scientific Concept of Development & Harmonious Society," Xinhua, December 31, 2005.
4   "China Strives to Narrow Yawning Income Gap for Social Equality," Xinhua, September 30, 2006.
5   *Cost of Pollution in China: Economic Estimates of Physical Damage,* The World Bank and State Environmental Protection Administration, P. R. China, 2007.
6   Fu Shuangqi, Ding Yimin, Wu Chen and Yue Deliang, "Premier: China reports drops in energy consumption, pollution in 2007," Xinhua, March 5, 2008.
7   "Hu Jintao's report at 17th Party Congress," Xinhua, October 15, 2007.
8   "Algae outbreak sparks water panic," *China Daily, May* 31, 2007.
9   Author's meeting with Cai Wu, Beijing, March 2006.
10   Author's meeting with Xing Bensi, Beijing, April 2008.
11   Author's meeting with Huang Jiefu, Beijing, June 2008.
12   Author's meeting with Song Jian, Beidaihe, August 2009.
13   *People's Daily* - http://english.peopledaily.com.cn/leaders/vpresident.html.

Snapshots of Economic Reform

Politburo member Liu Yunshan tells a story which sums up his own experience of the impact of reform: in 1982 he was a mid-level official in Inner Mongolia, when he and his colleagues received a directive from Beijing insisting that within 20 years they must increase the standard of living in Inner Mongolia to that of Mongolia, across the border. Liu, who later would become the region's deputy Party secretary, recalled: "We were so poor and ill-equipped at the time, it sounded like an impossible dream—we hardly knew how to react!" Yet in 2007, when President Hu Jintao visited Inner Mongolia "he saw how people from Mongolia now come across the border to Inner Mongolia to buy goods and services, and even for healthcare and education! That," Liu added, "is the power of reform."[1]

★ ★ ★

According to Gao Shangquan, former vice minister of the State Restructuring Commission, the flaws in China's planned economic system were glaring: "Enterprises had no sovereignty, no decision-making power," he says. "Their personnel, finance, equipment, and raw materials were entirely controlled by their ministry. To do anything, enterprises had to get ministry approval."[2]

Professor Gao gives an example of two factories in Shenyang, Liaoning Province: a transformer plant, belonging to the First Machine-Building Ministry, and a copper smelter, belonging to the Ministry of Metallurgy. "They were literally next door to each other," he relates, "but they never communicated, much less did any business together. The transformer plant needed copper, of course, but the copper had to be allocated by its ministry in Beijing, which shipped it to Shenyang from Yunnan Province almost 2,000 miles away." Meanwhile, Gao says, "the copper produced by the smelter was distributed to other places across China by its own ministry. For the two factories to do business would have saved significant effort, time and expense. But they had zero independence—they couldn't even work with their next-door neighbor!"

A similar contradiction of the planned economy were construction crews, which were administrated by ministries, not by cities or provinces, the result of which was inefficiency to the point of comedy: factories were factories, but each ministry had its own crew that traveled around the country and didn't know much about local conditions.

In another example of the planned economy, Gao recalls an extremely hot summer in Shanghai in the middle 1950s. In order for workers to continue working in the wilting heat, enterprises had to reduce the temperature. But to buy a fan, he says, firms "had to file reports with seven regulatory departments in their ministries. When they finally got the required seven stamps of approval, the summer was over."

Under the planned economic system, the government decided the price of every item. "A box of matches sold at 2 *fen* [less than one penny]," Gao explains with a smile. "If we wanted to hike the price, we would have to take it to the State Council for discussion." Gao recalls a survey of workers in Shandong: "One of the questions was: 'If somebody steals from your factory, what would you do?' Three options: pretend I didn't see it; stop him; or, if he steals, I steal. Of the 300 surveyed, 220 chose the first option. Only 13 chose the second."

★ ★ ★

Transforming a planned economy into a market economy was an unprecedented challenge, particular in the mid-1980s as reform ventured into urban areas. In September 1984, 200 young economists gathered in Hangzhou, Zhejiang Province, for what would become an historic conference.[3] The main organizer was a 36-year-old rural policy expert, Wang Qishan (who some 24 years later would become vice premier). The issue was fundamental for market economics: pricing.

Debate was heated. Some advocated a step-by-step approach, adjusting prices incrementally. Others opted for a "big bang," freeing all prices at once. The former maintained control and stability but was fragmented and took time; the latter was rapid but could be unpredictable and destabilizing (the "big bang" freeing of pricing would have disastrous consequences in Russia and Eastern Europe).

Dr. Hua Sheng, then an economist at the Chinese Academy of Social Sciences (CASS), along with four colleagues, had a radical idea. It was called a Dual-Track system and would, for each product, maintain fixed prices for production up to a planned quota, free prices for production greater than the quota, and reduce the quota each year. "The Dual-Track system introduced market mechanisms gradually," Hua reflects 25 years later. "It exemplified how China adapted economic theory to the country's special conditions, developing systems with Chinese characteristics."

After the Dual-Track system was explained to Premier Zhao Ziyang, it was approved as national policy in only about three weeks. Implemented in 1985, it lasted until 1992.

Hua Sheng's family had been well-to-do prior to the Communist Revolution and had some association, however remote, to the Kuomintang— each of which, during those terrible times of extreme zealotry, were life-shattering stigmas. As a result, in 1968, at the beginning of the Cultural Revolution, when he was 15 years old, he was one of the first to be sent down to the countryside.

In 1988, Hua wrote a paper on ten years of reform, offering three possible scenarios—turmoil, stagnation, high growth. What he did not predict was that all three would occur in succession: turmoil soon thereafter in June 1989, stagnation until late 1992, and high growth through 2008.

Also in 1988, Hua left China for the UK, where he continued his economic research at Oxford and Cambridge. When he returned to China in 1994, CASS refused to take him back because he had worked for the then discredited Zhao Ziyang. Hua had no option but to struggle to start his own business. In 2009, Hua had a group of successful companies, including a private university of which he was president. He continues to write economic papers which often take issue with government policy.

★ ★ ★

China's economic reform, so far, has consisted of five main stages. The first, beginning in 1978 and lasting until about 1985, focused on reform of the agricultural economy. The outcome was unambiguous, surprising even its proponents—the efficiency of agricultural production improved dramatically and the living standards of peasants increased.

The second stage, from 1985 until 1989, shifted reform to the cities, triggering complex problems. Urban reform was not as easy as expected, because it involved the emergence of different markets (labor, financial, housing), the start of state enterprise reform, and adjustments to the system of pricing. Trouble came quickly: first inflation, and then corruption—which became widespread, as government officials and enterprise managers formed unholy alliances, exchanging illegal payments for preferential treatments.

In the third stage, from the Tiananmen tragedy in June 1989 until early 1992, a conservative resurgence slowed reform and emphasized social stability. China's growth slowed too, due to international boycotts protesting the bloody crackdown as well as domestic policy restraints.

The fourth stage, beginning in mid-1992 after Deng Xiaoping resuscitated reform during his Southern Tour, featured almost complete concentration on economic growth, with the greatest concern being inflation (especially in 1993-1994). This sustained phase, covering President Jiang Zemin's two terms, energized China's historic economic resurgence. Macro-economic controls were developed and micro-economic restructuring of enterprises instituted.

The fifth stage, beginning in 2002 when President Hu Jintao assumed office, set other national objectives in addition to economic growth, in order to deal with emerging problems. New policies focused on economic imbalances, environmental pollution, and sustainable development.

Stages one, two and four centered on increasing quantity, whereas stage five stressed increasing value. In its early stages, reform developed outside the existing system—town and county enterprises emerged, private businesses established—without radically disrupting the old ways or uprooting China's socialist economy. The fourth stage tackled the most intractable problems of the traditional system. The fifth stage with its host of complex problems may be the most challenging—yet it should not be forgotten that it is only because of its remarkable successes achieved in the past that China could even be in this position.

★ ★ ★

The full name for China's reformed economy is Socialist Market Economy with Chinese Characteristics. Foreigners may assume that this mouthful is nothing but a linguistic smokescreen to conceal China's embarrassingly overt embrace of capitalism. The "socialist" descriptor, it is said, preserves Marx and Mao and thus maintains the Party's legitimacy.

But how do Chinese leaders continue to justify the Communist appellation when its foundational economic theory never worked in China historically, is being repudiated in China today, and has proved bankrupt everywhere it has ever been tried? Keep in mind why Chinese leaders believe that they need to maintain one-party CPC rule. This is the best way—perhaps the only way, in their opinion—to guarantee stability to their country and pride to their people.

While the CPC still weighs how much traditional socialism to retain and how much Western-style capitalism to adopt, this question has become one of economic optimization, not political ideology. However, most Chinese leaders, certainly Deng Xiaoping, really did continue to believe in the primacy of socialism, with market modifications, as the human ideal.

The chosen phrase allows nicely for ambiguity: if you are more disposed to capitalism, then read "market economy"; if you tilt toward socialism, then read "socialist." But there is more to these historically-baggaged words. If "capitalism" is defined as the industrial-revolution style of worker exploitation, or its harsh 19th and early 20th century manifestations in America and Europe, then China, indeed, is not promoting "capitalism." Similarly, if "socialism" is defined as the goal of a reasonably balanced society and the strategy of strong government macroeconomic controls, then China, indeed, is not abandoning "socialism."

The "socialist" modifier does in fact give a somewhat accurate description of China's current economic policy, even if only to differentiate it from Western-style capitalism. Chinese leaders wanted to preserve a high degree of central control for reasons of stability and to temper the increasing disparity between rich and poor. (To Jiang Zemin, the word "socialist" was not superfluous, not like "legs added to a snake," he said, but more like "eyes added to a painted dragon, which enables it to fly"—"eyes" meaning that the nature of China's market economy was socialist.)

The second descriptive idea is "Chinese characteristics," which gives policymakers the literary license to incorporate into the socialist market economy elements of capitalism, particularly free-market economics. "Chinese characteristics" adds both flexibility and mystery, enabling China to differentiate its form of self-defined socialism from classic 19th century Marxism and from the 20th century Bolshevik/Soviet catastrophe. China does differ substantially from other countries: huge population; diverse geographies and ethnic groups (56); strong cultural and historical traditions; and entrepreneurial instincts of its people. These differences demand the idea of "Chinese characteristics," which give the Chinese socialist economy its distinctive market flavor.

What's happening in China, like what's happening in most countries, is that developmental models are modified continuously to suit changing realities, without concern for political categories or labels. Sometimes markets should dominate; sometimes governments must intervene—witness the 2008-2009 global financial crisis. Optimizing development is 21st century; political theory is 19th century.

★ ★ ★

Tiananmen tragedy may ultimately be seen to have forced China to focus on economic reform. Certainly it resulted in a consensus that political reform must evolve gradually, with stability maintained and assured. At the same time, the events of 1989 seemed to teach China's leaders the lesson that militaristic solutions were archaic and counterproductive, hard-line approaches could only be temporary, and reactionary policies were not in the Party's interests. CPC rule would now depend on what it did for the people—how it improved their lives—which in turn would depend on economic reform and development.

Foreign conventional wisdom is that Chinese leaders reform the economy in order to protect their positions—so that destabilizing protests would not reoccur. In my opinion, however, almost all China's current leaders genuinely desire real reform—and this was largely true even in the past when reformers used the "self-preservation argument" to influence their more conservative colleagues to embrace change.

★ ★ ★

Reform was never easy and there have certainly been times when leaders have taken risks to ensure that it stayed on track. In April 1999, for example,

Premier Zhu Rongji went to Washington, seeking to reach agreement on China's entry into the World Trade Organization (WTO).[4] As Zhu told the Politburo: "We have been negotiating for thirteen years. . . . Black hair has turned white. It is time to conclude negotiations."[5] Yet joining the WTO remained controversial in China. Conservatives warned that waves of foreign competition, required by WTO rules, would put millions of workers out of their jobs and onto the streets, leading to social unrest. In addition, foreigners would soon dominate key industries, such as finance and retail.

President Jiang Zemin and Premier Zhu, however, were unified in their belief that the benefits to China of joining the WTO would outweigh its costs. They argued internally that China's accession would increase foreign investment, stimulate good Chinese companies to become better, and force inefficient enterprises either to meet the demands of the market or go mercifully out of business. Jiang even sought to open China's sensitive telecommunications market, which he called "stiff and ossified," adding that "it has a bureaucratic style, it goes for industry monopolization, it makes enormous profits but has no concept of providing services. Foreign capital must be brought in."[6]

Still, the debate, which had simmered for years, intensified in the context of Zhu's American mission. Some Party leaders tagged the trip "high risk," given what they saw as recent vitriolic "China-bashing" in the US—on everything from trade to spying—which they believed had "poisoned the atmosphere." Even Zhu Rongji himself said later that he had not wanted to go to the U.S. at that time, because the situation was not conducive to success.

With his engagingly direct style, Zhu Rongji might well have been a hit in America had he not arrived at such an inopportune moment. Unfortunately, though he offered greater concessions on opening China's markets than many in his country thought wise, and laid all his political capital on the table in one big bet to get China into the WTO, Zhu saw his best offer spurned by President Clinton, who was under political pressure to reject what he knew to be the right decision. The result was that Zhu was diminished in his own country, and the U.S. government undercut someone whose intrinsic interests were reasonably resonant with its own.

Clinton "quickly realized his error" and "called Premier Zhu in New York . . . to make a commitment to get China into the WTO by the end of the year"—but the damage had been done.[7]

"When we were about to return to China, President Clinton called, hoping to resume negotiations," said Song Ning, Zhu's speechwriter. "But it was not suitable to talk any more. So Zhu said 'No,' suggesting we should recommence talks in Beijing in the future."

Former U.S. Treasury Secretary Robert Rubin had a different recollection: "We had reached agreement when Zhu was in Washington, but we thought we'd have a better chance with Congress if we'd wait a few weeks to get out of the spotlight. But somehow," he said, "to our collective embarrassment, our agreement was leaked on the Internet—we never did figure out how the leak happened, and we certainly didn't anticipate the reaction in China."[8]

In fact, it was a U.S. government website that unilaterally disclosed the confidential list of agricultural products on which Beijing had supposedly made concessions, either by allowing them into China or granting tariff reductions. Zhu Rongji insisted he had categorically rejected the list during negotiations.[9] But the public revelation caused great stir in China, where people assumed that Zhu had indeed made those concessions. Nationalistic politics in Beijing, animated and energized by Clinton's mistake, were taking over, assaulting Zhu and buffeting Jiang. The unauthorized 17-page "Sino-U.S. Joint Statement" was instantly translated and distributed to China's senior leaders. The Chinese were outraged at the posting of their so-called "concessions" online, and assumed that the Americans had done it deliberately.[10]

"The reaction was as strong as a 6.0 [Richter-scale] earthquake," recalled an insider close to Zhu. "Rumors flew thick and fast in Zhongnanhai, and people ignorant of the true facts even said, 'How can Old Zhu have done such a thing?'"[11] Internet articles and student demonstrators labeled him a "traitor." Zhu himself said, "The Americans look down on us Chinese."[12]

Zhu Rongji would later correct misunderstandings, emphasizing that he took no initiative on his own. All WTO decisions were made by the CPC Central Committee and even the decision that Zhu should visit the U.S. was made by President Jiang.[13] But when, three weeks after his trip, American bombs destroyed China's embassy in Belgrade, killing three journalists and triggering an outpouring of nationalism, anti-American fervor weakened Zhu further. A combined opposition of broad nationalism (popular, intellectual, military), self-protecting bureaucracies, Leftist ideologues, and political rivals coalesced into a potent force that almost blocked Jiang's and Zhu's strategic vision for China.

In the following months, Jiang assumed a more nationalistic posture in internal meetings, directing harsh rhetoric toward America,[14] while Zhu kept a low profile, amid rumors that he had quit or been sacked. Finally, in August 1999 Jiang publicly renewed his call for deeper reforms, signaling that China was ready to resume talks on joining the WTO. Jiang confounded his critics by reaffirming his support for Zhu and for their mutual policy of reconciling with the U.S. and pursuing China's WTO entry.

At the APEC summit in New Zealand in September, Presidents Jiang and Clinton held a two-hour discussion, described as "very productive, very friendly, and quite comprehensive"[15]—though Jiang lectured Clinton on Taiwan and gave him as a gift a book denouncing Falun Gong, which some American officials took to be in bad taste.[16]

In 2000, in another positive development in Sino-American relations, the U.S. House of Representatives passed legislation authorizing permanent normal trade relations (PNTR) with China. Supporters of the bill argued that by opening China's domestic market to American products, American values would be exported as well. Those who opposed the legislation usually cited China's human rights abuses, but their underlying motivation was more often pressure from American labor unions, which feared loss of jobs. Its passage ended the 20-year-old annual review of China's trade status, reinforcing U.S. support for China's WTO entry.

On November 10, 2001, at the WTO meeting in Qatar, China's accession was unanimously approved, the culmination of its 15-year quest to join the global body. Jiang Zemin said that China, "as a member of the WTO, will strike a carefully thought-out balance between honoring its commitments and enjoying its rights."

★ ★ ★

Prior to China joining the WTO, Chinese scholars focused on forecasting the impact of membership. The general consensus, according to Wang Loulin, former vice president of the Chinese Academy of Social Sciences, was that there would be three phases. In the first, which would last for two-to-three years, there would be little change. In the second phase, which might last for three or more years, academics predicted that the effect would be more negative than positive, as Chinese companies struggled to compete against their larger, stronger foreign competitors. It would only be in the third phase, six or more years after WTO entry, when China would reap the benefits of internationalization.

But subsequent to joining the WTO, China achieved astounding economic success, the benefits far outweighing the costs. These achievements would become Jiang Zemin and Zhu Rongji's legacy. According to Wang Loulin, "we were all surprised to see immediate positive results in terms of international trade and foreign investments with no negative period at all. China's economy, propelled by trade and investments, grew at a speed unseen in our history." Indeed, Wang added, "We've noted the demonstrations against globalization in other countries—and we Chinese are baffled by it because we've experienced only the benefits." However, he acknowledged, "with the financial crisis beginning in 2008, many challenges lie ahead."

★ ★ ★

Certainly China's economy has entered uncharted territory. The reform of Chinese currency, the value of the RMB *yuan* relative to the dollar, and its restricted convertibility, became a hot political issue in America as China's trade surpluses, and America's trade deficits, skyrocketed. China's foreign reserves, $165 billion in 2000, exceeded $1 trillion in 2006 and reached $2 trillion in 2009.

The results were calls in the U.S. Congress for legislation to impose punitive tariffs (of up to 27.5%) on Chinese goods. But such tariffs would have proved counterproductive. They would have insulted China and created anti-American feelings, particularly among students; and though they might have temporarily helped certain workers in some American industries, most American jobs would not have reappeared. American job losses, while real and painful, were not very directly linked to Chinese imports. Even without China, manufacturing would simply go to other countries, like Mexico or Vietnam, wherever labor costs were low. But tariffs would reduce standards of living for all Americans—since so much of what Americans buy is made in China.

In July 2005, China ended its fixed-rate exchange, and allowed its currency to float within a limited band. Over the ensuing three years, the RMB appreciated about 20%. But issues were complicated, much more so than speeches of some U.S. legislators would suggest. (U.S. policy should certainly encourage China to continue to open its markets, and build on progress made—by 2005, 49,000 American companies had invested $51 billion in China.)

Similarly, in China, issues are complex. On the one hand, it's true that if the currency appreciates, it cuts into the already thin profit margins of Chinese exporters. On the other hand, if the RMB is artificially low, this increases inflationary pressures in China—which is always a concern. (China had to devalue its currency in the early 1990s, but then resisted pressure during the Asian crisis in 1997-1998 to devalue it further, a bold, responsible move which helped stabilized Southeast Asia.)

Likewise, too much money coming into the country, via exports and foreign investments, is not always a good thing for China. The danger of such massive inflows of capital is that they will be spent on inefficient projects, with growth-fueled ebullience driving investment frenzy. Shanghai's real-estate market, for example, became overheated and inevitably declined. This caused great concern, but it was simple economics: when too much cash is chasing too few good properties, real-estate prices rise, and can create a self-perpetuating, pyramid-scheme-like perception of rapidly increasing value—but such "bubbles" inevitably collapse.

And when national growth is generated by excessive capital investment, it is a warning sign that the system is fragile. China needs to derive more of its growth by domestic consumption. After all, economic growth is vital for maintaining employment. (China needs economic growth of at least 7-8% per year.) There are only three fundamental ways by which an economy can grow: consumption by people; investments by business (foreign and domestic) or by the government (primarily infrastructure); and exports. China's growth has been supported by the latter two: investment and exports. Now consumption is top priority for China's leaders—to boost the economy, raise living standards, and make the nation more self-reliant.

At the risk of over-simplifying—and prior to the 2008 financial crisis—the Chinese people saved too much and spent too little; whereas the American people spent too much and saved too little. Hence, America's gigantic trade deficit with China—which reached $273 billion in 2010. When Americans buy cheap Chinese products, they raise the American standard of living but also increase the American trade deficit, which the Chinese then finance with their trade surpluses: America sends China its cash in exchange for Chinese products, and then China sends this cash, which is now China's cash, right back to America to purchase U.S. government debt, which helps finance the U.S. deficit. If this system sounds stable, it is not. Imbalances are in neither country's long term interest; moreover, the financial crisis is effecting fundamental change.

The reason the Chinese people have such a high savings rate—as much as 25% of their post-tax income, among the highest in the world—is anxiety over healthcare and retirement pensions, because in the new market economy these are no longer fully subsidized as they once were.

The Chinese government is seeking to encourage greater consumption, by providing such social welfare, so people do not have to save out of fear they will be unable to pay their hospital bills or support themselves in their old-age. And demographics may shift spending patterns. Young people, who do not know past traumas and have known only a vibrant economy, see no reason why they should deprive themselves of what they want today.

★ ★ ★

Wu Jinglian, a distinguished economist, spelled out China's challenges in a 2008 article in *Caijing* magazine. Nicknamed endearingly Market Wu for his early and intense call for China to adopt a market economy, Wu praised the era of reform and opening-up as having "basically changed the course of Chinese history," but raised a number of concerns. China's social, political and economic reforms, he said, were "unbalanced," because "policy cannot keep pace with the demand for further change." As a result, he suggested, "fundamental problems such as resource consumption, environmental degradation, economic inequality, political corruption and the widening gap between rich and poor are becoming increasingly acute and attracting criticism from the public."

The outspoken Wu asserted that many of these problems stemmed "from flaws in the economic and political system." He stressed that "the power of resource allocation is too concentrated in the hands of government officials," while progress toward democracy and the rule of law was "sluggish." He implored leaders to "quicken the pace of political reform" and to fulfill Party promises to "build a country with rule of law."[17] "A modern market economy needs to have the superstructure guarantees of constitutional government, democracy and rule of law," he asserted. "We can no longer afford to tarry and wait." Wu charged that without checks and balances corruption had flourished, claiming that illegal commerce could account for up to an astonishing 30% of GDP.[18] Key tasks for future development, he said, included:

- Speeding up economic transformation—balancing consumption, investment and export; combining manufacturing and service industries, and moving toward an economy based on technology, talent, education, and managerial innovation.

- Building balanced relationships throughout society, especially between rural and urban areas, central and local governments, and humanity and nature.
- Creating more social wealth by improving people's lives and assuring social fairness and equality.

Wu stressed that the key to success was to rely even more on the market to allocate resources. He called for further reforms, including enhanced property rights, allowing rural residents to own land, and permitting more people to make income from their property; continuing the privatization of state-owned companies, and opening monopolized industries, including financial services, to private business; and further developing an open, competitive and ordered modern market system, by promoting regulatory reform, eliminating administrative interferences, and ending administrative price fixing.

Wu acknowledged that "China's Party and government leaders have instituted a series of reform measures to eliminate these problems," and noted that the 17th CPC Congress had "called for an 'expansion of democracy to assure that the people are masters of their own country.'" He added his own opinion, that "the path to realizing economic reforms is through reform of the Party," and that "the first step is to expand democracy within the Party, which will then lead to democracy in society. Such political reforms as these," he stressed, "are the basic guarantee for the future progress of economic and other societal reforms."

Endnotes

1 Author's meeting with Liu Yunshan, Beijing, December 2007.
2 Author's meeting with Gao Shangquan, Beijing, February 2008.
3 Author's meeting with Dr. Hua Sheng, January 2009.
4 The WTO is the international body established to promote and protect world trade, and includes all provisions for commerce in goods, services, and intellectual property. China's bid to gain accession to the WTO had been a long march, an arduous 15-year process.
5 Nathan Zong (editor), *Zhu Rongji in 1999 (I)*, p. 38.
6 Ibid., 51.
7 Joseph Fewsmith, "China and the WTO: The Politics Behind the Agreement," The National Bureau of Asian Research, November 1999, http://www.nbr.org/publications/report.html. Fewsmith states that the source of Zhu's problems lay first in the enemies he made among China's bureaucrats as he moved to restructure industry and government; "and second, Zhu became the scapegoat for discontent with Jiang Zemin's policy decisions." Jiang's "harsh rhetoric" in internal meetings asserted that "U.S. imperialism will not die" (an evocative expression used by Mao Zedong) and called "for 'biding time while nurturing grievances'."
8 Author's interview of Robert Rubin, 2003.
9 Song Ning.
10 According to Joseph Fewsmith, "the posting was widely seen in China as a way to publicly hold the Chinese government's feet to the fire, an action bound to evoke a hostile response."

"Worse," he suggested, "the posting allowed public opinion to play a role in China. Large enterprises and provinces which would be affected by China's entry [to the WTO] began to calculate "the impact on themselves. With the posting, the Chinese government lost control of the flow of information." Fewsmith, November 1999.

11 Ibid., 49.
12 Nathan, Zong (editor), *Zhu Rongji in 1999 (I)*, p. 48.
13 Song Ning.
14 Joseph Fewsmith, *China Since Tiananmen: the Politics of Transition* (New York: Cambridge University Press, 2001), 213.
15 David E. Sanger, "Clinton and Jiang Heal Rift and Set New Trade Course," *The New York Times*, September 12, 1999; AFP, September 11, 1999.
16 Robert L. Suettinger, *Beyond Tiananmen: The Politics of U.S.-China Relations 1989 – 2000* (Washington, D.C.: Brookings Institution Press), 2003, 406.
17 Willy Lam, "Intellectuals Lobby for Political Change as Party Marks 30th Anniversary of the Reform Era," *China Brief*, December 19, 2008.
18 Money.163.com, December 15, 2008; Chinareform.org.cn, October 10, 2008.

The Countryside is Core

In 2007, farmers accounted for 41% of China's workforce, yet agriculture contributed only 11% of China's GDP. And since the ratio of rural to urban populations was 55% to 45%, this meant that 55% of the population generated only 11% of GDP. The great disparity in per-capita GDP between urban and rural areas is China's severest problem of reform.

"Historically, few countries would still be plagued by agricultural issues by the time they have reached the middle phase of industrialization," said Lu Xueyi, a rural expert at the Chinese Academy of Social Sciences (CASS).[1]"The fact that China is still dealing with agriculture is a sign that the countryside-farmer situation has never been properly handled."

And it's not for lack of government concern, Lu stressed. "In China, agriculture and farmers are prioritized," he said. "At the National People's Congress, the first issue leaders report is always countryside-rural development, and yet after 30 years of reform, and so many discussions, the problems persist. So it's self-evident that the causes are structural and deeply entrenched."

Lu, then, highlighted four critical achievements: First, China, which was struggling to feed itself, is now self-sufficient in most items except soybean; the shortages which plagued all socialist countries have been solved for the first time. Second, the living standard of farmers has been significantly raised; sufficient food and clothing is no longer an issue for the vast majority. Third, farmers can move freely around the country—hence the vast migration of farmers into cities seeking jobs; this would have been unimaginable before (even romantic relationships, Lu notes, had to be between people in the same production team). Fourth, rural infrastructure, including power plants, roads, public transportation and even computers, has developed rapidly.

Even so, on an absolute basis, rural incomes remain far behind urban incomes. "Farmers have been largely left out of China's economic boom, and have not received what they deserve," Lu says. "Urban residents should not be the only ones to benefit from economic development."

"We have two different market economies, one in the cities and the other in the countryside," Lu asserted. "I describe China's system for dealing with urban and rural areas as 'one country, two approaches'."

There's no doubt that China's senior leaders recognize that rural-urban disparities are now the country's most invidious and intractable problem. "The imbalance in rural-urban development is worsening and taking on many forms," acknowledged Hui Liangyu, China's vice premier responsible for agriculture, in 2008.

Zhu Zhixin, vice minister of the National Development and Reform Commission, admitted that rural public services were deficient, especially in education, culture and healthcare. For example, 80% of schools in poor repair were in the countryside, he said, and 60% of hospitals at township level needed upgraded facilities such as X-ray machines. More than 250 million rural residents did not have access to safe drinking water, nearly 100 towns had no roads, and there were 2 million people without electricity.[2]

To make matters worse, the lawful rights and interests of rural residents were often infringed, with farmers frequently unable to get due compensation in cases of government land acquisition, Zhu said, acknowledging that "there have been frequent disputes over land acquisitions in recent years."

★ ★ ★

In 2006, in response to this deepening bifurcation in Chinese society,[3] President Hu Jintao and Premier Wen Jiabao unveiled the New Socialist Countryside, which was set as a primary objective of the 11th Five-Year Plan (2006–10).[4] Its goals were: advanced production; improved livelihood; civilized social conditions; clean and tidy villages; and efficient management. Its components included: water conservancy facilities; road construction; more clean fuels such as marsh gas and solar energy; completing the rural power network; improving rural education (including nine-year compulsory education); improving rural public healthcare; providing more access to culture (libraries and sports facilities); and enhancing rural social security systems.

Lu Xueyi was one of several experts with whom President Hu consulted.[5] "Rural problems are tricky," Lu noted. "Government regulations are always meant to help farmers, but the practical results always seemed to widen, not narrow, the urban-rural gap. This was partly because, historically, the people who drafted the regulations were mostly from the cities." Lu added that President Hu "feared that cadres might abuse their power when enforcing these regulations."

The government committed huge investment—an extra $750 million—to implement the New Socialist Countryside. Measures included abolishing the agriculture tax, increasing direct agriculture subsidies, guaranteeing free education, a new co-operative Medicare-like system, and more social security. President Hu stressed that it was time for industry to recompense agriculture, for the cities to help the countryside.

★ ★ ★

Rural welfare also highlighted the 3rd Plenary of the 17th Party Congress in 2008. It promised to establish a modern rural financial network, and invest more in rural public and social services. And it set a goal to double the per-capita disposable income of rural residents by 2020. China's leaders hoped that the measures would help increase rural consumption, since the global recession meant that exports alone could no longer drive economic growth.

The Party also emphasized that "rural cultural development is of great importance to building a new socialist countryside."[6] This included the directive that TV, radio, movies, and the Internet should be more accessible in rural areas, and that more cultural centers and libraries should be set up in villages. It specified improvements in education, especially for "left-behind-children" whose parents were working in the cities; enhanced, safe and inexpensive medical services; and the construction of a comprehensive social welfare system, including old-age insurance. And it urged urban organizations to spread scientific knowledge in the countryside, in order to help farmers break away from superstitions and respect gender equality in a harmonious society.

The Plenary's most important decision, however, was a landmark policy to allow farmers to "lease their contracted farmland or transfer their land-use rights." Farmland in China, by law, had long been collectively owned; in recent decades it was allocated out to farmers in small plots on 30-year lease contracts. Under these far-reaching reforms, markets would be created for the lease of contracted farmland and transfer of farmland-use rights, enabling farmers to sub-contract, lease, exchange and swap their land-use rights, or join shareholding entities with their farmland. The reforms aimed to enhance peasant wealth without abandoning state ownership.

Financial exploitation of farmland, especially as land values increased, was the key issue.[7] Because many farmers were migrating to cities, they wanted to sell their leases or to sublease their land. Prior, they were technically not allowed to do so without government approval. Yet many did so anyway, arranging informal transfers, subleases in essence, in "gray" transactions— which often led to confusion and problems over these rights.

Problems had also been brewing for years in cases where land was expro-priated for development, usually by investors allied with local officials, and where peasants felt they were not properly compensated. Such rural land disputes, a leading cause of demonstrations and protests, were also rooted in the ambiguous legal status of peasants' rights. According to Zhang Xiaoshan, chief of CASS' Rural Development Institute, "the land tenure system was advantageous for local cadres and entrepreneurs because they could obtain land, often agricultural land, at a very low cost. They would then convert the agricultural land into non-agricultural use so as to attract foreign investment to build industrial parks, recreational sites, luxury housing, and the like."

Indeed, Zhang says, China's cheap land, like its cheap labor, was a major factor in drawing foreign direct investment into the country. "But the added value created was enjoyed only by entrepreneurs and often [illegally] by local officials," he noted. "Farmers would receive very few, if any, financial benefits. Most social conflicts in China have occurred in rural areas as a result of land appropriations." One solution, he suggested, would be to require that a portion of the added value made from land should go back to the grassroots, and be used for improving infrastructure and elevating people's livelihood.

The 2008 reforms set up a "strict and normative" land management system, which would give peasants the legal right to benefit financially from their land through leasing and transfers. Rural citizens could now legally transfer or rent their 30-year land leases to large companies or other individuals or even use the land as collateral to support mortgages or other loans. This would yield several benefits: farmers would gain new funds, enabling them to start new businesses; many leases would be bought by larger entities, boosting the creation of modern agricultural organizations with sufficient critical mass to invest in new equipment and technologies, produce foods more efficiently, and compete better in domestic and global markets; and larger, more modern farms would also be better able to produce healthier, non-polluted foods, a serious concern in China.

(China commentator John Pomfret noted that one reason China's food-safety problems have been so grave is that because land was leased and not owned, and divided up in small plots [called "noodle strips"], investment was not rewarded. There was no incentive for an "organic" farmer not to use pesticides or a small-scale cattle rancher not to sell cattle which had died from disease. Creating bigger farms would enable production to be rationalized, and goods to be produced more cheaply, efficiently and hopefully more safely—essentially applying the China factory model to the countryside.[8])

Economists lauded the new measures as a major breakthrough in land reform, comparable to those initiated by Deng Xiaoping 30 years earlier, and they credited President Hu for delivering on his promise to increase the incomes of farmers, and mitigate standard-of-living disparities between rural and urban areas.

But there had been opposition, which had delayed enactment of the new law for years. While some critics argued that the reforms did not go far enough, the most vociferous cries came from the left, railing that state ownership of rural lands was one of socialist China's core precepts and this reform, while not eliminating it, did undermine it. Others contended that in practice the new policy might lead to the emergence of a few big landlords and many landless farmers with no means of making a living. It could also provide a financial incentive for converting arable land into non-farm use, which could threaten the country's food supply.

To ease such fears, the CPC Central Committee required that the country would carry out "the most stringent farmland protection system" and urged local authorities to guarantee that China's area of farmland did not dip below the minimum line of 1.8 billion mu (300 million acres) set by the government.

★ ★ ★

The new land reforms were also designed to smooth the movement of people from the countryside to China's towns and cities. China's leaders believe that urbanization is key for solving China's rural problems. Some 400-500 million people are expected to be transferred from rural to urban areas over the next two decades or so—the largest planned migration in human history.

China's urbanization lags behind its industrialization. While major industrial countries experienced a gradual decrease in the number of rural laborers during their periods of industrialization, China saw a sharp increase: from 1953, when China started its industrialization, to 2006, the number of rural residents rose by 447.65 million, an average annual growth of 8.5 million. "This is very rare anywhere in the world," said rural scholar Lu Xueyi.

Now, however, China's urbanization is in high gear.[9] At the end of 2007, China had 655 cities (an increase of 462 from 1978); 83 cities had between one and two million people (there were 19 in 1978) and 36 had over two million (10 in 1978).[10] Twenty megacities exceed 5 million. The poster child of urbanization is Shenzhen, which grew from an agrarian population of 310,000 in 1979 into a metropolis of over 10 million. The number of small towns rose from 2,700 in 1984 to more than 19,000 in 2007 At the current rate, China will reach the world average rate of urbanization, about 50%, by 2010,[11] and perhaps 60% in 2025 and 70% in 2030. This means that by 2030 China's urban residents would top one billion people; some observers fear the country is "approaching the limit of its tolerance" of urbanization, particularly with the growing income inequalities and deepening social fissures they are causing.[12]

According to Lu Xueyi, China's urbanization faces major problems. First, instead of moving to local small towns, most farmers migrate to major coastal cities where jobs pay better. In fact, Lu says, China needs local urbanization: building small towns promotes sustainable development and can absorb surplus rural laborers (while the "floating population" of migrant workers in the larger cities cause many problems); China needs more middle class consumers to boost domestic demand; moreover, small towns protect against food shortages because in emergencies workers can return to the farms quickly.

What's more, urban authorities tend to believe that migrant farmers retard local development and thus take measures to prevent them from moving in. Urban citizens also, seeing their cities as already overpopulated, oppose further waves of migrating workers. So the reality is that farmers, who do the most menial and tiring jobs, face endemic discrimination. (Indeed, in the past, the derogatory term "vagabond" was used in central government documents to identify migrant workers.)

Lu stresses that "I've talked with leaders face-to-face and argued that, in essence, the key is the farmers themselves, not agriculture, which is what the farmers do. When farmers' problems are properly settled, I said, the country's agriculture industry will develop naturally."

★ ★ ★

During the early transition to a market economy, once farmers were able to feed their families, they wanted to increase their incomes and improve living standards by engaging in non-farming activities. This led to the development of township and village enterprises (TVEs), the small local enterprises—mainly in agri-business processing and light manufacturing—which absorbed millions of unemployed or barely employed rural laborers, and became an important driver of the Chinese economic miracle. Many of China's small towns evolved from TVEs, which triggered waves of small town construction.

TVEs benefited from assistance from the State Science and Technology Commission (SSTC). In the 1980s, its thoughtful and dynamic chairman, Dr. Song Jian, launched the Sparks Program to disseminate scientific knowledge and new technologies in rural areas, with the aim of changing agriculture production methods and improving the performance of local industry. Thousands of scientists, agronomists, and engineers were invited to serve as magistrates of counties and mayors of small cities. About one million engineers and technicians went to the countryside to help peasants cultivate crops, rear animals, and establish small-scale TVEs.

More than 70,000 Sparks Program projects were developed and over 85% of all rural counties were involved. Many new industries emerged, with millions of TVEs created each year. By 2000, the number of TVEs reached 27 million, employing 130 million peasants, who thus became industrial workers without their leaving their home towns. In some provinces, such as Jiangsu and Shandong, TVEs accounted for about 30% of the rural workforce. In 1998, the output value of TVEs amounted to one third of China's GDP.

In the late 1980s, CASS researcher Zhang Xiaoshan traveled to Wuhan to visit TVEs. "Wuhan in August is called the 'big stove' because it's very hot, like a steam bath," he recalled. "In one TVE, the huge indoor factory had only three small fans; it was extremely hot—I was soaked with sweat. Dozens of young people, mostly girls, were making clothes for South Korea," he said. "They were paid per piece—the conditions were poor but they were working very hard."

"I thought to myself, here was the source of the Chinese economic miracle," Zhang mused. "It was founded on the labor of millions of Chinese people.

They received low salaries yet still they labored long. Cheap labor, cheap land, good policies and good infrastructure united to transform China."

★ ★ ★

One bright spot is the port city of Ningbo in Zhejiang Province, where, for five years, the increase in rural income has exceeded the increase in urban income. As Party Secretary Bayin Chaolu, an ethnic Mongolian, told me, "About 80% of rural residents live comfortable lives; Ningbo's per-capita GDP is $10,000. The reason we're closing the urban-rural income gap is that our overall plan integrates rural and urban areas so that urban areas promote rural areas. Indeed, 75-85% of rural income comes from manufacturing or service sectors."[13]

For example, in the showcase village of Tengtou, local enterprises—all of them collectively not state owned (including a large garment factory and eco-tourism)—generate about $500 million in annual revenues, enabling each of Tengtou's 341 families to have their own large modern villa. Although the quasi-utopian Tengtou cannot be duplicated often or easily, it serves as an ideal if not a prototype. (Tengtou Party leaders promote Three Firsts and Four No's, reflecting the Communist ideal. Three Firsts means whatever the Party requests villagers to do, Party members must do first; whatever Party members do, Party leaders must do first; and whatever Party leaders do, the Party secretary must do first. Four No's means Party leaders do not get more stock than other villagers, do not take highest wages, do not take largest bonuses, and do not live in best houses.)

Linked to Shanghai to the north by the spectacular Hongzhou Bay Bridge, the longest sea-crossing bridge in the world (22 miles), Ningbo seeks to "realize complete modernization," to attain the social and economic level of developed countries. To achieve this, rural urbanization is required.

★ ★ ★

For Zhang Xiaoshan, one solution to the countryside problem is to change redistribution mechanisms. Now, he says, "we can use the profits of reform to compensate the people whose interests were harmed during reform. This is our strategy."

But Zhang stresses that structural problems remain. "How to compensate the losers? How to take care of vulnerable groups? How to strive for fair distribution while maintaining economic incentives? This is our big challenge," he said, noting that "Everyone wants more in their own pockets; vested interests create rigid structures. . .That's why after 30 years of reform the task ahead is still tough."

Zhang believes that China has "too many large-scale 'transforming' mega-projects, but lacks general, systemic transformations." Bringing real change to redistribution systems, he stated, requires "giving more autonomy to local governments to implement reform." It also requires "regular, systematic, and transparent financial activities." At the moment, he suggests, there are conflicts between "central government ministries with too much power" and "local sectors and institutions with much to do and very limited power." He adds: "Sometimes central ministries control all the resources and have monopoly power; sometimes they serve as both player and referee."

The solution, Zhang argues, is to set aside certain fundings just for local use. Currently, local authorities must go to central ministries to fund budgets and projects, and thus they have to use all possible means to gain approvals. "And it's always the crying baby who gets more milk," says Zhang: "The system is irregular and leads to corruption. Even though we have reduced the number of ministries, they still have too much power."

Zhang appreciates central government concerns that if they apportion general funds to local governments to allocate, there will be local corruption, but he says local empowerment must be "the direction for development—with the precondition that democratic processes and financial transparency at local levels must be greatly improved."

Furthermore, Zhang continues, "we've always stressed physical capital, such as roads and other infrastructure, but we now pay more attention to human capital. Since 2006 we've improved rural education, eliminating fees for textbooks and enrollment. Still that's not enough. We should promote diversified social and economic organizations in the countryside and encourage cooperative relationships among farmers, local officials, and entrepreneurs. A harmonious society requires balance among different groups; otherwise a harmonious society is impossible."

Noting that many Westerners "criticize Chinese society for not giving citizens human rights," Zhang offers that "it's a matter of viewpoint. Is the bottle half empty or half full? For me, it's half full. Go back 30 years: no one could have imagined that China could become what it is today." Nevertheless, he emphasizes "we still have a long way to go." Zhang offered a daunting list: further land-tenure system reform, rural financial reform, organizational reform, shifting of population, and migrant worker issues (e.g., equal treatment and labor contract law).

His comments echo the remarks of former CPC General Secretary Hu Yaobang, who famously said: "If we don't solve the problem of rural areas, and the problem of peasants, the Four Modernizations will be empty talk."

Endnotes

1 Lu Xueyi.
2 Xie Chuanjiao, "Bridging urban-rural gap is 'historic task'," *China Daily*, September, 4 2008.
3 The income gap between urban and rural residents increased from 2.57:1 in 1978 to 3.22:1 in 2005.
4 "Your guide to 'new socialist countryside'," *China Daily* and *People's Daily*, March 8, 2006.

5 The group that met with President Hu had seven persons, including Yang Yongzhi (former vice minister of agriculture), Wan Baorui (director of the Chinese Academy of Agriculture), Xu Hulin, Chen Zhangliang, Lin Yifu, and Lu Xueyi (the narrator).

6 "CPC pledges to improve social welfare of rural residents," Xinhua, October 20, 2008.

7 Andrew Batson "In China, Leaders Turn Focus to Farmers' Plight," *Wall Street Journal*, October 10, 2008.

8 John Pomfret, "Is China Dismantling Its 'Socialist' Countryside?" Pomfret's China, *The Washington Post*, October 8, 2008.

9 "Decoding China's Urbanization," *Beijing Review*, No. 28 July 10, 2008.

10 Li Jianmin, "The Ascent and Plateau of China's Urban Centers," *China Brief*, December 19, 2008.

11 According to criteria before 2000, people with urban identification and living in urban areas were counted as urban citizens and those living in urban areas but without urban identification were not urban citizens. In addition, college students who came to cities for education were not viewed as local residents. Only those who managed to find jobs were counted as residents. And based on these criteria, urban citizens accounted for 30% of the total. In short, the criteria can be dual: the first is to live in cities; and the second, to possess urban *hukou*, or urban identification. Having a job in a city does not necessarily make you an urban citizen—you also need to be able to enjoy the welfare provided exclusively to urban citizens.

12 Li Jianmin, *China Brief*, op. cit.

13 Author's meeting with Bayin Chaolu, Ningbo, February 2009.

14

Rebalancing Imbalances

In Mao's China, equality prevailed—most people only encountered others who lived in similar conditions, earned similar incomes. Everyone shared, as it were, the same "iron rice bowl." What hierarchical differences existed in society was based on political stature rather than economic strength. Now, after three decades of reform, China has its own class divisions, just as Western countries do. Rich people drive foreign cars, own several houses, frequent expensive restaurants and clubs, and send their children to private schools. In Beijing or Shanghai it's common to see Mercedes and BMWs, even Porsches and Ferraris—driven by young people—while along the streets crowds of migrant workers struggle to find decent jobs so they can provide basic healthcare and education for their children. (Envy in China is known as "red-eye disease"—it has become a pandemic social malady and it worries China's leaders.)

Not unexpected given China's immense transformation, the system has been chaotic and often unregulated, and some people have become wealthy by exploiting the chaos and loopholes, not to mention frequent corruption. Examples have been buying state-owned assets at inside ("fire sale") prices, government contracts in non-competitive bidding, sweetheart loans from government banks, importing goods with lower-than-official tariffs, exporting goods at very low costs in order to expatriate wealth, and circulating money from inside China to outside China and then right back in again to take advantage of incentives given to "foreign" investors.

The government recognized these and other such improprieties, and they have tightened regulations and enforced laws. They have also sought policies, such as redistributions via taxation and social programs, to alleviate extreme disparities between rich and poor. The issue is social justice: how to allocate wealth fairly; how to balance urban and rural sectors, coastal and inland regions; how to raise the prospects of the poor.

China's wealth gap is undeniable and dangerous. The top 10% controls close to half the country's wealth while the bottom 10% earns barely 1% of total income.[1] Poverty is exacerbated by unemployment, which in China is notoriously hard to estimate (figures ranged from the government's "below 5%" to 10-15%, estimated by scholars—all higher, obviously, with the global recession.) An official State Council report had 23.65 million rural residents living in abject poverty in 2005, but the U.N.-sponsored China Human Development Report (also 2005) estimated that 300-400 million rural Chinese were living in or near poverty.

Income inequality is an explicit target of President Hu Jintao's campaign to build a Harmonious Society, the cornerstone of his political philosophy. In his report to the 17th Party Congress (2007), Hu said: "Equitable income distribution is an important indication of social equity . . . A proper balance will be struck between efficiency and equity in both primary distribution and redistribution, with particular emphasis on equity in redistribution." He stressed that "vigorous efforts will be made to raise the income of low-income groups, gradually increase poverty-alleviation aid and the minimum wage." Hu listed measures to achieve these goals: "We will increase transfer payments, intensify the regulation of incomes through taxation, break business monopolies, create equal opportunities, and overhaul income distribution practices with a view to gradually reversing the growing income disparity," he pledged.

Wealth-reallocation policies targeted the countryside: elimination of the (hated) rural tax on farmers; increased incentives for investments in less-developed areas; increased education for rural areas; fee exemptions and subsidies for students in poor counties; and increased minimum living guarantees.

★ ★ ★

Even though all areas of China have benefited from economic reform, coastal regions benefited much more than inland regions—with an estimated 6:1 or even 8:1 ratio between the per-capita GDP of the richest and poorest province/region. Such gross income inequalities, and resultant social disparities, have led to dissatisfaction and restiveness.

Rectifying imbalances has been an explicit focus of China's leaders. In 2000, President Jiang Zemin launched the Great West Development Strategy, allocating money and resources to China's poorer and historically more neglected central and western regions. The future of China's reform—indeed, the future of China itself—Jiang said repeatedly, would depend on transforming the growth-poor, resource-rich Great West, home to most of China's 55 ethnic minorities, into prosperous economic zones.

"For President Jiang," observed Zeng Peiyan, then minister of the State Development Planning Commission, "creating regional balance in China's development was an important guiding principle. He worried that geographic imbalance could affect national unity and social stability."[2] Economists too warned that if China's west did not close the gap with its east, the country's goal of becoming a mid-level developed nation by mid 21st century could not be achieved.

Jiang called for China's citizens to be "daring" and "resolute" in building the country's west, which comprised ten provinces and autonomous regions, including the Chongqing municipality, and covered 56% of China's territory. Jiang urged the wealthier coastal provinces to provide financial, technological, and managerial assistance to the poorer western ones. "The development of the west," he assured them, "will also bring new market opportunities to the east." And he endorsed a kind of "big brother" system, in which China's most successful cities would partner with needy provinces—starting with links between Shanghai and Xinjiang and Shenzhen and Guizhou.

Still, Jiang counseled patience. Though he envisioned initial success in five to ten years, he emphasized that "the great development of western China is a grand strategy for a hundred and a thousand years," and would take "the sustained efforts of many generations." Nevertheless, the initiative would become one of Jiang Zemin's prime achievements. As Zeng Peiyan put it, "moving from slogans to action was exhilarating—especially after years of dreaming about it!"

The Qinghai-Tibet Railroad, for example, was a visionary plan first put forward in the 1950s but which had never been implemented because of inadequate technology and funding. Jiang resurrected the idea, saying that the railroad was necessary to spur economic development, establish east-west communications, and improve living standards of minority ethnic groups in the regions. (The plan was not without its foreign critics, who suspected that China's primary motivation for undertaking the hugely expensive project was to Sinicize Tibet and dominate South Asia.)

At the same time, such rapid development risked creating unexpected problems. Jiang was especially concerned about the environment and indigenous minorities—and even asked Zeng Peiyan to visit the US to learn from the American experience in developing its West.

★ ★ ★

Balancing reform by building up less-developed regions has been a prime strategy of President Hu and Premier Wen. Prime initiatives were the Central Province Strategy and Revitalize the Northeast campaign, while continuing the Great West Development Strategy. The Party's 11th Five-Year Plan stresses balanced and sustainable growth, and seeks to shift economic activity to northeast, central, and western provinces where new urban centers will be created, while encouraging coastal provinces to concentrate on advanced technology.

To this end Chinese leaders have been wooing multinational companies to look beyond coastal regions and move their factories inland, and the government has been investing heavily in bridges, expressways, and power plants to make inland regions more attractive. Such areas certainly have advantages. Workers in Sichuan Province, for example, made little more than one-half the wages of similar workers in Shanghai or Guangzhou (2005).

China's northeast, meanwhile, had no shortage of industrial infrastructure—after all it had been the heartland of the country's initial industrialization.

In the early years of New China, workers in the northeastern provinces of Heilongjiang, Jilin, and Liaoning had earned relatively high wages and were among the most favored in China. Some 70% of production in the northeast came from state-owned enterprises (SOEs), compared to about 20% in Guangdong and even less in Zhejiang.

Yet therein lay a sad irony: the very fact that the northeast built the Chinese economy in the 1950s, when the coastal provinces of Guangdong and Zhejiang were little more than fishing villages and small farms, meant that it was ill-suited for the market economy. By the 1990s its large-scale SOEs in steel and heavy industry—coal, chemicals, steel, trucks—were struggling, and the northeast endured a protracted period of decline.[3] Almost 30 million workers were laid off, resulting in unemployment rates of 20%. In its heyday, the northeast contributed more than 20% of China's economy; in recent years the figure dropped below 10%.

For the Revitalize the Northeast campaign, President Hu worked with Premier Wen and then Liaoning Party Secretary Li Keqiang. SOEs were merged, restructured, and sold off; pillar industries (shipbuilding, autos, petrochemicals) were renewed and new industries, such as software, tourism, and even organic farming, encouraged. SOEs divested noncore businesses, shed their debts and welfare burdens, including non-economic assets such as hospitals and schools, and thereby became more attractive for investment. Local governments did their share by providing land at rock-bottom prices. The northeast had a well-educated and experienced work force which earned as little as a third of its peers in Shenzhen.

Yet not all areas of the country have the same advantages. The challenges were highlighted at the 11th National People's Congress (2008), when Hu Jintao joined the delegation from the Muslim-majority Xinjiang Uyghur Autonomous Region and expressed "great hopes" for Xinjiang's development. He stressed that China needed to develop its medical and healthcare system for the "countryside, grassroots, farmers and herdsmen," to "provide schooling opportunities for their children and make it convenient for them to see doctors," adding "together with the cultural activities in rural areas, medical care is what the farmers and herdsmen need most."[4] Hu also encouraged bilingual teaching in order to "cultivate more talented people well versed in both Han and Uyghur languages and with wide vision—who could work not only in other provinces in China, but also in other countries."

Again, China's conundrum is that the country needs growth, and growth comes most efficiently from those areas that are already developed—the coastal and urban areas—which further widens income disparity. How can China maintain its required growth and at the same time shrink income disparity? Government programs for less-developed areas, such as investment incentives, tax benefits, special loans, can be structured, but the task is to increase real productivity, not just spend money.

★ ★ ★

Migrant workers are a particular concern. In 2006, the rural population stood at 949 million, accounting for 72% of the national total.[5] But over the decades of reform, vast numbers of farmers have descended on China's cities and towns in search of jobs, mainly in factories, construction, service industries and other physical-labor-based occupations. This "floating population" grew from 70 million people in 1993 to at least 140 million by 2008—more than 10% of China's population, and about 30% of the total rural labor force. Some estimates put the number at 150-200 million, or even higher. Certainly it is the largest peacetime migration in human history—and forecasts (made prior to the global slowdown) predicted at least 250 million by 2025.

According to China's Census (2000), 65% of migrant workers are "floating" within their home provinces and 35% across provinces. Most migrants are young, with those between 15 and 35 accounting for 80% of the total.[6] But such massive relocations have also produced side effects, including significant social dislocations. The crime rate has surged: in cities like Beijing, Shenzhen, and Guangzhou, 75-95% of crimes are committed by migrants.

For the migrants, meanwhile, life is often far from happy. Though they can make more money—usually sending this money back to their families in rural areas—their lives can be harsh and oppressive. Without social networks, they are easily exploited by city people. Young rural maids being raped by their employers is tragically not uncommon.

While making my PBS documentary *In Search of China* in 2000, I spoke to rural migrants, such as construction workers. Some lived in parking garages and started their work day at 5am. Many worked 12-hour shifts. One laborer told me "There are no holidays. We work Saturdays and Sundays. I don't eat or sleep very well." Still, he added, "I have to make the best of it."

One woman explained that she had a son back home in the countryside: "He's four years old," she said, "I've only seen him once in three years. I stay in Beijing to earn money for my little boy's education." A man who was separated from his wife was similarly pragmatic: "I've been married one year," he said, "but I don't miss my wife, because it's useless to miss her."

Others were almost defiant: "We out-of-towners are willing to suffer and take on dirty and tiring jobs," said one migrant. "This is our strength. Lots of laid-off locals complain that we're taking away their jobs. Good! Because it means they realize we're improving ourselves."

The grimmest problem for China's leaders, particularly with a slowing economy, is how to prevent migrant workers from turning into a disruptive force. Millions of rootless people living on the fringes of society can threaten national stability.

★ ★ ★

Since the earliest days of the Communist era, China's population has been roughly divided into rural and urban, through a system known as household residence registration.[7] Every family was issued a household residency registration book, called a *hukou*, which recorded the details of all family members. This provided access to consumer resources—coupons to buy food or clothing—and social services: you needed a *hukou* to apply for jobs, to go to school. In fact the *hukou* controlled almost every aspect of people's lives—including movement: if you left the place where you were born, and were unable to obtain a *hukou* in the new place, you simply could not survive. And transferring a rural *hukou* into an urban *hukou* was almost impossible.

When China's first Special Economic Zones were established, they needed cheap labor to attract foreign investors. Since most people in those cities were already employed, peasants were only too willing to leave their exhausting work in the fields for wages which, though low, were higher than elsewhere. But because the *hukou* of rural migrants were tied to their home villages, when they moved to the cities they had no legal rights: their housing options were restricted, their families were not eligible for urban social services, and their children could not go to school. Their labor was needed—but the residency rules inadvertently made them into second-class citizens.

Since then, economic reform has gradually weakened the residence registration system. With money, anyone can access most services. Indeed, some cities encourage rich people from other areas to make investments locally by giving them temporary, or in some cases permanent, residence registration. In the countryside too, the system has been collapsing: if local people or peasants travel to new places, it has become impossible to track them.

Now, as social reform catches up with economic development, China's leadership has begun to adjust the *hukou* system to alleviate the problems of migrant workers. The aim is eventually to provide the floating population with social services, including schooling, health care, and insurance. In 2008, the Party pledged to "abolish the urban-rural, two-tier structure and to integrate the economic and social development of cities and villages," suggesting abolition of the *hukou* system, but setting no timetables.[8] Experimental programs testing urban-rural integration have already been introduced in several cities and provinces, enabling rural residents to move and work anywhere they like within those administrative boundaries. In Chongqing, full urban-rural integration was targeted for 2020; the goal was to reduce the percentage of Chongqing residents living in agricultural counties from 55% to 30%.

China's leaders have made the issues of migrant workers a focus of their domestic agenda. It is not a problem that will be solved quickly, but it is a problem that must be solved for China to emerge as a moderately well-off country, which is leadership's stated goal.

★ ★ ★

Providing a welfare system to help the urban unemployed is a further challenge. In the old days of the "iron rice bowl" people not only had stable jobs but also stable lives. College, high school and vocational school graduates had work assigned to them by the government—with permanent job security and welfare; the flip side was, regardless of whether you enjoyed your job or not, you had to stay in it, usually for a lifetime.

Now, following reforms, workers find their own jobs. But they can be fired. Many employees are on fixed-term contracts; when these expire the employer may decide not to renew. By the same token, employees can quit at any time and accept a better job elsewhere. Most young Chinese like this kind of freedom. But older people who have worked in state-owned enterprises (SOEs) are not used to such uncertainty. If they are fired, it's hard for them to find new employment—many do not possess the skills to survive in a technological economy. There is also the added psychological trauma of being abandoned by a company that was supposed to have been one's guardian for life.

A further problem was that China had no urban welfare system separate from SOEs. The system itself was the "safety net." Hence, even when workers were laid-off, they still remained attached to their SOEs—and in the absence of an alternative social welfare structure, their former employer was still responsible for providing them with minimal living expenses. (Mainland Chinese visiting the U.S., and seeing the Social Security and local unemployment welfare systems, would sometimes joke that America was the real socialist country.)

In recent years, China has begun to establish social security and pension systems. All employers are now required to set aside money in a social security fund, to be used for living, medical and pension expenses of terminated employees. Social security for China's citizens is essential for reform to continue.

★ ★ ★

In 2008, the *Pew Global Attitudes Project* conducted perhaps the most comprehensive survey of Chinese public opinion ever. It found broad overall satisfaction with the direction of the country and state of the economy—as noted, in both categories China scored the highest in the world. Nevertheless the report's authors noted that "the Chinese people may be struggling with the consequences of economic growth. Notably, concerns about inflation and environmental degradation are widespread."

And while most Chinese embraced the free market, the survey highlighted considerable concern about rising prices, economic inequality, and other endemic problems. Equity and fairness was also an almost universal worry. Almost half of those surveyed said that healthcare was difficult to afford. Anxiety over unemployment and working conditions were extensive.[9]

Despite widespread complaints about corruption, most people (65%) believed China was doing a good job on issues that were most important to them. About seven-in-ten among high-income (72%) and middle-income (71%) respondents gave the government a positive review. Poorer Chinese gave the government somewhat lower grades (59%). Ratings also varied by region, with those in eastern China giving the government more favorable marks (75%) than those in central (60%) or western (58%) regions.

Compared with the findings in Western countries, the survey revealed absolute differences (e.g., corruption was a bigger concern in China) and relative differences (e.g., air pollution was considered a bigger problem in China than healthcare, the reverse of the situation in America). Environmental concerns were striking—in response to apprehensions about air pollution (74%) and water pollution (66%), as many as 80% of Chinese thought protecting the environment should be made a priority, even if this resulted in slower growth and a potential loss of jobs.

The findings underscored China's unique situation and the challenges facing the country's leaders. (In 2009, China enacted one of the world's most stringent automotive fuel economy standards, requiring each automaker to reach a corporate average of 42.2 miles per gallon by 2015—18% higher than what President Obama announced for America.[10])

★ ★ ★

It's true that many of China's current problems are the inevitable side effects of rapid economic development, which, of necessity, had to occur in an unbalanced way. There is no way around this stage of development—and China is not unique in now having to deal with an accumulation of these problems.

But China is compacting the process of transformation—which took developed countries, including America, over 100 years—within just a few decades. Western experiences are helpful references but not absolute standards. For example, income disparities are particularly disruptive in China because of the stark contrast with the social homogeneity during the first three decades of Communist China where almost everyone was equal. (In other countries, from Western Europe to India, although income disparities are significant and troubling, they have existed for generations and are therefore not as disruptive.)

The American experience, in the "robber baron" era (late 19th and early 20th centuries) also has parallels with China's experiences: a very few people controlled a great deal of the wealth, and as a result millions of common workers were paid poor wages, had few benefits (e.g., no healthcare), and labored under intolerable conditions.

As a result, countervailing forces developed. Monopolies were broken in America just as they are being broken up in China. Critical in America was the development of competing social institutions, especially labor unions. In China's socialist system, however, the emergence of labor unions once seemed unthinkable. Since the State owned all the enterprises and represented all the people, labor unions seemed a contradiction in principles. Yet with the growth of private companies and foreign-funded ventures, the

Chinese government no longer owns all the businesses and hence must do more to protect the rights of workers.

Similarly, China must find fresh ideas for enabling diverse social institutions, including nongovernmental organizations (NGOs), to compete in society so that government is not burdened by constantly having to make all the micro-decisions adjudicating and balancing the myriad of complex, interdependent, and competing issues which make up modern societies.

As Chinese society continues to mature, and as China's leaders grow more confident in the Chinese people's commitment to stability (as standards of living rise across the country), it is to be hoped that various competing forces—labor unions, NGOs, a diverse media—can emerge and become, in essence, a partner with government in administering society for the benefit of all.

Endnotes

1 Dorothy J. Solinger, *Far Eastern Economic Review*, "The Scorned and the Forlorn,", June 2008.
2 Author's meeting with Zeng Peiyan, 2002.
3 *BusinessWeek*, July 19, 2004.
4 "Grinding the Rust Off China's Northeast," Xinjiang Television, March 8, 2008.
5 Interview with Lu Xueyi, *Beijing Review*, July 10, 2008.
6 "China's floating population tops 140 million" *People's Daily*, July 27, 2005.
7 Registration of citizens is not a new idea in China—it started in the Qin dynasty (221-206 B.C.), under China's first centralized imperial government.
8 Willy Wo-Lap Lam, "Hu's New Deal and the Third Plenary Session of CCP's 17th Central Committee," *China Brief*, Volume VIII, Issue 20, October 23, 2008.
9 The *Pew Project* found that the biggest problems were, in descending order: rising prices ("a very big problem": 72%; "a very big problem" or "a moderately big problem": 96%); rich/poor gap (41%, 89%); corrupt officials (39%, 78%); air pollution (31%, 74%); unemployment (22%, 68%); water pollution (28%, 66%); corrupt business people (21%, 61%); crime (17%, 61%); conditions for workers (13%, 56%); quality of manufactured goods (13%, 55%): old age insurance (13%, 53%); healthcare (12%, 51%); safety of food (12%, 49%); education (11%, 42%); traffic (9%, 39%); and electricity shortages (4%, 27%).
10 Keith Bradsher, "China is Said to Plan Strict Gas Mileage Rules," *The New York Times*, May 28, 2009.

How Reform
Permeates All Society

With reform, Chinese society has grown far more complex. Economic growth has given new opportunities, raised expectations, and created new trends.

To take one example, in 2007, 1.4 million Chinese couples divorced. This was more than four times the number in 1980.[1] Sociologists attribute the rising divorce rate to China's fast-changing society, more intense work lives, and challenges to traditional concepts of marriage. Extramarital affairs are increasingly common.

Divorce is also easier. In 2003, the procedure was simplified, allowing couples to divorce within a day at a cost of about $1.50. Previously, couples required permission from employers or community committees to get divorced, and many stayed together to avoid such public embarrassment.

As divorce becomes more common, its social stigma diminishes. No longer must wives suffer in silence as they endure boorish, brutish, domineering, indecent or unfaithful husbands. Furthermore, Chinese women are now more independent, financially and mentally. As one expert put it, "People are looking for marriages of higher quality. The things couples compromised on ten years ago aren't tolerated today."

Some scholars and policymakers warn that increasing divorce will lead to social instability, and have called for reversing the reforms and making divorce harder. Others, however, argue that because divorce frees people from misery and depression, divorce serves society more efficiently, and that, for children, a bad marriage is not better than divorce.

The growing acceptance of divorce in China changes the relative status of women. Women are taking an increasingly active role in public policy debates, including the ease of divorce and whether "guilty parties" should be punished by law. A nascent Chinese women's movement has begun.

★ ★ ★

Throughout Chinese history until modern times, women had lived in the shadow of men, subservient and dependent. A cruel expression of this unequal relationship was the custom of foot binding, an ancient practice considered the epitome of feminine beauty that caused life-long disability.

The communist revolution in theory gave women many rights. Mao Zedong declared that women "hold up half the sky," and his pronouncement, personified by his noisomely ambitious wife, Jiang Qing, had significant impact on women in the cities. In rural areas, however, most women continued to be treated poorly. Their education lagged behind that of men, and they faced more behavioral restrictions.

With economic reform, women began entering the labor market and finding new opportunities. China's educated urban women now have few limits, and women occupy senior positions: government ministers, corporate leaders, rocket scientists, even army generals. Liu Yandong is State Councilor responsible for education and science and technology; Wu Yi was the former vice premier in charge of trade relations (she also had responsibility for the SARS epidemic); Xie Qihua was chairwoman of Shanghai Baosteel Group; and Yang Mianmian is the president of Haier Group (Chapter 21). Chinese women hold about 20% of the seats in the National People's Congress and its advisory body.

And more women are also starting their own companies: perhaps because novel and untraditional, private business seems to be the playing field most level for women, who now run businesses ranging from flower shops, furniture stores and real-estate firms, to engineering services, technology companies and Internet ventures.

Some women have certainly struggled in the new economy—particularly those who worked for decades in state enterprises, where new emphasis on efficiency has resulted in many women (often a majority of the workforce in such factories) being laid off.

For me, the growing confidence of women, particularly of the young generation, was highlighted by the 20-something female assistant manager in a Legend (now Lenovo) factory. Asked what she would do if Legend failed to reward her financially or give her the promotions she deserved, she replied that this was unlikely since Legend had treated her well. "But," she added with gritty self-assurance, "if they fail to do right by me, then I'll quit and get a better job." She was speaking on camera—I was filming with a crew from CCTV, the government broadcaster—and for all she knew, she would be on CCTV's evening news.

For rural women too, economic reform has brought unprecedented opportunities. Many have left home to find work—and often, economic independence from fathers or husbands. It's a phenomenon that has shaken the traditional male domination of rural society, as young migrant women in Beijing made clear:[2]

"There is a deeply rooted mentality in the village to treat boys better than girls," said one girl. "Therefore girls' education is taken lightly. It's felt that an investment in a girl's education will be lost because they'll marry and move out." In Beijing, however, she noted, "there's no such discrimination."

Increasingly, country girls are marrying city boys—another way in which the separation between countryside and cities is breaking down, and another challenge to traditional rural attitudes. One migrant woman stressed that "Back home, your parents probably decided whom you would marry. But now you're in the city, a new world, and you find yourself wanting to marry somebody else. Falling in love is not about seeking a marriage partner. It's about seeking yourself."

But rural women are often vulnerable; market economics can make them cheap labor: young rural girls generally work as babysitters or maids for middle- and upper-class families in the cities; in restaurants and hotels; or in shops and factories. City life can be hard, and their low status puts them at risk of being exploited. Sexual harassment is a perennial problem.

In response, women's groups have begun to take action to help rural migrants. In Beijing some urban women set up an organization called Rural Women Knowing All, which helps young migrant women adjust to city life. At one Sunday workshop, the young girls were told what the famous female author, Bing Xin, had said: "You are a human being first, and then you are a woman." The girls said that they had never heard such ideas before. Yet for all the problems migrant women faced, one of the leaders of Rural Women Knowing All was upbeat: "Economic reform has greatly benefitted rural women," she said. "They're getting the chance to change their fates and lead lives very different from those of their mothers."

China's official women's organizations, government controlled, have also begun tailoring their missions to meet the needs of women in today's society— a position advocated for years by Chinese feminist scholars. Programs to protect rural women from physical hardships and psychological stress have been established.

★ ★ ★

Advocates of women's rights have also sought to stamp out the killing of baby girls—often by drowning or abandonment—a hideous practice rooted in China's feudal past which still occurs in remote rural areas, though far less than in the past. The government forbids such acts, and has instituted programs to change underlying attitudes.

One factor in the re-emergence of female infanticide was China's One Couple, One-Child policy. Introduced in the late 1970s to stem China's then runaway population explosion, the policy is said to have prevented about 500 million births.[3] (In 1982, Chinese households averaged 4.4 people; in 2005, the average was 3.1.) The policy is credited as facilitating the Chinese people's increasing standard of living, particularly in education and healthcare.

While the policy has been extraordinarily successful in achieving its intended purposes, there have been unintended side effects. These include forced abortions and sterilizations (as local leaders conform to Beijing's directives) and, predictably, a dangerously imbalanced sex ratio as families, employing ultra sound technology, choose to abort girls out of a traditional preference for male heirs (seen as providers for the family).

The social significance of China's One-Child Policy are the more than 100 million children with no siblings, raising special problems of the only child. According to Xie Lingli, director of the State Family Planning Commission, single children face five main obstacles in their lives: personality, psychology, emotional quotient, living environment and independence.

Surely the One-Child Policy has emphasized education. It is common for parents and both sets of grandparents to dote on the single child, showering him or her with educational aids (computers are essential). Many Chinese now send their children to special schools to learn music and art when they are very young—two- or three-years-old. And in an increasingly competitive society, many people see education as another kind of investment—which will give their child more earning power in the future. Single children in China today are called, for good reason, "little emperors and empresses."

And the One-Child Policy has affected China's demography—exacerbating the nation's growing problem of an aging population. In 2006, China had more than 150 million people over the age of 60, including at least 50 million widows and widowers. Senior citizens made up about 12% of the population, even more in some cities—and by 2025, the elderly population may account for 20%. China is becoming, by international standards, an "aging country." This may be seen as a sign of social progress, but it brings with it a range of social problems.[4]

★ ★ ★

The rise of the middle class has been a profound factor in China's transformation. From virtually nonexistent at the end of the Cultural Revolution in 1976, the middle class today is estimated at between 125 million (the population of Japan) and over 300 million (larger than the population of America).

China's National Bureau of Statistics defines middle class as households with annual incomes ranging from RMB 60,000 (about $8,750) to RMB 500,000 (about $73,000). Its members include company managers, technicians, teachers and educators, government employees, and private business owners—largely professional white-collar workers as well as private entrepreneurs.[5]

A McKinsey forecast estimates that by 2025, 90% of urban Chinese households will have incomes of greater than RMB 25,000 a year, and about 70% more than RMB 40,000.[6] The McKinsey model predicts that by 2025, the upper middle class, with annual household income of RMB 40,001 to 100,000, will comprise a staggering 520 million people—more than half of China's expected urban population—with a combined total disposable income of RMB 13 trillion (almost $2 trillion).

The upper segments of the middle class—the "new social strata"—include entrepreneurs, academics and self-employed intellectuals. This class is growing and irreversibly altering society: successful entrepreneurs now participate as delegates in People's congresses at local, provincial and national levels, while some have become members of the Communist Party. And while China's middle class is broadly seen as supportive of the government and CPC, which has facilitated its emergence, its members increasingly seek to protect their own interests and lifestyles.

★ ★ ★

"Insurance is a social stabilizer," says Yang Chao, chairman of China Life, the world's largest insurance company by market capitalization (around $100 billion).[7] Yang, who has a UK MBA, describes the growth of insurance in China as an "awakening lion" or a "tiger descending from the mountains."

China Life has 160 million policy holders (individual and group life, annuity and long-term healthcare), serviced by 120,000 employees and 700,000 agents. Yet insurance in China, Yang says, is "still at a low level in terms of penetration."

Demographics drives insurance as China's population urbanizes and ages. When millions of peasants migrate from rural to urban areas, leaving their villages, they need to find new ways to fulfill their traditional obligations of caring for their aging relatives. Similarly, China's One-Child Policy leaves increasing numbers of the elderly with only one child to support them. In both cases, insurance can fill the gaps.

"Insurance makes people more confident in the future," Yang says, "which means they are more willing to spend in the present."

Chairman Yang, who personifies China's new standard of executive excellence—"international understanding with domestic experience"—talks about three stages in China Life's branding: from famous brand to quality brand; from industry brand to social brand; and from domestic brand to international brand. A false rumor that Yang was leaving China Life in 2007 caused a drop of $15 billion in market value.

★ ★ ★

Sometimes, social change finds its expression in small ways. In 2007, for example, China's nascent animal rights movement claimed victory, after rescuing 415 cats, which were due to be slaughtered for their fur and meat, at a market in Tianjin. About 100 pet-loving protesters of the Love Kitty group, including local people who had lost their pets and suspected the animals had been abducted by furriers, surrounded the market and confronted the stallholders.[8] Professor Lu Di, founder of the China Small Animal Protection Association (CSAPA), who tried to mediate between the two sides, reported that demonstrators who forced their way inside the market found cats crammed inside tiny wire cages about 10 cm high.[9]

The rescued cats were taken to CSAPA headquarters in Beijing by dozens of volunteers, many of them students, in what was the largest animal rescue operation this part of China had ever seen. It was a symbol both of the changing attitude of Chinese society towards animals and their welfare, and of the willingness of citizens to organize on issues they care about.

★ ★ ★

Middle class opposition to pollution and other environmental intrusions is becoming increasingly vocal. In Chengdu, Sichuan Province, citizens marched through the streets to stop construction of a $5.5 billion petrochemical plant backed by PetroChina, China's largest state-run oil company.[10] One protest leader was Fan Xiao, a civil servant geologist in Chengdu. His government paycheck did not deter him from relaying an environmentalist mobile-phone mass message: "Protect our Chengdu, safeguard our home-land," it said. "Avoid the threat of pollution. Restore the clear water and green mountains of Sichuan."

In Shanghai, citizens staged a "walkabout" in the city center, to oppose plans to extend the maglev, the world's fastest train, through their middle-class neighborhoods. They were upset, like their peers in the West, because they feared that the intrusive trains would decrease property values and disturb tranquility.[11]

Such activism reflects both a surge in environmental awareness by members of the new social classes, and the willingness of middle-class Chinese to mobilize when the health of their families—or the value of their properties—is threatened. Many believe that only the middle class is strong enough to make the government listen to its requests, or risk finding those requests mutate into demands. Assuming current reforms continue apace, China's massive middle class will demand more transparency and accountability, which will likely lead gradually but inexorably, to a more open and tolerant civil society.

★ ★ ★

China claims to be a "multi-national unified state," with 56 ethnic groups, the largest by far being the Han which accounts for about 91.5% of the population. All together the other 55 ethnic groups, referred to as "minority nationalities," count just over 100 million citizens, constituting about 8.5% of China's total. Among China's minority nationalities, the Zhuang is the largest, with more than 15 million people. Only 17 minorities have a population of above 1 million. Almost all of China's 55 minorities have their own spoken languages, and 21 of them have their own writing systems.

China's minorities are distributed over expansive areas. Although less than one-tenth of China's population, minorities occupy over half of the country's area. (Autonomous ethnic regions make up about 64% of China's total land.) However, since 90+% of China's population is Han, even in ethnic autonomous regions, Han people are usually the majority. Yunnan is the most ethnically diverse province in China, with 25 indigenous minorities.

Ethnic groups live in compact communities which often extend into different provinces. For example, of the 4.5 million Tibetans only 2 million live in Tibet; the others live in Gansu, Qinghai, Sichuan and Yunnan provinces. Many minority regions are located in remote areas on China's frontiers, which are important for national defense and developing friendly relations with neighboring countries—107 of China's 135 border counties are ethnic autonomous, and more than 30 minority nationalities live "shoulder-by-shoulder" with the same ethnic groups in China's neighboring countries.

Most minority areas have backward economies, due to their out-of-the-way locations, sparse populations, and poor transportation access. About 12 million rural Chinese living in absolute poverty -- half of the country's total—are in ethnic minority regions.[12] With reform, progress has been made, but compared with the places where the Han live, the minority regions have not developed anywhere as rapidly.

China's minorities generally believe in some kind of religion; Islam and Buddhism are the strongest (also Christianity). In addition, some minorities also maintain their original belief systems, such as ancestor worship, witchcraft and shamanism.

After the founding of New China, the Chinese government formulated favorable policies toward ethic groups. China has five autonomous regions (Guangxi Zhuang, Inner Mongolia, Xinjiang Uyghur, Ningxia Hui and Tibet) and 124 autonomous counties. China's Constitution states that "In the struggle to safeguard the unity of the nationalities, it is necessary to combat big-nation chauvinism, mainly Han chauvinism, and to combat local national chauvinism. The state will do its utmost to promote the common prosperity of all the nationalities."

To support minority development, the government gives aid in finance, materials and technology, and provides continuous cultural subsidies. The government also seeks to prevent small minority groups from vanishing by recording their endangered languages and by conducting bilingual school education to protect their cultural heritage.

Quan Zhezhu, of Korean ancestry and minister of the CPC United Front, is one of the highest-ranking minorities in the Chinese government. I asked him about his status.[13]

"An ethnic minority cadre needs to grow by study and work, just like everyone else," Quan said. "Special treatment doesn't get the job done. The first barrier one faces is language: Chinese is not the native language of many ethnic minorities. For me, I have to use Chinese and Korean interchangeably. In regions where ethnic minorities are concentrated, ethnic languages are used in parallel with Mandarin Chinese ["Putonghua," the common language] for documents and speeches. In this way, the ethnic culture is respected and protected and national unity is recognized and promoted. Years ago, when Vice Premier Zhang Dejiang was Party secretary of Yanbian Korean Autonomous Prefecture (Jilin Province; population about 2 million). I worked under him as mayor and I had to deliver the government report in Korean, otherwise Koreans would be unhappy. In Party congresses when delivering a speech, Zhang Dejiang would begin and end in Korean. He studied Korean."

"I've never felt discrimination against me," Quan said. "For example, the Communist Youth League of China is a mass organization. Generally speaking, the head of a mass organization must be a person from the majority ethnic group in that region. Therefore in Yanbian, the heads of mass organizations must be Koreans. When it comes to the whole Jilin Province, the Koreans are not the majority ethnic group, but as a Korean I was still the head of Jilin Youth League. As an ethnic minority in a region where that ethnic minority is concentrated, one may get some special treatment, but you must have what it takes. You can't be a figurehead. When I was in the Jilin government, I was promoted to vice governor at the age of 40, which is something very few Han [Chinese majority] people are able to do."

Quan asserted that ethnic issues in China are economic not political. "Economic inequality, which is real, is the product of history," he said. "One reason is that most minority groups dwell in remote areas; another is that their education is poor. So to work for ethnic equality means to focus on economic development. The problem is not ethnic discrimination. In many countries, there is discrimination against ethnic minority groups. But in China, the less population an ethnic group has, the more preferential its treatment. Much of the world's turbulence and turmoil is caused by ethnic and religious strife."

★ ★ ★

Indeed, ethnic conflict in Llasa (2008) between Tibetans and Han Chinese, and in Urumqi (2009) between Uyghur Muslims and Han Chinese, brought the turbulence-and-turmoil message home hard to China. The riots (or uprisings) underlined the stark fact that while China's leaders have thought they were dealing effectively with minority concerns by providing economic subsidies and making capital investments, and therefore by increasing standards of living, they were not.

The worst carnage befell Urumqi, the capital of Xinjiang Uyghur Autonomous Region, where about 200 people were killed and over 1,700 injured in the deadliest "mass incident" in China since the 1989 crackdown in Tiananmen Square. Triggered by an ethnic brawl in far-off Guangdong Province, where in a local dispute over an alleged rape Chinese workers attacked Uyghur workers in a toy factory dormitory (killing two), what began as a peaceful protest in Urumqi, according to Uyghur sources, turned violent after confrontation with police. According to government reports, rampaging Uyghur thugs attacked Han Chinese people and properties in a coordinated fashion at some 50 locations simultaneously—burning buildings, torching cars and buses, looting stores, attacking police, and chasing and beating passers-by ("trying to kill any Han Chinese within sight").[14]

According to foreign analysts, the violent boil over was the long-simmering product of what many Uyghurs perceived to be the progressive "colonization" of their historic lands by Han Chinese (after decades of government-encouraged immigration, Han Chinese had become a slight majority of Xinjiang's 20 million people and 75% of Urumqi's 2 million). The result, some Uyghur leaders charged, was suppression of the Uyghur culture, marginalization of the Uyghur language, and limitation of the Uyghur Muslim religion—as well as endemic discrimination against Uyghur natives on their own soil.

Chinese government sources had most of the dead as Han Chinese—one body count numbered 137 Han and 46 Uyghurs—proof, the government said, that Uyghurs had mounted the initial attack on defenseless Chinese. Uyghur leaders vehemently disputed the official count, claiming untold hundreds of allegedly unreported Uyghur fatalities. Some witnesses reported that marauding Uyghur gangs demanded that random people of all ages speak the Uyghur language, beating or killing those who could not. The weapons of choice were often heavy stones; the anatomical targets, heads and chests.

A Chinese government press release blamed "premeditated and organized crimes of violence, directed and instigated by separatists abroad and organized and carried out by separatists inside the country." It singled out "The World Uyghur Congress headed by the ethnic separatist Rebiya Kadeer. . . . [who] directly instigated, orchestrated, directed and staged these highly violent crimes."

Xinjiang Party Secretary Wang Lequan, the most senior government authority in the region, stated that "The riot has destroyed the spiritual support with which the terrorist, separatist and extremist forces cheated the people to participate in the so-called 'Jihad.'"[15] Two days later, after Han Chinese mobs, armed with lead pipes, clubs, shovels, machetes and meat cleavers, sought vigilante justice and invaded Uyghur sections of Urumqi, Secretary Wang also condemned the Han Chinese counterattack, appearing on television to beseech troubled citizens. "If now groups of Han people are organizing and targeting innocent Uyghurs," he appealed, "won't this unreasonable act also bring sadness to the masses of all ethnicities?"[16] Only after thousands of armed police occupied Urumqi, locking down the city, was calm restored.

Acknowledging that the Chinese government "blamed me for the unrest," Rebiya Kadeer, a businesswoman who has lived in the U.S. (Virginia) after being released from a Chinese prison in 2005, wrote, "It is years of Chinese repression of Uyghurs . . . that is the cause of the current Uyghur discontent." Advocating "self-determination with genuine respect for human rights and democracy" she called for "a dialogue based on trust, mutual respect and equality."[17]

In the aftermath, hundreds were arrested, mostly young Uyghur men. Secretary Wang Lequan described the dragnet as a "life and death struggle," while Uyghurs called the crackdown indiscriminate and discriminatory. At a news conference, Urumqi Party Chief Li Zhi stated, "To those who have committed crimes with cruel means, we will execute them"—a vow broadcast repeatedly, causing widespread fear.[18] A government report noted that among the alleged ringleaders, were several women in long, black Islamic garb and black head scarves who issued "commands" to rioters (picked up on surveillance cameras). Most hoped that religion would not come into the conflict.[19]

But come what may, China's leaders, led by President Hu, were determined to continue their long-standing policies: Assure stability at all costs. Maintain economic growth for the benefit of all citizens in the context of the Scientific Perspective of Development. Support minority peoples, cultures, traditions and religions in the context of a unified country and a Harmonious Society.

★ ★ ★

In a disaster of a natural kind, in the 2008 Sichuan earthquake, the town hit hardest and in total ruin, Beichuan, was a center of the Qiang minority, which all together constitute barely 200,000 people. In fact, Beichuan was the only county in China that was designated a "Qiang autonomous county," a status achieved in 2003 in an atmosphere of greater concern for minorities.[20] Now the entire country is determined that Beichuan must be reborn as a Qiang autonomous county, even though it must be rebuilt in a different area.

Three months later, at the wondrous opening ceremony of the 2008 Beijing Olympics, each of China's 56 ethnic groups marched proudly into the National Stadium. Though the earthquake would never be forgotten, China's Olympics, with all its ethnic groups represented, symbolized their common confidence in a bright future. The stunning grand finale was when Olympic gold medalist gymnast Li Ning traversed the upper roof of the "Bird Nest" in the magical style of a kung fu master just prior to his lighting the Olympic cauldron. Li Ning, a national hero for winning six medals at the 1984 Olympics in Los Angeles, and a successful entrepreneur, is a member of the Zhuang minority.

Endnotes

1 Xinhua, January 25, 2008.
2 Interviewed for my PBS special, *In Search of China* (2000).
3 Xinhua, September 24, 2007. There are exceptions for ethnic groups, rural families and families where both parents are themselves only children.

4 Li Jianguo, *China Today,*

5 Solinger, *Far Eastern Economic Review.*

6 Diana Farrell, Ulrich A. Gersch, and Elizabeth Stephenson, "The value of China's emerging middle class," *The McKinsey Quarterly,* June 2006. At current exchange rates, these incomes may seem below middle-class level, especially compared with the world's most developed countries, but in China absolute income underestimates purchasing power. For example, Chinese households with an income of RMB 100,000 (about $15,000 at current rates) can have lifestyles similar to American households earning $40,000.

7 Author's meeting with Yang Chao, Beijing, May 2009.

8 Humane Society International, June 6, 2007.

9 Jonathan Watts, "Chinese animal rights victory takes cats off the menu," *The Guardian,* February 13, 2007.

10 Edward Wong, "In China City, Protesters See Pollution Risk of New Plant," *The New York Times,* May 6, 2008.

11 Jeffrey N. Wasserstrom, "China's middle class rising," *International Herald Tribune,* January 21, 2008.

12 Xinhua, March 30, 2007.

13 Author's meeting with Quan Zhezhu, Beijing, June, 2008.

14 "Truth of July 5th Violent Crimes in Urumqi and Chinese Government's Position," Press Release of the People's Republic of China, July 7, 2009. "Facts show July 5 riot 'far beyond ordinary violent matter'," *People's Daily,* July 19, 2009.

15 "Xinjiang Party chief slashes riot which kills 140," Xinhua, July 6, 2009.

16 Shai Oster and Jason Dean, "Ethnic Tensions Escalate in China's Xinjiang Region," *The Wall Street Journal,* July 8, 2009.

17 Rebiya Kadeer, "The Real Story of the Uighur Riots," *The Wall Street Journal,* July 8, 2009.

18 Andrew Jacobs, "Countering Riots, China Snatches Hundreds From Their Homes," *The New York Times,* July 20, 2009.

19 "Viciousness of rioters 'unexpected,' *China Daily,* July 20, 2009.

20 James Macartney, *The Times,* May 21, 2008.

16

Here Come the Lawyers

Despite reform of China's economic and political life, and relaxation of personal strictures and social controls, serious problems of human rights remain. Any who try to organize opposition to the Communist Party are restricted, detained, or jailed. Trials have been perfunctory, sentencing severe. Though less capricious and harsh than in the past, they are still designed to intimidate others from threatening political stability. The government's justification is the argument that, traditionally in China, the collective success of society is given priority over the individual rights of the person. Similarly, the rights of victims of crimes are more important than the rights of criminals who committed the crimes.

Such attitudes are reflected in the prevalence of capital punishment. In the West, the ultimate penalty of death is largely limited to premeditated murder— and administering it for any crime, no matter how heinous, remains controversial. In China, however, 68 offenses, including nonviolent crimes such as tax evasion and pornography distribution, have carried the death penalty,[1] and executing offenders for economic crimes is widely supported by the general public.

It's a reminder of the explanatory strength of the twin guiding themes of pride and stability. If the good of the collective exceeds the rights of the individual, then when the pride and stability of the country are undermined, the individual must be eliminated. Economic crimes (corruption) hurt the nation's pride by impeding China's economy and ruining China's image; they threaten stability by delegitimizing the government.

Still, most executions are for murder, robbery and drug trafficking. The exact number is considered a state secret. Estimates from independent organizations have varied widely—between 1,000 and 10,000 per year. There's general agreement that China executes more criminals than any other country, perhaps more than all other countries combined. Between 1990 and 2000, Amnesty International claimed to have documented almost 20,000 executions, a figure government sources call "exaggerated" and critics claim is low. Until recently, most death sentences were carried out swiftly, generally within a few weeks of sentencing, often publicly in front of crowds, with the condemned paraded through town to open fields or courtyards. Typically, they were executed with a bullet to the back of the head.

The Chinese government defends its right to "strike against serious criminals such as drug traffickers" and to publicize the executions as a deterrent to others. In 2001, for example, a Strike Hard campaign was launched amidst mounting concern about crime, including crimes previously unknown in Communist China, such as bank robberies carried out by armed gangsters. According to *People's Daily*, Strike Hard focused on violent crimes: "explosions, murders, robbery, kidnapping, poisoning; gang crimes and crimes with Mafia features; thefts and other crimes that affect the public security." An overwhelming majority of the Chinese people supported the Strike-Hard campaign and applauded the use of capital punishment.

"No government wants to use the death penalty more than it has to," said Liu Hainian, a law professor. "The government wants to reduce the use of the death penalty, but it has to fit with China's reality. We cannot cause harm to people's lives and property."

Yet China's leaders recognize that in building a civil society, the rights of all people deserve protection, especially from uneven and unfair application of law and punishment. In recent years, officials have been examining the rules and process of capital punishment, considering how best to reduce the categories of crimes punishable by execution—although severe cases of corruption, bribery and national security violations would still lead to death sentences.

In an important reform, from January 1, 2007, all death sentences handed down by provincial courts have to be reviewed and approved by the Supreme People's Court. Each death sentence is now reviewed by three judges, who are required to check facts, laws, criminal procedures, and precedents. The purpose, according to *China Daily*, is "to rein in irresponsible use of capital punishment at local levels . . . the Supreme Court has the obligation to make sure every death sentence it approves can stand the test of time."[2]

The Supreme People's Court had loosened its control over death penalty cases in 1983, amidst an earlier Strike Hard campaign against soaring crime. Over the years, local differences emerged: for a similar felony, a defendant might be sentenced to death in one province but jailed for life in another. Mistaken convictions, caused by lax supervision, were obviously irreversible.

Now, with reform permeating Chinese society, authorities advocate "killing fewer, and killing carefully." China's former Chief Justice Xiao Yang said in 2008 that although the country retains capital punishment, it should be applied only to "an extremely small number" of serious offenders, stressing that Chinese courts at all levels should "adhere to the policy of balancing severe punishment and leniency."[3]

Xiao Yang said that, after the Supreme People Court took back from provincial courts the power of reviewing death sentences, capital punishment has been "strictly, cautiously and fairly" meted out to "the very few number of felons who committed extremely serious, atrocious crimes which lead to grave social consequences." He noted that the Supreme People's Court rejected 15% of death sentences for technical reasons, including facts to be clarified, lack of evidence and procedural faults.[4] As a result, Chinese courts handed down about 30% fewer death penalties in 2007 compared with 2006.

A *China Daily* editorial praised the change, saying: "It is good to have fewer people on death row. After all, few crimes deserve the ultimate punishment. And this country's judicial philosophy has an expressed commitment to helping erring souls to correct themselves. It is encouraging to see the drop in death sentences in the provinces." It suggested that "incorporating both leniency and severity—with the accent on leniency—is a break from China's traditional emphasis on harshness in law enforcement. The general appeal for leniency in criminal justice and, more specifically, the call for prudent use of the death sentence are both indications of civilized law enforcement . . . . There is no remedy for execution."

The method of execution is also changing. In 2008, half of the country's 404 intermediate people's courts—which carried out most of the executions—were using lethal injections rather than gunshots.[5] Lethal injection, a judicial official said, was "considered more humane."

The Chinese justice community generally agrees that while the death sentence is at present still necessary to serve as a deterrent against crime (to maintain social stability and protect national security), China should reduce the number of executions until the death penalty is finally abolished "when conditions are ripe." Former Chief Justice Xiao Yang himself has said that abolishing capital punishment, or strictly limiting the use of the death sentence, is a global trend and that "China is also working toward that direction." But he stressed that the goal cannot be achieved overnight. "We cannot talk about abolishing or controlling the use of death sentences in the abstract without considering ground realities and social security conditions," he said, referring to the strong belief among the Chinese people of the concept "an eye for an eye and a life for a life."

★ ★ ★

President Hu Jintao has emphasized that strengthening the rule of law in China must be a hallmark of his administration. In 2006, he told the Politburo that the rule of law was fundamental to the way in which the nation was governed, and that, under Party rule, this should enable the people to be "masters of the country."[6] The Party should govern and construct the country according to the law, lead the people in making rules, and set good examples in obeying rules. Politburo members attending the meeting were given a lecture on the rule of law by legal scholars.

In his report to the 17th Party Congress in 2007, Hu Jintao mentioned "the rule of law" 13 times. He called for "ensuring that all citizens are equal before the law" and stressed the need to improve the "quality of judicial, procuratorial and public security personnel, to ensure that law enforcement is strict, impartial and civilized" and to step up public education campaigns "to increase public awareness of law and promote the spirit of the rule of law, creating a social environment in which people study, abide by and apply laws of their own accord."

In this context, Hu exhorted the Party to "respect and safeguard human rights, and ensure the equal right to participation and development for all members of society in accordance with the law."

★ ★ ★

Lawyers have entered into the life of ordinary Chinese people as a means of protecting their rights. In the future, most Chinese families will have a "four-two-one" structure—four elderly, a middle-aged or young couple, and one child. Leaving economic difficulties aside, taking care of senior citizens will become a formidable task, since middle-aged couples all have their own jobs and old people often suffer from a host of age-related diseases requiring increasing levels of care, from hypertension and arteriosclerosis to paralysis and senile dementia.

In Chinese culture, taking care of the elderly is a strong tradition. But as Chinese society continues to age and the size of Chinese families continues to shrink, a large number of parents who have only one child will enter old age facing an "empty nest." Over time, aging parents are progressively less likely to live together with their offspring, who due to the mobility enabled by reform may not even live in the same city, so that the ideal of "four generations living under the same roof" will become a description of history not a portrait of the present.

Many senior citizens find their lives dull and depressing. Following the modernization of the cities and urbanization of the countryside, many high-rise buildings have sprung up. Life in these massive edifices differs dramatically from life in one-story house neighborhoods of the past where residents had close relationships with their neighbors in the old alleys. People are no longer satisfied with merely having enough food and clothing. With a lack of entertainment and human interaction, they feel lonely and bored.

In modern society, people of different age groups differ greatly in lifestyle, such as hobbies and habits, so that the generation gap can cause conflict. After their offspring grow up, some old people must leave home because of crowded housing; others are willing to continue to labor as servants or babysitters for their children, an odd reversal of roles, and many are sad that their offspring do not care for them according to Chinese tradition.

There are problems of medical care and upkeep support. Since most Chinese senior citizens who live in the countryside don't have pensions, more than 90% must rely on their own old-age work or on help from family or relatives. Sadly, it is believed that among the senior citizens living in the countryside, 3% are maltreated by their offspring. The living conditions of the old people in towns and cities are much better than those in the countryside, but they have their own difficulties—their biggest complaint is "the fixed pension and price fluctuation." Some retirees are worse off still, with no guarantee of pension since the state-owned enterprises for which they had worked are in debt.

China's transition from a planned to a market economy has generated many urgent problems that demand attention so the problems of senior citizens are often neglected. China does not yet have enough apartments designed specifically for the elderly; the special needs of old folks are seldom considered in city planning.

Yet older people want to be productive. Many are busy working on the streets, in workshops, on construction sites or in designing offices. They have formed a gray-haired work force. Mr. Sun, senior editor for a newspaper before retirement, was famous in press circles for his writings. After he retired, he accepted the task of cooking and taking care of his grandchild. Though he worked hard, he was not familiar with household chores. The other family members were not satisfied with his work, and he himself felt helpless. He decided to change his life and found employment with another newspaper. He became responsible for three pages, which he edited well and became popular with readers. Mr. Sun commented, "My aim in returning to the post of editor is simple. I must say goodbye to the days of cooking around the stove and running after my grandson. Those days are unbearable to recall."

There are many similar cases. When the Zhejiang Provincial Museum announced that it was going to hire 12 workers for its exhibition hall, 2,200 retired people responded. Many of them said that getting a job was more difficult than college entrance examinations.

The Chinese people take seriously their tradition of respecting and pro-tecting the old, and in response, a new branch of science has emerged—socio-gerontology. Old-age welfare and medical insurance reforms need to be accelerated and a social system must be formed, combining social insur-ance, relief, welfare, and special care. Only in this way can China prepare for the coming of the aging society in the 21st century.

The reform and opening-up of China has influenced all the Chinese people's modes of thinking, behavior and lifestyle, and this includes senior citizens, who are no longer the conservative group they used to be. On the contrary, since they were subject to so many restrictions when they were young, now that they have the chance, they are even more eager than young people to express themselves and try their hands at new things. In a way, their "return to youth" epitomizes the new era.

★ ★ ★

In 2008, China had more than 130,000 lawyers working in 13,000 law firms, and their numbers were growing.[7] There were also about one million legal consultants.[8]

Criminal law is an important part of legal and judicial reform. A 2007 amendment to China's Law on Lawyers made it easier for attorneys to meet criminal suspects and obtain evidence (once judicial organs finished their initial interrogation or "taken mandatory measures"). It also entitled defense attorneys to access all files and materials relating to the case, and enabled them to speak with their accused clients without being monitored. Defense attorneys may also apply to people's courts to provide evidence, collect evidence themselves from relevant parties, and use courts to compel witnesses to testify.

The amendment also offers protection to lawyers, specifying that remarks made by defense lawyers in court cannot lead to prosecution—provided they do not threaten national security or slander others.

In what some observers characterized as a "left turn," China's Chief Justice Wang Shengjun, appointed president of the Supreme People's Court in 2009, called for "three supremes" in judicial policy—Party interests and public opinion as well as legal rules—rather than upholding the rule of law, as in Western systems, as the neutral and absolute adjudicator of disputes. Chief Justice Wang asserted that the courts had a key role in preserving social stability and national security, a policy which "strengthens ties between local courts and the local Party structure"—and erodes prior progress toward judicial independence.[9] Other observers, recognizing social dangers of slowing growth caused by the global financial crisis, opted to give China's leaders some slack during this difficult period but cautioned that close monitoring was required.

★ ★ ★

Provinces suing each other over various conflicts are another example of the growing role of the rule of law: for example if a company owned by one province purchases a company owned by another province, then decides to downsize the facilities of that company or to transfer the workforce to its home province, a lawsuit may result. Such suits, whatever their legal merits, evince the growing diversity, dynamism and pluralism of Chinese society (and are also a reminder that the Chinese government these days is no longer an undifferentiated monolith.)

Similarly, in 2008, China International Television Corp., a subsidiary of CCTV, filed a revealing lawsuit against a Chinese Internet firm for rebroadcasting the Olympic torch relay without permission. In pre-reform China, the government could have simply shut down the offending firm and incarcerated its managers. Now CCTV, even though it is the government broadcaster, must file a lawsuit, much like its counterparts must do in the West.

In addition, private citizens are starting to sue the government in a meaningful manner. In theory, Chinese citizens have had this right since the founding of the People's Republic, as successive versions of the nation's constitution have always propounded the political doctrine of "people's sovereignty."[10]

In practice, however, such rights were virtually meaningless—until recently. In 2008, for example, five citizens from Hunan Province took their county government to court for denying them access to information, the first such action under new national regulations on public disclosure.[11] The five were retired staff of a state-owned water plant, and had challenged the legality of a deal under which the local construction bureau turned the plant into a joint venture with a private investor. The county government had investigated the workers complaint—but then withheld the results. Immediately after the disclosure regulation took effect, the workers went back to the county government. Even though their application for disclosure was again rejected, the case was publicized, which increased public awareness of the right to demand government transparency and to initiate lawsuits against the government.

The legal rights of ordinary citizens were also set to be expanded by an anticipated amendment to the State Compensation Law, allowing people to sue government departments for "emotional harm."[12] For years, legal experts argued that the existing law needed amending to cope with increasingly complicated scenarios. Comparatively low compensation standards and the failure to cover mental anguish had reduced its practicality and undermined its authority.

Several such cases were widely reported, triggering healthy debate. Take Ma Dandan, a 19-year-old girl from Shanxi Province, who in 2001 was wrongly accused of prostitution and detained by local police for three days. Ma asked for compensation of RMB 5 million—but was awarded just RMB 74 ($10.80) in salary compensation, and nothing at all for damage to her reputation and mental state. "The absence of compensation for psychological damage is a big shortcoming," said Ying Songnian, a Chinese legal expert, adding that the harm done by government departments is often too grave to be redressed in civil lawsuits, as individuals tend to be vulnerable in the face of authority.

In another new use of the courts by individuals to advocate public policy positions against government institutions, Ding Ning, a resident of Harbin in Heilongjiang Province, filed a lawsuit in 2005 against a subsidiary of the huge China National Petroleum Corp. (CNPC). The company was being held accountable for polluting the Songhua River, the city's major water source, following an explosion at its chemical plant.[13] Ding accused the CNPC subsidiary of contaminating the river and harming Harbin residents. He told the media that the normal life of local citizens had been interrupted by the sudden water cutoff: many had rushed to stockpile bottled water; schools had been suspended and hotels temporarily closed. Ding asked for compensation of only RMB 15 (less than three dollars); what he really wanted was a formal apology from the corporation, and for this to be published in major newspapers. "My fellow residents and I would value a formal apology," he explained, "while the monetary compensation is only symbolic." (A CNPC executive quickly and publicly apologized.)

It's clear that Chinese citizens are becoming increasingly aware of their legal rights—and increasingly assertive in exercising them—and that this will increasingly pressure China's leaders to enable practical implementation of the rule of law to match the theoretical emphasis they place on it. As *China Daily* pointed out: "To sue the government is a civil right granted by a law-ruled society to its citizens."[14]

Endnotes

1 Robert Verkaik, "China spearheads surge in state-sponsored executions," *The Independent,* March 24, 2009.

2 "Fewer Death Sentences," *China Daily,* June 8, 2007.

3 "China rejects 'strike hard' anti-crime policy for more balanced approach," Xinhua, March 14, 2007.

4 "Top judge: death sentences meted out only to 'tiny number of felons' in China," *People's Daily,* March 11, 2008.

5 "Lethal injection to be used more," *China Daily,* January 3, 2008.

6 "President Hu Stresses Rule of Law in Government ," Xinhua, July 4, 2006

7 Ministry of Justice; "China to amend law to help lawyers obtain evidence, open individual law firm," *People's Daily,* June 25, 2007.

8 Only a small fraction of these one million legal consultants working on legal matters were trained at the graduate level and have formal, bar-like certifications—as is required for the appellation "lawyer" in most developed countries.

9 Thomas E. Kellogg, "The Death of Constitutional Litigation in China?" *China Brief,* Volume IX, Issue 7, April 2, 2009.

10 For example, the 1982 Constitution stated that individuals had the right to charge any state organs or officials if these infringed upon their rights or lawful interests, and that the government must compensate citizens if their lawful interests were harmed by governmental infringements. Xuxin Wang, "Suing The Sovereign Observed From The Chinese Perspective: The Idea And Practice Of State Compensation In China," *The George Washington International Law Review,* 2003.

11 Zhan Lisheng, "Workers sue govt for denial of information," *China Daily,* May 7, 2008.

12 Xie Chuanjiao, "Legal redress for victims of mental trauma," *China Daily,* May 7, 2008.

13 "Citizen sues China petroleum for polluting river," Xinhua, November 25, 2005.

14 "Don't shut the legal options," *China Daily,* August 1, 2008.

Facing Up to Corruption

Corruption is ubiquitous in the Chinese system and noxious to the Chinese people. It pervades all levels of commerce and government and has proved intractably and maddingly resilient. At best, corruption is a drag on the economy and a scourge on society. At worst, it threatens not only economic development, but also political stability and the legitimacy of the State. Corruption distorts economic decisions and undermines the rule of law, both of which are essential for a stable, prosperous society. It illegally transfers resources from society to individuals, effectively stealing from everyone, and leeches efficiency out of the economy by enabling risky ventures to go forward. Corruption, rightly, engenders public anger.

No political system is immune to corruption. ("Crony capitalism" was blamed as a prime cause of the Asian Financial Crisis of 1997.) Corruption is endemic in human nature: where it can exist it will exist. When societies move from public to private ownership, when vast state resources are privatized, fortunes can be made with astonishing speed—such that powerful behavioral forces can overwhelm morally weak officials who are tempted to "share" some of the spoils. Not only do such officials see others making a great deal of money very rapidly, often by corrupt means—and getting away with it—but they also see their own positions of power being eroded over time. This combustible mixture of envy, jealousy and anxiety, may lead them to fall victim to base instincts.

Many believe that a deep cause of current corruption in China is the continuing corrosive impact of the Cultural Revolution, which destroyed traditional Chinese culture and destabilized Chinese society—so that there remains little natural immunity to diseases of greed and personal aggrandizement.

Many conservatives in China, however, place the blame squarely on the market economy. And indeed, there is no question that free markets, which encourage individual initiative, enhance opportunity for corruption, and that corruption has spread as China has implemented market reforms (it is remarkable how the economy has grown in spite of it).

Nevertheless, the solution, as China's leaders believe, lies in deepening reform, not backtracking from it. Senior leaders do not whitewash the problem: they are aware of its gravity and are very serious about curtailing it.

Both President Hu Jintao and former President Jiang Zemin have fiercely fought corruption, seeing it not only as immoral, corrosive and inimical to socialism, but also as perhaps the largest obstacle blocking China's efforts to reach its full potential as a great nation. And for decades, a Politburo Standing Committee member has been placed in charge of the CPC Central Commission for Discipline Inspection (CCDI), which is responsible for rooting out corruption within the Party. In the late 1990s, Premier Zhu Rongji instructed investigators to "grab the big and release the small," offering immunity to those who took small bribes, if they agreed to cooperate and turn in the big bosses. A kind of witness protection program was established to protect informants, a rare occurrence in China's justice system. "I have 100 coffins," Zhu said famously, "99 for corrupt officials and one for myself."[1]

★ ★ ★

Exemplifying corruption's enormity, 1999 was quite a year. About $15 billion dollars in funds for poverty relief, resettlement or water projects were misused or embezzled. This outright looting of state property included $600 million from the Three Gorges Dam project, China's controversial effort to build the world's largest hydroelectric generating facility—that 12% of the entire budget to relocate 1.13 million people was embezzled in a single year indicated the scale, and the ease, of corruption. (Stolen money was used to construct buildings, finance companies, and invest in the stock market.)[2]

One of the most egregious corruption cases occurred in the port city of Xiamen in Fujian Province; involving untold billions of dollars in smuggling, it was China's biggest such scandal in 50 years.[3] The smuggled items ranged from shoes to petroleum and luxury cars (on which 100% tariffs were avoided). Multiple branches of the Party, government, and military cooperated with the Yuanhua company, which at the peak of its crimes supplied much of China's retail petroleum market. Three ministerial officials, 26 government department directors and 86 county officials were caught in the crackdown. (It is not without significance that the official appointed Fujian governor in 2000 to clean up the mess was Xi Jinping.)

In 2000, the deputy governor of Jiangxi Province, who had amassed $650,000 by demanding 90 separate bribes, became the highest-ranking official to be executed since 1949. "For such a flagrant criminal," commented *People's Daily*, "only the death penalty is sufficient to safeguard national law, satisfy popular indignation, rectify the Party work style, and fight against corruption," adding that "in socialist China there is no special citizen in the eyes of the law, no special Party member in the eyes of Party discipline, and no one can escape the punishment of the law if he has broken the law, no matter how high his position or how powerful he is."[4]

As anti-corruption campaigns continued, 110,000 Party members were punished for corruption in 2005 and 97,260 in 2006, when 3,500 Party officials were prosecuted, including seven at or above the level of minister or governor, and 10,883 cases of commercial bribery were investigated involving about $500 million. According to Liu Fengyan, a CCDI vice secretary, common practices of corrupt officials included (in 2007): purchasing commercial housing at far below market price; using borrowed houses and vehicles and failing to return them; gambling or seeking illicit profit from gambling; and using others to invest illegally in the stock market. Liu stressed that the Party will take firm action to prevent the exchange of money for favors, tackle waste and extravagance, curb building and renovating government offices, eliminate sightseeing trips masquerading as "government-sponsored tours," and promote a thrifty style of work among Party members.[5]

Zhang Huixin, another CCDI vice secretary, noted that the organization relied largely on reports from the public to trace corrupt officials. "They are very helpful in offering first-hand clues," he said.

And there have been signs that the anti-corruption campaign is deepening. In the past the Party's approach to corruption was summed up by the Chinese proverb "to kill only mosquitoes and flies, but not fight tigers."[6] Now however, times have changed and "tigers" are being hunted. Between 2002 and 2009, the Party punished several very high-ranking officials, including Shanghai Party Chief Chen Liangyu, China's top statistician Qiu Xiaohua, Beijing Vice Mayor Liu Zhihua, Shanxi Governor Yu Youjun, China's top drug administrator Zheng Xiaoyu, Sinopec (Asia's largest oil refiner) Chairman Chen Tonghai, and Chairman Li Peiying of Capital Airports Holding (which runs 30 airports including Beijing's showcase international airport).

Chen Liangyu was the most senior official to fall in a corruption scandal in a decade; a former Politburo member, he was sentenced to 18 years for channeling public funds, including Shanghai's pension fund, into projects to enrich his friends and relatives. Liu Zhihua was in charge of Olympic construction and convicted of accepting $1 million in bribes over seven years; he was given the death penalty with a two-year reprieve. Yu Youjun, who had just been appointed Minister of Culture, was sacked for family-related corruption which had occurred years earlier; although he was not imprisoned, this "rising star," who once enjoyed senior leader support, had a precipitous and apparently permanent fall. Zheng Xiaoyu was implicated in a string of bribery cases that may have resulted in tainted pharmaceuticals; the court rejected his appeal for leniency, ruling that he was a "great danger" to the country and its reputation, Zheng was executed in 2007. Chen Tonghai, the CEO of Sinopec (2008 revenues of $160 billion), took more than $28 million in bribes; he was sentenced to death with a two-year reprieve for assisting prosecutors with other investigations (Xinhua wrote that the case had sounded an alarm for the country's state-run company leaders). Li Peiying, who ran the $15 billion conglomerate that serviced 30% of China's air passengers, embezzled about $12 million and accepted about $4 million in bribes; stating that his crimes had caused the nation severe financial loss, the court sentenced him to death and Li was executed in 2009. The cases continue.

★ ★ ★

In his report to the 17th Party Congress, President Hu Jintao said the CPC had zero tolerance for corruption, and would intensify its crackdown. "The CPC never tolerates corruption or any other negative phenomena," he stressed, adding that "resolutely punishing and effectively preventing corruption is crucial to popular support for the Party, and to its survival." Pointing out that fighting corruption will be a protracted, complicated and arduous battle, Hu called for combining punishment with prevention to address both the symptoms and causes of corruption. He also lashed out at officials who were extravagant and wasteful as well as corrupt, reserving particular criticism for Party leaders who used their position to enrich themselves.

Addressing the Discipline Commission (2007), Hu said the Party faced an "arduous fight against corruption." He told the 110 CCDI members to continue investigating "major and high-level corruption cases," and sternly punish crooked officials. And he said Party cadres must "improve their work style"—which implies being conscientious, diligent and upright, modest in lifestyle, frugal and prudent, hard-working, and focused on helping the people rather than on one's own advancement.[7]

In 2008, 33,546 corruption cases involving 41,179 officials were under investigation.[8] There was special concern that the massive investment in reconstruction following the Sichuan earthquake, and the major economic stimulus program in response to the global financial crisis, would lead to an upsurge of bribery. Officials called for greater vigilance and severe punishment for offenders.[9] Guangdong Provincial Party discipline chief Zhu Mingguo, for example, announced that severe penalties would be imposed on officials overspending on government cars, conferences, entertainment, overseas travel and other administration expenses.[10] Officials were proscribed from lavishing public money on personal gifts, bonuses, dining, travel and entertainment. In 2008, almost 400 officials in Guangzhou were charged with corruption.

Several cities are now requiring officials to make public declarations of all their assets and the financial dealings of family members. The anti-corruption regulation of Liuyang, Hunan Province, states "Officials must detail their income such as salaries, bonuses, subsidies, allowances, remuneration from part-time work, housing rents and even cash gifts and presents from others." They must also report overseas travel, use of public vehicles, whether their spouses or children live abroad, and any income or gifts from weddings, funerals or other occasions. The details are made public in newspapers, on television and online.[11]

Predictably, similar initiatives have been thwarted by unsympathetic officials across the country. Nonetheless, all officials generally now operate under stricter rules governing conflicts of interest, such as funneling business to companies run by relatives, and the use of hefty expense accounts.

Even when egregious violations are eliminated, gray areas remain. In one city I visited, for example, a certain hotel where local officials were hosting lunch was of five-star standard—but it had deliberately not been rated, I was told, because if it formally had those five stars, officials would be barred from eating there on the government tab. Similarly, while I appreciate being treated to dinner, I sometimes sense that I can be a legitimatizing opportunity for local officials to enjoy a good meal. Once, prior to an evening return flight to Beijing, I tried to beg off an early dinner, having had a late lunch—until I realized that the officials, who had worked long and hard, were anticipating the repast (quite deservedly, I thought).

★ ★ ★

Corruption flourishes in the dark crevices that are shielded by the shadow of authoritarian protectionism. Only the bright light of an investigative free press, operating without restriction or fear, and the enforcement power of a truly independent judiciary, operating under a rule of law, can root out, if not stamp out, corruption. Only the media has the motivation, temperament, manpower and resources to expose corruption optimally. The Chinese government has been using the media to publicize its anti-corruption work and, within limits, has cautiously permitted (and on occasion even encouraged) investigative reports.

In the late 1990s, Chinese social critic He Qinglian, an economist and journalist, published withering criticisms of corruption, which she defined as "power going to market." Her iconic book, *The Pitfalls of Modernization*, dealt with systemic problems of corruption at local levels. How she was able to live and publish in China during those years was something of an enigma. It's possible that the answer lay in the fact that He Qinglian, without political position to protect or sensitivities to respect, was able to say what some leaders themselves would have liked to have said.

In 1998, I interviewed He Qinglian in a tranquil park on the outskirts of Beijing. I found her to be, on the one hand, incisive, rigorous, relentless, and fearless, and, on the other hand, dogmatic, mordant, supercilious—and rather intoxicated with celebrity status. I enjoyed our talk.

He Qinglian asserted that corruption was having a profound impact on China, undermining reform and development—both by venal officials stealing state funds, and through shoddy construction projects which could lead to the collapse of public structures such as bridges and schools (which later occurred, notably, tragically, in the Sichuan earthquake).

In her opinion, the roots of China's rampant corruption lay in the political movements of the Mao era. "I have never felt that our moral degradation began with economic reform," she said, "it began much earlier. Various political movements, especially the Cultural Revolution, eviscerated traditional Chinese moral principles, most of which were based on the teachings of Confucius—for example, loyalty and trust. One of the ugliest and cruelest things that happened in the Cultural Revolution," she stated "was that the government encouraged people to betray one another by informing on one another. That alone destroyed much decency and virtue." Thus, He Qinglian said, "the Chinese people who emerged at the end of that terrible time were not the same kind of people as the ones who welcomed the Communist victory of 1949. They had become a people with no shame."

She acknowledged that "once economic reform was implemented, people became obsessed with money," but stressed: "Reform was not the problem—the real problem was what the earlier political movements had done to the people's character. . . . The market economy simply provided an opportunity for people to express the lack of values that had been engendered earlier."

Another factor, she noted, was that when reform began, "the gate to the wider world opened." People who had spent decades preoccupied with class struggle suddenly "realized that all the people in the world who they had been told needed their help to be liberated actually lived better lives than they did. In the meantime," she added, "corrupt government officials were setting a negative example, misusing power—and getting away with it. The people also discovered that in such a system, being good didn't pay off. So some people followed the example of their bad superiors."

In He Qinglian's opinion, the behavior of officials was the key factor: "In China we have a saying that 'if the upper beam is not straight, the lower ones will go aslant.' If rulers want to end corruption among the people, they must set the proper example themselves," she stressed. "If they ignore laws in the name of making money, the people will do the same. When officials are not punished for wrongdoing, it leaves the impression that it's OK to do wrong. That's why morality and ethics have deteriorated to such a degree in this country. Now, at all levels, people are risking prosecution to make money illegally."

She acknowledged that gaps between rich and poor exist in every society, but argued that, while in other countries "that gap has been created by many generations of wealth accumulation, in China it has been created by the commercialization of power." Thus, she said, "the normal order has been destroyed, and the pain we are experiencing is the result. As reform continues, pain will continue. It cannot be any other way."

He Qinglian emphasized that "I'm not saying we don't want the government involved in running society. The issue is *how* it should be involved. Government should be involved only in the areas in which it has competence, and leave the rest alone. That by itself would significantly reduce corruption. Society, then, might move closer to normalization." Two years after our meeting, in 2000, He Qinglian was demoted from her job as a journalist in

Shenzhen, and censors banned her sensational though scholarly works. In 2001, Ms. He left China for America. The silencing of one of corruption's most severe critics, at a time when the government was cracking down on corruption, underscored that, for China's leaders, the watchword remained stability. It also revealed the limits of media openness on the subject and highlighted a continuing conundrum for China's leaders: If reporting is too timid, corruption will remain concealed and flourish. If reporting is too intense, social confidence and central authority may be undermined. For China's leaders, it is a conundrum which is not soon going away.

Endnotes

1   *Time Asia*, November 2, 1998; Willy Wo-Lap Lam, *China Brief*, January 17, 2002. There are several variants of this well-known quote—Lam states it goes back to the middle 1990s—but an original source is not found. Another sardonic statement that Zhu allegedly made was at a convention of entrepreneurs (September 2001), where the premier supposedly blurted out that his enemies would "get me after my retirement."

2   "China's Three Gorges dam hit by 600 million-dollar graft scam," Agence France Presse, January 21, 2000.

3   "An Actual Record—'Xiamen Yuanhua Smuggling Case' Published," *People's Daily*, April 29, 2001. The smuggled goods were worth 53 billion yuan (about $6.4 billion) with a customs-duty evasion of up to 27 billion yuan ($3.25 billion). Foreign sources put the value at north of $10 billion.

4   "People's Daily Commentary on Hu Changqing Case," Editorial, *People's Daily*, March 9, 2000.

5   "CPC resolute in combating corruption in past five years: official," Xinhua, May 12, 2007.

6   Peter Nimerius, "Daring to Fight Tigers: Anti-Corruption Work in Contemporary China," 1997.

7   "Hu Jintao vows full-fledged crackdown on corruption" Xinhua, January 10, 2007.

8   "Net 'major force' in monitoring corruption," *China Daily*, March 26, 2009.

9   Xinhua February 23, 2009.

10 "Party must give 'good example' to avoid social unrest," AsiaNews.it, January 22, 2009.

11 Fiona Tam, "Hunan officials told to list assets," *South China Morning Post*, April 1, 2009.

Values and the New Social Contract

For all the vast economic changes brought about by reform, the greatest change in China has not been economic. The truly greatest change has been the transformation of the *spirit* of the Chinese people—how they think and how they feel—and the sense of confidence they have in their country and their future.

Change has been dazzling—not just in the construction of new buildings and modern cities but more importantly in the psychology and culture of the people, and in the new conviction that change itself is possible. Before reform, no change was possible; after reform, no change seems impossible. And, in the process, the values of the Chinese people have shifted.

Citizens at all levels, from farmers and factory workers to intellectuals and entrepreneurs, think differently. Before the market economy, for example, salespeople in stores didn't bother to assist customers; you had to ask several times before anyone would show something to you. The staff couldn't have cared less whether you bought anything—it didn't matter to them; either way they were paid the same, there was no measure of success, and they couldn't be fired.

Nowadays a salesperson's sales directly affect his or her pay: indeed, customers are sometimes intimidated by sales people who surround them, fighting to sell them anything and everything in the store.

The slogans are different too. Using slogans to form a collective psyche and forge common goals has long been part of Chinese culture, and they are still found everywhere, on building walls and factory floors, strung over the façades of public buildings and adorning the interiors of concert halls. But instead of proclaiming "Workers of the World Unite" or some other Marxist-Maoist-proletarian dictum, the slogans in today's China are focused on making people more market conscious: they proclaim the importance of the market, urging companies to compete, workers to serve their customers, and, well, everyone to get rich.

"Never Say No to the Market," Haier's slogan, is one of my favorites. Another, hanging from the ceiling of a textile factory, was written in bold, striking characters three feet high and ran for 50 feet. But it was not ranting about "U.S. Imperialism" but proclaiming "Get the South Korean Order Out in 30 Days!"

The method of communication is the same, because the underlying cultural basis is the same. But there's irony in the fact that public slogans, that traditional mechanism of collective control, now focus on making people more market-oriented and independently minded—because market-economy success requires individual initiative and creative competitiveness—which undermine that collective control. (One young executive with a science doctorate from a foreign university ridiculed the imposed necessity of "studying aphoristic, simplistic slogans in endless, wasted hours." Better to empower the best people to do their best work, he said. "The government should stop supervising businesses they cannot understand. China will either move forward or fall behind.")

Certainly there is a new spirit of individual freedom in China. Today's young people put themselves first—and since self-interest energizes free markets, this new spirit augurs well for China's continued development.

But what happens to Chinese culture in the process? Traditionally, China has been a collectivist country, unlike America, which was founded on "rugged individualism." Collectivism in China has existed since the time of Confucius—the highest good being to contribute to society. Nowadays, however, many people focus on making money. When today's young people stress the self, they are flouting Chinese tradition.

Yet elements of that tradition remain strong: people are still attached to their families and friends. And it's an oversimplification to conclude that everybody in today's China just wants to make money. And indeed, just because people want to make money doesn't mean that they are not contributing to society.

The *Pew Global Attitudes Project* found broad public acceptance of the transition to free markets: seven in ten people said they were better off in the new economy, even though this meant some would be rich while others poor. (This sentiment held across demographic groups, with even those in the low-income category believing in the benefits of free markets.)

The social changes in Chinese society that have accompanied economic development received more mixed reviews, however. Many (59%) worried that their traditional way of life was being lost.

★ ★ ★

Many in China also lament a deterioration of morals, reflected not only in extreme problems like corruption, but also in a decline in civility and courtesy. In 1998, President Jiang Zemin began a campaign to encourage good manners. It was initiated with a front-page commentary in *People's Daily*, entitled "On Stressing Decorum," which quoted Confucius, Deng Xiaoping, and Jiang Zemin, and urged people to speak to each other in a more civil fashion.[1]

"Our country has always been known as 'a land of propriety'," the commentary read, adding that "stressing civility and decorum is a fine tradition of our nation." Referring to the Confucian code of ethics, the standard of ancient Chinese gentility, it blamed the Cultural Revolution for the breakdown in contemporary manners. During that period, it said, ultra-Leftists had characterized behaving with civility, decorum, and according to the law as "bad things," and had equated good manners with feudal, capitalist, and revisionist ideals. A polite person, allegedly, was a bourgeois person.

As a result, the article said, "the fine moral heritage of ancient times and the fine achievements of other countries in building civility and decorum," had been "blindly negated" by "the long-lasting influence of Left ideology." But *People's Daily* stressed that such attitudes did not reflect true Chinese culture. Decorum, it said, was "not just a formality. It is an indispensable, important component of the effort to build socialist spiritual civilization."

Equating good manners with good socialism was a significant move towards embracing traditional culture, which had been in danger of disappearing during the era of rigid Communism. Now *People's Daily* advised that a return to past ideals would "enable our country to stand like a giant among all nations of the world with a highly civilized spiritual outlook."

The county of Zhangjiagang in Jiangsu Province was lauded as a model of such "decorous" living.[2] Here, rules and norms of behavior were codified in a Civilized Citizen's Study Book which all citizens were required not only to memorize and follow but also to post them on the walls of their homes and offices. The book listed the "six musts"—which included advice on how to speak correctly and apologize properly—and the ten "must nots"—ranging from offensive language, lewd acts, and quarreling, to the flouting of traffic laws and other "uncivilized" conduct. It also gave instructions in personal hygiene—urging citizens to wash their hands before eating or after visiting the toilet, take regular baths, trim their nails, and not to spit. The region's spotless and odor-free public lavatories were given as a model for the rest of the country to emulate.

★ ★ ★

A good illustration of changing relationships is between Chinese mainlanders and Chinese from Taiwan and Hong Kong. In the early reform era, the relationship was one of unequal power. The vast material disparity meant that mainlanders generally felt inferior—and were often made to feel so—due to their lack of expertise, financial resources, and management experience.

Now, after almost three decades of double-digit growth, mainlanders are an equal party. Shanghai business executives do not feel inferior to anyone, certainly not those in Taiwan or Hong Kong—or in London or New York, for that matter. Power has shifted: China now comes to virtually any negotiating table as a proud equal.

Individual stories echo this national transformation. In the mid-1980s, in still-poor, agrarian Dongguan in Guangdong Province, a low-level government worker had a second child and was fired for violating the rigid one-child-per-family policy. Unemployed and desperate, he was forced to do odd jobs servicing private companies just springing up in the area. Today Dongguan is one of China's wealthiest cities and he is a millionaire. His four-person family owns three cars. Now here's what's most telling. His older daughter, Kelly, worldly-wise and fluent in English, earned a master's degree from the prestigious London School of Economics. After graduation, she chose to eschew attractive offers to remain in England, and returned to Dongguan to work for the local government. A career within the official system, Kelly believes, offers her best opportunities for personal development and social contribution.

Her case is a good example of how, despite the struggles of the reform era, most Chinese believe that Communist Party rule is essential for the nation's continued development. For China's leaders, serving such people epitomizes the nation's new social contract.

★ ★ ★

Here's how the social contract works. The Chinese people now live, work and dress as they like (and do so with diversity, style and flair), choose more or less whatever entertainment appeals to them (foreign movies, local rock stars, a multiplicity of publications and television channels), and discuss whatever they like, even criticizing the government—as long as they do so privately. They may even sue the government before a judiciary that is slowly becoming independent. The one proviso is that they do not challenge the primacy of the Communist Party, or form organizations that could become sources of alternative, independent political power.

To many Westerners, this "one proviso" flouts democratic values and violates human rights—invalidating the social contract. To most Chinese, the Party's monopolistic hold on power is an acceptable part of the social contract, and to many it remains essential for proper statecraft at this time.

That's the deal, in essence, which the Chinese people—particularly the educated urban elite—have struck with their government. The contrast between the attitudes of the intelligentsia toward China's leaders in the late 1980s and early 1990s, and the views of most such people today, is startling (and to traditional Western liberals, disheartening). Then there was smoldering resentment; today there is affirmative agreement.

In the heady days of early 1989, prior to the crackdown in Tiananmen Square, politics was the hot topic, openly discussed at virtually every gathering. After the crackdown, politics was forbidden discourse for years. In 1990, it was rare for Chinese people to speak about politics in the presence of other

Chinese. I had surmised that the old fervor was just below the surface—bubbling, as it were, building.

In 1994, returning after a two-year hiatus, I was surprised to find that politics was no longer so interesting to my Chinese friends. They didn't seem to care to talk about Tiananmen anymore. The focus was economics. "I am perfectly happy for this government to remain in absolute control," one of my formerly politically active friends confided, "as long as they leave me and my company alone so we can make money." The market had opened, bringing previously unimaginable opportunities. Economic gain was the new goal.

Nowadays, the Tiananmen movement is seen by many as representing the past. To be sure, many say, the government acted improperly, overreacted—but the students of Tiananmen, they also believe, were not being realistic.

So now the Chinese people have become realistic. China's urban elites, the country's intellectual and professional leaders, still expect progressively greater degrees of freedom, and look forward to a future when full democratic principles and individual rights will prevail. Yet they stress social stability, and insist that reform needs a peaceful, stable environment to flourish. Thus they accept the new social contract, and do so not reluctantly, giving the government credit for having delivered on its part of the bargain.

This applies to many former student protestors, now in their 40s. Recently, I've begun to sense a re-emergence of political interest among such people—but these days it's a more refined political sensibility, more sophisticated, more sensitive to the need for gradual change, and always, above all, prioritizing stability as a primary good. Perhaps it's the predictable maturing of radical students into mainstream business people with vested interests in the status quo. Perhaps it's the maturing of Chinese society itself.

As one Party chief of an academic institution confided, "If I myself don't understand Marxism, don't believe in Marxism, how effective can I be in indoctrinating our students?" Yet he adamantly insists that the Communist Party must continue to be the ruling party. "Western-style democracy could fragment China," he says, adding, "If China had free elections, our president could be Zhao Benshan"—an immensely popular farmer-actor known for his homely comedy skits.

There's no question that the relationship between the Communist Party and those it governs has, over the decades of reform, changed fundamentally. It used to be that the Party set strict, often stern, ideological rules and the people had to comply or else face punishment. Now roles have, up to a point, reversed: the Party serves the people. If it does not, its power would dissipate, perhaps evaporate. The continuing success of reform, many now say, is the Party's sole claim to monopolistic legitimacy. This is the other side of China's new social contract.

★ ★ ★

This new pressure on China's leaders can be seen in their response to trouble. The number of "mass incidents"—public disturbances involving crowds of people (riots, protests, demonstrations, mass petitions)—grew rapidly from 8,700 in 1993 to 32,000 in 1999, 60,000 in 2003, 74,000 in 2004, and 87,000 in 2005—an alarming tenfold increase during the dozen years of China's greatest economic development.[3] Better communications played a part—mobile phones are efficient gatherers of the disaffected—but there was no doubt that such cases were increasing not only in number but also in seriousness. They arose from diverse local problems—principally illegal land seizures, judicial injustice, non-payment of salaries and corrupt practices of local officials—which created tension and led to clashes.

Concerned, China's leaders determined to pay more attention to public opinion. In 2008, the Party and the government announced jointly that officials could be sacked from their posts, and expelled from the Party, for poor handling of public grievances.[4] This was the first time the central authorities had announced administrative as well as Party-level penalties for such offences. And in 2009, a large-scale campaign was launched to "retrain" local ("grassroots") personnel including civil servants, police officers and judges. The CPC Organization Department, led by Politburo member Li Yuanchao—who called on cadres to "have a better grip on the situation and a deeper understanding of the grassroots"—dispatched some 10,000 inspectors to ascertain the well-being of peasants and the "governance capability" of grassroots officials.[5]

New rules were issued to check the use of heavy-handed tactics by local officials. Now they can be reprimanded for mishandling public grievances, especially if these snowball into mass incidents, and those who abuse police force and use weapons wantonly face severe punishment. Other proscribed behavior includes delays or neglect in addressing public complaints, and implementing policies which go against the public interest. The rules have teeth: following a mass disturbance in Guizhou Province, where 10,000-30,000 people marched in the streets, torching police cars and government buildings protesting the death of a teenage girl, the local Party chief and county head were both fired.[6] Recognizing that some officials lacked necessary legal knowledge and always took a hard line toward the people, the new rules sought to change such attitudes.

According to Minister of Public Security Meng Jianzhu, who oversees law-enforcement, "police officers should avoid being carried away and becoming emotional when facing complicated situations. . .[and] should avoid using excessively strong language or employing undue force." Meng, also a state councilor, advises grassroots police: "A minor incident should be solved within the village; even a major incident should be tackled within towns and townships. Do not let [societal] contradictions go all the way up to the central authorities."[7]

★ ★ ★

Another area of public concern is industrial safety. China's single-minded rush for economic development led to industrial accidents becoming horribly common—as company managers and local officials often turned a blind eye to unsafe conditions in their drive to achieve production goals and hit profit targets. Between 2001 and 2004, China suffered about a million work-related accidents and nearly 140,000 deaths each year. Coal mine deaths alone were officially over 5,000 per year, and many believed the real number was 10,000 or more.[8] Xinhua acknowledged that "quite a large number of enterprises have distorted the relationship between work safety and economic gains."[9]

In light of President Hu Jintao's heavily promoted philosophy of Putting People First, this abysmal safety record was intolerable and embarrassing. In 2004, the government adopted People First, Safety First as the theme for its third National Work Safety Month, and in 2006, it announced a five-year initiative to improve workplace safety, encouraging workers to report unsafe industrial conditions.[10]

In 2008, workplace fatalities were 91,172, and total industrial accidents were 413,700, both figures down for six years in a row and over 50% below their earlier highs. Coal mine deaths dropped to about 3,200, an improvement though still unacceptably high. China closed 1,054 illegal coal mines in 2008. Yet the government admitted that almost 80% of the country's 16,000 mines were still illegal, and that these provided 35% of China's coal production—and accounted for more than 70% of the deaths.

★ ★ ★

China's leaders were personally involved following the horrific earthquake which struck Sichuan in southwest China on May 12, 2008. Within moments, Premier Wen Jiabao appeared on CCTV and assured his countrymen that the government would lead the people to win the battle against the devastation. "Confronted with the disaster, we need composure, confidence, courage and an effective command," Wen said soberly.

Two hours later China's premier was in the air, flying to Sichuan on a hastily prepared plane. During the next four, gut-wrenching days, Wen visited almost all of the worst-hit counties, walking over rocks and tiles, comforting weeping children and encouraging rescuers. He stressed that the highest priority was to save lives, and he pressed officials and troops to implement rescue-and-relief work.

A journalist traveling with Wen posted the following blog: "Wen's entourage reaches a school in Dujiangyan where 300 students are supposedly buried. Rescue efforts are faltering. Trying to coordinate another rescue attempt, Wen falls. Minutes later his arm is visibly bleeding. A medical worker tries to put a dressing on the cut, but Wen pushes him or her away."[11]

Minutes later, Wen heard that 100,000 people were trapped in the mountains, after the only bridge to the region collapsed, making access impossible and blocking rescue work. The premier shouted into his cell phone: "No matter what, I want these 100,000 people out of danger. That's an order."

It was "the first time I've seen 'Grandpa' this fierce," the journalist blogged, referring to Wen by his endearing nickname.

Back in Beijing on May 16, Wen called numerous meetings to coordinate the massive task. Some were high level and conceptual, like preventing epidemics or providing temporary housing; some focused on critical needs such as securing milk powder for infants or the proper handling of victims' corpses. Overall guidelines were set, and detailed instructions given—such as sending 6,000 temporary houses within two days, and ordering rescue teams to reach all remote quake-hit villages within 24 hours.

No sooner had Wen left the quake's epicenter than President Hu arrived. Addressing traumatized people standing along the road, he said: "We will make every effort to rescue stranded people, treat the injured and make proper arrangements for the victims, as well as help you to rebuild your homes." He encouraged them to be strong, reassuring them that "the whole Party, army and all the people have been mobilized to support quake-relief work."[12]

Meeting a father and his injured daughter, who were taking refuge in a tent, Hu said: "We know you've suffered. . . . We feel your anguish." He then went to Beichuan Middle School, where the quake destroyed all the main buildings, crushing and killing about half of the more than 2,000 students and teachers. Knowing there were still 300 people buried in the ruins, Hu said, "Saving lives is still an urgent task. As long as there is a glimmer of hope, we should rescue them by every possible means."

Premier Wen Jiabao visits earthquake victims in their temporary housing at Jiuzhou Stadium, Mianyang, Sichuan Province (May 13, 2008; Xinhua News Agency, Yao Dawei).

Ten days after the earthquake, Premier Wen flew to Mianyang, one of the worst hit cities, and inspected by helicopter the "quake lakes," formed by landslides that blocked rivers. There was growing danger that these would burst, sending tidal waves of water and mud cascading over villages, compounding the tragedy. Careful planning was needed to drain the lakes by controlled measures, and Wen's background as a geological engineer meant he was ideal for leading the effort.

A few weeks later, Premier Wen traveled to Shaanxi and Gansu, two other earthquake-affected provinces. Visiting a rural primary school, temporarily housed in a large tent, he told the students: "The earthquake is a most vivid, most realistic lesson, a lesson that you will never forget. You have gone through so much and heard many stories from others. All of them reflect the strength and solidarity of the people of our nation, and the spirit of friendship they demonstrate when they help each other. You are all very strong in the face of the disaster. Hardship only makes one stronger."

The Chinese people were captivated by their leaders' response to the crisis. All media was in constant-coverage mode, and internet blogs were afire. One online forum was called "Premier Wen, we love you." In awkward but heartfelt English, one Chinese publication put it this way: "A premier of China cannot be copied elsewhere."

The speed and competence of the Sichuan earthquake rescue-and-relief efforts won the world's admiration. But in China, where it came soon after tensions with the West over riots in Tibetan areas, the government's response to the earthquake was seen by many Chinese as proof that foreign criticism of their country's human rights record was unfair. When I expressed my condolences to a Chinese friend, a sometime critic of the government, he replied with vigor: "The West attacks China for its human rights policies, but what about the rights of the earthquake victims? What other government could have responded so rapidly, so efficiently, saved so many lives?"

Liu Yunshan, CPC Publicity Department head, enriched this argument when I met him some five weeks after the quake. "In this month alone, the Politburo Standing Committee has already held five specific meetings to discuss earthquake relief work—several late at night," he said. "The West is always attacking us on human rights—but these meetings, and the monumental relief work we have done, reflect our deep respect for human rights!" Liu said China welcomed "constructive and good-intentioned criticism," but stressed that "We Chinese resent it when some Western politicians and media make irresponsible remarks about China. There is no way we will accept accusations with ulterior motives. Obviously," he acknowledged, "China still has many problems. We have a population of 1.3 billion. It's only reasonable to have many problems. We have to work very hard to overcome these problems. But the trend is positive: our problems are 'growing pains.'"

And there is evidence that many in China support the view that the kind of response shown after the earthquake would not have been possible with a governance system of competing political parties. It ties in to the argument that, with 1.3 billion people in grossly disparate stages of development, protecting lives and providing basic living requirements is the highest priority, and for this, a strong government with a single ruling party is required.

★ ★ ★

Indeed, the readiness of Westerners to criticize China for human rights violations frustrates or infuriates many Chinese, even those of liberal leanings. Westerners extrapolate from the infringed rights of isolated individuals—dissident scholars, activist lawyers, religious leaders, wayward bloggers—to the well-being of all Chinese society, and thus tend to equate life in China today to life under authoritarian regimes with which Westerners are familiar, such as the police-state communism of the defunct Soviet Empire, North Korea or Mao's rigidly closed society.

Yet to do so is to miss the new individual freedoms in China, and to overlook the distinction, obvious to most Chinese, between voicing private opinions and organizing public demonstrations. (For example, organizing to oppose apparently non-political matters, such as local land appropriations, is deemed a far greater threat than individual expressions of antigovernment complaints.)

Religion reflects the new reality. Though it is not overtly encouraged, the government is increasingly appreciative of the positive role that religion can play in the personal lives of some of its citizens. The government does not coerce either belief or non-belief in God, though it does watch out for "cults" which might cause social turmoil or personal injury.

Back in the 1950s, everyone read Mao's little red book—in some sense it was the Chinese Bible. Now, while Mao's thoughts may be appreciated in their historical context or poetic beauty, they are no longer venerated, while actual Bibles can be found everywhere in China. And like people everywhere, some in China find comfort in the Bible; they form support groups, just as people do in America, to share their problems and explore their beliefs. "Underground" and "house" churches in China, religious groups not sanctioned by the state, are flourishing. But unless these worshippers sit themselves down in the town square, or prescribe dangerous behavior for their adherents, the government doesn't much mind.

Growing social freedoms were highlighted by the *Pew Global Attitudes Project*, presented earlier, which found that more than eight out of ten Chinese citizens were satisfied with their country's direction, the highest in the world. To a neutral observer, it may seem ironic, even astonishing, that countries like America, Britain, Japan, where the satisfaction level hovers around two to three out of ten, continuously criticize China and China's system of governance. Two factors may be working here.

Firstly, "satisfaction" is judged relatively, so that how one feels is measured more as a moving trend than as an absolute condition. A person who just lost one million of her ten million dollars invested in the stock market will feel worse than a similar person who just made one thousand on her investment of eight thousand dollars, even though the first person has nine million and the second person has nine thousand. That's human nature. In China, improvement has been palpable.

Secondly, in China, the satisfaction of the majority is overly weighted as compared to the rights of minorities. A Western democracy prides itself not in how it serves its majority but in how it treats its minorities. Is this a legitimate criticism of China, which has little tolerance for dissidents, and treats criminals harshly? Perhaps, but most Chinese people do not think so. They argue that it's easy for countries with much higher standards of living to be so magnanimous. Allow us to bring our living standards up to yours, they say, and we will be equally magnanimous.

Most educated Chinese are proud to be building their country, for the first time in centuries, into a respected and respectable nation, and are dumbfounded when all they have accomplished—including the freedoms they have won—remain unappreciated and often unknown. Some fall prey to conspiracy theories, imagining that America's motive is to keep China on the defensive, and that the US media's keen interest in human rights, which the Chinese consider biased and badgering, is simply a pretext.

★ ★ ★

Yet while it's surely true that China has made enormous progress in human rights, and that it fears that too-rapid change will threaten its vaunted stability, it's also true—and the country's leaders recognize this—that it must make additional progress. For China to claim its rightful role as a great nation, it will need the maturity and self-confidence to grant its citizens greater freedoms of expression.

So how do China's leaders see their mission today? Many foreigners assume that their primary interest is to maintain power for the sake of power itself. I believe that senior Chinese leaders today are honorable and patriotic people, whose primary interest lies in the well-being of their citizens and the development of their country, and that they are serious about wanting to develop a real democracy consistent with Chinese realities (Chapter 39).

Their aim is not to emulate a Western-style system, but nonetheless to give substantial powers to the people, and to build a civil society—a Harmonious Society—in fact as well as in words. In such a society, the role of government is to create an environment in which citizens have comfortable livelihoods, live their own lives, and solve their own problems with minimal interference. It is a society where the ruling party and the government serve the people, not the other way around.

I also believe China's leaders recognize that the full economic energies of the Chinese people will not be realized until increased political freedoms, including freedom of the press, are realized, and that such freedoms are necessary for China to reach its rightful position in the world, as a leading power and a proud people. Again, pride is a prime guiding principle.

However, China's senior leaders also feel that Western-style freedoms must be restricted until they are sure that they can maintain social stability, the second prime guiding principle. If Western-style democracy were to come too soon, they believe, the country, with its huge and diverse population, might well be torn apart by political infighting. The key is to continue to raise the standard of living for all Chinese: once the majority of the population, including 900 million peasants and migrant workers, are enjoying reasonably good lives, there will be every incentive for the citizenry to maintain the status quo, and the forces of chaos and fragmentation will have no grounds to foment trouble.

To some Westerners, the bargain may sound Faustian—to compromise human rights and freedoms for the sake of national pride, national stability, and economic gain. Yet most Chinese—especially the educated—still view the rights of the collective as more valuable than those of the individual, and believe that such rights are best protected by the maintenance of social stability and the continuing preeminence of the Party.

Notwithstanding widespread disregard (and even contempt) for the Party's past ideological excesses, many Chinese citizens still respect the Party's avowed responsibility for the people's welfare. Moreover, the Party offers "socialism with Chinese characteristics" as a framework for social conscience—and an expression of Chinese nationalism.

Wang Chen (center), director and minister of the State Council Information Office (Beijing, October 2008).

In 2009, China issued its first National Human Rights Action Plan—a lengthy document with sections on Economic, Social and Cultural Rights; Civil and Political Rights; and Rights of Ethnic Minorities, Women, Children, Elderly People and the Disabled.[13] Calling human rights "a long-cherished ideal of mankind and also a long-sought goal of the Chinese government and people," the document promises to "ensure people's civil and political rights" through improving democracy and the rule of law.

"It's dedicated to improving human rights through solving actual problems," said Information Minister Wang Chen, whose office issued the action plan "in accord with United Nations Human Rights declarations."[14] "It serves as a strong propeller to push forward China's human rights cause," Wang said. Intriguing was the subheadline in the official Xinhua announcement: "China has a long road ahead in its efforts to improve its human rights situation."

In another example of China's media calling for greater human rights for common people, a 2009 Xinhua commentary excoriated incompetent officials who blame mass-incident demonstrations and protests on "people ignorant of the truth being manipulated by schemers." The state news agency wrote that "Blaming people for not having all the facts is no different from saying they are unable to distinguish right from wrong, and that is simply untrue." Xinhua then proceeded to give warning that officials who let protests spin out of control would be punished.[15]

Endnotes

1   *People's Daily*, "On Stressing Decorum," January 25, 1998
2   Jasper Becker, *The Chinese* (Oxford University Press, 2002), 99-101.
3   Although the government ceased releasing official statistics in 2005, other sources reported 90,000 "mass incidents" in 2006 and more than 80,000 in 2007 (Joseph Fewsmith, "Social Order in the Wake of Economic Crisis," *China Leadership Monitor*, No. 28).
4   "Officials face sack for bad public work," *China Daily*, July 25, 2008.
5   Willy Lam, "CCP Campaign for a New Generation of 'Red and Expert' Officials," *China Brief*, Vol. IX, Issue 13, June 24, 2009.
6   Joseph Fewsmith, "An 'Anger-Venting' Mass Incident Catches the Attention of China's Leadership," *China Leadership Monitor*, No. 26.
7   Willy Lam, June 24, 2009.
8   January 17, 2009; Xinhua, January 28, 2009; BBC News, August 29, 2006.
9   Xing Zhigang, "China's mining sector sounds the alarm," *China Daily*, December 3, 2004; Cui Xiaohuo, "Coal mine deaths fall to 14-yr low," January 17, 2009; Xinhua, January 28, 2009; "China to tackle workplace deaths," BBC News, August 29, 2006.
10 "China to tackle workplace deaths," BBC News, August 29, 2006.
11 Jonathan Ansfield, "Wen Jiabao: Man of the Moment," *Newsweek*, May 17, 2008.
12 "Chinese President encourages quake victims to overcome difficulties," Xinhua, May 16, 2008
13 "China publishes national human rights action plan," Xinhua, April 13, 14, 2009.
14 One example in the Human Rights Action Plan was safeguarding detainee's rights, especially relevant after media reports and public outcry over prisoner maltreatment and deaths. According to the plan, corporal punishment, abuse, insulting detainees or extracting confessions by torture will be strictly prohibited.
15 "Xinhua calls time on protest blame game," *South China Morning Post*, July 30, 2009.

Part III

Doing Reform

Provincial Pictures of Reform

From outside, China is often perceived as one huge mass, homogeneous and undifferentiated, all the same across the vast country. This is wrong. In fact, China is heterogeneous, varying greatly from region to region.

Relationships between the provinces and the central government have not always been harmonious. There is a natural tendency for local officials everywhere to promote their own areas, even if their plans are not in the best interest of the country as a whole. But in China, in the early reform era, central government control was weaker than in other countries, certainly weaker than it is today, and provinces were much freer to flout Beijing's directives and get away with it—for example, not paying proper taxes or not repaying state-funded loans.

In those days, when provincial leaders met national leaders, it was not uncommon for them to express total support for Beijing's policy, then find a way to show that their particular province was in a unique situation, or had special difficulties, which meant that the policy could not be implemented there. Sometimes these arguments had merit; often they did not.

The story is told that at a 1994 conference of provincial governors, a time of dangerous economic overheating and inflation, President Jiang Zemin and Vice Premier Zhu Rongji asserted their austerity policy and denounced local protectionism.[1] Jiang set the tone by asking one governor the price of a *jin* [just over a pound] of eggs in his province. "A little more than three yuan," the governor answered. Zhu Rongji interrupted: "I don't think so," he said. "I was there a few days ago; the price was over five yuan."

Every governor was asked to report his province's inflation and growth rates for 1994 and to forecast rates for 1995. Each of them gave an inflation rate that was no higher than the growth rate. The figures were not only implausible, they were impossible—since for the entire country inflation well exceeded growth. That evening Jiang asked his staff to write a tough commentary for *People's Daily*, instructing the regions to "defend consciously the authority of the center."

In the years that followed, provincial independence has been largely reined in. Yet they continue to operate in vastly different circumstances. And local leaders, appropriately, seek solutions suited to their areas. It makes provincial governance challenging—and a proving ground for future national leaders.

As noted earlier, in 2005 and 2006 I had the exhilarating (and exhausting) opportunity of visiting more than 35 Chinese cities, meeting local leaders in different sectors and ordinary people from all walks of life. In early 2009, I again made extensive trips to several key provinces and municipalities—including Guangdong, Zhejiang and Tianjin—meeting political and business leaders, and speaking with common citizens and the media, particularly in light of the devastating financial crisis. Both the cacophony of local issues and the commonality of national concerns were revealing.

★ ★ ★

Several of these trips were to east China's Zhejiang Province. In February 2005, and again in March 2006, I met Xi Jinping, then provincial Party secretary, at the West Lake Guest House in Hangzhou, Zhejiang's capital. In

Xi Jinping, Party secretary of Zhejiang Province (later Politburo Standing member, vice president of China, and secretary of the Secretariat), with Robert Lawrence Kuhn and Adam Zhu (left) (February 2005).

May 2006, I (with Adam Zhu) advised the province on its 2006 US-China Zhejiang Week activities, which were linked to Secretary Xi's visit to the U.S, and aimed at promoting Zhejiang's development. Such independent initiatives by individual provinces epitomize the creativity, resourcefulness and freedom of thinking which China's local governments must develop to compete in the global economy. It is also a sign of China's increasing pluralism.

Zhejiang has about 50 million people, modest for a Chinese province, but its per-capita GDP is the nation's highest. In 2005 it reached $3,400. And as new Zhejiang Party Secretary Zhao Hongzhu noted when I met him in 2009, the figure has kept increasing, reaching $6,000 in 2008.[2]

In fact, for 30 years or so, GDP growth averaged a sizzling 13% annually. Secretary Zhao explained how an agrarian province with few resources had become an economic powerhouse—emphasizing the role of system reform and the emancipation and innovation of ordinary people.

The prime generator of Zhejiang's success has been private companies. The province is highly entrepreneurial—and not burdened with heavy industries of the past, which have stymied other provinces. Of Zhejiang's 680,000 enterprises, 500,000 are private. The private sector contributes 70% of total output value, pays 60% of local taxes, and provides 90% of all jobs. This entrepreneurial approach has had a significant influence across China, where it is known as the Zhejiang Model.

Under Xi Jinping's leadership, the province pioneered integration of private and public sectors; deepened governance reform with modern systems, checks-and-balances, transparency for selecting officials; and worked to ameliorate imbalances among social groups. Maintaining harmony between business owners and migrant workers, crucial for both economic development and social well-being, is a continuing concern. For example, Zhejiang eliminated China's long-established residency requirement [*hukou*] so that people from rural areas could move into urban areas without loss of social services. This was significant.

Opening-up has been equally critical. According to Secretary Zhao, about 4.5 million Zhejiang people do business outside the province, and about 1 million do so abroad; Zhejiang companies trade with virtually every country on earth, and have 3,500 offices in 110 countries; likewise, 84 of the world's 500 largest corporations have formed 200 joint ventures in the province. In response to the financial crisis, Zhejiang launched 81 investment projects and provided financial support to small and medium-sized companies, while seeking to upgrade its industries.

An analysis by the Chinese Academy of Sciences of the quality of financial assets of 291 cities in China concluded that of the top 13 cities, nine were from Zhejiang, including the number one and two in the entire country: Hangzhou and Wenzhou.[3] Of the 500 largest privately-owned companies in China, 118 were headquartered in Zhejiang, the most of any province.

Zhejiang's development is palpable—not only in the economic prowess of its manufacturing plants but also in its cultural vitality, new roads, and enhanced school systems. All children receive a complete education: 15 years of schooling, three years of preschool through high school—the first province to do so.

The province is on the leading edge of copyright enforcement, taking an aggressive stance against piracy—because its leaders want to uphold the law and protect foreign companies, and also because Zhejiang companies have developed strong local brands and demand protection.

Yet Zhejiang's success makes further changes necessary, indeed inevitable. Much of its transformation, like that of China as a whole, was founded on low-cost production. In Zhejiang's main industries, such as textiles and clothing, low wages for workers were decisive in building international market share. This resulted in some (entrepreneurs) becoming rich, causing severe economic imbalances.

Now, President Hu Jintao's goal of constructing a Harmonious Society requires that society be rebalanced, which means that workers' salaries must increase. This will make it increasingly difficult for China in general, and Zhejiang in particular, to remain a low-cost producer. Thus innovation is essential to maintain growth, by moving up the value curve and producing higher margin goods. It's a national objective set by President Hu and taken seriously in Zhejiang. Companies are now formulating transformational strategies, such as via automation, proprietary brands, or company retail stores. It's something they know they must do.

When I met Party Secretary Xi in Zhejiang, he emphasized that "the key," to implementing national strategies "is how to apply the spirit of the Party's guidelines to the realities of the local area, so as to formulate specific policies which can be implemented effectively." Thus in Zhejiang, "meticulous investigation" of the Scientific Perspective on Development had resulted in what Xi dubbed the Double Eight Strategy, which referred to the province's eight competitive advantages, and eight measures for action which would result in "a better Zhejiang." President Hu's vision of a Harmonious Society, meanwhile, had inspired Secretary Xi to propose several systematic initiatives like Safe Zhejiang, Cultural Construction, and Political Construction, which emphasized the rule of law and opened the Party's governance mechanisms.

Such local interpretation of national goals meant, according to Xi Jinping, that "we are laying a solid foundation on which we can build full-scale modernization...in line with the realities of Zhejiang." In addition to increasing per-capita GDP, Xi stressed that they were enhancing culture and education, developing the countryside and underdeveloped regions (including improving rural healthcare), and focusing on energy conservation. "We hope to decrease our current energy consumption per GDP unit by 15%," Xi said. By 2010, he announced, "we are expecting that all of Zhejiang's indexes will have reached or surpassed those set by the state as signifying a well-off society," Xi said.

He acknowledged that because of Zhejiang's leading economic position, "we are now encountering some problems ahead of other provinces, such as environmental issues, resource sourcing and allocations, and the demand for upgraded industrial talent."

Solutions included greater innovation to improve core competitiveness, and "strengthening education and training programs to cultivate qualified talent (and also importing talent from other places)," Xi noted. And he stressed the need to "coordinate and balance" various interests, in order to build a harmonious society "in a phase characterized by rapid economic growth and conflicts between interest groups."

Zhejiang's statistics, current and forecasted, were impressive, but more so were Xi's passion and commitment. Not only did he know plans and details, he loved discussing them. To conclude our meeting, he invited me back, suggesting that we have more detailed discussions, horizontal by geography and sectors, and vertical over time. The opportunity did not arise, as within a year, Xi Jinping was appointed Party secretary of Shanghai and then elevated to the Politburo Standing Committee and elected vice president of China.

★ ★ ★

Liaoning Province in China's northeast faced different issues. As an old industrial center which had fallen behind during China's reforms, it had

Li Keqiang (center), Party secretary of Liaoning Province (later Politburo Standing member and executive vice premier) (Shenyang, May 2005).

massive state-owned enterprises (SOEs) which were structurally ill-suited for a knowledge-based, consumer-driven market economy.

When then Party Secretary Li Keqiang (now Politburo Standing member and executive vice premier) championed President Hu's new national policy of Revitalizing the Northeast, he faced the challenge not only of revitalizing SOEs, but also of creating a fertile environment for private businesses.

Within two weeks of arriving in 2004, Li Keqiang left his footprints across the province, visiting one city almost every day.[4] His plan was to build Liaoning's economy on three economic pillars—the Jinzhou Bay region in the southwest; Shenyang, the capital, in the center; and Dalian, the flourishing city on the sea—and to connect Liaoning's five ports.

In the two major urban clusters, Shenyang and Dalian, Li targeted specific categories where world-class industry could develop, such as equipment manufacturing. He also advanced new rural construction and environmental protection. A major initiative was to renovate Liaoning's poor residential areas, the large-scale shantytowns, so that 1.2 million people could move into new homes.

The tale of two Liaoning cities, Anshan and Dalian, gives sense of Secretary Li's achievements. Anshan, in central Liaoning, was once renowned as "China's capital of iron and steel," but the large plants were archaic and losing money, and the hard-working people were suffering. When I visited Anshan I was moved by citizens' commitment to rebuild their city. I could sense annoyance that others might think that their falling behind economically was somehow due to their lack of intelligence or dedication, rather than the product of historical circumstances. Anshan had played a major role in China's initial industrialization and Ashan residents felt they should be appreciated for that contribution—but they also recognized that historical contribution is easily forgotten, and were determined to create anew.

The city's central squares were filled with large abstract sculptures—dramatic works of arresting artistry, daring shapes and colors and surfaces and angles. Of all the cities I visited in China, Anshan, despite its economic woes, had the most innovative public art. The sculptures seemed to radiate, well, confidence. Combined with the people's spirit, they symbolized Anshan's hope. And under Li Keqiang, the city's industrial revitalization began with mergers and restructuring of major steel plants.

Dalian, on a peninsula between the Yellow Sea to the east and the Bohai Sea to the west, has become one of China's most energetic areas. From high tech to high fashion, Dalian is a pioneering metropolis; it has become China's leading center for IT outsourcing, and in 2007 was the inaugural venue of Summer Davos—the World Economic Forum's annual meeting of New Champions (emerging companies). The setting was a natural way for Li Keqiang, virtually certain to become one of China's top leaders in 2012, an opportunity to meet with foreign dignitaries and heads of multinational corporations.

During the 17th Party Congress (2007), before his widely anticipated promotion to central leadership was announced, Li Keqiang spoke with the media. Pleasant, confident and relaxed, though side-stepping personal questions about his own career (slightly apologetically), he stressed that: "With the support of media friends, Liaoning people hope that we can realize the great rejuvenation of Liaoning!"

A former leader of Peking University's student union, Li pointed out that even senior officials "also need to study while we are working. Otherwise, our work will lack originality." His comment was noteworthy for two thoughts: first, "originality," the key word; and second, how originality happens, not by accident or genius, but by "study." It reflected President Hu's push for China to become creative and innovative, to use new thinking to solve complex problems now manifest in virtually every area of national development.

★ ★ ★

In Jiangsu Province, then Party Secretary Li Yuanchao recognized that even in one of China's most prosperous provinces, income disparity was a serious problem (between the regions north and south of the Yangtze River), and

Li Yuanchao, Party secretary of Jiangsu Province (later Politburo member and head of the CPC Organization Department) (Nanjing, March 2006).

that economic development must be balanced with cultural development to create a truly "well-off" society.

Li's "Jiangsu vision" included international and regional cooperation, an emphasis on science and technology, sustainable development, culture and all-around human development. Li called Jiangsu a "microcosm of China itself," and his coordinated growth strategy provides a model which helps other provinces deal with diversity and complexity. During the market reform process, Jiangsu transformed an economy where state-owned and collective enterprises accounted for 90% of capital into a mixed economic structure, where state-owned, private, and foreign-funded enterprises compete equally. In 2008, Jiangsu's GDP was about $435 billion, with over 700 enterprises invested by 280 of the world's top 500 corporations.

Jiangsu's Four Priorities are enriching the people, developing science and education, consolidating environmental protection, and reinforcing resource conservation work. In 2006, Jiangsu's 119 colleges and universities provided higher education to 36% of its college-age youth. Emissions of main pollutants decreased by 3.3% compared to the year before. Energy consumption per unit of GDP, a scrutinized statistic, fell by 4%.

The provincial government's policy of the Three Haves and Four Ensures (Chapter 11) transformed 152,000 barely habitable grass huts into brick houses in three years. For those with per-capita living space of less than eight-square meters, the Nanjing municipal government reduced their rent, granted rent subsidies, or provided them with new apartments at low rent. Though still a work-in-progress, the average per-capita living space increased to 12-square meters.

Perhaps nothing says more about Jiangsu's achievements than the fact that one of its cities, Yangzhou, won the 2006 UN Habitat Scroll of Honor Award, the world's most prestigious human settlement prize, awarded for improving the living conditions of urban centers, and implementing sustainable development. It recognized Yangzhou (former President Jiang Zemin's hometown) for its "conservation of the old city and improving residential environment."

Within just five years, Yangzhou (population 1.28 million) transformed itself into a clean, modern city. The municipality invested $2 billion to construct infrastructure, and guaranteed the supply of water, electricity and gas to the poor. Cooperating with local real-estate companies, it offered land buyers low prices and waived government fees to enable land ownership.

Ji Jianye, the Yangzhou Party secretary, pledged to "accelerate the construction of Yangzhou into a city of wealth, harmony, beauty and rule of law." Notably, modernization was achieved while conserving its intangible cultural heritage. "Human beings are at the center of concern for sustainable development," Ji emphasized.

Secretary Li Yuanchao kept a low-profile when inspecting Jiangsu. He traveled with few people and requested simple receptions. Often he wouldn't even inform local officials when he would visit. He liked speaking directly to the people. He would often walk the streets and lanes of Jiangsu cities, inquiring about people's lives and work. At convenience stores, he would ask customers about commodity prices and quality. He would converse with shop owners about their revenues and management styles.

In 2003, Li led a Jiangsu delegation on a research visit to Zhejiang Province, the center of entrepreneurship in China.[5] Li recognized that Jiangsu needed to learn from Zhejiang, its neighbor and sometimes rival, about private sector development and the entrepreneurial spirit. That year Li characterized the new Jiangsu Spirit—entrepreneurial spirit, innovative spirit, and strive-for-excellence spirit—and the Three-Create Spirits—create businesses, create novelty, and create excellence.

★ ★ ★

In Shandong Province, with more than 90 million people and China's second largest GDP ($603 billion in 2010), former Party Secretary Zhang Gaoli (now Politburo member and Tianjin Party secretary) built on traditional strengths by leveraging the province's industrial power, and capitalizing on its rich culture and civilization. (Shandong was the birthplace of the great Chinese philosophers Confucius and Mencius.) Zhang's goal was to enrich reform by balancing material and spiritual civilization.

An economist by training, Zhang Gaoli had come to Shandong in 2002 from Shenzhen, where he was Party secretary. Zhang has asserted that any idea that is in line with international practice and conducive to innovation and development may be tried—and tried boldly.

Yet while stressing that building the economy is the top priority ("without development there is no way out, without growth we would have no material strength and no problem could be solved," he said), Secretary Zhang also believes that "human development should be coordinated with nature so as to achieve sustainability," and that "our social development is lagging behind our economic development." He said "there are still many unbalanced, uncoordinated elements in Shandong's economy" and he insisted "we must have the vision to strive for coordinated, sustainable, and balanced development of society, economy, regions, human being and nature."[6]

Shandong was a pioneer in attracting investment to drive economic growth—it was the first province to top RMB 1 trillion in investment. Secretary Zhang focused on this personally, using his natural skills as if he were a high-powered investment banker. He called for Shandong to increase its special relationship with nearby South Korea and Japan, and in 2004, he led a delegation to Sweden, Denmark, and Austria, visiting multinational corporations (Ericsson, Volvo, ABB). Several large-scale projects resulted, including advanced technologies in energy-conservation and sustainable development.

Yet Zhang also sought to balance the province's future growth by increasing domestic consumption, developing the service sector, and strengthening the local financial industry. And he stressed that Shandong, with a large rural population, could not neglect the rural economy: "We encourage specific practices that are optimally suited for different regions, whether forestry, fruit trees, vegetables, and pasture land," he explained, "so that we can increase the output value per unit area of cultivation and increase farmers' incomes."

Zhang emphasized that his government had appraised each of the province's 140 counties: "We used dozens of indexes—economic, social, education, healthcare, and the like," he said. "This facilitates optimizing strategies as well giving awards." As a result, Shandong counties were categorized into three tiers: 30 developed; 30 underdeveloped; 80 in-between—and appropriate strategies devised for each.

Zhang Gaoli enumerated six principles of provincial leadership: 1) seek new ideas actively; 2) create favorable environments (stable and harmonious); 3) think clearly about complex problems (e.g., optimizing industrial structure); 4) have flexible systems (encompassing all aspects of society, including culture, media and sports); 5) be down to earth, do practical things, always follow through; and 6) build a strong team. "Results count more than words," he told me more than once.

"I always tell my co-workers that opportunities are everywhere," Zhang concluded. "If you are quicker in seizing the first opportunity, you will have advantages in seizing future opportunities."

★ ★ ★

For China's inland provinces, however, opportunities are not always so obvious. Jiangxi is a good example: a land-locked, mid-sized province of 40 million people, it sits in the shadow of its highly developed coastal neighbors—Guangdong, Fujian, and Zhejiang.

During his posting as Jiangxi Party secretary, Meng Jianzhu, now a state councilor and minister of Public Security, sought to accelerate development by, first, an unwillingness to accept second-class status, and second, empowering and energizing officials to think creatively, and not be afraid of introducing innovative ideas and taking careful risks.

The core of the strategy was to leverage Jiangxi's competitive advantages, such as lower labor costs, natural resources, rich history, and magnificent scenery. Poyang Lake, for example, is the largest freshwater lake in China, and home each winter to more than 4000 white cranes, 95% of the world's population—symbolizing the region's environmental excellence.

When I visited in 2005, I found Jiangxi to be second-to-none in "can-do" enthusiasm and optimism. It was evident in formal meetings with senior leaders and informal conversation with common people. One didn't hear excuses in Jiangxi. Though in times past some blamed the province's lagging development on its rich provincial neighbors—siphoning off foreign capital and poaching talented people—Jiangxi people now seemed ready to make their own mark. The province's economic operating principle was Help Investors to Succeed—and it was striking that the province's top officials did not see it as beneath their dignity to attend to detail personally, including working with potential investors on specific projects.

In Henan, then China's most populous province with almost 100 million people, Party Secretary Xu Guangchun was implementing the nationally-mandated Central Strategy. In addition to developing Henan's agricultural industries, he focused on stimulating new industry, in particular on leveraging Henan's central location—the province is almost equidistant between East and West, North and South—as a logistics and distribution center.

Attempting to break out of limitations imposed by its land-locked location, Henan introduced some radical policies. In 2008, Shangqiu city launched an initiative to encourage residents to start private businesses.[7] Under the banner of "greatly emancipating minds," it offered civil servants, often the most capable people in local areas, financial incentives to resign from their government posts and become entrepreneurs. They were offered a lump sum of their average monthly salary in the previous year multiplied by five times the number of years they had served, and they were allowed to register a business with zero capital.

The policy reflected the extent to which officials were prepared to go to promote new thinking. But it was not without controversy. Commentators complained that it would enable officials nearing retirement to enrich themselves without having to do any work, and that it might violate regulations

Yuan Chunqing, governor of Shaanxi Province (Xi'an, August 2007).

Han Zheng (right), mayor of Shanghai, with Robert Lawrence Kuhn and pianist Dora Serviarian Kuhn (Shanghai, January 2005).

restricting conflict of interests. "Emancipating the mind," pundits wrote, should not be used as a magic password to skirt the law.

Other central provinces are also seeking ways of catching up with coastal regions. In Hubei, Party Secretary Luo Qingquan stressed that in the wake of the financial crisis, the province should do its best to "turn challenges into opportunities and translate pressure into motivation," promoting integration of industry and agriculture, and capitalizing on its "late-start advantages." Governor Li Hongzhong stressed that Hubei must play the "central region card," leveraging its position in the center of China, and encourage foreign capital to transfer industry to the province from coastal areas in order to lower labor costs.

All over China, provincial leaders are seeking approaches best suited to their local situations—and showing a willingness to be flexible and innovate. Yuan Chunqing, the governor of Shaanxi, for example, has called for more "green investment" and urged local governments not to sacrifice the environment on the altar of economic growth. He stressed that officials should assess the environmental impact of investments, especially energy exploration projects, and that China's underdeveloped western regions must be on guard against industries seeking to transfer pollution from eastern regions.

In Fujian Province, Party Secretary Lu Zhangong focused on building up the West Taiwan Strait Economic Development Zone. Its importance lay not only in helping to develop Fujian's economy, but also because Fujian was on the "front line" of "peaceful integration with Taiwan," and thus vital for regional stability. I was struck by Secretary Lu's energy and joy in promoting Fujian; if he'd been born in the West, and hadn't gone into politics, he could well have been running a major advertising company.

In Shanghai, Mayor Han Zheng has promoted the Four Leads (taking the lead in changing the development mode, enhancing independent innovation, implementing reform and opening-up, and building a harmonious socialist society). He has also focused on the Four Centers strategy, which involves Shanghai becoming an international center for finance, shipping, trade and economy—and on the goal of making Shanghai a "modern cosmopolitan city" by 2020.

Reforming China's provinces requires massive transformation, and, inevitably, all will not be linearly positive or trouble free. As such, honest mistakes should not damper creativity or reduce capacity for risk. To construct President Hu's Harmonious Society, creativity and risk are essential.

Endnotes

1 *Lien Ho Pao* (Hong Kong), January 8, 1995, 7 (BBC).
2 The large jump in GDP per capita in dollar terms between 2005 and 2008 is caused by the appreciation of Chinese currency as well as GDP annual growth.
3 Li Yang and Robert Lawrence Kuhn, *China's Banking and Financial Markets: The Internal Research Report of the Chinese Government*, John Wiley & Sons, 2007, Appendix, 14-1.
4 Caijing, October 25, 2007.
5 Author's conversation with Qiu He, Kunming, October 2008.
6 Author's meeting with Zhang Gaoli, Jinan, June, 2006.
7 Wu Zhong, "China's 'cats' mistake cream for mice," Asia Times Online, June 13, 2008.

20

Regional Dragonheads: Pudong (Shanghai) and Binhai (Tianjin)

China's new economy has three engines—three "dragonheads" facing the sea —which drive development of the southern, eastern and northern regions of the country. They are the legacy of three generations of leaders: in the 1980s, Deng Xiaoping developed China's south coast, the Pearl River Delta, centered on Guangdong Province; in the 1990s, Jiang Zemin built up the Yangtze River Delta on China's east coast, centered on Shanghai and including the neighboring provinces of Jiangsu and Zhejiang. In recent years, Hu Jintao has focused on revitalizing the northeast, building up the northern Bohai Sea coastal region, centered on Tianjin.[1]

Each of these "dragonheads" has a vitalizing "eye": Shenzhen in Guangdong; Pudong New Area in Shanghai; and, most recently, Binhai New Area in Tianjin. Each was created as a radical vision of economic development; each highlights China's determination to transform itself with unprecedented scope and speed. Pudong is an amazing story.

★ ★ ★

Shanghai is the world's fourth largest metropolis and China's leading economic and financial center. The name Shanghai means "on the sea," and the city lies close to the East China Sea just south of the Yangtze River estuary. Another river, the Huangpu, runs through the city, dividing it into two parts, Puxi on the west bank and Pudong on the east.

In 2001, when Shanghai hosted the annual APEC summit meeting of Asia-Pacific leaders, pictures of the spectacular skyline of Pudong financial district were beamed around the world. Yet only a decade earlier, Pudong was little more than a large expanse of farmland, crisscrossed by narrow roads and dotted here and there with run-down housing, old warehouses, and wharves along the river.

Zhao Qizheng, who became director of the Pudong New Area in 1993 and later nicknamed the Godfather of Pudong, knows how it all came to be.[2] (A reporter once remarked that Minister Zhao was "better known for his knowledge of markets than Marx." Zhao sort of liked that.) What follows is largely his story.

Pudong epitomizes Shanghai's short but fabled history. In the early 20th century Shanghai was the most prosperous city in Asia, a vibrant international community, the center of finance and trade. Shanghai was known as the Pearl of the Orient, the Paris of the East, and a paradise for risk-takers. By the 1980s, however, it had fallen on hard, dark times. From the Japanese invasion and civil war, to central planning and the Cultural Revolution, events seemed to have conspired to turn the formerly grand city into an isolated, dilapidated relic.

Under the planned economy, Shanghai was required to transfer most of the wealth it created to Beijing: indeed, prior to 1990, fully one-sixth of the central government's revenue came from the city. Shanghai's own budget, meanwhile, was barely enough to support municipal maintenance at minimum levels. Core infrastructure badly needed upgrading; basic facilities were operating at a loss. The result was overcrowded housing, traffic jams, poor communications and pollution.

Something was wrong. While other areas, particularly Guangdong, were developing rapidly, Shanghai was not designated a Special Economic Zone, and its economic star, which had shone so brilliantly in the past, dimmed further—its role in China's economy turned from vanguard to rearguard. Shanghai was likened to a "heavily loaded cart pulled by an old cow." Its growth rate in the 1980–83 period was barely half that of the country as a whole, and far less than that of the SEZs.

In 1984, Deng Xiaoping stopped in Shanghai after inspecting Shenzhen and found the contrast between the two cities stunning. Before reform began, Shenzhen had been a shantytown; now it was a vigorous, burgeoning metropolis. In contrast, the infrastructure of once-proud Shanghai could not even support the needs of its own people.

Deng criticized city officials. "I come to Shanghai every year," he said. "What I see is always the same. Can't you move faster? Next time I come I expect to see major changes!"

China's leaders wanted to resurrect the city. But the problems were political as well as physical. So severe was the stagnation in local government that it had acquired a scornful name: Shanghai Comprehensive Syndrome. When Wang Daohan attempted to promote progressive ideas during his term as mayor in the early 1980s, the city's left-leaning Party secretary responded by ordering an investigation into the *World Economic Herald,* a newspaper which was an enthusiastic advocate for reform—whose honorary chairman was Wang himself. The investigation amounted to little, but it evidenced the political divisions.

In 1985, Jiang Zemin was appointed Shanghai mayor and faced many difficulties, the most pressing being shortages of basic necessities such as food and housing. One priority was improving the transportation system. "We must change Shanghai's three faces," Jiang said, introducing plans to build a new railway station, expand the international airport, and construct a passenger ship terminal.[3]

The new mayor's most far-ranging project, however, was laying the groundwork for the future Pudong New Area, an experiment in massive regional development which would have national significance. Jiang placed former Mayor Wang Daohan, his long-time mentor, in charge of drawing up preliminary plans.[4]

Less than a year into his term, Jiang unveiled Shanghai's Comprehensive Plan, which focused on three geographical areas: the central urban area which included the vast Pudong region east of the Huangpu River (Pudong literally means "east of the Huangpu"); seven satellite cities and towns; and various other outlying towns and villages.[5] The central city would be linked with these outlying areas by high-speed trains and highways, while ring roads would connect the satellite cities. Industry would gradually expand outwards from the core, while counties and towns would develop their own businesses, mainly processing plants for vegetables, eggs and poultry. "In the next five years," Jiang declared, "Shanghai will experience the greatest changes and fastest development in its history."

When Deng Xiaoping made his annual Chinese New Year's visit to Shanghai in 1990, Wang Daohan emphasized the urgency of developing Pudong.[6] Deng concurred. "I'm retired now, but I implore you to develop Pudong." And he added, "Shanghai is our trump card. We must boost Shanghai into the fast lane."

When Deng returned to Beijing, he spoke with central leaders, now led by Jiang Zemin. Deng said "I worry a great deal" about China's decreasing speed of economic development [less than one year after June 4, 1989], and he called on senior leaders to determine which areas were best suited for large-scale development. He then added, "It will be a shortcut for us to develop Shanghai."

It marked the start of Pudong's development. In April 1990, just two days after Vice Premier Yao Yilin submitted his in-depth report, the Politburo authorized the development of Pudong. Premier Li Peng announced to the world that building Pudong was not just a local plan, but a major strategic decision of the central government. The entire decision-making process, from Deng's internal admonition to the public announcement, had taken less than two months—unprecedented speed for such an important policy.

Deng wanted to use Pudong to jump-start the economy which had stagnated since the late 1980s. Developing Pudong was also a way to break the international community's economic blockade of China, imposed after the Tiananmen crackdown. Bringing Shanghai, China's largest economic center, into play signaled to all nations that China's reforms and opening-up would now advance to a higher level and with a broader scope.

In December 1990, Shanghai Mayor Zhu Rongji appraised plans for Pudong. Work would start with the Lujiazui Financial and Trade Zone, which would become a new symbol of Shanghai, integrating China with the world and the present with the future. Situated in the bend of the Huangpu River, just opposite Shanghai's famous Bund, it was only 1.7 square kilometers in area, but as with Wall Street or the City of London, it was prime property.

In January 1991, Deng Xiaoping inspected Shanghai and expressed regret that he had not enabled the city to develop earlier: "Pudong should have been developed years earlier, like Shenzhen," Deng said. Nevertheless, he insisted that "Pudong's aim can be higher" than Shenzhen's, predicting that "the later will surpass the earlier."[7]

It was a clarion call for Shanghai's revival. And the city rose to the task, proudly proclaiming its ambition: "Develop Pudong, revitalize Shanghai, serve the whole nation, and become oriented towards the world." No longer the rearguard of China's reform and opening-up, the city began to resume its rightful role as leader.

But if Pudong was to attract substantial foreign investment, its laws and processes would have to conform to international standards. For investors to feel confident, they would require not only first-class facilities and tax preferences, but also effective and clean government. This meant transparent and standardized administration.

Such large-scale construction and massive investment made corruption a real danger. (There is a Chinese saying: "When high-rises go up, some cadres go down.") To reduce bribery and other illegal practices, Pudong instituted a series of measures which came to be known as the "three high-tension lines," namely:

- No official could single-handedly set the price of land or authorize preferential treatment.
- Contracts could be awarded only through open bidding, and determined collectively on the basis of expert appraisal.
- No official could direct business to relatives or friends.

The Pudong government also appreciated that foreign investors were concerned about security—personal security, funds security, and intellectual property rights (IPR). Early on, in 1994, China's first basic-level IPR court was established in Pudong. Over the next dozen years, the court handled more than 2,000 foreign-related IPR cases, punishing violators and protecting investors.

From the beginning, Pudong leveraged its favorable policies and open markets to attract state-level financial markets, including the Shanghai Stock Exchange (which now accounts for about 80% of the nation's total stock trading). Equally important in making Shanghai an international financial center, the central government over the years granted it favorable allowances including: foreign capital to invest in the financial services sector; foreign financial institutions to carry out RMB transactions; Pudong (along with Shenzhen) to operate offshore financial businesses on a trial basis; and the Shanghai Futures Exchange to develop new products, such as fuel oil futures.

Master architects came to perform on this vast international stage, creating majestic and arresting works, including the breathtaking Oriental Pearl TV Tower, Jinmao Tower, and World Financial Center. Pudong International Airport, an intended hub for the entire Asia-Pacific region with capacity to handle 100 million passengers annually, was designed by French architect Paul Andreu in the shape of a roc (an enormous legendary bird) spreading its wings in flight; Andreu also designed the all-glass-exterior Oriental Art Center, shaped like an iris flower in full bloom. Former UN Secretary General Boutros Boutros-Ghali described Pudong as "an international Olympics in architectural design."

By 2008, after 18 years of development, Pudong had undergone earth-shaking transformation—pioneering new forms of urbanization, industrialization, and internationalization. (Pudong's GDP leapt from RMB 6 billion in 1990 to RMB 500 billion targeted in 2011.) Shanghai had become a world-class metropolis, an international city the equal of any in the world. Jiang Zemin described Pudong as "the epitome of Shanghai's modernization, and a symbol of China's reform and opening-up."

In 2009, the State Council approved Shanghai's grand masterplan to become a "global financial and shipping center by 2020."[8] It was a dramatic, game-changing decision. Faced with the worldwide financial crisis, China's leaders designated Shanghai as a "dual center" of finance and trade, solidifying the city's national leadership, and extending its ambitions internationally. Shanghai's targets were Tokyo, London, and New York.

New policies included tax rebates and exemptions, relaxing of financial restrictions (e.g., foreign companies could issue RMB bonds), gradual convertibility of the Chinese currency, new financial markets, and an initiative to attract 1,000 world-class professionals from abroad (offering housing, healthcare, education, and residence rights). In addition, three megaprojects were under consideration—a spectacular Disneyland, the Beijing-Shanghai high-speed railway, and a large commercial aircraft factory (in addition to the 2010 World Expo)—all of which would drive city industries.

Throughout the 1990s, Shanghai had been known as the "head of the dragon," the Chinese media's description of the nation's economic center. After 2002, with President Hu and Premier Wen balancing regional growth by developing central-western and northeastern areas around Chongqing and Tianjin, the phrase faded from official use. In 2009, with deep symbolism, Shanghai was again the "head of the dragon."

Not everyone backed Shanghai's resurgence. At first, some Beijing departments blocked Shanghai's "dual center" move, but it was eventually settled through "many rounds of negotiation and consultation." Promoted by Shanghai Party Secretary Yu Zhengsheng, the municipality's blueprint was supported by senior leaders Wu Bangguo, chairman of the National People's Congress, and Vice President Xi Jinping, both of whom are former Shanghai Party secretaries.

Some experts believe that designating Shanghai as a "dual center" is as important as Deng Xiaoping's decision to develop Pudong. The ultimate goal, says one Shanghai scholar, "is to challenge American financial hegemony."[9]

★ ★ ★

Nonetheless, as Beijing sought to balance regional development, what was being planned for Tianjin in northeast China was equally spectacular.

Zhang Gaoli had had two major successes as Party secretary (Shenzhen and Shandong)—building robust, sustainable economies and improving quality of life—when, in 2007, he received an urgent telephone call. "It was night—I had no advance knowledge," he recalled, "and almost the next day, I was on my way to Tianjin."[10] Zhang had been appointed Tianjin's Party secretary, with a brief to transform the city, China's fifth largest, from a regional industrial center into an international economic metropolis.

Zhang Gaoli, Politburo member and Party secretary of Tianjin Municipality (former Party secretary of Shandong Province) (Jinan, May 2005).

It had been in 2006 that China's leaders anointed Tianjin, with an area of about 4,600-square miles and a population of about 12 million, to catalyze the revitalization of China's entire northeast—a major strategic objective of President Hu and Premier Wen Jiabao, a Tianjin native. Tianjin was mandated three goals: an international port and logistics center, serving more than a dozen provinces in China's northeast, central and western regions (and even beyond into Russia, Kazakhstan and Mongolia); the economic engine for developing China's northeast, featuring state-of-the-art manufacturing and research; and an ecologically friendly city providing hospitable environments for its citizens.

The central city is historic. Although Tianjin suffered the indignation of having been sliced into nine concessions by foreign invaders, the different cultures that took root, combined with the dominant Chinese culture, provides a unique civilizing experience.

To empower Tianjin, China's leaders made the strategic decision to promote the rapid development, independent innovation, and ecological excellence of Tianjin Binhai New Area (TBNA). Located along 95 miles of Tianjin's eastern coast, TBNA may be the world's most ambitious regional development, a hypermodern metropolis of breathtaking dimensions. Viewing a sprawling model of the 876-square miles at 1:750 scale, one gasps at the vast vision—with specialized areas for hi-tech industry, marine economy, advanced manufacturing, eco-city, seaport logistics, seaport-based industry, and coastal leisure and tourism. TBNA is home to over 90 multinational corporations, including the Airbus A320 assembly factory. The Central Business District, surrounded by water, will feature some 40 contemporary structures, some of which are architectural marvels. Many provinces are constructing major buildings to support their own local companies doing business in Tianjin. According to plan, as Shenzhen drove Guangdong and Pudong New Area drove Shanghai so TBNA will drive Tianjin.

TBNA Governor Guo Lijun gives TBNA's four critical success factors: transportation (connecting adjacent and distant cities, provinces and countries); industries (major plants are supported by smaller companies in surrounding provinces); talent (42 universities nearby); and coordination with other provinces (e.g., raw materials, such as tomatoes from Xinjiang and soybeans from Heilongjiang can be processed and exported efficiently). Governor Guo notes that Secretary Zhang Gaoli expects local leaders to work 24/7.[11] "We must have passion for our work; enthusiasm for our career; and care for our people," Guo says, quoting Zhang.

"We seek best practices and invite top talent from across China and around the world," Zhang tells me (2009). "We stress dedicated work (5+2 days per week), honest performance, innovation, and unity among our officials. Our work environment is harmonious. We apply the directives of central leadership to Tianjin realities. We'd go nowhere if we ignore reality or fear innovation. Even with the financial crisis, Tianjin will grow rapidly. Tianjin will drive China." (In the first half of 2010, the GDP of TBNA exceeded, for the first time, the GDP of Shanghai Pudong New Area.)

"TBNA is our first priority and plays the flagship role," Zhang explains. "Our city planning coordinates TBNA, Tianjin city proper, and surrounding counties. We're highlighting Tianjin's different cultures, such as Italian architecture. We'll have coordinated design on both sides of the Hai River, integrating classic and modern styles. In two years we have RMB 1 trillion (almost $150 billion) invested, including aerospace (Airbus, helicopters, rockets), autos, hi-tech, petrochemicals, pharmaceuticals, and the Sino-Singapore eco-city. Ecology is critical. It would be terrifying to sacrifice the environment for growth. Ninety-eight percent of Tianjin's citizens are satisfied with the environment; in 2008, they planted 2.7 million trees."

Focused and determined, Zhang concentrates on people's jobs and living conditions. "For two years, we've had 20 policies per year to improve citizen's lives and we're ready with the third batch," he says. "We've built 130,000 apartments for low-medium income families, created 380,000 jobs, and provided good medical and pension benefits, including for farmers."

As for problems, Zhang cites Tianjin's service sector, the lack of financing for small and medium-sized enterprises (SMEs) as well as the broad impact of the financial crisis. "We must use our financial reserves to expand infrastructure and boost domestic demand. We'll support SMEs in difficult times. We'll not let good companies go out of business. Tianjin is ideal for Beijing scientists and engineers to commercialize their innovations."

Secretary Zhang promotes a "down-to-earth workstyle of intense effort and low profile." His motto: "Do more. Speak less."

To know what's really happening, Zhang says that "you must go yourself." Zhang is known to "ambush" his subordinates, visiting them unannounced in their offices. "I'm not interested in 'reports'," he states, "only results."

When Zhang heard that two old ladies did not have heat, he investigated himself and found that several dozen were suffering. When visiting a market serving lower-income citizens, he found that those with government subsidies had more vegetables in their baskets. When discovering that a village entertainment area for the elderly was too narrow, he ordered it enlarged—and returned to inspect the expansion.

To those who would confine Tianjin's impact to China's northeast, I offer this advice: visit Tianjin's Urban Planning Museum—Secretary Zhang insisted that I go (on my way to the airport). It is a masterpiece of design that lays out the vision of Tianjin, China's third dragonhead, as a 21st Century metropolis for the world.

Endnotes

1 In addition, the Chongqing Municipality, a catalyst for developing western regions, was fast-tracked in the 11th Five-Year Plan (2006–2010) by large investments and favorable policies.

2 Zhao Qizheng was deputy mayor of Shanghai and the first director of the Administrative Committee of Pudong New District from 1993 to 1998. Much of the following material is

taken from Zhao Qizheng's book, *The Shanghai/Pudong Miracle*; additional material from the author's communication with Zhao and others.

3 Yang, *Biography*, Chapter 5. These included building 50 million square feet of residential areas, passenger bridges at key traffic intersections, and a tunnel under the Huangpu River; erecting hotels, apartment buildings and office buildings for foreign businessmen; developing a subway and elevated rail system; and connecting Shanghai to its neighbors by freeway.

4 Author's meeting with Wang Daohan, Shanghai, 2002.

5 Yang, *Biography*, Chapter 5.

6 Wang Daohan.

7 The policies introduced in the Pudong New Area were by and large similar to those in the SEZs already established. However, because the level of preferential treatment in Pudong was slightly lower than in the SEZs, it was named the Pudong New Area rather than Special Economic Zone. Another reason for the different designation was because preferential policies practiced in Pudong, especially those relating to finance and taxation, did not apply to the entire city of Shanghai, whereas the policies in the SEZs were applicable to the cities as a whole.

8 Cheng Li, "Reclaiming the 'Head of the Dragon': Shanghai as China's Center for International Finance and Shipping," *China Leadership Monitor*, No. 28.

9 Ibid.

10 Author's meeting with Zhang Gaoli, Tianjin, 2007, 2009.

11 Author's meeting with Guo Lijun, Tianjin, 2009.

What to Do with State-Owned Enterprises?

21

The reform of state-owned enterprises (SOEs) has been an enormous challenge for China's leaders. During the high season of the planned economy there were almost 400,000 SOEs. Collectively, they accounted for well over half (perhaps 70%) of all the labor and capital utilized by Chinese industry but produced well under half (perhaps 40%) of the output. There is no clearer measure of SOE inefficiencies. SOEs came into existence to produce products according to directives from central planners sitting at desks in ministries in Beijing. They didn't have marketing and sales departments because they didn't market or sell anything—and they measured their "revenues" by how much their factories produced, not by how much they sold. Thus they had no incentive to make quality products: It made no difference whether SOE products were ineffective, despised and unused, or effective, loved, and demanded—as long as production quotas were met.

At the beginning of SOE reform, it was thought that perhaps 10,000 SOEs would be retained by the state. By the mid-1990s the number was reduced to 1,000, and in the late-1990s an official told me that the optimum number of SOEs should be "about 500." By 2008, the 500 contracted to about 150. By controlling these remaining giant enterprises, the government hopes to direct the economy, thus giving some continued meaning to China's "socialist" label.

★ ★ ★

China's first Law of Enterprise Bankruptcy was passed in 1986. Yet for most people it was an alien and shocking concept. Since the founding of the People's Republic, for 40 years, there had been no major bankruptcy in China.

The catchphrase "iron rice bowl" refers to entire lives that were guaranteed under the socialist system; people not only had stable jobs but also stable living. Under socialism, every worker, manager or laborer, had lifetime job security—work, wages and benefits. They worked for one enterprise and that enterprise took full and permanent care of them, through retirement to their deaths. A bowl made of iron will never break.

Under the state-owned system, SOEs maintained elaborate social facilities; everyone was guaranteed not only a job but also food, clothing, a place to live, healthcare and medical services, workmen's compensation, retirement pensions, and a grave site. Yes, many enterprises had enterprise graveyards, as well as nurseries, for literal cradle-to-grave care. I recall being startled on an early trip to China when I was taken to visit the "factory cemetery." (Workers' benefits came from the *danwei*—the work unit within the SOE.)

For workers used to the iron rice bowl, bankruptcy was a shattering blow. And nowhere was hit harder than China's rust-belt northeast—Manchuria. (After the 1949 revolution, the government, supported by the Soviet Union, made Manchuria the base of China's heavy industry. But what worked for a while in a planned economy did not work at all in a market economy. Massive SOEs were inefficient and uncompetitive—and by the late 1990s, they began shedding workers in large numbers.)

The Acheng Sugar Factory in Harbin, Heilongjiang Province, was China's first sugar company, founded almost a century earlier. Acheng had become a pillar of the planned economy, the largest sugar plant in China, producing 3,000 tons of beet sugar a day. But it was old, burdened with debt, and unable to compete with more efficient producers. In 1998, Acheng became China's first major bankruptcy, putting 4,500 employees out of work.[1] At the time China had no social system to care for laid-off workers. In the depths of a harsh Harbin winter, the personal tragedies were heartbreaking.

"This is the work of the market economy; the winners stay, the losers are gone," reflected Acheng President Zhang Xiaoqin, just after his company's bankruptcy was approved by the court. "According to the natural law, the first to be born is the first to die. Bankruptcy is a new thing for our country, but in the market economy, bankruptcy is a normal thing."

Creditors had to write off $85 million, but the human tragedy was far worse. Zhang pledged that "my next step will be how to settle with the workers. If the workers are not properly taken care of, history will view me as a sinner." Yet in dramatic scenes captured for my PBS special, *In Search of China*, agitated Acheng workers charged into his office. "I haven't been paid for 25 months," said one. "I've lost my job, I've nothing to eat," said another; "We've worked like donkeys our whole lives and now they kill the donkeys." "When you have nothing to eat, death is the only solution," added a third. Workers demanded that Zhang "face the people."

"We're all in the same situation," Zhang responded, "we're all unemployed— my grandfather, my father, myself, even my children have worked here. Now everything is gone. You think being a factory chief is easy? These three years have been like 30. I didn't get paid a penny either. I hope you won't forget me," he added. "Whether or not we can be reborn, we have to make the effort."

★ ★ ★

Allowing bankruptcies was a risk—unemployed workers could trigger social turmoil—but it was a risk China's leaders had to take to secure long-term economic stability.

In 1998, I met Shao Ning, director-general of the Department of Enterprise Reform at the State Economic and Trade Commission (later vice chairman of the state-owned Assets Supervision and Administration Commission). Shao coordinated government decisions as to which failing enterprises would be allowed to go bankrupt. The Acheng Sugar Factory, he said, had gone bankrupt for two reasons: one was the rising price of sugar beets; the second was that it had many surplus and retired workers, which increased its operating costs—the factory could no longer compete in the market.

The factory's management had worked hard to change the way its employees thought about bankruptcy, he said. "The decision to file for bankruptcy was passed through a committee of employee representatives."

I asked Shao about the growing gap between rich and poor. "From the inception of the market economy, the wealth gap has been growing," he said. "This is natural. I think the divergence between rich and poor can actually help improve economic efficiency." In traditional Chinese culture, he noted, "egalitarianism did not play a significant role. It came to prominence," he said, "with the communist idea of 'equal distribution', which was an idealistic and influential tenet of the planned [socialist] economy."

Shao said he believed in communism, then added: "Ideally, communism is supposed to be built upon a very wealthy society—one that has been created by hard work and to which everyone contributes. Given the mindset of our society and the current level of development, I'm not sure that kind of egalitarianism is realistic. We think, based on current levels of economic development, that stressing greater distribution efficiency and creating a fairer society are the best ways to go."

Indeed, he emphasized, "a reasonable gap in wealth is normal, and it shouldn't have negative effects on traditional Chinese culture," though he acknowledged that "if the gap becomes too great, it will become an issue of fairness, and that could affect stability. The government," he said, "should actively redistribute some of this new wealth by levying higher taxes on the rich."

Asked about negatives of a market economy, Shao suggested that an American would know the downside better than he. He was more knowledgeable, he said, about negatives of a planned economy, which he was quite ready to articulate: "The primary negative of a planned economy," he said, "is its decision-making apparatus. When the central government makes a plan, it affects the whole country. Such plans cannot possibly predict changes in demand across the whole country, because so many variables affect this. That's why many of these plans fail."

A second negative, he said, was the "lack of motivation on the part of people at all levels. In a centrally planned economy," he explained, "nobody's personal interests are served by implementing the plans, so it's very difficult to motivate people. For these reasons, efficiency in a planned economy is less than optimal." Another problem, he suggested, was "commissions" (kickbacks) in the purchasing process.

★ ★ ★

The late 1990s were a crucial period in SOE reform. Yet while some managers struggled with productivity and markets, particularly after Premier Zhu Rongji set tough guidelines for SOE transformation in 1998, others reveled in their newfound freedom to maneuver. These were the people who re-revolutionized China, like Wang Hai, president of China's largest shoe manufacturer, Doublestar.

Headquartered in Qingdao, Shandong Province, Doublestar has world-class facilities, 3,000 chain stores, and healthy profit margins. With operations in tires, clothes and other industries as well as in shoes, the Doublestar Group is a trans-national business with 40,000 employees and 140 operating entities. Before reform it was a money-losing, medium-sized enterprise making inferior rubber shoes.

Much of the transformation was due to Wang Hai, Doublestar's CEO for 30 years, who started his career as a soldier with a gun, not an MBA with a calculator.

"In the early 1980's, Doublestar was making shoes that nobody wanted," Wang Hai recalled, when I met him in 1998. "No one knew that this was due to market problems. I had no idea what the market was either," he added. "So I said to myself, 'If I can make shoes, why can't I sell them?'"

So Wang did something unprecedented for a Chinese factory manager. "I carried shoes on my back to the department stores, trying to get sales," he said. "I was probably the first factory director in the country to sell shoes to the stores. Nobody could believe it. I was treated with contempt. Even my employees said I wasn't doing my job," he added. "They said, 'Why is a factory chief peddling shoes?!' What they didn't know," he explained, "is that I was trying to understand how the market works."

Wang Hai's salesmanship was novel because the old system was rigidly hierarchical, with clearly defined roles: senior management should never deign to do menial things like "selling." But Wang Hai's success came from the fact that he viewed a CEO's job as selling, just like a salesperson. In essence, Wang Hai reinvented the wheel, rediscovering techniques that a planned, command economy had discarded. A born salesman, who speaks his mind freely no matter who is listening, he flourished with reform.

"A reporter once asked me if I wore my own shoes," Wang told me, "so I quickly took off my shoe to prove to him that I always wear Doublestar. Of course," he added, "I know that to take off your shoes in public is very impolite, but I'm the president of the company. If I don't wear my own shoes, I'm not qualified to be a shoemaker!"

For Wang Hai, being a good salesman and being Chinese went together. He integrated Chinese tradition, modern enterprise management, and his own philosophy of market, management and life. Doublestar's culture, formulated by Wang, was founded on The Rule of Our Service: 200% Service and The Rule of Our Work: Seriousness. Practicality. Innovation.

"I found that some of our Chinese culture can be applied for purposes of management," said Wang. "But what I take is not superstition. Superstition means I do nothing but pray all day long, recite the scriptures and be a vegetarian—and while I pray, the shoes just come out of the Buddha's ass."

Nevertheless, dominating a yard in the Doublestar headquarters compound was an enormous Buddha. Not far away, tucked in a corner, was a large Santa Claus. "Putting Santa in the corner emphasizes that our Buddha is better than your Santa," said Wang with a twinkle. "This is to encourage us. Historically, Westerners treated Chinese badly. This is to remind us of that history, and also to punish them!"

The Santa also had a practical use. "There's a bathroom inside it," said Wang, laughing. But he quickly returned to his theme of China's revival:

"On the surface of the earth, only the Chinese have defeated the Americans," he said. "The first time was in Korea and the second was in Vietnam. I missed Korea, but I didn't miss Vietnam." Wang, it turned out, had been among Chinese troops sent to Vietnam to assist communist forces fighting Americans. "I was in Vietnam in 1965-1966," he explained. "I was about 25; we were the first group to enter Vietnam—we even had to wear Vietnamese clothing. So I have experience in both the battlefield of the market and the battlefield heavy with the smoke of gunpowder."

Wang said that the lessons he had learned in the army helped him in his business career: "To be successful on either of these battlefields, you first need to have the will to defeat your enemies," he said, adding, "I could have been a goddamn general in the Red Army, and I'm absolutely confident that I would have commanded very well in war. But I ended up being a shoemaker—shoemaker is the tougher profession!"

Wang Hai's commanding personality was in evidence when I witnessed him screaming at one his executives about a new product. "What the hell is this?" he yelled. "How can you do this? You'll ruin the stores! How can you ask me for four million at once! Do you think I can just print money? This is an international joke! Take it away!"

Catching up with the just-berated executive, I asked whether Wang had ever criticized him like this before. "I've had worse," the executive replied, more calmly than I expected.

Wang Hai knew I'd asked about the little scene. "To yell at the employees is the best way for me to release the pressure," he said; "that's why I'm always so healthy."

Wang's combative talents were also required in his dealings with bureaucrats in Beijing. One clash had come over his claim that Doublestar was the world's leading shoe brand. "If you go by population and market share," Wang insisted, "I am the world's most famous brand. The funny thing is that our own government is giving me trouble. They asked, 'Who approved your claim that Doublestar's the world's most famous brand?'" Wang's reply had been typically blunt. "'Bullshit' I told them. 'Do the world's most famous brands need approval? Who approved Nike? Did they vote for Pierre Cardin in the UN?' We give respect to artists, politicians, scientists," he went on. "We should also give respect to entrepreneurs. We've got to be taken seriously. I think the government is having trouble understanding who we are."

Certainly at that time, the government's attitudes to entrepreneurial managers like Wang Hai were ambiguous: it needed them to make SOEs profitable, but it had yet to provide them with the kind of personal financial incentives common to executives of large international companies, due to a lingering sense of socialist equality. (Despite revisions to this policy, even as of 2009 compensation for heads of Chinese SOEs was still significantly lower than that of their worldwide peers.)

Wang Hai was not afraid to vent his frustrations. "All of this, the entire company, is my creation," he said. "But even though our stock is traded publicly, I don't own any of it." I asked if he thought this was fair: "No, of course it's not fair," Wang shot back, "but there isn't absolute fairness in this world."

Wang Hai was appointed by the government and served at its pleasure. Did he think he had sufficient freedom to run the company as he wished, I asked, goading my new friend.

"I do not," he replied. "It'll take a long time for this to come true. Why do I say this? Because the company was born in a planned economy. It's still an SOE and thus not truly free." In fact, Doublestar needed government approval for many things, from firing employees to getting loans.

Wang Hai clearly had little faith in bureaucrats. Asked to comment on Premier Zhu Rongji's then-recent (1998) pledge to make most SOEs profitable within three years, he was similarly blunt—even though he was speaking in front of Chinese TV cameras:

"The way they think will never change," he said, "what they're running is still a planned economy. Their approach can't work. It's bullshit. The officials send somebody down to the factory, and you know his opinion is no good—but if you don't do what he says, that's no good either. Saying it's a market economy is a joke," he went on. "The government is full of hot air."

"In my opinion," Wang added, "SOEs are hopeless. If there were no entrepreneurs to make them ready for the market, they would never survive."

★ ★ ★

Yet times were changing—and so was the thinking of some bureaucrats. Zhang Ruimin, for example, started out as a mid-level official in the Qingdao municipal government, an unlikely incubator for a free-market visionary. In 1984, at the age of 35, he took over the nearly bankrupt Qingdao General Refrigerator Factory. His resume hardly suggested great success—he had missed out on college because of the Cultural Revolution. But Zhang had been reading western management books by night, and harbored a peculiar belief that Chinese companies could produce goods of world-class quality.

From the beginning, Zhang was a fanatic about quality and appalled at the low-quality of his company's products. Famously, he took 76 faulty refrigerators and ordered the company's workers to smash them to pieces with sledgehammers—leading the destruction himself. The workers were distressed: this was 1985, when a refrigerator cost two years wages. But Zhang Ruimin did not waver. "If we don't destroy these refrigerators today," he said, "what will be shattered by the market in the future will be this enterprise!" This singular act impressed on employees that poor quality would not be acceptable—and marked the beginning of the company's turnaround. Zhang reinforced the message with an aggressive Western-style quality-control program. (The hammer wielded by Zhang is now on display in Haier's exhibition hall as a witness to history and a warning to posterity—a symbol of what happens to bad products.)

Today Haier Group, as it's now known, is the world's third largest white-goods home-appliance manufacturer—making refrigerators, freezers, air conditioners, washing machines, kitchen appliances, and other products.[2] It is the domestic market leader in nine products and China's top global brand. Haier has 240 subsidiary companies and more than 50,000 employees throughout the world—including in the U.S., where it has a $30 million factory in South Carolina and a 30-35% market share of small refrigerators. Haier's 2008 global revenue was almost $18 billion.

In 1998 I visited Haier's campus-like facilities in Qingdao—Tsingtao in the older spelling—a beautiful city on the Yellow Sea leased to the Germans in 1898 to build the famous brewery of the same name—and was struck by Haier's corporate slogan, Never Say No to the Market, festooned everywhere. President Zhang Ruimin, who was showing me around, explained:

"This slogan is to remind our employees that we are servants of the market, and we should always supply our best service to the market," he said. "Some employees tend to think that it's the market that needs us, not we who need the market." Another example of Haier culture was the Demerit Board, devised by Zhang, which sat prominently near the company cafeteria and listed the names of employees, including senior executives, who had been responsible for various kinds of failures. This was no joke: repeat offenders faced consequences.

Zhang told me that Haier's goal was to become one of the world's 500 largest corporations. At the time, it seemed an impossible dream, reflecting Chinese pride more than economic reality. I was wrong.

As we toured Haier's multi-story headquarters, we came upon an area which looked oddly out of place. Zhang said that it was the Activity Room of the Communist Party and he invited me into what seemed an anachronism—a room out of the 1950s, decorated with red flags. Along the walls were pamphlets and magazines preaching proletarian doctrines, and on the walls large photographs of Marx, Engels, Lenin, Stalin and Mao.

Haier Group—market-savvy, technically astute and financially strong —exemplified the new, successful Chinese enterprise. Yet the Party operated a parallel organization within Haier, just as it does within most large enterprises and the government itself. Around 10% of Haier employees were Party members, Zhang said, and around 90% of its management. Didn't this send a powerful message to Haier employees that they had better join the Party in order to advance into management, I asked?

"Not necessarily," Zhang responded. "Young people have their own ideas. Some don't want to join any party, they just want to build their careers; some want to go abroad." The percentage of senior management who were Party members would drop, he said. "Already some of our executives are

Zhang Ruimin, chairman and CEO of Haier Group, in the Communist Party room at Haier headquarters, Qingdao, Shandong Province (April 1998).

not Party members, especially those who are young." (Three of Haier's four divisional presidents were in their early thirties.)

And Zhang emphasized that Party activities within the company had changed: "In the past they took place during work. Now they only happen after work," explaining that "Party members are required to set a good example for other workers. Especially when conditions are tough, we require Party members to contribute more. For example, when we acquire other companies, Party members volunteer to do extra work, such as integrating our corporate culture." (Zhang was obsessive about inculcating Haier's culture into all acquisitions.)

It was hard not to feel a certain irony standing in the Party's Activity Room speaking with the Haier CEO about executive compensation, stock options, market preeminence, mergers and acquisitions. Yet there was less contradiction here than first appeared. Chinese communism, except during Mao's later life, was more nationalistic than economic. Foreign domination was the gut issue, not exploitation of the working class—with the real goal being Chinese honor and pride, not state ownership of production. And so perhaps communism had its place in China's development, as the nation entered the competitive fury of the global market.

Haier's ownership had something of China's socialist system. Technically it was a "collective," not an SOE, meaning that it was owned by the employees rather than the state. Yet, for years, the employees had no sense of their ownership and didn't receive dividends, all of which were retained in the company. And the government could still act as if Haier were an SOE—for example, Haier was "asked" to acquire a poorly performing enterprise in order to save jobs and prevent unemployment, even though the industry, pharmaceuticals, was far from its core business.

Yang Mianmian, then Haier's executive vice president (now its president), emphasized that the company's slogan, Never Say No to the Market, informed every aspect of its operations: "We display it throughout our factories and offices," she said. "The market is all-consuming to us, and we inculcate that sense in all our employees." She added: "We emphasize serving our customer: we think *for* our customers—we think of things that may not occur to them. In a competitive market, success depends on who knows customer needs better . . . If we know Chinese needs better than the Japanese and Americans do, we will beat them in the Chinese market," she explained.

To this end, Yang explained, the development of new products was carried out by the same departments which were responsible for selling them—the refrigerator division was responsible from start to finish. The focus on transferring Haier's corporate culture to new acquisitions, meanwhile, enabled the firm to manufacture products outside its core business, she said: "In the past, a company that made refrigerators couldn't possibly make television sets—now we can acquire a television company and we can make television sets."

Yang, who trained as an engineer, was one of a surprising number of female senior executives in China. She noted that "in Chinese traditional

Yang Mianmian (left), vice president (later president) of Haier Group; Chinese on the window: Never Say No to the Market. Qingdao, Shandong Province (April 1998).

culture, women are seen as weak, not capable." But, she stressed, "the market economy gives unprecedented opportunity to women."

Yang, who had children and grandchildren, said she had a happy family life. "I don't have much time with the family, so I accept the lowest status," she said. "I don't get into many conflicts because I usually listen to everyone else." However, she added, "I do cook sometimes. I grew up in Shanghai, and Shanghai people are very picky about their food. I'm a good cook—every time I make dinner, the family eats a lot."

But she acknowledged that "when career and life are in conflict, I subordinate my life to my career. Only when the 'company's kitchen' sells well will my family's kitchen have everything," she explained, adding, "The balance between life and career is always imperfect, but I do my best."

Yang also emphasized her desire to enable company workers to share in its profits, explaining: "I want workers to own shares individually."

Eight years later (2006), Qingdao Haier, the publicly listed home-appliance arm of Haier Group, announced a stock option incentive plan to reward management.[3] The exercise of share options over the seven-year term amounted to 6.69% of the company's existing shares, and was contingent on the company hitting profitability targets. President Yang Mianmian received 3 million options, or 0.25% of the company's shares. In 2008, she ranked no.17 on Fortune's list of the 50 Most Powerful Women in the business world.

★ ★ ★

Another path to business success in China was epitomized by Lenovo, which by 2007 had become the world's fourth largest personal computer maker, and, with $17 billion in revenues, was among the Fortune 500. In 2004, in a high-profile acquisition, Lenovo bought the personal computer division of IBM, which was three times its size and had operations in more than 100 countries.

Liu Chuanzhi, founder and chairman of Legend Holdings, Lenovo's predecessor, explained that the company was founded in 1984, with an investment of about $23,000 from the Chinese Academy of Sciences, which controlled China's best research institutes. In the past, Liu said, these had "made some of the most advanced machines in the world—but they didn't commercialize them." As market reforms took root, however, "we started to think about turning our technologies into merchandise: Previously our achievements were evaluated by our publications and scientific awards. Now we're evaluated by our products and profitability."

Having started out assembling foreign computers, "in 1990 we decided to build the Legend brand," he said. "By focusing entirely on the Chinese market, and by providing value and specialized service to our Chinese-speaking customers, we gained competitive edge. Our market share went from zero to 7% in 1996 and to 20% [1998]." Most of Legend's 11 original founders had by this time retired, replaced by younger people: "The computer and information industries require original thinking, unfettered by years of status-quo mentality," Liu insisted.

Yet he still felt limited by the company's status as an SOE. "In America, entrepreneurs like Bill Gates enjoy complete decision-making power," Liu said. For a state-owned business to develop in a dynamic, demanding market, was, he said, "very difficult."

"How can Legend attract the most capable, creative people?" he asked. "When Legend makes large profits, most goes to the state. In China, privately owned companies are more advanced than SOEs," he added. "Logically, Legend should be much more developed than private companies, because it's backed by China's best high-tech institutes, but Legend is not as developed as it should be. The system is the issue."

The company did have some advantages over traditional state enterprises, however. In 1994, Legend employees received 30% of the shares, which Liu said had made it easier for its older founders to retire: in typical SOEs, managers resist early retirement because they would lose most of their benefits. "Since Legend's founders had shares, they were happy to give their positions to younger people who could make the company more profitable," Liu explained. "The better Legend does, the more money they make."

At that time Liu Chuanzhi himself owned the right to share dividends—but not the right to sell these shares. I asked how he felt about receiving far lower compensation than an American CEO.

"I'm a product of the Cultural Revolution generation," Liu reflected. "Just after I graduated from college, the chaos started: my first ten years were totally wasted—and even the next period, when reform developed slowly, was not terribly productive. So in 1984, when we were asked to start the company, I was very happy," he said. "I just wanted to do things. I didn't even think of making money. Four years later, in 1988, Legend had about 1,000 employees. My entire motivation was my responsibility for those people. Now," he explained, "as Legend has become the biggest PC manufacturer in China, I feel proud to be contributing to our national industry." And he added: "As for money, Bill Gates is donating his wealth to charity—my income is enough to live a good life."

But Liu acknowledged that such attitudes, though common among his generation, was not consistent with market economics. "For the younger generation," he continued, "their incomes should correlate with their contributions." And he agreed that CEOs owning shares in their companies reassure investors of their common interests in share prices.

"In fact," he said, "when I consider whether Legend should invest in a private company, I also want to know how much stock its CEO owns. But I'm an SOE entrepreneur, so my situation is different."

I understood, I said, but added mischievously: "When I hear that you own significant stock, that's when I'll invest in Legend!"

"I hope you tell this to our nation's top leaders," Liu replied, laughing. "It's very important, I agree. When foreign institutions or even local Chinese companies consider buying Legend stock, they also want to know how much stock I own."

In 2000, President Liu was granted stock worth $14 million. Upon hearing the news I felt obligated to purchase some shares.

I then met "Michael," who was Legend's vice director of new business development, responsible for strategic acquisitions and investments. He was 26-years-old. I asked whether it was risky for a giant corporation to put so much trust in someone so young. "I don't think so," he answered softly. "The information industry is young and changes rapidly. It needs fresh ideas and innovations." And he added, "I'm confident because I'm competent." As for potential investments, Michael said that Legend studies them very carefully: "An opportunity may also be a trap," he said. Michael's dream was to start his own company.

At one of Legend's factories, I met a 25-year-old female deputy general manager who, only three years after college, was responsible for 600 production workers, mostly male and older. She earned far more than her parents, both government officials. It was a common phenomenon, she said, noting that there were many women in managerial posts at the company. Legend's staff earned up to half their salary from bonuses (they were sworn to secrecy about compensation.)

I sought out an official at Legend's Communist Party branch, an agreeable fellow named Li, and asked him how Communist ideology meshed with the needs of a world-class computer corporation. "The Party branch can unite the workers to complete tasks so that the corporation can make more profit," he told me, stressing that "Our thoughts have been liberated by reform. Now we're more concerned with corporate development, because that helps the workers. Party and corporation are the same." Wouldn't this just make the shareholders—the capitalists—richer, I asked. "Socialism wants to make profits, too," Li replied.

★ ★ ★

In just five years since its formation in 2004, China National Chemical Corporation (ChemChina) has become China's largest chemical company (19th in the world). Founder and President Ren Jianxin built ChemChina, which is anchored by BlueStar Group (Ren's original company), with about 100 M&A transactions and 85 major construction projects.[4] (Twenty-five years ago, Ren started BlueStar with a government loan of about $1500; ChemChina's 2009 assets were about $23 billion.)

For Ren, innovation is key, both self-generated and acquired—"especially for tackling the financial crisis" (ChemChina ranks 4th among all SOEs in patents owned). Epitomizing China's new generation of industrial leaders, he believes that internationalizing drives innovation and compels managerial transformation—and ChemChina's process is on-going, with acquisitions in France and Australia, a high-profile strategic investment from Blackstone Group, and explorations worldwide. Ren recognizes the challenges of cross-cultural M&A and seeks to learn from these acquisitions: he likens buying foreign companies to "hiring foreign teachers."

Sustainable development and environmental protection now dominate mindsets. "'Chemical production equals pollution'," Ren admits; "this is our reality." Yet this also brings opportunity, he believes, since "major sources of economic growth are the safety, energy-saving, pollution-reduction and emission-reduction businesses." The basic chemical business is our foundation, he says, "while life science, material science and environmental science form a '3+1' industrial pattern."

Ren requires all ChemChina companies to "benchmark themselves against the world's leading chemical producers in executing our 'zero-emission' strategy." He calls for "rigorous measures" to save energy, reduce emission and "prevent pollution from the very source of production in a bid to change the old practice of 'treatment after pollution'." The goal, Ren says, is "sustainable business" that creates value for customers and shareholders, and enhances the environment and society.

★ ★ ★

Gree Electric Appliances Inc. of Zhuhai in Guangdong Province has become the world's largest residential air conditioner manufacturer, surprising many. The company was formed around 1991 when Chairman Zhu Jianghong restructured several inefficient SOEs.[5] A small, nameless factory with 200 employees and annual production of less than 20,000 units, Gree was an unlikely candidate for global air-conditioner leadership, particularly in technology where the Japanese and American giants enjoyed what seemed to be unassailable dominance. Gree is now a multinational enterprise with 40,000 employees and annual production of 20 million units,

Owned 64% by the government and 36% by other parties, including management, Gree is proud that its R&D is now second-to-none. "We have 2,000 research engineers, including foreign experts, and invest RMB 1 billion [almost $150 million] in R&D annually," said Chairman Zhu. "A company without core technology is one without a spine; when one has no spine, one will never stand. If no technology, then no competitive products, no market share. Production alone makes no sense."

Zhu recalled that in its early days Gree had to purchase technology from other countries, which turned out to be self-limiting, even a trap. "We imported machines from Toshiba but when they had problems the Japanese technicians wouldn't come to the Mainland, only to Hong Kong, and we had to take instructions verbally," Zhu said. "It was humiliating."

"Another time, we needed to import quality-control equipment but the Japanese supplier deliberately withheld the latest technology," Zhu continued. "I came to realize that if we could buy 'advanced' foreign technology, that just meant it wasn't advanced anymore."

"Even worse was when we needed a multi-unit control system and were willing to pay a very fair price of RMB 300 million, but the Japanese turned me down cold before I'd even finished making my request," Zhu said, evincing residual anger.

"I became determined that Gree must break their monopoly by having our own technology, our own patents," Zhu asserted. "What took the Japanese 10 years to develop, we did in one year. Moreover, our heating unit would function at -25° C whereas the Japanese unit was limited to -15° C."

Zhu concluded with unalloyed pride: "I had wasted 18 years in fruitless SOEs before starting Gree and I can now say with confidence that Gree's refrigeration technology is the most advanced in the world. We possess about 1500 technical patents. We are selling air conditioners, with energy-saving technologies, in Japan."

★ ★ ★

Wahaha Group, based in Hangzhou, Zhejiang Province, is China's largest beverage company (bottled water, milk drinks, soft drinks, fruit juices). It has grown from a small distributor of health supplements for children into a market-dominant firm whose 2009 revenues were almost $6 billion. Wahaha CEO Zong Qinghou is a tough-minded, high-profile entrepreneur who led a management buyout and became one of China's wealthiest persons. (Zong topped Forbes' 400 Richest Chinese list in 2010 as the richest person in China; his personal fortune, primarily his ownership in Wahaha, was worth around $7-8 billion.[6]) Zong is all action, no pretense, and his story exemplifies the emergence of powerful Chinese companies.[7]

Impatient with organic growth (and the complex rules for land utilization), he acquired the much-larger Hangzhou Canned Food Factory (1991), an almost-bankrupt SOE, which he turned around in 100 days. It was not without difficulty: employees protested and boycotted and the media criticized the minnow-swallowing-whale transaction.

Although his negotiations with the government required that the new company need only retain 500 of its 2,000 employees, Zong did not want to lay off anyone and determined to develop new products instead. Realizing the huge potential of China's beverage market, he changed direction. Moreover, he capitalized on leaders' strategy to move industries inland, setting up Wahaha's first bottling plant in Chongqing in central China. Wahaha now has plants in all provinces except Hainan and Tibet.

President Zong gives five reasons for Wahaha's success: focus on core business; manage growth, never over-expand, keep cash high and debt low; develop proprietary products every year through R&D and top talent; strong distribution system; and a corporate culture that encourages career advancement and financial participation for its 10,000 employees. The compensation of Wahaha employees averages over RMB 100,000 per year and many own cars. Wahaha provides housing or matching grants to buy houses; reimbursement of education costs; and first-rate healthcare. After spending time and money training its workers, Wahaha does not want to lose them, either to competitors or because they return to their hometowns. "By providing workers housing," Zong says, "they can get married in the city." But, he adds, "the Wahaha model is not widely applicable."

Zong has strong opinions and isn't shy in sharing them. "Under the old ideology, when wealth was shared by everyone, wealth was enjoyed by no one, because when working for the state, few worked hard," he said. As if answering criticism that great personal wealth—for example his own—was inimical for China, Zong responded, "The wealth really belongs to the country anyway; after all, how much can I eat, spend. But personal incentives are what build enterprises and national wealth. Look at Europe. With all its equality and benefit programs, it's in decline. The whole continent can go bankrupt!"

At the same time, Zong recognizes that China's biggest problem is economic imbalances which retard domestic consumption. "If China gets wealth distribution right," Zong says, "China can grow for 20-30 years no matter what happens to the rest of the world." Zong implores the government to lower corporate taxes so companies can pay their workers more and thus drive domestic consumption; establish a minimum wage; and, critically, provide for education, healthcare and retirement.

On the other hand, Zong blames the media for sensationalizing income disparity by casting a suspicious eye on wealthy people. "The media stirs up anger and protests and creates local 'bandits' who demand equality without working," he says. "People without knowledge can be misled."

Wahaha may be more known in the West for its titanic legal battle with French food giant Groupe Danone, its erstwhile joint venture partner, a struggle that reflects both the increasing importance of the Chinese market and the growing aggressiveness of Chinese companies. In 2007, Danone, the world's largest yogurt maker, initiated action to stop Wahaha from producing and marketing what Danone said were identical products outside their joint ventures.[8] Danone charged that Zong had established over 80 unauthorized companies using the Wahaha brand name illegally. Zong charged that Danone had invested in numerous competitors. At least 25 lawsuits and arbitrations raged on five continents, including a personal lawsuit against Zong's wife and daughter.

The joint venture, once called a "showcase" by *Forbes*, had deteriorated to the point where protesting Wahaha employees shouted nationalistic slogans of wrath outside the five-star Shanghai hotel in which Danone executives were staying, and Danone accused Zong of looting company assets. Each side tried to buy out the other; valuations were quite literally oceans apart.

Chinese courts sided with Wahaha Group's claim to the trademark. A Swedish arbitration tribunal rejected Danone's attempt to prevent Wahaha Group's expansion. In 2008, the warring sides, pressured by their respective governments, agreed to suspend the legal war and negotiate.

I asked Zong Qinghou about the lawsuits. I wasn't so much interested in discerning truth as in how this Chinese entrepreneur thinks. The following is not meant to be balanced.

"Danone cheated and bullied us," Zong begins, with no nuance. (He characterized the joint venture contracts as "unequal treaties," invoking the image of foreign oppression during China's century of humiliations.) According to Zong, Danone effected "a bad-faith takeover" by buying out a third partner in a "stealth transfer of ownership."

"We wanted to grow rapidly, which is why we brought in Danone," Zong says. "But they courted us, not we them. We set four terms: we operate the joint venture; we use our own brand; no layoffs of employees; and provide a pension plan. I was chairman and CEO but at the first board meeting I was stripped of power. The board had to approve all expenditures over RMB 10,000 [$1200]; when I traveled I had to get their consent. But then Danone appointed a person who gave me latitude and we had huge growth, with about 40 ventures in 11 years."

"Danone invested less than RMB 1.4 billion and has received about RMB 4 billion in dividends," Zong states (as if subsequent high returns should justify changing the original legal arrangement). "Danone tried to buy us out at book value, but I refused," he says. "They wanted our company for free. Then they violated the non-compete and tried to constrain us from doing business. But our employees boycotted them."

Zong asserts that Danone invested some RMB 3 billion in competitors. "Although I tried to help, they lost money. Then Danone sent reports to the government—central, provincial, municipal—accusing me of misappropriating assets. They wanted to put me in jail for life! When they lost their case under Chinese jurisdiction, they accused the Chinese judges of being uneducated and biased and they filed suit in the U.S. My daughter was studying in Los Angeles; they sued her for $100 million. They used all means possible against us, including high-powered PR firms and lobbying by the French president. They've lost every case."

"I've lost track of what Danone is doing in China," Zong concludes. "Wahaha is doing very well. We are responsible to our employees and our country."

Wearing an ordinary suit with no hint of wealth, much less great wealth, the gritty Zong Qinghou could pass for a low-level, old-style Chinese manager. But appearances mask his determination and when he speaks he is forceful and resolute and not fearful about criticizing the government. "I warned against China's austerity program [in 2007 and early 2008, right before the financial crisis]," Zong says, "the switch from credit crunch to huge stimulus was swift."

Zong rails against China's corporate tax. "Paying so much tax prevents companies from investing in R&D and upgrading facilities. It's sometimes better to sell the plant for real-estate!" He deplores government bureaucracy. "It's impossible for Beijing-based officials to allocate resources efficiently for the entire country. They make so many wrong policies; that's why they zigzag so much. Deng Xiaoping had it right: Whatever benefits the people is good."

Zong's rejects multi-party democracy. "I've been to Taiwan. They spend so much time and money on elections, wasting both. When politicians get elected they only focus on paying back election debts or preparing for the next election. Nobody cares about the people."

His advice on China's international communication is tinged with nationalism. "Our government is too sensitive to criticism," he says. "We can't simply copy foreign practice. We have our own realities in China. The West doesn't understand. We should ignore the criticism, not change because of it. We must do what's good for China."

★ ★ ★

Sheng Huaren was chairman of the State Economic and Trade Commission in 1998 when Zhu Rongji issued his famous edict about making SOEs profitable in three years. Sheng, a former head of Sinopec, China's largest petrochemical company, reflected that although "SOEs are the pillars of China's economy and were the central point of the reforms, there were no precedents, no models. The big step," he went on, "came when these SOEs became responsible for their own profit-and-loss. We found that we needed much work in the areas of law (e.g., well-defined property rights), management independent of government, and a scientific system of decision-making. All this was new and, to many, daunting."

Reforms of the state sector continued. In 2003, Li Rongrong, director of the State-owned Assets Supervision and Administration Commission, which oversees China's large SOEs, sounded like a market-share-obsessed management consultant when he warned SOE executives, "If you cannot be one of the top three firms in your sector, be prepared to be acquired by some other firm."[9]

In 2006, China's Enterprise Bankruptcy Law was enacted. The new law, which foreign legal experts agreed had a high degree of sophistication, is similar to Chapter 11 of the U.S. bankruptcy code in that it allows insolvent companies to remain in business under court supervision while attempting to reorganize and pay their creditors.[10] It also, for the first time, empowers foreign owners and creditors to assert rights to assets they hold in China and to pursue legal claims in an orderly fashion when businesses fail. "It is an announcement to the world that global commerce can be conducted in China and China is part of the global economy," said Thomas Lauria, chairman of the global financial restructuring and insolvency group at New York-based law firm White & Case.

The new law also gives priority to lenders with secured claims, putting them senior to company employees, a critical and necessary reform in China where workers' rights are appropriately sensitive. (Previously, employees of failed companies came before creditors on claims to collateral, even though the creditors held the collateral, thus discouraging businesses from extending credit and lenders from issuing loans.)

In 2008, the government announced that it would merge about 20 of its remaining SOEs, bringing the number of state-controlled enterprises down to about 130.[11] Beijing stated it intended to reduce the number of large SOEs to as few as 80.[12]

Endnotes

1   I credit the story of the Acheng Sugar Factory bankruptcy to Li Qiang, CCTV's briliant director with whom I worked on my PBS documentary, *In Search of China*. Li Qiang and his crews spent many months in Harbin, braving subfreezing temperatures and poor living conditions to capture the heartbreaking story of China's first major bankruptcy and the resulting human tragedies.

2   The name "Haier" is German in origin, the product of an early joint venture with a German company to acquire world-class technology. The Chinese bought out the Germans but the name stuck.

3   "Haier Launches Stock Option Plan," *China Daily*, December 26, 2006.

4   Author's meeting with Ren Jianxin, Beijing, May 2009.

5 Author's meeting with Zhu Jianghong, Zhuhai, February 2009.
6 "Wahaha's Zong Qinghou heads how new Forbes China Rich List," *People's Daily*, October 28, 2010.
7 Author's meeting with Zong Qinghou, Hangzhou, February 2009.
8 "Danone Loses Claim Against Chinese Partner Wahaha," Bloomberg News, July 14, 2008.
9 Barry Naughton "The State Asset Commission: A Powerful New Government Body" *China Leadership Monitor* No. 8, Fall 2003, p. 5–6.
10 Shu-Ching Jean Chen, "China's Bankruptcy Big Bang," *Forbes*, June 12, 2007
11 Adam Chen, "Sasac to group 20 firms under asset manager," *South China Morning Post*, July 21, 2008
12 Jamil Anderlini, *Financial Times*, August 20, 2008.

22

The Private
Business Revolution

In 2007, the registered capital in China's private sector hit a milestone: RMB 10 trillion (almost $1.5 trillion), symbolizing spectacular transformation. Unambiguously, the private sector has become the engine driving China's growth. China had 5.5 million private enterprises and 27.4 million individual businesses, which together accounted for 61% of China's enterprises by revenue. Twenty-eight private enterprises each had total assets of over $1.5 billion, and 93 had total assets of over $730 million.

Private companies and individual businesses accounted for 40% of China's GDP, while in its broad sense, the non-state sector (private, individual and collective) accounted for 65%. Critically, of the increment in GDP, 70-80% comes from the non-state sector. Private companies are expanding into heavy industry, chemicals, infrastructure, public utilities, and capital markets.

The non-state sector accounts for about 80% of China's total non-agricultural employment. It has become China's seat of innovation. Since reform began, 70% of technology innovations, 65% of invention patents, and 80% of new products have come from medium and small-sized enterprises, of which over 95% are private. In 2008, there were about 150,000 private technology companies in China.

★ ★ ★

Simon Chen, founder and chairman of Evoc Intelligent Technology, an award-winning computer systems company in Shenzhen, exemplifies private sector innovation. In 1991, Chen was working for the Ministry of Aerospace and sent to Shenzhen. In 1992, after Deng Xiaoping's Southern Tour, Chen "jumped into the sea," as the expression goes, and started his own business.

"At the time, the accepted way to start a business was to enter into a joint venture with a state-owned company," he recalls. "To form a private company was not allowed. But a local official told me to come back in ten days, and for whatever reason, I was able to form one of the first private companies in Shenzhen."

Initially, growing the company was hard. "Banks wouldn't provide loans," Chen says. "We struggled for years." Later, China Development Bank started making loans to high-tech businesses, and the State Science and Technology Commission began to offer grants. "Now we're appreciated," says Chen, adding enthusiastically: "It's been 30 years since reform began. Give us another 30 years. Chinese companies will surprise the world."

Huawei Technologies, China's largest telecommunications equipment maker, grew 46% in 2008, notwithstanding the global recession, booking $23 billion in contract sales. While rival firms expected 2009 to be a depressing year, Huawei forecast 30% growth to more than $30 billion.[1] Once criticized as a second-rate company that copied foreign technology—it lost a narrow judgment to Cisco in 2003—Huawei has become an innovation leader, surpassing former leaders such as Nortel, Nokia and Alcatel-Lucent in its drive to become the world's telecom-gear champion.

With more than three-quarters of its business coming from international markets, Shenzhen-based Huawei is the dominant telecom supplier to the developing world and is penetrating North America and Europe. In 2008 Huawei was the world's top international patent seeker and *BusinessWeek*'s first annual list of "The World's Most Influential Companies" named Huawei number 3, after only Apple and Google.

However impressive its technologies, marketing and systems—Huawei's worldwide intranet command center rivals NASA's mission control—what impressed me most was something more subtle. I was holding a simple Huawei marketing brochure showing a map of China and surrounding countries when faint writing caught my eye. Along the China-India border, there is a disputed region in the Himalayas over which the world's two most populous countries fought a hot war in 1962, with large-scale combat at altitudes above 14,000 feet. A half century on, the territorial dispute still smolders, particularly in India.

So here's the conundrum: Huawei is a Chinese company that wants to do big business in India; in China, borders are sensitive because they reflect sovereignty, and in India there is enduring conviction that China is occupying Indian land. What to do? The Huawei map simply describes the realities on the ground in a way that both sides can accept. The disputed territory, controlled entirely by China, is demarcated by the objective statements "Chinese line of control" (closest to India) and "Indian claims" (farthest into China). In a gentle tilt toward India, the shading of the disputed territory looks like India, not like China. Huawei's first foray into India, I'm told, was not successful; the second time they got it right.

Two other Shenzhen-based companies are also shaking up their markets: Mindray in cost-efficient healthcare (patient monitoring equipment and ultrasound diagnostics) and Fantawild (Shenzhen Huaqiang Group) in digital entertainment and theme-park technologies. The Fantawild Park in Anhui Province, driving distance from Nanjing, Hangzhou and Shanghai, is said to be the largest on earth and to feature advanced technology. The company itself is built on a Disney model, and although still minuscule in comparison, Fantawild seeks to challenge Disney in technology, content, and theme parks. Fantawild's 4D films provide multi-modal sensory experiences, such as chair movements, air pressure and water sprays, amplifying the impact of 3D motion pictures. Before one dismisses Fantawild's ambition, remember Huawei!

★ ★ ★

China's private sector was given a significant boost in 2007, when the National People's Congress passed perhaps the most controversial law since the Communist Party took power in 1949—a landmark Property Law, which for the first time gave explicit legal safeguards to forms of private property.[2] The Property Law was adopted after an extraordinary 14-year debate, some of it incandescently hot. It was to have been passed in 2006 but had to be pulled due to extreme opposition by conservatives.

China's leaders promoted the new law to facilitate the continuing expansion of the private sector. Prior to its enactment, citizens could buy and sell private property freely, but its legal status remained murky. The new law reassured entrepreneurs and the growing middle classes—both essential for China's growth and for sustaining CPC authority—that their accumulating assets were secure and not subject to political whim and caprice.

And this was precisely the reason why the bill had elicited such sharp opposition. Left-wing critics, mainly academics and former officials, contended that the CPC was wrenching itself off its ideological foundation, which was based on public ownership. One of the petitions against the law, signed openly by hundreds of professors and retired cadres, argued that, by equating private property with public property, it overturned the basic system of socialism, and would worsen endemic inequality.

The official line, however, stressed that the Property Law was a milestone in managing State affairs according to law. *People's Daily*, the Party's mouthpiece, stated that "the Property Law sends out a strong signal that China will deepen its reform and opening-up process"—though other Chinese media recognized that enforcing the law would prove as critical as its enactment. One local newspaper called the law "only a fine start in a more arduous journey to protect citizens' property."

★ ★ ★

The Youngor Group, one of the world's largest men's garment manufacturers, is headquartered in Ningbo, Zhejiang Province, China's second largest port. With its strong brands, Youngor is China's market leader in suits and shirts, and with the acquisition of Smart Shirt from US-based Kellwood Corp., Youngor gained an American distribution network. The company employs over 50,000 people and had 2008 sales of about $3 billion.

Chairman Li Rucheng founded Youngor in 1979, investing RMB 20,000 after having left his rural hometown. For several years he produced OEM garments for companies in Shanghai. Margins were very low, of course, so Li decided to develop his own brands. He found capital and technology in Hong Kong and Macao and took dead aim at besting Shanghai brands.[3]

Today, 90+% of Youngor's sales are of its own brands and almost 80% of distribution is through company-owned stores or counters in department stores. "Our brands can generate gross margins approaching 70%," he says, "compared with the cut-throat OEM business where we struggled to squeeze out 20%." The increasing recognition of Youngor brands internationally fulfills Li's life-long dream.

"Capital no longer constrains our expansion," Li notes. "Management is our major challenge, particularly international executives working multiple cultures. Part of the value of our Kellwood acquisition is the 80 American and 300 Hong Kong employees."

"Ideas can be leveraged," Li reflects. "'riding the right trend', companies must find their own way. Every company is unique."

For years, Youngor was weak, the poor relative, compared to leading international apparel companies (for which Younger manufactured garments), but now some of those same companies come to Ningbo to ask for help. "I wish I could spend more time with you," Li Rucheng told me after our detailed discussion, "but I'm negotiating with a French company that wants us to purchase them." Li then paid me the ultimate compliment: "I don't remember spending so much time with a visitor without getting an order."

★ ★ ★

The growing status of China's private sector was again highlighted in 2008, when private businesses made significant donations to relief efforts following the May Sichuan earthquake. "All I've been thinking about is earthquake relief work," said Quan Zhezhu, Party secretary of the All-China Federation of Industry and Commerce (ACFIC), when I met him in June. "Private sector donations in money and materials already exceed $730 million, accounting for over 20% of the total," he noted.[4]

Six private companies had donated over $15 million, Quan said, the largest being China Oceanwide at $36 million. Quan, whose organization represents the interests of private companies in China—under Party guidance of course —said it was a sign that, "after 30 years of reform and opening-up, many private companies are starting to take social responsibilities seriously. They used to be very passive—now they're more proactive."

There were two main reasons for this, he suggested. "In the early years, entrepreneurs' main objective had to be profit-seeking," Quan said. "They had no choice—starting and building a business is hard, risky work. Now enterprises are becoming more mature, with increasing economic capabilities. The other reason is gratitude: such enterprises are the largest beneficiaries of new policies."

There was another factor too: successful private companies were now in the spotlight of public opinion. "If the public thinks that some are not 'doing their fair share', society will condemn them," Quan noted. "Take Wang Shi, chairman of Vanke, [China's largest publicly traded property developer] who is now under heavy fire for being too stingy." When Vanke donated under $300,000 to quake-hit areas, there was a barrage of criticism in the media, and an outcry from netizens in blogs; Vanke's share price dropped and Wang Shi was compelled to apologize and dramatically increase his donation to almost $15 million.[5]

Quan stressed that charitable donations should be voluntary, but successful private companies do have social responsibilities. Nevertheless, he emphasized that "the first and primary social responsibility that companies have is to build their businesses and make them robust: if an enterprise does poorly and lays off workers, society suffers. A good, strong company creates more wealth for the country, makes its employees more secure, and produces high-quality products for consumers." Thus, he said, it was understandable that "companies facing business or financial trouble could not afford to be socially generous—and it would be wrong if they were."

For other enterprises, such as those which cause pollution—ceramics factories, for example—"their major social responsibility is not donation but transformation," Quan said—either to clean up their act, or to close down. "Social responsibility is not just a matter of charity," he added. "It also concerns enterprise development, moral standards, and corporate culture." Environmental protection and resources conservation are issues that cannot be shirked, he said.

Quan Zhezhu spent his career promoting market-economy ideas, often before their time. An ethnic Korean, he was born in Yanbian, Jilin Province, near the North Korean border. (Yanbian is a Korean Autonomous Prefecture, home to many of China's two million ethnic Koreans, one of the country's larger and most prosperous minority communities.) "My father was a pediatrician; my mother a teacher," Quan said, adding. "Koreans attach great importance to education; my parents encouraged me to study hard—but because I was so naughty, my mother quit her job to take care of me."

In 1988, Quan called for a shareholding system to enable accountability. In 1999, as Jilin's propaganda chief, he caused controversy by asking "What makes a good book?" and by providing his own unorthodox answer: "It's not what leaders say. It's not what scholars say. It's what people say, and people vote with their pocketbook. Revenues determine good books."

When Quan first came to ACFIC, public attitudes toward private business people were rather negative. "There was an assumption of 'original sin'," he said, "the accusation being that entrepreneurs generally made their first 'pot of gold' by exploiting loopholes in the law." Now, however, China's leaders see the private sector as vital. "This used to be a backwater organization," he said. "Now ACFIC, supporting the private sector, is the frontline of China's development. [Politburo Standing members] Jia Qinglin, Xi Jinping and Li Keqiang are all extremely supportive. Whenever I ask for a meeting, they accommodate me," he explained. "In May [2008] I met with [Vice-President] Xi Jinping to discuss ACFIC work and personnel."

"Central leaders focus on how best to foster a strong private sector," Quan continued, "and we're determined to support and serve the private sector. We have challenges. Private entrepreneurs are emerging as a 'new social stratum'—they're a new social class, there's no denying it. They are not exploiters of workers as in the past but rather builders of a new socialist society."

"ACFIC is increasingly important to the Party. I'm sure of this," Quan added. "In fact, the reason I'm a minister in the Party's United Front Work Department in addition to my directing ACFIC is because as a non-government organization ACFIC cannot issue directives, such as to provincial leaders. As a minister I am empowered to issue major directives."

"I listen to entrepreneurs; I want their candid thoughts," Quan stressed. "They have no pretense; they get right to the point; they've no time for empty words. When I speak, if they don't think what I'm saying is useful, they go to sleep or walk out."

According to Quan, China's entrepreneurs came from diverse backgrounds: rural people, so-called "farmer-entrepreneurs" who started

Quan Zhezhu, Party secretary of the All-China Federation of Commerce & Industry (June 2008).

township enterprises; urban unemployed; former civil servants, scholars from scientific and technological institutes, laid-off SOE managers; returned overseas Chinese; and college graduates—some of whom cannot find jobs and have no choice but to start their own businesses.

In Quan's opinion, much work must be done on the structure, strategy and management of China's private enterprises, many of which grew out of family businesses: as a result they suffer from closed ownership, irrational corporate governance, and high risks in decision making.

"I support family businesses," Quan explained, "but I'm against patriarchal management. Company ownership should be open and diversified so that the modern corporate system can be introduced. A mixture of owners," he stressed, "gives vitality. It creates natural checks-and-balances, helping to correct errors and catch and reverse bad decisions. With different owners, the decision-makers can listen to different or even opposing opinions."

Above all, Quan suggested, "a proper system is more important than a competent person, and professionalism trumps academic smarts." Many Chinese entrepreneurs failed because they had allowed success to go to their heads, he said. "Basking in compliments, applause and worship, they lost touch with reality and started to make mistakes. And if there is no modern corporate system in place, when the boss goes down, the enterprise goes down with him."

Quan emphasized that success in increasingly competitive markets meant the ability to "change before change becomes essential—to adapt to change, to be good at changing." But he warned that enterprises should be wary of over-diversifying: China's private firms tend to be small in scale, yet engage in diversified industries, resulting in lower proprietary content in their products and depressed competitiveness. "Most Chinese enterprises don't have what it takes to diversify successfully," Quan argued. "If you diversify blindly, the larger the scale, the higher the risks. An enterprise should first concentrate on one thing and build a strong market position."

There are two other "common shortcomings" in the corporate cultures of Chinese private companies, he added. One is a lack of employee participation. "Corporate culture is not 'boss culture'," Quan explained, "but something co-created by both decision makers and staff."

The other was "the absence of a recognizable 'personality'—a bona fide corporate culture," he said, "is one that cannot be easily copied by other companies. It should be unique." Most Chinese private firms, however, do not have proprietary, market-recognizable brands, forcing them to compete at the lower end of the industrial value chain where margins are always tight. Enterprises need to bolster their image: "The reputation of an enterprise is also a kind of productive force and can decrease certain costs," Quan emphasized. "Corporate culture and credibility sustain enterprises."

In Quan Zhezhu's opinion, the first 30 years of China's reform were, in essence, the "first act" for the private economy, when it often relied on favorable policies. Now the private sector is entering the "second act," in which it must solve comprehensive problems, especially for small and medium-sized firms (SMEs).

★ ★ ★

China has about 40 million SMEs, the vast majority of which are very small and run by individuals.[6] As in most free-market countries, SMEs have become the Chinese economy's most dynamic sector, accounting for some three-quarters of the urban labor force and driving innovation.[7]

But Chinese SMEs are also vulnerable. They typically make products for export: after the RMB began to appreciate (about 20% in three years), their products became more expensive for overseas buyers. Facing fierce global competition, SMEs had to decide whether to raise their export prices in foreign currencies, which would depress sales, or maintain prices and watch their profit margins erode—and in many cases evaporate. To make matters worse, the stunning global financial crisis of 2008 substantially reduced foreign demand and many SMEs were devastated. Tens of thousands went out of business. The hardest hit were those in labor-intensive sectors such as textile and garments.[8]

Furthermore, China's large banks have historically not supported private companies, especially SMEs, which are often starved for capital. But China's leaders now recognize SME importance, and as part of the 2008 economic stimulus package, introduced new policies to support and strengthen SMEs, especially those involved in exports that provide so many jobs in coastal regions.[9] Included were measures to stimulate banks to lend to SMEs. (By mid 2009, China's four largest state banks had outstanding loans to SMEs approaching $1 trillion, a huge increase).

China Construction Bank is pioneering greater SME lending. CCB President Zhang Jianguo, who began his career as a loan officer, wrote two town-hall-like letters to employees encouraging them to turn the financial "crisis into opportunity" (the word in Chinese means both) by "pro-actively reaching out to SMEs during this shaky period."[10] The best SMEs are flexible, high-growth and generate jobs, the English-speaking Zhang says, and "they will be the next wave of bank revenues."

So this is the moment to "grab the best," he adds, stressing "Own the client!" Reflecting his down-to-earth pragmatism, Zhang draws an analogy with a banquet "where first-comers scoop up all the top-quality food." He attributes CCB's SME success to intense analysis, excellent IT systems, and dedicated teams that know SME managers.

(Recognizing the ever-present threat of corruption when dealing with SMEs—some entrepreneurs try to bribe loan officers—Zhang quotes the Chinese saying, "Walking along the river, it's hard not to get your shoes wet." The antidotes, he says, are special task-forces and training to resist temptation.)

A long-discussed SME Board on the Shenzhen Stock Exchange—Growth Enterprise Market—was anticipated to open in late 2009. With looser rules, it would provide access to capital for high-growth, largely high-tech SMEs.

Ironically, just as China's economy is increasingly dependent on private business, private business is facing its most serious challenges. But at least these days China's leaders are paying close attention and have committed their support.

Endnotes

1   Kirby Chien, "China Huawei '08 contract sales up 46 pct to $23 bln-report," Reuters, January 7, 2009.

2   Mary-Anne Toy, *Sydney Morning Herald*, March 17, 2007.

3   Author's meeting with Li Rucheng, Ningbo, February 2009.

4   Author's meeting with Quan Zhezhu, June 2008, January 2009.

5   Diao Yang, *China Daily*, June 6, 2008.

6   Xin Zhiming, *China Daily*, September 12, 2008.

7   My interest in Chinese SMEs stems partly from my early work on American SMEs when I was at MIT in 1979-1980. At the time, the conventional wisdom was that only very large and very small companies would survive, and that most mid-sized companies would disappear. My research showed that this easy generalization did not hold in many specific industries and instances, and that many SMEs would "flourish among giants"—the title of one of my books (Robert Lawrence Kuhn, *To Flourish Among Giants: Creative Management for Mid-Sized Firms*, John Wiley, 1985).

8   Wang Lan, *China Daily*, August 5, 2008.

9   These initiatives included guidance to commercial banks to increase loans to SMEs, rebates of value-added taxes, tax credits for fixed-asset investments, requiring local governments to buy SME products, subsidies and loan guarantees (e.g., for acquiring new technologies), legalization of informal sources of credit (e.g., credit clubs and private moneylenders, on which many SMEs rely for their capital), various funds dedicated to SMEs (e.g., for international marketing), and establishing a bank that would specialize in SME lending. (Barry Naughton, "A New Team Faces Unprecedented Economic Challenges," *China Leadership Monitor*, No. 26.)

10 Author's meeting with Zhang Jianguo, May 2009.

Banking Reform: The Largest Assets and Greatest Risks

In the late 1990s experts feared that the Chinese banking system, burdened by incalculable amounts of bad debt, could cause the collapse of China's entire economy. The fear was expressed not only by China's foreign critics, but by domestic officials and economists too.

In 2008, of the world's top five banks by stock market capitalization, *three* were Chinese. The world's number one valued bank was the Industrial and Commercial Bank of China (ICBC); its value peak of more than $300 billion was 40% higher than any other bank. How did this happen?

Historically, Chinese banks were more funding agents of government subsidy than prudent lenders of commercial credit. They functioned as cash-transferring funnels, into which the state treasury poured money in order to prop up inefficient state-owned enterprises (SOEs), which lost money constantly but provided employment. In a planned economy this actually made sense, but with the transition to a market economy, it had become a severe liability.

Change began when the government removed the bad loans from major banks' balance sheets, put them into special-purpose companies (which would hold and sell off these bad loans), and recapitalized the major banks with tens of billions of dollars of fresh capital. The government also brought in foreign financial institutions as minority investors, to help change the banks' management style and create a credit culture. This transformation, while still on-going, has been a great success. Banks are now broadly accountable to commercial economics not government orders.

Liu Mingkang, chairman of the China Banking Regulatory Commission (CBRC), which is responsible for overseeing all banking institutions in China, told me his personal story of banking reform.[1]

Liu Mingkang, chairman of China Banking Regulatory Commission (Beijing, April 2008).

As with virtually all China's reforms, Liu emphasized the Party Plenary in 1978 as the "demarcation line in China's banking history." At the time, he was a steel worker in Jiangsu Province. "I got the news on the radio and realized that China would see a huge change, because the focus had shifted to economic development and modernization," he recalls. "Right after that, I was recruited by the People's Bank of China, the Central Bank's Jiangsu branch."

In 1979, the government broke up the "all-in-one" banking system. Previously there was only one bank in China—the People's Bank of China (PBOC). "But PBOC itself said, 'No, it's not enough—we should not be the only bank in China," Liu says. "The first step was to create a bank that specialized in rural financing: we separated out the Agricultural Bank of China (ABC) from the PBOC. Then we separated out the Bank of China (BOC) to specialize in foreign exchange business—foreign trade payment and settlement, trade financing, and shipping insurance. We called these 'specialized banks', he says. "This was vital."

Next was the People's Construction Bank of China, later renamed China Construction Bank (CCB), which specialized in large-scale infrastructure financing. Then in 1983 the State Council decided that PBOC should only maintain the Central Bank's role. One year later, the Industrial and Commercial Bank of China (ICBC) was separated from PBOC, taking all industrial and commercial banking operations and services, including the savings business. ICBC immediately became China's largest bank. Thus by early 1984, China had one central bank and four specialized banks.

"This was certainly progress, but there were some odd consequences," says Liu Mingkang. "Take a specific construction project. Through the construction period and up to the commissioning date, China Construction Bank would be responsible for originating loans. After the commissioning date, all accounts would be switched to Industrial and Commercial Bank of China. And if there was any foreign exchange involved, such as for imported items, then that part would be handled by Bank of China. The cash flow would have to be divided into two streams: one to repay the loans from BOC, and the other to pay back ICBC's working capital and loans. And if there were any additional money, this would be repaid to CCB for the original construction loans."

As a result, Liu says, "CCB complained, saying, 'I'm hatching all the eggs, but, when they become chickens, they go first to your courtyard. Where is my turf?!' This reflects our banking structure at that time."

Nonetheless, from 1984 to 1997, there was relative stability in China's banking system. "The government was busy from 1989 to the mid-1990s with two issues," says Liu Mingkang. "After the political event in 1989, China faced huge downside risks, with heavy foreign and domestic pressure. But thanks to Deng Xiaoping's Southern Tour [*Nanxun*] in 1992, reform and opening-up were put back on track." The second issue, Liu explains, was the subsequent overheating of the economy, which resulted in high inflation (1993-1995). "Every province wanted to develop instantly," he notes. "They were willing to try all sorts of things and the central government could hardly control them. Prices were going up very quickly; the Central Bank was running out of cash; some food prices doubled or tripled. The government instituted stringent measures to rectify market disorders and cool down the economy. It was a huge economic and political battle."

During this period, banking reform moved forward ponderously. But China's leaders gradually realized that the four specialized banks could never turn themselves around and become real commercial banks if they were still required to issue policy loans, with little chance of being repaid. So when Zhu Rongji came to Beijing as vice premier, he reignited banking reform by setting up policy banks. In 1994, three policy banks were formed: first was the State Development Bank, now called the China Development Bank (CDB); second was the Export-Import Bank of China (Eximbank); and third the Agricultural Development Bank of China (ADBC).

The great benefit of these policy banks was that they transformed the four specialized banks. By transferring government-dictated loans, the specialized banks could focus on commercial loans and begin their journey of conversion into real commercial banks. A whole new vocabulary emerged, as bankers now had to begin talking about capital adequacy issues, non-performing loans and their classification, risk management, and independent due diligence—all of which are needed for banks to be truly commercial.

1995 could be described as China's "year of financial law": new laws enacted gave the Central Bank and the four commercial banks the legal basis to operate on their own. And as their business boundaries blurred with each passing day, these previously specialized banks started to compete in more diversified markets.

But after a year of high growth and low inflation in 1996, China was buffeted by the Asian Financial Crisis. "In November 1997, China held a financial conference at which we instituted a whole series of reforms," Liu Mingkang recalls. "We put in place banking, insurance, and stock market policies. For China's state-owned commercial banks, policies targeted tightening credit, enhancing internal controls and reducing non-performing loans ratios."

Significantly, Liu says, "the government was preparing to pump money into the four commercial banks to build up their capital adequacy ratios." In fact, "the real purpose of that conference was to 'clean the courtyard', making the four commercial banks accountable for their future decisions and behavior, and putting them all on the same playing field, so that they could compete with one another."

China's banking industry was "in heaven," Liu notes, with great enthusiasm that reform and restructuring would move ahead. This new freedom to cross the old "borders" of their former specialized areas meant that "the Agricultural Bank of China staff were very happy," says Liu, "maybe the happiest people in the banking industry. They said, 'Now we can take off our straw shoes and wear shiny leather shoes, enter the urban market, do business with rich people and compete with our friends at BOC and ICBC!'"

The next major step in banking reform came in 1998, when the Ministry of Finance injected RMB 270 billion ($32.5 billion) into the four commercial banks to augment their capital.[2] In addition, the government urged banks to carve off their non-performing loans (NPLs).

"At the time I was in charge of almost all regulatory and supervisory work at the central bank, under Governor Dai Xianglong," says Liu Mingkang. "The four presidents of the four big commercial banks were always coming to us making excuses. They were passionate: 'We have heavy legacy burdens from history. They were caused not by our mismanagement but by loans required by the state and imposed on us,' they told us. 'We can show you the certificates and instructions from government departments, or from VIPs. . .' Listening to all the excuses was very interesting!"

"But Zhu Rongji, who had just become premier, was fed up with excuses," says Liu. "He said to the bank presidents, 'Let's say goodbye to all these excuses. No more government-dictated loans. I'll give you money in one shot. Carve off all your existing non-performing loans—I don't care where they came from, but I do care about your future behavior. I'll get proper benchmarks to measure your performance from here on. [For new bad loans] I will hold accountable those who are responsible'."

In 1999, RMB 1.4 trillion ($169 billion) in non-performing loans were carved off from the four commercial banks. Four state-owned asset management companies were established to manage and/or sell off these bad loans.

"You loaned your money to your customers," Zhu told the banks, explaining his decision to set up these independent companies, "but when those loans became bad, it's better to let someone else blow the trumpet."

According to Liu Mingkang, "Premier Zhu encouraged us to speak with people from RTC [the Resolution Trust Company which managed the U.S. Savings & Loan bailout between 1989 and 1995.] We heard mixed stories from the former RTC chief about their experience—there were threats and coercion, including a bullet in an envelope. The RTC people taught us lessons they learned," he adds, "but our Chinese side took their experiences too lightly. The reason was that, at that time, our overall system had not changed; the legal framework was not yet in place; the hazards [conflicts of interest] between commercial banks and asset management companies were still present. The RTC people said, 'You need integrity and need guts.' But our Chinese listeners needed something more."

In one meeting with the four major banks' presidents, Premier Zhu invited them to explain to him the difference between the Chinese banking system and the Canadian banking system. A few days earlier, Zhu told them, he had received a delegation of Canadian bankers, and had asked them, "What is your non-performing loans ratio?" (Zhu asked this question every time he met foreign bankers.) Everybody told him, "2% or less."

At the time, according to Liu Mingkang, China's non-performing loans were between 26% and 30%, though the real number was "much higher."[3] In early 2000, for example, when Liu became president of Bank of China (BOC), he discovered that "the non-performing loans ratio of our banking industry was 33-34%." And, he adds, if the NPLs carved out when China set up the asset management companies in 1999 were included, a further 9% to 10% should have been added, bringing total non-performing loans to over 40%! In fact, Liu recalls, "the NPL stock of the Chinese banking industry amounted to RMB 3 trillion ($362 billion) nationwide."

"Premier Zhu was determined to bring discipline and integrity to business in China," says Liu. "I reported to him several times in person. He was extremely intense and could be harsh. He told bank executives, 'After three years, if you can't bring your NPL ratio down, you must quit your job.'"

"But in the end the NPL ratio was still high," Liu recalls. "The problem was systemic. During Premier Zhu's term [1998-2003], bank presidents were still thinking about market share, deposit earnings, loan expansions, and so on. In those years, the capital adequacy ratio was not accurate. Furthermore," he notes, "it was easier to reduce the NPL ratio and approach the benchmark, because China was booming and so the total amount of loans was becoming larger and larger! So the NPL ratio is not enough." Later, Liu says, Wen Jiabao, who succeeded Zhu Rongji as premier, emphasized that he used "dual benchmarks": "'One is the NPL ratio', Premier Wen told me. 'The other is the total amount of NPLs. We should reduce both'."

In 2003, Liu Mingkang was appointed chairman of the newly established China Banking Regulatory Commission (CBRC), an independent body set up to take over the supervision role from the Central Bank. Premier Wen summoned Liu to his office in Zhongnanhai to discuss his new role. It was a Sunday afternoon and Wen's first sentence was, "For 14 years, I've worked every weekend. So don't be surprised that I called you on a Sunday."

Liu, who had been both a regulator and a banker, stressed that he would "'grasp the two ends and bring the middle forward.'" The first "end" was the big four state-owned commercial banks: "We must grasp these firmly," he told the premier, "by diversifying ownership, bringing in sound corporate governance, building up internal control systems, and learning from all practices and experiences which are useful to transform these four banks into real commercial banks—not just by continuing to inject money into them." If the big four banks, whose market share at that time was approaching 60% [later down to under 50%], could be turned around, Liu said, "then the whole financial market and the whole banking industry would be brought into discipline."

The second "end" to be grasped, Liu continues, was rural financing reform, "which we had to improve to support and motivate the farmers to till their land and produce grain and food to feed our 1.3 billion people. Premier Wen's face lit up and he nodded," Liu recalls.

The "middle" which needed to be pulled along consisted of China's many stock-holding banks, city commercial banks, city cooperatives, and non-banking financial institutions, such as trust companies, leasing and financing companies. "They also needed reform to adopt modern corporate philosophy and carry out prudential operations," Liu states. "I said to Premier Wen, 'What I need is policy'."

Premier Wen concurred, telling Liu that "to reform our system, we need to enhance sound regulation, and to cultivate talent." In Liu's opinion, the root of China's problem was that, from 1949, its banking industry followed the Russian model. "Nobody could talk about diversifying ownership or commercializing SOE banks," he explains, "because it would seem as if you were shaking the pillar, the foundation, of the whole socialist system. But Premier Wen was committed to deepening reform and clearly defining property rights —this was brand-new policy."

Wen Jiabao suggested starting reform with one bank, and asked the amount of each bank's non-performing loans. Bank of China and China Construction Bank had less NPLs and were better capitalized than Agricultural Bank of China and ICBC, Liu told him.

In fact, Bank of China (BOC) had the least NPLs because, in 2002, with Premier Zhu Rongji's approval, Liu Mingkang, then BOC chairman, had merged Bank of China Hong Kong with 13 smaller banks to form a new entity. It was the first large overseas M&A in the Chinese banking industry and it attracted international attention and awards. After the merger, ownership was diversified from 100% Beijing-owned to about 65%.

"The initial public offering (IPO) in the international capital markets was a great success," Liu reports. "The price/book ratio was 20% higher than the market average of other similar banks. We had carved off the non-performing assets and made the action transparent by using independent directors, auditors, and assessors to help us. Also, we introduced strategic investors for the first time in Chinese banking history."

Then someone suggested starting reform with only one SOE bank—such as Bank of China—in order to get experience on a trial basis. But Liu Mingkang said: "If you want to have babies, you should have a couple of them so that they can compete with each other and you can compare them. A single baby will be spoiled." So reform started with China Construction Bank and Bank of China." (Later, Bank of Communications was added so that there were three banks in the first round of restructuring.)

According to Liu, Premier Wen told banking leaders, "For all of us, including myself, this is a war with our backs to the water—it's a game we can't afford to lose. We must guarantee success." Once work began, it moved swiftly. From Wen Jiabao's declaration of the start of reform to the injection of capital, took just over one year. A new era of China's banking history had arrived. The essential steps included:

- Ownership change and diversification, the first of its kind.
- Sweeping restructuring, injecting capital and carving off bad assets.
- Cooperation with foreign institutional strategic investors brought in world-class experts and advisors. There was natural tension here. On the one hand, China was loathe for Western financial institutions to dominate its finance and banking sector. On the other hand, it desperately needed Western expertise and experience (as well as capital): running commercial banking, managing credit facilities, controlling risk.
- A new approach was taken for non-performing loans. The government bought 100% of the "total loss" category, but only 50% of the doubtful category, so banks had to recover the other 50% of these loans. Furthermore, NPLs were allocated by competitive bidding not private negotiations. And some asset management companies were allowed to repackage and sell NPLs, nourishing market mechanisms of asset management.

ICBC, China's largest bank, followed as the fourth bank to be reformed. "It was the biggest success of all," says Liu. "We diversified ownership by introducing foreign institutional strategic investors who helped the bank restructure corporate governance and risk management, and develop wealth management and modern retail services like bank cards, online-banking services, and so forth. It was a brand-new approach through which the banks could turn themselves around."

In Liu Mingkang's view, restructuring Agricultural Bank of China, begun in 2009, would mean "the end of the era of wholly state-owned banks." Likewise, the largest state policy bank, China Development Bank, would have to be "100% commercial" Liu adds. "Our work never stops."

How can ABC continue to wear the "hat of agriculture" (focusing on rural work) and be economically viable? According to Liu Mingkang: "They will start from day one by establishing an independent strategic business unit (SBU) for rural finance, which will have separate accounting, cost/profit analysis, training methods, and incentive and motivation schemes. If it turns out that this line of rural business needs some subsidies," he adds, "this could be quickly measured, so that the Ministry of Finance can comfortably support the rural SBU without the confusion and moral hazards of allocating subsidies to the entire bank."

Liu stresses that Premier Wen Jiabao's commitment and encouragement played an important part in China's banking reforms. "He likes to sit down and talk with us," Liu says. "We pick the most important issues where we need his guidance."

Liu describes how "peer group comparison puts heavy pressure on Chinese banking executives. The Chinese people care a good deal about their 'face'," he explains, "so peer group comparison is very powerful.

Liu notes that "Every time I meet with a bank chairman or president, they say, 'Chairman Liu, we've made progress. This year we're No. 2, rather than No. 5.' So they care where they stand. Moreover," he adds, "our banks now have diversified board members and highly professional independent directors, most of whom are overseas returnees. When we bring in strategic partners, we require that they send the experts we need." Transparency is also now taken seriously, Liu says. "We tell board members what we find. So the overseas directors immediately question the majority-representing directors here in China, asking, 'Why didn't we know this? What happened? And what's your plan to rectify or mitigate the risks noted by CBRC?'"

And, Liu emphasizes, "We also tell them that if you do not correct yourself in a timely fashion, we will report these issues to the SEC in Hong Kong (where the banks are listed). We must be responsible to public investors worldwide."

"Initially, we had to push the banks," Liu recalls, "now they're pushing us. They ask CBRC's help to build better systems, for example. We kept them busy at first; now they keep us busy."

"The pressures on my shoulders are heavier than ever," Liu says, "because all the current question marks require fundamental change in the legal framework, accounting systems, and taxation systems."

Looking back on what he called "remarkable" changes, Liu notes that "Five or ten years ago, everyone said that China's banks were on the brink of bankruptcy. Today [2008], we have a long queue of investors waiting to get a stake in a Chinese bank. 'Let me have one,' they say. And if you give them one, they say 'Let me have another'!" Yet just a few years earlier, he comments, when China Construction Bank was first seeking strategic investors, "it went first to its domestic friends, but the answer was 'No'—nobody liked Chinese banks, not even the Chinese! So CCB went to Bank of America and others; the negotiations were very hard."

Subsequently, Liu says, some people suggested that Chinese banks had been sold too cheaply. "They didn't know the reality," he asserts. "Why weren't there any Chinese strategic investors? As one CCB executive put it, 'domestic investors all turned their backs to me.'"

Now, Liu says, China's banking industry is confidently moving forward with the market approach, though he is quick to add "Having said all this, I don't mean to imply we're perfect. We still have difficulties and challenges." The biggest, he says, "remains corporate governance. We've taken bold steps, but they're not sufficient. The credit culture is still very weak in China. It must be nourished: discipline, incentives, education, cultivation—it's a huge endeavor."

The Chinese banking industry could "never be fully successful," Liu adds, unless it "moves forward side-by-side with domestic reform, especially of large SOEs. The Chinese banking industry cannot thrive by itself," he explains. "And we still find interference from some local governments."

Furthermore, even after all the reforms, Liu stresses that there is still need for "a massive change of culture in banking service. Most Chinese banks are still not focused on delivering value," he says. "The Customer is King is still only a slogan. Banks must deliver what customers, clients, businesses, and markets request." Staff quality is another problem, he says. "I think the top executives of the large SOE banks have the right capabilities. But they cannot yet access the talent market, especially internationally, to recruit and retain the best people."

"So while we have a very warm heart," Liu concludes, "we must always keep a very cool head!"

Speaking assertively during the global financial crisis with both head and heart, Liu Mingkang criticized the U.S. and other developed countries for not doing enough to detoxify bad bank assets. He said solving global banking problems was essential for economy recovery. "Toxic assets must be immediately resolved world-wide. Absent a radical carving off of toxic assets in one go, the picture will never be good," Liu stressed, noting that, in contrast, China's banking system is "sound and solid."[4] How the world had turned!

★ ★ ★

According to one insider, the person primarily responsible for the remarkable transformation of China's banking system, particularly the resolution of some $865 billion in bad loans, is Zhou Xiaochuan, governor of the People's Bank of China, China's central banker. At the time, Zhou was said to have "one of the toughest jobs on earth."[5]

"I attended the major meetings," the insider told me passionately; "I know what happened—Zhou deserves the credit."

Educated as a chemical engineer with a PhD in economic systems engineering (Tsinghua University), Zhou is an erudite economist lauded for his intellect and diplomacy and called "China's most able technocrat." (He has written a dozen books and 100 academic articles.)

Moreover, Zhou has had perhaps the broadest experience in China's financial sector, with leadership positions in foreign exchange and securities regulation (he attacked corruption at listed companies). As president of China Construction Bank (1998-2000), he oversaw creation of the asset-management companies to work out the banking system's bad debt.

In response to the financial crisis (2009), Zhou stirred controversy by calling for a new "super-sovereign reserve currency" which, over time, would replace current reliance on the U.S. dollar. The goal, Zhou wrote, is to "create an international reserve currency that is disconnected from individual nations and is able to remain stable in the long run."[6]

★ ★ ★

Chen Yuan, the son of late Party elder Chen Yun, has been governor of China Development Bank (CDB) since 1998. "I've tried very hard to convert CDB from a 'bad bank' into a 'good bank'," he says. "When I took office, CDB had only RMB 500 billion in loans, of which more than 33% were non-performing. Working to correct that," he acknowledges, "has been difficult. I've tried to change the CDB culture and the attitude of government agencies with which we work. I've tried to build strong ties with local governments. The story sounds simple, but I've spent a great deal of time thinking about how to make a good loan and a good bank."[7]

Chen Yuan's own story began in 1988, when he joined the People's Bank of China, and was sent on a two-week training program in the U.S. "My classroom was Washington and New York. I visited the Fed, the Treasury, investment banks and commercial banks. They were my teachers. I learned supervision, risk management, payment services, and financial products. Breaks between meetings were the best time to learn." Indeed, he adds, "every time I'm in the U.S. I learn."

At the time, Chen was in charge of information technology at PBOC, and visited the computer center of the New York Fed. "That was when I decided to significantly improve our system, which was quite underdeveloped," he says. "Now the PBOC system is probably No. 2 in the world. Each day on average we transact RMB one trillion [almost $150 billion]. I'm proud of that."

After becoming CDB governor, Chen Yuan focused on the fact that all CDB borrowers had local governments behind them, whether directly or indirectly. He told local officials: "CDB will provide more loans provided that you provide sound, resilient governance and introduce financial criteria into your system." The officials were very happy to hear this, Chen recalls, since they had no other access to debt capital: "Commercial enterprises can go to commercial banks for loans, but local infrastructure projects, such as highways and urban utilities, cannot get loans from commercial banks—because these loans are long-term by necessity, and there are no qualified borrowers."

To overcome such structural obstacles, Chen Yuan pioneered a new system, requesting that local governments inject their high-quality assets into a commercial entity, which could then, as a more credit-worthy borrower, construct local infrastructure projects such as power plants, airports, seaports, and telecom systems.

"The mechanism worked well," he says. "In a few years, we built a nationwide system. Every province followed the model and could borrow a large amount of money from CDB."

In terms of capital investment in China, CDB accounts for around 30% of the market (in the past it was 40%). Chen says, "Now we're undergoing new reforms to make ourselves more commercial. Perhaps we will list in the public markets."

Chen is tough-minded about the continuing need for reform, stressing capital markets and monetary policy. "China needs more sophisticated capital markets, to provide debt as well as equities," he explains. "Our legal system is still not conducive and the capital market itself is volatile because investors are immature. China's financial system relies too heavily on banks."

According to Chen, "financial globalization and China's integration with the world economy" has created an excellent opportunity for CDB to become "much more active in international markets." His words are not idle: in 2007, CDB paid $3 billion for a 3% stake in UK lender Barclays, and regular rumors allege new CDB targets.

★ ★ ★

Pan Gongsheng sits at the center of China's banking restructuring. He coordinated ICBC's historic 2006 IPO—which raised $19 billion, the world's largest ever—and he now manages Agricultural Bank of China's (ABC) restructuring and eventual IPO.[8] With a doctorate in economics and postdoctoral work at Cambridge, Pan was, in his words, "the practitioner" at ICBC under the visionary leadership of Chairman Jiang Jianqing. "When we began," Pan recalls, "we were focused on reducing non-performing loans. We weren't thinking about an IPO, but the results exceeded our expectations."

Now, Pan says, "I'm fortunate to be working on ABC—we concentrate on China's rural areas, which is China's top strategic priority because of severe imbalances in society and because it will be our country's economic engine of growth for the next 30 years."

ABC is the last of the four major banks to be restructured. With its vast rural footprint, it is also the most difficult. And because 800 million farmers and China's food supply depend on it, it is perhaps the most important.

As for investors' prospective concern that because ABC must support agriculture and farmers, it might be compelled to undertake business that is not economic, Pan smiles and says, "I expect this question on every stop of our [IPO] road show." The answer, he says, is "strategic, mid-to-long-term, and macroeconomic in that ABC will benefit most from the government's epic process of urbanization." As harbinger, Pan notes that ABC today is profitable in rural areas of developed provinces.

Yet Pan is prudent and cautious. "Just because Chinese banks have the highest market cap, doesn't mean their performance is uniformly excellent."

★ ★ ★

Investment banking (IB) has contributed significantly to China's economic transformation, largely by providing foreign capital to Chinese enterprises through initial public offerings (IPOs). No one knows how IB works in China better than Margaret Ren, one of Asia's premier bankers, who speaks of "five phases."[9]

The first phase, 1990-1997, was experimental, she says, and publicly listed medium-sized basic-industry companies (Ren led several milestone deals—railways, coal mines, petrochemicals). The second phase, beginning around 1997, targeted telecommunications (the lead was China Telecom, the name later changed to China Mobile—Ren was financial advisor to the telecom ministry); these were the first restructurings and IPOs of China's "pillar industries,"

Margaret Ren, international investment banker and daughter-in-law of former Party General Secretary Zhao Ziyang, with Robert Lawrence Kuhn (Beijing, July 2007).

which later included the major oil companies, PetroChina and Sinopec (this was also the period when technology and new media firms were irrationally hot). The third phase, beginning around 2003, focused on financial institutions, commencing with China Life (Ren was a lead banker) and then the major state banks. The fourth phase, beginning around 2005 when China was booming and reaching critical mass, greatly expanded the kinds of companies going public, including manufacturing, textile, retail, real estate, etc.

"Now we're looking at a new, fifth phase of investment banking," Ren says. "Chinese executives are more educated, knowledgeable; many speak English and can read research reports themselves—so they require more sophisticated services, especially after the global financial crisis and realignments." Financial advisory alone is no longer sufficient, she asserts. "The new IB model embeds funding capabilities and high-level political access and sensitivities as well as global intelligence and financial expertise."

"With the new model," Ren stresses, "IB opportunities are substantial."

Among the companies with whom she works, three chairmen told her that they had the world's largest market capitalization (in 2009) in their respective industries: ICBC in banking, China Life in insurance, and PetroChina in energy. For someone who was born in underdeveloped Gansu Province—who had experienced China's destitution before reform and witnessed China's struggles through reform—who became a medical doctor in Shanghai and then a pioneering investment banker raising international funds for Chinese enterprises—there was satisfaction in recognizing how far China had come and in playing a part in the historic process.

"It's astonishing how Chinese companies have become global leaders," Ren says.

Endnotes

1 Author's meeting with Liu Mingkang, April 2008.
2 ABC received RMB 93.3 billion; ICBC, RMB 85 billion; CCB, 49.2 billion; BOC, 42.5 billion.
3 The larger NPLs were based on a more accurate, five-category loan classification system versus a four-category system.
4 Andrew Batson, "China Urges Action on Toxic Debt," *Wall Street Journal*, June 12, 2009.
5 "Zhou Xiaochuan: Governor, People's Bank of China," *BusinessWeek*, July 12, 2004.
6 Zhou Xiaochuan's father, Zhou Jiannan, was vice-minister of the Machine-Building Ministry who, in 1962, gave the 36-year-old Jiang Zemin the seemingly impossible job of converting the power plant at the First Automotive Works in Changchun from coal to crude oil in three months (during Mao's disastrous Great Leap Forward)—a task that Jiang, for the rest of his life, would call his proudest achievement. Zhou Jiannan, who died in 1995, had been so impressed with Jiang that he helped arrange his promotion, a key link in the long chain of events that would culminate in China's presidency. Kuhn, *The Man Who Changed China*.
7 Author's meeting with Chen Yuan, Beijing, June 2008.
8 Author's meeting with Pan Gongsheng, Beijing, May 2009.
9 Author's meeting with Margaret Ren, Beijing, May 2009.

24

Reforming Science & Technology with Sparks & Torches

For a millennium or more, China led the world in science and technology. The four great inventions of ancient China—papermaking, printing, gunpowder, compass—did not appear in Europe until hundreds of years later. China's historic and prodigious creativity can be appreciated by the sheer enormity of the book series *Science and Civilisation in China*, Joseph Needham's magisterial opus of 24 massive volumes.

In Needham's words, "One after another, extraordinary inventions and discoveries clearly appeared in Chinese literature, archaeological evidence or pictorial witness, often, indeed generally, long preceding the parallel, or adopted inventions and discoveries of Europe."

There were dozens of other advances made in China long before they were developed or copied in the West: abacus, astronomical clocks, non-throttling horse collar, wrought iron, wheelbarrow, chain drive for irrigation pumps, suspension bridge, segmental arch bridge, seismograph, decimal system, fishing reel, sternpost rudder, gimbals for use in rough seas, umbrella, first flying things (kites and lanterns), helicopter rotors and propellers, rockets and multi-staged missiles, matches, brandy and whiskey, playing cards, porcelain, paper money, perfumed toilet paper, and more.[1]

Subsequently, in the late imperial era, China's science and technology fell far behind that of the West. And despite the emphasis on modernization in the early Communist period—which included China's atomic bomb—the political turmoil of the Maoist years hardly encouraged creativity.

In the reform era, however, all of China's leaders, from Deng Xiaoping onward, have stressed science and technology. Jiang Zemin, Hu Jintao and their colleagues were trained in science and engineering; they are highly conversant with science policy and the application of science to industrial enterprise.

At the 2007 Party Congress, Hu Jintao stressed the task of making China a leader in independent innovation. "This [innovation] is the core of our national development strategy and a crucial link in enhancing the overall national strength," he said in his agenda-setting speech. Hu pledged to increase spending on innovation, and make breakthroughs in key technologies vital to economic and social development.

Hu acknowledges that there remains a large gap between China's scientific and technological level and that of the world's most advanced countries. But speaking to China's scientific elite (2007), Hu put the scientific world on notice of his nation's vaulting ambitions: "We are ready for a fight to control the scientific high ground and earn a seat on the world's high technology board," he said.[2]

In 2006, when President Hu held a summit with President Bush, he made a point of visiting Bill Gates at Microsoft headquarters in Seattle, where he reiterated that China would move against software pirates. "China is focused on and has already accomplished much in creating and enforcing laws to protect intellectual property (IP)," Hu said. "We take our promises very seriously." Significantly, he stressed that enforcing IP protection was necessary not only to protect foreign companies, but also "as we strengthen our innovation ability." It was a vital point: China's enforcement of IP rights was now essential for its own innovative companies—which are so central to China's future.

Amid laughter, Hu described himself as a "friend of Microsoft"—because "I am dealing with the operating system produced by Microsoft every day." Gates then took Hu for a whirlwind tour of the Microsoft campus, where they watched business technology demonstrations and toured Microsoft's Home of the Future. In the kitchen, the counter displayed a recipe in Chinese for making focaccia bread, prompting Hu to ask if you still need a housekeeper if you have such advanced technology.

★ ★ ★

China's rapid development of science and technology owes a great deal to the vision and leadership of Dr. Song Jian, who was chairman of the State Science and Technology Commission (SSTC) from 1985 to 1998, a critical period. Perhaps unique among China's senior leaders, Song is a true scientist.[3]

It was under Dr. Song's auspices that I came to China for the first time in 1989, and I am honored to call him my mentor. I meet him on almost every trip I make to China, and we discuss latest scientific theories from cosmology to consciousness (and some international affairs). I also had the pleasure of helping him found Beijing Institute for Frontier Science, which publishes *Frontier Science* magazine and looks to over-the-horizon science and technology.

In Song's opinion, whereas China has long needed to stress applied science to feed and clothe its vast population, now that China has obtained a

Dr. Song Jian, former state councilor and chairman of the State Science and Technology Commission, with Robert Lawrence Kuhn (Beijing, September 2002).

higher economic level, the country should begin to refocus on basic science in the grand tradition of Chinese civilization.

Song's political career began in the 1980s when he worked in the aerospace ministry (he had been director of research and then deputy president of a key institute for defense-related space and sea flight). "My specialty was guidance systems, altitude control, and mathematics," he says.[4] "My boss in the ministry was Dr. Qian Xuesen [perhaps China's most distinguished scientist, who had been deported from America in 1955 on spying charges, which later proved to be false]. In 1981, I was appointed chief engineer of the ministry. It was a vice ministry-level position and I was sure it was the pinnacle of my career. I love science and technology, especially space science and technology." (In "retirement," Song wrote a comprehensive book about space for general audiences.)

But several years earlier, at a Party conference on China's population policy, Song had become known to China's top leaders. "I became 'almost famous'," he says, "because my colleagues and I projected China's population growth over 20-30 years, which no one else had done." In 1980, an article about Song's research published in *Guangming Daily* became a nationwide sensation.

"Our prediction showed that if we didn't control or curb the population growth rate, China's population would double in 20 years, and in another 20 years would double again," he says. "This would be catastrophic; it would be impossible to feed so many people." Song's research triggered new policy.[5] (To this day, Song believes that one of China's biggest achievements is its successful control of population growth.[6] The average number of children born per woman dropped from 6.0 in the 1970s to below 1.8 by the 1990s— below the replacement level of 2.1. As a result China's population should stabilize at 1.5 to 1.6 billion within 30 years, according to Song, and after that, it may decline—"if that is what people then will want to do.")

In 1984, China's then leaders Hu Yaobang and Zhao Ziyang appointed Song as chairman of the State Science and Technology Commission (SSTC), with responsibility for China's entire science and technology communities and activities. It was a startling promotion and totally unexpected—Song was at a conference in Budapest when he was summoned back to Beijing to be given the news at the airport!

The job had its challenges. A week after his appointment, Song was summoned to the leadership compound at Zhongnanhai by Xi Zhongxun, a senior Party official (the father of Vice-President Xi Jinping). "We had a long talk and he gave me detailed instructions on what I should do," says Song. But, he notes, at the time "there was dispute among leading cadres, especially of the older generation, as to whether science policy should be oriented to economic development. Their argument was that economics was not the goal of science: Science was enlightenment, something higher, something almost holy—not something utility-oriented."

These disagreements meant that, even though senior leaders headed by Deng Xiaoping agreed that science should serve the economy, they couldn't proceed without consensus. So Xi Zhongxun told Song Jian, "Your task is to find a way through the barrier." Song, however, politely refused Xi's request, saying that his long-standing respect for the older revolutionaries would make it impossible to "battle or argue with them."

Song stressed his support for using science and technology to help "our industry to develop," and promised to "faithfully follow the decisions of the Central Committee," but added that while he would report to the elders about new directions, he could not "ruffle the feathers of old revolutionaries." He hoped they would agree, but if not, he would report back to Xi, to ask his guidance.

"My comments did not please Xi," Song recalls. "We argued a bit, though he wasn't angry. He just smiled and said: 'No, your position is wrong. Your task is to struggle with them. Their thinking is old, not applicable today. We should open new ways of thinking!'"

Eventually, after Song continued to resist, Xi told him: "'OK, Song, your position might be right. Go on, try your best.'" In the event, Song's reasoned approach was enough, and the Party elders supported the new policy. "I think they appreciated the younger generation, and didn't want to argue with us," Song says.

★ ★ ★

Song Jian's first major initiative at SSTC was the Sparks Program which called upon China's scientific and engineering communities to help rural areas improve agricultural yields and establish low-tech light industry for township and village enterprises (TVEs, Chapter 13). Song submitted the idea in 1985, and quickly received positive responses from Premier Zhao Ziyang and Wan Li, who was vice premier responsible for agriculture. Song recollects that Wan Li told him "'It's a great idea. If the SSTC can mobilize China's scientists and engineers to go to the countryside to help the farmers, create new business, new crops, new vegetables, and new agricultural products, and to make people rich, that's very important.'"

At around the same time, in the mid 1980s, a group of scientists proposed a coordinated initiative to jump-start development of China's high-tech industries. The program was approved in March 1986 (and hence known as the 863 Program). Its aim was to support hi-tech research and innovation in academic institutions through special grants, focusing on 20 themes in biology, spaceflight, information technology, laser, automation, energy, new materials, and maritime technologies.

Then, in 1987, Song and SSTC proposed the Torch Program, a new initiative for hi-tech industrial development. Launched in 1988, this "national guideline program" included projects to commercialize hi-tech products; management systems suitable for hi-tech industries, and, crucially, hi-tech industrial development zones across the country. The Torch Program achieved success in many fields: new materials, biotechnology, electronic information, integrated mechanical-electrical technology, and energy-saving technology.

Song's aim was for "scientists within research institutions and universities to work with industry." It was no easy task: as Song puts it, "scientists usually do not want to go to companies or factories to work with business people, and besides they're not much welcomed there either. So how could we commercialize their discoveries? That was the reason we decided to open a third way: private hi-tech enterprises."

But promoting such private enterprises was a challenge politically. Song and his team submitted proposals to Zhao Ziyang and Hu Yaobang, centered on encouraging professors and researchers to leave their ivory towers and go into the market to create their own enterprises. Ultimately, it catalyzed the development of Beijing's Zhongguancun Street, which became the center of high-tech companies particularly in computer technologies.

"Many young scientists left their institutions with dreams of owning their own shops," Song recalls. "They sold microchips, small computers, software, and so forth. Nobody paid much attention to them—academic science leaders assumed that they were incapable of producing serious research. But," he adds, "five to seven years later, by the early 1990s, people began to realize that many of these young scientists and engineers were creating their enterprises based on their own knowledge, discoveries, and new achievements."

The Torch Program faced other challenges: Song's central idea was the science park—new technology development zones which would be built around China's most important research universities nationwide.[7] He modeled the idea on similar parks abroad, particularly in France and North Carolina's Research Triangle. "These new zones would be magnets to attract young scientists and engineers to come together and develop collectively," Song explains. "We wanted to create 'critical mass'—a place where they could work in proximity and set up private enterprises in different disciplines."

But capital was a problem. Almost no one had enough money to start a business. "We asked our universities and research institutes to provide some investment," Song says. "We got China's industrial ministries to put up some money. We understood that hi-tech entrepreneurship was a new kind of managerial system—it had to be non-governmental, and avoid the planned economy style. 'Let the engineers and scientists make their own decisions,' I said at the time. 'Let these smart, passionate young people decide what to do, what to produce, how to sell it, and whom to employ.' That was the goal of the Torch Program."

Even so, taboos at the time about private enterprise meant that "we couldn't openly and blatantly announce our intent to create private businesses," Song recalls with a smile, "because some would take political 'pot-shots' at us. So what we said in public was that we should 'transfer our high-tech achievements to the market'. And the means of putting this into practice was to create the new science parks."

Song and SSTC sent telegrams, detailed and (apparently) authoritative, to provincial leaders announcing the science parks. They covered ten points, explaining the purpose of science parks and their usefulness to China, advising how to organize and implement them.

Yet soon after, Song was warned from higher up that SSTC did not have the right to issue instructions or guidelines to provincial governments. But then something odd happened: nothing!

"After my 'confession', no one criticized me," Song recalls. "Moreover, no one refuted the points in our telegram to provincial leaders. Everyone in Beijing was silent, everyone pretended that they hadn't heard about it," he says. And in the provinces, "no one had any idea that I had been criticized by the central government and told to stop building science parks. Provincial leaders were excited and made building science parks a priority!"

Construction of the parks began swiftly, in Xi'an, Chengdu, Nanjing, Guangzhou, "and even Beijing," says Song. "The Beijing park was close to us at SSTC, and we had many colleagues working there, so we didn't need to issue written instructions—we just talked with them almost every day!" Soon afterwards, the Torch Program won general acceptance. "It was a very happy result," Song says.

According to Song Jian, who in 1986 was promoted to state councilor, the Torch Program's most significant achievement was in telecommunications. In 1985, China couldn't produce programmable electronic switchers (the heart of telephone exchanges). Every system had to be purchased from AT&T or

Ericsson at a cost of $150 per phone line—but only a very few cities had enough foreign currency to buy them. Most still used antiquated, quasi-mechanical systems, which could take minutes to get connected. Everybody knew they were terrible, and China's entire communications industry suffered.

In the early days of the science parks, Song recalls, "We found two young people aged 25 and 27, and absolutely unplanned, they announced a new design for these switchers. They didn't follow the AT&T or Ericsson system—they invented a new one." The designers, he adds, "told me it was easy—they simply used a microprocessor in a unique way!" As a result, China soon became a major producer of programmable switchers for telephone systems. "Their products sold in China at RMB 100 per line, more than ten times cheaper than the foreign counterparts," Song notes. "The CEO of AT&T told me, 'We never expected that your young people could do that; their system is better than AT&T's. So what can we do?' he said. 'Pack, and go home!'"

Thanks to such innovation, by the mid-1990s China was turning out 80 million lines per year, produced primarily by new startups based in Shenzhen, Huawei and ZTE, which, Song notes proudly, were "two of the Torch Program's first creations." "They now out-compete American companies in many markets," he adds. (Lenovo, original name Legend, was another Torch Program beneficiary.)

★ ★ ★

But despite the early successes, Song was not satisfied. At that time, no central leader openly recognized private business, or even wanted to touch the subject. At a high-level conference where Song predicted that the "non-governmental sector" would play a critical role in China's development, someone challenged him openly, 'We don't find what you're talking about in our Constitution—there are no references to it in Marx and Engels.'"

Song had to find new ways to promote his ideas. "By the early 1990s China was already building science parks, but we needed to build faster," he recalls. "I had the duty to help the nation achieve its developmental goals. I brainstormed with our science communities."

In late 1992 a debate among leaders changed the course of science and technology in China. Everyone recognized that without strong science and technology China's development would go nowhere. The issue was not whether to promote science and technology but how best to do it. The traditional approach was to stress large, state-owned enterprises (SOEs), leveraging China's industrial strength. But Song advocated small, entrepreneurial companies, leveraging China's young scientists.

According to custom, a national plan for the following year, prepared by then Vice Premier Zhu Rongji, was to be discussed at a Politburo meeting, presided over by General Secretary Jiang Zemin. As part of the 1993 plan, Song Jian suggested that China should encourage the development of hi-tech, entrepreneurial, start-up companies by accelerating and expanding several dozen industrial science parks to house them.

At the meeting Song explained to senior leaders how difficult it was for scientists to work within the confines and strictures of SOEs. "In SOEs' seniority-based hierarchy, how can young people ever get a chance to do anything original, to challenge accepted ways and norms?" he asked. "Young people are unlikely to be respected, no matter how good their ideas. If we're serious about innovative science and technology, we need to break the old mold," he implored the Politburo. "Why not free China's best and brightest young scientists to create dynamic start-up businesses on their own?"

As the presiding official, Jiang Zemin did not enter the discussion but listened intently and took notes. Finally he spoke: "I agree with the proposal by Comrade Song Jian," Jiang said, counseling the others, "You shouldn't so staunchly oppose this idea. Let them give it a try. Maybe it will work; maybe it will be important. Our most talented young people should by all means do this. After some years we can review the program and judge it properly."

★ ★ ★

Another step forward came in 1995. As SSTC chairman, Song Jian was responsible for the annual conference on science and technology and for helping to prepare President Jiang Zemin's speech. Months earlier, Song had sensed that China was ready for the third and final step in elevating science and technology to a core national strategy. The first step, the Sparks Program for developing rural and township enterprises was a decade-long success, and the second, the Torch Program to start new hi-tech companies, was showing progress. What was needed now, Song concluded, was to institutionalize the strategy.

Song sent President Jiang a letter which proposed "the establishment of a national strategy for revitalizing the nation through science, technology, and education." The proposal was approved by the Politburo Standing Committee, and at the May conference, Jiang announced the national strategy to Revitalize the Country through Science and Education.

"I was very pleased," Song recalls. "Chinese scientists had been discussing such a grand vision for years. Now we had a leader who believed that what we were doing was essential for our country's future. President Jiang was highly supportive of our scientists. He never interfered with our work, and he made sure that other Party or government officials didn't either. Speaking as a politician," he adds, "Jiang told me that pure scientific research is 'none of our business.' And speaking as an intellectual, Jiang had great interest in our projects."

Jiang Zemin's commitment to science—and scientists—was highlighted in June 2000, when he wrote a guest editorial in *Science,* perhaps the world's most prestigious science magazine. He stressed the importance of basic science and the personal freedoms required to do it well: "We are encouraging scientists to conduct basic research in the fields where the needs of the state intersect the frontiers of science, and we applaud those who are driven by curiosity to pursue pure research," Jiang wrote. "We recognize and respect the unique sensitivities and sensibilities of scientists; we understand that scientific creativity is the very source and lifeline of a knowledge-based economy."[8]

He concluded with a sweeping vision of China as a proud member of the world community: "By seeking common ground and common interests, I firmly believe that international scientific exchange and cooperation can transcend any differences in social systems, economic models, cultural traditions, and levels of development. The advancement of science in China is essential not only for China's welfare but also for that of the whole world. Chinese scientists look forward to joining with their counterparts in other countries in contributing to humankind's common cause. It is our solemn commitment that China's scientific development shall benefit all peoples."

In an interview with *Science*, published the same month, Jiang expressed his hope that China's scientific glory was not only historic. "The Chinese people have every reason to be proud of their ancient tradition of civilization," he said, "but on the other hand, we should not stop learning—not even for a single day—from all the fine traditions of the world. Confucius once said, 'Whenever there are three people walking together, one of them is bound to be able to teach me something.'"

★ ★ ★

By 2006, a total of 53 national hi-tech development zones and 62 science parks had been set up in major cities across China; 548 business incubators were operating; 45,828 startups had been nurtured (generating annual revenues of $538 billion); and the development zones employed 1.5 million people. Many overseas returnees established new companies, and many enterprises entered international markets.[9]

Companies in science parks now contribute a sizable part of central government revenues, generating about one-fifth of China's entire GDP. "Today, personal computers, telecommunication equipment, new materials, biotechnology products, pharmaceuticals, and new agricultural products are widely available in China's domestic market and are being exported to world markets," Song emphasizes. "They have grown to become major industries. Their export-import volume was almost $200 billion, which was more than the whole country's total in the 1980s. China has become one of the world's leading science and technology nations. In supercomputers, we're no. 2; telecommunications, no. 1; life sciences / biotechnology, almost no. 3. What progress we've made!"[10]

★ ★ ★

Recently, Song says, there was debate about whether and how China's science and technology strategy should change to meet the challenges confronting the country. What was not debated, he emphasizes, was President Hu Jintao's commitment that science and technology were China's highest priority.

"Today's sweeping technology revolutions worldwide were catalyzed by new discoveries in basic science," says Song. "But it was only in the late 1980s that we reached consensus that basic research is the driving force behind the progress of civilization and the cradle for nurturing the young scientific elite. China now has distinguished scientists in nearly 200 national laboratories and sponsors 50,000 research teams."

China's leaders, especially President Hu and former President Jiang, have supported science not only because of what it can achieve in practical terms, but also because of what it means intrinsically. This deep commitment to science is significant for China's future: a society that appreciates science and scientists is not, in my opinion, one which can be, or remain, very much authoritarian. And a country whose leaders are so serious about science is one which will likely contribute much to the world.

Endnotes

1 Jonathan D. Spence, "The Passions of Joseph Needham," *New York Review of Books*, Volume 55, Number 13, August 14, 2008.
2 David Barboza, "China's Ambition Soars to High-Tech Industry," *The New York Times*, August 1, 2008.
3 Dr. Song Jian is an academician of both the Chinese Academy of Sciences (CAS) and the Chinese Academy of Engineering (CAE), and a foreign member of the U.S. National Academy of Engineering and the Russian Academy of Sciences. His doctorate is from Moscow National Technical University and he specialized in control theory, system engineering, and aerospace technology.
4 Author's meeting with Song Jian, Beijing, June 2008.
5 Eric Mueggler, "Cybernetic Birth Control," *Science*, Vol: 321. 22 August 2008.
6 Song Jian, "Awakening: evolution of China's science and technology policies," *Technology in Society* XXX, 235-241 (2008), Elsevier.
7 Dr. Song Jian conceived the strategy for developing science parks around key universities in China with the advice and counsel of Dr. George Kozmetsky, who was a catalyst in building Austin, Texas as a center of science and technology. Dr. Kozmetsky, co-founder of Teledyne Corporation and long-time dean at the University of Texas, received the National Medal of Technology award in 1993. Dr. Kozmetsky was my mentor in America and he introduced me to Dr. Song Jian.
8 Jiang Zemin, "Science in China," *Science*, June 30, 2008.
9 Song Jian, 2008, op. cit.
10 Author's meeting with Song Jian, Beidaihe, August 2009.

25

Education: When Reform and Tradition Clash

China's emphasis on science, technology and innovation has gone hand-in-hand with rethinking the nation's education system to meet the needs of a knowledge-based economy. The slogan Revitalize China Through Science and Education is no coincidence.

In theory China offers all its citizens "basic education." For most children, this means nine-year compulsory schooling, which was implemented in most areas by around 2001. And the goal to eliminate illiteracy among young and middle-aged people has been largely realized.

As the new century began, China set itself the target of elevating the country's basic education to the standard of the world's developed countries within a decade. It was an ambitious goal: in 2008, over 200 million students were enrolled in kindergarten through senior secondary school, and many difficulties beset the education system, particularly in rural areas where schools experienced chronic funding shortfalls and some teachers went for long periods without pay.

Beginning in 2002, the government began to address the situation, allocating $730 million to improve basic education in impoverished rural areas (2002-2007). It meant, for example, that teachers no longer had to worry about their salaries, since they were now paid by state finances.

There was other issues, most significantly, growing complaints about the over-rigid nature of teaching. It was an issue with a long history: for over 2,000 years in feudal China, anyone who wished to enter into the upper class of imperial officialdom had to pass difficult and highly structured examinations, which required spending years or even decades of preparation (e.g., learning complete works of the Confucian classics by rote memory). And for all the changes in China, traditional attitudes died hard. More often than not, learning in China's schools was limited to book knowledge, with students enduring numerous, high-stress examinations.

Teachers as well as students had long criticized such "ossified teaching methods" for overburdening students with homework, cramming too many technical facts into them, and forcing them to focus blindly on high grades in exams.[1] As one teacher put it, "most students are turned into 'docile machines' fit merely for exams." Professor C.N. Yang, a prominent Chinese-American scientist and Nobel Laureate noted that students from China, though outperforming American students in rudimentary knowledge, found difficulty in working out novel, creative ideas. This, he said, would weaken China's competitiveness.

The stress imposed on students was highlighted in 2000, when a series of school-related cases of violence gripped public attention.[2] In one, a middle school student killed his mother with a hammer "because he could not bear his position in class and the pressure from his parents." In another, two young students hacked a fellow student to death. And in a case of parental rage, a father incited a group of people to beat up his child's teacher.

President Jiang Zemin, described these reports as "really shocking," and called for broader concepts of education, which would not concentrate excessively on academic achievement to the exclusion of other skills. Jiang called on schools to reduce homework, teach courses that would create "a spirit of innovation," and move from "exam-driven education" to "quality education."[3]

Stressing the value of developing "well-rounded individuals" with improved "moral, intellectual and fitness levels," Jiang insisted that "we cannot shut up young students in books and rooms all day; we must let them take part in some social practice to broaden their vision and enhance their social experience."

Jiang's ideas provoked controversy as well as praise. Education in China had a long tradition and many were wary of change. Nevertheless, as one education official put it, the existing system was "divorced from reality and needs to be improved."

China began experimenting with new methods, relieving students of the psychologically toxic burden of all-deciding examinations. Proposed changes included replacing the long-standing grading system (1-100 with 60 as passing) with a more lenient five-level system; university entrance based not only on a student's intellectual achievements but also on his or her moral and physical education; and less homework, to give students more time after school to learn about society, enjoy culture and appreciate nature. New courses in information technology and social practice were also added. The idea was to arouse students' interests and to develop their all-round abilities.

Many educators welcomed the changes. Students were learning more by surfing the Internet, visiting libraries and museums, and participating in various extra-curricular activities, an education official in Ningxia said. "It's really remarkable that many students are learning to think independently and more often daring to speak out what's in their minds."[4]

Those who devised the changes believed they could have major impact on Chinese society. "The core of curriculum reform is to enable, through education, new, advanced cultures and concepts to spread in schools and society at large, to build among the Chinese people a cooperative and constructive partnership of democracy, equality, dialogue, consultation and mutual understanding," said a professor from the Ministry of Education. "It helps the learner develop the ability of critical analysis, problem solving, communication and cooperation."

Some academicians did express concerns, however, worrying for example that the new textbooks were too easy to learn, particularly in subjects like mathematics. But supporters of the reforms argued that the new textbooks would benefit the majority of students, not just the "smartest" few: "The old curricula seem to have been designed to 'screen' the students, to differentiate the 'superior' from the 'inferior' through assessments," said the Ningxia official. "In the new curricula, assessments are used as feedback to help teachers and students improve their performances."

By 2005, 95% of the students in grade one of primary schools were using the new curriculum. Zhu Muju, an official in charge of elementary education at the Ministry of Education, emphasized that the reform was designed to "bring forth a new generation of high-caliber citizens, people who are competent enough to serve China's modernization drive."[5]

This "competence-oriented education," she said, would "eventually do away with the kind of education which is irrelevant to the practical needs of society and meant for nothing but preparing students for examinations."

★ ★ ★

Reform has also come to China's university system. Until the 1990s university disciplines or majors were modeled on the Soviet system of the 1950s. Extreme specialization, especially in the sciences, was the order of the day, and educational breadth had no place. More than 600 separate subjects were available for undergraduate majors.

Beginning in 1997, scholars revised the entire system, reducing the number of subjects to 270, and making broader-based, integrative, cultural knowledge central to university education ("whole-person education"). Today, in most Chinese universities, students must acquire cross-disciplinary knowledge through coursework outside their major concentrations. University lecturers are encouraged to work at or near the academic frontier and to teach students state-of-the-art knowledge using modern methodologies.

China's goal is to bring 100 Chinese universities up to world-class standards during the 21st century.[6] To that end, salaries of university lecturers have increased many fold since the 1990s and are now at middle or upper-middle levels of Chinese society—a marked contrast from Mao's days, when knowledge was denigrated and the income of intellectuals, even when they weren't being persecuted, was often lower than average.

To former State Councilor Song Jian, China's development in science and technology has been entirely dependent on the country's educational system, particularly on the great improvements in higher education. From 1980 to 2006, the number of universities in China increased 2.5 times (to 1,867) and enrollments soared—undergraduates rising nearly 20 times (to 5.5 million); graduates over 25 times (to 3.8 million); and postgraduates 100 times (to almost 400,000).

Also significant are the huge numbers of young people studying abroad. Between 1978, when the government first began sponsoring students to go overseas, and 2006, some 1.67 million Chinese students had enrolled in universities in 108 countries. By 2006, only 275,000 had returned to China, but Song Jian stresses that many of those who did return became leaders in R&D, teaching, and the creation of hi-tech enterprises. "The policy of unrestricted access to overseas education is instrumental in China's drive toward modernization," he says. As of 2006, there were 583,000 students studying abroad, and government guidelines were to welcome them back to China when they graduated—though the final decision rested with the students themselves.

By 2005, the number of graduates with majors in natural sciences and engineering exceeded 1.5 million (two-thirds were engineers), far more than any other country. In total, there were 35 million science and technology-related human resources in China, of whom 14.5 million held bachelor degrees or higher. The young science-technology workforce was growing rapidly: 60% of team leaders were 45 years old or younger.

Tellingly, in a 2009 international computer competition—sponsored by the super-secret U.S. National Security Agency (for obvious reasons)—China fielded the most finalists (20), well ahead of second-place Russia (10) and far ahead of America (2). The worldwide winner of the algorithm-coding contest was a Chinese 18-year-old student.[7]

★ ★ ★

Focusing on education as a means of fulfilling China's destiny as a nation, and of realizing the potential of its citizens, is something which President Hu Jintao keeps emphasizing. Himself a graduate of Tsinghua, China's leading science and technology university, Hu believes education can raise moral standards, enhance cultural awareness and increase scientific expertise.

He has thus made showing support for education part of his public persona. On the 110th anniversary of Peking University in 2008, Hu visited the campus to offer his congratulations and chat with students. "College life is a golden time in a person's life," he told them. "You should make the most of this time to study hard, think hard and practice hard." Elite educational institutions should bear the responsibility of making scientific breakthroughs and fostering talent for the country, Hu added, emphasizing that Peking University should build itself into a world-class institution.[8]

Hu also stresses equality in education, for example by helping needy families and eliminating unreasonable tuition fees. Similarly, teachers in underdeveloped regions should be assisted in their work and their lives, and their initiative encouraged.

President Hu epitomized his commitment on International Children's Day (2007), when he visited a kindergarten and primary school for the children of farmers and migrant workers in a small town in southern Beijing.[9] He joined children in working with toy bricks, playing basketball and skipping rope. He told them that they should make good use of their school time and grow up to be knowledgeable, honest and healthy. The president also made a point of paying his respects to the school's teachers, expressing appreciation for their dedication to rural education.

Chinese leaders are aware that upgrading rural education is vital if China is to address imbalances among regions, classes and sectors, the country's most corrosive problem. It will take at least decades, and likely generations, to equalize rural and inland areas with urban and coastal areas in terms of infrastructure and high-paying jobs, but equality in education can arguably be achieved much more rapidly, and can help to readjust social imbalances. People of every class and culture are united in desiring more for their children than they have for themselves, and they are willing to make economic sacrifices to give their offspring a first-class education.

In 2006, China began eliminating tuition and fees for rural students during their nine-year compulsory education; students from poor families also received free textbooks. (In 2007, 150 million students had benefits of $2.4 billion.)[10] In addition, substantial resources are being allocated to electronic (distance) education, particularly in science and technology, so that remote areas can have equal access to education. Providing its rural and inland schools with personal computers and internet facilities will play a major part in fostering curiosity and creativity, as well as in building knowledge and skills. Nothing can bring about equality faster. Nothing more properly expresses President Hu's Scientific Perspective on Development.

Endnotes

1 "Quality Education, Focus of China's Educational Reform: NPC," Xinhua, March 9, 2000.
2 Xinhua, March 1, 2000 (BBC).
3 Zeng Peiyan.
4 Wang Jing, "Curriculum Reform of Elementary Education in China,"*China Features*, May 9, 2005.
5 Xinhua, September 29, 2005.
6 "Higher Education Reform in China Today," Ouyang Kang, *Policy Futures in Education*, Volume 2, Number 1, 2004; pp. 141–149.
7 Patrick Thibodeau, "China dominates NSA-backed coding contest," *Computerworld*, June 8, 2009.
8 "Chinese President urges college students to turn patriotism into diligence in study," Xinhua, May 4, 2008.
9 "Chinese president visits rural children on International Children's Day," Xinhua, June 1, 2007.
10 China.org.cn, November 7, 2007.

Healthcare and Medical Reform: One Doctor's Story

In China's reforms, if the economy was the leader, healthcare was the laggard. The transition to a market economy spelt the end of the old system in which healthcare was provided by the state, often through state-owned enterprises. But introducing state-backed medical insurance programs, needed in a market economy, has been a slow and agonizing process. Even today patients generally must pay prior to treatment and only a fraction of medical costs are covered by insurance.

This state of affairs affects public sentiment: the *Pew Global Attitudes Project* found (2008) that about half of those Chinese surveyed (48%), and a majority (54%) of low-income respondents, said they found it hard to afford healthcare. People feel they must save up for medical emergencies, and this cautiousness contributes to China's relatively low rates of consumer spending.

There was widespread agreement that the results of healthcare reforms, which included commercialization of medical care, were little short of disastrous. Just how serious the situation had become was laid out by China's Ministry of Health itself, which outlined healthcare's major challenges (2007). These included: Collapse of the primary healthcare system and rise of profit-oriented state-owned hospitals; declining public access to healthcare; demographic transition to an aging society with old-age diseases, and fewer young people to take care of older people; industrialization and emerging health risks from environmental and work-related factors; growing disparities and inequalities in healthcare coverage, efficiency, and quality (by region, classes and gender); rising costs, due to advancing technology and specialization; widespread cases of irrational and illegal incentives, such as overcharging, bribery, and kickbacks; deterioration of the doctor-patient relationship; and perhaps most serious of all, inadequate healthcare financing and insurance—80% of the rural population and 50% of the urban population (largely migrants) were entirely uninsured.

China is now striving to build a "well-off society in an all-round way," but it is clear that, without a modern and affordable universal healthcare system, this is impossible. China's leaders know this. As a result, massive healthcare reform and transformation is a national priority.

Reporting to the 17th Party Congress (2007), Hu Jintao called for everyone to have access to basic medical services and to enjoy improved levels of health. He proposed measures including: separating government administration from medical institutions, management from medical care, medical care from pharmaceuticals, and for-profit from nonprofit operations; improving disease control and prevention, and capacity to respond to public health emergencies; improving professional ethics and workstyle of health workers, and quality of medical services; ensuring food and drug safety; launching sanitation campaigns and developing healthcare programs for women and children.

In 2009, China committed to spend $123 billion on medical reforms over three years. The goal was dual: to improve healthcare by reforming public hospitals, which are often criticized for poor access, high fees, inadequate services, and indifferent care; and to stimulate domestic consumption by increasing participation in medical insurance systems to 90% of China's total population by 2012. In the plan, every village would have a medical clinic and every county at least one hospital by 2011.

The timing, soon after the eruption of the global financial crisis, was no coincidence: China's capacity to boost domestic consumption, essential for protecting the country's economy, was highly dependent on citizens feeling confident that healthcare was affordable.

Minister of Health Chen Zhu, meanwhile, set out specific milestones for healthcare reform: by 2010, establishing the framework of a healthcare system covering urban and rural residents and achieving universal coverage; by 2015, raising China's healthcare level to the top of developing countries, and by 2020, raising healthcare levels of China's eastern and some western regions to approaching that of medium-developed countries.

★ ★ ★

Achieving such goals requires talent, creativity, and commitment. Yet there is reason to hope, offered by the presence in China of medical professionals such as Professor Huang Jiefu, a world-renown hepatic surgeon and China's vice minister of health.

Professor Huang, a specialist in organ transplants, hit the headlines in 2005, when he confirmed to a startled audience at a World Health Organization (WHO) meeting on transplantation in Manila that "The majority of the organ donors in China at this stage are still executed prisoners."[1]

"Perhaps it was WHO strategy to select me to chair the meeting," Dr. Huang reflects. "Perhaps they were saying, 'Let's see what's going on with the Chinese government.' Afterwards, the WHO official in charge of organ transplantation, a good friend, said, 'Jeffrey [his English name], you are the first Chinese official to say this.'"

"I was heading a Chinese delegation that had seven other members," Huang recounts. "All were friends as well as colleagues and they worried about my openness and honesty. They said to me, 'Jiefu, you made a big mistake; you took too much risk although you told the truth.'"

It is hard to overstate the sensitivity of the subject—China's official representatives had long denied, often with indignation and outrage, international allegations of links between executions and organ transplants, of organs being taken from prisoners who had not given consent, and most controversially, of prisoners being executed "to order." Such a public statement from a senior Chinese official was therefore a stunning development—not least to Dr. Huang's colleagues in China's Ministry of Health.

"Before I went to Manila," he says, "I was given some 'talking points', denying the [organs-from-executed-prisoners] charge as nonsense."

But Huang had gone through the traumatic experience of China's struggle with SARS in 2003, when a ham-handed attempt at covering up the severity of the epidemic had, as he puts it, "made the whole world angry, isolating China." Such cover-ups, he decided, were wrong. "I checked with no one," he says, of his decision to speak out in Manila. "It just came from the bottom of my heart . . . I thought, well, I'll just take a risk. We learned the lesson during SARS . . . I did what I thought was right for China."

Professor Huang's message to his foreign peers at the meeting, many of whom were friends, was that the Chinese government was "making great efforts to change this situation and our organ transplant program will follow the guiding principles set by WHO." China, he said, "realized the weakness of its organ transplantation system. We had rules on paper requiring prisoners' consent, but the rules weren't fully enforced. So with the reform and opening-up of our society, and with political reform, I said that China eventually will abolish the practice of using the prisoners' organs [without real consent]. But that couldn't happen overnight and I asked my audience's patience. Change takes time . . . We still had many patients dying and needing organ transplants, and we urgently needed to establish an organ transplantation system."

Dr. Huang's public pledge to seek the highest human ideals was, in my opinion, one of China's most significant reform breakthroughs ever. And indeed the story of the life and work of Huang Jiefu, an unassuming man with a ready smile, is a striking example of just how much China has changed— and a confidence-builder of why further change is likely.

Born in 1946 in Hunan Province, Huang excelled in math and physics and dreamed of becoming an engineer. But in 1961, his father, a factory

Dr. Huang Jiefu, vice minister of Health (Beijing, June 2008).

accountant, died suddenly of hepatitis B. "My father's will asked that I become a medical doctor 'to cure illness and save people's lives,'" he recalls. And so, in 1963, after passing the national entrance examination with high marks, Huang enrolled in one of China's four key national medical universities, Zhongshan (Sun Yat-sen) Medical College in Guangzhou. In his third year, however, the Cultural Revolution broke out, and Huang and his fellow students were sent to the countryside to "receive reeducation from peasants." In practice, they, and several teachers, worked in county hospitals.

"The chaos enhanced my understanding of politics and society," Huang recalls. "And, because my parents were neither workers nor peasants, I wasn't eligible to join the Red Guards and seldom participated in any political movements. So I could concentrate on my clinical education and saving lives."

After returning to medical college in 1969 and graduating a year later, Huang was again sent for "re-education," this time in Yunnan Province, where he worked as a miner and a doctor at the same time. He labored in an iron ore mine—but his medical skills were also in demand: "If there was an emergency, if an injury occurred, I was the doctor," Huang explains. "I founded a small hospital with eight medical students and several nurses, and we served miners and farmers." His dedication paid off when local leaders recommended him for surgical training at Kunming Medical College.

Huang remained convinced that the political situation would one day change, he says, "so I concentrated on studying and improving myself."

Deep in the countryside, he taught himself English. "Even in the early 1970s, I felt that China should open to the western world," he says. "There were no learning materials so I listened to the Voice of America and imitated the pronunciation. I found a small dictionary and every day memorized 100 words."

After Deng Xiaoping's return to power, and the reopening of formal university education in 1977, Huang took postgraduate work at Zhongshan Medical College. Of 96 applicants for liver surgery, Huang was the one admitted.

News of the first liver transplants, performed in the U.S. in 1963, had generated enthusiasm in China, Huang says, but China's first clinical trial of 56 human cases (1977-1983) had been a failure. And so in 1984 Huang was sent to Sydney University to study liver transplantation and hepato-biliary surgery under world-renowned professors.

When his scholarship from the Chinese government ended, he won an Australian fellowship. Life was good: "My wife and my daughter moved to Australia," he says. "We had happy times: our living environment was excellent: we had a private apartment with a swimming pool. I was well-paid as a surgeon and my young daughter spoke English. My wife was content. I enhanced my surgical technique. I played tennis and had many Australian friends."

But in 1987, Huang's old colleagues at Zhongshan Medical University, and his mother, asked him to return to China. Despite his wife's reluctance, he says, "I persuaded her that we should go back, to serve our country and to be with our family, teachers and classmates." It was a time, he notes, when "most Chinese students were fixated on going abroad and staying abroad, and so everybody said, 'Jiefu's stupid, why did he come back?'" And the first years back home were, he admits, "very bad: China was not so open and policies for returning scholars were not like they are nowadays. We had sad stories: my daughter couldn't speak Chinese well and no Chinese school would take her, so I had to use some 'social connections' and pay some 'fees'." And if life in a 16-square-meters dormitory room wasn't bad enough, all the family's property was stolen soon after their return. "It was terrible," Huang recalls.

Huang, however, was "still determined to serve my country: I worked with several returning scholars to promote liver transplantation and achieved success in 1994." And gradually Huang advanced, receiving better working and living conditions. By 1996 he was president of Zhongshan University of Medical Sciences, and the following year, at the 15th Party Congress, he was selected as an alternate member of the CPC Central Committee—the only one of China's 1,000 university presidents to be awarded such status.

Such official endorsement, Huang says, "encouraged me to initiate some reforms, based on China's situation and what I had learned in the West. From 1996 to 2001, Zhongshan made great achievements in education, research and clinical practice." Huang himself became the leading figure in liver transplants in China, performing more than 500 transplants ("most of my patients are still alive"), publishing over 500 papers and editing 16 books. He had guest professorships at Harvard and MIT.

In 2001, he was offered the post of China's vice minister of health, in charge of medical research, education and international cooperation. "Initially I was reluctant to go into government, because my life's objective was to cure illness and save lives," Huang says. After talks with the CPC Organization Department, however, he received special permission to continue his surgical practice while serving in government, and was made director of the Department of Liver Surgery of the influential Peking Union Medical College. "Every week I select one or two tough cases and perform the surgery," Huang explains, adding "This is unique. The arrangement reflects the open-mindedness of our central leaders, and the spirit of reform: they also want me to keep in touch with ordinary medical professionals."

When SARS broke out in 2003, Professor Huang was involved in its control and prevention. "I knew that SARS was a very severe outbreak of a very unusual virus," he says, "and I insisted that we shouldn't cover it up. We should tell the truth."

His performance led to his elevation to leadership of the very special Bureau of Healthcare, which is responsible for the medical care of China's senior leaders. For a scholar returned from abroad to be given such responsibilities, Huang says, was a sign of the "progress that reform has brought to China," and of growing "democracy and freedom." The increasing recognition of intellectuals, he says, just a few decades after the Cultural Revolution—when China's intellectuals were ranked as the "the stinking ninth," the worst category of "class enemies"—"exemplifies how our senior leaders appreciate knowledge and talent. So I'm confident that our country will become more open, more democratic, and more advanced."

In Huang's opinion, the changes regarding organ transplantation is one of the best examples illustrating China's increasing reform, openness and integration into the international community.

Throughout the world, he relates, the first organ transplants used executed prisoners as donors, but from the 1980s an ethical and voluntary organ donation system was developed in many countries. In China, however, as a developing country, "our legal system and healthcare administration lag behind our technical medical progress," Huang notes. Moreover, there were "social and cultural taboos constraining organ donations," not least the Confucianism tradition that people should "keep their body intact as a demonstration of filial piety," even after death.

For all these reasons, "China has not yet established an effective organ donation system," Huang explains. And, he adds, "at present, the 'brain death' concept has not been legalized in China. So the primary source [of organs for transplant] has been from executed prisoners." In theory, the government requires written consent from prisoners or their families, but, Huang concedes, "it's a huge country and there are loopholes."

In this under-regulated environment, China has faced constant criticism over two issues: allegations of commercialism and trafficking of patients, so-called "transplant tourism;" and the use of executed prisoners as sources of donor organs without proper consent.[2]

Huang stresses that China is grateful for foreign support for "the healthy development of organ transplantation," but he says some of the attacks have been "ruthless and vicious . . . They only see problems and exaggerate them. They ignore the bright side." Still, he acknowledges, "some lower-ranking Chinese officials have made matters worse by totally denying the problem, saying, 'No, China has not used any organs of executed prisoners.'" And in general, Huang says, "China's transplant surgeons want to save lives, and have avoided dealing with sources of organs. Nobody in China likes to talk about sources of organs, making the international community very suspicious."

It was against this background that Huang Jiefu made his courageous remarks at the 2005 WHO meeting, acknowledging, with precision, that "at the moment, 95% of the organs for transplantation came from executed prisoners." He explains that his "first reason for making the announcement was the lessons and reflections from the SARS outbreak [in 2003]. When President Hu and Premier Wen were dealing openly with SARS, they set good examples for me."

Huang stresses that "As surgeons, we must abide by the ethical standards practiced by the international community. As doctors, we follow the Hippocratic Oath. We should do everything that is good for patients. We cannot cheat society. If we doctors don't tell the truth," he adds, "if we allow malpractice and unethical activities to go on, it will rot our whole profession. Under-the-table dealings would make organ transplantation the most corrupted profession in China." And, he adds, "If we have to get everything [we say] checked [with superiors], it would be impossible to effect change. There has to be a first person to tell the truth."

Friends and colleagues were apprehensive. But according to Huang, "a very high-level leader" [he wouldn't give the name] defended him in a very high-level meeting, saying "Jiefu is a very good intellectual and a very sincere surgeon. What he said came from the bottom of his heart as a medical professional. We don't demand that he be a rigid political official."

It was a revealing comment, suggesting that China's senior leaders are far more enlightened than popular perception would have them. And Huang's future promotion within the ministry reinforced the message, though he says that this was because of his work looking after senior leaders during the SARS crisis. (Dr. Huang successfully handled difficult and sensitive medical situations. Otherwise he might not have won such trust from China's leaders.)

What's more, Huang says, he received strong backing from medical professionals and organizations. "China's transplant community is the main strength impelling reform," he says. "Most transplant surgeons knew we must change and regulate our practice based on ethical guidelines prescribed by WHO. We had to face our problems."

Top priority, he explains, was that "a legal framework for organ transplantation was urgently needed—to standardize professional behavior; to establish responsible medical criteria for screening potential organ recipients and donors; to restore equilibrium between the extreme demand for organs and their limited supply; and to protect the right of donors, whether living or deceased."

In two years, according to Huang, much happened—"We mobilized the Chinese Medical Association and the Chinese Doctors' Association. We held conferences, seminars, and round-table discussions. We set criteria and standards for liver, kidney, heart, and lung transplants."

In 2006, an Organ Transplantation Summit was held in Guangzhou, under Professor Huang's leadership and with WHO support. A joint declaration announced five initiatives: creating a legal framework for national oversight; establishing credentials for Chinese transplant staff and regulators; banning the purchase and sale of human organs; preventing organ trafficking and transplant tourism; and establishing national self-sufficiency in sourcing organs that includes deceased and living donors. At the time, Huang said it would take five years to implement these initiatives, which were well-received internationally, and gradually establish China's new organ transplantation system.

"China must be a responsible member of the global family," Huang asserts. "We are stakeholders. From our progress in organ transplantation, one can see Chinese leaders' determination and vigor in promoting reform in medicine and healthcare."

Asked whether it was really possible that China's senior leaders had not known what was happening with executed prisoners, Huang is vehement. "They had no idea," he insists. Someone needed to tell them the truth, talk to them honestly. I let President Hu Jintao know the full truth of the matter, and he was quick to make a decision: legislation must be enacted so that organ transplantation practice would be governed by laws and regulations. 'Organ transplantation must benefit the people, while preventing others from exploiting our problems,' Hu said." It was, in Huang's view, a sign of "the attitudes, the openness, of our leaders."

Under directives of President Hu, a State Council meeting presided over by Premier Wen passed the Human Organ Transplantation Act (2007). It established formal regulations and procedures for transplant quality, transplantable organs, transplant tourism, and sources of organs and rights of donors. It set down strict rules regarding the use of organs: there must be uncoerced, written consent from organ donors or their families; transplant surgeons are barred from interacting with potential donors, donors' families, or donors' care team, until death is declared and consent is obtained; in obtaining donors' or donors' families' consent, all must respect human freedom and dignity and not exploit vulnerable individuals. Red Cross societies will help publicize the need for organ donations.

The act was unprecedented, a milestone. It won appreciation from the international transplant community and the WHO. And it led to practical changes: "It used to be that foreign patients would come to China to receive organ transplants—every year, more than 300 patients from Japan, South Korea, and other countries," Huang acknowledges. "This is now banned in China. Without special approval, there are no organ transplants for foreigners."

In 2008, Professor Huang Jiefu (Jeffrey) received the President's International Award from The Transplantation Society (TTS), the world's leading transplant community. In its formal notification to Huang, TTS noted "the favorable changes and good progress in the regulatory development related to organ transplantation in China . . . The Transplantation Society is most impressed with the enormous energy and thought that you have personally devoted to organ transplantation in China, and the substantial changes you have brought about in the recent years."

Addressing 4,300 attendees at the TTS World Congress in Sydney, Huang reported that over 11,000 cases of various organ transplants were performed in China each year, placing it second among all countries. His presentation included a slide with the bold title "All 5 Stigmas in One Place"—under which Huang spelled out the areas for which China had been criticized in the past: Utilization of executed organs without proper consent; commercialization of transplant services; organ trafficking and tourism; no accreditation system for organ transplantation; and no regulation for allocation of organ donors.

Now, Huang Jiefu emphasized, the overall mission was to provide high-quality transplant services for recipients, to maintain highest professional standards for transplant services—and to ensure that organ transplantation conformed to medical ethics guidelines. The former countryside doctor and iron-ore miner had reformed China.

Endnotes

1 Author's meeting with Dr. Huang Jiefu, Beijing, June 2008. The November 2005 WHO event was the Consultation Meeting on Transplantation with National Health Authorities.

2 The Falun Gong movement, outlawed by the Chinese government, claimed that thousands of practitioners had been sent to "concentration camps" throughout China, and that many had been killed for profit through the live harvesting and sale of their organs. (Thomas Lum, "China and Falun Gong," CRS Report for Congress, August 11, 2006.) Many of the claims were based upon allegations about a camp in Sujiatun, in Shenyang in north-east China. The Falun Gong accusation was repeated in a report by two Canadians, though American officials investigating the area on two occasions—the first time unannounced—"found no evidence that the site is being used for any function other than as a normal public hospital" (Kilgour-Matas Report—http://www.investigation.redirectme.net/).

27

Media and Publishing Reform: Hidden in Plain Sight

On May 12, 2008, a devastating earthquake hit Southwest China's Sichuan Province. The next day, Chinese media reported 12,012 deaths, 9,404 people buried in the debris, 7,841 missing, and 26,206 injured. From then on, the media released precise new numbers every day; by July 2008, 69,227 were confirmed dead and 374,176 injured, with 18,222 still missing.

The rapid and accurate reporting helped reassure citizens that the crisis was under control, and prevent the spread of rumors. Coverage on state broadcaster CCTV, meanwhile, was dynamic, much like 24-hour cable news channels in America, replete with maps, graphics, pundits, and breaking news stories.[1]

This transparency and openness, so critical in a crisis, was in stark contrast to the not-too-distant past when the Communist Party deemed any "negative news," such as natural or human-caused disasters, to be inappropriate for public consumption. Why agitate the people, was the patronizing attitude; keep them oblivious, blissful and productive.

But in an age when mobile phones and the Internet give all citizens instant access to real-time information, such control is no longer possible. These days China's leaders know that if the official media does not report a story, it's likely to be reported by these unofficial "media," which could lead to inaccuracies and rumors disseminated widely.

To prevent this, honest reporting is now generally seen as desirable. Significantly, not long before the earthquake, a new "government information disclosure" law put more onus on officials to release data deemed relevant for the public interest.

The earthquake also represented something of a breakthrough in China's attitudes to reporting by foreign media. According to Wang Chen, head of the State Council Information Office (SCIO), "When the Sichuan earthquake occurred, the central leadership decided to adopt an open policy towards foreign reporters and allow them to go into affected areas." Many foreign reporters, unable to get to the quake areas due to frequent aftershocks and flight cancellations, turned to SCIO for assistance. "Three days after the earthquake, we arranged for over 50 foreign journalists to travel to the quake areas," Minister Wang says. "We provided five buses, arranged local support, and prepared water and food. At the peak, there were more than 800 foreign journalists in the earthquake zone."

Wang stresses that "We didn't cover up in any way: we believed that only if we enabled reporting in an accurate, timely manner would we win the world's sympathy and support. And because of our almost real-time coverage, people from all over the world sent supplies like tents and even rescue teams. Openness and transparency played a key role."

There were tensions: "Some local residents, especially parents of students who had been killed in their collapsed schools, had complaints," Wang says. Some foreign journalists, he alleges, "tried to incite these distraught people, instigating them to complain to the president." And he notes, "the local government set guidelines, and if journalists were caught violating them, their cameras were confiscated. In some instances, we had to intercede to stop physical confrontation—we got their cameras back."

Despite this, Wang says "most journalists were professional and conscientious and reported in a truthful, objective manner. Though there were negative, critical stories, we kept an easy attitude. Firstly, there were errors and problems in our relief work, so we should allow the press to point them out and criticize them. Secondly, even if criticisms were not so accurate, we could still learn from what they said. And although we did oppose groundless rumors, which came from very few reporters, even with those who acted in conflict with journalistic ethics, we took peaceful approaches to dissuade them; we had no physical confrontations."

It was, Wang Chen suggests, evidence that "China's opening-up policy is deepening." He stresses that SCIO's new principle is that reporting should be "accurate, timely, open, transparent, and orderly." And he's pleased that the new freedoms for foreign journalists introduced, originally temporarily, for the Beijing Olympics, were subsequently made permanent. These allow foreign journalists officially accredited in China to conduct interviews without applying for permits, and to travel around the country without having to seek permission from local authorities. Some restrictions remain, such as unaccompanied travel to certain areas (e.g., Tibet and military regions), but the measure has been welcomed as another sign of China's commitment to continue forward on its long, sometimes winding road to open up to the world.

Minister Liu Binjie, head of China's General Administration of Press and Publications (responsible for all print media), emphasizes that openness is the antidote to potentially poisonous rumors. "Our mistakes in the past resulted from hiding," Liu says. "That's why rumors were rampant. If we didn't inform the public about, say, the death toll of a disaster, people would start making up their own numbers and stories. It's high time we changed our thinking."[2]

What's more, even where there are still restrictions in place, the Chinese media these days is not always as obedient as in the past. In the immediate aftermath of the Sichuan earthquake, numerous local media organizations from across China, responding to intense interest of their audiences, defied government instructions that only the big four state-level media (People's Daily, Xinhua News Agency, China Central Television, and China National Radio) could send reporters to the earthquake areas. Rogue reporting teams were enterprising and persistent, generating stories that circulated broadly, particularly through the Internet.

★ ★ ★

Media in China was always sensitive. From the founding of the People's Republic, the media was seen as the mouthpiece of the Party, tasked with presenting news and information that supported the Party's rule of society and view of the world. Social stability and national pride were guiding factors motivating media control. And while it's obviously still true that Chinese journalists do not have the same freedoms as do their Western counterparts, progress is being made. While Chinese media still cannot oppose central leadership or Party rule, they are now often ready to take on local government in cases of corruption or incompetence—and especially if locals try to cover up errors or accidents.

Change in the media has been a gradual, stop-start, and sometimes frustrating process. Even very early in the reform era, journalists sometimes sought to push accepted limits. When Minister Wang Chen was a reporter with the influential *Guangming Daily*, there was a story in Shanxi Province (1979-1980) where funds from the state budget, designated for education, were diverted to build houses for officials. Teachers whose salaries were cut off as a result wrote to *Guangming Daily*. "We discovered that the accusation was true," Wang Chen recalls. "We published our investigative report and it had national impact."

In another case, an overseas returned scientist in Fujian Province was suspended by the local government after it discovered he had sold his research commercially (early-1980s). "The local government put up obstacles but we wrote a front-page story," Wang Chen notes. "General Secretary Hu Yaobang read our report and issued a directive that such intellectuals must be reinstated."

Chinese media grew freer in the late 1980s under General Secretary Zhao Ziyang, but then after the Tiananmen crackdown in 1989, the conservative resurgence stifled the media back into almost its pre-reform rigidity. But by the late 1990s Premier Zhu Rongji was saying that the media served as society's "watchdog," criticizing the mistakes and excesses of government. Premier Zhu made it known that he was a fan of CCTV's investigative news programs, which exposed corruption and other abuses of power. It made sense: with such a huge governmental apparatus at federal, provincial, municipal, and local levels, it is impossible for central leaders to find all cases of corruption, incompetence, and bureaucratic tyranny. Only the media could root out such pervasive problems.

When told that CCTV news was 30% negative and 70% positive (itself a remarkable shift from the all-out propaganda of the past), Premier Zhu said that 49% negative and 51% positive would be fine by him.

When President Hu Jintao assumed power in 2002, he had fresh ideas about how the media should change. For the first time, he asked that the press report each time the Politburo met, making governance more transparent—a rather radical move in China where senior leader activity was traditionally secretive. Hu also told media officials that television news allocated too much time to leaders attending meetings and going on routine tours. He called for more "real news content" and stories of human interest, and less coverage of the mundane comings and goings of senior leaders, which he criticized internally as "wasting time." (Such ideas worried Party officials, and the Propaganda Department issued a directive to newspapers not to "misunderstand and distort the meaning of Hu's statements" about the press.[3])

Minister Liu Binjie confirms that Hu Jintao pays much attention to China's media industry. "Shortly after Hu took office, we reported to him and asked his directions," Liu says. "He instructed that China's press and publications should observe the Three Closenesses: close to reality, close to life, and close to the people . . . He recognized that our news was far away from the people and the people didn't like it," Liu adds. "He suggested that we start with 'real news.'"

One of Hu's innovations was to downplay the tradition of listing every leader in attendance whenever a political meeting was reported, with special care taken to present them in their official rank order. "TV news would read out the names of all members of delegations," Liu Binjie recalls. "If, on a given day, the (then) seven members of the Politburo Standing Committee all had reportable activities, then CCTV's evening 30-minute news [China's leading news program], would *exceed* 30 minutes to give every one of the seven leaders five minutes— and there would be no time for other news! Viewers were annoyed."

From 2003, news coverage of routine conferences, foreign affairs activities, and leaders' speeches was simplified and shortened, with regulations limiting the number of words, lengths, and page arrangements for leadership coverage. Prominent pages in newspapers and prime time slots on radio and TV were reserved "for the people." It was a profound change, according to Minister Liu, "which was appreciated by journalists and reporters, who want to work on real news. President Hu," he adds, "supports our work."

Furthermore, increasingly pressured by the reforming market economy, the media landscape was becoming fiercely competitive. Newspapers that didn't give readers what they wanted suffered financially and could go out of business.

★ ★ ★

Media changes were evident in the coverage of two crises in 2003. One was defused quickly. When home-made explosions occurred at China's most prestigious universities, Tsinghua and Beijing, panic was averted by rapid and complete news reports. *People's Daily* commented that media "transparency played the greatest role in stopping the spread of rumors and avoiding panic."

The other crisis, however, became a stern lesson in the pitfalls of media control.

When the frightening new epidemic known as Severe Acute Respiratory Syndrome (SARS) broke out in late 2002, China's state-run media, under directives, first ignored the threat and then, when that became impossible, downplayed it.

But containment was impossible: in the new, open era, the highly contagious disease traveled swiftly between countries. By not warning its neighbors, China had inadvertently allowed the epidemic to spread, exposing people beyond its borders to illness and possible death.

Originating in Guangdong Province, the disease next erupted in adjacent Hong Kong and then jumped north to Beijing. News of the contagion was suppressed until February 9, 2003—and then again after February 25, in order to prevent the unpleasant tidings from affecting the annual legislative sessions in early March. And so, as SARS cases multiplied, China's newspapers described the situation as being "under control," "diminishing," and "no longer a threat." Some Western critics charged that the government seemed more interested in stopping the flow of information than in preventing the spread of disease. Chinese media accused their Western counterparts of exaggerating the problem in order to embarrass China.

On April 4 the minister of public health, Zhang Wenkang, claimed in a widely reported news conference that the epidemic in Beijing had been "effectively controlled." In televised remarks, he assured the public that there had only been 12 cases of SARS in the capital. Many people knew better, and some refused to remain silent about it: several, including a former chief of surgery, went public with their revelations, giving the whistle-blowing scoop to Western media.

Suddenly, Beijing was awash with rumor, and travelers en masse canceled their trips. Mounting public pressure at home and abroad soon forced China's leaders to change their policy. On April 17, President Hu Jintao ordered that the government "should never cover up the spread of SARS." Hu and Premier Wen Jiabao demanded that China's medical establishment tell the truth and that China's media establishment report the facts. They warned that officials who misled the public would be punished severely.

A news conference was hastily scheduled for April 20, to be conducted by Minister of Health Zhang Wenkang, and the mayor of Beijing, Meng Xuenong. Neither showed up. Instead, the executive vice minister of Health appeared and announced that the number of SARS cases in Beijing was more than *eight times higher* than had previously been stated—346, not 42. As for the missing minister of health and mayor of Beijing, a terse statement issued by Xinhua explained their absence: they had been fired.

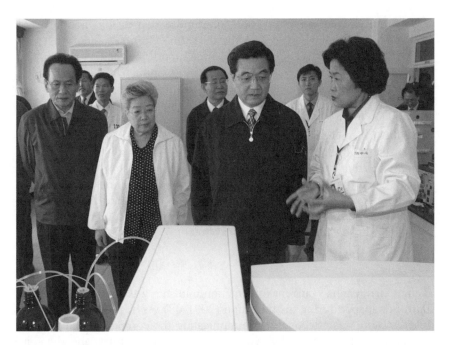

President Hu Jintao in Tianjin during the SARS epidemic, inspecting the prevention and treatment of SARS, with Vice Premier Wu Yi (second from left) (May 1, 2003; Xinhua News Agency, Lan Hongguang).

Analysts were dumbfounded. Zhang Wenkang was a friend of former President Jiang Zemin, who had brought him to Beijing from Shanghai. Meng Xuenong was a former Youth League compatriot of Hu Jintao, a rising star barely three months on the job. But where the legitimacy of the government—and by extension, the stability of the country—was at stake, action had to be taken.

"Zhang Wenkang and Meng Xuenong Are Sacked for Negligence" ran one headline. The *New York Times* called the announcement "a rare, blunt and very public admission of failure if not deception."[4]

In truth, it was the system, which sought to preserve order at all costs, which was at fault, not two individuals: most likely there had been near unanimity among China's senior leaders, who, not realizing the severity of the disease, agreed to downplay it so as not to cause panic at home or damage abroad.

Literally overnight, SARS stories monopolized China's news and the people's psyche. As the SARS toll mounted, Beijing was enveloped with anxiety. Schools were closed, college students confined to campuses. Some hospitals were quarantined, while others refused to admit patients suspected of being infected. Some people stockpiled groceries and holed up in their homes; others fled the city.

Yet, though media reports were now more depressing, people were, ironically, more encouraged. For the first time Chinese readers felt they were getting the truth. Capitalizing on the mood, the media grew bolder. *Southern Metropolis Daily*, Guangdong's most popular newspaper, called for a "breakthrough" in how the government dealt with crises and information. (Though punitive action was later taken against *Southern Metropolis Daily*, ostensibly for other matters, and media repression continues, history will likely record that SARS was a significant, albeit unpleasant and halting step toward a more open and free media in China.) Further evidence of greater openness came soon afterwards, on May 2, when the media reported that a mechanical failure had destroyed a Chinese Navy submarine, killing all 70 seamen on board. It was unprecedented for the government-controlled press to report military disasters, especially during the festive May Day week.

★ ★ ★

Wang Chen, China's current Information minister, was president of *People's Daily* newspaper during the transition (2001-08). As he puts it, "In the past, *People's Daily* was effective in communicating the correct political orientation and in reporting on the general secretary, the premier, and the spirit of the CPC Central Committee. But our work had been relatively weak in serving the people."

Wang's new approach, based on Hu Jintao's philosophy, meant that "*People's Daily* enhanced its role in public supervision. We added letters from readers. We began to do investigative journalism," he says. "Instead of avoiding hot, controversial issues, we went head-to-head with them." Stories the paper broke, he says, included "the rampant construction of theaters across the country," as cities around China sought to keep up with Beijing and Shanghai. "Some cities could barely afford to complete construction of their theaters, much less have enough money to maintain them," Wang notes, adding that *People's Daily's* reports affected senior leaders.

The paper also exposed how many companies, in order to save money, only turned on their environmental protection equipment just before government inspection teams arrived; its reports led to a tightening of controls. *People's Daily* also disclosed a coal-mine flood that killed 81 miners in Guangxi Province (2001). But local officials, led by Wan Ruizhong, the Party secretary, covered up the accident, continuing to deny it when investigation teams arrived, bribing survivors and threatening journalists with violence. Analysis determined that the flood had been caused by mismanagement and poorly conducted explosions. Eventually the story was revealed and several officials punished. For his role in the cover up, and for taking bribes, Wan Ruizhong was executed.

Wang Chen explains that, during times of national transition, principles are often in conflict, and emphasizes the press's role in providing oversight and supervision. He notes too that *People's Daily's* circulation increased from 1.7 million to 2.3 million under his editorship—evidence of the paper's enhanced relevance for readers. Today, even editors of official government media must be concerned about market response.

★ ★ ★

Media reform also means that government subsidies are no longer handed out, so that newspapers, magazines, and radio and television stations, like other enterprises, must compete in the marketplace for revenues. To continue to exist, they must attract audiences and advertising. In market economies, consumers are kings.

Apropos, and another watershed in China's media coverage, this time of foreign affairs, came with the Iraq War in 2003. The Xinhua News Agency, long seen as a turgid government servant, delivered up-to-the-minute stories on everything from breaking battlefield news to diplomatic activities. Saddam Hussein's brutality, mass graves, and the extreme repression were reported—hardly the old way of glorifying a long-time trading partner and anti-American ally. In a market economy with multiple news sources, Xinhua had no choice. If it didn't start offering truth and reasonable balance, audiences would turn elsewhere.

Similarly, China Central Television carried the U.S. invasion of Iraq live and uncensored on its flagship Channel 1. For the first time in its history, CCTV was broadcasting real-time feeds from CNN and Fox News, taking raw footage straight, including from embedded reporters, and providing real-time translations. This unprecedented coverage gave millions of Chinese a broader and more nuanced view of the world than they had ever before been allowed to see.

In 1978, China had less than 2 million TV sets and only one TV channel. "Today (2008), China has 1.2 billion TV viewers and CCTV alone has 18 public channels and numerous digital pay channels," according to former CCTV President Zhao Huayong. CCTV also has interactive TV, HDTV, and mobile TV, and is developing new media such as Web TV and IPTV. Every day almost 700 million watch CCTV programs. When major events occur, such as the Sichuan earthquake, 85% of the population turns to CCTV. CCTV has been named one of the world's top 500 brands (71st in 2007).

★ ★ ★

The growing power and freedom of China's media, and its role in protecting the public interest, were underscored during 2008 by several seemingly unrelated events. The first involved photographs of a supposedly rare tiger, which a farmer in Shaanxi Province claimed to have taken in the local woods.[5] Trying to claim $150,000 in reward for finding an endangered South China tiger in the wild by brandishing dozens of digital photos, the farmer found support from local Shaanxi forestry officials (who were only too happy to boost tourism). "After the careful examination," they announced publicly, "experts confirmed the authenticity of the photos. This means the tiger has been found again after more than 20 years."

But when the photos were posted online, they ignited a firestorm among China's savvy netizens. Why was the tiger so shiny? Why always staring right into the camera? Why did its position never change? Soon someone discovered an old poster which was shockingly similar to the "wild tiger." The "discovery" was fake—literally a "paper tiger" propped up among trees.

The Shaanxi officials finally admitted the hoax, and the farmer was arrested on charges of fraud. But public anger was directed at the officials, who soon found out how much China had changed as bloggers accused them of intentionally disregarding the truth in their desire for money. As the *Southern Metropolis Daily* put it, "a small number of officials ignored science, common sense and seething public opinion to play with the public trust. When the wisdom of the people stripped away the emperor's new clothes, the officials lied and used bureaucracy to keep the truth from coming out." Shaanxi authorities eventually got the point: they held a disciplinary meeting and required thousands of officials to attend. And in the end, public opinion won as a dozen officials were punished.

Such online public scrutiny has become increasingly common. A year earlier, online outrage over child slave labor in rural factories forced the government to investigate illegal labor practices. The public was enraged that such feudal practices could be happening today, and officials were punished for negligence if not complicity.

Another case where the exposure of fakery aroused public debate occurred at the Olympics. Chen Qigang, the opening ceremony's chief musical director, revealed in an interview that the picture-perfect little girl who had sung "Ode to the Motherland," Lin Miaoke, had lip-synched the song. It had actually been sung by another girl, Yang Peiyi. Chen said that a senior official had felt that Lin Miaoke's voice was not good enough for the ceremony, but that Yang Peiyi did not look quite right. By using both girls, "we combined the perfect voice and the perfect performance," Chen said.[6]

China's internet community went aglow. The general consensus was that the two separate roles should have been announced openly. Online anger was directed at the organizers for keeping the secret, not at Lin Miaoke, whose self-assured performance as she soared on wires above 91,000 enchanted spectators was praised.

Soon after the Olympics, a far more serious case of fakery erupted, with the revelation that many Chinese dairy companies, seeking to cut costs, had not only used diluted milk to make infant milk powder, but also added melamine (an industrial additive used to make fertilizers and plastics) in order to boost its nitrogen content and achieve an artificially higher protein count in testing.[7] About 300,000 babies fell sick, many with kidney stones and kidney failure. Over 50,000 were hospitalized, hundreds in serious condition, and several died.

The contamination was soon found in other milk products, far and wide, including in yogurt in Hong Kong. Sanlu Group, one of China's largest dairy companies, was the first company found to be selling melamine-laced milk (it later went bankrupt). Almost 10% of milk tested from China's two leading brands—Mengniu and Yili—revealed traces of the same contaminant.

Parents were furious and the Chinese media, reflecting public anger, vigorously publicized and castigated the tainted brands. Xinhua revealed that Sanlu had known about the contamination from consumer complaints for 10 months before it recalled the products, and had repeatedly tried to hide information about contaminated dairy supplies from the public.[8]

The relentless media coverage led to product recalls, regulation tightening, and the firing of officials, including the mayor of Shijiazhuang, Hebei Province, where Sanlu had its headquarters, and the head of the national quality inspection agency responsible for food safety.[9] President Hu Jintao reprimanded officials for not properly safeguarding the public interest, warning that "some leaders lacked a sense of responsibility."[10]

Soon afterwards, in a nationwide media campaign to heighten safety awareness, President Hu was shown on CCTV inspecting a dairy farm in Anhui Province:[11] "Food safety affects people's health," Hu told the head of the dairy company, shaking his finger. "You must learn the lesson from Sanlu's experience, and improve your management to ensure that all products that reach the market are up to the standards."

Other cases sprung up. Chinese media revealed an attempted cover-up by local officials when a deadly landslide of illegally dumped mining waste entombed a village in Shanxi Province. The Shanxi governor, Meng Xuenong, was forced to resign to take responsibility. (The decent but wildly unlucky Meng, who was not personally involved, had only recently been rehabilitated after his scapegoated dismissal as Beijing mayor during the 2003 SARS crisis.)

I've had my own experiences with an increasingly confident Chinese media. In 2005, while touring and researching China I also promoted my biography of President Jiang Zemin, and met many local reporters. Some asked probing questions, including one who stood up in a press conference to enquire bluntly whether I wrote the book in order to help my business in China.

While some in the audience looked askance at the reporter for asking what they perceived to be an impertinent question, I thanked him, telling the assembled journalists, "This is precisely the kind of investigatory question that Chinese reporters should be asking. Conflict of interest is a professional disease and the only effective medicine is either voluntary full disclosure or involuntary media exposure." My questioner had, I noted, increased my confidence in China's media.

I then explained that I wrote the book because I wanted to learn about eight tumultuous decades of contemporary Chinese history, and to tell the true story of China to the world—and that I was fortunate not to worry much about financial matters. "But make your own judgment," I stressed.

I then addressed the probing reporter: "I'm often asked how my writing and business intermix. Some pose the question as you did—asking whether I wrote the biography of China's leader to *boost* my business. What's fascinating is that others pose the opposite question—'Dr. Kuhn, now that you've written the biography of Jiang Zemin, who is China's *former* leader, aren't you worried that your business will *suffer*, because China now has a *new* leader, Hu Jintao?"

I wasn't worried, I assured the audience; I love learning about China and communicating what I learn—with a touch of my own "spin." I concluded by again thanking the reporter for his honesty and courage.

All these incidents highlight the increasing investigative prowess and reporting confidence of the Chinese media, which now covers incidents ranging from natural disasters and industrial accidents to tainted food and bad drugs, often uncovering human error or negligence. One consequence of China's more assertive media is that officials are now more vulnerable —whether local leaders who do not follow central policies, or try to cover up problems, or higher officials who have to bear responsibility for whatever happens "on their watch." Officials at all levels are becoming more vigilant, knowing that if serious problems occur, the media will report them, the public will demand truth, and they will be held accountable. The Chinese media is starting to affect governance. This is progress.

★ ★ ★

Not everyone is convinced. Certainly not the energetic and acerbic Chinese journalist He Qinglian, who wrote in 2004 that China's "much-lauded economic modernization has allowed the government to camouflage its pervasive control under the glossy façade of consumerism, with a shift from ham-fisted censorship to an elaborate architecture of Party supervision, amorphous legislation, stringent licensing mechanisms, handpicked personnel and concentrated media ownership."[12]

He Qinglian cited cases of intimidation of journalists and gave examples of restrictions on media ownership. There was no doubt truth in what she wrote—yet similarly, there is no doubt that Chinese media is in historic flux. Four years earlier, for example, in 2000, I had organized a private conference, with China's Information Minister Zhao Qizheng, on Media in America, in which Chinese officials and media leaders took part, along with American journalists, academics and diplomats.

The very fact that such a conference could be held was itself testimony to China's reforms. Yet Chinese officials still feared going down the road of U.S.-style press freedom. A state editor asserted that absolute freedom of the press erodes objectivity and encourages subjectivity. One Beijing professor said that while he appreciated press freedom, if it were suddenly allowed in China precisely as it operates in America, the country could be torn apart.

Other participants worried that an American-style press law would not only create political instability, but also shower China with crass entertainment.

Certainly there remains media censorship in China. I know some of the censors personally. Most believe that they are maintaining standards of a civil society. Others are embarrassed with their role and hope for more media freedom.

Publications Minister Liu Binjie suggests that "Foreigners surmise that China censors every piece of news and every book. That would be impossible—we have so much news and so many publications!" Every day in China, he says, "more than 60 million people are saying something in their real names at meetings, in newspapers, on radio, television, and the Internet. That's more than the total population of Britain!"

In 2008, Liu met former U.S. President Jimmy Carter, who commented on how much China had changed, particularly how the Chinese people were now able to openly discuss issues like housing, demolition and relocation, prices, and the like. "I told President Carter that China had been openly discussing all these issues for a good while," says Liu. "It's nothing new. He just hadn't understood what was going on in China until then, nor do most in the West."

Liu Binjie, who has overall responsibility for China's print media, stresses "I only take action on matters that violate relevant laws and regulations, such as fabricated news that undermines public interests." As an example,

Liu Binjie, director and minister of General Press and Publication (GAPP) (Beijing, June 2008).

he gives "the Cardboard Steamed Buns incident," in which a TV journalist faked a story that claimed to show an unlicensed snack vendor in Beijing selling steamed dumplings stuffed with cardboard soaked in caustic soda. The journalist was later jailed because, according to Liu, the story "falsely accused and severely damaged the food industry."

Another type of case where he will take action is "when journalists blackmail enterprises if those enterprises don't buy ads from their newspapers or TV stations, such as by threatening to expose informants' letters to the public. Blackmailing behavior will be severely punished."

But in general, Liu stresses that while overseeing legal regulation of the industry, "we don't interfere with specific content creation and news reporting. Freedom of news and speech are safeguarded as stipulated in our Constitution." What is prohibited, he says, is content which would "bring about public damage." This ranges from Hitler's books, proscribed in China "by requests of other countries," to pornographic publications that would "hamper young people's development."

Liu acknowledges that "media regulation is far from perfect," and calls for "a comprehensive legal system to protect the rights of citizens, journalists, media, and media companies." For example, he says, "some interviewees make trouble for journalists. China needs a sound legal system. It is still our weak spot."

China's leaders would prefer the media to focus on failings of local governments rather than question policies of the central government (as would leaders of every country). Yet the genie of increasing media freedom is likely only to grow stronger, and China's media will probably continue to open wider. The result may not be an Americanization of China's media but a distinctive Chinese system that reflects the values and interests of its people.

But censorship is always at the ready and often not subtle. When Iranian citizens erupted in protest, braving government crackdown, after the rigged re-election of Iran's hard-line, theocratic president, Mahmoud Ahmadinejad (2009), China hit the delete button. With uncomfortable echoes of Tiananmen Square (1989), the Iranian demonstrations went largely unreported in China's media. China's leaders believed that the "vulnerable period" caused by the global economic crisis was not the time for the chaos of revolution, especially "color revolution." China's online discussion boards, however, sparked with sympathy for (and envy of) the Iranian protestors, and while tens of thousands of their comments were removed by censors, many netizens tinted their online offerings green, the color of the Iranian opposition, in defiant support. Some official Chinese commentators hinted darkly that Western forces, rather than grassroots Iranians, were behind it all.

Notwithstanding censorship, it's striking how well informed the Chinese people are. Over the years, they have learned how to take the increasingly free news they do get, discern concealment and spin when added, and discern a close approximation of truth. (The joke is told that the 30 minutes of

CCTV's evening news has three ten-minute blocks: "Our leaders are working;" "Chinese people are happy;" "Foreign people are not happy.")

★ ★ ★

Insatiable desire for information of all kinds has engendered the flourishing of an expanding publishing industry catering to varied tastes. In 2007, for example, *Global People* magazine, published by *People's Daily*, asked me to write an article on Hillary Clinton, in which I explained why she had become the most polarizing politician in recent memory. It aroused high interest and typified the approach of *Global People*, a glossy, personality-focused publication. The story of the magazine's launch is a microcosm of reform.[13] Magazines in China are strictly regulated: each one requires a "number" (i.e., license) from the General Administration of Press and Publication, and new numbers are rarely issued. Thus to start a new magazine is a challenge, even for government agencies: one generally needs to take over an existing magazine, use its number, and begin publishing with fresh content.

Global People was no exception. *People's Daily* took one of its existing magazines, an ideological publication, and changed it completely, bringing in one of its top editors, Liu Aicheng, whose previous jobs included head of international news and U.S. bureau chief. Liu wrote that "*Global People*'s mission is to satisfy the great desire of the Chinese people to learn about and adapt to the outside world . . . It focuses on 'celebrities' broadly conceived: fascinating individuals—politicians, business leaders, entrepreneurs, scientists and artists—who make a difference or who have vital stories to tell."

Such personality-based reporting would, until recently, have been forbidden, according to Liu—not least *Global People*'s stories on the private lives of former Chinese leaders. One story called "The Truth about Mao Zedong's Financial Property," described Chairman Mao's income and the life of his family members, through interviews with his former chief of staff and close confidantes. Another revealed the reasons why Deng Xiaoping never went back home after joining the Communist Party; while an interview with Hu Yaobang's son yielded previously unpublished stories about the former CPC leader.

As for domestic reporting, Liu stressed that "*Global People* does not shirk from exposing China's negative side. One story exposed the no. 1 corrupt official in Hebei province; another featured investigative reports of China's top financial evaders, the worst delinquents on taxes, debt payment, and the like." The magazine also published a sensational cover story on the corruption scandal of former Shanxi Governor Yu Youjin—which became the magazine's best-selling issue. Inconceivable in the past, the expose tested the limits of media today.

The changing attitudes of China's leaders to the media were brought home to me by reactions to the Chinese translation of my biography of former President Jiang Zemin. One of the nation's current leaders told me it had made an important contribution to reform by portraying a Chinese leader as a normal human being. "China has had a tradition," he said, "of making of our leaders either gods or devils. In truth, they are neither—they are human beings."

In internal discussions among senior leaders, the biography, which had been controversial, was also cited as a good example of the benefits of openness. Jiang Zemin himself was quoted in the Chinese press as telling a friend, "The author wrote objectively; he didn't try to beautify me. But," he added, "he got my wedding date wrong."

★ ★ ★

Publishing in China is surprisingly diverse. Prior to reform, there were few publications other than textbooks and Mao Zedong's works—and foreign publications were strictly controlled. Now, according to Publications Minister Liu Binjie, China has the most book publishing houses of any country in the world (573); publishes the most new book titles per year (234,000); and prints the most books (6.4 billion). "We have 9,468 periodicals and printed 2.85 billion copies in 2007," he adds, plus "1,938 newspapers with an annual circulation of 42.45 billion—an average daily circulation of 100 million—making China the world's no. 1 newspaper publisher."

Furthermore, China imports about 3.5 million books every year, and some 5,000 periodicals and 400 newspapers continuously. "It reflects significant changes in leadership's guiding principle on press and publications," says Liu Binjie. In the old days, he explains, "these were expected to serve political purposes. This is no longer true. Now our fundamental objective is to enrich people's personal, spiritual and cultural lives. In the past," he adds, "we stressed one uniform voice, view, and culture. Now we respect differences and advocate diversity. Cultures are diverse, and people's needs are different. Uniformity cannot satisfy all needs."

Liu stresses government support for translations of foreign works. "All the best works of the world should be available in the Chinese market in a timely manner," he says, adding proudly that, on occasion, China's best-seller book charts are now no different from those of New York, Paris, and London. The Harry Potter books, for example, were released in China on the same day they were released in other countries.

China participates in the world's 47 largest international book expositions, involving over 100 Chinese publishing houses. By taking part, China is learning ways of doing business and increasing cross-cultural communications. Both are crucially important to Chinese leaders, who authorize government subsidies to support participation. The annual Beijing International Book Fair, meanwhile, which houses some 500 Chinese book publishers and 1,300 publishers from 51 countries, has become the largest copyright trading event in Asia; in 2008 about 5,000 copyrights deals were signed.[14]

State control of the publishing industry has been diluted: in the past, all news and publishing enterprises were affiliated with specific Party or governmental departments. As a result, according to Liu Binjie, "they only served the purposes of those departments." Many of these enterprises have now been turned into "genuinely independent market entities."

Links between newspapers and ministries have also been severed. Previously, each ministry had its own papers, but Liu notes that "in 2004 we separated out over 700 newspapers and publications which solely served the Party or government." He emphasizes that such changes have "significantly increased the independence and credibility of the press." Reforms of the old geographically based publishing system are also planned. Traditionally, every province and large municipality had its own publishing company, which dominated the industry in that region and did little business in other regions. For Chinese publishing companies to operate with efficiency and compete against foreign multinationals, however, they now need to have a national presence.

"Our next step is to promote merger and acquisitions, reorganization, and ownership reform to further restructure the industry," says GAPP Minister Liu. Diverse ownership of publications—until recently the government was the only owner/investor permitted—allows publishing houses to raise funds through different channels, including going public.

Liu cites textbook monopolies as another historical "blockage," which is being broken through open bidding involving numerous publishing houses. Boundaries between different media are also being removed, to promote multimedia business, and integrate digital publishing, Internet and electronic media with traditional media.

(These reforms echo those mooted in the late 1980s, when General Secretary Zhao Ziyang asked Du Daozheng, a veteran journalist and former-leftist-turned-reformer, to restructure GAPP.[15] "I wanted to establish new regulations—the principal issue was whether private entities should be allowed to operate newspapers," Du recalls. However, he was dismissed in 1989, following suppression of the student protesters.)

Liu Binjie notes that many opposed the reforms. "Some worried that foreign and private capital in press and publications would endanger our cultural security," he says. "Others assumed that none of these now-independent companies would publicize government policies or advocate public welfare anymore, because they would only be focused on the market and making money."

Liu, however, was confident "that modern corporate structure would improve China's publishing industry's performance and not affect China's cultural security. Investors only care about the returns they get on their investments," he states. "They wouldn't interfere with editorial." His judgment, he says, has been corroborated by the success of listed publishing and media companies. "It's only a matter of management," he says. "Capital doesn't control content. We're now cultivating strategic investors who add managerial, marketing and operational value."

China has about 60 periodicals in partnership with foreign publishers (sharing local copyrights). The roster includes *Vogue, National Geographic,* and *Readers' Digest.* "Foreign companies need China's market and resources," says Liu, "while China needs foreign experience and brands. Cooperation is mutually beneficial."

Minister Liu is forthright about China leaders' determination to optimize market mechanisms. "We saw how the publishing industry works in other countries, using the market, and it dawned on us that our industry needed to change," he says. "If the government's objective is to hold our ground, then if we lose the market, we lose our ground. Therefore," he says, "my stance is that 'To gain market is to gain ground; to lose market is to lose ground'."

A senior leader joked that this had become "Liu Binjie's signature quote." But, Liu insists, "this is really what I think. I do not enforce mandatory control, but stress that problems be resolved through development. This is the opposite of China's approach in the past."

Liu notes that the industry's top priority is "to develop compelling content." The news, he says, should reflect social events and people's lives in an accurate and timely manner; publications should showcase creative achievements—both in China and throughout the world. "Innovation and development" should be emphasized, he adds, pointing out that the government has set up funds to support original content creation in books, animation and cartoons, and game products.

High-tech is a priority. "I'm personally pushing the digitalization of media," says Liu. "We aim to catch up with our foreign counterparts. We support digital publishing, and introduced favorable policies to boost R&D for on-line gaming." Liu is proud that China hosts the world's largest game industry conference in Shanghai (Chinajoy), and has gone from being heavily dependent on imported cartoons to where 70% of product shown on television is domestically produced (though in part due to restrictions on foreign content which even officials admit has led to rushed, low-quality Chinese productions).[16]

In tandem with these initiatives, Liu asserts that China is taking action against piracy. "Copyright-related work is progressively more important in our country, its role in the national economy is increasing," he says. Almost a billion copies of illegal publications were seized in five years, he notes, and 104 illegal CD production lines closed down, while campaigns were launched to combat Internet piracy and promote usage of genuine software.

China has also opened its printing sector to foreign capital and technology; more than 2400 Sino-foreign joint ventures have been established, bringing in advanced printing and copying equipment—and these enterprises have not only taken the lion's share of the domestic printing market, but also turned China into one of the world's largest printing bases. (Over 40 American periodicals are printed in China.)

GAPP Minister Liu Binjie sums up reform by emphasizing that "the most significant change in the industry is not the growth in economic prowess, but in the transformation of people's spiritual worldview and the regulatory system. China's press and publication industry is not 'locked behind closed doors' the way it used to be," he adds. "Instead, our industry is now more integrated into the world." (GAPP 2009 guidelines called for state-owned publishing houses to convert into stock companies, merge into large groups and expand overseas, in order to provide the public with richer content and to compete in worldwide media markets—initially Chinese language, ultimately all languages. Significantly, international strategic investors and public listings were encouraged.)

And Liu is confident that these changes are just the beginning. In the future, he says, "we will witness great strides in our industry's industrialization, marketization, and internationalization. I believe that, in 25 years, Chinese media will be able to meet the people's spiritual and cultural requirements. While safeguarding social and public interests," he suggests, "Chinese media will be more recognized and understood by the West. I think there will be 5-6 top Chinese media companies enjoying international fame. That's the plan. In 25 years China will have media companies like News Corp. Perhaps sooner."

Endnotes

1 Jonathan Ansfield, "Wen Jiabao: Man of the Moment," *Newsweek*, May 17, 2008.
2 Author's meeting with Liu Binjie, Beijing, June 2008.
3 Elizabeth Rosenthal, "Chinese Legislature Meets to Appoint Leaders," *The New York Times*, March 5, 2003.
4 Erik Eckholm, "China Admits Much Higher Number of SARS Case," *The New York Times*, April 20, 2003.
5 AP, July 4, 2008.
6 Vivian Wu, "Perfect young singer lip-synched in opening ceremony, says director," *South China Morning Post*, August 13, 2008. Rohan Sullivan, AP, August 13, 2008.
7 Edward Wong, "Mayor in China fired in baby formula scandal," *The New York Times*, September 19, 2008.
8 David Barboza, "China Says Complaints About Milk Began in 2007," *The New York Times*, September, 23 (also 24, 26) 2008.
9 "China's Tainted Baby Formula Scandal Widens," Forbes.com, September 17, 2009; "Top Heads Roll In China's Tainted Dairy Products Scandal," Forbes.com, September 22, 2008.
10 Jim Yardley, "China Seeks to Calm Fears Amid Dairy Scandal," *The New York Times*, September 21, 2008.
11 Raymond Li, "Hu urges dairy industry vigilance on symbolic visit," *South China Morning Post*, October 1, 2008.
12 He Qinglian, *Media Control in China*, HRIC, 2004.
13 Full disclosure: I am Senior International Adviser to *Global People*; I helped with its start-up and have an interest in the magazine.
14 Zhu Liyong, "Spread the Word," *China Daily*, September 9, 2008.
15 Du was editor of the liberal magazine *Yanhuang Chunqiu* ("Spring and Autumn of the Chinese People")—EastSouthWestNorth, http://zonaeuropa.com/20070604_1.htm; author's meeting with Du Daozheng, Beijing, April 2008.
16 Duncan Hewitt, "A State of Fantasy," *Newsweek*, 2007 - http://www.newsweek.com/id/32897.

28

How Telecommunications and the Internet Changed China

Nothing has changed China more than its swift embrace of telecommunications reform and the spectacular development of the Internet. The process has not been smooth—but it has propelled economic development, enabling China to leapfrog other nations, and it has radically changed the lives of ordinary people.

Again, the transformation was unprecedented. In the 1980s, having a telephone at home was a privilege reserved for the elite few. As Wu Jichuan, China's former telecommunications minister, puts it, "Before reform, the total number of phones in all China was less than in Hong Kong—it was unimaginable that ordinary Chinese citizens could have a telephone. In 2009, we exceed one *billion* phones, with many ordinary citizens owning multiple phones."[1]

Wu Jichuan was a key figure in bringing China's antiquated communications networks into the modern era. An early computer user himself, he led the restructuring of the industry during his period as minister of Post and Telecommunications (1993-1998) and minister of Information Industry (1998-2003). The process of change was complex and often controversial, with frequent conflict between traditional and entrenched bureaucracies and the demands of modern technology and financing.

Wu pioneered innovative funding policies—indeed telecom was the first industry in China to use foreign funds.[2] "The first phase was telecom infrastructure in Guangzhou, Shanghai and Tianjin," Wu recalls. "Suddenly people were waiting in line to get telephones."

Minister Wu played a central role in breaking up China's telecom monopoly, in order to infuse the industry with competition and vibrancy. Originally, all telecommunications in China were owned and operated by China Telecom. In 1994, another company, China Unicom, was separated out. And a milestone event occurred in 1997 when China Mobile, a portion of China Telecom, went public.

Yet changes in ownership were controversial. An early telecom joint venture in Shenzhen with the UK's Cable & Wireless was blamed for causing a security breach, after confidential conversations about a proposed nuclear power station were leaked. The foreign stake was bought back.

And, as Wu Jichuan recounts, implementing the decision to list China Mobile "wasn't easy. No so-called 'pillar industry' had gone public; telecom would be the first," he says. "The rules prevented foreigners from owning telecom; there was worry that China's security could be jeopardized." The problem, he explains, was that "some officials didn't yet understand the difference between ownership and management, so they assumed that capital would control management and compromise security." With the benefit of hindsight, however, Wu expresses satisfaction that foreign ownership "has never interfered with management." And he is proud that the market capitalization of China Mobile—$190 billion in early 2011, after peaking at about $400 billion—is the largest in the telecom industry worldwide.

And reform continued, as China Mobile and China Satellite (1999-2000), and later China Netcom (broadband services), were split off from China Telecom. There was also a decision to separate fixed-line services into separate enterprises covering north and south China, which Wu describes as "debatable." "I did not think that the network should be broken," he says, "but senior leaders did."

There were twists and turns: at one point China's railways set up its own telecom company. But eventually, in 2008, a series of mergers and transfers left China with three strong telecom companies: China Mobile, China Telecom, and a strengthened China Unicom. Wu Jichuan displays the instincts of his industry when asked whether these three companies represent the final division. "How can we know?" he says. "Telecom is a dynamic industry. If changes are needed, changes will happen. The market will decide."

As minister of Information Industry, Wu Jichuan did his best to calm irrational enthusiasm for new technologies. He is credited with preventing the Internet bubble from harming China—famously warning against overvaluations at a Goldman Sachs meeting in 1998—for which he earned the nickname "Minister No" (a pun on his name) "I knew we should focus on the real economy," Wu says, "not the virtual one." And when 3G licenses came up for sale, Wu stopped China's telecom companies from "overbidding before the public could pay for the service—that's what hurt many foreign companies," he says.

(Indeed, so essential did Wu become for foreign confidence in China's telecom industry that once, when rumors circulated that he had resigned, he visited investment banks to prove he was still in charge. Wu's expertise surprised even George Soros, the legendary investor. "Soros seemed shocked that he could discuss funds and investments with a minister of the Chinese Communist Party!" recalls Wu.)

Now retired, Wu suggests that China's leaders should pay more attention to telecom. "It combines national infrastructure, major industry and high technology," he says. "Development and regulation are key. You must get both right!" And he stresses that a fast-changing industry "needs a strong legal framework to provide service, protect privacy and maintain order. Enabling market development and securing network safety are key."

China's telecom law, Wu notes, "has been ready for ten years but it's still not enacted." The cause of the delay, he says, is territorial not technical: China's powerful State Administration of Radio, Film and Television (SARFT) opposes the law (or seeks exemption from it), Wu says, because, as technologies converge, it hopes to develop its own telecom network using cable and satellite infrastructure. "SARFT thinks that if technology can transmit pictures, the network should be theirs," Wu asserts. "There is convergence between telecom, Internet and media—but SARFT doesn't want to be merged."

Wu points to Shanghai as a model of revenue-sharing cooperation between the local telecom company and SARFT. In other areas, however, "there is competition." It only adds to his conviction that China needs both a telecom law and an independent regulatory body. "China must figure out jurisdictions and optimum structure," Wu asserts. "In my opinion, SARFT should regulate telecom resources and infrastructure, while an independent body should regulate telecom operators. All telecom should be under the same law."

(In 1996, in early preparation for China's first telecom IPO, Minister Wu said to investment banker Margaret Ren, who advised the ministry, that consumption had no turning back. Wu compared mobile phones, the IPO's focus, to indoor toilets. All toilets used to be outdoors, but once indoor toilets were installed, people would never again tolerate going outside. The same, he said, would be hold with mobile phones.)

★ ★ ★

President Hu Jintao gave his first Internet interview in 2008, to people.com .cn, a website managed by *People's Daily*. By reaching out to Chinese netizens, Hu acknowledged their acute and increasing influence on society—and on policy. More than 300 questions were submitted via online bulletin boards. Three were chosen for Hu to answer: "Do you usually use the Internet?"; "What online content do you look for?"; "Do you read opinions and suggestions from netizens?"

In the live video broadcast, Hu replied that although he was too busy to surf the web every day, he tried to find time to read domestic and international news on the Internet. He said he finds out people's concerns by reading their views online, especially netizens' suggestions for the Party and state.[3] "I'm very concerned about various problems and opinions raised," Hu said. "To do a good job, we must listen to the people and rely on their wisdom."

Many netizens praised Hu's appearance, particularly for paying attention to their opinions—though true to the Internet's DNA, contrary opinions were voiced too, most calling for increased freedom of speech and less Internet policing.

★ ★ ★

The Internet presents a paradox for China's leaders, a finely-honed balance for weighing national pride against social stability. On the one hand, they recognize that free access to information is essential for technological advance, competitive success in world markets, and the spiritual enrichment of the Chinese people. On the other hand, they worry about potentially disruptive consequences of such free access, which can deliver malicious, salacious and seditious information. Hence the dilemma: restrict information and retard progress? Or remove restrictions and risk instability?

In the Internet's early days, opinions varied. In 1998, meeting in Shenzhen with provincial propaganda officials, Propaganda chief Ding Guangen stated that the Internet should become "the mouthpiece of the Party" (echoing the motto of *People's Daily*). Similarly, Chinese officials at one point sought to create a "Chinese intranet"—a wholly enclosed national system, fire-walled off from the global Internet. Wiser heads prevailed: Such a firewall would have been impractical to build, hopeless to maintain, and vulnerable to being breached by ever more sophisticated technology. Worse, it would have retarded Chinese knowledge.

Since then, China's Internet policy has been a sometimes contradictory process of evolution. Attitudes to foreign investment are one example: initially, the government took a hands-off approach ("Let the market decide"); then came a sudden switch to prohibiting any foreign ownership whatsoever; then, under pressure from WTO entry requirements, it had to permit up to 50% foreign ownership of any Internet-related company. There were also rules restricting loosely defined "state secrets" from being distributed through Internet news services or chat rooms; requiring the release of commercial encryption codes (enabling government access to e-mail and other data transmissions); and requiring web-blocking software filters to be pre-installed on all personal computers (delayed and in limbo after a torrent of protests from international business associations and Chinese computer users, although some PC vendors were "voluntarily" installing the "Green Dam Youth Escort" software). All the while, various ministries and agencies jockeyed for influence, seeking authority over jurisdiction and policing.

China's leaders insist that they are committed to the Internet's role in enabling China's citizens to speak their minds, but they nonetheless remain convinced that, for social stability, websites considered to be politically disruptive, pornographic or otherwise undesirable should be blocked. It's an unending and thankless endeavor: an arms race of software technologies where clever individuals can outwit government minions.

"There should be order on the Internet; disorder would thwart Internet growth," states Liu Yunshan, China's Publicity (Propaganda) minister. But he stresses that China's "laws and regulations are not there to limit the Internet, but to facilitate its development. As long as you act within the legal framework, you are totally free on the Internet—you have freedom of speech." Indeed, if China were controlling every aspect of the net, "how," he asks, "could we have five million websites and 80 million blogs? Who's monitoring them all?"[4]

★ ★ ★

Cai Mingzhao, vice minister of the State Council Information Office (SCIO), and the Chinese government's lead official for Internet content, has been intimately involved in the Chinese Internet since its earliest days.[5] Around 1986-1987, Cai says, a Chinese journalist visited the U.S. and published a series of reports on the "information revolution." These caused a stir in China, and caught the attention of senior leaders. At the time, Cai was vice president of Xinhua News Agency's Jiangsu branch. "We started to think about what information really was and to develop information products and services for enterprises, much as Reuters was doing," he recalls. "As journalists, we were very excited."

According to Cai, by the time Hu Qiheng, vice president of the Chinese Academy of Sciences (and sister of Hu Qili, then the reformist minister of Electronics Industry), visited the U.S. in 1994 and signed an agreement with the National Science Foundation to introduce the Internet into China, intellectuals, officials, and the press were eagerly anticipating the information revolution. In Cai's words: "We passionately embraced the advent of the Internet Age."

At around this time, Cai Mingzhao was promoted to serve as Xinhua's secretary-general in Beijing. In 1995, a Xinhua manager in Hong Kong informed Cai that he wanted to start an Internet company.[6] "I was in charge of the company," Cai said, "and gave the green light to the website, which was the predecessor of www.china.com."

In discussions with American investors, the Xinhua company suggested setting up an independent network in China connecting to the international Internet via an interface, which would allow China to filter out harmful information. "This concept was supported enthusiastically by the American investors," Cai recalls: "It would be vetoed by Americans now, but it was endorsed by them then!" Though initially, Cai says, "we did want to set up a physical [and isolated] network in China . . . later we found the plan to be too expensive, redundant and unrealistic. The plan was abandoned and the current structure adopted."

Wall Street bankers/investors showed an interest in China.com and several met Premier Zhu Rongji. "They immediately asked whether Zhu supported

Cai Mingzhao, vice minister of State Council Information Office with Bill Gates at the first Sino-US Internet Forum held in Seattle (November 2007).

China.com going public," recalls Cai, who was in attendance. Premier Zhu said, "Of course, otherwise I wouldn't be meeting with you!"

In 1999, China.com listed on NASDAQ, the first Chinese Internet company to do so. The IPO raised almost $100 million—a figure which had a great impact on the Chinese Internet industry. "People started to regard the Internet as a goldmine," Cai says. "It took only a handful of people, computers and servers to raise hundreds of millions of dollars. It was a miracle!" Indeed, he adds, "I'll tell you a little secret: At that time Xinhua had 7,000 employees and over 2,000 of them didn't have their own apartments. We sold a small part of our shares in China.com and received hundreds of millions of RMB. In one shot, we had the money to build houses for all those staff!"

China.com paved the way for other Chinese Internet companies, such as Sina, Sohu, and Netease, to list on NASDAQ. And in 1998, after Cai Mingzhao became vice president of Xinhua, he decided that in order to create Internet momentum, all of Xinhua's news should be posted on its new website, Xinhuanet.com, first.

"This was very controversial because the news was meant to be sold," Cai recalls. "If the news was to hit Xinhuanet.com first, how could we make money from it? I said that we should look into the future and see the Internet's growth potential. I believed that although we might lose some small clients initially, we would ultimately win huge markets."

Now, Cai says, Xihuanet.com "has become the most influential of Xinhua's departments, and has created far more revenue than all those small clients could have ever done." While not the largest website, it remains politically influential: "All important news is carried first by Xinhuanet.com."

The one event which accelerated Internet development, Cai recounts, was the bombing of China's embassy in Belgrade in 1999. Three journalists, including Xinhua's correspondent, were killed—but *People's Daily's* correspondents survived and sent back reports. Normally, Cai says, "we would have to wait until the next day to read the reports in the newspaper, but no one wanted to wait. So the reports were run on the *People's Daily* website. This," he says, "was the breakthrough. Before this, the website would only repeat the news from the previous day's newspaper. This was the first time the website ran reports earlier than the newspaper."

As a result, many Internet users were drawn to the *People's Daily* site. Soon afterwards, it opened a bulletin board system (BBS), the precursor of the current *Qiangguo Luntan* (Strengthening the Nation Forum) for people to post their opinions. "Within a month, more than 80,000 comments were posted," notes Cai. "At the time this was a huge number—and it made the BBS China's most influential forum."

As people came to realize how swiftly the Internet could disseminate virtually real-time news, Internet growth in China accelerated sharply. The best-known websites, including Sina, Sohu and Netease, started to focus on news. Thus China's Internet has followed a different developmental path than that of the U.S. or Europe: news as the main content, and portals (information supermarkets, basically) as the primary mode of entry.

Today, Minister Cai says, most of China's influential websites carry news, with such sites accounting for 95% of China's total page views. "This has dramatically affected the whole Internet socio-ecosystem, patterns of spreading news, and traditional news systems," Cai observes. "This alone, to a certain extent, shows that China's Internet environment is relaxed—otherwise, there wouldn't be so many sites because the news wouldn't be as compelling."

Cai also emphasizes that the Internet has made it much harder for abuses or problems to be concealed, even in remote corners of China. "In the past, when there was no Internet, local officials could cover up problems or unpleasant events," he says. "But now any incident that happens at any time in any place can be propagated on the Internet in no time and to every place. It's almost impossible to effect cover ups."

The swiftness of the Internet, and mobile phones, in spreading news and information—genuine or false—compelled China's leaders to establish a "spokesperson system," particularly after the SARS outbreak in 2003. "Through SARS, leaders came to understand that open information was critical for defusing public crises," Cai explains. Now each ministry or government agency has a trained spokesperson who releases information to the public at regular press conferences (coordinated by SCIO).

BBS growth has also transformed public discourse in China. These days, websites in China must have an accompanying BBS; there are also specialized BBS sites—about 600,000 by 2008, some with thousands of sub-forums. The outspoken opinions—some slanderous, some malicious—initially "caused great concern for a traditional and conservative country like China," Cai explains, adding, "Now that a balance has been found, some of the negative aspects have been curbed." But Cai Mingzhao denies that the bulletin boards are "censored." "My response," he says, "is 'OK, how [do we do it]? I'm the one responsible and I'm not capable to do it. My total staff in the Bureau of Internet numbers only 20. So I say, 'If you know how to censor BBS, you can have my job!'"

Instant messaging has also helped transform communications: China's most influential platform is Tencent QQ, with 820 million registered subscribers and 636 million active user accounts (2010). Blogs have expanded rapidly too, numbering some 80 million. "All these types of communications deepen connections between people," Cai comments. "And all were unimaginable before the Internet."

Commercial use of the Internet, such as online job hunting, day trading, e-banking, and shopping, remains lower in China than in other countries, accounting for less than 20% of total traffic. But Cai Mingzhao believes this will enlarge rapidly, driven by economic growth and by the Internet becoming more integrated into society. An outstanding example is Alibaba.com, the privately-founded Chinese B2B site, which now has a vast global reach: 24 million small and medium-sized enterprises (around 60% of China's total) have registered on Alibaba. Cai predicts that, in ten years, "the story of China's Internet will be about how it drives economic growth."

★ ★ ★

The Internet is also a change-maker in promoting citizen participation and social justice. When prison officials claimed that a prisoner's death was accidental, bloggers revealed that he had been beaten to death and exposed the cover-up. When after three deaths from rabies in Yunnan Province, local officials slaughtered 50,000 dogs—most bludgeoned to death, including pets in front of their owners—animal rights activists went into online outrage and demanded change.

And when a local Party official in rural Hubei Province tried to rape a 21-year-old karaoke-bar waitress after she had refused sex, and she defended herself with a pocket knife, accidentally killing the official, she was arrested and seemed surely headed for prison. But an online furor erupted, with over four million hits, suddenly making her a national folk hero—lauded for representing exploited women resisting above-the-law officials. In a surprisingly rapid verdict, the local court, pressured by public opinion, ruled that she had acted in self-defense and freed her.[7] Two other officials present at the attempted rape and fatal stabbing were fired.

★ ★ ★

Regarding the government's role in administering the Internet, Minister Cai says, "We've tried hard to find the right approach."[8] The Internet is new for all countries, he notes, "everyone's trying to figure it out. In recent years we visited over 20 countries, including the U.S., U.K., Germany, France, Italy, Japan, Russia, South Korea, India, Singapore, Australia, Mexico, and Brazil. We genuinely want to learn from them. In a way, China's current mode is a fusion of experience from various countries integrated with China's basic national conditions." China's approach, he says, is the Three Accords: "in accord with the natural law of Internet development; in accord with China's basic national conditions; and in accord with international common practice."

Cai states that "when the Internet came into China, China wasn't ready for large-scale information for the masses. The Internet pushed China into an information society while it was still undergoing industrialization," he adds. "Therefore we encountered some problems that Western countries had not encountered. There is simply no one-model-fits-all."

For example, he says, China's unique period of social transition from a planned to a market economy occasionally makes some forms of censorship necessary. This transition can bring tensions, he says, and "the Internet's power can magnify these tensions." Cai gives examples of payoff discrepancies for laid-off workers in different enterprises and different geographies, and of different levels of compensation for people relocated for the construction of various dams at various times. If these differences are highlighted online, he says, it "could upset people and cause instability—and even turn regional issues into national problems. So we are cautious," he says.

Cai also suggests that because China's market economy is still in its preliminary phase, self-regulatory mechanisms are lacking. Some enterprises, he says, deliberately create pornographic content on their websites to attract more traffic. This should be a self-discipline issue, he notes, "but since the websites themselves aren't yet doing it, the government has to step in. I often joke with websites, 'When you can behave yourself and self-administrate, the government will be happy to step back and rest.'"

Cai stresses that regulatory measures and actions are specific for "certain periods of time and target specific issues. They're for the transition," he says. "If China is to effect a smooth transition to its new system, we must ensure that conflicts'—'legacies' of the old system—are not amplified by the Internet."

He appreciates, he says, that "my American counterparts hold that the government should not be much involved in Internet administration. An important reason, they say, is that the Internet is a virtual environment." Yet nowadays, Cai states, "the Internet has become such an indispensible element of society—of politics, economics, and culture—that the government must shoulder administrative responsibility."

Cai highlights "a worldwide consensus" that the Internet has problems. In China, he says, these "range from pornography, gambling, and fraud to personal attacks, libel, fabricated news, rumors, vilification, and the like." But he stresses that 99% of the websites which China blocks are pornographic. "We act mainly on pornographic websites, as well as on gambling, fraud, and cult websites such as Falun Gong," he says. "All are done in a legal framework. There are hundreds of thousands of pornographic websites in the world; we can only block those that target Chinese."

However, Cai insists, "We're not blocking websites that criticize the Chinese government." Indeed, he says, "sometimes Chinese netizens are more outrageous in criticizing our government than foreigners!" And he stresses that China's regulation of the Internet "is not about controlling how people think or curtailing their freedom of speech." Anyway, he adds, "there simply is no effective mechanism to control how people think. We're just trying to mitigate social conflicts, trying to prevent their exacerbation on the net."

According to Cai, the State Council Information Office (SCIO) does not itself do any actual blocking: "We provide guidelines," he says, "and then each ISP [Internet Service Provider] makes judgments. When many people report on the same website, say providing Chinese-language pornographic content, ISPs may block it." Given more than 4,000 ISPs in China, he says, "it's hard to estimate how many websites are blocked. And the number changes all the time. But definitely we're not blocking *tens* of thousands of websites, as foreign media has charged. It's simple logic," he argues. "If we really were blocking that many websites, China's Internet would be extremely slow. We've probably blocked several thousand websites, 99% of them being pornographic."

Overall, Cai says, the government's position has three main planks: "First, legislate laws and regulations; second, establish guild self-discipline mechanisms (try to solve problems through self-regulation); and third, rely on netizens to monitor websites themselves. The Internet Society of China has founded a Report Center for Illegal and Unhealthy Information, which reviews netizens' reports and, when necessary, asks relevant websites to take action." (The Report Center, opened in 2004, averages about 200,000 reports a year—most were about pornography, though gambling and fraud were increasing.)

Cai says he welcomes constructive criticism of China's Internet policy from experts. "Even if their criticism might be harsh," he says, "we would still take it seriously and try to improve." Other critics, he says, "don't know the Chinese language and never surf the Chinese Internet," and base their criticisms "on sheer hearsay." Such people, he says, "I invite to China to speak with us; they are surely welcome." Of those who "criticize out of a political agenda," however, Cai is rather dismissive. "I met an American congressman who accused China of being unwilling to allow its citizens to criticize it on the Internet," he says. "I asked him, 'Have you ever been to China? 'No, I haven't, he said.' 'Do you understand Chinese? 'No, I don't.' In the end, I said, 'If you take your own words so lightly, then I will take them lightly as well.'" And he added, "Those ignorant American congressmen just have no clue. I once joked that if the U.S. government could find an official who has been in charge of the Internet for 14 years, I'd love to debate him."

In late 2008, China began blocking some Chinese-language news websites operated by foreign media, including Voice of America and the BBC, and, apparently, *The New York Times* website. A Foreign Ministry spokesman defended this action, saying that some websites had gone afoul of the law by (somehow) "recognizing" Taiwan's independence. A few days later, China unblocked *The New York Times*. Government officials did not offer explanations—but China watchers saw the tightening as a prophylactic to contain social instability during the economic downturn.

There was less ambiguity about a crackdown on major Chinese websites soon thereafter. The sites, including search engines Baidu (with two thirds of China's search traffic) and Google (about one fifth) and major portals like Sina.com, were accused of "violating public morality and harming the physical and mental health of youth and young people" by spreading pornography and encouraging vulgarity.[9] The very public campaign was announced by the Ministry of Public Security and six other government agencies, and police officers were shown on national television confiscating electronic equipment. According to official sources, the 19 websites and Internet operators named had not properly responded to warnings from censors.

SCIO Vice Minister Cai Mingzhao was widely quoted as saying "Some websites have exploited loopholes in laws and regulations. They have used all kinds of ways to distribute content that is low-class, crude and even vulgar, gravely damaging mores on the Internet." He instructed officials to "fully grasp the gravity and threat of the vulgar current infesting the internet" and warned lawbreakers of "stern punishment."

Reading these quotes, I felt a certain sadness for Cai, whom I count as a friend. Anyone who would read his words in isolation would be likely to form adverse opinions of the man and his motives—if I didn't know him, I would too. I recalled Cai's personal comments: "Chinese regulators are people who love the Internet," he said. "I established two websites, China.com and Xinhuanet.com. We're professionals. We're not haters of the Internet.

We're lovers. But," he added, "China is in transition and we must protect our people."

I also recalled Cai's comments at a U.S. Internet Forum in 2007, when he told the audience how, when his older brother was at Stanford 20 years before, he would be happy to receive one letter from him every month. "Now my son is studying at NYU," Cai said, "and we can chat on MSN every day. It's like we're in the same room!" Spontaneously, he added, "I thank America for having invented this great thing called the Internet, and I thank Microsoft for inventing this great thing called MSN." When Cai finished, the MSN president ran up to him and said, "I didn't expect that you, a Chinese government minister, would use MSN!"

Weighing up the evidence, I believe that China's leaders appreciate the Internet, especially for accelerating China's development. They hope only to restrict its destabilizing influences long enough for China to emerge as a civil society with sufficiently high standards of living that all citizens will have a stake in maintaining stability.

Endnotes

1 Author's meeting with Wu Jichuan, Beijing, February 2009.
2 The first loan, with a 30-year term (with a 10-year grace period), came from a Japanese fund (Xieli) in the mid-1980s.
3 S. L. Shen, "Chinese leaders embrace the Internet," UPI, June 23, 2008
4 Author's meeting with Liu Yunshan, Beijing, June 2008.
5 Author's meeting with Cai Mingzhao, Beijing, June 2008.
6 A joint venture with Peter Yip, a Hong Kong investor, was established to run the website. Xinhua and Yip jointly invested HK$1 million, and owned 60% and 40% of the JV's shares respectively.
7 Michael Wines, "Civic-Minded Chinese Find a Voice Online," The New York Times, June 16, 2009.
8 According to Cai Mingzhao, there are five governmental bodies regulating the Internet in China: State Council Information Office (SCIO); Ministry of Information Industry; Ministry of Public Security; State Administration of Radio, Film and Television; and Ministry of Culture. "Our major responsibility at SCIO is to review websites' qualifications for carrying news and then issue permits so that we can protect Intellectual Property Rights," Cai says.
9 Chris Buckley, "China targets big websites in Internet crackdown," Reuters, January 5, 2009.

29

Diversity of Culture; Question of Censorship

In the U.S. president's State of the Union address, it's rare that culture is mentioned at all, much less given prominence. In his report to the 17th Party Congress, President Hu Jintao highlighted culture: "The great rejuvenation of the Chinese nation will definitely be accompanied by the thriving of Chinese culture," he proclaimed.

Hu stressed that Chinese culture has been an "unfailing driving force," enabling China to safeguard its unity and progress from generation to generation. And he pledged to vigorously develop the "cultural industry"—a broad term covering all media and entertainment sectors.

Li Changchun, China's senior leader responsible for culture and ideology, calls for Chinese artists to "innovate and create more outstanding works to meet the people's demand" (said while visiting distinguished old artists during the Spring Festival, a grand Chinese tradition).[1] He also encourages China's artists and writers to create more works for children, and to "bring Chinese culture to the world," making it "a positive factor in deepening understanding, friendship and cooperation."[2]

But how? A planned economy and a controlled media does not creativity inspire.

China's Minister of Culture, Cai Wu, stresses that the nation now has what he calls "a unified, open, competitive, and orderly socialist cultural market," covering "performing arts, entertainment, audio and video products, internet, and animation products."[3] According to Cai, China is now developing its cultural industry through market mechanisms—encouraging innovation, performance targets, enterprise evaluation, competition and incentive systems; promoting diversification of ownership; rationalizing state-supported culture schools and troupes (some forced to become self-supporting); encouraging strategic investors to boost competitiveness, promoting economies of scale and specialized industrial clusters; developing emerging sectors such

Cai Wu, minister of Culture (center), and Theodore Forstmann, Chairman and CEO of IMG (left) (May 2009).

as internet, gaming and animation; promoting cultural interaction with other countries; and magnifying the influence of Chinese culture.

For example, many arts organizations have been revitalized through changing ownership and introducing corporate structure: After the Beijing Children's Art Theater was transformed from a state agency into a for-profit company, the number of annual performances rose from 100 to over 400 (within four years), and performance-generated annual revenue soared from under $150,000 to over $7 million.

In 2007, China produced almost 1,000 movies and TV dramas; its cinemas attracted 200 million people; and 460 million people watched half a million performances by professional cultural troupes. A priority is bringing quality cultural offerings to rural areas, including more libraries and mobile-stage vehicles to enable live performances.

Sports are an integral and growing part of China's "cultural industry." The Chinese people are enthusiastic sports fans, but the business of sports has remained behind the curve of reform. Change is coming, however: the international success of Yao Ming at the Houston Rockets has been a catalyst, and the NBA is now developing commercial opportunities in China. China Central Television formed a joint venture with IMG Worldwide, Inc., the global sports and entertainment company, to create, develop and promote world—class sporting events and TV/multimedia sports programming in China; it will bring the best of world sports to China and take the best of China's sports to the world—and serve as a platform for corporate sponsors. (Theodore Forstmann, the private equity pioneer, is chairman/CEO of IMG.)[4]

Jiang Heping (third from left), managing director of CCTV Sports and chairman of CCTV-IMG Sports Management; Ted Forstmann, chairman and CEO of IMG (third from right); Adam Zhu (far right); Yang Bin (second from left) and Ruan Wei (far left) (Beijing, May 2009).

Jiang Heping, president of CCTV Sports, and chairman of the CCTV-IMG joint venture, stated, "China's abundant sports resources and huge market give us an enormous opportunity for growth, and makes sports one of China's key competitive industries worldwide." A *Hollywood Reporter* story exemplified worldwide interest in China's sports industry—and they quoted me accurately when I said, "This deal is in keeping with Hu Jintao's political philosophy to create a Harmonious Society. If you are a rich person in Shanghai or a poor person in Lanzhou, everybody in China can enjoy sports on the same level."[5]

★ ★ ★

As recently as the 1970s, "there was no such profession as 'writer'" in China, notes Tie Ning, a novelist and president of the Chinese Writers' Association. "Works of prose were assigned by the Party or government for political purposes," she says, "and groups of writers were organized so that such works were written collectively under an alias."[6]

Change began in 1978, when 35 popular Chinese and foreign books were reprinted and hit bookstores nationwide. They included *The Arabian Nights, David Copperfield, Anna Karenina, Les Miserables,* and *The Divine Comedy.*[7] For a decade or more, such masterpieces, along with classic Chinese literature, were castigated as capitalist or feudal and banned. When they finally re-emerged there was a veritable stampede to purchase them.

But political zealotry would not die quietly: in 1979, Zhejiang People's Publishing House republished *Gone with the Wind*, the great American novel of the Civil War, and demand was so great that the print run was increased from 100,000 to 600,000. China's political policemen were less enthusiastic. In caustic critiques they warned that "Socialism, too, would be 'gone with the wind'." Deng Xiaoping had to intervene, telling visitors from Temple University (Philadelphia) that the novel was "well written."

That same year, Deng addressed the 4th National Conference of the Representatives of Literary and Art Workers in which he confirmed the change of atmosphere, emphasizing that "The Party's leadership over literature and the arts is not expressed by giving orders, or demanding that literature and the arts succumb to temporary, specific, or direct political tasks—but rather by helping writers and artists to use their talents to enable literature and the arts to prosper, to elevate quality, and to create new works that match the great works of Chinese history based on the law and characteristics of literature and the arts."

Deng displayed striking sympathy for artists and appreciation of the creative process: "Literature and arts are complicated spiritual work and therefore call for individual creativity from writers and artists," he said. "The questions of what to write and how to write should be explored and gradually solved by writers and artists themselves in their artistic practice. We shouldn't intervene in this respect." Political leaders and writers and artists should exchange views "in an equal manner," he added, stressing that the Party "will guarantee support from every aspect, including material support, to ensure that writers and artists can give full play to their wisdom and talent."

Deng noted that China was a vast nation with different ethnic groups, and that its people had "different occupations, experiences, education, customs, cultural traditions, and artistic tastes." As long as people were "inspired or entertained" by a piece of writing, or could enjoy it or learn from it, Deng said, then such writing was acceptable—no matter whether it was "grand or delicate, serious or humorous, lyrical or philosophical." The era of art as a pure political tool was over.

At the time, 1979, Tie Ning was 22 years old, and had just returned from "reeducation" in the countryside during the Cultural Revolution. An amateur writer and magazine editor, she recalls Deng's speech as "very inspiring." It "affected the entire artistic and literature community," she says, "and motivated me and writers of my age."

Tie Ning had begun writing diaries in the early 1970s—though, in the frigid climate of the Cultural Revolution, when "libraries and bookstores were forced to destroy the classics," these were "more like self-critical confessions," she says. "My parents were intellectuals, so I felt inferior to others and very depressed, and constantly confessed my 'faults' in my diaries. Even

Tie Ning (left), president of the Chinese Writers Association, in a yurt at the Xilin Gol Grassland of Inner Mongolia.

if I hadn't done anything wrong, I would make things up so I could criticize myself."

Prior to reform, life was harsh: Tie Ning's mother, having been sent down to work on a farm, got in trouble for visiting her family in Beijing without first obtaining permission. Even hairstyles were regulated. "During the Cultural Revolution, girls could only have straight hair that did not exceed shoulder length," she says. "As soon as reform started, I went straight to the beauty salon to have my hair permed. The curls looked hideous, but I was just happy to have the option of being able to perm my hair."

What impressed her most when reform began, she says, was "the upsurge in the thirst for knowledge. Humanitarianism and respect for human beings were reinstated. Thousands of people were reading the same novel," she recalls. "People were queuing up in front of book stores. Every new arrival, whether it was philosophy, science, literature, or even a textbook, would sell out immediately. Libraries were running out of books!"

Literature, Tie says, was "in the right place at the right time to soothe and heal the wounds: it reflected on the past, and pushed reform forward. It spoke for individuals and as a result writers were respected." And, she adds, "When China began to open its door, literature was there to introduce China to the outside world and rebuild China's image."

A wave of new writing emerged. Public enthusiasm was such that, as she puts it, "some of our novels were able to change people's destinies." Tie Ning herself won national acclaim in 1982 for her prize-winning short story "Ah, Xiangxue," which relates the adventures of a country girl, living in the mountains of North China, who dreams about the outside world and waits every night for a train which stops at her village for one minute, like waiting for a lover—one day she gets on the train by mistake. Tie says she later met a poet who chose to work for the railways after reading the story—and a senior executive at the Shanghai Futures Exchange told her that "Ah, Xiangxue" had inspired him to work his way out of his poor mountain village.

Tie Ning continued writing stories and novels, winning awards and becoming one of China's best-known writers.

★ ★ ★

But China's cultural renaissance has not been without limits. In 1996, President Jiang Zemin addressed 3,000 of the country's leading writers and artists, a group inherently wary of government influence. Rather than simply offering bland words of welcome, he chose to give a speech that revealed his own inner conflict. Jiang loved poetry and music all his life, calling literature and the arts "the torches that guide the national spirit." One of his old friends was Ba Jin, the great novelist, whom he knew from Shanghai; Jiang also liked performing with artists: at the convention he stepped up on stage and sang along with famous singers. Yet in his talk, Jiang struggled to balance the desire for intellectual freedom with the need for social stability: as a state leader, he feared the chaos that dissenting views could cause.

"On the one hand, we should point out that literary creation greatly requires writers and artists to give play to their personal creativity," he said. And, echoing Deng Xiaoping, "the question of what and how to write can only be probed and gradually resolved by writers and artists themselves in their artistic practice."[8]

But on the other hand, he said, "we should also urge literary workers who hold themselves responsible to the people to unswervingly adapt to the needs of the vast numbers of the masses,...pay close attention to the social effects of their own works in a serious and responsible manner, and provide the people with the best spiritual food."

Jiang stressed that it was "impossible for literature and the arts to be separated from politics, especially when facing the pressure of the dominant position of Western countries, and when dealing with the infiltration of Western ideology." Indeed he seemed to fear that Chinese culture—and the Communist Party's values—might be swamped by western influences: He warned against "all kinds of decadent cultural influences of capitalism and the exploiting classes," and urged Party branches to "improve" their supervision of literature and the arts. "If we lose the ability to create our own things, blindly worship things foreign, and copy indiscriminately the capitalist value outlook of the West," he said, "we will end up imitating every move of others and eventually turning into a dependency of others." China's literature, he said, needed "ideological and cultural independence."

It was part of Jiang's campaign to instill "spiritual civilization" in China, and counteract Western influence. That same year, the government banned 4,000 product and company names which "sounded Western." Jiang also authorized the construction of a library of modern Chinese literature.

In subsequent years such xenophobic campaigns diminished, perhaps as China's leaders grew more confident in their country's resurgence. Indeed, Yu Long, the conductor of the China Philharmonic Orchestra and artistic director of the Beijing Music Festival, argues that "the decade between 1992 and 2002 was one of the great revivals in Chinese cultural history. People talk about China's economic resurgence; I believe our cultural resurgence is equally important." Since the 1990s, Yu notes, classical music has flourished in China, growing faster than anywhere else in the world, and producing famous performers like Lang Lang and Yundi Li. For this, Yu credits Jiang Zemin, "whose passion for the arts, especially classical music, had national impact."

And these days, Zhao Qizheng, who was spokesman for the 2009 session of the 11th CPPCC, sounds relatively relaxed about foreign influence. He says that "the essence of Chinese culture is in no danger because of market reform—it's strong enough to absorb the great traditions of Western culture—science, skyscrapers, dance, music, clothes, and so on." All such things, he says, "invigorate us."

★ ★ ★

As if to confirm the elevated status of writers, the novelist Tie Ning became an alternate member of the powerful CPC Central Committee (2002). The following year she spoke during a group discussion that included several leaders, stressing that China should not develop the economy at the expense of the environment and making her point in an unusual manner. According to analysis, she said, "the Renminbi [Chinese money] has more bacteria than any other currency in the world." She said this showed that "while the Chinese economy is buoyant, we should be concerned about our hygiene."

"The difference between politicians and statesmen," Tie told the group "is that politicians only think about next elections while statesmen think about next generations." Tie says she had expected to be rebuked for her words—but in fact she was praised for them.

She also observes that speeches by senior officials have become "shorter and more substantive than before. They surface real problems and we voice real opinion—we say whatever we want to say." Another difference that the ever-observant Tie Ning noticed on the Central Committee related to music. "In the past, the background music played during voting periods were songs with strong tempos, which stirred excitement and jangled some nerves," she said. "But recently, the music was changed to 'Jasmine Flower', a Chinese folk song which is lyrical, mellow and easy-rhythmed. It's a detail few caught but I think reflects some sort of change in the Party's mentality."

In 2006, Tie Ning was elected the minister-ranked president of the Chinese Writers Association, the first female (and the youngest person) to hold the post. The Association groups 8,000 of China's leading writers, who must qualify through their work. Tie insists, however, that her official status has not limited her freedom to write. "As a writer, my soul is free. My writing is independent. Nobody forces me to write, neither am I restricted by anyone," she says.

China's literary world has become increasingly variegated since the 1980s, no longer dominated by a few veteran masters. Tie Ning notes the rise of new generations of writers, whose interests are often far removed from those of their elders.

"Young writers born in the 1980s are thriving," she says. "They're free to choose their subjects, genres, and stories, and ways to present them; they promote their works in a market-driven manner. It reflects the freedom Chinese writers enjoy."

Money now matters. Before reform, according to Tie Ning, "authors were ashamed of talking money. Only 'merchants' talked money, they believed. With the market economy writers came to understand that money wasn't shameful. Poverty wasn't glorious, wealth no sin." Nowadays, Tie says, "writers recognize their rights, especially after China's entry into WTO."

These changes have gone hand-in-hand with the commercialization of China's publishing industry (Chapter 27), and some young writers have become celebrities—and rich—as a result. Others, however, complain that in the process literature has lost its idealism. Indeed, Chinese writers find themselves being chastised by the public for their lack of social responsibility, shallow understanding of social changes, and deliberate avoidance of social conflicts.

Yet behind the euphoric freedoms and heady commercialization lurks the undeniable and perhaps undiminished threat of censorship. How does Tie Ning respond?

"If you want to talk about censorship," Tie Ning said to me pointedly, "you're talking to the wrong person." The Chinese Writers' Association's role, she states, is "to service writers, not to regulate them," and to "help writers develop their creative capabilities and artistic sensitivities"—stressing "We censor no one."

It's obvious, Tie says, that China now has "far more freedom in speech, media, literature, and arts" than 30 years ago. Literature was critical for "healing wounds caused by past political movements," but today, "The ubiquity of the Internet" means that "people have much more freedom…It seems as if all

Chinese are writing something on the web. They write whatever they want to write. The Internet has enabled ordinary people to voice their opinions."

Tie Ning argues that "there is no absolute freedom anywhere in the world. Freedom shouldn't be used in ways that hurt others and harm society. It's true with every country, not only with China." Tie Ning emphasizes that China is a society increasingly based on the rule of law and thus "writings advocating pornography, violence, cults, anti-humanity and anti-science [screeds] are prohibited. Writers should show respect for religious beliefs," she adds, and should avoid "personal attacks against and defamation of real-life figures in books and articles," which these days could—and often do—lead to legal proceedings.

At the same time, Tie says, there is more tolerance. For example, she points out, "We are much more open about sex. Chinese readers have become more sophisticated and mature; they can discern the difference between the artistic expression of sex in literature and the vulgar exploitation of sex in pornography." And in general, she adds, even writers who cause controversy are no longer in danger of being "physically punished" as in the past, and have not been "struggled" or "pressured in their writing."

Tie Ning says that Chinese writers today actually face "much bigger challenges" than censorship. She recalls a visit to China by Kenzaburo Oe, the Japanese Nobel Laureate in Literature. "He admonished our writers to write more, and not to be distracted by all the features and facets of contemporary life," Tie says. "I was shocked and awakened by what Oe said, and I rededicated myself to helping writers write. Frankly, in today's China, censorship is not writers' primary problem. Commercialism and distractions are far more insidious."

In an article in *The American Scholar*, titled "Censor in the Mirror," Ha Jin, professor at Boston University (originally from Harbin in northeast China), describes censorship in China as "a powerful field of force" which "affects anyone who gets close to it."[9] Above all, he highlights the insidious impact of "self-censorship": "It's not only what the Chinese Propaganda Department does to artists," he notes, "but what it makes artists do to their own work."

Ha Jin, who won the prestigious National Book Award in 1999 for his novel *Waiting* (which he wrote in English), cites his own experience. In 2004, he signed a contract with a Shanghai publisher which planned to bring out four volumes of his fiction and a collection of his poems. However, he says, "the editor in charge of the project told me that he couldn't possibly consider publishing two of my novels, *The Crazed* and *War Trash*, owing to the sensitive subject matter. The former touches on the Tiananmen tragedy, and the latter deals with the Korean War." As a result, when Ha Jin came to select and translate his own English poems into Chinese for the poetry volume, he says "I couldn't help but censor myself, knowing intuitively which ones might not get through the censorship." Disheartened by the realization, he found himself unable to go ahead with the project: "To date, I haven't translated a single poem, though the deadline was May 2005," he notes.

Ha Jin asserts that "self-censorship is a necessity for most Chinese writers"—not least for those who receive salaries or benefits from the Writers' Association. He quotes the Chinese saying, "If you eat others' food, you cannot talk back to them." Ha Jin stresses that China needs its "own original cultural and material products," without which, he argues, "a country can never stay rich and strong." A nation's real wealth, he stresses, "is the talent of its people. In the case of China, the way to nurture that talent is to lift the yoke of censorship."

Tie Ning's husband, Hua Sheng, a liberal economist and entrepreneur (Chapter 12), told me he wanted to answer Ha Jin. "Frankly, we can't be sure whether the sudden and complete 'big bang' elimination of censorship would be good or bad for China," Hua says. "And *because* we can't be sure, that's why it should be done step-by-step. Censorship has always been part of Chinese civilization," he adds. "And just as President Obama invoked the founding fathers in his inaugural address, we Chinese may not be able to hold together and advance by cutting off our traditions overnight. In Chinese history, too much radical change has taken us backwards; the past 60 years have taught us that, for China, gradual change is the best change. If I had to list Chinese writers' problems in order, censorship would fall somewhere between second and fifth."

Tie Ning sums up her views on censorship by combining two Chinese sayings: "Bystanders see a more complete picture and can be more objective—but only the foot knows if the shoe really fits."

★ ★ ★

One area of China's culture which has almost totally shed the old system of rigid controls is fine art. Not long ago, China's avant-garde artists were regarded with suspicion; with minimum money and no support, many were living illegally in run-down neighborhoods, seen by their neighbors as "jobless loafers."

Today, some of these same "loafers" are international stars: With little off-limits, contemporary Chinese artists are now producing diverse and often controversial works. The popularity of their art has skyrocketed, attracting interest from western collectors, curators and critics.[10] Works by artists like Zhang Xiaogang, Fang Lijun, Liu Xiaodong and Yang Shaobin sell for big sums at international auctions.[11]

Indeed few aspects of Chinese life better characterize the nation's tectonic shift away from its collectivist past to a more individualistic future than contemporary art. Artists have their own signature theme or style, such as old photos on canvas by Zhang Xiaogang; harmless hooligan-like men with shaved heads by Fang Lijun; and red-hued violence depicted by Yang Shaobin. "Every artist has in his mind an individual style. It's the key of contemporary art," says Yang Shaobin.[12]

One of the biggest stars is Yue Minjun, who paints himself laughing at the world—and gets paid very well for it. Yue's paintings often consist of groups of figures with his own laughing face—during military exercises, flying on backs of geese, and laughing at historic world events. His painting, "The Pope," a giggling Yue dressed as the Pope, sold for over $4 million at Sotheby's London auction (2007), setting a new record for Chinese contemporary art.

Yue Minjun sums up the changes in China's art world: In the days of the planned economy, he recalls, "the elite powers decided what the people should do and say: the people should all make steel because the country needed steel, or should weave cloth because of a shortage of cloth. Society was run from top to bottom." Now, he says, artistic creation "starts from a single individual. Every artist tries to express his individual experience and thought."

Highly trained artists have been the norm in China for centuries. Experts believe that the Chinese system, with ancient roots and contemporary vision, will continue to engender young artists taking their works in new directions.

★ ★ ★

Internationally, cultural communication has become an important part of China's overall foreign policy. As of 2008, the country had established 89 cultural departments in embassies and consulates in 78 countries worldwide, signed intergovernmental cultural cooperation agreements with 145 countries, and held almost 800 annual cultural exchange programs, including cultural tours (e.g., Chinese Culture's Tour of Africa) and cultural years (e.g., Sino-French Culture Year). If culture was becoming the new battlefield among nations, from this "war" all the world benefits.

Endnotes

1 "Senior official Li Changchun visits old artists," *People's Daily*, January 23, 2006.
2 *People's Daily*, March 25, 2008.
3 *Qiushi* (Seeking Truth) magazine, July 17, 2008.
4 Full disclosure: I structured the CCTV-IMG deal (2008) and am a partner in the joint venture.
5 Jonathan Landreth, "CCTV forms venture with IMG, *The Hollywood Reporter*, July 31, 2008.
6 Private communication with Tie Ning, Beijing, September 2008; entire section.
7 Qin Xiaoying, "When books indicated the dawn of a new era," *China Daily*, January 17, 2009.
8 *People's Daily*, May 21, 1997.
9 Ha Jin, "The Censor in the Mirror," *The American Scholar*, Autumn 2008.
10 Chelsea Mason, "Contemporary Chinese Art: Generating Debate and Sometimes, Staggering Prices," US-China Today (University of Southern California), August 11, 2008.
11 David Ebody, "Chinese contemporary art prices skyrocket," *Art in America*, May 2006.
12 "Chinese Contemporary Art Comes out of the Shadow," Xinhua, September 25, 2007; entire section.

30

How China's Leaders Love Film

In 2010, China produced about 500 films, putting it number three in the world in movie output (behind India and America). In terms of total audience, China was number one. China's box office reached almost $1.5 billion, a jump of 61 percent over 2009.

"These are good times for China's film industry," says Liu Yunshan, head of the Party Publicity (Propaganda) Department, which has ultimate responsibility for culture and film. "The industry is expanding: our technology and our quality are both improving." Even the worldwide slump doesn't diminish his enthusiasm: "During economic downturns films are relaxing and relatively inexpensive," he says.

China's film industry has a long tradition. The country's first movie was made in 1905. By the 1930s Shanghai was a vibrant film production center, with dozens of studios. Later, after the 1949 revolution, the industry split: many directors and stars relocated to Hong Kong; those who remained in China found themselves increasingly required to serve political masters. Nonetheless, film has remained a central part of China's culture No national leaders anywhere in the world have attached as much importance to motion pictures as have China's leaders.

"The Chinese always say that they grew up watching movies and learned so much from them," says Zhao Shi, vice minister in the State Administration of Radio, Film and Television (SARFT) responsible for the film industry (2008).[1] That the nation's senior leaders take the industry seriously was highlighted in 2007, when Sun Daolin, a famous veteran actor, passed away in Shanghai. President Hu Jintao and former President Jiang Zemin both sent their condolences. Yu Zhengsheng, Shanghai's Party secretary, attended his memorial service. "Some people were surprised to see China's senior leaders pay high respect to an actor, but all Chinese people love our motion picture artists," explains Zhao, who is herself a former film director and later deputy head of the influential Changchun Film Studio. (Such adoration can be excessive. One insider noted that "star-struck officials find it hard to distinguish the human actors from the characters they portray." Thus, some "greedy actors" have become "lobby-ists for costly projects or personal promotions!")

Yet only a few decades ago, China's movie industry had been decimated. "In Mao's era, movies [supposedly] served farmers, workers, soldiers, and most important, leftist politics," says Zhao Shi. While some creative, though "politically correct" films were made during the 1950s and early 60s, by the Cultural Revolution years, the industry was, in Zhao's words, "constricted with ideological rigidity."

Ironically it was a former Shanghai movie actress, Mao's villainous wife, Jiang Qing, who, along with her leftist allies in the Gang of Four, who did the decimation. A self-styled Great Flag-bearer of Proletarian Culture, Jiang Qing ordered the detention and punishment of many of her old colleagues. For seven of the Cultural Revolution's ten traumatic years, not a single motion picture was made in China. The only approved entertainment was the eight "model operas," personally selected by Jiang Qing (later made into movies).

As in so many areas, Zhao Shi cites Deng Xiaoping's 1978 speech on "emancipating the mind" as a turning point. Previously, she says, arts and literature had been seen as "weapons to fight the enemy." After China abandoned class struggle, however, arts and literature were to serve the people. "Get rid of the fakeness, exaggeration, and meaninglessness that had characterized movies during the Cultural Revolution," Deng said. "Make movies that reflect reality."

The years that followed, from 1979 to early 1990s, were the film industry's first phase of reform. It was, Zhao says, a period of "freeing the imagination"—in some cases literally: "A host of renowned movie artists were liberated from labor camps," she notes. Once they returned to work, the industry resurged. The creative energy was palpable."

Veteran directors were revitalized. Xie Jin, head of Xi'an Film Studio, made movies such as *Hibiscus Town* and *The Wrangler*. Middle-aged directors such as Li Qiankuan (*The Birth of New China*) became the backbone of the industry. And the so-called "fifth generation" began their rise to prominence, with Chen Kaige's *Yellow Earth* and Zhang Yimou's *Red Sorghum* winning international awards.

Movies now reflected the lives of ordinary people, showing respect for their values and dignity. And the response was spectacular: television had not yet occupied China and watching movies was, for many, the main form of entertainment. Cinema audiences peaked at 29.3 billion in one year—a world record of more than 30 films per person.

The second phase of film-industry reform, Zhao Shi says, was from early 1990s to early 21st century. Later than other sectors, the movie industry began transitioning from a planned system to a market system in 1993 with the distribution sector: the China Film Corp.'s monopoly was eliminated, as were quotas, which had assigned every studio a fixed number of films to produce.

Zhao Shi (left), deputy Party secretary and vice minister of State Administration of Radio, Film and Television (SARFT); and Zhang Pimin (right) SARFT vice minister responsible for the film industry (appointed in 2009) (Beijing, June 2008).

In 1995, China's movie market was opened and ten Hollywood films were imported. China could only afford old films, not new releases, but the impact was huge. The imported movies attracted large audiences and thus put severe pressure on China's state-owned film studios, which were plagued by inefficient systems, insufficient investment, backward technologies, over-staffing, and low production quality. Suddenly, China's combined annual output of about 100 movies only accounted for less than 20% of the nation's total box office revenues, with the ten Hollywood films taking 80-90%!

The survival of China's film studios was at stake. But Zhao Shi stresses that leaders believed "only through opening-up, competition, and coopera-tion would China's film industry develop. To meet competition from abroad, we would have to develop ourselves," she adds. "Some called the Hollywood imports 'wolves'—but I proposed that we must 'dance with the wolves!'"

Steps were taken to boost the domestic industry: in 1996, regulations stipulated that Chinese movies must account for two-thirds of total screen-ing time, says Zhao. "We also instituted favorable financial and tax policies to support domestic films, and initiated the convergence of television and film." Notably, SARFT launched CCTV-6, a dedicated movie channel, which catapulted TV movies in China. "Today China produces over 1,000 TV movies annually," she notes, "and CCTV-6's audience is 800 million."

Significantly, ownership was reformed, with film studios allowed to bring in outside capital to help fund productions. Initially, this capital came from other state-owned units; private capital would come later. The first state-owned joint-stock film company, Beijing Forbidden City Film Co., was formed by departments under SARFT in 1997. But in 2000, Xi'an Film Studio formed a company with 30% private capital (from several private companies in Shenzhen). It was controversial—so much so that Zhao Shi says friends warned her it would be politically risky to attend the opening ceremony. Nevertheless, Zhao, who had studied how the shareholding system could work in the film industry, says "We supported it as a pilot."

Indeed, at a Party meeting in 1999, Zhao Shi became the first Chinese official to describe motion pictures as an "industry," something which had previously been considered sensitive. By 2002, China's leaders affirmed publicly that the nation should strengthen its "culture industry."

And from 1998 onwards, SARFT began to form large film groups, such as China Film Group and Shanghai Film Group, creating market entities to produce, distribute and screen movies. These new companies established modern corporate structures and conducted ownership reform.

China also allowed foreign companies to form joint ventures in technology segments of the film industry, though not in production. Zhao stresses, however, that "We do permit foreign capital to jointly produce a specific film"—though rules for such co-productions require that the film's content should relate to China; it should suit the tastes of Chinese people; it shouldn't contain anything that would be condemned by a third country; and Chinese actors should account for at least half the cast (except in the case of co-productions with Hong Kong). And like all films in China, co-productions need to be reviewed by the censorship committee.

As Zhao Shi puts it, "We are opening the Chinese film industry in a gradual, orderly manner."

In terms of content, the government offers "guidance" to the industry; for example, with its Fine Works campaign (late 1990s), which encouraged movies with patriotic and politically positive themes. These included the *Big Turning Point* , *The Opium Wars* and *Fatal Decision* with corruption as its theme. (The latter was so admired by President Jiang Zemin that he ordered the whole Politburo watch it.)

On the lighter side, China produced its first New-Year comedy—*Party A, Party B* by Feng Xiaogang—in 1997, and New-Year comedies have now become an annual institution. "We've also presented many diverse, independent movies, not only mainstream films," Zhao says.

China's film industry has now "entered the era of industrialization, digitalization, and modernization"—reform's third phase. The industry, she says, is in "a virtuous circle of healthy, rapid development," with a competitive market and business model which no longer relies solely on box office, but includes revenue from TV, DVD, audio/video products, and online transmission.

To no small degree, China's film industry was transformed by the country's entry into WTO in 2001. To honor its commitment, China must import 20 revenue-sharing movies from other countries each year, instead of 10, with American movies taking the lion's share. In addition, China must import 30 non-revenue-sharing movies every year. The new rules brought more choice for cinema-goers—and forced the domestic film industry to become more modern and competitive.

Zhao Shi recalls how, in past years (when China's film industry was floundering), she would visit the U.S. or Singapore and see people queuing up to buy tickets outside cinemas. "I would be very envious," she says. "I wanted to see such long queues in China. Now," she adds proudly, "I do! Chinese blockbusters are extremely popular: young people regard movie-going as a fashion."

★ ★ ★

One man who has literally lived the triumphs and tragedies of China's film industry is Li Qiankuan, the well-known director and long-time head of the Changchun Film Studio. Li, and his wife and co-director Xiao Guiyun, were, as he puts it, "lucky to help produce the first feature films after the worst of the Cultural Revolution," working as assistant directors on one of the four films made in 1973—after seven years when China produced no movies.[2]

Making movies then meant grappling with ever-present—but ever-shifting—ideology. In the mid 1970s, Jiang Qing, Mao's notorious wife, commissioned a film about the Liaoshen Battle (1948), in which the Communist People's Liberation Army (PLA) surrounded Changchun, forcing the Nationalist Northern China Army, with 100,000 troops, to surrender. During pre-production, in October 1976, however, Jiang Qing was arrested. Li and Director Zhao Xinshui pressed on with the project, but faced a dilemma in how to depict Lin Biao, the PLA commander-in-chief in the Liaoshen Battle, who later died in a plane crash after a failed coup attempt against Mao in 1971. Lin was, as Li puts it, "much reviled at the time."

Li and Zhao won backing from the then commander-in-chief of the Shenyang Military Region, General Li Desheng, to portray Lin's handling of the battle in an accurate light. "History is history," General Li told them. "We shouldn't use what happens today to twist what happened yesterday. We shouldn't be afraid of anything." But when they submitted their proposal in 1977, censors turned it down.

Li's attempts to produce another film about Lin Biao's later plotting, did initially receive approval—from Hu Yaobang, who would later become CPC general secretary. Li visited Hu in October 1976, mentioning that though the Gang of Four had just been arrested (October 6), the Ministry of Culture held a conference to honor Jiang Qing three days later. When Hu Yaobang heard this, Li recalls, "he laughed so hard that he had to lie on the sofa." Hu pledged to support the film—and Li even attended the Gang of Four's trial as part of his research. But the Film Bureau under the Ministry of Culture did not give approval. It didn't express disapproval either—but Li says "the ambiguity was too risky and I had to give up."

According to Li Qiankuan, it took until 1980 before the "spirit of reform and opening-up reached actual film productions." But when the opportunity came, China's film studios were quick to seize it: "Although materially we were poor—my monthly salary was only RMB 62—we were very enthusiastic," Li recalls. "We worked very hard. All we wanted was to make good films. We didn't care about money. *The General with a Sword*—Li's first collaboration with his wife, Xiao Guiyun, released in 1981—set a box office record."

Film reform was a gradual process, says Li, and old ways did not disappear quickly. In 1983 Li directed *On the Bank of Yellow River*, a film about the lives of farmers in Shandong over previous decades—and the changes brought by reform. The film touched on the catastrophic Great Leap Forward and the Cultural Revolution. Li's aim, he says, was to show how these political campaigns "had affected the countryside," and "make people appreciate Deng's reforms."

Li's film depicted a district Party chief, who, during every political movement, "would speak the truth and was therefore constantly demoted," and a more senior county Party chief who "always told lies and was therefore frequently promoted." It also featured a farmer who deprived himself of food in order to save the district Party chief from starvation during the famines.

When Film Bureau screened the film, "the censors were deeply moved and even cried," Li recalls. "They said 'It's a good movie: the direction, script, cast, music, language are all excellent.' But they wouldn't allow it to be released." The problem was that in the film, the character of the farmer eventually starved to death. Li says the Film Bureau told him, "'In China's New Society, no one should starve to death'. Only if I 'revived the farmer' would the movie be approved for release!"

"I said to the censors: '30 million people starved to death in reality, and you won't let just one die in my movie?' They said, 'If he died, then the New Society would be the same as the old society.' I said it was not about 'New Society' or 'old society'. If a human being didn't eat for weeks, he would die—it was a medical matter, not a political one!"

Li refused to compromise—"I wouldn't flout history," he says—and sought help from senior leaders, but Deng Liqun (head of the Propaganda Department) agreed with the censors that "There *should* be a difference between the New Society and the old society," while the vice minister of Culture reflected official fear at the power of cinema: "A director creates images and images can be penetrating and influential," he told Li. "The Party has many scars. But let's leave all these scars in the past. You can't rip off scars and rub salt into the wounds."

But Li refused to quit. After receiving letters from Shandong farmers asking why the film hadn't been shown yet, Li took a risk, bringing the film to Shandong and screening it for farmers: "Thousands came and they cried and cheered. They said the movie helped them understand that we should never make the same mistakes."

Inspired by the farmers' words, Li arranged for retired Party elders to watch the film. After the screening, Li recalls, "all of them cried; then they erupted into applause." Finally, after multiple reviews by senior leaders, the film was released in 1985, accompanied by a front-page story in *People's Daily*, which described it as a "movie that can serve as a textbook for rectifying Party ethics."

Li notes that sensitivity about films reflected the fact that, "in Mao Zedong's era, many political movements began with movies—people with political agendas picked on 'flaws' in these films and turned them into 'class struggles'." Such accusations would "bring catastrophe on the directors, playwrights and actors." After reform, he says, this no longer occurs: "Even for my so-called 'problematic films', though they were not allowed to be released for some time, I wasn't disgraced with a political 'hat' [disparaging label] as would have happened in the past," he notes. "Chinese society was relaxing; the general environment was friendly."

But Li Qiankuan again faced difficulties in trying to combine positive political messages with accurate portrayals of his characters when he made his epic *The Birth of New China* in 1989. The story of the Communist victory over the Nationalists in the Civil War, it included three major battles, and climaxed with Mao's declaration of the People's Republic of China on the Tiananmen Gate. It was a glorious, politically correct film—with just one problem: Li had chosen to portray Chiang Kai-shek, Mao's adversary, as a normal human being, rather than the one-dimensional thug mainland filmmakers had depicted in the past.

Censors said they would not release the film, which was planned as part of the People's Republic's 40th anniversary celebrations on October 1, 1989—unless he "brutalized up" the generalissimo's character. Li refused. "People asked me bluntly if I harbored 'warm feelings' toward Chiang," he recalls. In the aftermath of the Tiananmen crackdown, he says, "it was a dangerous accusation," and the chances of the film being shown seemed slight: "It's always risky for government functionaries to sign off on controversial films," Li says. "The safest and easiest thing for them to do is to kill them."

Li and his wife, who was co-director, spent a depressed summer waiting: "We literally couldn't eat or sleep," he says. "I felt like a parent who was watching his child die and wasn't able to prevent it." Eventually Li Ruihuan, a popular senior leader, intervened. Known among artists and intellectuals for his open views and quick wit, he suggested that Director Li appeal directly to the new CPC general secretary, Jiang Zemin.

In August the movie was screened in Zhongnanhai, attended by Jiang, Li Ruihuan, and others, including five military leaders. Li was asked to give a 15-minute introduction. "My wife was nervous about what I might say," he remembers. "She worried that, as a director, I always spoke with authority and demanded obedience, and that I scowled a lot! She kept warning me to sound humble and smile. 'These people are *really* China's leaders, she said, not a bunch of actors costumed up to look that way!'"

Li explained to the assembled dignitaries that "as an artist I take up the camera with a passion for my craft and a responsibility for my country." The film, he said, reflected his commitment to being "both objective and artistic." His inspiration, he told them, had come from listening to a veteran general explain the terrible hardships suffered by those who had fought to establish the People's Republic. "I told him that I looked forward to the day when I could reenact the historic moments, particularly when the Red five-star flag was raised over the pavilion in Tiananmen Square," said Li.

Jiang Zemin asked Li to sit next to him, questioning him throughout the screening. At the end he patted Li's hand, praised his filmmaking abilities, and explained to the other leaders the innovative techniques that the director had revealed to him about the film—including Li's use of genuine old newsreels intermixed with his own reconstructions of newsreel footage: "I was fooled," said Jiang. "He's obviously a talented director." Jiang then explained that, since he was not a military man, he would like to hear the opinion of the "revered military leaders" in the room.

Various suggestions followed, but none on the character of Chiang Kai-shek as portrayed in the movie. Finally Jiang expressed his own opinions: he noted that "our young generation tends to make horizontal comparisons, across geographies. They see America and Europe as advanced and Hong Kong and Taiwan as prosperous, and they become envious." However, he went on, "Our young people are not good at making vertical comparisons, across time periods. To appreciate how far China has come, one must appreciate how backward we once were and how difficult our road has been. On our Red five-star flag there is blood of millions of martyrs."

It was the green light for Li's film—and a sign that despite the turmoil of preceding months, and the conservative retrenchment, Jiang would not simply adhere to established norms. Indeed, Li Qiankuan describes Jiang's personal intervention, and the fact that he took the time to watch and debate a film in such circumstances, as "unprecedented." (There was one other problem, however: Mao's wife Jiang Qing, featured in two scenes, was so detested that Li Ruihuan advised Li Qiankuan to cut her character out. Li, grudgingly, agreed.)

The film went on to win the Golden Rooster, China's version of the Academy Award, and to be recognized as one of the most important films in the history of Chinese filmmaking.

Such success did not prevent Li Qiankuan from facing further difficulties. From 1992 to 2002, the Politburo member responsible for propaganda and culture was the generally conservative Ding Guangen. After Li directed *The Chongqing Negotiation*, the story of the cease-fire talks between Chiang Kai-shek and Mao Zedong in 1945, Ding voiced several complaints: "First, he asked why, when word came that the Anti-Japanese War had been won, was 'Yan'an [the Communist HQ] at night, while Chongqing [the Nationalist HQ] during the day?'" recalls Li—who says that that's when the news actually arrived in these respective places, and adds wryly: "Apparently, irrespective

Film Director Li Qiankuan (right)), president of the China Film Association, with Sun Feihu (left), who played Chiang Kai-shek in *Chongqing Negotiation*, and Xiao Guiyun, Li's co-director and wife, at Chiang's residence at Deanli, Chongqing (1992).

of history, Ding still stuck to the caricatured "three prominences principle" that the Party should be 'bright, tall, and face upward'; while the enemy should be 'dark, short, and face downward'!"

Ding also complained that the Shaanxi farmers seeing Mao Zedong off at the airport were turbaned with white towels, and that this was undignified. ("A local custom," says Li.) And Ding questioned why the Nationalist officials wore smart uniforms while the PLA soldiers wore old-fashioned, shabby yellowish cotton-padded trousers. ("That's the history," Li smiles.)

Ding's opinions "caused a minor uproar in the film community, including outbreaks of ridicule," Li Qiankuan recalls. Eventually, Li wrote a letter to Jiang Zemin explaining the film and asking him to inscribe the Chinese characters for its title. Jiang agreed, and the film was shown to members of the Politburo, who praised it—a sign, Li says, that it "had passed censorship and was ready for release." (For some reason, Jiang never made the actual inscription, but his affirmation to do so was power sufficient.)

(Li notes that later Ding Guangen told him "I supported *The Chongqing Negotiation*. Of course, I am also a film-goer, so shouldn't I be allowed some personal opinions, director?" Li says, "I laughed with him but didn't respond. To be frank, without reform, those 'personal opinions' could have killed the movie and put me in big trouble.")

Propaganda chief Ding caused another stir in 1993 when he instructed the media to avoid showing the Party in an unflattering light. *Farewell My Concubine*, directed by Chen Kaige and starring Leslie Cheung and Gong Li, and winner of the Palme d'Or at the Cannes Film Festival, was banned in China. Although approved by China's Film Bureau, it was pulled after a private screening for the Politburo, during which some members reportedly walked out. (In addition to the film's sexual content, including homosexuality, its main character is seen to suffer as much persecution under Communist rule—during the Cultural Revolution—as under the Nationalist regime and Japanese occupation.)

And Li Qiankuan faced similar problems in 1994 when his film, *The Victory of the Kunlunguan Battle*, was banned. Again the problem was that it focused on the Nationalists, in particular General Dai Anlan, who led his troops to defeat the Japanese invaders. "The Anti-Japanese War was fought by the whole nation, including the Nationalists," notes Li. "General Dai was a Chinese hero who later died in Burma fighting the Japanese. Mao Zedong and Zhou Enlai sent their condolences. But the movie was banned anyway—the censors said that 'the Nationalists had no right to be featured in a movie'!"

But Li remained undeterred. The first time I met him, in 1997, he explained that it was his dream to produce a television drama series on the Korean War. Li believed that America and China would become partners in peace in the 21st century and thus it would be instructive to reflect back on the one time we were enemies at war. He envisioned an epic work—30 episodes, giving perspectives from all sides: Chinese, American, Russian, North Korean, South Korean. The script, Director Li claimed, would "respect history." The Chinese would reveal their highest-level deliberations; Russian archives had been tapped; scholarly American books were being consulted. CCTV, the producer, said it would offer "full and objective depictions."

The Korean War would have the largest budget in CCTV history, thousands of extras. The Chinese military and Dalian city offered assistance: MacArthur's Inchon landing would be staged when it actually occurred (September 15); battles would be taped in the rugged terrain of Manchuria, just across the border from North Korea, in the frozen snows of dead winter. American actors would be involved, and 25% of the production would be shot in English.

Moved by the spirit of Director Li's vision, my partner Adam Zhu and I decided to assist in the production as advisors. I was concerned about whether CCTV could produce even a modestly accurate or "balanced script" or would give a demonized or cartoonish characterization of America and Americans (which I could not countenance). I liked Li's desire to explore the emotions and tragedies of war, by infusing the series with personal stories of American and Chinese characters. "A soldier in war is a soldier in war," as he put it.

Suddenly, however, without explanation, the production came to a halt—evidently after a directive from on-high. But CCTV kept lobbying for permission—and after about 30 months they were able to proceed: there was no formal decree of permission; it seemed more an easing of a decision to block than an affirmative decision to encourage.

We arranged for Director Li and the CCTV team to work with a Hollywood casting agency; they auditioned over 100 American actors for about 12 major roles.[3] Dozens of scenes were shot in the U.S. scenes set in Korea or Japan were shot in China.

(Director Li was asked, while in Los Angeles, whether *The Korean War* reflected a Chinese bias. "Of course it does," he said with a straight face, then added, with a grin, "I'd be very pleased to make another version reflecting an American bias, if you find me the investors!" Li told me he thought the film would surprise Western critics.)

Information Minister Zhao Qizheng was surprised to learn of this Chinese-American cooperation in producing *The Korean War* and he marveled at its historical irony. How forever impossible this series would have seemed three decade ago, he said, and how symbolic it was of progress in China-U.S. relations and of the power of art. Zhao said he wanted photos of the Chinese crew filming *The Korean War* with American actors on location in Los Angeles. He planned to label these photos, "Who Could Have Thought It?"

This story does not end happily; actually, it doesn't end at all. Li Qiankuan completed *The Korean War* in time for its scheduled release on CCTV in 2001. But it was not shown, then or since—and no one has ever really explained why. Despite its huge budget, all 30 episodes sit in some CCTV vault. Continuing tensions on the Korean peninsula are the likely reason. Even if that's the case, says Li, the series is an artistic expression, not a historical document, and deserves to be seen. He has written letters; spoken to friends. Everyone who has screened the series likes it. In classic bureaucratic fashion, no one has said that CCTV cannot broadcast *The Korean War*, but after more than seven years, no one has yet said that they can.

★ ★ ★

To all who know him, Li Qiankuan's devotion to Chinese film is a joy to witness. In 1998 he organized a letter signed by 20 noted film artists seeking President Jiang Zemin's support for a national film museum, asking him to "dissolve all the red tape" which had been holding up the long-delayed project. Aside from his personal contacts, Li knew Jiang had shown interest in the film industry, visiting China's main movie studios in Beijing, Shanghai, and Changchun.

Again Jiang gave tacit support, forwarding the letter to Ding Guangen, requesting that he "study the project and take care of it." Jiang added, "Please inform me of the final decision." It was not an overt directive, but, according to Li, "in China we all know what that phrase means." Land near Beijing airport was set aside, and finally, in 2005—the 100th anniversary of China's film industry—the China Film Museum opened.

And in recent years, Li Qiankuan's status has reflected growing official respect: He was among the artists acclaimed as "having made great contribution to the nation," and he became chairman of the China Film Association.

"Jiang Zemin calls artists 'engineers of the soul,'" Li notes. "He wants Chinese artists to not just keep up with the world's advanced culture—he wants them to pioneer and extend it. 'Outdated ideology,' Jiang said, 'must not restrain China's artists. They must catch up with China's rapid reform and opening-up.' Though we all recognize that there are certain limits in Chinese society," Li adds, "these are changing too. Jiang loves to be with artists; I've been to his home many times."

And under Jiang's successor, Hu Jintao, Li sees progress continuing. "His administration has been promoting the film industry," Li says. "I know Hu personally: he loves films." Significantly, Li notes, new talent now has better chances to flourish, as the stifling influence of bureaucracy diminishes. "The seniority system has been shredded," Li says. "If you're talented and capable, then you'll have opportunities to shine."

There is another side to this new freedom, Li acknowledges. These days, "as long as you have money, you can make a film, which has resulted in an increase of bad films." But overall, he says, "the thinking and spirit of the film industry has been improving."

★ ★ ★

Zhao Shi, vice minister of film, says that "China's leaders attach great importance to constructing both material and spiritual civilization. Now that we've made great material progress, people have higher aspirations, particularly the satisfaction of spiritual needs—and here film can contribute."

"When I took office, film screenings in rural areas had hit rock bottom," recalls Zhao Shi. "In the 1990s, commercialization had taken hold and farmers were still watching 1960s movies." But she believed the tradition of traveling rural film shows was worth reviving, particularly in light of President Hu's philosophy: "If China's film industry couldn't provide 800 million farmers with quality films, it would be dereliction of our duty," she says. "The countryside needs culture; the farmers need movies." There's no doubting farmers' enthusiasm, she adds: "Sometimes when a movie is shown in one village, people follow the screening team to the next village to watch it again."

Making movies accessible to farmers was a massive challenge—not least because China has about 640,000 villages. Yet after a county in Shanxi Province set a goal of "one movie per village per month," Zhao turned this into national policy. To fund 7.7 million film screenings every year, they arranged to split costs between central and local governments, with Beijing paying higher percentages for less-developed provinces.

One key is government investment in digital film technology. Zhao recalls visiting the countryside in 2003 and being appalled at the poor quality of the 16mm films: "The people were so happy [about the film show] that they welcomed us with song and dance," she says. "But when the movie was screened, the picture was so shaky and the voices so distorted that I wanted to hide." Rural digitization uses special screens and film-quality transmission via satellite. It means, Zhao says, that "we no longer buy prints and carry them to the countryside—villages order movies via the Internet."

Foreigners are often surprised that the government invests in films for farmers, Zhao says. "It reflects Hu Jintao's policies of Putting People First and building a New Socialist Countryside."

Zhao Shi calls digitalization "the driving force of reform in China's film industry"—The National Digital Movie Production Base, which SARFT helped China Film Group set up outside Beijing, is Asia's largest movie base, and includes one of the world's largest soundstages.

As China's film industry becomes more successful, it grows more confident. Zhang Yimou's *Hero* has had major success both internationally and in China, where it set a box office record of RMB 250 million. Independent productions are now increasingly common. "If foreign movies are wolves, then we've learned from the wolves," says Zhao Shi with a smile.

Endnotes

1 Author's meeting with Zhao Shi, Beijing, June 2008. In mid 2009, after almost 14 years as vice minister of SARFT responsible for the film industry, Zhao Shi was promoted to deputy Party secretary, and vice minister, of the State Administration of Radio, Film, and Television (SARFT); and Zhang Pimin, formerly deputy director of the SARFT Film Bureau was appointed as SARFT vice minister responsible for the film industry. (Previously, Zhang was president of Xi'an Film Studio.)

2 Author's meeting with Li Qiankuan, Beijing, April 2008.

3 Several thousand American actors responded to the casting call, from which the casting agency chose about 100 for formal auditions. Several American character actors were selected (MacArthur was the most difficult role to cast). In the spirit of full disclosure, the lead American role, a fictionalized reporter named Kinsky, modeled after the war correspondent Marguerite Higgins, was played by Daniella Kuhn, the author's daughter, whose previous credits included *Patch Adams* and *Traffic*.

31

Why Religion Became Important

The *Daodejing* is the scriptures of Daoism, China's indigenous religion—profound, concise, wise, mysterious. In 2007, I took part in the International Forum on the *Daodejing*, a gathering of religious leaders and scholars from China and abroad in Xi'an. I spoke on the relationship between science and religion, particularly cosmological models and ultimate origins, a topic of lifelong interest.[1]

I had been invited to the forum by Minister Ye Xiaowen, director of the State Administration of Religious Affairs (SARA). It reflected China's growing interest in state-of-the-art ideas, and increasing freedoms to explore spiritual pursuits. Indeed, I had previously been asked to write an article for *China Daily*, entitled "Does God Exist?"—a brief introduction to the modern debate.[2]

The forum, supported by President Hu Jintao, was part of a broader trend. The previous year, China had hosted an international Buddhist conference. Both were evidence that Hu's approach to religion went beyond non-hostility and tolerance—and represented recognition by China's leaders that religion has legitimate, continuing and perhaps ineradicable roles in human affairs.

It's a significant turnaround. Rather than trying to suppress religion, as traditional Marxism propounded, and thus drive people into depression or cultic religions, China's leaders have now determined that it is best to appreciate and respect legitimate religion within a stable and civil society. Certainly, the ethical and social teachings of *Daodejing* can support a Harmonious Society—President Hu's stated aim.

Confirmation of religion's changing status in China was confirmed when the Politburo held a meeting dedicated to the study of religious issues. President Hu reiterated the Party's policy of promoting freedom of religious belief, saying that "The Party and government shall reach out to religious believers in difficulties and help them through their problems." He also supported self-governance for religious groups—while requiring law-abiding management of religious affairs, and encouraging believers to keep their patriotic tradition and help develop Chinese society.[3]

At around the same time, China established training programs for religious professionals, covering subjects such as world religions and ethics, and practical courses in management, psychology and law. And in 2007, the Party for the first time included the word "religion" in its Constitution: "The Party strives to fully implement its basic principle for its work related to religious affairs, and rallies religious believers in making contributions to economic and social development." President Hu commented that, "We shall fully understand the new problems and challenges to manage religious affairs so that we can do it right." According to Ye Xiaowen, by inscribing its principles regarding religion in its Constitution, "the Party showed its commitment to guaranteeing religious freedom."[4]

China's leaders, though members of a party whose official creed is atheism, now recognize the reality that, no matter pressures to the contrary, human beings will seek and believe in religion of one kind or another—and, significantly, that if religious opportunities are not provided by proper institutions, shady or shadowy institutions will fill the vacuum.

Some among China's leaders go further still. They see in China's traditional religions—Confucianism, Daoism, Buddhism—vehicles to promote Chinese culture globally, and thus boost the nation's international influence. (Harvard Professor Joseph Nye Jr.'s concept of "soft power"—expanding national influence by means of culture or ideology—is taken seriously by Chinese leaders and intellectuals.)

★ ★ ★

Attitudes toward religion in China are based on a long and complex history. Zhuo Xinping, director of the Institute of World Religions at the Chinese Academy of Social Sciences, and China's leading scholar of Christian studies, suggests that, because Christianity has deep roots in Western civilization and played a decisive role in its development, "the importance of religion in society, especially Christianity, is obvious to Westerners." In China, however, he says, the nature and status of religion has been a source of controversy at many stages in the nation's history.

Professor Zhuo, an advocate of cross-cultural communications, stresses that China historically has been a religious country, with a rich tradition infused by Confucianism, Daoism, and Buddhism (which came to China from India about 2,000 years ago and was eventually enculturated).

However, Zhuo says there is "still debate among Chinese scholars as to whether or not Chinese civilization was religious. Some argue that China was the only country in the world that had no religion at all. The claim is that China had philosophy, not religion—and this was an advantage, because religion starts with belief whereas philosophy starts with suspicion.[5]

At the same time, Zhuo stresses, China has a tradition of government management of religion, stretching back to ancient times. In the Qin (221-206 BC) and especially the Han (206 BC—9 AD) dynasties there were agencies for religious affairs. In the Tang Dynasty (618-907), there were even departments for various religions—with Buddhism and Islam ranked higher than Christianity due to their larger sizes. According to Zhou, China had neither a "unity of religion and politics," as in some Islamic countries, nor a "separation of religion and politics," as in some Western countries. "In China, politics stands higher than religion," he says. "This is our tradition."

The history of Christianity in China has been particularly tortuous. The first Christian mission was in the Tang Dynasty, but it brought a Persian form of the religion that was criticized as heresy by the Catholic Church. The second mission was in the Yuan Dynasty (1271-1368), when Catholic missionaries made the treacherous journey via the Silk Road, and established Beijing's first Diocese. They were treated well—the emperor gave them salaries. But within 100 years the Yuan disappeared and along with it the missionaries.

It was not until the late Ming Dynasty (1368-1644), and the arrival of Jesuit missionaries like Matteo Ricci, that Christianity began to have real impact in China. With their beards and long hair and interest in Confucianism, the missionaries were initially welcomed, and several became friends with Chinese emperors. Problems began, however, when some Catholic missionaries asserted that Confucianism was a religion and went to Rome to implore the Pope to stop Chinese Catholics from embracing Confucianism. Jesuit missionaries requested tolerance for Chinese rituals and customs, and in the early 1700s, the Pope and Holy See sought compromise, allowing Chinese Catholics to honor both systems.

But under attack from some Catholic priests, the Pope later changed his mind, disallowing Chinese customs. Emperor Kangxi (1661-1722) was furious. Seeing political motives, he decided that Catholics in China should obey Imperial not Papal authority. Missionaries were forbidden. Many moved to Macao and Hong Kong; those who remained were no longer missionaries per se, but were regarded as scientists, artists, and scholars, who served the emperor for their own interests. A precedent was set: if a religion had dangerous implications, Chinese political authorities would move against it.

When Christianity came to China for the fourth time, in the 19th century, the "friendly mission" was no more. The "unequal treaties," which forced open various geographies of China after its defeat in the Opium Wars, also forced it to accept the so-called "freedom of Christian mission in China." Missionaries returned, but the circumstances created a legacy of bitterness and distrust. According to Professor Zhuo, "This cast a great dark shadow over the Christian mission in China. Christianity was branded an alien or foreign religion, a symbol of 'cultural imperialism,' the face of colonialism. There was a famous saying: 'One more Christian means one less Chinese.'"

A series of nationalist movements, from the late 19th century onwards, sporadically targeted these "foreign religions"—and in some cases the missionaries themselves were attacked. By the 1930s the mood had mitigated: Nationalist leader Chiang Kai-shek even announced that he had become a Christian convert, while his rivals, the Communists, sought to reach out to various sectors of society, including religious groups, in the run-up to the 1949 revolution. The CPC's first Constitution, passed in 1945, stipulated that citizens had the freedom of religion.

But soon after the founding of the People's Republic, pressures grew for Chinese Christianity to be "self-supporting, self-governing, and self-propagating"—independent of foreigners—and there were calls for foreign missionaries to be expelled. In 1954, the official Chinese Protestant Church's Three-Self Patriotic Movement was established. Islam, Buddhism, Tibetan Buddhism, Daoism and other religions also conducted restructuring. (After the Korean War in particular, the U.S. government disallowed financial support to Chinese churches.)

China's relationship with the Vatican was occasionally tense. In 1947 and 1949 the Vatican ordered that no Catholic should join or sympathize with a communist party. In the early 1950's, the Chinese Catholic Church still sent the names of its candidates for bishops to the Vatican. But the Pope criticized them sharply, stating that Chinese Catholics were no longer Catholics, and he excommunicated the lot of them

According to Professor Zhuo, in 1957, the Chinese Catholic Church cut off all political and economic ties with the Vatican; on religious matters Chinese Catholics continued to obey the Holy See and Pope, he says, but they would now elect their own bishops and priests without the Pope's permission—though they still held out hope that one day their religious relationship might be normalized.

During the early decades of the People's Republic, and especially during the Cultural Revolution, there was virtually no religious freedom. Afterwards, Zhuo Xinping says, "Leadership realized that mistakes had been made. With reform, change began. Religious freedom was emphasized again; many religions came to new life. We spoke about a so-called 'religious renaissance' or 'religious revival' in China."

There were even signs of a rapprochement with the Catholic Church. In 1983, Pope John Paul II sought to talk to Chinese leaders directly, and from 1986 there were frequent communications between the Vatican and the Chinese government. In 1999, the Pope stated that relations between Chinese Catholics and the Vatican should not undermine the independence and sovereignty of China, and hopes of an eventual normalization remain. (The road has not been smooth, however. In 2000, for example, the Vatican canonized several missionaries of whom China disapproved and the Chinese government protested.)

★ ★ ★

Ye Xiaowen, director of State Administration for Religious Affairs (second from left) attends the China Bible Ministry Exhibition in Atlanta, with former President Jimmy Carter (third from right) (May 2006).

Perhaps the one closest to the development of religion during China's reform era—particularly the evolution of senior leaders' thinking about religion—is Ye Xiaowen. When we spoke, Minister Ye had been director of the State Administration of Religious Affairs for 14 years—a long time for a senior official to remain in one position.[6] But Religious Affairs is no ordinary post—it's a sensitive brief, and China's leaders know that not just any competent administrator can handle it.

Ye Xiaowen comes from a poor teacher's family in Hunan, and grew up in Guizhou. Sent down to work as a farmer during the Cultural Revolution, he never stopped studying, and after Deng Xiaoping reopened China's higher education he needed only one year at college before jumping into a postgraduate program in Marxist philosophy. When academic disciplines were revived, Ye Xiaowen was selected to study sociology, which had been suppressed for 20 years.

Later, Ye wrote a long article on the history of sociology in China, and its contemporary relevance, and this enabled his becoming vice director of the Institute of Philosophy of the Guizhou Academy of Social Sciences. In 1985, Hu Jintao was appointed Guizhou Party secretary. Soon afterwards, Ye Xiaowen was made secretary of the Guizhou Communist Youth League, and five years later he was promoted to the Youth League's United Front Department in Beijing. One of his tasks was to understand why some young people were becoming religious believers—and to convince them not to believe in religion, but to join the Communist Youth League.

In 1992, Ye traveled to villages in China's northwest to conduct research. "I was shocked by what I found," he recalls. "Many outstanding young people were devout religious believers. I had to think: why was the appeal of our strong Party less than that of these much weaker religious groups?" At that time, he notes, "I believed that the religious young people had misunderstood religion and had simply, in their youth, chosen the wrong path."

An article he wrote after this visit, reflecting on religion and its legitimacy, attracted widespread attention, including from Chinese religious leaders— and before long Ye was put in charge of the State Administration of Religious Affairs. (Ye's given name "Xiaowen" means "small articles." Strangely enough, Ye laughed, "my career has been catalyzed by 'small articles'.")

Ye, who still describes himself as "one-half scholar and one-half official," stresses that part of his job is "to educate our own officials." Some, he says, "tend to regard religion as simplistic and therefore use simplistic approaches to deal with religious issues. They must understand religion's complexity."

For years, he says, "our incorrect and vacillating policies have been a result of our lack of understanding—you don't have to tell U.S. officials that religion has mass appeal and is going to be around for a long while." In China, however, Ye says he must explain to his colleagues "how religion is compatible with socialist society, and how to cultivate a correct view of religion. It's been a challenge," he acknowledges, though he feels he has succeeded.

Ye, who has been criticized for his forthright approach to sensitive issues, says "I'm outspoken . . . but if the Party wants to understand religious affairs correctly then we have to articulate the issues and problems."

"Historically," he says, "the Party's dominant mentality was that religion was backward and fatuous. Early CPC leaders believed that religion was a short-term phenomenon and believers were just small numbers of uneducated or superstitious people." Frankly, he says, they felt that "religion should not be allowed to influence China's youth. 'We hope that young people become atheists' was their view."

It was, he explains, an attitude born of traditional Marxism. "In its infancy, the socialist movement was critical of religion. In Marx's eyes, theology had become a bastion protecting the feudal ruling class in Germany. Therefore the political revolution had to start by criticizing religion. It was from this perspective that Marx said 'religion is the opium of the people'."

Another factor in China's suspicion of religion, Ye adds, was the general perception that "Western countries not-so-friendly to China, who had used Christianity as a vehicle to invade China in the past, were now again employing Christianity to infiltrate China in order to overthrow the Party." Ye notes that religion played what he describes as "a famously significant part" in the overturning of former socialist countries, such as Poland, Romania, and the Soviet Union, "by stirring up trouble." This, he says, "is one reason why religion continues to concern us. Therefore we stress the principle of self-governance, self-support, and self-propagation."

Ye Xiaowen makes it clear, however, that the antipathy shown towards religion during the Cultural Revolution was categorically wrong. "Religion was regarded as something exceedingly bad," he says. "People were forbidden to have any religious belief. Religion was crushed."

In the reform era, however, he says officials began to rethink their attitudes: "To bring order out of chaos, we had to." This meant a gradual revision of traditional Marxist attitudes, Ye explains. "If we still acted on what Marx said, we'd encounter great difficulties. If we still considered religion to be 'opium', then all believers would be 'drug addicts' and all clergy 'drug traffickers'!"

According to Ye, Deng Xiaoping stressed that China shouldn't use administrative force to regulate religions but nor should religions engage in any fanaticism. Ye recalls that former U.S. President Jimmy Carter told him he had asked Deng three religion-related questions when they met. Deng told Carter "he would think about them and answer them the following day." In response to the first question, "Could the Chinese people have freedom of religion?" Deng said, "Sure." To the second question, "Could Christians print and distribute Bibles?" Deng said, "No problem."[7] But to the third question, "Would China welcome missionaries to China for proselytizing?" Deng said, emphatically, "NO!"

Nevertheless, Ye says, Deng did not give any explicit directions for how the Party should deal with religion. Now, Ye announces, "I'm pleased to tell you that this problem has been resolved."

The first step, Ye relates, was taken by Deng and Hu Yaobang, who commissioned an article that acknowledged the legitimacy of religions. Published in 1982, it declared that the CPC must genuinely implement its policy of freedom of religion, but it also predicted, based on Marxist theory, that as the socialist cause advanced, the religious cause would retreat, and religion would "shrink."

As a result, Ye says, "China worked to 'shrink religion' for more than 25 years."

"But what were the results, he asks? "Anyone can see," he answers, "that, notwithstanding high economic growth, religions are growing not shrinking."

★ ★ ★

One defining moment in the attitudes of China's leaders to religion came in 1999. Early in the morning of April 25, a startling, bewildering challenge to the Marxist view that religion would wither emerged as if from nowhere. Without warning, more than 10,000 practitioners of a quasi-religious sect known as Falun Gong materialized in Beijing, and surrounded the government compound at Zhongnanhai. Buses had entered the capital before dawn carrying protesters.[8] Sect members filled nearby sidewalks, five and six deep, sitting silently, many in meditation.

Falun Gong, which literally means "the Practice of the Wheel of the Dharma," was founded in 1992 by Li Hongzhi, a middle-aged former grain clerk and soldier who claimed to be a master of the ancient art of qigong (which professes to use breathing and meditation to channel energy and improve one's health). Li, who by 1997 had moved to America but remained Falun Gong's absolute leader, combined concepts from qigong, Buddhism, and Daoism with his own mystical theories to form what he proclaimed to be an "advanced system of cultivation and practice" leading toward enlightenment. Some followers claimed to feel the "dharma wheel" whirling in their bellies—which Li professed to install telekinetically into the abdomens of practitioners as a way to collect cosmic forces and expel bad karma—and devotees were told to harness this power, rather than use medicines, to cure disease.

The practice of Falun Gong included sets of exercises, performed to Chinese music, involving lotus postures and hand movements. With its syncretic belief system of quack health claims, psychic fantasies, and amalgamated philosophical-theological ramblings, Falun Gong might be likened to an Asian combination of L. Ron Hubbard's Scientology, Mary Baker Eddy's Christian Science, and Madame Blavatsky's Theosophical Society—a New Age cult, if you will, with Chinese characteristics.

The movement had spread through word of mouth, and in just a few years its membership climbed into the millions. By 1999, foreign media suggested it might have as many as 70 million practitioners; government counts put the number of confirmed believers at about two million. Whatever the real number, prior to the April demonstration some senior leaders had never even heard of the movement, while others were rumored to have relatives who were practitioners.

Officials from the State Council Appeal Office, a bureau that handles public complaints, met with the demonstrators, a resolution was reached, and the crowds dispersed quietly. The crisis seemed over. But senior leaders were astounded to learn of Party cadres among the demonstrators, even an official from the State Security Bureau—and the protest went unreported by state media for two days.

President Jiang Zemin was stunned. "How could it be that in one night the Falun Gong just appeared?" he asked Shen Yongyan, his lifelong friend in Changchun.[9] "Did they come from under the ground? Where was our Public Security? State Security?" Shen told Jiang of a female vice president at the automotive plant where Jiang had once worked, a graduate of a prestigious institute, who practiced Falun Gong. "She had hypertension," Shen says, "and because she refused medical treatment, she died of a cerebral hemorrhage. Jiang knew the woman and was dumbfounded."

"How could so many intellectuals practice Falun Gong?" Jiang asked Shen. "What can these people be thinking?" From the outset Jiang saw the sect's slogan of "truthfulness, benevolence, and forbearance" as deceptive and cunning, and an attempt to usurp the Party's moral authority, and he attributed the sect's growth to negligence in ideological work.

In a May memo, shortly after the NATO attack in Yugoslavia, Jiang observed wryly, "If Falun Gong masters can foresee everything, why didn't they predict the bombing of our embassy?"[10] In July, the Ministry of Public Security issued an edict: The Falun Gong was "an unlawful organization that has to be outlawed." Party members were forbidden to participate on penalty of expulsion. An arrest warrant was issued for Falun Gong founder Li Hongzhi, who was accused of spreading "superstition and malicious fallacies to deceive people, resulting in the deaths of many practitioners." Hundreds of practitioners were hustled into custody.

In August the Party linked the campaign against Falun Gong with ongoing efforts to reinvigorate itself with Marxist and socialist ideology. But it also motivated leaders—Jiang Zemin in particular—to pay more attention to religion and belief.

★ ★ ★

In December 2001, President Jiang convened a three-day National Work Conference on Religious Affairs, with the aim of devising China's policy on religion for the new century. It was the largest, highest-level, and most significant gathering on religion that the Party had ever held.

As a lifelong socialist and rational man of science, Jiang had, in the past, found himself mystified by the appeal of religion, with all its presumptions, imaginations and superstitions, and had subscribed to the classic Marxist view that religion's influence would gradually diminish and ultimately wither away. Instead, he now saw, religion had grown ever more potent, even as educational levels had risen—not only in China but all over the world.

(A 1997 government estimate put China's religious adherents at about 100 million for the five officially recognized religions—Buddhism, Daoism, Islam, Catholicism, and Protestantism; nongovernment estimates later posted much higher numbers: 200 million or even 300 million depending on definitions, including more than 100 million Buddhists, almost 50 million Daoists, 21 million Muslims, and 70-80 million Christians—the majority Protestant, Catholics likely being under 10 million. Whatever the numbers, everyone agreed believers were increasing.[11])

Accordingly, Jiang revised his attitudes, particularly after the Falun Gong shock. Religion was a power that needed to be recognized, appreciated, controlled and focused. What's more, part of Jiang's rationale for the Communist Party to remain the ruling Party, as outlined in his theory of the Three Represents, was that it must "represent" the "overwhelming majority" of the people. To be consistent, then, the Party could hardly disregard 10% or 20% of the population. Jiang also concluded that most believers were also loyal citizens, who were contributing to building the country.

A radical change had taken place in Jiang Zemin's thinking. As his philosophy was evolving towards "ruling the country by virtue," he now felt religion could become a more central element of society, supporting both his vision for a moral and civil society and his desire to repulse destructive elements such as Falun Gong.

Visiting a Buddhist temple in 2001, he had even asked the senior monks for their ideas on channeling "young people's interest in religion." Jiang also spoke about an episode in his own life, which he described as a "fateful encounter": "I once practiced the kind of meditation you just described," Jiang told one of the Buddhist masters. "It was during a very difficult period, in the late 1950s [when Jiang was highly stressed working at First Automotive Works]. I had severe gastric disease and practiced meditative sitting for three months—it seemed to cure my ailment," he went on. "Meditation can lead one to serenity; it is very marvelous indeed."[12]

In his speech to the Conference on Religious Affairs, Jiang recognized the relevance of religion, acknowledging its contributions to social stability and warning against underrating its role in world affairs. He praised the "broad believing masses" for their support of the nation and highlighted the social function of religion, such as in disaster relief. And he encouraged participants to "make socialism and religion adapt to each other."

"Asking religions to adapt to socialism doesn't mean we want religious believers to give up their faith," Jiang stated.

Jiang also warned, however, that no one would be allowed to "abuse religion" in order to sabotage the Party, socialism, or national security—an overt reference to Falun Gong and other unauthorized religions—and he cautioned against "infiltration of foreign forces cloaked in the mantle of religion."

At the same time, new rules allowed churches and other religious organizations to register directly with the state as independent entities, rather than as part of one of the official "patriotic" religions. In this manner, various groups among China's unofficial "house churches" (see below) could gain a form of official recognition—and avoid punishment—without having to subsume their identities to religious groups with which they did not identify. On the other hand, those choosing not to register could find themselves subject to even more constraints. In short, Jiang was promising freedom of religion—so long as those religions were under the authority of the state, which was entirely consistent with Chinese tradition.

Balanced as Jiang was seeking to be, this new view of religion was attacked from both sides of the political spectrum. Left-wing purists saw any accommodation with religion as yet another example of Jiang's anti-Marxist revisionism—which they felt was eviscerating the Party's core beliefs. Rightist liberals criticized Jiang for not going further and removing virtually all restraints on religious freedom.

Ye Xiaowen summarizes Jiang's speech with two concepts: religion's mass appeal and its long-term existence. "Among all aspects of humanity, religion is unique in its complexity and power," says Ye: "Socialism must tackle religion." He notes that the speech was Jiang's "own brainchild—he even drafted it himself." The day before the conference, Jiang had called Ye to his office to iron out the final draft. Vice-President Hu Jintao and other leaders were also there.

During the half-day discussion, Jiang stressed that "We have to affirm the positive role of religion. As the ruling party," he added, "we have to make full use of religion's contributory role." But, he asked Ye, "How should we explain this? Did Marx say anything about this?"

Ye replied that Marx had said a few nice things about religion, "but not many." He told Jiang, "Marx noted that 'Religion is the sigh of the oppressed creature, the heart of a heartless world, just as it is the spirit of spiritless conditions.'" However, Ye stressed, Marx went on to say that "Religion is the *opium* of the people," and described it as "imaginary flowers on the chain," which didn't bear fruit, and therefore were not good flowers.

According to Ye, President Jiang responded: "If Marx didn't say many good things about religion, then we will say them!" He said that religion had both negative and positive roles, and the key for the Party's work was how to leverage the positive roles. It was, Ye says, a turning point. "Marx had never said that religion could play a positive role in society, but now the CPC was saying that it could. The CPC was in essence endorsing religion!"

Jiang's speech also contradicted communism's traditional view that religion would eventually shrink and die out; he raised the idea that the ultimate demise of religion might go beyond the demise of classes and countries. This was, says Ye, "a pretty big deal for the CPC at the time: the CPC had held to the orthodoxy that, after the demise of classes and countries, communism would be realized. Now the general secretary was effectively saying that religion would coexist with communism."

It was, says Ye, "a powerful proposition"—and Jiang Zemin had felt it necessary to get approval of the Politburo Standing Committee. Some members, Ye says, suggested Jiang should not include this unprecedented statement in the speech. "Are you sure about it?" they asked. Jiang sought advice, and Ye organized a team to check whether Marx or Engels had ever said anything remotely like this—but could find no such reference.

"However," Ye recalls, "as a philosophy major, I was good at deduction. I took some remarks of Marx and Engels and wrote four full pages of analysis demonstrating that Jiang's conclusion was proper and could be included in the speech. For example, Engels indicated that as long as there are problems, there will be religion."

At the conference the following day, Ye Xiaowen noticed that Jiang Zemin placed these four pages beside him when he made the speech, and when he came to the abovementioned conclusion he stressed that "I have proof, but because the deduction is too complicated, I'm not going to read it—but it agrees with Marxism."

According to Ye, Jiang's speech emphasized China's commitment to change. "I am a Marxist. The essence of Marxism is change," Ye says. "Barack Obama beat Hilary Clinton by stressing change. The Marxist in China today is not a stubborn, dogmatic, and outdated 19th-century old man, but a dynamic, pro-change, young thinker. We have a flexible approach: for words Marx said, if they are still applicable, we will use them; for things he didn't articulate clearly, we will spell them out; for what he didn't say, we will boldly come up with something new."

★ ★ ★

Several years later, President Hu Jintao incorporated religion into his vision of the Scientific Perspective on Development and his ambition of building a Harmonious Society. Ye Xiaowen set out Hu's four basic guidelines for religious work:[13] First, freedom of religious belief is a fundamental right of citizens, embodying the Party's people-oriented policy and its respect for human rights; second, religious affairs must be handled according to law—the government cannot use executive power to either eradicate or encourage religion, but no person or organization should use religion to oppose the Party's leadership and the socialist system, or to endanger national unity, ethnic solidarity and social stability; third, uphold the principle of self-administration: Chinese religious affairs should be run independently by Chinese believers, not subject to foreign domination, and should resist religious infiltration by foreign forces, though equal and legitimate religious exchanges with foreign countries are encouraged; fourth, adapt religion to socialist society: give full play to religion's positive role in promoting economic and social development, and promote a harmonious society through religion.

Ye notes, however, that "there still remains much to be explored" regarding religion's growing role in society. "In a market economy people are encouraged to pursue wealth and possessions," he says, "but we have to face two challenges. The first is that China's traditional belief system and values are heavily shaken. When working competitively, people may feel empty and confused and choose to believe in religion. Then," he adds, "how do we view this phenomenon and how do we guide and regulate it?"

The second challenge, according to Ye, "is that a market economy requires trustworthiness. If a person only knows how to make money and cannot be trusted, he or she will be difficult to deal with. But if a person has no sense of business, then society would stagnate. How do we combine business sense and trustworthiness in one person?"

Ye cites my own partner, Adam Zhu (whom he knows well) as "a good example." Adam, he says, "is a successful businessman, but the reason I consider him as a genuine friend is because he is trustworthy. As a Christian, he knows God is watching over him."

Ye notes that if he wants to get officials to pay attention to his message about religion, "I have to quote Marx frequently in my speeches." It might seem odd to foreigners, he says, but "historically, senior leaders haven't spent much time on religious affairs. I'm just a vice-minister-level official in charge of religion, what can I say on my own? Would people be convinced by *my* words?"

Nevertheless, Ye says that China's leaders are increasingly conscious of the centrality of a moral framework. "President Hu has three phrases which I respect: 'Ponder the harm of greed; cultivate integrity and ethics; maintain a heart of self-discipline'—we must restore China's grand traditions of culture and civility."

All this means, Ye says, that there is now fertile ground in which religion in China can grow. "According to our government's orthodox vision, China's future will witness the renaissance of Chinese culture, core values and common ideals, socialism with Chinese characteristics, patriotism, and collectivism. I am all for these," he states, "but I believe that the real renaissance will be a fusion of multiple cultures—more of a harmonious, cohesive culture in which religious culture will play a significant role."

He predicts that, "in 20 years, religion will be integrated into society and positively affect its cultural and moral functioning. Now it's still too weak to do that." Ye's theory is that "The future of religion in China is more cultural, moral, and ethical than holy and spiritual. Religions that have prevailed in China are more rational and humane instead of fundamentalist and evangelical," he notes. He envisions what he calls a "virtuous circle" for China's religious believers: "Obey the country, and the country will treat you well. Adapt to society, and society will be tolerant toward you. Mix with the culture, and culture will comfort you."

Ye defends himself against criticisms that, as an avowed atheist, he is hardly qualified to be in charge of religion: on a visit to the U.S., he says, he was frequently asked, "What is your religion, 'Mr. Director-of-Religious-Affairs?'" His answer was that "In China, the director of sports does not play sports; the director of tobacco does not smoke; and the director of religious affairs does not believe in any religion." When critics suggested that, because he was not himself a believer, he "wouldn't respect or treat religions very well," Ye was ready: "As minister of Religious Affairs, if I believed in Christianity, the Buddhists might not be pleased; if I believed in Buddhism, the Muslims might think I was biased. Because I have no personal religious affiliation, I can respect and serve every religion equally."

Indeed, Ye suggests that part of his job is preventing religious tension and pre-empting insults to various religions. China's relationship with its Muslim population has been a sensitive one, for example. (Some Muslims in the northwestern region of Xinjiang have espoused violent opposition to Beijing's rule—which in 2009 erupted in the deadly Urumqi riots.) And Ye suggests that careful handling is required.

A case in point occurred in 1995, the year of the pig in China. Newspapers published articles praising the traits of pigs; some joked that Muslims didn't eat pork because they were descended from Zhu Ba-jie (a pig character in the classic Chinese novel *The Monkey King*), which caused Muslims to protest in street demonstrations. The government fired several newspaper editors after which Muslim anger died down.

But on the eve of the 1995 Chinese New Year Gala on CCTV, the nation's most watched extravaganza, Ye was asked to attend the rehearsals to make sure that nothing offensive would be broadcast. He was horrified to see a gigantic pig head hanging above the stage, and demanded that it be replaced. Then, however, he noticed more than 100 children holding lanterns in the shape of a pig's head. The gala was the next day and it was impossible to change the lanterns—so Ye asked CCTV to use only long shots of the children, so that viewers could not recognize the pig heads.

At other times, though, Ye says the challenge comes from religious extremists. For example, he discovered that one Imam had defined *jihad*, in a sermon, as "war against China." After consulting with the president of the Islamic Association of China, Ye organized authoritative Imams to write an exegetical book of the Qur'an, which gave "the proper understanding." Copies were given to Islamic communities for free. Eventually, over 20,000 Imams were given training based on the book. Anyone who failed their tests would lose the Imam title.

★ ★ ★

Professor Zhuo Xinping argues that China has now entered its "best time of religious freedom." He acknowledges that "of course, this comparison is from a Chinese, not a Western, perspective." But he still expresses "disappointment" that foreign criticism of China's handling of religious affairs has, he says, "intensified" in recent years. "I understand that Westerners are not satisfied with our progress," he says, "but that's because they inappropriately evaluate our status in terms of their own history and religious conditions."

The frequent foreign criticism, Zhuo recognizes, accuses China of persecuting those involved in Protestant "house churches" and the "underground" Catholic church" (which pays allegiance to the Pope and not to Beijing) and, in some cases, of imprisoning pastors and clergy.

"'House churches' and 'underground churches' are not the same thing," he says, "and it's a mistake to conflate them." "House churches" (religious groups set up unofficially in homes and other places) emerged during the religious revival of the reform era: some were established by foreign Christian missionaries, of different denominations, who returned to China unofficially—and did not accept the authority of the Three-Self Patriotic Movement, the official "post-denominational" organization which since 1958 had represented all Protestant denominations in China. Other house churches were set up by Chinese returning from overseas who had become "new Christians" and didn't relate to the government-approved Church. Other groups had no foreign influence, but simply wanted their own "free-style tradition."

The problem was that according to Chinese law, all religious organizations must be registered by the government. Some house churches applied for registration—which the government has not approved, though it has considered the question seriously. According to Professor Zhuo, if the government registered house churches, the official "post-denominational" church would be undermined. But Zhuo stresses that, although they are technically illegal, the government's attitude toward house churches is generally tolerant, and there is dialogue. (The Chinese government's approach toward benign house churches echoes the U.S. military's "don't ask, don't tell" approach toward gay and lesbian personnel.)

As for the "underground" Catholic Church, Zhuo says that tensions remain because its believers' loyalties are split—between the political authority of the Chinese government and the religious authority of the Pope. When these two authorities do not disagree, there are no problems. When they do disagree, there are problems.

Whatever the case, Zhuo suggests that foreign criticism can be counterproductive. "We need friendly support from abroad," he says. "If China's reform is praised, this facilitates faster reform. On the other hand, if our reform is criticized, then China might hesitate to take further reforms and perhaps even take steps back. The international atmosphere is important."

But Zhuo emphasizes that China's leaders have had an evolving view of religion. He identifies three stages. In the first, religion was viewed with suspicion, as a form of political power, and measures were taken to control it. In the second stage, from the early 1990s, religion was viewed as a cultural phenomenon. This was, in a sense, progress, Zhuo says: since culture is relatively neutral, it helped remove the largely negative historical evaluation of religion (Christianity in particular.)

Now, he says, we have entered the third stage: religion as religion. This means, Zhuo explains, that "we should recognize the spiritual potential of common people. 'Religion as religion' allows everyone a spiritual life or spiritual pursuits. That's the difference between religion and other kinds of culture."

It's a transition in progress. And Zhuo points to the fact that religious leaders now serve in high-level positions in government as another sign of religion's increasing influence. (The former head of the official Catholic Church, Bishop Fu Tieshan, for example, was vice chairman of the National People's Congress, a position higher than minister; when he died in 2007, President Hu and Premier Wen attended his funeral.) And Zhuo rejects suggestions that this merely confirms government control over religion: "It's a two-way street," he says. "Religious leaders can give closer advice to the government. Moreover, the status of religion in society is elevating. These are very positive changes."

As for the possibility that at some future date, the Communist Party might permit religious believers to become members, Zhuo says that, "as a scholar I am quite open to this question," though he acknowledges that, "Of course there are different opinions." Zhuo notes that in the Russian Revolution, Vladimir Lenin said that religious believers and priests could join the Party, and he never said Party members had to give up their religious beliefs.

Indeed, Zhuo suggests, "Communism and religion are different kinds of 'faith'"—one political and one spiritual. "They are different categories," he says, "you can't compare them. So they have no contradiction if you hold both of them."

Professor Zhuo himself encourages new thinking on religion in China: in 2002, he organized China's first forum on the relationship between science and religion.[14] He explains that, in the past, "many Chinese thought that religion and science stand in mutual opposition. The assumption," he says, "was that with more scientific knowledge, there would be less religious belief. But after China's opening," he notes, "Chinese scientists found that many famous foreign scientists were religious believers. This puzzled them and lead to serious study."

The science-religion dialogue probes the nature of existence, the methodology of discerning knowledge, and humanity's place in the cosmos. That such issues are now being discussed in China is a sign of a new willingness to take religion seriously, not only as a cultural phenomenon but also as a potential window on reality. It's all to the credit of "emancipating the mind."

Endnotes

1 The author is creator, writer and host of *Closer To Truth: Cosmos, Consciousness, God*— a public television series—www.closertotruth.com. "Why This Universe: Toward a Taxonomy of Possible Explanations," Robert Lawrence Kuhn, *Skeptic* magazine, Volume 13, Number 2, 2007 - http://www.closertotruth.com/pdf/Why_This_Universe_-_Kuhn_-_Skeptic_Mag_13-2_-_Spring_2007.pdf.

2 Robert Lawrence Kuhn, "Does God Exist?" *China Daily*, December 2, 2006.

3 "Hu stresses full implementation of free religious policy," Xinhua, December 19, 2007.

4 Author's meeting with Ye Xiaowen, Beijing, June 2008.

5 Zhuo Xinping notes that it was Matteo Ricci, the 16th century Jesuit missionary, who stressed that Confucianism should not be considered a religion. The reason, Zhuo says, is that such a conclusion was necessary for Ricci's proselytizing work: "The best way for Ricci to convert Chinese intellectuals was to allow them to keep their Confucian tradition, but at the same time ask them to accept the Christian faith and become Catholics," Zhuo explains. Moreover, the Catholic Church could not accept converts who believed in another religion as well—and so "the only way he could do this was to claim that Confucianism was not a religion," thus allowing many Chinese intellectuals to become "Confucian Catholics." Some Chinese scholars too saw Confucianism purely as a philosophy—though they, unlike Ricci, believed that this meant it was superior to Catholicism.

6 Ye Xiaowen.

7 According to Ye Xiaowen, China had about 16 million Protestant Christians and had printed 42 million Bibles (with state subsidies).

8 Falun Gong protestors were angered by what they claimed to be police brutality in breaking up a previous protest in Tianjin (which had targeted an academic who had criticized Falun Gong as a superstitious movement.)

9 Shen Yongyan.

10 Seth Faison, "Ex-General, Member of Banned Sect, Confesses 'Mistakes,' China Says," *The New York Times*, July 31, 1999.

11 According to Professor Zhuo Xinping, the State Council asserted in 1997 that there were 100 million religious believers in China. Interestingly, that same figure, 100 million, was given in the 1950s by Premier Zhou Enlai. In 2007, East China Normal University surveyed 5,000 people from different places in China and concluded that there should be about 300 million religious believers in China. The number 200 million appeared in

China Daily and provoked discussions among scholars. Their consensus was that if 200 million number represents only the five officially recognized religions, it's an overestimate; if it includes all religious believers, it's an underestimate—especially considering the large numbers of believers in folk religions. Some put the number of Chinese folk religion believers alone at nearly 300 million. With all these diverse statistics, what's clear is that scientific research is needed. Professor Zhuo gave his personal estimate: without folk religions, fewer than 300 million believers; with folk religion, more than 300 million.

12 Vivien Pik-Kwan, "Jiang urged temple to boost religion, says monk," *South China Morning Post*, June 21, 2002.

13 Ye Xiaowen, "How to implement the Scientific Development Perspective in Religious Work," *Qiushi* (Seek Truth) *Magazine*, June 2, 2008.

14 The forum was supported by the John Templeton Foundation and co-sponsored by the Center for Theology and the Natural Sciences in Berkeley, California, which was founded by Robert John Russell, a minister with a Ph.D. in physics.

32

Foreign Policy Breaks Free

"China's relations with the world are undergoing historic change," said Foreign Minister Yang Jiechi in 2008. "We know very well that China's diplomacy shoulders historic responsibility to promote world peace."

It may have sounded like little more than rhetoric, but China's foreign policy today is indeed a world away from that of a few decades ago.

Wang Guangya, China's vice foreign minister and former ambassador to the United Nations (2003-2008), recalls that when he joined the diplomatic service in 1972 all world problems had to be understood through the "theory of confrontation" between two superpowers, the United States and the Soviet Union. "Every event, no matter where in the world or what local complexities were involved, had to be analyzed in terms of this fundamental confrontation," he explains. "Moreover," he adds, "there was also the pre-programmed idea that, while both the U.S. and USSR were always evil, the USSR was always the larger evil."[1]

By the late 1960s, the USSR, once China's "Big [Communist] Brother," had become China's primary enemy, and armed border clashes in 1969 almost erupted into full-scale war. Around this time, Mao Zedong and Zhou Enlai commissioned four retired generals to assess the international situation. Their advice was that the Soviet Union was the most serious threat to China—a conclusion which was to shape the mindset of a generation of diplomats. It meant, according to Wang Guangya, that China's diplomats "did not so much analyze international events as describe them in terms of preset concepts or doctrines."

The Four Old Marshalls suggested that China should reopen communications with America—leading to Sino-U.S. rapprochement and President Nixon's historic trip to China in 1972. (It was a fortuitous development for Wang Guangya too. As China's leaders realized that they required knowledgeable diplomats to work with the West, Wang was chosen to study at the London School of Economics in 1974, one of the first class of Chinese

Wang Guangya (right), China's Ambassador to the United Nations (later executive vice minister and Party secretary of Foreign Affairs), and Cong Jun (left), minister counselor in China's Mission to the UN (Wang and Cong are husband and wife), at the Chinese Mission to the UN (New York, September 2008).

officials since the Communist revolution to receive a Western education. At the LSE, Wang met and married fellow student Cong Jun, an elegant woman who speaks fluent English and has held diplomatic posts in her own right, including ambassador to Estonia and minister counselor in the Chinese UN Mission. "Common people in China today have consumer rights," says Cong. "For example, they're concerned about pollution and hold many peaceful demonstrations to protest real or potential environmental damage." Cong Jun is the daughter of Chen Yi, one of the Four Old Marshalls.)

Wang, who since late 2008 has managed foreign affairs activities for China's senior leaders including President Hu, notes that control over policy and decision-making in China's foreign affairs has always resided with the country's top leaders: from Mao Zedong and Zhou Enlai in the first generation, to Deng Xiaoping, Jiang Zemin, and now Hu Jintao.

Under Deng, Wang says, reform of China's foreign policy really began: "Deng believed that the world was not entirely dominated by U.S.-USSR confrontations and that another world war was not inevitable (Mao's core conviction was that another world war *was* inevitable). To avoid war in a nuclear age was essential, Deng stressed."

As a result, Wang adds, Deng advised flexibility in China's diplomacy—because China needed international peace and stability for its economic and social development. "China's vision of reform," Wang emphasizes, "was strategic as well as economic." (Indeed Minister Wang, who graduated from the Johns Hopkins' School of Advanced International Studies—and is known to correct his English translators—stresses that reform and modernization is linked to foreign invasion and domination in the late Qing dynasty: "We had no choice but to reform," he says, "otherwise we could be defeated again. For China, reform means national survival as well as domestic prosperity.")

★ ★ ★

Deng introduced a series of strategic adjustments to China's diplomacy, according to Foreign Minister Yang Jiechi.[2] Along with prioritizing peace and development, Deng called for an independent and non-aligned foreign policy. China should not have a "one-line strategy," and should not form alliances with any country or group of countries—not even for ideological reasons. He called for China to play a positive and expanding role in global and regional affairs, and to promote pragmatic cooperation (particularly in economics) with developing countries.

Deng also encouraged dealing with "historical issues," the Chinese euphemism for long-term serious disagreements. These included border disputes with neighboring countries, such as territorial sovereignty in the South China Sea, and importantly, promoting the "one country, two systems" principle for the return of Hong Kong to Chinese sovereignty. (Deng proposed this idea in 1982, and would later extend it to include Taiwan, in order to promote reunification. As early as January 1979, Deng sent a Message to Compatriots in Taiwan, transforming China's unification strategy for the island from bellicose "armed liberation" to nuanced "peaceful liberation."[3])

There were big bumps in the road, notably after the Tiananmen crackdown in 1989, when, according to Yang Jiechi, China had to combine principle and flexibility to resist international pressure and "break Western sanctions." In late 1989, Japan took the lead in restoring assistance to China; by late 1990, Western European countries resumed high-level visits; and following the Sino-U.S. summit in 1993, there was no longer an "abnormal situation" in Sino-U.S. relations.

China focused on the major powers. In 1996 China and Russia began exploring a strategic partnership, and in 2001 they signed a "good-neighborly treaty of friendship and cooperation." And in 1997, America and China agreed to build a constructive strategic partnership which aimed for long-term cooperation rather than confrontation.

A favorable neighboring environment was another priority. China resumed diplomatic relations with Indonesia (1990) and Vietnam (1991), each freighted with historical baggage (an alleged Communist coup attempt in Indonesia in 1965 and a fierce border war with Vietnam in 1979). And while maintaining traditional friendly relations with North Korea, China also normalized links with South Korea. In Central Asia, meanwhile, China established the Shanghai Cooperation Organization, which includes Russia, Kazakhstan, Kyrgyzstan, Tajikistan and Uzbekistan, and stresses mutual security.

China also began participating more broadly in international affairs; for example, joining UN peacekeeping operations. China is a primary member of Asia-Pacific Economic Cooperation (APEC), the forum for Pacific Rim countries to discuss common concerns, and strengthened ties with developing countries, particularly in Africa. The China-Africa Cooperation Forum was established—its first meeting in Beijing in 2000 was attended by nearly 80 ministers from 45 African countries.

There was certainly continuing emphasis on defending national sovereignty, territorial integrity and national dignity, and promoting reunification. This included the return of Hong Kong and Macao; repeatedly thwarting the Taiwan separatists; and countering various "anti-China" proposals at UN agencies.

"Our mindset today is completely different," says Vice Foreign Minister Wang Guangya. "We analyze situations in terms of real facts, reach our own conclusions—and take responsibility for them." Wang stresses that "because of this new freedom, amplified by a more complex world, Chinese diplomats have harder jobs. Each issue," he says, "requires its own, often sophisticated and subtle analysis; for example, Russia-Georgia disputes. China's leaders expect its diplomats to give their candid assessments of situations and come to reasoned, rational, right judgments. That puts extra pressure on us. There are no pre-arranged conclusions in search of justifications." Wang, whom the *New York Times* described as "one of the UN's most adroit diplomats,"[4] adds that, with regard to "China's diplomatic policy today, I won't say that ideology counts for nothing, but its influence today is far less than in China's pre-reform past."

★ ★ ★

After the tragic events of June 1989, a frost descended on Sino-American relations. Even in 1993, when presidents Jiang Zemin and Bill Clinton met for the first time, they simply talked past each other, and the chill could not be concealed. Further tension erupted in 1995, and again in 1996, when China—angered by what it saw as moves by Taiwanese President Lee Teng-hui toward the bright red line of independence—launched surface-to-surface ballistic missiles into the sea surrounding Taiwan. The U.S. Seventh Fleet, with two aircraft carrier battle groups comprised of 40 warships, responded by patrolling the northern end of the Taiwan Straits.[5]

Former U.S. Secretary of State Henry Kissinger, who met with Jiang Zemin at this time, says that the Chinese leader, whom he knew and admired, wanted "to get the confrontation behind him in a way compatible with Chinese self-respect." During the 1996 crisis, Kissinger recalls, "President Jiang chose a very Chinese way of letting me know that events wouldn't spin out of control. I told him that when I saw Chairman Mao, he said that China can afford to wait 100 more years to resolve the Taiwan situation; I asked Jiang: 'Is that still true?' The president answered, 'No, it's no longer true. That was 24 years ago—now we can only wait 76 more years!'"[6]

The ice was thawed by October 1997, when President Jiang embarked on a landmark eight-day visit to America. Although he had met President Clinton on four prior occasions, the trip marked their first formal head-of-state summit. Despite controversies, its success exceeded expectations.

A positive note was struck early on during a White House tour, when Clinton showed Jiang an original manuscript of Lincoln's Gettysburg Address. The Chinese leader's face lit up: he had memorized these words as a child and quoted them ever since—now he began reading them aloud.

At every stop on his tour—Hawaii, Washington, Philadelphia, New York, Boston, and Los Angeles—Jiang was met by protesters, mainly human rights activists and supporters of Taiwanese and Tibetan independence. But Jiang, who wanted to reach out to the American people, was well-prepared. At his press conference with Clinton, he alluded to the protesters delicately: "I have been immersed in an atmosphere of friendship from the American people," he began. "However, sometimes noises came into my ears." Noting that he was aware "that in the U.S. different views can be expressed, and this is a reflection of democracy," Jiang quoted a Chinese saying—"'to see something once is better than hearing about it a hundred times.'" "I've gained real understanding of this during my current trip," he said.

When Clinton chided China for not tolerating political dissent, Jiang cited "different historic and cultural traditions, different levels of economic development, and different values," and said "It is just natural for our two countries to hold different views on some issues . . . The concepts of democracy and human rights and of freedoms," he averred, "are relative and specific ones, determined by the specific national situation of different countries."

Jiang gamely endured a grueling breakfast encounter with 50 members of Congress, including its harshest, most vociferous China critics. They hit all the hot buttons—human rights, religious freedom, weapons proliferation, harvesting human organs from executed prisoners. Jiang defended China, saying that "never before has Chinese society been as prosperous and open as today." He added that his government intended to "expand democracy . . . and build a socialist country under the rule of law." And he voiced the hope that "more Congress members will visit China."

President Jiang Zemin and President Bill Clinton hold a joint press conference at the White House in Washington, D.C., during Jiang's state visit to the United States, (October 29, 1997; Xinhua News Agency).

From Washington, Jiang made a fleeting stop in Philadelphia, where he spoke at two universities, visited Independence Hall, and met city leaders— plus personal meetings with an old friend and an esteemed teacher (to whom Jiang apologized for not coming sooner). "The city got a taste of the unexpected from Jiang," Philadelphia reporters wrote. "A more Americanized, personable, and English-savvy pol than many . . . were expecting."[7]

Days later, Jiang gave a major address at Harvard University. In an overt rejoinder to President Clinton, who had said China was on "the wrong side of history," he asserted that China's policies were "all based on both reality and history." Switching to English for part of his speech, Jiang praised America for its "pragmatic attitude and creative spirit" and noted that, "in our cause to further open up and achieve modernization, we have spared no efforts in learning from all the fine cultural achievements of the American people." However, he stressed that, just as "sunlight is composed of seven colors, so is our world full of colors and splendor." And, he added, "We should respect and learn from each other."

Jiang took his audience on a tour of Chinese history and culture. He quoted the Daoist philosopher Zhuang Zi on the nature of "limits" (what other national leader refers to calculus in a foreign policy speech?); he spoke of how ancient Chinese astronomy integrated the universe and humanity; of various schools of philosophy, and China's contributions to mathematics, music, and medicine; and of China's many inventions, which, he said, had "changed the face of the world."

He emphasized China's traditions: solidarity and unity; maintaining independence ("After 100 years of struggle," he said, "China has stood up again as a giant"); love for peace ("We will never impose upon others the kind of sufferings we once experienced."); and constantly striving for self-perfection. And he expressed the hope that "younger generations of China and America will understand each other better, learn from each other, enhance the friendship, and strive for a better future."

Not everyone agreed: throughout his speech there was a constant low-level background noise of muffled screams and rants from demonstrators outside the theater. Jiang again stressed that he now had "more specific understanding of American democracy" and added with a smile, "Although I am 71-years-old, my ears still work very well . . . I believe my only approach is to speak even louder."

Before reading out pre-selected audience questions, Ezra Vogel, director of the Fairbank Center for East Asian Research, stressed that "We hope that President Jiang will remember that Harvard is a place where democracy works." The first question, from the Joint Committee for Protesting Jiang Zemin's Visit to Harvard, noted that Jiang had "asked the West not to engage in confrontation but dialogue" and asked: "Why does he refuse dialogue with his own people? Why did the Chinese government order tanks in Tiananmen Square on June 4, 1989, and confront the Chinese people?"

Jiang responded by emphasizing the diversity of China, the difficulties of running such a large country, and the various channels leaders used to learn people's views. Then he added: "It goes without saying that, naturally, we may have shortcomings and even make some mistakes in our work. However," he added, "we have been working on a constant basis to further improve our work."

It was a vague-sounding comment—but it made headlines: Was Jiang hinting that China's actions in Tiananmen might have been "mistakes"? Either way, in the context of the question, his answer seemed to break from the canned rhetoric of the past.

★ ★ ★

Cordial Sino-U.S. relations continued through 1998, when President Clinton made a reciprocal visit to China—speaking to students, attending church, and holding a press conference with President Jiang live on Chinese television. But the following year events took a sudden downturn. The NATO military campaign, led by the U.S. to stop Yugoslavia from ethnic cleansing in Kosovo had already aroused anger in China when, on May 8 1999, disaster struck.

It was a day that Wang Chen, then editor-in-chief of *Guangming Daily*, will never forget. Around 8:00 am he received an urgent call: "Something has happened to our newspaper's two reporters in Yugoslavia." Wang rushed to his office. "Communications were cut off," he recalls. "We had no idea what was happening. Around noon, the vice foreign minister called and told me that there had been a bombing, people had been killed. Soon he called again and said that two of my journalists, Xu Xinghu and Zhu Ying, a married couple, were dead."

A U.S. B-2 stealth bomber had mistakenly bombed the Chinese Embassy in Belgrade, destroying the building and killing Xu, Zhu and another Chinese journalist.

"I was shocked and terribly sad," says Wang Chen. He had worked nightshifts with Xu, who was 31, and knew him well. "Xu was a dedicated, scrupulous young man," he says. "His wife, Zhu Ying, worked in our advertising department and was very pretty. Her father used to be a diplomat and her mother was a teacher. Just before they were sent to Yugoslavia, I'd joked with them: 'You've been married for over a year now; it's high time you had a baby.' Zhu Ying smiled," Wang recalls, "and replied: 'You're sending us to Yugoslavia. We can't have a baby now.' When I knew they were dead," Wang says, "I was grief-stricken, in utter anguish. I shed tears on camera." Wang had to visit Zhu Ying's parents to tell them of her death. "Her mother was devastated and cried inconsolably," he says. "She was jumping as she was crying; I'd never seen that before."

President Jiang Zemin and all seven Politburo Standing members came to *Guangming Daily* offices to offer their condolences. Jiang had responded rapidly: within an hour of the blast he convened an emergency meeting with all relevant leaders. Wang Guangya recalls the delicate balance that needed to be struck.

"China would have to respond sharply," he recalls. "Our sovereignty had been violated and the norms of international law flouted." What's more, he says, "We recognized that this incident would send shock waves through the populace, especially the young people. Students would surely react. The Chinese public would be watching us."

At the same time, according to Wang, Jiang did not want to condemn America excessively and damage relations. "Jiang believed that although China had suffered a great wrong, we shouldn't jeopardize our future by an out-of-proportion response," Wang says. Our biggest worry, he stresses, was "that our own students could overreact."

We all recognized, he recounts, that "the major challenge we faced was not how to deal with the Americans—that we could handle—but how to deal with our citizens, particularly our students, how to prevent counterproductive behavior, how to persuade them not to overreact."

After he had listened to input from everyone at the meeting, Wang recalls, "it was left to President Jiang to weigh the long-term interests of the country against the short-term emotions of the people."

Together China's leaders planned a course of action. They would cut off negotiations on China's entry into the World Trade Organization (WTO), suspend military and arms control talks with Washington, and demand that America compensate China for losses sustained in the attack. Vice President Hu Jintao would make a televised address with two purposes: to express how seriously the Chinese government viewed the incident—and to urge citizens to exercise restraint in their reactions.

As predicted, the Chinese people cast the bombing as a national insult, and virtually everyone assumed that it had been done deliberately. Across China, furious students took to the streets. Angry crowds formed outside the U.S. Embassy in Beijing, where the U.S. ambassador to China, James Sasser, was holed up as a virtual hostage. "Tell the U.S. government the Chinese people are not easy to humiliate," a middle-aged man shouted at a Western reporter. "China is not Kosovo, and it is not Iraq."

It was widely assumed in the West that Chinese leaders were orchestrating and stirring up the protests. Commentators said China's government was using the crisis to promote nationalistic fervor and divert students' attention from domestic problems. Western media, discovering that Party-supported student unions had rented the buses to transport students to the U.S. Embassy, took this as prima-facie proof. Yet while the facts are undisputed—the Party did rent the buses and transport the students—the motivation of China's leaders was, according to insiders, to contain the protests, not to exacerbate them.

Leaders say they decided to take students directly to the embassy district in order to avoid having masses of young people marching across Beijing, drawing workers and ordinary citizens to join their cause, as had happened in 1989 (indeed the sensitive 10th anniversary of June 4 was within weeks). The government certainly didn't want protesting students passing by its headquarters at Zhongnanhai, or heading there directly to vilify their "weak" leaders for not "standing up to America."

Even so, China's leaders underestimated the depth of the people's fury. "At the Foreign Ministry," recalls Wang Guangya, "we received avalanches of biting, hostile criticism. Mountains of letters piled up, our switchboards were jammed, and our ministry's website was almost incapacitated with e-mails. A few," he says, "would have had us declare war on NATO or America, or retaliate with missile attacks against NATO's headquarters."

Jiang Zemin did not escape censure. It was no secret that he and Premier Zhu Rongji believed that good relations with America were necessary (a position with which some of their colleagues, especially Li Peng, disagreed).

To many Chinese, their president seemed inordinately quiet, even reticent, in the face of the American outrage. Public expressions of disgust at Jiang's apparent passivity spread. Not all the protest banners condemned America; some now ridiculed their own leader. One read "Slave of the American Master." Another said, "Jiang Zemin—the Turtle That Pulls in Its Head"—a particularly odious remark in Chinese. To all who remembered Tiananmen Square a decade before, it seemed ironic: then Chinese students had appealed to America for help against their own leaders; now they were lambasting their leaders for being pro-American.

Across China, angry crowds grew more raucous. Students and workers continued hurling rocks and garbage at the U.S. Embassy, smashing the few remaining windows. A college student besieging the embassy insisted, "Even if the government forbids protests, we'll still demonstrate until the Americans give us a good answer."

Jiang Zemin had expected that public anger would peak early and decline quickly. But he now found himself walking a thin line, as he sought to appease an irate public without alienating an apologetic America. He still called for economic progress and social stability.

Moderation, however, was not popular. The Chinese people, long wary of foreign aggression, had the bombing as an egregious affront. At least 90% did not believe NATO's explanation that the bombing had been an accident (a statistic borne out by my conversations with well-educated Chinese. It seemed implausible, they said, that a country as technologically advanced as America could make such a stupid mistake. When I suggested to a senior defense-industry executive, a sophisticated and savvy fellow, that the bombing was an accident—the result of "old maps"—he shot back an instant "impossible," and what had been a friendly conversation turned frosty. My argument, a good one I thought, that the scoop-seeking American press would have long since ferreted out a deliberate plot—if such ever existed—did not cut much ice in China, perhaps because of an inherent skepticism that the press could thwart its own government.)

The Chinese media sought synergy with public anger. Every newspaper devoted multiple pages to the bombings, expressing identical views—often using identical turns of phrase. The headlines screamed "Shock, Outrage, Protest" or "The Bomb Attack Was Premeditated," as the Chinese press spoke with a single stentorian voice. Television programs that normally attacked corruption now vilified America.

To the West, it looked like an orchestrated propaganda campaign; the bombing seemed a handy excuse for Chinese leaders to do what many Westerners feared they wanted to do all along—promote nationalistic aggressiveness. The opposite was true, however—the public was dictating what the media broadcast and published. The headlines and outrage gave the masses precisely what they wanted to read and hear, just as the market-driven press does in the West. Expert opinion that the bombing was intentional only confirmed what most Chinese already believed: that America sought to contain and control China and would stop at nothing to do so.

In this tense state of affairs, the challenge for Jiang Zemin was not only to preserve social stability—it also involved sustaining his personal power. He had to wonder whether his conservative colleagues, perhaps in concert with elements in the military, could turn the rapidly growing anti-American demonstrations against him. Some were now speaking with open nostalgia for Mao Zedong, praising his actions in thwarting the U.S. during the Korean War. "Now everyone is saying Mao was great after all," asserted one army colonel. "Let the world's proletariat unite and smash U.S. imperialism. The embassy attack woke up the Chinese people; it should also wake up Jiang and Zhu."

Jiang now realized that the Party had to take the lead in expressing such nationalism or risk losing control of the volatile situation. (The irony of the situation was not missed by China's leaders. For years Americans had criticized China for not being responsive to its people's wishes. Now, listening to public opinion would mean taking an even stronger anti-American stance.)

Faced with the unnerving prospect of raging protesters on the streets, Jiang moved to channel the outrage rather than oppose it, seeking alignment between protesters and government. State media praised the students. Jiang refused to take a hotline call from President Clinton, who telephoned to offer his apologies.

"I was dumbfounded and deeply upset by the mistake and immediately called Jiang Zemin to apologize," remembered Clinton, who called the tragic bombing "the worst political setback of the [Yugoslav] conflict."[8] But China's leadership had decided that any U.S. apology must be made officially as a nation, not exchanged privately between leaders.

While other Chinese leaders kept a low profile, Vice President Hu Jintao appeared on national television, condemning the bombing as a "criminal act" which violated international law. Hu, the youngest senior leader, sought to encourage students, yet at the same time calm them. He said the Chinese government "firmly supports and protects . . . all legal protest activities," but also added that it would "prevent overreaction." It was the first time most Chinese people had heard Hu speak; he projected a confident, resolute image.

Soon after, at an emotion-laden ceremony, President Jiang welcomed home embassy staff members from Yugoslavia, and conferred the title of "revolutionary martyr" on the three dead journalists, who were buried at the prestigious Babaoshan Revolutionary Cemetery. Jiang praised the Chinese people's indignation, which he said evinced the "great patriotism and cohesive force" of the Chinese nation, and stressed that China "can never be bullied."

Jiang accused America of pursuing "power politics" and, for the first time in years, described America as "hegemonist"—a derogatory term straight out of Cold-War communist lexicons. He said that the U.S. must "make formal apologies, thoroughly investigate the bombing and punish those responsible," warning "otherwise the Chinese people will never let the matter go."

At the same time Jiang asked the Chinese people to channel their rightful ire into building the country's economic strength. He asserted that social stability must be maintained, noting that China had to be "vigilant to the attempts of hostile forces from both home and abroad to create chaos and undermine the socialist modernization drive."

Finally, after a week of tense non-communication, President Jiang accepted a telephone call from President Clinton. During the 30-minute conversation Clinton again expressed his sincere regrets for the tragedy and offered his condolences.

Clinton later recalled: "I apologized again and told him that I was sure he didn't believe I would knowingly attack his embassy. Jiang replied that he knew I wouldn't do that, but said he did believe that there were people in the Pentagon or the CIA who didn't favor my outreach to China and could have rigged the maps intentionally to cause a rift between us. Jiang had a hard time believing that a nation as technologically advanced as we were could make such a mistake." Clinton then mused, "I had a hard time believing it too, but that's what happened."

Clinton promised that the bombing would be investigated and the results revealed. Jiang "took note" of the regrets and the promises—a diplomatic expression that suggested Beijing was finally willing to acknowledge Clinton's repeated apologies. Stating that the protests were spontaneous, Jiang told Clinton that it was up to America to repair damaged ties.

The heat of the crisis began to dissipate the following day when Clinton's apology was featured on the front pages of all the national newspapers. In fact, Clinton had publicly and repeatedly apologized earlier, and had sent a formal letter to Jiang expressing "regret and condolences on behalf of the American people." The delay in reporting the apologies was seen in the West as proof that China's leaders encouraged the violent protests; in truth the outrage had come first from ordinary citizens, not from their leaders. The four-day lapse between the first American apology and the Chinese media's reports, insiders reveal, gave the people a chance to express and dissipate their nationalistic anger. By the time the apology was finally reported, passions had run their course and the population could accept resolution.

The U.S. paid $4.5 million in compensation to the victims, and an additional $28 million to rebuild the Chinese Embassy. Wang Chen, then editor-in-chief of *Guangming Daily*, recalls "I went to Xu Xinghu's hometown and arranged the renovation of his parents' house. They lived in the countryside and led a difficult life. We used around RMB 2 million [$241,000] of U.S. payments to make life a little better for his parents."

In retrospect, the crisis confirmed that China's leaders could no longer control their own people as they had in pre-reform times. China's foreign policy now had to take into account public opinion.

Nevertheless, Western fears that the bombing would set back U.S.-China relations for years and bolster conservative factions in the Party proved misplaced. In fact, Jiang Zemin used the crisis to strengthen his leadership and his reform-minded agenda.

In mid-June, only a month after the bombing, the American side of the story was presented in a complete and relatively balanced manner on CCTV's national news. "Most Chinese people believe the bombing was deliberately planned," said one government adviser confidentially. "We needed time to release that kind of emotion."

Yet Chinese people's attitudes to America remained complex. During the protests at the U.S. Embassy, one undergraduate berated a reporter about America's condescending assertion that its political system should be imposed on all countries. When the reporter asked how long his protest would continue, the young man matter-of-factly replied that he couldn't stay much longer—he had to go home, he explained, to study for his upcoming GRE, the entrance exam for American graduate schools.

Like many peoples, many Chinese aspire to live in ways similar to Americans, even as they resent the power that they believe America holds over them.

★ ★ ★

Less than two years later, the flames of Sino-U.S. tensions were fanned again when, on April 1, 2001, a U.S. Navy EP-3E Aries II surveillance plane collided with a Chinese PLA F-8 fighter jet over the South China Sea. The Chinese plane disintegrated and went down into the ocean. The pilot was seen descending with an open parachute, but was never found and presumed to have perished. The American aircraft sustained damage to a wing and engine, declared an emergency, and landed—without prior permission—at the nearest airstrip, on a military base in China's Hainan Province.

The American crew blamed the Chinese pilot, Wang Wei, for the collision, accusing him of being a "dangerous daredevil" who twice brought his faster aircraft within feet of the EP-3E, before finally striking their propeller with fatal results. The pilot of a second Chinese fighter, however, insisted that the U.S. spy plane had veered, suddenly and deliberately, into the Chinese jet, shredding its tail.

The next day President Bush, barely two months in office, demanded immediate U.S. access to the plane, which Washington said enjoyed "sovereign immunity," and requested that it be returned "without further tampering."

The accident came at an awkward time for President Jiang. He was about to depart for Latin America, where he was seeking political support as well as promoting trade; and Beijing's bid to host the 2008 Olympics would soon be put to a vote.

But public sentiment in China was hostile. Echoing the outcry of two years earlier, ordinary citizens accused Jiang Zemin of being weak: "he doesn't dare fart unless America agrees!" said one young woman; "Chairman Mao would have fought to make the Americans apologize," said a middle-aged man.[9]

Sensing the hardening of popular opinion, Jiang blamed the U.S. and demanded an apology. However Washington insisted the U.S. had "done nothing wrong": "We have nothing to apologize for," said Secretary of State Colin Powell, "we had an emergency."

Once again Jiang was pressured from both sides. Every day the American crew was "detained" was another black mark against China in world opinion, while the lack of a U.S. apology made him seem ever weaker to his own people. From Argentina, he insisted that China "never gives in to any outside pressure on issues of principle related to China's state sovereignty and territorial integrity." Critics abroad speculated that Beijing's Olympics bid could be in jeopardy.

Searching for the smoothest way out of the crisis, Jiang devised a common-sense analogy: "I have visited many countries and seen that it is normal for people to ask forgiveness or say 'excuse me' when they collide in the street," he said. "But the American planes come to the border of our country and do not ask forgiveness. Is this behavior acceptable?"[10]

In the first crack in the hostile atmosphere, U.S. diplomats were permitted to visit the plane's crew and reported them to be in good health. The next day, in a parallel show of goodwill, Colin Powell expressed "regret" for the loss of the missing pilot.

The Chinese Foreign Ministry now conceded that the actual collision had occurred outside Chinese air space, though it stressed that the U.S. plane had subsequently penetrated Chinese territory illegally. In his first conciliatory statement, President Bush expressed his own "regret" over the loss, adding, "Our prayers go out to the pilot and his family." But he still stopped short of making a formal apology.

Jiang Zemin, touring South America, remained measured, suggesting that two such important countries "should find an adequate solution to this problem."

Finally, after more than a week, diplomats worked semantic magic. The U.S. wrote a letter which expressed "sincere regret" over the missing Chinese pilot, said the U.S. was "very sorry" for entering China's air space without permission, and admitted that the landing in Hainan did not have verbal clearance. Unusually, the wording of the letter—agreed after hours of haggling—was negotiated entirely in English, allowing the Chinese what one American diplomat called "a little more wiggle room" in providing their own translation.

China quickly claimed that Washington's double use of the word "sorry" in the letter amounted to an apology, and the next day, Beijing announced that the Americans would be released on "humanitarian grounds"—though the spy plane would have to be disassembled into boxable pieces before it could be taken back home.

The West, in general, appreciated President Jiang's handling of the crisis. *The New York Times*' former Beijing correspondent Nicholas Kristof suggested America was lucky that "Jiang Zemin used his influence to tamp down Chinese populist anti-Americanism." He speculated that another kind of [pre-reform] Chinese leader, "trying to arouse public anger, might have put the American spy plane crew on trial and executed the captain."

While the Chinese media toned down its anti-U.S. rhetoric (two weeks after the collision), many Chinese again berated their leader for backing down. *People's Daily* called on the public to "turn patriotic enthusiasm into strength to build a powerful nation," but Chinese websites were flooded with indignation. One e-mail offered this analogy: "If someone peeps at your wife when she is having a bath and your son goes out to drive that person away but instead he is beaten to death, what would you do?"

Again, the people were welcome to vent their rage, but only within a controlled context and only for a limited amount of time.

★ ★ ★

Five months later, on September 11, 2001, at midnight in Beijing and noon in New York, just hours after the horrific attacks on America, President Jiang Zemin sent an urgent message to President George Bush, expressing "sincere sympathy" to the U.S. government and people, and condolences to the family members of the victims." He was one of the first world leaders to do so.

The next evening Jiang spoke with Bush and pledged, "We are ready to provide all necessary support and assistance to the U.S. side." That same day, at the UN, China voted for the U.S.-sponsored resolution against terrorism, describing the attacks as "an open challenge to the international community as a whole."

Shortly afterwards, China dispatched 32 counterterrorism specialists to the U.S., and provided unprecedented access to China's detailed intelligence about the Taliban and Osama bin Laden's al-Qaeda network. To the surprise of many, Chinese officials handed over a treasure trove of information on international terrorist groups in two publicized meetings and subsequent undisclosed ones.

It was a stunning turnabout in U.S.-China relations. Over the next months, as America planned its counterattack, China raised no objection to the arrival of U.S. forces in Central Asia, and the Chinese military, at America's request, moved listening stations to the Afghanistan border to monitor Taliban and al-Qaeda communications. China also closed its borders with Afghanistan and its longtime friend Pakistan to prevent terrorist leaders from using China as an escape route, and it quietly encouraged Pakistan and Central Asian nations to cooperate with America.

Such proactive behavior was all the more remarkable considering China's policy of not violating national sovereignty. In an unambiguous signal of support, China allowed a U.S. aircraft carrier to stop in Hong Kong en route to attacking Afghanistan.

"The United States is not China's enemy now," one Chinese scholar concluded, "and probably never will be."[11] In a high-level briefing for senior officials, the scholar had offered China a stark choice: the U.S. or Osama bin Laden. "We chose the U.S.," he confided to the *Washington Post*, explaining that while "some Chinese intellectuals and officials reacted gleefully to the attacks," President Jiang realized that China's long-term interests lay with Washington. In return, America seemed willing, at least momentarily, to table its own anxieties about a "China threat" in order to focus on the immediate dangers presented by radical Islam.

To China's leaders, China's cooperation with America had a larger arc. It was as much about the country's international emergence as a great power as about a parochial battle against a common foe. Real-world circumstances—from its economic surge to its successful Olympic bid—were bringing China closer to America and Europe.

★ ★ ★

China's position on North Korea—its close neighbor and long-time socialist ally—has also evolved. For Beijing, it's a matter of natural loyalty, a corollary of pride, to support the regime of strongman Kim Jong-Il, who became North Korea's Dear Leader after the death of his father, Great Leader Kim Il-Sung, in 1994. At the same time, China's leaders began to fear that North Korea could collapse, creating untold collateral damage in China—including a potential flood of millions of refugees.

Worse still, a nuclear North Korea was all negative for China: not only would it threaten world stability—a prerequisite for China's continued economic development—but it might also give Japan—or even Taiwan—occasion, or excuse, to also go nuclear.

Thus in recent years President Hu Jintao has been a consistent supporter of the Six-Party Talks, which have sought to eliminate North Korea's nuclear capacity. Several rounds of talks from 2003 produced little real results—and in October 2006, the rules of the game changed when North Korea detonated a small nuclear device. Supposedly, Beijing was given only 20 minutes' advance notice—and immediately notified Washington.

During the fifth round of talks in February 2007, North Korea finally agreed to shut down its nuclear facilities, in exchange for emergency fuel aid and normalization of relations with America and Japan. Confirming the seriousness of the situation, in June 2008, Vice President Xi Jinping made North Korea his first visit abroad. There were public expressions of harmony—but in fact China wanted progress in ridding North Korea of nuclear weapons. Indeed, Xi explicitly linked the strengthening of cultural and economic ties between China and North Korea to "co-operation in the Six-Party Talks on the DPRK [North Korean] nuclear issue."

And according to China's Vice Foreign Minister Wang Guangya, whereas in the past China "would have come to the traditional conclusion of defending North Korea no matter what, now we can debate the issues, which are complex." North Korea does still have loyal supporters in China, Wang says—but "the fact is that North Korea building a nuclear weapon is not in the interest of China or the world." Wang stresses that "North Korea is like a good friend with bad behavior—we're still good friends but we try to stop the bad behavior. What's good for China," he adds, "is not ideology but practical results."

Yet after many times threatening to renounce its pledges to abandon nuclear ambitions, in April 2009, just hours after the UN imposed sanctions on the authoritarian state for its multi-stage rocket launch, North Korea defied the world by restarting its nuclear facilities to harvest weapons-grade plutonium—and in May it tested its second nuclear weapon, this one more powerful. For China's leaders, North Korea was a migraine.

★ ★ ★

One issue on which China's position remains unwavering, however, is Taiwan—which China asserts is and always has been part of its sovereign territory. No leader of China could ever appear "flexible" on "Taiwainese independence" and expect to remain a leader—the people would not permit it. Over the years, no issue has been a greater source of Sino-U.S. tension.

The replacement of Taiwan President Chen Shui-bian, who was overtly pro-independence, by the Nationalist Party's Ma Ying-jeou in 2008 ushered in a new era of cross-Straits cooperation. Later that year, the two sides, after decades of posturing, implemented the Three Direct Links—postal service, transportation (air flights and shipping) and business links (trade, investment, finance)—a major boost for cross-straits economic ties.

President Hu Jintao marked the 30th anniversary of Deng Xiaoping's Message to the Compatriots in Taiwan by offering a six-point proposal which mainland analysts described as "strategic guiding principles" and which even China's critics recognized as likely to encourage cross-strait harmony and promote normalization of relations. Stressing economic development more than political unification, Hu called for: firm adherence to the "one China" principle; strengthening commercial ties; promoting personnel exchanges; stressing common cultural links between the two sides; allowing Taiwan's "reasonable" participation in global organizations, such as the World Health Organization's annual assembly (a breakthrough since China had long resisted Taiwanese participation in multilateral bodies, particularly those connected to the UN); and negotiating a peace agreement.[12]

Nevertheless, Hu made it clear that China had not moved at all on its basic position that relations between the mainland and Taiwan—whether good or bad—are "purely China's internal affairs," adding: "No foreign country is allowed to interfere."

Moreover, according to Foreign Minister Yang Jiechi, safeguarding national sovereignty and security—by containing Taiwan independence, Tibet independence and East Turkistan separatist activities—is top priority for China's diplomacy. Other areas of focus, especially since 2002, include: maintaining stable relations and strategic dialogues with the major powers—America, Russia, European Union and Japan; expanding cooperation with China's neighbors, notably India, Indonesia, and Kazakhstan, and developing joint exploration of the (disputed) South China Sea; deepening ties with developing countries (aside from links with Africa, China also set up the "China-Arab Cooperation Forum," and expanded relations with Latin America, especially Brazil).

Other key goals include playing an increasingly active role in multilateral diplomacy, and helping to solve global and regional hot issues. China is also focusing on economic diplomacy, promoting regional cooperation and bilateral free-trade—as well as securing foreign energy resources and supporting Chinese enterprises in going abroad. And there is new emphasis on public and cultural diplomacy, aimed at developing worldwide appreciation of Chinese culture, through festivals and other activities abroad, and by establishing "Confucius Institutes" and Chinese cultural centers in many countries.

How China's status in the world has changed! As Yang Jiechi puts it, China's diplomacy is likely to face "unprecedented opportunities—and challenges" in the coming years.

Endnotes

1　Author's meeting with Wang Guangya, New York, September, 2008; whole section
2　*People's Daily* - http://world.people.com.cn/GB/8212/14450/46162/8053694.html.
3　Russell Hsiao, "'Six-Points' Proposition to Taiwan," *China Brief*, January 12, 2009.
4　James Traub, "The World According To China," *The New York Times*, September 3, 2006.
5　Kuhn, *The Man Who Changed China.*
6　Author's meeting with Henry Kissinger, New York, 2002.
7　*Daily News* (Philadelphia), October 31, 1997
8　Bill Clinton, *My Life* (New York: Alfred P. Knopf, 2004), 855.
9　"Communist leaders feel force of the patriotism they nurtured," *The Independent*, April 13, 2001; Calum MacLeod, UPI, April 12, 2001.
10　"Jiang Zemin: Crew Safe and Sound, US Arrogant Conduct Unacceptable," *People's Daily*, April 6, 2001.
11　John Pomfret, "China Sees Interests Tied to U.S.; Change Made Clear In Wake of Sept. 11," *Washington Post*, February 2, 2002.
12　"Taiwan calls for new ties," *Straits Times*, January 2, 2009.

What does Military Reform Mean?

When armed pirates from Somalia operating in the North Arabian Sea attacked and captured merchant ships for ransom, including Chinese ships, the Chinese Navy deployed two destroyers and a supply vessel about 5,000 nautical miles from the mainland to join the international community in protecting commercial shipping. Chinese officials said the operation underscored the need to build a long-range navy capable of protecting national interests.

At around the same time, there were assertions that China would be constructing its own aircraft carriers. A defense spokesman suggested the strategy was as much about China becoming a modern, growing nation, as about any specific military aims. "An aircraft carrier is a symbol of a nation's comprehensive strength," he said.[1]

Observers, however, were struck by the bellicose tone of commentary in the official *Liberation Army Daily*. One general admonished the PLA to abandon the old strategy of "building a peace-oriented army at a time of peace" and to "prepare for battle, fighting wars, and winning wars."

A well-known military analyst declared that "China cannot emerge in the midst of nightingale songs and swallow dances"—a reference to idyllic peace being a fairytale. China, he wrote, needed to "hack out a path through thorns and thistles" in its ascent to great power status. "When a country and a people have reached a critical moment, the armed forces often play the role of pivot and mainstay," he asserted. Reducing international concerns about a "China threat" was apparently not the man's job.

Most mainland Chinese believe that powerful, modern armed forces are necessary to safeguard national sovereignty—the century of invasion and foreign subjugation still resonates in their collective consciousness—and this includes maintaining the country's territorial integrity and assuring ultimate reunification with Taiwan. Mainlanders desire reunification with an emotional depth that surprises foreigners—they view Taiwan, where Chiang

Kai-shek's Nationalists retreated after losing the Civil War in 1949, as the last vestige of foreign plots to fragment China and keep it weak.

The threat of separatism in Tibet or Xinjiang (China's mainly Muslim north-western region) is taken equally seriously. For most Chinese, these are foundational issues of the nation's integrity and dignity—and necessitate a strong military.

★ ★ ★

Commemorating the 80th anniversary of the People's Liberation Army (PLA) on August 1st 2007, President Hu Jintao emphasized the PLA's historic contributions. He highlighted its role in the War of Resistance against Japanese Aggression, stressing that it had defeated "enemies from both within and outside the country," and "effectively destroyed various separatist schemes and sabotage that threaten the national security and unity."

But Hu, also chairman of the Central Military Commission (CMC), emphasized that in the modern era "our people's army has also made important contribution in safeguarding world peace through extensive exchanges with foreign counterparts, active participation in UN peacekeeping missions and international disaster relief operations, and enhanced international counter-terrorism cooperation."

Speaking with 29 foreign navy delegations at celebrations marking the PLA Navy's 60th anniversary (2009), President Hu pledged that "no matter how much China develops," it would never be a threat to other nations.[2] Observing the dramatic "fleet parade" of 25 Chinese naval vessels, including two nuclear-powered submarines capable of launching ballistic missiles far from the country's shores, Hu, dressed formally with dark suit and white gloves, asserted that "For now and in the future, China will not engage in military expansionism or in an arms race."

It was only the fourth naval review since 1949 and the first to invite international ships, including a U.S. destroyer. Military analysts agreed that the rare display of openness reflected China's growing prominence and self-confidence in world affairs.[3] But they disagreed why China chose, as its first nuclear submarines ever displayed publicly, two 20-year-old Long March submarines rather than the newer and more advanced Jin-class submarines. Some suggested that China didn't want to flaunt its top weaponry and appear to be going global as a military power; while others suspected that China was still being opaque and deliberately secretive.

★ ★ ★

The true nature of China's military today is an issue of international concern and debate. The overarching, sacrosanct principle is that the Party controls the army: China's civilian leaders maintain absolute authority over military decisions, which both prevents military adventurism and helps secure the Party's ruling position.

"Upholding the Party's absolute leadership is our army's political superiority and its unchanging quintessence," said General Li Jinai, PLA political commissar and close to CMC Chairman Hu. "We must take the Party's will as our will, the Party's direction as our direction."[4]

In December 2008, Hu introduced "the core values of military personnel," extending to the PLA his "socialist core values system" (essential for building a Harmonious Society).[5] Featured was a 20-character slogan: "being loyal to the Party [uphold the Party's absolute leadership over the armed forces], deeply cherishing the people [share weal and woe with the masses], serving the country [defend the country's sovereignty, security, and territorial integrity as well as the state power], showing devotion to missions [perform the sacred duties of revolutionary soldiers . . . .be proficient in military skills], and upholding honor [cherish and defend the honor of the country, the military, and military members; put honor ahead of one's life . . . and strictly observe military discipline]."

★ ★ ★

As for military reform, the PLA has undergone substantial changes during three decades—and is now smaller and far more modern. According to

Senior Colonel Yang Guihua, Colonel Li Zhen and Senior Colonel Bao Guojun (left to right), General Political Department and Academy of Military Sciences, People's Liberation Army (PLA) (Beijing, October 2008).

Senior Colonel Yang Guihua, director general of War Theory and Strategic Studies at the Academy of Military Sciences, PLA transformation began in 1978 and can be analyzed in four phases.[6]

The first phase of PLA reform, which lasted until 1984, focused on recovering from the damage of the Cultural Revolution and beginning modernization—in particular mechanization. Prior to 1978, the PLA was largely dependent on horses, mules and some motorcycles. The army's size was reduced in 1980, and then again in 1982, from 6 million to 4.3 million soldiers (mostly eliminating non-military units such as engineering). The Central Military Commission, the PLA's highest authority, was founded during this period. And the PLA's approach to war preparedness changed as well, from a strategy of "active defense and enticing the enemy into our territory so as to defeat them" to one of "active defense" alone.

Most significantly, according to Colonel Yang, "our philosophy of war changed from revolution and war to development and peace." He ascribes this decision to Deng Xiaoping and other leaders, who concluded that China's national security environment had changed radically.

The second phase occurred between around 1985 and 1992 when improving relations with major powers (America, Russia, Japan), and a growing conviction that an invasion by foreign forces would not happen, led to a formal decision to shift from preparedness for major warfare (nuclear war), to army construction under peaceful conditions.

China remained vigilant about regional armed conflicts, but leaders downsized the army by another one million, which they viewed as contributing to world peace; it also reflected Deng's conviction that the PLA needed to become more efficient through downsizing and armament enhancements. Group armies and the air corps were formed. General infantry units were reduced and replaced with technical forces. "We didn't see horses and mules anymore!" notes Colonel Yang.

In the third phase of PLA reform, China's leaders discovered that despite PLA efforts to reduce the huge quality gap between itself and the armed forces of developed countries, the gap was, in fact, only widening. "The 1991 Gulf War was the advent of a brand-new form of hi-tech warfare and mode of military operations," says Colonel Yang. "We realized that China had to conduct revolutionary transformation to keep pace." Thus between 1993 and 2004, China progressively embarked on a new strategy to strengthen the army through science and technology.

The PLA was further streamlined, cutting another 500,000 soldiers between 1997 and 1999, and reconstructed to wage hi-tech warfare; notably, from 2000, it started to focus on "information warfare" (as seen in the Kosovo and Iraq wars). Somewhat earlier, beginning in 1990, China began participating in international peacekeeping operations under United Nations auspices. (Since 1990, China has participated in 16 peacekeeping operations.)

In its fourth phase, commencing around 2004 and continuing, PLA reform accelerated. A further cut of 200,000 soldiers brought the PLA down to

2.3 million. Significantly, President Hu called for "Four Innovations"—in military technology, organization, weaponry, and management—with the objective of building an "informationized army so as to win information wars."

At the same time, the PLA increased its international cooperation. China has participated in anti-terror exercises with Russia, Pakistan, and the central Asian member countries of the Shanghai Cooperation Organization; in search-and-rescue exercises with France, Britain, and Australia; and in military exercises with various countries. PLA personnel now visit other countries and go abroad for advanced study. "Such military exchanges enhance mutual understanding and trust," says a PLA officer who earned a master's degree in the UK.

In addition, under directives from China's civilian leaders, the PLA is developing strategies for an enlarged mandate, called "historic missions for the new stage in the new century."[7] This includes not only international peacekeeping, but also "non-traditional security" operations such as anti-terrorism (and anti-separatism), disaster relief (earthquakes and floods), economic security (protecting resources), public health intervention (quarantines), and information security (cybercrimes).

Other duties, categorized in China's 2008 Defense White Paper as "military operations other than war," include anti-piracy patrols, national and local construction, environmental protection, social support, and controlling social disturbances.[8]

Such activities are part of the PLA's tradition. In the 1950s it established construction regiments with 400,000 troops, and since the mid-1980s it has participated in thousands of projects, from building canals and roads, to energy plants, water conservancies, and installing long-distance optical cables. PLA units also handle tasks in landscape engineering, curbing environmental pollution, local construction, building small hydropower stations and Project Hope schools in the countryside, and providing poverty relief.

Fighting disasters has also long been part of the army's tradition: Tangshan Earthquake in 1976; forest fire in northeast China in 1987; floods of 1988 and 1998; and paralyzing snowstorm and devastating Sichuan earthquake of 2008.

Underreported in the West, the PLA in recent years has devoted more attention to the well-being of its soldiers. Colonel Yang stresses that "It is glorious for soldiers to serve their country—but we also need to ensure that they can survive in society when they conclude their military service, which is especially important for young recruits." Soldiers are offered training to help them develop commercial skills, he says, along with assistance for "their personal development and even their families." In the past, says Colonel Yang, the army neglected the psychological support of soldiers. Today, he notes, "all units above the regiment level have psychologists in their health departments. Moreover, we train grassroots officers in psychological methods to help solve soldiers' psychological problems."

★ ★ ★

The reform of China's military faced its gravest test in the late 1990s—and it had nothing to do with warfare. Since the mid 1980s, the military had become increasingly involved in commercial activities. Begun innocently enough to supplement dwindling budgets, PLA business interests had become a world of their own, mushrooming into vast networks of thousands of loosely connected enterprises and companies. These included hotels, nightclubs, karaoke bars and golf courses, as well as pharmaceutical firms, cellular phone networks, electronics distributors, stock brokerages and even cosmetics suppliers. The military owned two of the 12 teams in China's professional basketball league.

As many as a million enlisted soldiers—almost a third of China's armed forces—and 70% of PLA's facilities were said to be involved in commercial work. And some of the military's business activities were not-exactly legal. Smuggling by military-related enterprises cost China between $12-25 billion per year in unpaid duties. In some cities, army (or police) companies distributed illegal satellite TV dishes. Rogue PLA elements sold pirated music, movies and software.

To President Jiang Zemin, who was also chairman of the Central Military Commission, PLA commercialism was disruptive and debilitating for two reasons: they diverted the army's focus away from defense, and they increased the army's independence of civilian control. At best, they entailed conflicts of interest, bred corruption, and brought the PLA into competition with civilians. Moreover, they were insidiously corrosive of the military's ability to defend the nation. As Jiang told General Xiong Guankai, deputy chief of the General Staff, "An army under the threat of corruption will not be best able to defend the country."[9]

Still, Jiang had to make sure that he had the support of PLA leadership before taking action. In July 1998, acting in his capacity as CMC chairman, Jiang ordered that "Companies operated by units under the military and armed police forces must earnestly conduct housecleaning, and shall, without exception, no longer engage in commercial activities, effective immediately." The army, he said, should be supported by national defense expenditures.

According to General Xiong, the decision took "vision, bravery, and guts." Many influential people stood to lose a great deal of money and power from the policy change. Jiang, who as a non-military man had worked for years to build support and loyalty within the military, was now risking his credibility.

There was opposition. Some senior generals were concerned that "accounting and inspection" regimens would upset army morale—and some Politburo members were said to harbor doubts about the decision, fearing disorder in the military. Jiang compromised some, withdrawing his call for investigating the army's past activities—though he continued to insist on separating the military from commerce. And by late 1998, the government and the military had largely agreed to the terms of the separation.

General Fu Quanyou, chief of the General Staff, called on "every unit and every cadre" to implement the decree "without conditions." In the end the transition progressed relatively smoothly: "Since the army is a military organization and used to obeying orders rapidly, President Jiang's policy could be implemented much faster than it could in the Party or the government," noted General Xiong. Another senior officer said the decision was eventually "supported by the vast majority of the PLA: we recognized that operating businesses was a huge distraction," adding "the army had no experience at doing business and was not very good at it—many military companies were losing money." (One five-star hotel was always full and never profitable; owned by the military it gave away too many freebies.)

* * *

On orders of Mao Zedong in the 1950-60s, China's defense industries were built largely in remote, inland, often mountainous regions—Mao's theory being to safeguard China's nascent military manufacturing from anticipated attacks from the Soviet Union or United States. With the introduction of "smart bombs," witnessed in real-time operations on international television during the first Iraq War (1991), and then brought home shockingly after the U.S. bombing of the Chinese Embassy in Yugoslavia (1999), Chinese leaders realized that the old notion that inaccessible geography could protect China was meaningless in the modern world. What's worse, a defense-industry executive told me, "In converting military factories to civilian uses, we face terrible disadvantages due to the difficult access, poor roads, and long distances—the legacy of this anachronistic theory."

Other defense-industry traditions were also outdated. "We used to think that China's weapons systems production needed to be vertically integrated, from mining the iron ore and making the steel to designing the systems and producing the machinery," the defense executive said. "But when we visited foreign defense contractors, we were surprised to find how specialized they were—and how small some were—but with technologies and efficiencies much higher than ours." Nonetheless, he added with pride, "in some military categories, we have achieved world-class capabilities, such as tanks (Type 99), mobile artillery and short-range ground-to-ground rockets."

Around 1999, China's monopolistic defense industries were broken into independent units with the expectation that market competition would generate better technologies and higher efficiencies. "This was silly," the defense industry executive remarked, "it only fragmented technologies and generated redundancies. We in the industry knew that the split-apart 'companies', particularly in aerospace, would have to be put back together—which ten years later was just what happened when China Aviation Industry Corp [AVIC] I and II were re-merged in 2008." In the interim decade, he added, "no one knows how much resources were wasted. Now our leaders are making a similar mistake by creating a new company to build civilian jumbo aircraft. Military and civilian aircraft use the same technologies and even the same parts," he stressed. "Our leaders don't seem to realize that Mercedes-Benz makes good military vehicles."

"Boeing advised China's aviation industry to separate our military and civilian businesses," the executive continued, "and when we didn't agree Boeing sought to convince China's senior leaders that only if we segregated civilian aerospace businesses from their military counterparts could Boeing be permitted to transfer technology to us. But we felt that Boeing, which itself had both military and civilian businesses, wanted AVIC to waste resources, so we'd never be an international competitor."

★ ★ ★

The changes in the PLA were highlighted by the U.S. Department of Defense in its 2008 Annual Report to Congress on "The Military Power of the People's Republic of China." The PLA, the report said, "is pursuing comprehensive transformation from a mass army designed for protracted wars of attrition on its territory to one capable of fighting and winning short duration, high-intensity conflicts along its periphery against high-tech adversaries—an approach that China refers to as preparing for 'local wars under conditions of informatization.'"[10]

Driving PLA modernization, the report stated, were a set of tactical and strategic contingencies: shorter-term concerns about Taiwan and possible tactical consequences in the Taiwan Strait, and longer-term concerns about possible strategic conflicts over resources or disputed territories.

China's rapid rise as a regional power with growing global influence was, the report said, "an important element in today's strategic landscape." It stressed that the United States "welcomes the rise of a stable, peaceful, and prosperous China." But it also raised concerns that "much uncertainty surrounds China's future course, in particular in the area of its expanding military power and how that power might be used."

For the moment, it concluded, "China's ability to sustain military power at a distance remains limited," but it suggested China was the country with "the greatest potential to compete militarily with the United States and field disruptive military technologies that could over time offset traditional U.S. military advantages."

The heightened pace and broader scope of China's military transformation in recent years was said to be fueled by "acquisition of advanced foreign [mainly Russian] weapons, continued high rates of investment in its domestic defense and science and technology industries, and far-reaching organizational and doctrinal reforms of the armed forces." It specified China's modernized nuclear force with new DF-31 and DF-31A intercontinental-range missiles which enhanced "China's strategic strike capabilities;" and China's emergent "anti-access/area-denial capabilities," including advanced cruise missiles, medium-range ballistic missiles, anti-ship ballistic missiles [targeting aircraft carriers], and the 2007 successful test of a direct-ascent, anti-satellite weapon. The extension of China's military capabilities into space and cyber-space were noted. And in citing China's cyberwarfare capabilities, the Pentagon reported that U.S. government computers were the target of "intrusions that appear to have originated" from China, although there was no evidence the military was involved. (The PLA has set the goal of "winning informationized wars by the mid-21st century."[11])

The Defense Department report expressed discomfort at what it said were actions by China "that appear inconsistent with its declaratory [peaceful] policies," and "the lack of transparency in China's military and security affairs." These, it said, posed "risks to stability by increasing the potential for misunderstanding and miscalculation," which could lead to unintended conflict. And in an apparent hint at some kind of new arms race, the report concluded that: "This situation will naturally and understandably lead to hedging against the unknown."

And the report also warned that "China's leaders may overestimate the proficiency of their forces by assuming that new systems are fully operational, adeptly operated, adequately supplied and maintained, and well integrated with existing or other new capabilities." Such overestimations and "misperceptions" it said, "could lead to miscalculation or crisis."

★ ★ ★

In fact, numerous published articles in the Chinese press, civilian and military, suggest that Chinese leadership is well aware of PLA strengths—and weaknesses, especially in relation to American military forces.[12] Lt. Col. Dennis Blasko, a former U.S. defense attaché in Beijing, has noted that official Chinese publications have stated on more than 20 occasions (2006-2008) that "the level of our modernization is incompatible with the demands of winning a local war under informatization conditions and our military capability is incompatible with the demands of carrying out the army's historic missions." Specifically, this referred to personnel, training, logistics, and comparative technology levels.

Funding is also a problem. *Liberation Army Daily* suggested (2006) that "the contradiction between the needs of military modernization construction and the short supply of funds will exist for the long run."[13]

China's military budget is a topic of interest internationally, especially for those concerned about a looming "China theat." Since 1998, the Chinese defense budget, as officially announced, has increased more than four-fold. But according to Colonel Yang Guihua, much of the PLA's annual double-digit growth has been "compensatory," making up for years of substandard investment to provide proper living conditions for soldiers— new barracks, new uniforms, upgraded salaries, and better food. (Experts at the Academy of Military Sciences argue that during the first decade of reform, 1978-1988, military spending actually suffered negative growth, because China had to concentrate on economic development; in the second decade, 1988-1998, military budgets were about flat. Now, with China's economic strength increasing, they say, military budgets are "catching up," after years of neglect.) Moreover, Colonel Yang insists that "PLA budgetary growth is in fact slower than the growth in national fiscal spending."

"We cannot allow our soldiers to continue to suffer," says Colonel Yang. He recalls the late 1980s, when he was stationed in China's northeast (Manchuria), where the winters were bitterly cold: most of the barracks had no heating, and the only warmth came from coal fires. "Showering was impossible because of the ice," he says. Life on border patrols was even worse: "A company under my command lived in rooms constructed with dried mud bricks," Colonel Yang adds. "The bottom halves of our rooms were dug into the ground so as to provide some insulation. In the middle was a large oil-barrel-turned-stove in which we burned wood—we didn't even have coal. More than 20 soldiers huddled in one room to maintain warmth. Border patrols were on horseback."

Real growth in military budgets, however, escalated rapidly after 1995 when China became increasingly concerned about "Taiwan independence." "We had to speed up PLA development in order to safeguard national sovereignty," states one senior officer. Soldiers now have computers and communications equipment. Training exercises have been upgraded in speed and realism, including larger, coordinated, multi-service maneuvers and live-fire operations.

Yet in response to the Western criticism that China's true military budgets exceed published budgets—possibly by far—one officer says: "Our military spending is 1/20 of that of the U.S. We have to use it to support 2.3 million soldiers and much-needed infrastructure improvement. Furthermore, the total annual PLA budget is RMB 300 billion, which is not very much when you convert it into dollars [less than $45 billion]. How many planes or ships do you think we can buy?" he asks.

"Our budget is approved every year," adds another PLA officer, "and we cannot hide or change it," adding, "Maybe the only thing we don't declare is the money parents send to their soldier sons to buy food."

Still, he notes, "if there is no trust, no one will believe us no matter what we say."

★ ★ ★

China leaders do seem to have a realistic appraisal of their country's relative military strength. In his 2007 Army Day address, President Hu Jintao acknowledged that China is still not up to leading developed nations in state-of-the-art science and technology.[14] There is no question, however, that China is determined to raise its level, and build a very strong military. For China's leaders, this is non-negotiable. The focus is on high-tech weapons, information warfare, and elite, mobile forces that can respond to diverse national security emergencies.

As for fighting wars, Hu was authoritative and confident, but not belliger-
ent or cocky. He said that the PLA must "effectively manage crises, uphold
peace and forestall war, and win the war should it occur." Informatization,
he said, would help "ensure that our armed forces are capable of winning
warfare in the information age."

Chinese officials generally emphasize that the nation's strategy is a defensive one. No other nuclear state in the world, they assert, has announced
publicly that it wouldn't be the first to use nuclear weapons. Other than participating in UN peacekeeping operations, they claim, China hasn't stationed
a single soldier on foreign soil. The Great Wall, they say, symbolizes China's
historic defensive policy.

When pressed about why China is developing a "blue-water navy," which
by design projects power far beyond one's own borders, one PLA officer
emphasizes that "we still adhere to the coastal defense strategy [set in the late
1980s]. We'll not compete with the U.S. or other countries for hegemonic sea
power, and this policy would continue to be true even if we were strong. We
support cooperative sea power." Some Western countries, he says, question
China's motives as "an excuse to develop their own military forces." (What
is left unsaid, however, is the conviction that, should Taiwan declare independence, the PLA Navy would need the capability to attack and invade the
"renegade" island across the 112-mile-wide strait.)

And what about that aircraft carrier, perhaps several of them, on the
drawing boards? According to Chinese Defense Minister Liang Guanglie,
"China will not remain the world's only major country without an aircraft
carrier." Come what may, China's leaders believe that the nation must master the technical and logistical demands of the most sophisticated modern
weaponry. The public is supportive. A poll of 20,000 Chinese netizens had
87% affirming that "China has long been capable of building aircraft carriers
but has been waiting for the right time to manufacture them."[15]

Nevertheless, China's leaders are unlikely to make the futile mistake of
the former Soviet Union, and bankrupt their economy in a vain and hopeless attempt to achieve parity with the U.S. They will keep a credible nuclear
arsenal with first-strike survivability as ultimate protection, and they will seek
to learn the lessons of asymmetric warfare. They believe that the best way to
avoid war is to be prepared to fight and win wars. And they also believe,
quietly, that the long future is on their side.

Endnotes

1 Willy Lam, "China Flaunts Growing Naval Capabilities," *China Brief,* January 12, 2009;
   whole section.
2 "Parade Marks 60 Years of Chinese Navy," Xinhua, April 23, 2009; "Spectacle at sea,"
   China Daily, April 24, 2009.
3 Jane Macartney, *The Times,* April 23, 2009.

4 Willy Lam, "PLA's 'Absolute Loyalty' to the Party in Doubt," *China Brief*, Vol. IX, Issue 9, April 30, 2009.

5 James Mulvenon, "Hu Jintao and the "Core Values of Military Personnel," *China Leadership Monitor*, No. 28 (Spring 2009).

6 Author's meeting with Yang Guihua, Beijing, October 2008.

7 Dennis J. Blasko, "The Pentagon-PLA Disconnect: China's Self Assessments of Its Military Capabilities," *China Brief*, Volume 8, Issue 14 (July 3, 2008).

8 Cynthia A. Watson, "The Chinese Armed Forces and Non-Traditional Missions: A Growing Tool of Statecraft," *China Brief*, Vol. IX, Issue 4; 2.20.2009.

9 Author's meeting with Xiong Guankai, Beijing, 2002.

10 Military Power of the People's Republic of China 2008, Annual Report to Congress, U.S. Department of Defense.

11 Blasko, *China Brief*, whole section.

12 Ibid.

13 Ibid. Jiefangjun Bao, August 8, 2006.

14 "Hu urges sci-tech progress for enhancing combat capabilities," Xinhua, August 1, 2007.

15 Cui Xiaohua, "Aircraft carriers needed: Minister," *China Daily*, March 24, 2009.

Telling China's Story to the World

In 2009, Politburo member Liu Yunshan, CPC Publicity head and directly responsible for China's media, said it was now "an urgent strategic task for China to make our communication capability match our international status. In this modern era, whoever gains the advanced communication skills and the powerful communication capability, and whose culture and value is more widely spread, is able to more effectively influence the world."[1]

China's leaders recognize the economic and political exigency of China's image, and they believe that the West—Western media in particular—at best oversimplifies and at worst deliberately distorts. Minister Liu promised China would raise the strength of its media, domestically and internationally.

When Wang Chen became minister of the State Council Information Office (SCIO) in 2008, he set new targets. These included: building an information-release system of press conferences and spokesmen; facilitating access and services for foreign journalists; enhancing international cultural exchanges; increasing publication of China-related books and magazines; regulating the Internet for "healthy and constructive growth" by blocking pornographic and other objectionable sites; and boosting Tibet-related communications.

Mediawise, China was considering multibillion-dollar moves to enhance its worldwide presence and influence. These included China Central Television's (CCTV) international channels in Arabic and Russian (augmenting English, French and Spanish); upgrading news bureaus (*People's Daily's* 72 domestic and foreign bureaus; Xinhua News Agency would double its bureaus to 180); and establishing a global, 24-hour, English-language satellite news channel (like Qatar's Al-Jazerra or even CNN and the BBC), run by Xinhua.

CCTV President Jiao Li said that, in comparison to Western media, Chinese media was relatively weak, well below China's relatively strong position in economics and international affairs. Soon after taking office, Jiao, who

Politburo member Liu Yunshan (center), head of the CPC Publicity Department, and Wang Chen (right), minister of State Council Information Office (Beijing, January 2009).

Jiao Li, president of China Central Television (Beijing, May 2009).

had been Publicity vice minister (and, earlier, Publicity chief of Liaoning Province where he pioneered media reform), set the ambitious goal for CCTV not only to continue its wide-ranging domestic growth—including revamping its news broadcasts—but also to develop innovatively as an international media company. "China must compete confidently in the global marketplace of ideas," Jiao said.

"China's voice in the world is still small, and international understanding of China is still limited," says former SCIO Minister Zhao Qizheng (1998-2005). He gives an example: "When I was in Vienna and some young people saw I was Chinese, they all crouched down and put their hands into a kung fu position." Zhao gives a wry smile: "Foreigners learn about China through martial arts films!" he says. "We have to do better!"

Zhao criticizes "sensationalized reporting about human rights in China" in the Western media. Every year, he notes, the U.S. State Department issues its "Country Reports on Human Rights Practices" which, he says, "criticizes the human rights situations in over 100 countries but never in America itself." China's human rights failings are emphasized, Zhao notes, but the content is "mostly untrue. We have problems, sure," he says, "but we are making progress every year." In response, China now issues its own White Paper on domestic human rights—and another reciprocal report on the "Human Rights Record of the United States." "We cannot always concede the high ground of human rights protection to the U.S." Zhao argues.

"There is a gap between how we Chinese see ourselves and how others see us," says former SCIO Minister Cai Wu (2005-2008). Cai believes that "The American media is mostly biased about China, presenting only our problems, and often in a biased way." In contrast, he says, "The U.S. is featured frequently in the Chinese media and the reports are largely objective and positive. We know the American political system, economic situation, and social life. But it's not reciprocal. Imbalances in mutual knowledge limit mutual understanding"[2]

Many of China's leaders—including the three most recent information ministers (each of whom I know)—concentrate on this "gulf of understanding" which exists between China and the West. Indeed, several have asked me to explain frankly why China's image was not good in the eyes of many Americans. I've offered a list of reasons, which, I said, heightened American concerns that China was a competitor and perhaps an adversary. Everyone recognizes that countries act in their own best interest, I began, but many Americans believe that China does so even when helping themselves hurts others.

The specific perceptions I described follow: China is an economic predator, using cheap, exploited labor to undercut prices and take American jobs, keeping its currency artificially low to eliminate competition; China supports energy-rich, rogue regimes to the detriment of international security (because it wants access to their resources and sells them weapons to weaken America); China is a repressive society, with a harsh judicial system and no press freedoms; China is a robotic society with automaton-like officials parroting the same phrases and concerned only with strengthening the nation not helping the people; and China has expansionist ambitions to extend power beyond its borders.

Chinese officials tend to respond by emphasizing national differences, which they believe hinder mutual understanding. Government ideas for changing foreign perceptions have sometimes betrayed a certain naivety. (For example, a proposal to launch a commercial magazine in America with the editorial purpose of improving China's image would be, I counseled, counterproductive—though a clearly promotional magazine might be fine.)

Sometimes, however, criticisms spur self-critical reflection. Cai Wu acknowledges that "Part of the problem is our fault. We Chinese need to learn how to communicate with foreigners so as to introduce our real situation," he says.

Cai outlines what he sees as cultural obstacles to communication: Westerners, he suggests, tend to look at issues "through specific examples and cases." Chinese officials, he says, tend to discuss issues "in a more abstract, general and theoretical manner"—in part because cultural attitudes incline them to be indirect, but also because of "the influence of the old political system." Thus, he notes, "foreigners think Chinese news reports and speeches are filled with 'clichés and empty talk',"—programmed and robotic—and may see Chinese people as evasive or deceitful. Cai also suggests that Chinese officials avoid going into too much detail because "they believe it may make them appear 'pompous'!" Chinese people, on the other hand, "may see Americans as haughty and arrogant."

What's more, Cai adds, "Westerners tend to focus on individuals when studying social development, while the Chinese, by tradition, tend to focus on organizations and institutions," and believe that the needs of society as a whole are more important than the ideals of individual human rights. "We must learn to tell stories of people's lives," Cai advises.

Several leaders also suggest that Chinese officials are usually not adept at using humor. Self-deprecating banter or taking a light-hearted approach to serious issues feels unnatural to many, especially those of the older generation. Cai notes too that Chinese officials have been conditioned to present a "dour countenance" by a political system which, in the past, was driven by fear—where a single mistake could cost an official his job, if not his freedom. Thus, Cai suggests, Chinese leaders may appear more stiff, impersonal, and doctrinaire than they really are. (Current officials confide that under President Hu, there are greater tolerances: mistakes don't end careers, risks can be taken.)

Increasingly, senior Chinese officials have come to recognize that greater openness is the best policy. "We must tell the truth," says Zhao Qizheng; "if we don't, others will." Cai Wu says "We shouldn't beautify or belittle ourselves. Just stay truthful." And many cite Deng Xiaoping's maxim: "We can never boast; the more developed we become, the more modest we should be."

Information Minister Wang Chen suggests the following practical action: release authoritative information as early as possible, or else the rumor mill will start to whirl (e.g., dangerous products); strengthen communication with foreign mainstream media, by inviting more executives, editors, journalists, and hosts to China; enhance capabilities of China's own media; expand cross-cultural activities with other countries; and, Wang says, on issues which generate negative coverage, such as human rights, democracy, or religious affairs, China should present the positives, such as new human rights laws.

★ ★ ★

China's international image was put to the test in 2008. In April, as China looked forward to the Olympics, the Olympic torch relay was disrupted in several countries by large protests and even attacks, triggered by what the West perceived to be China's repression of recent protests in Tibet and which China said were instigated by errors and bias in Western media coverage.

Leng Rong, head of the CPC Party Literature Research Center and an old friend, told me soon afterwards that the protests in the West reflected a broader issue: "It's a battle of core interests," he said. "The rise of China, a socialist country, upsets the world balance of power." It was, said Leng, "a kind of clash of civilizations [as per Samuel Huntington]"—though he quickly added: "but it shouldn't have to be."

Leng suggested, in fact, that China "shouldn't take these kinds of problems too seriously." The torch relay protests, he said, "didn't scare us at all. We'll surely turn this page. It won't affect how we interact with other countries." However, he said, the protests were a reminder that "we have to improve our external publicity"—noting that "one of the Dalai Lama's significant advantages is that he is fluent in English . . . understands Western values and culture," and is thus "easy to communicate with." This, Leng said, "is China's weak spot."

According to Press-and-Publication Minister Liu Binjie, China learned lessons from these events. After the riots in Lhasa, he said, "It was a mistake to forbid foreign journalists from entering Tibet as soon as possible—this caused misunderstanding across the world. Even though we made great effort to clarify the facts and tell the truth," he adds, "we failed to get the right message across—[because] we failed to introduce transparency immediately. Even several weeks after the riot, we still restricted foreign journalists. Since they didn't understand what was happening in Tibet, the rumor mill worked overtime."

At the time, Liu Binjie was abroad, accompanying a senior Chinese leader. "When we compared notes with our foreign peers," he recalls, "we discovered that they had only twisted information and were clueless about the truth. We realized the sore need for further opening-up . . . . It was a major lesson learned."

Soon after, when the Sichuan earthquake took place, the Chinese government took the opposite approach, opening the area to foreign reporters.

Publicity Minister Liu Yunshan notes that at one stage some foreign media were evacuated from the quake area—but he stresses that this was "out of fear that 'quake-lakes' which had built up in the area could rupture, or that epidemics caused by decomposing corpses buried under the rubble could break out." From those dangerous places, he says, "We evacuated not only journalists, but also locals—we weren't covering up; we were responsible for everyone's safety."

With the more open approach, according to Liu Binjie, "the international coverage of the earthquake was accurate. Why did foreigners trust China on the earthquake but not on the Tibet riot?" he asks. "Transparency! If we had been open and allowed foreign journalists into Tibet and report on the riot first hand, most of them would have been able to discern right from wrong." Liu's motto, he says, is "Trust comes from transparency."

As noted earlier, a sign that China was serious about putting such ideas into practice came shortly after the conclusion of the Olympic Games, when the government announced that foreign journalists accredited in China would still be allowed to travel to different parts of the country without seeking permission in advance, as they had had to do before 2007. And Minister Liu Yunshan stresses that "We want more journalists to visit China, not less."

A defining test came in 2009 when brutal clashes between Uyghur Muslims and Han Chinese resulted in widespread ethnic bloodshed in Xinjiang Province, particularly in its capital, Urumqi. Literally the next day, SCIO Minister Wang Chen arranged for foreign and Chinese journalists to inspect the riot-torn areas. So fresh was the violence that hundreds of Uyghur protesters crashed the state-sponsored tour, and, while journalists watched, smashed the windshield of a police car.[3]

Reflecting back one month after the riots, Minister Wang reported that a total of 309 foreign journalists representing 147 news organizations from 28 countries went to Xinjiang, and that the SCIO held seven press conferences and provided substantial logistical support, including assuring the personal safety of journalists. (Some Japanese journalists were concerned that Uyghurs might mistake them for Hans and some European journalists were concerned that Hans might mistake them for Uyghurs!)

Wang summarized China's approach to the media with three points. First, stick to openness and transparency. "China is progressing in building our democracy," Wang said. "We are more self-confident, tolerant and open" —adding (with a smile) "….It's anyway impossible to cover up." Second, trust the power of truth. "The most convincing evidence is truth; only truth can persuade," Wang stressed. "One cannot 'tailor' truth to suit one's will." Third, truth must be released as soon as possible. "The only way we can get our story picked up is to tell the truth and tell it rapidly," he stated. "Western media is much stronger than China media and so for us to have a larger say in world opinion, to become a source of facts and a resource for reporting, we must publish our account quickly." (Note: The riots occurred on July

5, 2009. At 9:00 pm that same day, Xinhua released its first news bulletin, almost an hour before the international wire services. At 9:00 am the next morning, July 6, the State Council Information Office had a provisional media center in operation, and a few hours later, at 12:30 pm, they held the first press conference.)

Wang noted that even though some journalists filed stories that he said were untrue, he still insisted that "China still needed to be open and transparent." Minister Wang disputed accusations that "China's ethnic policy of 'autonomous regions' was a failure," and he cited as evidence China's substantial material support for minorities. As for "demolishing Uyghur homes and undermining Uyghur culture," Wang said that some buildings were razed "as a matter of public safety because they were old and dangerous in a region prone to earthquakes and fires." And as for the searing charge by Turkish Prime Minister Tayyip Erdogan that China's response to the riots was "a kind of genocide," Minister Wang calmly referenced Turkey's history of genocide against Armenians and Kurds. Though saddened by the tragic events in Urumqi, Wang was proud of China's new openness.

Perhaps the coolest high-level Chinese response to foreign criticism—in this case the Olympic torch relay protests—came from Vice President Xi Jinping. Xi was visiting Qatar at the time and told a group of Hong Kong reporters traveling with him, "We cannot worry too much whether people like the fact that Beijing is hosting the Olympics. The world is a big bustling place made up of all sorts of people and that's why it's so colorful. It's like a huge bird cage where all kinds of birds coexist. If you try to drive away the ones making the most noise, the cage would no longer be a bustling place and you would lose that wonderful variety and color. The key is to mind our own business well."[4]

If relaxed, self-assurance in response to controversy reflects how China's next-generation leaders think, this augurs well for the future.

★ ★ ★

China's leaders have at times broken through the stereotyped image of faceless, rigid bureaucrats. One notable occasion came in September 2000, during the UN Millennium Summit, the largest gathering of world leaders in history, when the leaders of the five permanent members of the UN Security Council met for the first time. President Jiang Zemin gave a short address to the UN General Assembly, focusing on safeguarding peace, promoting economic development, establishing a new world order, and strengthening the UN. And to coincide with Jiang's visit to New York, a series of events promoting Chinese culture were held.[5] Included were concerts, art exhibitions, and—the crowd favorite—fashion shows: pencil-thin Chinese supermodels modeling avant-garde gowns followed by clusters of elaborate and exotic costumes portraying China's numerous minority groups.

But truly groundbreaking was the appearance by President Jiang on CBS's *60 Minutes*—America's highest-rated television news magazine. The idea,

President Jiang Zemin (center) with four other heads of state at the United Nations Millennium Summit in New York; left to right: U.K. Prime Minister Tony Blair, U.S. President Bill Clinton, China President Jiang Zemin, French President Jacques Chirac and Russian President Vladimir Putin (September 2000).

suggested by Information Minister Zhao Qizheng, was a bold and risky one: the interviewer was the notoriously combative Mike Wallace and there were no restrictions—Wallace would choose all questions and select all footage.

It was a gesture of unprecedented openness for a Chinese leader. In a first for Western television, the interview was conducted at the seaside resort of Beidaihe, where China's senior leaders once planned the nation's business each summer. Jiang Zemin not only took questions on sensitive subjects, he also tried to answer some of them in English. (Wallace stressed in his introduction that he had only agreed to do the interview if Jiang would be "willing to level with us"—adding, in a tone of apparent surprise, ". . . and he was.")

On the embassy bombing in Belgrade the previous year, Jiang maneuvered deftly between not alienating the American public and not contradicting the Party line. Asked whether he still thought the bombing had been intentional, he replied: "I can only put it the other way round. The United States is a country that possesses technology at a very high level. Therefore, up to the present, the U.S. explanation of 'bombing by mistake' is not convincing."

Jiang also stressed his own government's role—not in fomenting the protests that followed, as many Americans believed, but in controlling them: "We guided the anger of over 1.2 billion people onto the track of reason," he said. "This was not at all easy."

President Jiang Zemin meets American business leaders at Lincoln Center in New York prior to a concert by the China National Traditional Orchestra. Left to right: Information Minister Zhao Qizheng, President Jiang, Culture Minister Sun Jiazheng, Chinachem Chairwoman Nina Kung Wang, and Robert Lawrence Kuhn (September 9, 2000; Xinhua News Agency).

Jiang seemed to enjoy the give-and-take. He stressed he wanted "mutual friendship and understanding," and a "constructive strategic partnership" between China and America. But when Wallace asked whether he agreed with a Chinese newspaper which had described America as a "threat to world peace," Jiang responded that "I do not like to use too much harsh language," but noted that America's economic and technology development were so advanced that they put the U.S. in an "advantageous position"—as a result, he added, "you often may take an attitude of not treating other countries very equally. . . . Those in power in the United States," he said, "are perhaps tinged with hegemony and power politics."

At the same time, Jiang displayed unexpected understanding that while China can be a convenient target in American election campaigns, American presidents, once in office, tend to recognize the importance of mutual respect and good relations.

President Jiang Zemin being interviewed by Mike Wallace for CBS's *60 Minutes* in the working summer resort of Baidehai (August 15, 2000; Xinhua News Agency).

Jiang was self assured without being cocky. When Wallace badgered him about Wen Ho Lee, a Chinese-American nuclear scientist who had recently been accused of spying for China, Jiang turned the tables and asked, with a twinkle in his eye, whether Wallace thought Lee was guilty. Since no one really knew the truth of this muddled and controversial case, Wallace was caught off balance: he offered the safety-net excuse that he was "not the one being interviewed," and quickly changed the subject. "This is the first time I discover you face difficulty to answer the question," said Jiang, in English, with a smile. (The charges against Lee were later dropped, with the U.S. judiciary reprimanding the U.S. government.[6])

Although Jiang's answers stayed close to official policy, he had a certain flair. On banning of Falun Gong, he insisted that "under China's constitution people have the freedom of religious belief," but said Falun Gong was a cult which harmed people's health and broke up families; as for the Internet, he stressed that China blocked certain websites to prevent pornography and certain political views which could harm society; on the press, he argued (awkwardly) that "we do have freedom of the press, but such freedoms should be subordinate to and serve the interests of the nation; how can you allow such freedom to damage the nation's interests?"

Nevertheless, in the face of Wallace's probing questioning, he won sympathy from viewers: after Wallace complained that his answers were too long, Jiang shot right back that his answers were about the same length as Wallace's questions, and that if Wallace wanted shorter answers he should ask shorter questions.

Wallace used humor to score points. When the president said, "I have a lot of friends among the leaders of both parties, Republican and Democrat," Wallace retorted with mock seriousness, "So you give money to both their campaigns?" The president then showed his serious side: "Are you just joking? We have never done such things. I have read the campaign platforms of both parties and whoever becomes president will be friendly [to China] because this is in the strategic interests of the whole world." When Wallace thrust with "That's spoken as a true politician; there's no candor in it," Jiang parried with, "I don't think that 'politician' is a very nice word."

Jiang gave the impression that, while he took his responsibilities very seriously, he didn't take himself so seriously. Never one to turn his back on a captive audience, he serenaded Wallace with "Song of Graduation," a melody from his youth sung during protests against Japanese occupation forces. Nor could he hide his pride and pleasure in reciting Lincoln's Gettysburg Address, which he so admired. "This had a great influence on students when I was young," he told Wallace.

Wallace seized the opportunity: why then, he asked, didn't Lincoln's ideal government "of the people, by the people, for the people" apply to China? Why didn't China allow free elections of its national leaders?

Jiang Zemin responded that even in America, some of what Lincoln described still remained only an ideal. He stressed that "different cultures and historic traditions, and different levels of education and economic development" meant that each country should have its own system.

Wallace hit back, describing Jiang as "a dictator." China's system, he said, was "'father knows best'—and if you get in the way of 'father'"—he made the sign of a throat being slit—"father will 'take care of you.'" Jiang responded, not without humor, that "Your way of describing . . . China is as absurd as the 'Arabian Nights'!"

Wallace countered that the famous image of the young man in front of the tank near Tiananmen Square in 1989 was a symbol of Chinese dictatorship. Interrupting his translator, Jiang said, in English: "I don't need translation. I know what you said—I'm very willing to answer these questions." Though he defended the crackdown by stating that certain people (whom he didn't identify) tried to "use the students to overthrow the government under the pretext of democracy and freedom," Jiang seemed to offer a modestly nuanced view. "In the 1989 disturbances," he said, "we truly understood the passion of students who were calling for greater democracy and freedom," adding, "in fact, we have always been working to improve our system of democracy."

It was the first time that a senior Chinese leader still in office had publicly expressed any sort of sympathy for the students. As for the man blocking the tanks, Jiang responded, "I don't know where he is now. Looking at the picture, I know he definitely had his own ideas." China, he said, respected "every citizen's right to fully express his wishes and desires. But I do not favor any flagrant opposition to government actions during an emergency."

The tank, Jiang noted, had "stopped and did not run the young man down." And he said the man had never been arrested.

Going one-on-one with Mike Wallace was daring and dangerous but Jiang Zemin's down to earth, open, and thoughtful tone scored well. He was sincere and direct, and came across as wanting America and China to be real friends and work together for the common good. Americans came away with a fresh opinion of China's leader as a real human being—and, by extension, a richer and more nuanced impression of China itself. *The Washington Post* selected the program as one of "This Week's Picks" of all American television. Even media maven Bill Clinton praised his performance, telling Jiang, "Mike Wallace is so mean to all the rest of us. He's purring like a little child [with you]. . . . I'm so jealous."[7]

★ ★ ★

Back in Beijing, some of Jiang's senior colleagues were less impressed. They thought his interview was demeaning and insulting. It was unseemly, they contended, for China's leader to be treated so disrespectfully and subjected to such hectoring. Moreover, they weren't pleased about some of Jiang's answers, particularly about Tiananmen Square. (When the transcript of Jiang's *60 Minutes* interview was published in China, there were notable excisions.) But Jiang was determined to communicate with an American audience. As he told Wallace at the end of the interview: "I'm convinced that this interview will further promote the friendship and mutual understanding between our peoples. I trust in that."

That China was prepared to be more open-minded in terms of managing its image was emphasized to me in the late 1990s while working on my PBS documentary, *In Search of China*, a co-production with China Central Television (CCTV)—and simultaneously on a parallel co-production for CCTV, entitled *Capital Wave*, which focused on American mergers and acquisitions. As I explained to one senior official, if our film appeared 100% positive about China, American audiences would believe 0% of it. On the other hand, I suggested, if it were 90% negative, the same audiences would likely believe the 10% positive part to be true. The percentages were an exaggeration, obviously, but my point was to elucidate the psychology of Western audiences.

In my contract with CCTV, it was agreed that each side would have veto power over both productions. On the M&A documentary, CCTV lived up to its end of the bargain—but I was worried about the English-language version, a warts-and-all depiction of China's transformation, which included some rather strong stories about China's problems, including bankruptcy and unemployment, migrant workers, rural women, the handicapped, and even the underground church.[8]

Indeed, one mid-level CCTV manager proudly announced that he would be the one to censor my PBS documentary. Yet to my surprise, he was swiftly derailed by his boss, a senior CCTV executive, who cleverly asked him why he thought he had the competence to evaluate an American program made for American audiences! In the end, CCTV never requested an advance screening. After it was broadcast, the documentary received favorable feed-back from CCTV and Chinese media officials.[9]

★ ★ ★

There is no doubt that China's central leaders are highly attuned to world opinion, knowing that China's image in the world directly affects the country's economic strength, political standing and social welfare—and they are increasingly desirous to listen to the views of others from afar.

Effective communications requires honesty and clarity. The place to start is for each side to explain, politely but forthrightly, how it truly feels about the other side. Being frank, even if uncomfortable, often stimulates constructive and converging dialog.

Chinese should appreciate that Americans are genuinely troubled by China's lack of democracy, human rights violations, support of dangerous regimes, and huge trade surpluses; this is why China's military buildup is worrying. Americans should appreciate that China's stability, essential for its continued reform, requires a different developmental path due to the country's different history and culture and its massive, disparate population; this is why China needs time to build its own kind of democracy.

Endnotes

1   David Barboza, "China looks to improve its image abroad," *International Herald Tribune*, January 15, 2009.
2   Author's meeting with Cai Wu, Beijing, March 2006.
3. Author's meeting with Wang Chen, Beijing, August 2009; Edward Wong, "New Protests in Western China After Deadly Clashes, *The New York Times*, July 8, 2009.
4. Ting Shi, "Vice-president takes the Games critics in his stride," *South China Morning Post*, June 25, 2008.
5   Adam Zhu and I were advisors to China's State Council Information Office.
6   In the end, Wen Ho Lee pleaded guilty to mishandling nuclear secrets, not to spying, and he was fined a token $100. The presiding judge in his case considered the government's treatment of the scientist so abusive that in an official statement to the court he offered Lee a formal apology and delivered to the government a harsh rebuke. Years later, Lee received more than $1.6 million from the federal government and five media organizations to drop his lawsuit that government leaks violated his privacy.
7   "Clinton Says Jiang Charmed US Interviewer on CBS," *People's Daily*, September 7, 2009.
8   Most of the stories in *In Search of China* were sourced and shot by Li Qiang, a dynamic and iconoclastic CCTV director.
9   *In Search of China* was broadcast on PBS nationally in the U.S. in September 2000; WETA in Washington, D.C. was the presenting station; I was creator and executive producer, Adam Zhu producer. *The Washington Post* featured it in "This Week's Picks," coincidentally the same week as President Jiang's interview on *60 Minutes*.

Part IV

Reform's Future

China's Future
Senior Leaders

In early 2009, articles featuring Vice President Xi Jinping and Li Yuanchao, head of the CPC Organization Department, appeared prominently in the Chinese press. The primary subject was a national campaign to study and implement President Hu Jintao's Scientific Perspective on Development. The campaign was led by a Central Leading Small Group, of which Xi was the head and Li his deputy. To China watchers, it seemed reminiscent of the time when Hu Jintao, then vice president, led the national campaign to study former President Jiang Zemin's Three Represents theory for modernizing the Party—a task considered part of Hu's preparation to become CPC general secretary.

As the leading member of the Secretariat, which manages Party operations, Xi Jinping is responsible for Party affairs; Li Yuanchao, likewise a member of the Secretariat, also focuses on the Party system. Their joint focus and coherent messages signaled how China's future senior leaders think.

"Do not be satisfied with the status quo." "Do not follow the beaten path." "Guard against formalism and mere process." "Achieve real results while avoiding superficial work." "Be innovative not conservative." These admonitions were sometimes attributed to both Xi and Li—even though they were not speaking together.[1] Topics covered in their various speeches included advice on morality and ethics, self-cultivation, multifaceted learning to improve capabilities; ensuring that work is based on reality and rejecting superficial activities; perseverance so as to "do well from start to finish"; and creating new ways of competitive advantage and economic growth.

China's leaders have always stressed the need for upgrading Party officials. Xi Jinping calls cadres education and training a fundamental, strategic endeavor. He sets requirements for cadres to emancipate the mind and focus on reform and innovation; enhance scientific, democratic, and legal governance; serve as role models of high ethics and integrity; be vigilant, clean and down-to-earth; and do real things for the people.[2] Cadres must learn the full knowledge necessary for their duties, Xi says, and make study a process for cultivating a global vision. They must make solving real problems the starting point of study, and apply what they learn in a principled, systematic, farsighted, and creative manner. Xi stresses that theory must match practice, study match application, and words match actions. Only if leading cadres study assiduously can they keep up with the times and assume leadership responsibilities.[3]

LiYuanchao, similarly, states that the Scientific Perspective on Development provides "the weapons" to overcome economic difficulties and to seek opportunities in crisis. He emphasizes talent as "the primary resource of scientific development," and establishes "democratic, open, competitive, merit-based" principles in selecting and promoting future leaders. In 2009, in response to the financial crisis, and in order to achieve "our goal of making China an innovation-oriented nation," Li instituted a People Plan to attract high-level personnel to China from overseas.[4] (Scientists, financial experts, entrepreneurs and top managers would be offered attractive government packages, including high salaries and relocation expenses.) Recognizing China's new place in the world, Li stresses training leaders with international knowledge and perspective—the "internationalization of the mind," he says, is a needed new way to "emancipate the mind."

Xi Jinping and Li Yuanchao, two of China's Fifth Generation leaders (following previous generations led by Mao Zedong, Deng Xiaoping, Jiang Zemin, and Hu Jintao), were always listed in this order, but often presented in parallel. Analysts took note, since both are expected to be among China's top leaders when the Fifth Generation assumes full power at the 18th Party Congress in 2012. Certainly regarding the Party, these two leaders seemed to be positioned as a single conceptual unit.

★ ★ ★

Whatever their precise positions after 2012, the new generation will likely bring fresh ideas, insights, and a rich range of experience to the pinnacle of China's governance. Leng Rong, the CPC Party Literature Research Center head who advises senior leaders, comments that "Our new leaders are young, intelligent, pragmatic, versatile, tolerant." In the past, he says, "some in older generations were blinded by ideology: they were fooling themselves about China relative to the West." Now, however, "times are different, our leaders are different—the new generation has an objective understanding of China. Xi Jinping is my age [born 1953]; Li Keqiang is younger still [born 1955]. Both have doctoral degrees." (Xi's doctorate is in law from prestigious Tsinghua University; Li has a PhD in economics from equally prestigious Peking University.)

Xi and Li were the youngest of the new Politburo Standing Committee (PSC) elected at the 17th Party Congress (2007). With nine members, including CPC General Secretary Hu Jintao, the PSC is the pinnacle of power in China. (On the PSC, where rank is significant, Xi is sixth and Li seventh.)

In March 2008, at the 11th National People's Congress, Xi was elected state vice president and, in addition to running the Party, he was given responsibility for Hong Kong and Macao affairs, and for coordinating the Beijing Olympics and Paralympics. At the same time, Li Keqiang became executive vice premier of the State Council responsible for broad areas of the economy, social services, and central government operations.

Both Xi Jinping and Li Keqiang have run two large provinces, adjudicating competing demands. Senior leaders today, they are widely expected to lead the country following the retirement of President Hu and Premier Wen Jiabao in 2012. To make Xi's status clear, Hu mentioned his name first when introducing "the relatively young comrades" on the new PSC.

Though China's future leadership line-up will not be finalized until late 2012, the general line of succession, involving top positions for Xi Jinping and Li Keqiang, and for other current leaders such as Li Yuanchao and Liu Yunshan, is clear. It was determined after sensitive inner-Party negotiations, compromise and ultimately consensus, and was designed to give the Party continuity and stability as it faces the future. Indeed it meant that, from the time of Xi's and Li Keqiang's appointment to the PSC in 2007, China would have, barring disruptive events, 15 years of predictable senior leadership: the five years until 2012 by led Hu, followed by two successive five-year terms led by Xi and Li and other Fifth Generation leaders. It was a leadership prepared to deal with the challenges of an increasingly complex society and interdependent world.

★ ★ ★

In addition to Xi Jinping and Li Keqiang, other senior leaders of China's Fifth Generation also bring diverse experience to government. They include Liu Yunshan, Li Yuanchao, Wang Qishan, Wang Yang and Bo Xilai. All are current Politburo members who are young enough to anticipate one or two more five-year terms.

Liu Yunshan, head of the CPC Publicity [Propaganda] Department, is already a two-term Politburo member, which is significant in China where seniority is highly respected. Born in 1947 in Inner Mongolia, Liu was a school teacher and manual laborer during the Cultural Revolution, and worked for seven years as a reporter before becoming head of the Inner Mongolia Bureau of Xinhua News Agency. After posts in the Communist Youth League, he eventually became deputy Party secretary of Inner Mongolia. He also studied at the Central Party School, and headed the Office of Spiritual Civilization under President Jiang Zemin.

Under Liu's leadership (since 2002), China's cultural industries—including media and entertainment—have been transformed, an underappreciated achievement considering ideological sensitivities and financial constraints.

While retaining the kinds of media controls deemed necessary to maintain Party rule and social stability, Liu Yunshan has nevertheless effected major change in terms of media modernization, marketization, sophistication and innovation. This restructuring, underreported in the West, has unleashed creative competition and enabled greater diversity. The Internet, new media, television, press, publishing and film have experienced great growth, in some cases approaching world-class standards in technology and content. Significantly, media enhancement benefits all citizens irrespective of class or income—critical in a nation where social imbalances are worrying. Liu has also enabled increasing openness in China's international communications.

Li Yuanchao, born in 1950 in Jiangsu Province, has had diverse experiences in central and provincial governments. He majored in mathematics, then taught, at Fudan University in Shanghai, before becoming a leader of the Youth League (1983-1990, initially under Hu Jintao), during which time he completed a master's degree in economics at Peking University. In the 1990s he spent six years in international communications, including three as deputy director of the State Council Information Office—and also earned a doctoral degree in "scientific socialism" from the Central Party School. (He also attended a training program at Harvard University.) Li served as vice minister of culture (1996-2000), before being appointed deputy secretary of Jiangsu Province and secretary of Nanjing, Jiangsu's capital. Li became Jiangsu Party secretary in 2003 and led the province through its greatest growth and reform (Chapter 19).

Wang Yang, born in 1955 in Anhui Province, is recognized as an aggressive and innovative reformer. A teenager during the Cultural Revolution, Wang worked in a food factory where he became workshop director. After teaching at a May 7 Cadre School (giving urbanites countryside lessons) and studying political economy at the Central Party School, he held various positions in Anhui Province, culminating in Party deputy secretary and deputy governor. He earned an on-the-job master's degree in engineering, and studied administration at the Central Party School, before becoming vice minister of the State Development and Planning Commission (1999-2003). After serving as Party secretary of the Chongqing Municipality, he was elected to the Politburo in 2007 and appointed Party secretary of Guangdong Province with a broad mandate to institute change. When the financial crisis hit in 2008, Wang Yang proposed far-reaching—and controversial—transformation (Chapter 38).

Wang Qishan, vice premier in charge of finance with major responsibility for China's economy, was born in 1948 in Shanxi Province and worked on a commune during the Cultural Revolution. He later took an undergraduate degree in history and worked for five years in the Shaanxi Provincial Museum before joining the Chinese Academy of Social Sciences, where he became a leading expert on rural development policy.

In 1989, his career changed dramatically when he was appointed vice governor of the Construction Bank of China. He later became vice governor of the People's Bank of China (central bank), and governor of China Construction Bank, before being appointed vice governor of Guangdong Province in 1997. In this post he oversaw the liquidation of the debt-laden Guangdong International Trust & Investment Co., a quasi-government enterprise—an unexpected decision which announced China's determination to allow market mechanisms to bring discipline to the financial sector. He subsequently served as director of the State Council's Office for Economic Restructuring; Party secretary of Hainan and mayor of Beijing (where he was also executive chairman of the Olympic Organizing Committee).

Wang Qishan is known for his humor as well as for his sophistication. When the Olympics was approaching, a distinguished American financier asked for his business card. "You won't need my card," Wang, then Beijing mayor, said with a smile. "If the Olympics is successful," he joked, "I'll be too high to help you—and if it's not successful, I won't have a phone!"

Bo Xilai, born in 1949 in Shanxi Province, is a charismatic, creative leader known as a "people's official" and "troubleshooter."[5] The son of Bo Yibo, one of the founding elders of New China (known as the Immortals), he did manual labor during the Cultural Revolution and then worked in a machine repair plant. He majored in history at Peking University and earned a master's degree in international journalism at the Chinese Academy of Social Sciences. From 1984 to 2004, he worked in Liaoning Province, serving as mayor and Party secretary of Dalian and then as provincial governor. He is credited with transforming Dalian into an ecologically inviting center of modern industry and fashion.

Known for his quick wit, maverick ways, international savvy, elegant attire, and personal flair, Bo Xilai is a media favorite who enjoys light-hearted banter with the press. In 2004-2007 he was China's minister of Commerce. In 2007 he entered the Politburo and was made Party secretary of Chongqing, a province-level municipality reporting directly to the central government and seen as the gateway to China's Great West.

Shortly after moving to Chongqing, Bo encouraged local officials to debate on live broadcasts, a pioneering move that encouraged government transparency and efficiency. When Chongqing taxi drivers struck over what they claimed to be high license fees, Bo negotiated directly with their representatives and reached a solution—he did not call out security forces and order a crackdown as other local leaders have done in similar situations. "Ordinary people are very rational and understanding," Bo said. "As long as you address the issue with trust and mutual respect, there's nothing that can't be properly solved."

All China's future senior leaders are proudly pro-business: they are energetic and innovative and like to make things happen. This new generation has one striking difference with previous generations. Previously, the majority of leaders were schooled in science and engineering—indeed, all nine members of the 2002-2007 Politburo Standing Committee were trained as engineers: President Hu in water conservation and hydropower, Premier

Wen in geology, Vice President Zeng Qinghong in automation, etc. Former President Jiang Zemin too was an engineer (electrical and power).

China's future leaders are trained largely in the social sciences—law, economics, history and journalism. When President Hu visited the U.S. in 2006, I wrote a commentary in *BusinessWeek* noting that the majority of American politicians were trained as lawyers, and suggesting that difficulties between China and America might lie less with cultural differences, and more with divergent ways of thinking between lawyers and engineers.[6] I was only half serious—but perhaps the broader training of China's future leaders may facilitate their dealing with complex, dynamic and subtly interconnected issues both domestically and internationally.

★ ★ ★

Li Keqiang, currently China's executive vice premier, has served in several challenging posts: he spent over five years (1998-2004) as deputy governor, governor and Party secretary of Henan Province, at the time China's largest with almost 100 million people; then three years as Party secretary of Liaoning Province, in China's northeastern rust-belt. (Running large provinces, with executive responsibility for tens of millions of people, has become the required career path for China's senior leaders.)

Son of a low-ranking official in Anhui Province, Li Keqiang worked four years after high school in a production brigade on a farm. He then took a degree in law at Peking University, and became head of the university's student union. After graduating in 1982, he was secretary of the university's Communist Youth League branch (CYLC). Between 1993 and 1998 he was the national CYLC's chief executive officer, while simultaneously studying for his doctorate. (During his early years in the CYLC he formed a close working relationship with Hu Jintao, its head in the 1980s.) In 1998, about three months after Hu Jintao became China's vice president, Li Keqiang was appointed vice governor, and later governor, of Henan—the youngest provincial governor at 43, and the first with a PhD.

In Henan, Li promoted agricultural modernization. By 2004, the year he left, Henan had become China's biggest producer of grain. Per capita GDP increased over 50% from 1998 to 2003. And significantly, given disparities between urban and rural areas, in 2004 rural income grew 14%, a higher rate than that of urban areas for the first time. Li Keqiang also brought order and organization to the flow of Henan's surplus agrarian labor force to richer provinces, and was on the front lines in fighting AIDS (which was riddled with blood-selling scandals and endemic corruption).

Li has been described as "low-key, clear-minded, responsive, prudent, and very tactful."[7] Meeting him in Shenyang, Liaoning's capital (2005), I was struck by his determination to try innovative ideas for resuscitating China's old industrial base—as part of China's Revitalizing the Northeast initiative—and his decisiveness in tackling seemingly intractable problems. Li's intelligence and commitment were self-evident and his tone and demeanor suggested he was confident he could get the job done. The key, he said, was to find market-sensitive ways to restructure large-scale state-owned enterprises while at the same time creating a healthy environment for private business to flourish.

★ ★ ★

Xi Jinping, China's vice president, likewise gained administrative experience in some of China's most important regions. He served for 17 years in Fujian Province, on the frontlines with Taiwan, working his way up from vice mayor of Xiamen to provincial governor; then spent over four years as Party secretary of Zhejiang, China's most entrepreneurial province; and finally served—briefly, due to his subsequent promotion—as Party secretary of Shanghai, China's commercial center.

Xi Jinping's personal motto is: "Be proud, not complacent. Be motivated, not pompous. Be pragmatic, not erratic."[8] His life experience is no doubt the reason.

The son of a revolutionary hero, Xi Zhongxun, who later became one of China's visionary reformists after the Cultural Revolution, Xi Jinping was born in June 1953 in the northwestern province of Shaanxi.

In 1962, when he was nine years old, his distinguished father, who had faithfully served Mao Zedong, was purged by Mao Zedong, publicly stripped of his positions and humiliated (Chapter 6). A few years later, during early convulsions of the Cultural Revolution, Xi Zhongxun was purged again, becoming one of the first senior figures to be disgraced. Jailed in one form or another for some 16 years, he endured protracted periods when he was subjected to withering criticism and severe physical abuse. His family was torn apart.

It was the time when China's urban "educated youth" were being sent down to the countryside, to learn from the peasant masses and to be "re-educated" through physical labor. And as the son of a reprobate and a prisoner—an "enemy" of Mao and of the revolution—Xi Jinping faced particular difficulties. In January 1969, when he was 15 years old, he was packed off to a small, remote mountain village in Shaanxi.

Xi Jinping spent the next six years in this harsh, poor rural area—chopping hay, reaping wheat and herding sheep as a member of a local work unit. He lived in a cave house, as was the local custom. But he adjusted well to his new life, impressing older colleagues with his enthusiasm to labor long and hard, and with his personal modesty. He built a reputation for endurance by winning wrestling matches with farmers, and by carrying "a shoulder pole of twin 110-pound buckets of wheat for several miles across mountain paths without showing fatigue."[9]

Xi did not lose his love of studying, however: by night, he would read thick books in the dim light of kerosene lamps. The locals liked to go to his cave to listen to his stories about history and the world beyond the mountains. Everyone, old and young, enjoyed chatting with him.[10]

In 1972, the 19-year-old Xi had become so respected by his peers that he was put in charge of Party-Line Education. In 1973, shy of his 21st birthday, he was made Party secretary of his production brigade.

To alleviate energy shortages, Xi started a biogas program for cooking, and he led commune members in building dams and fixing ditches. One winter, a ditch became filled with ice; if it wasn't cleared before spring, the ice would melt and the dam might collapse. Xi urged commune members to climb into the ditch to remove the ice. But no one budged: it was too cold. Xi said no more: he jumped into the icy water alone and started throwing out chunks of ice. Commune members then joined in.

In 1975, just after the reopening of universities, Xi was recommended to study at Tsinghua University. Before he left, every household in the village treated him to a meal. On the day he left, the whole village stopped work and came in a long line to see him off. After they had walked with him for five kilometers, Xi, moved, cried out: "You're so kind to me. I don't want to leave. Let me stay and spend my whole life here!" But one of his friends, a young farmer, shouted back: "You've got the chance to go to Tsinghua, you must go! And in the future when we come to Beijing we won't worry where to eat!" Only then did some of the villagers turn back—but dozens of young men walked with Xi the full 30 kilometers to the county seat. At night they slept on the floor in one room of a local hotel. The next day they all went with Xi to have their picture taken in a photo studio (for many, their first photo ever). Xi started to pay but his friends stopped him, pooling their money to cover the bill.

It's hard to imagine the impact on a child—or a teenager—of seeing his father publicly shamed. In 2003, speaking on CCTV, Xi referred to this period: "In the past, when we talked about beliefs, it was very abstract," he said. "I think the youth of my generation will be remembered for the fervor of the Red Guard era. But it was emotional," he added, "it was a mood. And when the ideals of the Cultural Revolution couldn't be realized, it proved an illusion."[11]

Yet, in retrospect, Xi was strengthened by the experience of these six years of hard rural life on the barren Loess Plateau in Shaanxi—and they would affect his later political career: although Xi is, technically, a "princeling," no-one could ever accuse him of being pampered—indeed, he is known for "never losing his common man's touch." (As one official Chinese source puts it, he was "born into the family of a former vice premier but tempered by hardships in the countryside."[12]) Xi himself has said that "Many of my practical ideas stem from my life during that period, which has influenced me every minute, even till today. To truly understand the common folk and society is the most fundamental thing."[13]

At Tsinghua, Xi studied chemical engineering (organic synthesis), graduating in 1979 at age 26. Tsinghua has produced many senior leaders, including President Hu Jintao and former Premier Zhu Rongji. (When asked to

Xi Zhongxun is appointed second secretary of Guangdong Province in April 1978. Xi (center, sixth from left) with family and friends at the Beijing airport before he leaves for Guangdong.

Xi Zhongxun (center, hidden by kids) and his family. Xi Jinping is third from the left (undated).

which political faction he belonged, Zhu famously joked, "the Tsinghua faction.")

Timing for Xi Jinping was fortuitous. A year earlier his father, Xi Zhongxun, had been rehabilitated and appointed Party secretary of Guangdong Province, where he pioneered reform and opening-up. In 1982,

Xi Zhongxun entered the Politburo and the Secretariat where he managed Party affairs and worked to rehabilitate people and restore systems devastated by the Cultural Revolution. (He also devoted himself to United Front Work, encouraging diverse constituencies, including minorities and religions, to participate in the process of governance under CPC leadership.)

During 1979-1982, the younger Xi served in the general offices of the State Council and of the Central Military Commission. This experience as an officer in active service gave him "special affection for the army." In subsequent years, wherever he worked, Xi would visit troops stationed there. (In 1988-1990, as Party secretary of Ningde Prefecture in Fujian Province, he often joined soldiers at night in watching open-air movies. Xi is one of the few leaders of his generation to have direct defense-related experience and military ties.)

After three years, however, he decided to give up his (relatively) comfortable life in Beijing and go down to the grassroots, and in 1983, Xi Jinping's political career began in earnest when he was appointed deputy Party secretary—and later secretary—of rural Zhengding County in Hebei Province. After two years focusing on rural issues, Xi, now 32 years old, commenced what would become 22 years of leadership in China's advanced coastal areas when, in 1985, he became vice mayor of Xiamen, an important city in Fujian Province across the Straits from Taiwan.

It was in Xiamen that Xi began to get noticed. One former colleague recalls him being "unusually easygoing and down-to-earth." He often wore simple windbreaker-jackets rather than Western business suits and traveled in mini-buses rather than chauffeur-driven cars. Xi's manner won raves from legendary Singapore leader Lee Kuan Yew, who described him as "a thoughtful man who has gone through many trials and tribulations. I would put him in the Nelson Mandela class," Lee proclaimed.[14]

In 1990, Xi became Party chief of Fuzhou, the capital of Fujian. Locals still remember Xi's work philosophy: "Do it now."[15] Officials, he said, should work quickly and efficiently to respond to problems. "Do it now" became the Fuzhou motto.

In 1999 Xi became acting Fujian governor, and in 2000 governor. Throughout his 17 years in the province, he dedicated himself to building a service-oriented government, to conserving the environment and resources, and to attracting investment from Taiwanese companies. As one local academic noted, "He liked to receive suggestions from experts. He was the first provincial leader to set up a team of counselors."[16]

In 2002, Xi left Fujian and became Party secretary of Zhejiang Province where he focused on resolving tensions between rapid economic growth and sustainable development. After instituting thorough study of Zhejiang's situation, Xi concluded that the province needed comprehensive industrial restructuring. He ordered local authorities to shut down or transition from highly polluting and energy-consuming businesses. And he introduced the Double Eight Strategy, designed to stimulate Zhejiang's economy and attract foreign investments—and to help the province compete for business against nearby Shanghai and Jiangsu (Chapter 19).

These strategies built Xi Jinping's reputation as an economic innovator and enabled Zhejiang to maintain rapid economic growth, while also improving quality of life for its citizens, rural and urban. New cultural performance troupes were established in music and dance, new roads were built, education enhanced. As for political reform, Xi, who speaks frequently of the "rule of law," instituted a system for public scrutiny of officials.

In meeting Xi Jinping in Hangzhou, Zhejiang's capital, I learned that in the province with China's highest concentration of private companies, Xi sought harmony between business owners and workers to ensure both economic development and social wellbeing.[17] His down-to-earth approach influenced the behavior of officials. Retired cadres in Zhejiang describe him as open-minded, a man of action without being ostentatious. To learn more about public opinion, Xi would frequent farmers' markets, board fishing boats, and visit coal miners in shafts hundreds of meters underground. Xi is also remembered for organizing the evacuation of a million people three days ahead of Typhoon Saomai in August 2006—the strongest storm to hit China in 50 years.

According to one Zhejiang official, Xi also "kept his reputation wholesome and clean, untainted by allegations of corruption."[18] Indeed, Xi, who is said to have "zero tolerance" for dishonest officials, has twice been called in to clean up after a major corruption scandal. The first time was in Fujian following the discovery of a massive smuggling ring run by Mafioso-like kingpin Lai Changxing. And in March 2007, Xi Jinping was appointed Party secretary of Shanghai, following the removal of his predecessor, Chen Liangyu, and the arrest of numerous city officials and businessmen, in a high-profile corruption scandal.

In Shanghai, Xi worked quietly to restore civic confidence in the demoralized city. Pledging to be "a good student, a good civil servant and a good team leader," he urged local officials to be stricter with themselves, and said it was up to everyone to "get results."[19] Reportedly, Xi refused the house originally provided to him as too large.

He also sought to refocus the city's orientation, calling on Shanghai people to be more open-minded, and to increase assistance to other regions of the country. Xi stressed cooperation with neighboring provinces Jiangsu and Zhejiang (from where he had just come), which had long resented the favoritism shown to Shanghai.[20] And he promoted the idea of "green, sustainable development."

Though he was only in Shanghai for seven months, Xi helped stabilize and reenergize the city. Now managed in accord with central government policy—his predecessor had often opposed Beijing's directives—Shanghai garnered more support as the nation's leading commercial and financial center. Xi's efforts were given a vote of confidence with a front-page story in *People's Daily*, titled "Glad to Hear Good Tidings from Shanghai."

This, along with national television coverage showing Xi Jinping walking closely behind Hu Jintao while he was visiting Shanghai, shortly before the 17th Party Congress in late 2007, was seen as corroboration of sudden rumors of Xi's coming elevation to the Politburo Standing Committee, and his being tipped as Hu's heir apparent.

Of the 25 members of the new Politburo elected in 2007, seven, including Xi, are offspring of former senior leaders (compared with three in the previous Politburo). While these so-called "princelings" are not a unified political faction, their shared backgrounds, training, values and interests encourage cooperation, and they are generally "pro-reform." However, being a princeling also has a downside. The Chinese public can be suspicious, if not downright critical, of those whose rapid "helicopter" ascent in their careers is seen, fairly or not, to be attributable more to their personal relationships than to their professional competence (though princelings are also recognized for their spirit of service, and for being less likely to fall victim to the temptations of corruption). In elections for Party bodies, such as the Central Committee, princelings often score poorly.

Yet Xi Jinping's approachable and amicable personality, and his well-known affection for common folk, made him popular among both Party rank-and-file and senior Party leaders. Indeed, Xi emerged as the consensus top candidate to be President Hu's successor following polling of leading Party figures on a short-list of potential candidates. The highly confidential survey was conducted person-by-person, and coordinated by then Vice President Zeng Qinghong, for many years chief advisor to former President Jiang Zemin (and whose father, like Xi's, was a veteran revolutionary leader.) Thus, when Zeng Qinghong retired in 2007 as vice president and head of Party operations, Xi Jinping assumed both positions.

Xi was soon active in his new roles. His first major assignment, to oversee the 2008 Beijing Olympics, was an unqualified success. Earlier that year, when unprecedented blizzards wreaked havoc, Xi went to snow-struck villages in Guizhou Province to visit local residents and make sure they could enjoy a safe Chinese New Year. Inspecting Hebei Province during the same period, Xi paid a special visit to his old colleagues in Zhengding County, where he had worked in the early 1980s. They were not surprised to find Xi to be the same person, still amiable and easy going.[21]

★ ★ ★

Xi Jinping is unusual among Chinese leaders in that, for many years, his wife was better known to the public than he was. He is married to Peng Liyuan, an extraordinarily popular singer. A member of the People's Liberation Army's (PLA) musical troupe, Peng is a soprano known for her starring roles in revolutionary operas and stirring performances of patriotic songs. She has headlined important anniversaries, such as the founding of the army and the return of Hong Kong, and has performed all over the world.

Peng's songs focus on ethnic or rural Chinese themes and generally reflect emotions of ordinary rural citizens. She herself grew up in the countryside, joining the PLA in 1980, 18 years old, as an ordinary soldier (she now holds the rank of major general). Soon she began performing at PLA performances to boost troop morale. In 1982 she came to national prominence when she appeared in the first Chinese New Year's Eve Gala on CCTV, singing her trademark *On the Land of Hope*. Peng, who holds a master's degree in traditional ethnic folk music, became a perennial favorite, and went on to appear on CCTV's New Year's Gala every year for more than 20 years—the most regular participant in the nation's most-watched show. (This stopped in 2008, soon after her husband's promotion.)

Peng Liyuan, legendary singer and wife of Vice President Xi Jinping, in the classic revolutionary opera, "The Daughter of the Party" (circa 1991).

Following a concert honoring People's Liberation Army soldiers for their relief work during the Great Flood of 1998, Central Military Commission Chairman Jiang Zemin comes onstage to sing with performers the popular patriotic song "Ode to the Motherland." Peng Liyuan is in the center (on Jiang's left). (October 8, 1998; Xinhua News Agency).

The love story of Xi Jinping and Peng Liyuan has been a favorite topic among Chinese.[22] They first met in 1986, on a blind date arranged by a friend. Peng, then 24 years old and already famous, initially didn't want to meet Xi: he was working in Xiamen, far from her home in Beijing, and the likelihood of a serious relationship was low. However her friend insisted that this man was simply "outstanding." Reluctantly, Peng agreed.

On their first date, Peng wore a pair of fat military pants; she wanted to see "whether the guy was only into looks." Upon meeting Xi, Peng was disheartened: he was dressed unfashionably and looked rather old (he was 33). But when he spoke, she found herself attracted. Xi, who said he rarely watched television, didn't ask her what songs were popular or how much her appearance fee was. He asked about vocal styles, and they talked a long time. Peng said later: "I was touched. I wondered, 'Is he the one I'm looking for? He's very simple and honest, but very thoughtful.' Later he told me that within 40 minutes he'd determined that I was to be his future wife."

On their second date Xi explained to Peng that he was very busy with his work and might not have much time to attend to a family. Peng was impressed by his dedication to his job, and told him: "Work and family complement each other. Only if you do your work well can you maintain a good family." They talked about history, China, international affairs, their goals in life. Xi told her that he thought they had both "suffered in life," but had maintained their "integrity and innocence."

Peng's parents, however, didn't want their daughter to marry an off-spring of a senior official, since they believed that "princelings were playboys." Xi reassured Peng that his father was a farmer's son, and "very approachable"—and that all his siblings were married to children from ordinary families.

Peng Liyuan and Xi Jinping married in a simple wedding in Xiamen on September 1, 1987. Travel wasn't easy at the time, and Peng needed a letter from the PLA's Song and Dance Ensemble to fly to Xiamen. When she arrived, Xi took her straight to a photo studio where their wedding pictures were taken. The marriage registration staff came to Xi's house and issued them a certificate. Xi, vice mayor of Xiamen, then informed his boss, the mayor, who invited all of Xiamen's leaders to have dinner together at Xi's place. Prior to dinner, none of them knew this was the actual day of Xi's wedding—nor that he was marrying the famous singer Peng Liyuan.

For many years, Xi and Peng were not able to live together full-time. He was working in Fujian; she was frequently on tour. (Indeed, four days after their wedding, Peng had to fly back to Beijing for the National Arts Festival, followed by a long-planned North American tour—the newlyweds didn't see each other for three months.) Xi however, always supported his wife's career. "The audiences need you," he told her. "I cannot let you leave the stage for me; that would be too selfish."

Peng, meanwhile, was not only dedicated to her own work but fearful of interrupting her husband's. "Sometimes when I went to see him, he would postpone meetings and his trips to the countryside so that he could be with me," she said. "I felt I was making too much trouble for him, so I seldom visited." Peng noted that "Jinping is a very nice person who never puts on airs: some of his classmates went abroad and became rich," she said, adding that "he could have gone abroad too, but he chose the hard way of becoming a public servant. Therefore I couldn't ask my husband, for example, to forsake the trust of the five million people of Ningde [where Xi was Party chief in 1988-1990] and just be my husband."

Peng would certainly visit Xi in Fujian when she had the chance, buying him food and cooking him meals. She once had her mother make him a cotton quilt because Fujian had cold winters and the houses had no central heating. But she was on tour at the time, and had to carry the quilt around the country before visiting her husband—much to the amusement of colleagues and members of the public, who were surprised to see such a famous singer carrying what seemed to be her own bedding on airplanes.

When Peng did visit, Xi would keep it secret, and not even take her with him to functions to which spouses were invited. "People would gossip if I took you," he told her. "It would have a bad influence." He also asked her not to perform concerts for her own financial benefit: "I am a cadre of the Party," he explained. "You should never do moonlighting performances."

Xi put high demands on himself too, even missing the birth of his daughter Xi Mingze in 1992 due to his devotion to his work. (Ningde was hit by a typhoon, and Xi, who was organizing flood-prevention measures, couldn't return for three days.)

Still, the couple has been happily married for over 20 years. They may have different interests: Xi reads political and philosophical books, while Peng enjoys arts and literature. But they like each other's company. Asked why she was always in high spirits, Peng once replied, "The secret lies in my family. If I weren't happily married, if I had a bitter heart, would I be able to shine and perform for everyone? Family is something a woman can rely on," she added. "It is a quiet, safe haven." Her family, she said, was "an ordinary and happy one."

According to Peng, Xi is "the most qualified husband for a woman and a most qualified father for our daughter," but he is also like a mentor to her: "Perhaps it's because of the age gap [Xi is nine years her senior]," she has said, "but he treats me like a little sister." Xi has acknowledged that he is protective of Peng, and never asks her to do household chores. "I've never done anything to help her career, nor could I," he has said. "So how could I ask her to do anything for me? As long as she's happy, I'm happy whether or not she does household chores."

Yet Xi is good at keeping his wife's feet on the ground. When Peng received her master's degree, she called to tell him the news. "Really?" Xi said, not sounding impressed. "How come you're not congratulating me?" Peng asked. "What's there to congratulate you about?" Xi responded. "I've many people here with master's degrees waiting for me to give them a job!"

The couple's daughter has also attracted headlines. In 2008, Xi Mingze, age 16, volunteered to work in earthquake-devastated areas of Sichuan, along with thousands of other volunteers. According to her mother, she took several days off from school, and worked with others to rescue the injured and counseled children at a collapsed primary school.

Asked by journalists whether she had been worried when her daughter volunteered, Peng Liyuan, who was giving special performances in the quake-hit areas, said, "The earthquake brought such catastrophe to people here. This is exactly where she should be." Her daughter, she added, had "matured so much during the seven days she worked as a volunteer. She not only learned, but also made friends with many local people. She told me the Sichuanese are 'as kind as the day is long; they cared so much about the volunteers, and they were as confident as ever,' she said. 'The disaster didn't knock them down.'"

Peng herself won praise in Sichuan for her human touch, singing impromptu songs for soldiers who hadn't been able to attend her performances and having her photo taken with them.

★ ★ ★

My own experience of Xi Jinping is that he is friendly, courteous, open-minded and engaging. A large man with a strong physical presence, he carries himself with the ease of someone comfortable with authority and empathetic with guests, and has none of the airs of an official impressed with his own status. Energetic and pragmatic, he now advises Party officials to embrace change.

That China's historic change has been primarily attitudinal was stressed by Xi, whose thinking is a bellwether of China's future. He ascribes China's "earthshaking change" to "the Chinese people's inspiration to rejuvenate the nation." And speaking to new members of the CPC Central Committee in December 2007, Xi urged them to "unswervingly continue to emancipate our minds and resolutely overcome the attitude of being satisfied with the status quo, the inertia of conservative and complaisant thinking, the fear of difficulties, and timid thinking . . . Emancipating the mind shall be reflected in our concrete work and in problem-solving."

Xi, like his father, is a strong advocate of pro-market reforms, stressing economic efficiency and further market liberalization, and has a long record of promoting the private sector. He has been described as the "candidate of China's entrepreneurs and growing middle class," those whose ideas, energy and dedication are building new companies, creating new jobs, growing the economy, and generating personal wealth.

Xi is well regarded by international business leaders as someone who understands international commercial practices. As a "pro-business campaigner," he attends high-profile events such as the Davos economic summit and counts global leaders as friends. On his first visit to China as U.S. Treasury Secretary in 2006, Henry Paulson made a very public first stop in Hangzhou to meet with Xi, before going on to Beijing. Paulson described Xi as a "guy who knows how to get over the goal line."[23]

★ ★ ★

When Jiang Zemin retired in 2002, it marked the first non-traumatic transfer of power on the Chinese mainland since the end of the imperial era. It also meant that a tumultuous age had passed into history: no future generation of Chinese leaders would have living memories of the brutal Japanese occupation or the debilitating civil war that followed. Post-Jiang leaders did not experience the idealistic days of Mao's revolution in the 1950s, and their recollections of the self-destructive Anti-Rightist Campaign and the Great Leap Forward are weak.

Although members of China's Fifth Generation of leaders did endure the Cultural Revolution, for most of them it was more a rural delay to their careers than a time of humiliation, persecution, or suffering. (Xi Jinping is an exception, having suffered, at least vicariously, through the persecutions of his father, Xi Zhongxun.)

Future generations of Chinese leaders will be both lesser and greater for this. Not having lived through those decades of true belief nor experienced the full mania of political zealotry, they may react more analytically and less emotionally to historically encumbered issues, such as Sino-Japanese relations, changes still needed in China's governance and the Communist Party, and making dispassionate judgments on still-sensitive matters of history, such as the Tiananmen crackdown.

The current generation, led by President Hu Jintao, has certainly made its indelible mark, and in the process, some of Jiang Zemin's policies and positions have been modified. Such change is inevitable—Jiang said so himself: just as his generation had surpassed its precursors, so too, he predicted, would his successors exceed him. And the same process of historical progression should continue into the future, when China's Fifth Generation assumes power.

President Hu has displayed all the characteristics of being the right leader at the right time. He has had the realism to deal with endemic and debilitating problems, the vision to devise the Scientific Perspective on Development, the inclusiveness to inspire people to work together, the close-to-the-people commitment to bring all citizens into the expanding tent of China's success, and the perspicacity to guide China as a responsible power in the international community.

As for the future, there are many inside China who, with good reason, worry about inequality and instability, and others outside who fear Chinese expansion and some kind of "threat." To address these understandable concerns is one reason that I have written this book. But if I were to answer in one sentence, I can think of no fact more dispositive, no argument more persuasive, and no harbinger of China's future more unambiguous, than the likely leaders of China's next generation—Xi Jinping, Li Keqiang, Li Yuanchao, and others. Fifth Generation leaders, with their education, their experience and their vision, should bring new ways of thinking to China—maintaining continuity, innovating policy, advancing development, reforming governance and modernizing philosophy.

Endnotes

1 Wen Hai, CPC News Network, April 15, 2009.
2 "To do a good job in the new round of cadre training in the spirit of reform and innovation, stressed Xi Jinping at the National Cadres Education and Training Working Conference," *People's Daily*, July 17, 2008.
3 "Leaders and cadres should study studiously, conduct themselves honestly, and do their work cleanly, stressed Xi Jinping at the opening ceremony of the Class for Further Studies and Training Class for Teachers, Central Party School," Xinhua, May 13, 2008.
4 Xinhua, April 6, 2009; *China Daily*, April 16, 2009.
5 Al Guo, "Chongqing's party boss dazzles with forthright maverick charm," *South China Morning Post*, March 10, 2009; following section.
6 Robert Lawrence Kuhn, "A Problem of Perception," *BusinessWeek*, April 24, 2006. There is no small difference in how engineers and lawyers think: engineers strive for "better," which can be the mortal enemy of "good enough;" lawyers prepare for the worst, even if such preparation makes the worst more likely to occur.

7   Wu Peng, "Debut of the 17th Politburo Standing Committee," *Caijing* magazine, October 25, 2007.

8   Ibid.

9   Geni Raitisoja, "Xi Jinping: President in 2012?," Radio 86, October 26, 2007 (Quoting *The Globe and Mail*).

10 *Qiangguo Luntan* (Strong China Forum), www.china.com.cn. July 17, 2008; following section.

11 Jonathan Watts, "Most corrupt officials are from poor families but Chinese royals have a spirit that is not dominated by money. Choice of 'princeling' as the country's next president came as a shock to many," *The Guardian*, October 26, 2007.

12 "Xi Jinping - Vice President," Xinhua, March 16, 2008; China.org.cn

13 Ibid.

14 Jonathan Ansfield and Melinda Liu, "Xi Jinping: China's New Boss And The 'L' Word," *Newsweek*, December 22, 2007.

15 "Xi Jinping - Vice President," Xinhua, March 16, 2008.

16 Li Fei of Xiamen University, quoted in Bill Savadove, "Xi Jinping: Man for all factions is tip for top," *South China Morning Post*, October 23, 2007.

17 Author's meeting with Xi Jinping, Hangzhou, March 2006.

18 Geni Raitisoja, Radio86, October 26, 2007.

19 "Xi Jinping - Vice President," Xinhua, March 16, 2008.

20 Bill Savadove, op.cit.

21 "Xi Jinping - Vice President," Xinhua, March 16, 2008.

22 "Peng Liyuan on a happy family life, Xi Jinping night reading," *Qiangguo Luntan* (Strong China Forum), www.china.com.cn. July 17, 2008; following section.

23 Geni Raitisoja, Radio86, October 26, 2007.

China's New Kind of Leaders

As Chinese society has become more complex, and the world more globalized, the nation's need for first-rate leaders has never been greater. Li Yuanchao, head of the CPC Organization Department, has stated bluntly that the Party and government should not settle for second-best when it comes to recruiting and promoting officials.[1] Not only has he argued that important positions can only be entrusted to people who are both "in line with the Party" and also "pioneering and innovative . . . perform actual work, and . . . are honest and clean and recognized by the people," he has also specified four types of officials the Party does not want.

The first category includes those who "abuse their power for personal gain." Such people, according to Li, tend to be "so selfish that they are blinded by greed," and use their power not to serve the public, but "as a mechanism to fish for money, pretty women, and political advancement . . . Every day, all they think about is how to realize a profit on their power and enable their relatives to benefit."

Second, Li criticizes those whom he describes as "personal network weavers and thrusters, who seize every opportunity to obtain personal gain. With their eyes set on the likes and dislikes of their superiors," he explains, "they rack their brains thinking of how to 'climb up' to higher positions. Through nice meals, drinking, and other networking activities, they cozy up to superiors, co-workers, relatives and fellow townsmen who are of use to them, aiming to weave a network of interwoven interests or a kind of fraternity." This, he asserts, "undermines the honesty and ethics of officials."

Third, he says, the Party does not want "benign and uncontentious people who are indifferent to matters of principle and are unconcerned about right and wrong." Such people, he warns, "vacillate or dissimulate" in order to protect themselves: "They know better than anyone else about improper conditions in their areas, but even if they know who is corrupt they don't dare reveal them." And, he adds, by keeping on good terms with everyone "at the expense of principle," their behavior "disrupts Party democracy, violates laws and disciplines, and dissolves the integrity, energy, and vitality of the Party."

Fourth, Li also rejects those "who don't perform concrete deeds" and just "muddle along," wasting "a whole day with a cup of tea, a piece of paper, and a cigarette. They spend more time on diversions than on work," he says, and are incapable of doing good things for the people.

China's new leaders are none of these.

★ ★ ★

In Chinese politics, the power of officials is often more related to their next position than to their current position—this is especially true toward the end of expected terms and surely as officials approach retirement. (Retirement is determined by age and by rank: vice ministers retire at 60; ministers at 65; Politburo members at 70.) To illustrate roughly: within two years of retirement, the half life of the effective power of some officials can be, say, about one year—meaning that every month or so their capacity to do things diminishes by about 4-5%. In a real-world example, the highly qualified protégé of a powerful minister of a central government agency was blackballed because the minister waited until near his retirement to recommend the promotion—and the minister's previously loyal subordinates deserted him, distancing themselves from the old regime in preparing for the new one.

Loss of power can be emotionally brutal. This is true in any human organization, but particularly so in Chinese state-run institutions, where senior officials control careers so strongly that employees feel compelled to switch loyalties to protect themselves. Senior officials can be highly respected, fawned over, one day, and utterly ignored, shunned, the next day. (Such personal loss is expressed by *Ren Zou Cha Liang*—literally Person Leaves, Tea [is] Cold—which means that when an official loses power no one remains to attend to him ["keeping the tea hot" represents caring and friendship]. The saying packs an emotional wallop in Chinese as it's based on a classic story of a faithful dynastic premier who after he is wrongly dismissed by the emperor becomes so distraught after his friends forsake him that he commits suicide.)

★ ★ ★

Thus in Chinese politics, youth is power. It was not long ago that rank in China's system was determined partly by seniority. Now, all things being equal, the younger leader is the advantaged leader. The Party's elite promotional policies—now based more on achievement and vision—assign future leaders sequences of positions in provincial and central government; individuals normally serve in several such posts, with increasing levels of responsibility, before being promoted to upper echelons of national leadership.

Thus, when *Global People* magazine, published by *People's Daily*, featured in 2009 five officials of full-ministerial rank who were born in the 1960s—and thus still in their 40s—observers took note.[2] (In China, to make full minister before age 50 signals fast-track ascent.)

Three of the members of China's so-called "Sixth Generation" of leaders were provincial-level governors: Hunan's Zhou Qiang, Hebei's Hu Chunhua, and Xinjiang's Nur Bekri. The other two were Agriculture Minister Sun Zhengcai and Lu Hao, Party secretary of the Communist Youth League of China (CYLC). Zhou Qiang and Hu Chunhua, also former CYLC heads, are considered protégés of President Hu Jintao, and candidates for the Politburo at the 18th Party Congress in 2012.

Hunan Governor Zhou Qiang has a master's degree in law and served in the Ministry of Justice prior to his appointment to run the CYLC (a full ministerial post) at 38. When in 2006 he became acting governor of the large central province of Hunan, with almost 70 million people, locals had their doubts: "We don't know what the country's youngest governor can do for us?" was the whisper in the streets. Yet, even into the strong headwinds of the 2008-9 financial crisis, Hunan had one of the best growth rates in China, well above the national average. Using a track-race analogy, Zhou suggests Hunan has an opportunity to exploit the financial crisis to catch, or surpass, more developed provinces: it's easier to pass your competitors, he says, "on the curves than on the straightaways."

"Zhou Qiang is a strategic thinker," said Li Xiaowei, chairman of Hunan Valin Iron & Steel Group. "He frames economic issues with strategic vision. For example, when we acquired Jiangsu Wuxi Iron & Steel Group, local provincial officials objected that we shouldn't be spending our capital in other provinces. But Governor Zhou supported us, asking 'How could multinational companies ever become multinational if they didn't make investments outside their home territories?'" Consistent in his principles, Zhou Qiang did not object when large SOEs from other provinces acquired smaller Hunan companies. "After all," Zhou said, "they still employ our local citizens and still pay our local taxes." In another example (2008), Governor Zhou affirmed Valin's decision to acquire 17% of FMG, the third largest Australian iron and ore company, counseling Valin Chairman Li to be "confident and persistent while being sensitive to find the best opportunity." The purchase proved to be one of China's few cross-border acquisition successes.

Zhou Qiang was given the UN's Champion of the Earth Award in 2005 for his long-term concern about environmental issues, including his "Protect the Mother River" initiative for the Yellow River (while he was at CYLC). A rigorous legal thinker, Zhou established five-step working guidelines aimed at reducing corruption during urban development—these included: research, expert review, public participation, legitimacy analysis, and collective review. The local media welcomed his plan, suggesting that "If local governments comply strictly with these provisions, Hunan Province will be a most 'peaceful' place." In 2010, Zhou Qiang was appointed Party chief of Hunan Province.

Hu Chunhua spent many years working in the Tibetan government (he is fluent in the Tibetan language), before assuming leadership of the Youth League. (He thus has both Tibet and CYLC experience in common with President Hu Jintao [no relation]). From a modest family, he won admission to Peking University's prestigious Department of Chinese Literature at the age of 16, the youngest in his class. When he became vice-chairman of the All-China Youth Federation, Hu was only 34, making him the youngest official of vice-ministerial rank in the country.[3]

Hu Chunhua is known for severely criticizing some CYLC officials for being "busy with social engagements" and "subject to all kinds of temptations from a variety of adverse influences." On becoming acting governor of Hebei in 2008, he had to cope with implementing security measures related to the Olympics (in nearby Beijing), the Sanlu melamine milk contamination scandal, and the financial crisis. Hu sought to "mobilize the enthusiasm, initiative and creativity" of the people, and expand domestic demand. He is said to work non-stop—in the first few months after assuming his post, he visited all of Hebei's 11 cities. In 2010, Hu Chunhua was appointed Party chief of Inner Mongolia Autonomous Region.

When Sun Zhengcai, who has a PhD in agriculture, was appointed agriculture minister in 2006 at the age of 43, he was the country's youngest full minister. Fellow students at China Agricultural University remember his good sense of humor, rigorous scholarship, and capacity to solve complex problems—and that his only hobby was basketball. An excellent English-speaker, he also studied in the U.K. He is a former head of Beijing's Shunyi district, where he simplified bureaucratic processes and increased efficiency in an area which combines industry and agriculture. Known for his direct style, Sun is seen as knowledgeable, with a strong sense of responsibility. In 2009, Sun Zhengcai was appointed Party chief of Jilin Province, becoming the youngest provincial Party secretary in China.

Lu Hao, appointed CYLC Party Secretary in 2008, is an economics graduate of Peking University who began his career in the textile industry, rising to factory director. He was then director of the famous Beijing-based Zhongguancun Science and Technology Park (China's Silicon Valley), before becoming vice mayor of Beijing in charge of industry (2003). His career has been marked by a series of "firsts." At 20, Lu was Beijing's first directly elected student union president; at 27, the youngest "number one" of a large state-owned enterprise (SOE) in textiles; at 32, the youngest department-level official in the Beijing Municipal government; at 35, the youngest vice mayor of Beijing; and at 41, as CYLC Party Secretary, China's youngest ministerial-level official. In each position, he has promoted innovation, and evinced a low-key, pragmatic workstyle. Lu came to the CYLC, untraditionally, from outside the organization, and has brought fresh ideas, including how to operate with reduced funding.

Nur Bekri, chairman of the Xinjiang Uyghur Autonomous Region, is a native Uyghur whose key tasks include combating Uyghur separatism. Born in a border area, his early life was difficult. After graduating from Xinjiang University (where he was CYLC secretary), he worked in various remote areas of the province, before becoming mayor of Urumqi, Xinjiang's capital, at 36. He was the youngest mayor of a provincial-level capital in China, and dedicated himself to the greening of barren hills (he was known as the "green mayor"). As Xinjiang governor, Nur promotes bilingual education to support Uyghur culture, but wields "an iron fist against terrorism" (including pre-emptive strikes), and has lashed out at Western countries "for instigating unrest in the area," saying "their schemes would never succeed because only very few people support separatism."

During the 2009 Urumqi riots, Bekri said police had exercised "the greatest restraint" as they sought to quell the violence. "In any country ruled by law, the use of force is necessary to protect the interest of the people and stop violent crime. This is the duty of policemen," Bekri told reporters, including Reuters, as he revealed that police had killed 12 Uyghur rioters.

★ ★ ★

Some of China's new leaders may surprise. In 2004, *Nanfang Zhoumo* (Southern Weekend), the often-daring magazine based in Guangzhou, published a long, startling article about a dynamic young official named Qiu He.[4] Entitled "The Most Controversial City Party Secretary," the article lauded the results of his reforms, which had radically transformed Suqian City, a poor area of wealthy Jiangsu Province, bringing rapid development and making it more democratic. Yet his "autocratic approach" was questioned and his "iron-handed" leadership criticized.

The article recounted various controversies, such as teachers going on strike over "investment tasks"; one-third of local officials seeking investment or developing business; or kindergartens and hospitals allegedly being "sold off"—a move that sparked especially heated debate.

"Standing behind all these controversies," the article said, was Qiu He, Suqian's Party Secretary, who, it claimed, "has hidden behind the scenes . . . and has never tried to explain his actions to the public." The reporter had spent nearly a month in the city interviewing local people, and expressed "confusion" at the diverse opinions regarding Qiu. Some Suqian officials were unhappy and resentful, describing him as "sometimes arbitrary, sometimes understanding, sometimes aggressive"; the common people, however, were near unanimous in expressing their support, praising him for doing "a lot of practical things, such as good law and order and economic development."

The article highlighted the paradox of "an autocrat who rode roughshod over those who opposed him, but promoted economic development and introduced, contrary to his own behavior, democratic methods," according to Joseph Fewsmith, who specializes in Chinese politics. But other media were less ambivalent: "*Focus Interview,* China's *60 Minutes*–like [CCTV] program, reported on him unfavorably three times," Fewsmith noted.[5]

Traditionally in China, high-profile publicity—even if entirely positive— can be politically destructive (unless mandated from above). After these reports, which depicted an official who seemed the polar opposite of the steady Party cadre maintaining stability, Qiu He's career might have been limited— or indeed over.

It was anything but. In fact, three months after the controversial article appeared, President Hu Jintao personally came to Suqian City, effectively giving Qiu's reforms his blessing—which triggered further debate about the "Qiu He phenomenon."

For years, Qiu did not speak with the media. But in an extensive interview— both verbally and in writing—he told me his story, which may reflect new directions in China's reforms.[6] (As Fewsmith puts it, "Known as an 'official with personality,' Qiu He stands out among the ranks of China's generally staid bureaucracy and makes us think about what types of officials might be promoted under Hu Jintao and what this means for the building of institutions in China.")

Qiu He was born in 1957, to a farmer's family in the Jiangsu countryside. In 1977, the national college entrance examination system resumed following the Cultural Revolution, enabling him to study at Nanjing Agricultural Institute. "Otherwise," Qiu says, "I'd have been a farmer." In the same year, he joined the Communist Party.[7]

Years later, after working in Jiangsu agriculture and science, Qiu studied in America, attending the University of Maryland (1995) and learning Western public management and market economics. It had a big impact: "I learned how to think about market economies," he says, "such as the kinds of measures and laws governments employ in regulating economies." Qiu recalls reading *Reinventing Government: How the Entrepreneurial Spirit is Transforming the Public Sector,*[8] a book Bill Clinton recommended to U.S. officials. "The book inspired me," Qiu says. "It taught me how to conceptualize a city or a region as if it were a large enterprise. One must think in terms of input-output ratios, return-on-investment (ROI), and cost-benefit analysis."

Qiu, who was reported to have read every edition of Paul Samuelson's classic text *Economics* (8th-14th), adds: "Public control should be as small as possible and market control as great as possible."[9] (In 2005, Qiu attended Harvard's Kennedy School of Government, where he studied market regulation, crisis management, and other areas. "What I learned provided new perspectives," Qiu says, noting, "Chinese people stress the benefits of learning from others. Although China and America have different national conditions and political systems, the laws of market economics, with its rules and regulations, have extensive applicability.")

In 1996, soon after returning from America, Qiu He was appointed vice mayor of Suqian City in north Jiangsu, and Party secretary of Shuyang

County (part of Suqian). Jiangsu was booming, but Suqian, with over 5 million people, was its poorest city—and Shuyang its poorest county.

Shuyang wasn't just poor, it was also filthy. On his first night in office, Qiu took a night walk through the county town, and was horrified to find piles of garbage in the streets; four times he stepped in human feces. The next day, he ordered more than 5,000 cadres to carry out sanitation work—in what Fewsmith called "a Maoist-style campaign"—and in two weeks brought dramatic change to the environment.[10]

It was clear, Qiu says, that basic changes were needed: "I come from a rural family," he says. "Shuyang's 1.72 million people were plagued with rural problems—I felt the connection." To tackle the region's problems, he states, it was necessary to "change how people think, their beliefs, ideas. That means more than all the fancy statistics."

The following year (1997), Qiu says he "encouraged cadres to participate in the process of beautifying their hometown" by taking part in a county clean-up in their spare time (weekends). He denies reports that officials were "forced" to join in, saying that he simply "set up volunteer teams so as to create an atmosphere of participation." Qiu quotes "an important theory in sociology: that participation rates equal satisfaction rates; more often than not," he explains, "a volunteer is a satisfied person."

Public order was also high on Qiu's agenda. After discovering collusion between criminals and police, he dismissed the Public Security head, rotated 41 station chiefs and arrested others, replacing all who were suspected of having criminal connections. In his first year in office, 240 corrupt officials were prosecuted.

Problems abounded: the county's finances were upside-down—annual expenses ($31 million) were more than double reported revenues ($14 million), and reported revenues were one-third higher than real revenues. Shuyang's roads were awful too: the county had only 56 kilometers of paved roads of which more than half were damaged. Only 28% of its villages could be accessed by anything like a real road.

Qiu took unprecedented action, launching an all-out drive to improve transportation—critical for building the economy. To fund road construction, Qiu took "loans" from local residents. Some reports claimed he withheld 10% of public employees' wages (including retirees). Qiu however stresses that: "it was a kind of lending mechanism for developing the city" which "went through all statutory procedures and was approved by Suqian's People's Congress." He also required local farmers to volunteer eight days of labor each year and to join road construction teams. (Qiu notes that it's common practice in China that people "sometimes have to do unpaid labor." What I did, he adds, "was to develop our city and the results proved its effectiveness.")

In three years, Shuyang built 424 kilometers of asphalt road, 156 kilometers of cement road, and 1,680 kilometers of gravel road, producing one of the best transport networks in northern Jiangsu. *Southern Weekend* called it a "miracle," saying it would have taken at least 50 years to achieve this by conventional means.

Qiu's urban reconstruction sparked controversy. To make way for new buildings, old ones were bulldozed. Some residents were angry: several traveled to Beijing to complain about Qiu and his methods, but to no avail. Qiu insists, however, that "what we bulldozed were illegal and temporary buildings" (i.e. built without building licenses), and that "we did so according to relevant laws and we went through due process." (Later, as land values rose, some of those same peasants thanked Qiu. "At that time, I was backward," said one former petitioner, "I couldn't see as far as Qiu He could."[11])

In 2000, Qiu He was named vice Party secretary of Suqian City and, eight months later, Party secretary. He continued his innovative, even daring initiatives, striving to "minimize the resources the government could control and maximize the resources the market could allocate," as he puts it. To boost the economy, he ordered that one-tenth of government employees leave their positions and go into business; some were tasked with seeking outside investment (with quotas of up to $600,000).[12]

Starting from 2001, he seemed to divest the city's SOEs—schools, township clinics, and hospitals. The move was unprecedented—and criticized vehemently by those opposed to such apparent privatization in a socialist country. Indeed, in 2003, an investigatory team from the Ministry of Health concluded that auctioning hospitals and clinics to private owners was unacceptable.

Qiu himself contends that "Suqian didn't sell a single school or hospital. We just separated governmental functions from enterprises' operations"—the "operations," not the entities, being put into private hands to enhance efficiencies. He admitted at the time that he felt "great pressure." But Qiu had his own backing. In 2000, the Jiangsu government authorized Suqian to "allow and support . . . a more flexible approach to explore a new road for faster development."

And Qiu continued to promote bold policies, convinced that major reforms were necessary, particularly in the healthcare sector: "There were numerous problems," he says. "Medical resources were insufficient—Suqian ranked last in Jiangsu in terms of per-capita healthcare assets and healthcare professionals. Supply and demand," he adds, "were mismatched: it was too difficult and expensive to see a doctor." What's more, he says, the fact that "there was no competition in a monopolized market," combined with "absolute egalitarianism and life-tenure," meant that healthcare workers "lacked incentive, were irresponsible, and had very bad attitudes towards patients."

After studying medical systems in other countries and consulting with experts, Qiu He says, Suqian "introduced competition into healthcare through market mechanisms, while guaranteeing public health services which are within the competency sphere of government." This approach, he says, was based on the Four Separations—"separation of regulation from operation, and medical treatment from healthcare, disease prevention, and medicines."

Hospitals and health centers were established in every township. The government ran the health centers: according to Qiu these were "responsible for disease prevention and control, healthcare, health education, sanitary supervision, countryside cooperative medical care management, and other public healthcare services," and did not charge for any of their services.

Suqian's 124 township-level hospitals, on the other hand, were privatized through open-bidding transfer of net assets, auction of intangible assets, joint-stock ownerships and trusteeships. In Qiu's words, "the government completely withdrew from operations of township hospitals and focused solely on public health." Qiu is blunt about the reasons for this decision: "When government runs hospitals," he says, "the poor suffer, the rich benefit, and the bureaucracy profits. Better to let the market function. The role of government should be to provide direct subsidies to the poor."[13]

The reforms, he says, were a success: "We greatly expanded the total quantity of medical and healthcare services. Suqian became the only city in Jiangsu with health centers, and dedicated staff for disease prevention, in every village (1,418)." By 2004, he notes, Suqian had medical assets of almost $200 million, more than double the 1999 figure—and two-thirds of this was private capital. Equally important, Qiu continues, the salaries of medical professionals increased steadily—and "their sense of risk, competition, responsibility, and ethics were all enhanced." Local people benefited directly: the city's medical costs dropped 25% to 50%.

Education was another of Qiu He's targets. Suqian ranked last in Jiangsu in college entrance examination scores. "Quality lagged far behind nearby areas," Qiu recalls. Not only were there insufficient resources, but existing resources were often wasted: "There was severe overlap," he says. "Remote areas were short of teachers while urban areas were overstaffed. Schools lacked energy and creativity." Suqian's future competitiveness, he believed, "depended on education: Education couldn't wait," says Qiu. "Education couldn't be conservative. We had to emancipate our mind and develop by leaps and bounds."

He instituted a policy known as One Guarantee and Three Relaxations. The government guaranteed and operated "compulsory education"—which in China consists of nine years of primary and junior middle school—and increased investment; but it loosened controls over pre-school, senior middle-school and vocational education, allowing "diverse" ownership: its operating slogan was "Industrialize non-compulsory education, privatize the industrialization—and standardize the privatization." Ownership of state-run high schools and vocational colleges was "diversified" away from government, while well-run public schools were encouraged to open their own private schools. As Qiu He puts it, "Our attitude shifted from 'solely relying on government' to 'being supported by government and implemented by society'."

Within just a few years, Suqian's educational level became no.1 in north Jiangsu. Senior high school attendance increased from 48% to 89%. The number of students qualifying for college increased 50%.

Qiu stresses that all his reforms have been "people-oriented"—and they stem from a clear vision: "Taking people's progress as our purpose," he says, "we must enhance people's longevity, employment, entrepreneurship, innovation, and competition." To develop these five capacities, he says, five changes are required: "turn the population into a workforce, turn the workforce into manpower, turn manpower into talent, turn talent into capital, and turn capital into wealth—so that in the end the wealth created will benefit the people."

Qiu He also instituted reforms in governance, pioneering Public Recommendation and Public Election—the solicitation of public opinion prior to the appointment or promotion of officials. Candidates' names were publicized, allowing any criticisms from ordinary citizens—particularly regarding corruption—to be investigated before candidates took office. Working efficiency was enhanced, and corruption was curtailed. The aim, according to Qiu, was to enhance democracy. "The premise of democracy is to safeguard the people's right to know," he says. "Democracy can be achieved only when the people are fully informed. These reforms guaranteed the people's right to know, right to participate, right to elect, and right to supervise."

The CPC Organization Department, he says, sent "multiple inspection teams" to Suqian and authorized the reforms, while Hu Jintao, then vice president, also gave "complete backing." Qiu further introduced a groundbreaking system of Public Recommendations and *Direct* Election for the selection of Party leaders at the township level, which he says "again prompted now General Secretary Hu to issue supporting instructions." (Suqian's transparent approach to local leadership was gradually rolled out nationwide.)

In a further attempt to "fight corruption and complacency," Suqian introduced a Public Scrutiny System, designed to "guarantee the people's right to supervise cadres' work and conduct," and make "power work in the sunlight." Officials who performed poorly could now find themselves relieved of their posts. Previously, Qiu notes, "we only appointed cadres; we never removed them—cadres had an 'entrance', but no 'exit'. Now we have both, and both are under the supervision of the people: the people can remove as well as appoint cadres [at this local level]."

The overall goal, he emphasizes, was to "enable real public participation in the process of governance." Qiu emphasizes, however, that his reforms were not copying Western models, but rather following the "socialist democratic road with Chinese characteristics, a system in line with China's national conditions." The reforms "addressed the prior 'information asymmetry' between people and officials," he says, "making the selection of officials more open and transparent, and genuinely turning the people into the masters of democratic politics."

Qiu He's radical policies stimulated growth, reconstructed the city, reduced poverty, cut crime, curtailed corruption, improved education, and structured a viable healthcare system.[14] In 2005, Suqian's GDP reached $4.7 billion, almost double the $2.4 billion in 2000 when Qiu arrived.

Looking back, Qiu says that "systematic innovation was key—we kept exploring courageously." He stresses that, even though Suqian was considered backward, "there are really no such things as backward people; there are only backward rules." Still, he says, "We were very cautious about every reform we initiated. For every decision, if we weren't 100% sure, we didn't do it. For a city of over 5 million people, failure was intolerable." His principle, he says, was "rational, rule-based, orderly, solid, and reliable." And he claims that all his reforms were introduced "on the basis of scientific argument and democratic decision-making."

In ten years in Suqian, Qiu says his goal was to "institutionalize" systems so that reform would never depend on any one person or small group of persons. The system he created, he says "connects the 'visible hand' of the government with the 'invisible hand' of the market—and the public watches, monitors and discusses it openly." Qiu quoted Deng Xiaoping: 'Good systems prevent bad people from doing bad things, while bad systems prevent good people from doing good things or even encourage them to do bad things."

In 2006, after his second period of study in the U.S., Qiu became vice governor of Jiangsu, a promotion that elicited much media comment. In December 2007, he was named Party secretary of Kunming, the capital of Yunnan Province. It made Qiu He, still only 50 years old, a national figure.

In Kunming, Qiu reformed SOEs, public utilities, administrative process, investment and financing mechanisms, personnel, and intra-party supervision, among other areas. In less than one year, he established 169 new "systems reforms."

But it was one of his first moves in Kunming that really caught public attention. Qiu decided to publish the phone numbers of 859 leading officials (including his own), 5607 mid-level officials, and 888 deputies to the municipal congresses, along with their responsibilities, in the *Kunming Daily* newspaper. (The newspapers sold out; more copies were printed the next day.) Officials' office numbers could also be obtained in bookstores and from directory assistance. Qiu instructed that random checks be made to assess whether officials were answering calls from the public. "Right now," he proclaimed, "the rate is above 96%."

Qiu stresses that his initiative was "nothing new"—he had done the same in Shuyang County (1997) and in Suqian City (2001). It was necessary, he says, because "Kunming's social, cultural and political environment—our 'soft' environment'—lags far behind people's demands." His aim, he adds, is "to improve political participation, social services, legal regulation, culture and morality," and "turn Kunming into a city 'most friendly for entrepreneurship, most civilized for people, and safest for living'—a city of low costs in production, administration, society and life. Publicizing officials' contact and job data was an important part of the process."

Chinese media commented that the action could "signal a new era in China's local governance;" articles suggested that Qiu's measures should inspire others in advancing democracy and the rule of law, and in placing governmental power under better public supervision. *Beijing Youth Daily* wrote that the initiative was "worthy of praise no matter whether it was a mere technical move or out of deep-seated political consciousness."[15]

And Qiu He believes that China's media organizations themselves can help promote such changes in society. "Reforms have helped media gain some independence from government so that they can serve as real watchdogs," he says, adding that this "improves Party ethics and morals, corrects poor cadre conduct, guides individual behavior, purifies civil customs, and establishes new attitudes." In particular, he notes, the Internet has "sharply advanced people's right to know, right to express, right to participate, and right to supervise. It not only promotes scientific and democratic decision-making, but it also helps leaders gauge actual conditions of society so that conflicts can be nipped in the bud."

As for media criticism of his own methods, Qiu says that "reform is about taking risks and even paying a great price . . . for the people's good. Reform is like revolution, and so is innovation. They involve the readjustment of interests," he explains, "which means that some people will be unhappy. Especially during transitions, we have to take more risks and pay higher prices. Continuous development can only be achieved through continuous reform and innovation."

As a result, he says, "It's normal that reform encounters objection and resistance—it makes me study harder and improve my work relentlessly." Actually, he adds, "We welcome disagreements and different opinions; they are in themselves a kind of supervision, [and] will only encourage us to correct any deviation in a timely manner and do a better job." (Actually, the Qiu He debate in the Chinese media was in itself a kind of reform, since it was essentially a relatively open discussion about different types of political approaches.)

Still, despite Qiu's general popularity at the grassroots level, controversy over his "authoritarian methods" has continued. Some critics have even suggested he promoted reforms simply to gain political advantage. Intellectuals, in particular, have accused him of a "dangerous resuscitation" of "one-man rule."

Cai Dingjian, a legal specialist, described Qiu's approach as "fearful." He acknowledged Qiu was a good person who had accomplished much for common people, but stressed, "While I appreciate some of his reforms, I cannot appreciate the tyranny of such a reformer."[16]

Cai likened Qiu's style to "rule by good man" or "rule by strong man"—characteristics of feudalism, he said, which have traditionally been admired by the Chinese people. However, he added, good results produced under "rule of man" were not necessarily good for the country or for the people.

"The tragedy of strongman politics," he warned, "is that good officials always want to do everything themselves, to change the fate of the people, and to become the savior of the people, but they don't let people grasp their own fates." Such absolute power, he said, can turn tragic—witness Mao Zedong—and so society needed to create institutions and not to rely on individuals.

Qiu himself doesn't respond to his media critics: "If I'd come out to clarify," he says of the controversy caused by the 2004 *Southern Weekend* article, "it'd have created more buzz, which would have distracted my energy and wasted my time." His guiding principle, he says, is to "keep my mouth shut, lower my head, do real work, and act like a sponge—so that even if I'm punched by a fist I don't move or change." Indeed, he asserts, "I'm far more concerned what the *people* say about me, because the people are what count. As long as the people recognize what I do and conclude it's correct, higher levels will support me."

Nevertheless, Qiu He says there were many "mischaracterizations"— because few of his critics "had ever visited Suqian. Some media criticize me because they jump to conclusions without understanding," he adds. "They confuse my intense focus on implementation with the 'rule of man', even though my methods are in line with 'rule of law'."

Qiu notes that "Legislation is done from top-to-bottom, while institutional innovation is done from bottom-to-top. What integrates legislation and institutional innovation," he says, "is policies, and what drives the implementation of policies is social mobilization. This is not 'rule of man'." He stresses that he has "put great effort into institutionalizing systems, rules and procedures that supersede individuals. I've established accountability systems, performance-pledge systems, and deliver-within-limited-time systems, using desired results to orient officials' work."

As for his authoritarian image, Qiu says "If we don't effect tough measures, more often than not, things don't get done. I think that's why I strike people as a 'tough, strong man'." And, he insists, "each situation demands its own real-time, actual-conditions response: what I did in my early days in Shuyang would not make sense today in Kunming," he acknowledges. "It wouldn't even make sense in today's Shuyang. But when I first arrived, it *did* make sense."

On the Internet, voices supported Qiu's implicit questions—"Can't one use 'rule by man' to promote 'rule of law'? Can't one use nondemocratic means to promote democracy?"[17] One blogger noted that between "rule by man" and "rule of law," there exists a large "gray area" that couldn't be avoided. He criticized intellectuals for focusing on dualities such as "democratic" versus "autocratic," and "'rule by man" versus "rule by law." The common people, he said, were more concerned about ideas like "order" and "chaos." Strong officials like Qiu He, he suggested, understood social psychology and were simply basing their methods on it: "Rule by man under public supervision," he argued, was a necessary albeit short-term strategy for crossing this gray area.

(It's a convincing argument: China is in transition from an authoritarian past to a more democratic future, and this process cannot be short-circuited.

For a people without democratic traditions, hundreds of millions of whom still aren't well-educated, a sudden "Big Bang" of Western democracy could cause chaos. Officials like Qiu He may be just what's needed to help smooth the transition to a society which is ruled by law and respects human dignity. Some of Qiu's methods may seem tough: publishing officials' phone numbers in Kunming, for example, was arguably an "authoritarian" decision—but it placed the government more under the will of the people, helped improve people's lives, and could have long-lasting democratic impact. Moreover, Qiu is a systems creator and institutions builder, which is the best antidote to "rule by man." If Qiu He is truly successful, there would be less need for future "Qiu He's"—the system itself, which he would have helped create, would have become self-regulating.)

And despite the controversy, Qiu appears to have enjoyed high-level backing. The significance of this has been debated. Does it mean that China's senior leadership now supports aggressive reformers—or is Qiu an isolated case? In this context, the opinion of Li Yuanchao seems significant. When he was Jiangsu Party secretary, Li was Qiu's ultimate boss. More importantly, as head of the CPC Organization Department, he is now the senior leader responsible for Party and government promotions. Li Yuanchao says without equivocation that creative, risk-taking reformers are favored: those who dare to take risks, to devise new solutions to old problems, will be rewarded. That, he says, is President Hu's conviction, and "that is my own as well."

President Hu's visit to Suqian, when Qiu He was still in charge there in 2004, helps reveal how China's leaders think. Qiu recalls how it all happened.[18]

In April 2004, a few months after he was first criticized in the media, Qiu was summoned to Nanjing, the provincial capital, by Party Secretary Li Yuanchao, and told that Hu Jintao would be visiting Jiangsu in about a week—and would come to Suqian. (Qiu would later learn that the CPC General Office in Beijing had rejected the original itinerary, and insisted that President Hu wanted to visit the poorest area of the province.) "Secretary Li told me that we needed to make sure that Hu received *real* understanding of Suqian's situation—our accomplishments, sure, but also our challenges and problems," Qiu recalls.

President Hu first visited Shuyang County, where Qiu He had previously worked. In one of Shuyang's townships, which had lifted itself out of poverty by encouraging farmers to grow flowers and plants, Hu met an elderly farmer in his greenhouse and learned how the town had set up specialized teams to provide technology, market data, and sales—so that farmers could focus on growing the plants. He also met a wheat farmer and heard how new rural tax-exemption policies had rekindled farmers' enthusiasm for growing grain.

In the evening, after meeting Suqian City leaders (and posing for individual photos with everyone, including those who served the leaders their tea), Hu suggested an unscheduled visit to the city's main commercial district, stating that he didn't want an entourage accompanying him, only a few close aides (despite concerns about security).

Qiu He (pointing), Party secretary of Suqian City, accompanies President Hu Jintao (center); Wang Gang, head of the CPC General Office (second from right); and Jiangsu Party Secretary Li Yuanchao (far right), inspecting Suqian City, Jiangsu Province (May 2, 2004).

Qiu He (left), Party secretary of Suqian City, accompanies President Hu Jintao (right) inspecting Suqian, Jiangsu (May 2, 2004).

In a Li Ning Sports shop,[19] Hu asked the salesperson about sneaker prices and Suqian's business environment. In a grocery store, he asked shoppers about increasing prices and food quality, and about their views of the city's leadership. He was told that although there had been some short-term pain at the beginning, citizens were now pleased with their city's achievements. Word of Hu's presence spread quickly, and crowds began to gather, including many children. Notwithstanding his staff's anxiety over his safety (and the crowd's), Hu wanted to "see more and talk to more citizens." He visited two more stores, staying for almost an hour in the last one, before finally agreeing to climb into the van (though instead of heading back to the hotel, he requested a drive around the city.)

After his talks with Suqian residents, Hu gave Qiu He positive feedback, noting that "It's important that citizens are happy with our reform policies." Qiu says he was pleased that China's president, "without any prearrangement, had direct contact with local people." During the visit, Qiu also briefed Hu on Suqian's reforms and innovations; Hu made a point of visiting a private school, and asked detailed questions about governance reforms.

According to Qiu He, President Hu "affirmed our reforms and was very interested in our initiatives. He encouraged us 'to press on bravely without looking back', and he said we should focus on execution and implementation." Moreover, Qiu adds, "Hu was very clear. He instructed us to further deepen reform and creatively explore new ways to build a well-off harmonious society."

Hu's remarks were significant. In a city whose controversial initiatives—from privatization of education and healthcare to public presentations of candidates for public office—were on the leading edge of reform (some would say *over* the edge), China's most senior leader was instructing officials to "further deepen reform" and "creatively explore new ways" to do so. (Indeed, Hu's exhortation in Suqian was reminiscent of Deng Xiaoping's in Shenzhen [1992, on his famed Southern Tour]. Shenzhen had been criticized by conservatives as the poster child of reforming too rapidly; Deng said Shenzhen was reforming too slowly.)

Qiu later learned that, before President Hu's visit, "supervisory bodies of the central government had secretly sent multiple inspection teams to Shuyang and Suqian to investigate our reform initiatives, interviewing local people." Thus, he says, "I believe that Hu's visit embodied his concern for Suqian and for me personally."

And following Hu's visit, other senior officials came to Suqian. The "Qiu He phenomenon" was not a side show in China's reforms; it had become part of the main event. In 2008, Qiu He was awarded the title of Outstanding Contributor to China's Reform.[20]

★ ★ ★

Also awarded the title in 2008 was Pan Yue, vice minister of Environmental Protection, one of a new generation of outspoken Chinese officials. Pan, who comes from a Party family (his father was a CPC military officer), has attracted much attention—and controversy—for his outspoken role in encouraging environmental debate in China. The British political magazine *New Statesman* named him its "Person of the Year 2007," describing him as "a rare, if not lone, public voice within the Chinese government warning that disaster threatens unless development is checked." *BusinessWeek* too described him as "a courageous voice."

Pan Yue has had a varied career. He was originally a journalist, working as deputy editor of *China Youth Daily*, and had stints in several government agencies before entering the environmental protection arena in 2003. A high-profile, innovative thinker, Pan Yue attracted attention in 1991 with a widely read article on "China's practical response and strategic choices following the sudden changes in the USSR," in which he emphasized the need to preserve the Party's power—but called for the Party to adopt "a social democratic perspective" based on support of the "middle-income class."

"The Party's claim that it should rule because it won the revolution is no longer adequate," Pan Yue, then 31, wrote. "Time has passed and popular support has declined." He proposed a political system that, while maintaining CPC leadership, would allow other "social groups" to "participate in the distribution of national wealth and resources" through multi-candidate elections for official posts. The only alternative to "reform" at the top, he warned, was a "violent revolution" from below, much like what had just happened across Eastern Europe.

Ten years later, in 2001, Pan Yue, then deputy director of the State Council's Economic Restructuring Office, issued an internal report entitled "Principles of Political Reform." Praising Jiang Zemin's Three Represents, Pan agreed that the CPC must continue its historic role as the ruling party so that economic and political reform could continue to progress, and that it should represent the interests not only of the Chinese masses but of the wealth-creating elite as well.

Rejecting orthodox Marxist-Maoist governing styles, he stated that reform must reach from top to bottom of society. With increasing globalization and advanced technology, Pan said, China could only advance if its intellectuals and entrepreneurs played a leading role. Radically, his report urged a separation between the ruling CPC and the executive branch of the Chinese government, and asserted that any modern party, even a ruling party, must act more as a social mediator between various interest groups than as a political monolith.

As expected, Pan Yue's report was attacked from both political wings: the Left (orthodox Marxist-Leninists) denounced it as deviating from socialist fundamentals, while the Right (liberal democrats) rejected its continued support for absolute Party rule.

It was in the field of environment protection, however, that Pan Yue made his most powerful and persistent impact. In 2005, he startled China's industrial establishment by shutting down 30 projects, with $14 billion in investments, ranging from thermal power to hydroelectric plants—for not filing proper environmental-impact statements.[21] Even though these high-powered projects got back up running with modest effort (by paying small fines), Pan succeeded in igniting national debate on whether China was sacrificing its environment on the altar of uncontrolled growth.

"The main reason behind the continued deterioration of the environment is a mistaken view of what counts as political achievement," he said, adding bluntly, "the crazy expansion of high-polluting, high-energy industries has spawned special interests. Protected by local governments, some businesses treat the natural resources that belong to all the people as their own private property."[22]

In an interview with *Der Spiegel,* Pan Yue went even further. "This miracle [China's economic growth] will end soon because the environment can no longer keep pace," he warned. "Acid rain is falling on one-third of China's territory, half of the water in our seven largest rivers is completely useless, while one-fourth of our citizens do not have access to clean drinking water."As if that were not bad enough, he added: "One-third of the urban population is breathing polluted air, and less than 20% of the trash in cities is treated and processed in an environmentally sustainable manner. Finally, five of the ten most polluted cities worldwide are in China."

Pan pledged to take action wherever possible. "Even though we have little power, we will close down illegal projects, including economically powerful steel, cement, aluminum, and paper factories," he said. "And we will ignore the agendas followed by influential officials and companies."[23]

However he stressed that environmental protection was hampered by a "lack of public participation in China," which he said lay "at the root" of the country's environmental problems. Only public opinion, he said, could ensure that anti-pollution laws were "properly implemented."

Friends describe Pan Yue as imaginative and determined; an informal, unstuffy figure, he is also a published poet. But he is no liberal democrat advocating Western-style free-market capitalism. On the contrary, he argues that the "fundamental cause" of the global environmental crisis is "the capitalist system," and he seeks reform within socialism. "China's circumstances, in particular imbalances among its population, resources and environment, mean that traditional western industrial civilization is not an option," Pan has said, adding "China is a socialist country and cannot engage in environmental colonialism, nor act with unilateral power, so it must move towards a new type of civilization."

And Pan suggests that recent ideas promoted by China's leaders, "such as . . . building a harmonious, resource-saving and environmentally-friendly society, have laid the foundation for doing so."[24] The Scientific Perspective on Development, he says, "seeks a comprehensive and sustainable change of politics, economics, society, culture and theory—a transformation of civilization." It is not, he adds, "simply a change in the mode of economic growth." The next decade, he says, "will be crucial in determining whether China can complete this transformation from traditional to eco-industrial civilization."

★ ★ ★

Yu Yibo, director-general of PetroChina's M&A department, personifies the sophisticated kind of overseas returnees that Minister Li Yuanchao encourages as part of his visionary program to upgrade China's future leaders. With a BA in oil exploration, MBA, and doctorate in finance (from Japan), Yu has managed numerous PetroChina financial transactions, including China's first public tender, delisting of Jilin Chemical in three markets (New York, Hong Kong and Shanghai), and major overseas acquisitions.[25]

Our acquisitions, Yu says, are "strategic and global, positioning PetroChina to become a world-class integrated oil company." For example, the purchase of Singapore Petroleum provides flexibility in distribution, product allocations, and pricing, and strengthens PetroChina's competitiveness in refining and sales.

Certain PetroChina technologies, such as abandoned oil field recovery, are strong, Yu says, but others, such as exploration analysis, are weak. He stresses that PetroChina is "determined to have state-of-the-art technologies in all relevant categories," noting, "we will use acquisitions to accomplish this." Although PetroChina's market capitalization is the world's largest, Yu says, "We still have work to do. We will enhance our technology—then really be number one."

For PetroChina to become world-class, and for China to continue developing for another 30 years, Yu states, "quality people are key." Therefore, Yu advocates that in selecting China's future leaders, their personnel decisions should be assessed. "People are the best test of leaders," Yu says. "In addition to traditional criteria, officials should be evaluated on how well the people they choose and promote perform."

★ ★ ★

Whatever their political views, there is no doubt that many of China's new leaders are becoming more sophisticated in issues of governance, and seeking new approaches. Zhang Xiaoshan, a rural expert, says many younger officials are capable, well-educated and think clearly. "If a county-level governor in China was appointed president of a small European country, they would do very well," he says with a smile. "Many local governors manage over a million people; a prefecture leader manages several million. These local leaders have great abilities and much experience."

However, he calls for better governance at grassroots levels. "Certainly local officials know reality better than central officials," says Zhang. "But if the system is wrong, the more capable they are, the more dangerous they are—especially if we don't have effective checks-and-balances mechanisms. Even though officials know what they should do, they might do the opposite."

The solution, Professor Zhang believes, is to provide greater public access to information, enhance the people's right to participate in decision-making processes, and make known how money is spent. "Such democratic participation is critical," he says, "to prevent local governments from misusing resources." In the end, he adds, "all reform comes down to political reform. We must trust our younger leaders."

"Compared to their peers abroad, Chinese officials are expert and very knowledgeable," observed Politburo member Liu Yunshan. "I've travelled to many countries and I can tell you this: Chinese officials, in general, are most proficient with data and analysis—they know intimately key numerical criteria and can provide detailed assessments spontaneously and without notes."[26]

It wasn't always this way. In times past, Chinese officials were chosen largely by communist ideology or political patronage. Now, though ideology and patronage remain, the most important criterion for promotion is professional competence. Chinese leaders attribute the sophistication of current officials to the increasingly meritocratic system in the Party and government. In addition, given China's traumatic history and long epochs of national inferiority, Chinese leaders say they are eager to learn and committed to excel. Many are also very intense. (And some sound like investment bankers!)

Endnotes

1 "Li Yuanchao on cadre recruitment and promotion," *People's Daily*, July 16, 2008.
2 *Global People*. April 22,2009.Willy Lam, "Hu Jintao Picks Core Sixth-Generation Leaders," *China Brief*,Vol. IX, Issue 10, May 15, 2009.
3 The All-ChinaYouth Federation is a federative body of Chinese youth organizations closely associated with the Communist Youth League of China.
4 Zhang Li, *"Zuifu zhengyi de shiwei shuji"* [The most controversial city party secretary], *Nanfang Zhoumo* (Southern Weekend), February 5, 2004.
5 Joseph Fewsmith, "Promotion of Qiu He Raises Questions about Direction of Reform," *China Leadership Monitor*, No. 17 (2006). http://media.hoover.org/.
6 Author's and Adam Zhu's meeting with Qiu He in Kunming, October 2008.
7 Kunming Government: http://en.km.gov.cn/ColumnInfo.aspx?cid524
8 David Osborne and Ted A. Gaebler, *Reinventing Government: How The Entrepreneurial Spirit Is Transforming The Public Sector*, Basic Books, 1992.
9 Fewsmith, *China Leadership Monitor*, No. 17 (2006).
10 Ibid. and Zhang Li, *Nanfang Zhoumo* (Southern Weekend), 2004; section
11 Ibid., quoting *Renmin Wang*.
12 Zhou Jing, China.org.cn, March 31, 2008.
13 Zhang Li, *Nanfang Zhoumo* (Southern Weekend), 2004.
14 Ning Song, "The Qiu He phenomenon: promotion of "official with a personality" evokes national debate". *Chinaelections.net* (February 25, 2008) at www.chinaelections.net.http://

en.chinaelections.org/newsinfo.asp?newsid515838; Fewsmith, "Promotion of Qiu He Raises Questions about Direction of Reform".

15 "Full disclosure: Public phone lists signal new era of China local governance," Xinhua, February 19, 2008.

16 Cai Dingjian, "*Women xuyao zenyang de gaigejia?*" (What type of reformer do we need?) Originally from *Xinwen zhoukan*, posted on www.polisino.org.

17 Fewsmith, "Promotion of Qiu He Raises Questions about Direction of Reform."

18 Adam Zhu, my long-time partner in China, was with Qiu He in Kunming when he gave me this account.

19 Li Ning is China's largest sportswear company, founded by the famous gymnast, Li Ning, who won three gold medals (six medals in total) at the 1984 Olympics in Los Angeles and who lit the flame hoisted high above the electrified crowds at the 2008 Beijing Olympics.

20 Zhou Jing, China.org.cn, September 29, 2008.

21 "A Courageous Voice For A Greener China," *BusinessWeek*, July 11, 2005.

22 Joseph Kahn and Jim Yardley, "As China Roars, Pollution Reaches Deadly Extremes," *The New York Times*, August 26, 2007.

23 "The Chinese Miracle Will End Soon," Spiegel Online, March 7, 2005.

24 "The Environment Needs Public Participation," China dialogue, October 27, 2006.

25 Author's meeting with Yu Yibo, Beijing, June 2009.

26 Author's meeting with Liu Yunshan, Beidaihe, August 2009.

37

China's Economic Future: How Far Can It Go?

In 2007, China became the world's third-largest economy, surpassing Germany. In 2008, China contributed 22% of world economic growth. In 2010, China's GDP reached $5.75 trillion (about $10 trillion in Purchasing Power Parity), overtaking Japan to become the world's second-largest economy. Sometime between 2020 and 2030, China's GDP is expected to exceed that of the U.S. and become the world's largest (though China's per-capita GDP would still lag far behind).[1] All recognize that China must play a larger role in global economic affairs, particularly after the financial crisis.

China's leaders have long sought to maintain economic growth in an optimum narrow band, ideally between about 8% and 10% per year—high enough to maintain employment and increase standards of living, and not so high as to overheat the economy and engender inflation.[2]

During 2007 and early 2008, however, the government faced the specter of overheating: growth exceeded 11-12% and inflation rose to almost 9%, the highest in 11 years. Global escalations in prices of energy, raw materials and food threatened to push prices higher still. At the same time, the gradual but unrelenting appreciation in the value of the Chinese currency, the RMB yuan, against the U.S. dollar—it rose 20% in three years—undermined the competitiveness of Chinese goods in world markets. Manufacturers of labor-intensive products, especially small and medium-sized firms, were hard hit—in the first half of 2008 alone, more than half of China's toy exporters closed shop. Most were very small, but it was a worrying trend.

Export-oriented companies were hurt further when the nascent worldwide recession was greatly intensified by the meltdown in financial markets. Foreign demand for China's products weakened, and in some cases collapsed. Suddenly, China's leaders' concerns flipped from how to dampen an overheated economy to how to stimulate a lagging one. The previous policy of monetary austerity was replaced by an expansionary policy designed to prevent massive job cuts. China's central bank cut interest rates for the first time in six years, and to boost lending, bank reserve requirements were reduced. As for industries affected by the slowdown, tax policies were changed to encourage investment. The window of China's economic future, for so long so clear, had begun to fog.

As the financial crisis worsened, China's State Council targeted ten areas for its massive $586 billion stimulus: affordable housing; rural infrastructure (roads, power grids); transport (railways, subways, roads, airports); health and education (including special education and cultural facilities); environment (pollution-control and energy-conserving projects, greenbelts); industry (high-tech upgrading); accelerated disaster relief; raising rural incomes; tax reforms; and finance (bank credit for smaller companies, financing for mergers and acquisitions to rationalize industries).[3] As part of the stimulus, China facilitated exports (tax rebates and trade financing) and restricted imports by proscribing government agencies from purchasing foreign products—thus inviting charges of "protectionism," which China itself had railed against in America's stimulus.[4] (Embarrassed by the charge of hypocrisy, China quickly blamed foreign media for misunderstanding China's efforts to boost domestic demand and stepped up supervision on construction projects.)

Reflecting China's maturing self-confidence, the measures outlined in the stimulus package were scrutinized in the media.[5] Dueling editorials in mainstream newspapers highlighted the debate swirling at the highest levels of government. Virtually everyone agreed that China must wean itself off its dependence on foreign exports and promote domestic consumption. But some argued that the stimulus should focus on promoting inland rural consumption, which would also work to correct China's internal economic imbalances. Others believed that, considering the seriousness of the crisis, the safest investment would be in the proven economic engines of the more powerful eastern coastal provinces, with their stronger, more market-savvy companies.

Li Keqiang, member of the Politburo Standing Committee and executive vice premier of the State Council, summarized China's leaders' thinking and action. "In the face of a complex and ever-changing international and domestic environment," he said in a speech at the Global Think Tank Summit in Beijing (July 2009), "the Chinese Government promptly and decisively adjusted our macroeconomic policies and launched a comprehensive stimulus package to ensure stable and rapid economic growth. We increased government spending and public investments and implemented structural tax reductions. Balancing short-term and long-term strategic perspectives, we are promoting industrial restructuring and technological innovation, and using principles of reform to solve problems of development."

Some Chinese commentators pointed out that the stimulus package in itself was insufficient to solve China's problems. "Its benefits are short term, perhaps two years," according to economist Hua Sheng (Chapter 12). He emphasizes that increasing domestic demand is more important than stimulating exports, "which are vulnerable to disruptions."

At this stage in China industrialization, Hua contends, domestic demand should already have been much greater. The underlying cause of the problem, he argues, is that urbanization lags well behind industrialization. While China's urban population, at 46%, superficially appears close to the world average of 50%, Hua points out that this includes some 200-300 million migrant workers, who do not have anywhere near the standards of living of permanent urban residents. Take away the migrant workers and China's urbanization drops to a debilitatingly low 28%, he says.

The key to solving China's economic problems, he argues, is thus to make "peasant workers" into real citizens. "By providing migrants with equal housing, medical care, education, and social security, they will drive domestic demand, and maintain China's high growth."

At the annual National People's Congress in 2009, the focus was almost entirely on the economy, and Premier Wen Jiabao increased government commitments to fund social programs in healthcare, education and old-age pensions. He also pledged to help laid-off workers start their own businesses by offering tax incentives and training. The idea was to give people confidence in the future so that they would spend rather than save.

China's leaders were so deeply concerned with the financial crisis that they began attending regular, private lectures by distinguished economists who offered varying solutions to China's structural problems. In meetings with senior officials I am always asked for my assessment, and peppered with probing questions.

Politburo member Liu Yunshan recalls that "Several years ago, Robert Zoellick, now president of the World Bank, advised us to open our financial and capital markets more rapidly. Can you imagine what would have happened to us?" he asks. "If we were totally linked, as many have implored us, what a disaster we would have! Chinese leaders continue to be cautious," Liu emphasizes. "Every decision we make, we try to base on reality. When Hank Paulson seemed to blame the worldwide financial crisis on China's high savings rate, we didn't know what he was thinking. President Hu has stressed that we will unswervingly stick to reform and opening-up; even if we have problems, we will persevere. Opening-up is our goal, but we must do it gradually."[6]

For China's economy, as for the world's, 2008 was turbulent. Prior, China's economic objectives had been easy to articulate, if challenging to implement. Short term: modulate an overheated economy to maintain continued growth. Long-term: restructure industry to move toward sustainable development, reduce pollution, and increase the value-add component of China-made products.[7] The financial crisis shuffled all the cards.

★ ★ ★

Politburo member Li Yuanchao suggests that one of the real lessons of the financial crisis is that economic imbalances between China and Western countries need addressing. He argues that "excess distribution" of assets and consumption of products in the West is a fundamental cause of world economic problems.[8]

"We have entered an era of globalized production, but world market systems, world financial systems, relations between countries, international political relations, and people's consumption psychology have not yet properly adapted to it," says Li. "Wealth in the world is uneven and not in accord with new realities. We need to adjust relationships between people's consumption and their production, and even how assets are allocated."

Specifically, Li Yuanchao points out that, "World manufacturing has shifted largely to developing countries. Yet in the transfer," he adds, "the wages of labor didn't much increase, primarily because the developed countries, mainly America and Europe, used the strength of their financial sector to increase their own considerable consumption and wealth (i.e., their possession of properties, including real estate, stocks, and the like)."

Thus, Li notes, "Over the five years 2002-2007, U.S. households enjoyed a rapid increase in net assets, while the production labor in developing countries did not." As a result, he says, while China is now the world's leading manufacturing power, and its labor wages have increased, the wealth of its people has lagged. Americans provide less of the labor, but own more of the wealth—even though "American productivity didn't much increase during this period."

"Why such an arrangement," Li asks pointedly? He cites the auto industry as an example: "Due to joint ventures and similar equipment, worker productivity in Shanghai or Nanjing is almost the same as in Detroit," he says. "However, U.S. household wealth doubled in five years, whereas in China, though they are growing, they aren't growing nearly as fast."

Noting that India and other Asian countries are also affected, Li asks: "Why the 'excess distribution' to Americans and Europeans?" He quotes Thomas Friedman: "'The World is Flat' in the production of goods," he says, "but uneven [pyramidal] in the distribution and possession of property." This imbalance, he suggests, made a crisis inevitable: "Of course the crisis is related to financial instruments, leverage and bubbles," Li adds, "but even without these triggers, it was bound to happen sooner or later."

While emphasizing his concern for both American and Chinese people, Li calls for adjustments in the accepted order. "American households' share of consumption and assets should be reduced and Chinese households' share should be increased," he says (though, on a per-capita basis, of course, Americans would still have far more).

I agreed that Americans spend too much and save too little while Chinese save too much and spend too little, and that to fix both sides of the equation should be a high priority for both countries—but that underlying reasons for the "excess distributions" are complex. In a globalized economy, new and attractive products and services—embedding knowhow, technology, branding, and all manner of value-added innovation—demand high percentages of created wealth.

From China's point of view, Li Yuanchao stresses that senior leadership is focused not only on boosting the Chinese people's consumption, but also on increasing the Chinese family's property—by means of, for example, speeding construction of low-income housing and broadening home ownership (a prime wealth-builder in most countries). He highlights the government's policy of subsidizing purchases by families in rural areas—covering, for example, 13% of the cost of electrical appliances such as television sets and washing machines. Currently, Li notes, "most rural families have a house but lack household items."

Li concludes by calling for America and China to work together as partners, using the financial crisis to promote commonality of interests, so that "the distribution of assets and consumption of goods are more harmonious and sustainable." He suggests that positives may emerge from the global slowdown. "The crisis is serious but in every crisis there is opportunity," Li says, stressing that such situations can be both "destructive and creative. After the Internet bubble burst, innovations followed. Out of the Great Depression, the automotive and aircraft industries emerged. Many industries and companies will suffer now," he acknowledges, "and some may disappear, but others will arise and the world will be stronger for this. As an optimist and idealist," he stresses, "I take such an attitude, though we must strive to reduce the suffering of our peoples."

★ ★ ★

For a world increasingly panicked at the prospect of the worst recession in a lifetime, such optimism, and the prospect of continued Chinese growth, has seemed like a lifeline in raging seas. A 2009 United Nations report described China as Asia's "locomotive" for global economic growth (corroborated by a surprisingly rapid and strong recovery from the world economic crisis, even as the U.S. and other leading economies stayed stuck in recession). Commenting on the report, Professor Wang Tongsan of the Chinese Academy of Social Sciences (CASS) said, "It is beyond doubt that China will play a more important role in the world economy as the U.S. and Japan experience setbacks."[9]

In 2007, before the financial crisis but amidst growing suspicions about the so-called "China threat," I put a list of questions about China's economic future to Professor Wang and his colleagues at CASS—those "inner sanctum" government forecasters, whose job is to provide leadership with best estimates of the future.[10] I gave them target years: China 2030 - 2035.[11] The results were interesting, not least because Professor Wang challenged his own researchers on their responses to several of my queries, and did so openly in my presence. (Good for China, I thought, open disagreement is progress!)

The forecasts assumed a significant slowing of China's growth, but Wang warned that similar estimates had proved wrong in the past, sometimes wildly so. In the 1960s, for example, Chinese forecasters assumed that China's GDP would roughly double by 2000—but in fact it grew almost

17 times, as reform leveraged China's huge population to create spectacular growth. The same conditions, Wang suggested, might still apply today, making forecasted numbers conservative. With that caveat, CASS forecasts for China 2030-2035 follows:

Economic System Reform: By 2030, researchers suggested, it would be basically completed. The major issue would be "adjustment of interests" among different classes.

Gross Domestic Product: The researchers forecast serious slowing of GDP growth by 2030-2035, giving estimates far lower than those made by Western economists. (It's worth noting, however, that CASS researchers significantly underestimated that *current* year, 2007. Indeed China's habitual underestimation of its own GDP indicates, I suggest, that foreign fears of China's "secret plans for world domination" are ill founded.)

GDP Sectors: Tertiary (service) industry would increase from 40% in 2005 to 48-49% in 2030-2035. Professor Wang, however, thought that it would rise to 55-60% in the target years. (This is significant because China's service industry must grow—reflecting a more consumer-oriented economy and reducing the country's excessive dependence on exports—if trade imbalances are to ease.)

Trade Surpluses: These were not expected to continue at today's levels, which have caused tensions. But researchers saw no dramatic change: they said China's share of world manufacturing would continue to increase, though its dependence on foreign trade must and would decrease as a percentage of GDP.

RMB Exchange Rate: Researchers asserted that, no matter the size of its trade surplus, China would never be bullied into revaluing its currency—although leaders appreciate constructive criticism (and perhaps pressure, too, if good-hearted, subtle and private). The RMB was expected to continue its slow rise, though nobody would hazard a guess as to its ultimate plateau. (After over a decade of being pegged at an exchange rate of RMB 8.28 to the dollar, in 2005 the RMB was allowed to float within tightly controlled ranges, and within three years had appreciated to about 6.8. But with the 2008 financial crisis, further appreciation, at least for a time, was halted. China's leaders realized that the "triple trouble"—worldwide slowdown, inflation, and currency appreciation—could devastate the economy. In June 2010, after China had sustained its economy rather remarkably through the worst of the financial crisis, the RMB was again allowed to float, though its modest appreciation did not much satisfy foreign critics.)

Competitiveness in Global Markets: Chinese corporations were forecast to reinforce their international competitiveness by higher R&D (leveraging increased government expenditures on science and technology), while still benefitting from comparatively low labor costs and huge economies of scale. Policy-makers know that China must move up the value chain: it cannot remain dependent on low-skilled, low-cost, low-margin manufacturing of textiles, toys, shoes, clothes and other simple goods—and redressing social imbalances will inevitably lead to rising labor costs.[12]

In 2010, there were 46 Chinese companies among the world's top 500 based on revenue (up from 22 in 2007). Forecasters predicted 30-40 more by 2030-2035—likely in telecom, petrochemicals, electric power, banking, autos, electronics, and computing.[13] (President Hu has pledged that China will "support domestic enterprises in carrying out international operations of R&D, production and marketing, and accelerate the growth of Chinese multinational corporations and Chinese brand names in the world market.")

Science and Technology Level: Strikingly, researchers predicted that the nation's level of science and technology would be hampered by what they called the country's "serious, systematic deficiencies," in particular the poor state of intellectual-property rights protection, and a shortage of top talent, caused by problems in the "existing talent nurturing system." It meant, they said, that China would have to rely more on overseas-trained professionals.

Intellectual Property Rights (IPR): Only if IPR were protected, researchers insisted, could China capitalize on its economies of scale in R&D to become a world innovation center and leader in technology. (Branded Chinese companies, like in software and clothing, are now also pressuring the government to crack down on piracy. The Chinese publisher of my biography of President Jiang Zemin, for example, stationed people to search out counterfeit copies, intercepted a railroad car that held thousands of bootlegged books, and prevented me from signing pirated versions.) In basic sciences, researchers said, China will still lag far behind the U.S.

Environment/Pollution: Pollution, researchers claimed, was at or near its peak. A national initiative to develop pollution-combating technologies, together with increasing public pressure to protect the environment, will reduce the impact of high-pollution products and mitigate pollution problems—though they predicted rapid growth in the number of automobiles. (In 2008, China manufactured 9.3 million cars, surpassing America.)

Sustainable Development/Alternative Energy: Advanced technology combined with decreasing demand for high energy-consuming products will gradually help China achieve sustainable development, CASS experts predicted. Alternative energies—nuclear, solar, wind, gas, and bio-energy—will enjoy expanding markets. (Greater international cooperation in energy technology will help—joint Sino-U.S. research on efficient, low-polluting coal, for example.)

Energy Efficiency: Here Professor Wang again questioned his researchers' conclusions that China's "energy utilization efficiency ratio" would fall dramatically.[14] Wang agreed there would be progress—since energy efficiency is a prime national directive—but doubted it would be so great. The researchers insisted that, because most of China's companies are "small with very low energy utilization," achieving a four-fold improvement is possible, given advanced technology and changing attitudes.

(High-level concern about energy efficiency was emphasized by an analytical paper by former President Jiang Zemin, published in 2008 in the *Journal of Shanghai Jiaotong University*, his alma mater. It analyzed global energy trends and their implications for environmental, economic and social development, focusing on China's opportunities and challenges. Jiang prioritized energy conservation, efficient utilization, low pollution, and advanced technology. He had consulted several technical experts, and corrected proofs of the article himself—evincing his concern that what he called China's "very grim" environmental situation should be addressed. For a retired senior leader to prepare an academic analysis of a critical problem is, to me, another signpost announcing how far China had come.[15])

Water Resources: Water shortages will constrain China's development—this was the one area where researchers saw no grounds for optimism, predicting that China's water resources would only deteriorate further by 2030–2035.

Education: China will relax restrictions on its education market, researchers forecast, which will enable "the fair competition between public education and private education."

Population: Slowing growth, from 1.31 billion people in 2005 to 1.47 billion in 2030 and 1.49 billion in 2035. (Researchers predicted that China's strict one-child-per-family policy will be gradually abandoned.)

Income Inequality: The Gini coefficient, which measures equality of income distribution in a country, tracks this most serious of China's problems. The coefficient is a scale of 0 to 1—"0" represents perfect equality (everyone has the same income) and "1" represents perfect inequality (one person has all the income). Higher than 0.4 is seen as threatening social harmony, and above 0.6 may predict social unrest. For decades (1950s-1970s), China was one of the world's most equal nations—a Gini coefficient below 0.3. Recently, the figure has risen sharply: from 0.35 in 2003 to 0.48 in 2009, higher than that of the U.S. (0.46).[16]

CASS researchers suggested China's Gini coefficient would decline to a remarkably low 0.26-0.28 by 2030-2035—but Professor Wang interrupted to express his disagreement with such optimism, suggesting that it would remain about the same even over this long time period. The researchers then clarified their position by explaining that 0.26-0.28 was "an ideal situation in a just society," but acknowledged that achieving this goal would depend on "long-term government policies."

The researchers also assessed the affect of various key strategic relationships on China's economic development:

United States: They predicted closer economic ties, and suggested that China and America will find more common interests in regional security and thwarting terrorism, while more efficient "crisis coordination systems" will engender more positive Sino-U.S. relations.

Taiwan: Relations between the mainland and Taiwan will become more equal, and hence more harmonious, with economic and trade cooperation replacing political disputes. (If Taiwan ever "loses the mainland," I was told, it will lose its economic basis.)

Africa and Latin America: China was predicted to enhance political relations, especially with larger countries in these regions (like South Africa and Brazil). However, if African and Latin American countries do not improve their manufacturing competitiveness, they would remain simply providers of commodities to China—a long-term asymmetry that could trigger anti-China backlashes.

Military Development: Researchers asserted it was naïve for foreigners to hope that China would not upgrade its military technologies and enhance its military power—though they stressed that if China has a "master plan," it is defensive, more of an "anti-domination master plan." China will produce more of its own military equipment, but even in 2035, they said, it will still be dependent on imports for its most advanced military systems—which may limit its options.

★ ★ ★

Whatever the accuracy of these predictions, there seems no question that China's continuing economic growth will lead to further expansion of its worldwide influence. In a globalized economy, Chinese enterprises will accelerate their international expansion, and will acquire increasing numbers of companies in developed countries.

Some liken Chinese acquisitions today to Japan's buying spree in the 1980s. This is wrong. Then, Japanese companies purchased foreign assets because they seemed cheap in comparison with "bubble" valuations in Japan's domestic real-estate and stock markets. Now, Chinese acquisitions are strategic in nature, and fueled by deep domestic markets which select and sustain superior Chinese companies. This Darwinian emergence is generating new species of Chinese industrial giants with robust and enduring strength, firms like PetroChina and Haier, which have entered into the world's top tier.

Such expansion stirs political sensitivities. For many Americans, Chinese takeover bids for U.S. companies exacerbate emotions already heated by trade imbalances and what they believe are unfair trade practices. Americans see China using low-cost government loans to finance acquisitions, thus taking unfair advantage of open American markets—while keeping American entry into China limited.

One example was a 2005 email sent by a Dell salesman which alleged that buying personal computers made by IBM—whose PC division was acquired by the Chinese firm Lenovo—was tantamount to "directly supporting/funding the Chinese government." The story, blasted by the Chinese media, led to a storm of outrage, and sent Dell into a whirl of damage control.[17]

The case which aroused perhaps the most ire, especially in the U.S. Congress, was the 2005 attempt by CNOOC, China's off-shore oil company, to acquire Unocal, the California-based U.S. oil company. Issues of

U.S. national security were raised. Yet, as I argued at the time, energy competition and Chinese purchasing are inexorable trends, and CNOOC's bid was more of an opportunity than a threat for America.[18] Chinese enterprises, even those controlled by the Chinese government, I suggested, should be rewarded, not punished, for following the rules and norms of international business.

The more such beneficial behavior is reinforced, the more China will continue to mature into a responsible nation. To frustrate its natural ambition, on the other hand, may be to retard its transition. American resistance to such cross-border acquisitions triggers hostile reactions in China, confirming embedded perceptions that the U.S. seeks to "contain China" and retard its growth and power. Chinese see bias, emblematic of a Western aversion to China's historic rise.

Similarly dark rumors about China's "master plan"—its supposed intent to control foreign assets as part of an insatiable desire to expand—surfaced in 2007, when China Investment Corporation (CIC), which manages $200 billion (about 10% of China's massive foreign exchange reserves of $2 trillion), invested $3 billion in Blackstone Group, one of the world's leading private equity firms.[19]

In fact, putting a small fraction of its foreign reserves into a top U.S. private equity firm was entirely logical for China. Led by its Chairman Lou Jiwei —a former finance minister who *Time* magazine selected as one of the world's 100 most influential people—CIC made the investment based on various factors, none of them conspiratorial or even particularly monumental, among them the simple fact that China's increasing participation in international capital markets required becoming more versed in the ways of Wall Street. (The deal was criticized in China too—particularly as Blackstone's stock price declined, losing as much as three-quarters of its value.)

Half a year after its Blackstone investment, CIC paid $5 billion for 9.9% of Morgan Stanley, one of America's premier investment banks, and, notably, there was hardly a ripple or rumor. Facing the ominous financial crisis, Americans suddenly saw Chinese investment as more savior than predator. Thus, as international investments by Chinese companies become routine, the West must learn to deal routinely with a nation which is now the source of so much of our clothes, furniture, toys, electronics—and, in the case of the U.S., our Treasury finance as well.

Chinese companies face their own challenges as they move into other countries—primarily cultural and organizational integration. We should welcome them to compete freely in our markets—just as we should insist that our companies compete freely in their markets. The closer Chinese companies, state-owned or private, work with American companies, the closer our common interests will be aligned. In addition to greater economic efficiencies, which will increase standards of living worldwide, the benefits may also include political and social reforms in China's increasingly pluralistic society.

(I gained insight into the growing strength of Chinese companies relative to the Chinese government—even when the companies are government-owned—when I was visiting a provincial capital and invited to dinner by the city's Party secretary. The CEO of a local state-owned company then suggested dinner on the same evening, explaining jovially that his casual pre-emption of the Party chief was "no problem." A few decades earlier he might have been jailed for such impertinence. As Chinese companies become stronger, they become independent centers of power and provide new checks and balances in China's governance.)

As China celebrated the 30th anniversary of reform and opening-up in December 2008, only two things economic seemed sure: the first was that the past had been the most remarkable period of sustained growth in Chinese history (and perhaps in world history); never before had so many people been brought up out of poverty so far so fast. The second was that the future would not emulate the past; never before had there been such complexity exacerbated by such uncertainty. That's the promise of New China's next 30 years.

Endnotes

1   2008 GDP: United States, $14,330 billion; Japan, $ 4,844 billion; China $ 4,222 billion; Germany, $3,818 billion. Using Purchasing Power Parity (PPP): China, $7,800 billion. CIA World Fact Book.
2   Barry Naughton, "A New Team Faces Unprecedented Economic Challenges," *China Leadership Monitor*, No. 21.
3   "China's 4 trillion yuan stimulus to boost economy, domestic demand," Xinhua, November 9, 2008.
4   Keith Bradsher, "As China Stirs Economy, Some See Protectionism," *The New York Times*, June 23, 2009.
5   Rodger Baker and Jennifer Richmond, "Internal Divisions and the Chinese Stimulus Plan," Stratfor, February 23, 2009.
6   Author's meeting with Liu Yunshan, Beijing, December 2008.
7   Barry Naughton, "A New Team Faces Unprecedented Economic Challenges," *China Leadership Monitor*, No. 26, Fall 2008
8   Author's meeting with Li Yuanchao, Beijing January 2009.
9   "China key to easing global recession," *China Daily*, January 17, 2009.
10 Robert Lawrence Kuhn, "What Will China Look Like in 2035?" BusinessWeek.com, October 16, 2007.
11 For the conspiracy-minded, what I was told may or may not be what China's forecasters really think. But these are real data points: for sure this is what they really told me.
12 David Barboza "China's Industrial Ambitions Soar to High-Tech," *The New York Times*, August 1, 2008.
13 Doug Tsuruoka, "Fortune 500 Gets A Makeover As Chinese Firms Grow Bigger," Yahoo! News, July 20, 2009 - http://news.yahoo.com/s/ibd/20090720/bs_ibd_ibd/200 90720general.
14 China's "energy utilization efficiency ratio" was forecasted to fall from 2.81 in 2005 to 0.73 in 2030 and 0.57 in 2035 (calculated on the number of 10,000 tons of coal-equivalents used to generate each RMB 100 million of GDP, at 1990 constant prices).

15 As to why Jiang Zemin chose a low-circulation academic journal for his energy-policy analysis, rather than more well-known print platforms, opinions differ. Some say Jiang has special feelings towards his alma mater, while others think that as a former leader he wished to avoid direct intervention in real-life affairs. Both may be true, but I would add a third reason: Jiang Zemin loves the academic world. In fact, right before unexpected events propelled him to political leadership in 1989, he was happily anticipating retirement and becoming a professor at Shanghai Jiaotong University (Kuhn, *The Man Who Changed China*).

16 Arthur C. Brooks and Charles Wolf, Jr., "All Inequality is Not Equal," *Far Eastern Economic Review*, June 2008.

17 "Dell in damage control mode after employee's email swipe at IBM," *Austin Business Journal*, June 10, 2005; *People's Daily*, June 2, 2005.

18 Robert Lawrence Kuhn, "Enter the Dragon," *The Deal*, August 15, 2005.

19 Robert Lawrence Kuhn, "Behind China's Investment in Blackstone," BusinessWeek.com, May 25, 2007.

38

Guangdong Visions

Guangdong Province has pioneered China's historic economic resurgence. Its 2010 GDP was $689 billion, a 12 percent rise over 2009 and its import and export value was $785 billion. If Guangdong were a country, its GDP would be in the top 20 worldwide.[1]

But China's leaders were not complacent. New times demanded new ideas. In December 2007, two months after being elevated to the 25-member Politburo, Wang Yang, the hard-charging Party secretary of Chongqing Municipality, was appointed Guangdong's Party secretary. His mandate: take reform and opening-up to new levels.

Secretary Wang seemed determined to change the fact that while Guangdong was the leader in economic reform, it was a laggard in social, environmental and political reform. Wang recognized such reforms could be a "bloody road," pointedly using Deng Xiaoping's famously colorful language about the challenges and obstacles to reform. Going further, Wang proposed that Guangdong should not only plan to outstrip the Four Tigers of East Asia (South Korea, Taiwan, Singapore and Hong Kong) in economic output, but also to match them in quality of governance.

Wang Yang laid out his objectives: maintain Guangdong's status at the vanguard of reform and opening-up; accelerate shifts to higher value-added products; improve socialist democracy and the protection of people's rights; improve local culture; improve residents' quality of life; and continue to strengthen Party organization. It was a reformist agenda—and it was also prime application of the Scientific Perspective on Development, and Wang Yang, who was a Youth League official in Anhui Province (1982-1984) when President Hu Jintao was running the national Youth League in Beijing, made sure everyone knew it.

In terms of practical action, Wang Yang began by setting 2008 targets for the province to cut energy consumption per GDP unit by 3.5%, and to cut pollutants (with specific emission targets for each), while calling for a (pre-financial crisis) GDP increase of only 9%, the lowest in years. Energy conservation and environmental protection were increasingly essential given Guangdong's high concentration of energy-hungry and environmentally unfriendly heavy industry, including petrochemicals, steel, automobiles and papermaking. Pollution, particularly of Guangdong's rivers, was a serious problem—and drinking water shortages were growing.

When, within a year, the financial crisis hit with tsunami force and terrifying speed, Guangdong was devastated. Thousands of its innumerable small factories producing goods for export cut back production or shut their doors; millions lost jobs.[2]

Concerned about stability, the watchword of China's leaders, Premier Wen Jiabao sought to ease hardships by supporting or subsidizing at-risk companies.

But Party Secretary Wang, age 52, the second youngest Politburo member,[3] had a different vision. Not fearing controversy, he argued that giving assistance to what he called "backward enterprises" would simply entrench Guangdong's traditional model of cheap manufacturing, low wages, low margins and high pollution.[4] Far better, he said, would be to leverage the unpleasant situation and do what needed to be done anyway: restructure Guangdong's economy, and move up the ladder of industrialization into more knowledge-based, high-tech, low-polluting businesses, with greater added value—and send the low-cost manufacturing to China's inland provinces. He used the colorful analogy of "emptying the cage, removing the birds" so that "new birds can come in and settle down."

Premier Wen responded by dispatching an inspection team to enforce his directives to shore up troubled firms. Yet Wang Yang maintained his call to upgrade the quality of technology and labor, and his conviction that the financial crisis could facilitate this necessary transformation.

It was a dispute which Guangdong's media downplayed, but did report. Such very public disagreement—some called it a "clash of wills"—was highly unusual and many saw it as a healthy development, evidencing a China of increasing maturity and self confidence, where the public participates in policy deliberations. Though Wang Yang seemed to be in the minority (at least publicly)—stability continued to be leadership's highest priority—he seemed unperturbed: Wang's vision for Guangdong reflected President Hu's vision for China. Several months later, Premier Wen made a high-profile visit to Guangdong and underscored innovation. "China should play a leading role in innovation worldwide," Wen said, signaling consensus.[5] Only in the free play of ideas among leaders holding opposing but defensible positions can optimum solutions be explored.

★ ★ ★

In early 2009 I spent a week in Guangdong, arranged by Secretary Wang's office, and I met separately with a range of locals, from business managers to migrant workers.[6] I had an organizing framework for my visit—the collision in China of three megatrends. First, the historical need to restructure industry, moving away from low-cost manufacturing based on cheap labor and up the value-added chain of knowledge, technology and branding (much as Japan had done in the 1970s and South Korea in the 1990s). Second, the social need to shrink widening disparities between classes and areas, particularly income gaps between urban and rural residents. Third, the imminent need to mitigate the deepening impact of the worldwide economic recession, which was causing company failures and massive layoffs. For all three seismic megatrends, Guangdong was the epicenter.

Even though China's economy is suffering, Wang Yang, like other Chinese leaders, rightly believes that the country is now stronger in comparison to the U.S., Europe and Japan. In our discussion, he begins by advocating that the West should come to know "the real, changing China" and to realize how "the Communist Party of China has been advancing with the times."[7] China, he says, is "on its way to modernization and therefore is gradually obtaining the capability of communicating with the West"—but, he adds, if "the West still doesn't understand China, it is neither good for the West itself nor conducive for establishing a Harmonious World." China's interactions and dialogs with the West must now be on an equal basis, he indicates—different than in the past. He stresses that at this critical juncture "the West must really understand China, and a good place to start is in Guangdong."

I begin by presenting to Secretary Wang my three megatrends. He agrees that these factors are all relevant to Guangdong's current situation, and after stating that "the contradictions of the traditional Guangdong Model are further exposed by the financial crisis," he gives historical perspective.

Wang Yang, Party secretary of Guangdong Province (Guangzhou, February 2009).

Wang explains that when Deng Xiaoping assumed responsibility for administering the state, "because China's economy was on the brink of collapse, providing food and sustenance for the Chinese people was the priority—so the fastest way of developing was the best way. And because China didn't have the technology, the funds or the talent required by a market economy, the fastest way was to open-up to the outside world." As a result, he says, Guangdong soon "became the workshop for Hong Kong. Little skill was required for manufacturing, processing and assembling."

But after 30 years, he observes, "while Guangdong's historical achievements cannot be denied, the drawbacks of its model are gradually emerging. First, rapid growth generally neglects the costs of resources, the environment, and worker health; rapid growth has caused environmental damage: air quality is almost intolerably poor, unprocessed water cannot be drunk. Second," he continues, "this model is excessively dependent on international demand, which in the current crisis threatens our economy. Furthermore, land is running out. Whereas Hong Kong developed only 25% of its land in a century, Shenzhen developed 37% in just 30 years, and Dongguan over 40%."[8]

The Guangdong model has made the province a magnet for migrants from other parts of China. One consequence, Wang Yang states, is that Guangdong has now become China's most populous province, with 95 million permanent residents, and, adding migrant workers, well over 100 million residents all together. The influx has contributed to social problems: A public security study found that more than 70% of suspects detained by police in 2007-2008 were migrants.[9] "We've had about 20 million migrant workers in Guangdong, of whom almost 70% have an educational level of middle school or below," he adds, before acknowledging that "our province has not fully taken up the responsibility of providing education, health, housing and other basic public services to these people."

Under Wang's leadership, the local government has taken steps to address the imbalance between locals and migrants. In 2009, for instance, Guangdong moved to improve conditions for migrant workers by replacing "temporary residential licenses" with "residential licenses"—a dramatic step giving them access to social insurance, vocational training, legal aid and other services. Defending earlier Guangdong leaders, Wang insisted that "if we had treated migrants the same as those with Guangdong residence, it would have been an unbearable burden."

It was evidence, he says, "that our growth model of 30 years, which enriched us rapidly, has come to the end of its cycle." In fact, he notes, previous provincial leadership and some scholars recognized years ago "that the traditional Guangdong model was unsustainable. But with the global demand for cheap, high-quality, Guangdong-made products still very high, it was not the right time to change."

By providing a catalyst for change, Wang said, the economic downturn is therefore helping the province make difficult changes. "So in this sense, Guangdong should *thank* the financial crisis," he says. "During the economic downturn, we've reached consensus on the need to transform our developmental model. The 'invisible hand' of the market is working." Therefore, he says, how Guangdong solves its problems is of significance to the entire country.

However, Wang Yang concedes that readjustment will not be easy. He asserts that "the roadmap is clear," and stresses that contemporary "economic transformation and industrial restructuring must be based on the requirements of the Scientific Perspective on Development." But he insists that it was necessary to "liberate our mindset," and overcome major obstacles, in order to implement such change. "Thirty years ago when we changed from class struggle to economic development, the main challenges were ideological," he says. "Now the main challenges lie in existing vested interests."

Such interests, Wang Yang suggests, include large numbers of Guangdong residents who became wealthy by renting or selling land, factories and houses to the cheap-labor manufacturers. "Farmers have become landowners," Wang states. "They enjoy lucrative incomes without doing anything. That's why they oppose changing the model. If we withdraw from low-end assembly, processing and trade, these farmers, and the rural cadres who live off these rentals, are the people whose lifestyles are affected first."

Achieving industrial upgrading and structural transformation would, therefore, mean tackling such vested interests, Wang explains. "Therefore our mission is a tough one. We must convince them that we must change. The old ways of consuming resources and importing labor will not work. Even if we wanted to continue with it, we'd be unable to do so—we're running out of resources and environmental capacity."

(Secretary Wang's commitment to good government was put to the test in 2009 by a raft of corruption cases involving high-profile, senior Guangdong officials, including Xu Zongheng, mayor of Shenzhen, one of China's most dynamic cities. Concerned that corruption was impeding reform, Wang reportedly energized the investigations—which may also have the added benefit of removing officials wedded to the status quo.[10])

Wang, who projects intensity and confidence, stresses that the government sought "to minimize the pain of the transformation." Following President Hu Jintao's directive for leaders to address the environment and inequality as well as to maintain economic growth (under the Party-promoting banner of Scientific Perspective of Development), he says, Guangdong developed a road map for reform and development of the Pearl River Delta. Approved by the State Council, this master plan has three main aims: enhancing independent innovation; transforming traditional industry; and establishing modern industrial systems. Wang's government has allocated $150 million to upgrade production at 1,000 local enterprises. "Once again, Guangdong is the pilot project for China," states Wang. "We must seize the opportunity of the financial crisis to shift our industrial structure." Doing so, he says, "will open wider markets."

Wang Yang suggests that restructuring would also benefit other regions of China. "For three decades, vast numbers of migrant workers from central and western regions have come to work in Guangdong, and it's thanks to their contributions that Guangdong has achieved rapid growth," he says. "So when designing the new strategy for Guangdong's transformation, of course we took into account these contributions."

Guangdong's approach, Wang Yang says, involves what he called "dual transfer." As the Guangdong government promotes the upgrading of local industry, it will encourage enterprises to transfer low-cost manufacturing to inland provinces. "This will reduce labor costs and improve the competitiveness of Chinese products in world markets," he says. "Equally important, workers will find jobs in or near their hometowns, reducing the social costs of not being able to take care of their families (as well as transportation costs), and bringing a huge improvement in their lifestyles." Such "transfers" would benefit Guangdong, he adds, "by reducing the population."

He draws an analogy of Hong Kong's relationship with Guangdong. "For 30 years," he says, "this could be described as 'the-shop-in-the-front-and-the-factory-in-the-back'—Hong Kong was 'the shop' and Guangdong was 'the factory'." Now, Wang Yang offers, "Guangdong aims to be 'the shop' and hopes central and western regions can be 'the factory'. Guangdong should move to both ends of the industrial chain: concentrating on R&D, design, marketing and sales at the commencement and logistics at the culmination." But, he stresses, the new relationship between Guangdong and inland provinces is not "a simplistic copycat" of past links between Hong Kong and Guangdong, saying "it should be an industrial division of labor on a higher level. . . . which, given another 30 years, will engender a very bright future with everyone sharing the benefits."

Such a transfer policy is not without challenges. One industry being relocated is the heavily polluting production of ceramics, which has long been centered in Guangdong's Foshan City. Wang warns that "the new home must prioritize environmental protection from the outset, or else they will only repeat the old [polluting] model." And, based on the experience of industries which had already moved inland, he acknowledges that "some receiving provinces pay more attention to environmental protection, while others, honestly speaking, only duplicate what the relocated enterprises had in Guangdong."

Still, Wang stresses that China's central and western provinces welcome the transfer strategy: "In 2008 most of them sent delegations to Guangdong to promote business and investments," he says. "Guangdong officials are also traveling there to seek their advice on regional cooperation."

I respond by suggesting that the degree of difficulty of the two kinds of "transfers" is quite different: moving manufacturing to central and western areas is not easy, but it can be facilitated by government incentives such as preferential tax policies. Transforming Guangdong into an innovation center, on the other hand, is more complex and less manageable, because in attempting to create value one has to face the chaos and capriciousness of the marketplace.

Secretary Wang acknowledges this challenge. "In fact," he responds, "it relates to the larger issue that we must first solve the problem of whether we need to change our developmental model, and then, second, figure out how to do it through building Guangdong into a center of independent innovation."

There was no doubt, he says, that "independent innovation has risks and cost; it is always harder than the cookie-cutting businesses of assembly, processing and trade." However, he adds, Guangdong could "be grateful to the financial crisis for making our enterprises recognize the importance of independent innovation. Such awareness is more effective than all our efforts. The first companies that went down," he notes, "were the cheap-labor OEM manufacturers. The companies that have their own design capabilities have been able to sustain themselves, despite the downturn. And those that have independent innovation strengths now have even more opportunities."

This confirms, Wang Yang muses, that "the market is always better than the government in teaching commercial players." Nevertheless, he stresses that "the government should follow the trends, conform to the market and help enterprises innovate"—adding "Guangdong attracts independent innovators because it's market-driven; technologies can be commercialized quickly." Wang Yang lists some practical steps which Guangdong was taking—these include:

- Protecting intellectual property rights by squeezing out piracy; preventing those who steal technology from enjoying its benefits.
- Instituting pre-tax deductions of up to 150% for investments in independent innovation (R&D).
- Supporting small and medium-sized firms by providing industry-focused public information. For example, in Zhongshan, a place known for lock manufacturing, a public technology platform has been set up for developing and testing new locks, which everyone can access.
- Attracting innovative talent from around China and abroad to start businesses in Guangdong: in 2008, Guangdong began offering grants of between RMB 1 million and 100 million.
- Establishing a new base of the Chinese Academy of Sciences in Guangdong, the third after Beijing and Shanghai.
- An "alliance for innovation" program at over 100 universities across the country to fund projects that could benefit Guangdong.

"No matter how tough the task, we are determined to develop Guangdong's capability for independent innovation," asserts Wang Yang. "Otherwise, in the world's industrial division of labor, we may remain manual laborers [field-hands or blue-collar workers] forever."

I ask him to predict Guangdong's situation in 10 or 20 years. Wang Yang pauses. "The world changes rapidly," he says after a moment. "But here's what I see: Guangdong's industrial structure will be fundamentally different: the service sector will be the mainstay of the provincial economy, and the manufacturing sector will be close to or equal to the world's most advanced." And he continues, "People will lead a more relaxed life. If you come to Guangdong in ten years, I will buy you a cup of coffee by the Pearl River, and I can guarantee there will be no more dusty air or smelly water. In short," he concludes, "after ten years Guangdong will be well along the road of scientific development."

"We're not interested in 'facelifts'," he emphasizes. "After the financial crisis we want a new Guangdong, not an expansion of the old one!"

⋆ ⋆ ⋆

As I traveled around Guangdong, before and after my meeting with Secretary Wang, signs of both the challenges which the province faces, and the transformations which the province desires, were everywhere to be seen. In my private conversations with local leaders, government and business, there was near unanimous support for Wang Yang's vision of how to transform Guangdong. All realized the difficulties and short-term pain, and the potential for instability, but nonetheless they felt that hard decisions made now would yield a much stronger Guangdong in the future.

Arriving in the provincial capital, Guangzhou, I meet Liu Zijing, president of the city's Baiyun Airport. In 2008 the airport handled 33 million passengers, almost 50 times the number in 1978, and, notwithstanding the financial crisis, Liu forecasts growth: 38 million passengers in 2010, 60 million in 2015, 70 million in 2020, and ultimately 100 million (requiring five runways). International routes from Guangzhou will increase from 57 in 2008 to about 90 in 2010, he says, reflecting the city's growing global clout. Federal Express's regional hub had already added 136 flights a week. And Liu echoes Wang Yang in highlighting the opportunities offered by the global situation:

"The economic downturn is bad, no question," he agrees, "but we now have more time to adjust, develop agilely, and improve our service quality. Developing too rapidly has been burdensome," he says. "We must prioritize environmental concerns, including noise control, energy-saving procedures, and treating waste water for use in landscaping."

And when I visit Guangzhou Party Secretary Zhu Xiaodan, he also emphasizes that the city has reached a turning point. Guangzhou's GDP increased 45 times over the three decades of reform, he says, while urban disposable income increased 55 times.[11] In 2008, Guangzhou's per-capita GDP reached $11,600. "Compared to some cities in Asia, we still have a ways to go," Zhu says, "but compared to where we were, we've done pretty well. The question now is, where do we go from here? What's our future and how do we get there?"

Zhu is quick to acknowledge that "we cannot deny that we've paid a heavy price for rapid growth." Intense development was crucial in the 1980s-1990s, he explains, "because China was so poor"—adding "we cannot blame ourselves for the inevitable problems." But now, he continues, "we cannot ignore

Zhu Xiaodan, Party secretary of Guangzhou, Guangdong Province (Guangzhou, February 2009).

social, political and cultural progress. If these are neglected—particularly social imbalances and environmental pollution—we will be blameworthy. We have a duty to our country and our children. To continue in the future as we have in the past would be irresponsible."

In practice, Zhu Xiaodan says, this means that "our central concern must be the people's welfare, their standard of living." In 2008, Guangzhou spent 69% of its budget on medical welfare, pensions, unemployment, and other initiatives such as providing culture to rural communities. "We strive to give rural and urban residents equal opportunities," he emphasizes.

And, citing the Scientific Perspective on Development as theoretical foundation, Zhu stresses that the city's economic development "could not continue in the old way, by simply consuming resources. We must transform our growth structure," he states, "and focus on the service sector—finance, technology, conventions, information, and creative work."

In fact, Zhu notes, Guangzhou's service sector is already relatively well-developed, accounting for 59% of GDP (2008)—second only to Beijing, while industry amounts to 38-39%. Because of this, he says, the impact of the financial crisis on Guangzhou has been "less serious than expected," affecting it less than nearby cities like Shenzhen or Dongguan. But Zhu isn't complacent: "more is required," he says.

"We used to say that 'without industry a city cannot become rich,' he recounts, "so cities pushed industrialization. We cannot deny that industrialization is the foundation of growth," he acknowledges, "but today, at least in Guangzhou, industrialization cannot sustain growth. We have too much manufacturing; even with treatment, pollution is unacceptably high."

"Our focus is to support companies at the high end of the value chain and to use industrial parks as a driving force," Secretary Zhu explains. "Companies which pollute or cannot transform will be phased out. We're transferring manufacturing firms to the city's outskirts and service firms to the city's center. There'll be no chimneys in the city!"

One business seeking to move up the value chain is Guangzhou Automobile Industry Group (GAIG), China's fourth largest car manufacturer, which targets 600,000 units a year in its joint ventures with Honda (Accord) and Toyota (Camry). When I visited, executives stressed that GAIG was committed to "self-reliant R&D and own-brand business," with plans to launch a "rationally-priced, good quality" own-brand passenger vehicle, and to focus on environmental protection, fuel economy and safety.

Zhu Xiaodan's vision is that Guangzhou will eschew heavy manufacturing, and encourage industries which rely more on innovation than investment, like biomedical and electronics. "We'll change 'Made in Guangzhou' to 'Created in Guangzhou,'" Zhu asserts. "We need more intellectual property, more of our own brands."

To help foster creativity, Guangzhou has established a "university city," known officially as the "Guangzhou Higher Education Mega Center," with backing from the ministries of Education and Science and Technology. Organized by Zhongshan University, one of China's top research institutions, this unprecedented academic center has a planned area of 16.6-square miles (including an entire island in the Pearl River), includes campuses of ten leading provincial universities, and anticipates 200,000 students, 20,000 teachers and 50,000 staff.

Guangzhou Secretary Zhu, like Guangdong Secretary Wang, sees the Pearl River, which winds through Guangzhou on its way to the sea, as a symbol of the city's vision to transform its development model and improve its environmental health. "When I was young, we could swim in the river," Zhu says. "But later, at its most polluted, it was black and smelly." Now, after preliminary treatment, water quality is improving, Zhu reports, "but it'll take years before we can swim in it again." In 2009 and 2010, he says, Guangzhou will invest almost $6 billion in treating the river. "Otherwise we'd be destroying our heritage—our ancestors have lived here for over 2000 years," Zhu notes, emphasizing "without clean water and air, sustainable development is meaningless."

Zhu describes the government's commitment, for example, to protecting Guangzhou's wetlands. The Nansha Wetland Park, home to thousands of diverse birds, abuts the city's expanding port and major enterprises including steel, petrochemicals and shipbuilding. A full 50% of Nansha District land will now be covered with forest or grass, incorporating wetland reserves, mangroves and coastal forests. And, significantly, a multi-billion-dollar refinery-petrochemical complex, a joint venture between Kuwait Petroleum

Company and Sinopec (Asia's largest refiner)—planned for Nansha for years and after significant investment—is being relocated.

"I think this reflects how Guangdong values environmental protection, the ecology and the opinions of our citizens," said Guangdong Party Secretary Wang Yang, speaking with foreign reporters. He attributed the rare reversal to "strong criticism from the community" and commented that "It was a very difficult decision to make because [the project] has been approved by the State Council and signed by the partners. We only have one planet to live on," he added, "and whatever we do at this end affects people at the other end."[12]

(My hosts arranged for me to cruise the Wetland waterways. After a quick, polite look, I attempted to beg off—I was on a search for panicked entrepreneurs and angry workers. But it proved awkward to refuse: I was escorted aboard a small boat and off we glided. After a few minutes brushing by the endless mangroves growing verdantly in the shallow waters, breathing the crisp winter air and gazing across the expansive greenery, I found myself starting to relax—and appreciating environmental activism. To minimize disturbing the birds, visitors are limited to 150 per day.)

★ ★ ★

In other parts of Guangdong, the financial crisis was more evident. I visited Dongguan, on the east bank of the Pearl River between Guangzhou and Shenzhen, home to the sprawling amalgam of endless factories and crowded dormitories which are the center of China's low-cost manufacturing base.

I was brought to see a medium-sized, Hong Kong-run company making substrates for IC wafers. The migrant workers lived cheek-by-jowl, six to eight in cramped rooms, but they had reasonable work hours, good-quality subsidized food, recreational facilities, and 100 computers for watching movies or surfing the Internet. (As it was picked by local leaders, this factory was no doubt as good as it got, but it did demonstrate that the government at least knew what it should encourage or enforce.)

This kind of industrial development has made Dongguan rich. An obscure rural county just 20 years ago, it now has 20 five-star hotels, behind only Beijing and Shanghai. Almost everything made here is for export—shoes and sweaters, toys and textiles, and every imaginable computer part (except microchips)—hence the recent devastation.

In Dongguan alone, at least one million migrant workers lost their jobs. When I was visiting (early 2009), no one knew where the bottom was or when it would come, and people at all levels, even wearing their best face for a foreigner with government connections, were apprehensive or scared.

But there is evidence that even Dongguan is trying to reinvent itself. Its Songshan Lake Sci-tech Industrial Park, which surrounds an 8-square-kilometer freshwater lake, and features hill vegetation and ecological wetlands, is populated by hi-tech companies, including leaders in batteries and power-supplies, all housed in architecturally inviting buildings.

And to the south, Shenzhen, the cradle of China's reform, is rapidly transforming itself from a city of cheap manufacturing to a modern metropolis focused on technology, innovation and service. Shenzhen-based Huawei has become the world's strongest telecommunications equipment maker, an icon of China's new enterprises.

But Shenzhen's future is more than just high technology. Local officials stress design and creativity in new products—not only hi-tech, but packaging, architecture and printing—as the city's direction for the 21st century. With more than 6,000 design companies and 60,000 designers, Shenzhen sets itself to become the "national innovation city" by 2015. In 2008, Shenzhen won the UNESCO City of Design award, the first city in China to win such a prize.[13]

Shenzhen is also known for its strong, vibrant and relatively free media. A huge media fund of RMB 20 billion (almost $3 billion) is in the offing, leveraging the city's strengths, and reflecting opportunities for reform and opening-up of China's massive media market.

Crossing to the west bank of the Pearl River, Zhuhai, bordering Macao, is moving even further away from the cheap-labor growth model. In part this is out of necessity: though it, like Shenzhen, was one of the first four Special Economic Zones established in 1980, Zhuhai's growth has lagged far behind.

Now the city's Party secretary, Gan Lin, focuses on leveraging Zhuhai's magnificent coastline and favored environment of water, air and mountains.[14] Describing it as a model city for President Hu's Scientific Perspective on Development, Gan seeks to limit Zhuhai's population growth, reduce pollution, and upgrade industrial structure. The aim is to eliminate low-end factories, and preserve more land for ecological purposes through restricting real-estate development and locating new industries only in industrial parks. Gan Lin believes Zhuhai can both grow and protect its environment, though he admits "it's a heavy task."

★ ★ ★

Guangdong's desire to be more than just a cheap manufacturing base is palpable. My tour guide was an insightful provincial official, Liu Geli, who sought to explore with me cultural differences between China and the West. He used the example of Dafencun Village, whose professional artists (many of whom are migrant workers) create remarkable reproductions of classic Western paintings as well as original works. The paintings are produced by teams of artists working in assembly-line fashion, with four or five artists sequentially painting each piece—one specializing, say, on faces, another on torsos, yet another on backgrounds, and so on. Liu said that while Chinese people admire such efficiencies, many Westerners are offended by the notion of "assembly-line art." He quoted one BBC reporter who was horrified at the revelation, calling it "awful" and certainly "not art."

On the other hand, as art, Chinese people generally do not appreciate oil paintings as much as Westerners do; for displaying in their homes or offices, Chinese prefer calligraphy and sketches. (One minister uses this example to explain why changing China's economy from export-driven to domestic-demand is not as simple as just redirecting marketing and sales from foreign buyers to Chinese consumers. In the worldwide recession, Dafencun Village struggled to shift its suddenly-surplus capacity to produce oil paintings for China. To sell designed-for-export products to domestic markets, they must first be tailored to local tastes or requirements.)

Early on, Liu asked me, among other questions, what I perceived to be Guangdong's negatives. I made the mistake of repeating the common perception in China—one perhaps tinged with envy—that while Guangdong is advanced economically, it is weak culturally.

From that moment on, Liu missed no opportunity to give me a crash course in Guangdong culture. It was as if I were taking sensitivity training for having uttered some politically incorrect remark. But my re-education regimen, to my surprise, turned out to be a treat.

In Guangzhou, Liu took me to the Chen Clan Academy, with its classic structure, ornate carved-stone windows and civic history. How did it survive the Cultural Revolution, which sought to destroy such relics, I asked? Liu smiled and explained that clever local officials had turned the Academy into a factory for printing Mao Zedong's books. Who would have dared to destroy Mao's books, he exclaimed!

Housed at the Academy is the Guangdong Folk Arts Museum. The intricate and elegant carvings in wood, ivory and bone, massively large or minusculely small, stop one's breath—they seem to defy all sense of the possible. Perhaps, I thought, this is a metaphor for Guangdong.

Endnotes

1 Based on Purchasing Power Parity, Guangdong as a country would be in the top 15.

2 It did not help that the precipitous downturn erupted while Beijing sought to slow torrid growth and restrict exports through macro controls.

3 The youngest member of the 17th CPC Politburo is Li Keqiang, born in July 1955; the second youngest is Wang Yang, born in March 1955.

4 Zhu Kuoliang, "Guangdong Province Media Reveals Premier Wen Jiabao Issues Ultimatum to Guangdong Province Party Secretary Wang Yang Regarding Economy," www.chinafree-press.org., December 4, 2008.

5 "Chinese Premier underscores innovation in Guangdong Province," Xinhua, April 21, 2009.

6 Much (but not all) of this entire section on Guangdong and Party Secretary Wang Yang was published in a five-part series in BusinessWeek.com. Robert Lawrence Kuhn, "Guangdong Visions: A Talk with Wang Yang," BusinessWeek.com, June 5, 2009; "Guangdong Visions: Responding to the Crisis," BusinessWeek.com, June 15, 2009; "Guangdong: Reenvisioning Guangzhou," BusinessWeek.com, July 6, 2009; "Guangdong Visions: Forging China's Future," BusinessWeek.com, August 5, 2009; and "Guangdong Visions: Transforming Cities, Appreciating Culture," BusinessWeek.com, in press.

7   Author's meeting with Wang Yang, Guangzhou, February 2009.
8   As Hong Kong is mostly mountainous, with much of the land undevelopable, while Shenzhen and Dongguan are mostly flat, the comparison is not entirely apt.
9   Ivan Zhai, "Guangdong to change system for migrants," *South China Morning Post*, March 31, 2009.
10 Also sacked were Chen Shaoji, chairman of Guangdong's CPPCC and former provincial deputy Party secretary; Wang Huayuan, former deputy Party secretary and head of Party Discipline Inspection Commission (then head of Zhejiang Province's Party Discipline Inspection Commission before his arrest), and Zheng Shaodong, former head of Guangdong's Public Security and Assistant Minister of China's Public Security.
11 Author's meeting with Zhu Xiaodan, Guangzhou, February 2009.
12 Tom Mitchell, "China bows to activist pressure on plant, *The Financial Times*, July 31, 2009.
13 "Pioneering Shenzhen gets UNESCO award," *China Daily*, December 9, 2008.
14 Author's meeting with Gan Lin, Zhuhai, February 2009.

39

China's Political Future: Is Reform Real?

I am convinced that on political reform there has been a major shift in how China's senior leaders think. Certainly there are limits, but less than before, and these too are instructive.

The belief system of China's leaders may be described as a hierarchy constructed on four levels. At its most fundamental level, there are twin pillars. One represents the Chinese people, their lives and welfare; China's leaders believe that their primary mission is to provide the basic necessities of life for China's vast multitudes, and that assuring such sustenance for all is a far greater good than allowing full political freedoms for some. The other pillar represents Chinese pride and patriotism and values and culture. These are the immutables, the foundation on which all else is built.

The second level, the action item, is the quality of life of the Chinese people, and how to improve it in the broadest sense. That's the reason why President Hu's Scientific Perspective on Development is now China's guiding principle for formulating and implementing policy. Economic development, which enhances standards of living and strengthens the country, is the primary objective, but it is not the sole objective. Harmonious balance between sectors of society, sustainable development and environmental protection are also essential.

The third level is Party leadership. China's leaders believe that given China's unique situation and special characteristics, only unopposed rule by the Party—without competing alternatives—can provide the national stability, unity, and vision needed to continue to improve the lives of the Chinese people, develop China's economy, enhance its civilization, and restore its pride. Without the Party's leadership, they believe, the country could disintegrate into chaos. Unabashedly, they reject Western-style democracy, because they are convinced that competitive elections would disrupt society, foment instability, and lead to all manner of trauma for 1.3 billion Chinese. Nothing, China's leaders say, can be accomplished without stability.

The fourth level is China's leaders' belief in contemporary socialism and ultimate Communism as a political ideology, particularly as Deng Xiaoping modified it, "with Chinese characteristics." But what this now means is fostering equality and fairness today, and posing a utopia of abundant material goods in the far future—not a rigid economic system of collective ownership and central planning.

The geometry of these four levels of belief is consequential: it means that the Party's role in leading China (third level) is more fundamental than any specific socialist or communist precept it espouses (fourth level). This was Deng Xiaoping's great intuition (and the opposite of Mao Zedong's, whose hierarchy of beliefs was arguably the reverse—Mao's commitment to Communism was so fundamental that he would enforce orthodox socialist policies no matter what the cost to the people, the country or the culture).

In other words, if China's current leaders experience a conflict between their practical goal of helping the Chinese people—or indeed their patriotic commitment to China—and some theoretical precept of socialism, helping the people—or love of the nation—will always win out. Take Hong Kong, for example: China's leaders' commitment to preserving Hong Kong's capitalist system and not interfering in the territory's affairs is a serious one, based not only on Deng's promise of "one country, two systems," but also on the simple fact that capitalism works in Hong Kong—and if Hong Kong prospers, so does China. China's leaders are proud patriots more than crusading Marxists, and want Hong Kong's international status enhanced not diminished.

★ ★ ★

Minister Leng Rong, the ideology scholar who runs the CPC Party Literature Research Center and advises senior leaders, sums up the Party's new pragmatism: "China is a highly diverse country with a huge population, undergoing rapid industrialization in a dynamic, turbulent environment," he states, "and under these conditions, the current system is in the best interests of the people. Any objective person could see that a Western political system would be bought at a price too high for China to pay. For China's overall benefit, the Party should continue to be the ruling party," he says, insisting "this is the only way to maintain stability and promote development."

However, Leng stresses that these days "we focus on the actual needs of the people and the nation. The only way the Party can continue to rule is if it serves the people's interest. Nothing else matters. This has always been true on paper," Leng adds, "but not always in reality. It used to be that the Party dictated what it wanted and the people had to follow." Today, he says, the change is dramatic. "Now the people assert what they need and want and the Party must provide and deliver it," he says, though he notes that

Leng Rong (second from left), vice president of the Chinese Academy of Social Sciences (CASS) (later director, CPC Party Literature Research Center), at the home of IMG Chairman Ted Forstmann in New York. Attendees from the left: Paul Gigot (*The Wall Street Journal*), Leng Rong, Maurice "Hank" Greenberg, Yang Yang (CASS), New York Governor George Pataki, Robert Lawrence Kuhn, Jim Hoagland (*The Washington Post*), Chinese UN Ambassador Wang Guangya, Tom Brokaw (NBC News) (November 14, 2006; Adam Zhu).

"it's never easy to satisfy everyone. Leftists say the Party has abandoned Marxism and serves the wealthy; Rightists insist that multi-party democracy is the solution."

"You don't have to hit us over the head with a baseball bat," Leng, who has become a good friend, tells me with a smile. "We believe in the universal values of freedom, democracy and human rights. We just need time to apply them to the realities of China with 1.3 billion people, the majority of whom still live in the countryside. Give us a chance to do it right. In our internal meetings, President Hu stresses democracy."

"We no longer argue over ' . . . isms', the political correctness of this or that policy," Leng continues. "Today [2009] the key drivers are Efficiency and Social Fairness." He describes the "active intellectual debate" that is "surprisingly strong" in contemporary China—with "democratic socialism," "new leftism," "new liberalism," and "new Confucianism" all vying to dethrone "socialism with Chinese characteristics" as the defining theory of state. "China's reality is triggering new thinking," Leng adds; "intellectual debate is healthy."[1]

★ ★ ★

For President Hu Jintao, the challenge is to maintain the Party's power and relevance within a rapidly changing society. In his speech to mark the 30th anniversary of reform (December 2008), Hu, significantly, said that a political party does not automatically remain progressive, and its ruling status is not obtained once and for all—just because a party has had power in the past does not mean it's only right and proper to have that power in the present, let alone in the future. "What we possessed in the past doesn't necessarily belong to us now," Hu said. "What we possess now may not be ours forever."

Hu offered a list of three "no's" for the Party: "no wavering"; "no relaxing of efforts"; "no being sidetracked." He urged his colleagues to promote further reform and opening-up, and stick to the path of "socialism with Chinese characteristics," in order to achieve countrywide modernization by mid-21st century.

To emphasize that China must keep on its current track, Hu used a colloquial expression: "*bu zheteng*," which triggered audible gasps and ripples of laughter from the huge audience in the Great Hall of the People.[2] Rarely used in formal speech, *zheteng* is a slang phrase meaning to do something useless, absurd or repeatedly without results, causing oneself (or others) unnecessary trouble, and generally wasting time (*bu* means "don't"). "*Bu zhetang*" may be rendered as "don't flip-flop," "don't mess around," or "don't make much ado about nothing." Parents say "*bu zhetang*" to young children so that they don't get themselves into trouble. Hu Jintao was effectively saying "Don't fuss over ideology"—the implication being that China would never again go back to debilitating political movements.

As Minister Leng Rong puts it, current leadership has "a fivefold mission" for China. "Economically, more wealthy; politically, more democratic; spiritually and culturally, more civilized; socially, more harmonious; environmentally, more friendly." He likens the method for achieving this mission to "a mathematical formula that must yield a specific output, the output being the people's benefit and the formula being the Party's actions. We in the Party," he adds, "must find the proper variables so that the formula will produce the output the people want." And he reiterates, "If the CPC does not serve the people's interest, it will no longer be the ruling party."

Such comments confirm that China's senior leaders are serious about bringing about profound, though gradual, political reform. Indeed, in his report to the 17th CPC Congress (2007), President Hu used the word "democracy" 61 times.

To most Westerners, democracy has a simple, one-dimensional test. If a country accepts multiple parties and offers free-and-honest one-person-one-vote elections for its most senior leader, then it's a democracy. If it doesn't, it isn't. China, Westerners believe, must be either democratic or dictatorial, and since it isn't the former, it must be the latter.

But this test is myopic as well as archaic—a black-or-white fallacy. Granted, Hu Jintao's kind of democracy provides neither for free elections of national leaders nor for multiple political parties—still, it mustn't be ignored. A process of change *is* under way: when China's leaders talk about democracy, it's shorthand for their commitment to promoting enhanced rule of law, protection of rights, diverse personal and social freedoms, and public participation in the process of governance.

Questions arise: Is Western-style democracy the highest good for all countries at all times? If public policy were truly dictated by majority rule, some countries, including several in the Middle East, would initiate more, not less, aggressive acts against their perceived foes (including America), even to their own detriment. One Chinese leftist intellectual said that he supported a "one person-one vote" democracy in China because he believes it would be the only way to *oust* his country's pro-American leaders.[3]

And to be consistent with democratic values, Western critics should ask what the Chinese people think. Are they clamoring for immediate transformation to Western-style politics?

Certainly, China's citizens face limits to their freedoms. Leadership's desire to maintain stability prevents political free speech, suppresses political dissidents, and enforces a notoriously harsh penal code. It also seeks to block any dissension, disagreement, personality conflict, or political struggle within the Party or government from being reported or leaked.

Yet most Chinese are not much troubled by such restrictions. They support severe punishment for crime, for example; and if one looks at most aspects of everyday life—where to live, work, travel; how to dress, whom to marry, what to study, think, say; how to make and spend money—Chinese people have more personal freedom today than at any other time in their very long history. The journalist Nicholas Kristof has written of the Jiang Zemin era that "China did not achieve political pluralism, but it did move toward economic pluralism, cultural pluralism, social pluralism."[4] As evidence, he pointed to China's large number of newspapers, publishing houses, TV stations, mobile phone users, and netizens. Those who still insist on classifying China as a repressive society must explain why, notwithstanding its limitations on political freedoms, China would be the first country of its kind to offer such vast arrays of information and expression to its citizens.

Indeed, the personal and social freedoms of most urban Chinese are now just about on a par with those of their counterparts in the West. Text messages disseminated on millions of mobile phones these days often include political and sexual jokes, the content of which, a few decades ago, few in China would have dared to utter even in the privacy of their own homes. More importantly, most of China's vast population is finally free from famine, pestilence, homelessness, illiteracy, and political mass movements—the physical and social scourges of past eras. Furthermore, the Chinese government is now conducting itself in ways normally associated with democratic systems, such as polling citizens to assess their attitudes and opinions.

To President Hu and China's new generation of leaders, transparency is a hallmark of China's incipient democracy (and one could argue that in a society governed with true transparency, the people are better served than in one where there are free elections but much remains hidden from public gaze.) This is not to say that China's governance has become transparent—but China's leaders have gone on record that such transparency is their goal and they have taken concrete steps in this direction.

★ ★ ★

Key to political reform is what the CPC calls "intra-Party democracy," a concept which indicates the type of society China's senior leaders are seeking to build. Primarily a system of laws and rules governing process within the Party, it calls for oversight of Party officials by Party members, and the progressive opening-up of inner workings of government—including the appointment of officials—to public access, scrutiny and critique.

Whether this will expand—to include, for example, truly free and secret elections among members of the CPC Central Committee to select the Politburo and its Standing Committee—remains to be seen. But, assuming no severe economic dislocations (which could trigger unrest and postpone progress), intra-Party democracy augurs well for a more democratic Chinese society. (That political reform is high on the agenda of China's leaders may surprise some, but it follows naturally from President Hu's philosophy of Putting People First, because democracy and individual rights are its natural requirements.)

Some elements of democracy have been developing, quietly, for years, through the system of grassroots elections in rural areas. "Village elections" originated in 1988 with the enactment of a law stipulating that village leaders should be elected directly by villager members for three-year terms, and that any villager aged 18 years or over has the right to vote or stand as a candidate. Since then, peasants across the country have participated in elections, usually with turnouts exceeding 90%.

Economic changes in the countryside, new affluence, and the emergence of joint-ventures all necessitated greater distributions of power. Local issues such as building roads and schools and distributing money and manpower could not be effectively decided in some county seat 100 miles away. And unlike appointed village cadres (who seldom considered villagers' interests and were often corrupt), elected cadres must satisfy their constituents and maintain popular support, as well as be responsible to higher authorities.

There have been, inevitably, problems with incipient rural democracy. Villagers don't always exercise their rights properly—some are indifferent and vote at random; others harbor grudges or sell their votes to the highest bidder. Candidates have rigged elections by voting-blocks, bribes or threats. Villages have become subject to nepotism or other factional interests. That's why many cadres at village, town, county and city levels say they oppose elections, arguing that peasants don't understand democracy, and that "elections manifest resentment against cadres and are too troublesome" and would cause disorder.[5] Some town leaders have refused to hold elections, saying they are "unsuitable to China's actual conditions."

A 2009 government circular urged candidates to practice fair play in direct elections of village heads amid complaints of bribery and other dirty tricks to win votes. The "bribery situation is grave and seriously harms the impartiality of election," it said, asserting that criminal penalties will be enforced on those who try to win votes from villagers with money, violence or intimidation, and to those who cheat in vote counts. Improving elections, the circular said, "will help ensure villagers to practice their rights and develop grassroots democracy."[6]

So progress continues. The media has helped by publicizing election irregularities and disputes, making it easier for villagers to plead their cases. Secret voting booths have helped too. Speeches and electioneering, along with question-and-answer sessions, educate voters and compel candidates to make and keep campaign promises.

And there have been concrete results. The village committee in Tuntou, Henan Province, for example, was forced to scrap plans to build itself a new office building and instead used the funds for two new school buildings, after a village meeting where locals voted in favor of prioritizing education. In Shuangwang in Hebei, indulgence in food and drink was common among local village cadres, but in the three months following public discussion of financial affairs—the results of elections—entertainment expenses dropped substantially. Public accountability is a hallmark of democracy.

★ ★ ★

Westerners remain skeptical whether China's leaders are really committed to political reform. But there is now a real road map, with steps so specific that it would be awkward for China's leaders not to carry them out. Basically, the plan is this: first, build democracy in the Party, and then expand it throughout society.

Shortly after the 17th Party Congress (October 2007), I had a private talk with Li Yuanchao, who had just been promoted to the Politburo. Now in charge of the CPC's Organization Department, Li had just published a provocative article in *People's Daily* on "Intra-Party Democracy," expanding on President Hu's call at the Congress for greater democracy.[7]

While many in the West see such theories and slogans as "empty rhetoric," experience shows that the political philosophies of China's senior leaders greatly affect current policies and future directions. According to Li

Li Yuanchao, Politburo Member and head of the CPC Organization Department (Beijing, January 2009; Adam Zhu).

Yuanchao, strengthening intra-Party democracy would "pave the way" for "people's democracy." Greater democracy within the Party, he explained, is the cornerstone of political reform: it empowers individual Party members, increases transparency, subjects higher bodies to supervision of lower bodies, introduces voting to prevent "arbitrary decision-making," solicits public opinion of candidates, and expands a system of direct elections at local levels. All of this would have been unthinkable until recent years.

Li's views reflected what President Hu and China's top leaders want to communicate to the world about political reform in their country—plans to which they are attaching themselves publicly. Li said that three decades of reform and opening-up had led to "the freeing of people's minds"—and helped develop "an environment that leads naturally to political reform and the development of democracy." And, he emphasized that China's reform had begun "as political reform in the Party, not as economic reform in society, as many foreigners may assume"—the core being Deng Xiaoping's decision "to change the Party's mission from focusing mainly on class struggle . . . to developing the economy and enhancing productivity, and to building a wealthy and stronger country." "This was *political* change," Li stressed.

While many of China's reforms had provoked "spirited debate in the Party," Li said, "the only reform that no one has raised any objection to is this fundamental change of the Party's mission from class struggle to economic development."

China's leaders, Li noted, "do agree that democracy is a fundamental political value." He cited President Hu's repeated references to democracy, and noted that "China has been examining the experiences of other countries in building democracy."

He insisted, however, that "China's democratic development should cater to its own conditions . . . In constructing democracy," he said, "we must take into account a country's history and culture. For example," Li continued, "in France, a man may have an open relationship with a mistress and still be elected president." But in China, he said, "such a man would be barred from being even a small town chief. In America," he went on, "many former presidents were wealthy. In China it's very rare to see wealthy officials. People would first investigate such officials and check the legitimacy of the source of their wealth."

Li Yuanchao pointed out that "historically in China, we have used two phrases to describe good officials or statesmen: *Qing Guan* and *Fumu Guan*." *Guan* means official; *Qing* means honest and upright. "These good officials," he explained, "don't have many assets, and don't use power for personal gain. In the U.S.," he noted, "a person with minimal assets might not engender confidence." *Fumu Guan*, meanwhile, turns on the word *Fumu*, meaning parent. The phrase had, Li said, the sense of "acting as if a parent. It implies that officials protect citizens as if they were their own children. In the U.S., if a government official administrates like a parent, he might be considered patronizing or have no sense of rule by law."

Thus, Li said, "to develop optimum political reform, we must take into consideration all of China's characteristics, such as its history and culture, and this includes the road along which we have come since the founding of New China and the beginning of reform and opening-up." He noted that there are differences between the political systems of western countries, such as the U.K. and U.S.—and he stressed that "the American political system should not be used to judge the Chinese political system. It's not realistic and it's not scientific," Li added. "China has its own ideas and ideals, and has every right to choose its own system. We have our own models and goals for political reform, and we will accordingly choose our own roads to reach those goals."

Li emphasized that "we will do what is in the best interests of our people— which surely includes the development of democracy and the rule of law." Hu Jintao, he said, had "clearly stated the universal values such as 'advancing democracy and protecting human rights' at the Party Congress. They are not just values accepted and appreciated," he stressed, "they are also practiced and realized."

Li said that after past centuries of foreign domination and domestic turbulence, and unending wars, "in the last 30 years China has been in the most stable period throughout its history, and has had more peace than it had had for hundreds of years."[8] He acknowledged, however, that "China's political and legal system is certainly not perfect, and we are certainly not satisfied. This," he said, "is why President Hu stresses advancing intra-Party democracy, which is the life source of the Party, and "democracy of society," which is essential." (Pointedly, Li added, "the experiences and lessons of the past prove this"—a reference to the chaotic catastrophes of the Cultural Revolution, when dictatorship trumped democracy.)

Only by fully advancing intra-Party democracy, Li Yuanchao insisted, "can the enthusiasm, initiative and creativity of Party members be maximized. Building democracy in the Party is the key to building a society that is a socialist democracy with Chinese characteristics." And he added, "regardless of the political system, the people must decide what is in their own best interests."

Li said that building "an effective democracy and legal system" must occur in an orderly fashion. "We must maintain stability," he said. "This is why we define reform as 'evolving revolution.' Not rapid, violent, or traumatic; not with one force confronting or toppling another force. It's an internal change," he explained, "which is consistent with the law of development."

In his much-discussed article in *People's Daily*, Li Yuanchao listed seven specific steps for establishing intra-Party democracy. The first was to respect the position of ordinary Party members as principals, and guarantee their democratic rights—including the rights of participation, election, decision-making, and supervision. Li noted that, during the Cultural Revolution, on the contrary, certain state leaders were seen as principals, and this was the root of those terrible times.

The second step involved increasing transparency in Party affairs, and creating favorable conditions for democratic discussions within the Party. Opinions should be widely solicited before important decisions are made, Li said, allowing broad participation and effective supervision by grassroots branches and Party members.

Li's other proposals included: implementing a system of Party congresses with fixed terms in selected areas on a trial basis, and requiring the Politburo to report regularly on its work to the CPC Central Committee and to accept its supervision—and likewise having local standing committees report back to their respective Party committees.

Li also called for local Party committees to vote on major issues and on appointing officials to important positions, in order to prevent arbitrary decision-making. He proposed reform of the intra-Party electoral system, with improved methods for nominating candidates and conducting elections.

Increased transparency, Li Yuanchao acknowledged, was "vital" for making this work, and to making intra-Party democracy efficacious, meaningful and lasting. If Party members were to effectively exercise their right to "vote, voice opinions, participate in decision-making, and supervise Party institutions," he said, they "must have access to true Party information." He claimed progress: "When officials are selected for positions, the process is now not opaque to the public as it once was—we conduct *gong shi* [soliciting public opinions] of the candidate, giving the constituency an opportunity to voice its opinions. Only if there is no serious objection does the candidacy convert to an appointment."

As for other practical steps, Li said that innovative measures were being used to expand intra-Party democracy at the primary level (grassroots Party organizations). "The election of township Party secretaries is a good example," he said. "Candidates are nominated by both the Party and all residents; then all Party members participate in one direct election to choose the town Party chief." This system, known as "two nominations, one election" was pioneered in Jiangsu when Li was Party secretary. Now, Li said, "its approach reaches 600,000 grassroots Party organizations in towns and villages across China."

He noted that political reform in Jiangsu had affected "three levels of government." The first was "the village level, generally a few thousand people, where the people elect village chiefs directly, much like people in the U.S. elect city mayors." The second was the township level, where the electorate, he said, was generally 20,000-30,000 people, of whom about 1,000-2,000 were CPC members. "It is no secret," Li said, "that the leader of the Party, the Party secretary, is the overall leader of the township, while the administrative leader, the governor or mayor, is often the Party's deputy secretary." For several years, however, he noted, "we have been holding pilot elections in which Party members elect Party leaders—in Jiangsu, nearly 100 townships elect Party leaders this way," he added, "especially in poorer areas, such as in Suqian City, where almost all the township Party leaders are elected. In Yangzhou, President Jiang Zemin's hometown, some rural leaders are elected. The process is working well." And in Nanjing, Jiangsu's capital, officials are now recruited from across the country, rather than just locally, which Li said improved the "quality, diversity and integrity of officials."

Li would not predict details of how such initiatives would change China (2007-2012), but he left no doubt that "grassroots democracy will have great impact." He also reiterated the Party's commitment to continuing change. "Many risk-taking reformers are now advancing in the Party," he said. "This inspires more people to move forward more aggressively. The fact that reform is progressing so rapidly—in fact more rapidly in China than in most of the rest of the world," he added—"is the result of our policy of promoting reformers."

To underline his point, Li Yuanchao noted that "In the last two decades the National People's Congress has passed over 200 new laws and developed a relatively comprehensive and increasingly sound legal system. We have amended our 1982 Constitution four times," he added. "Every five years we hold a National Party Congress and institute new reformist policies. In constructing a democratic society based on rule of law," he insisted, "China is doing in decades what it took Western countries centuries to do."

★ ★ ★

About half a year later, in mid 2008, the CPC granted enhanced power to its delegates, enabling them to participate in Party affairs more frequently and more authoritatively.[9] Under the previous structure, central and local Party committees, made up of leading Party members, took charge of Party affairs, while delegates met only every five years—and even then were little more than rubber stamps ratifying decisions that had already been made. The wide-reaching reform formalized a "tenure system" for delegates to Party congresses at all levels, which empowered their participation in Party governance and decision-making on an ongoing basis. They could now attend Party committee meetings at their own level and give feedback and suggestions, even on leading Party members.

"Previously, being a Party delegate was largely a ceremonial position without much substance," said Wang Yukai, professor of Party affairs at the National School of Administration. The new initiative, he added, would give Party delegates more power, and "subject the Party elite to greater accountability."

For example, the roughly 2,200 delegates to the National Party Congress (which meets only once every five years) are now permitted to attend plenary sessions of the Central Committee, the Party's core decision-making body, which are normally held once a year. Thus the 371 Central Committee members are now, in theory, more accountable to national Party delegates, and required to brief them on issues, decisions, and policy implementation.

Delegates at provincial and local levels now also play similar roles, which include participating in personnel appointments and evaluations. Furthermore, when Party committees are not in session, delegates may organize discussions on policies and launch research and investigations into Party issues and decisions—with the Party committees picking up the tab.

However, Professor Wang warned that the main challenge would be putting these ideas into practice—though the new initiative specifically gave notice that anyone found trying to obstruct delegates from carrying out their monitoring role, or to take revenge against them, would be punished.

With these reforms, China's leaders were announcing that they were serious about building intra-Party democracy—promoting transparency, widening participation in governance, accepting open debate, holding internal leadership elections, and encouraging decision-making by ballot. All, they believe, are prerequisites for developing democracy in the country as a whole.

★ ★ ★

Promoting intra-Party democracy means encouraging discussion and disputation within the Party. Debate takes place inside the one monopoly Party, rather than outside between competing parties, and because groupings of interests in the one Party can function like multiple parties—as these groupings strive to put forward their positions, expand influence, affect policy, and promote personnel—a rudimentary, proto-democratic version of checks and balances begins to emerge. Thus these jockeying groups, or factions, within the Party—as long as they are rational and collegial as well as partisan and competitive—help strengthen the development of Chinese democracy. (Political unanimity can exist only under the coercive thumb of an absolute dictatorship, which China used to be but is no longer.)

Leng Rong, the Party theorist, suggests that "The process of building consensus in the Party is not unlike the political process in the American system. Both take diverse, even divergent ideas," he says, "and drive toward a majority decision that almost everyone more or less accepts. The difference in China, of course," he adds, "is that with only one party, ideas are contested out of public view, but this too is changing as more policies are debated in the media, with even officials taking different positions."

In Chinese terms, it certainly represents progress. During his later years, Mao Zedong's views differed radically from those of the majority of the Party's leadership, but he still had the power to enforce his destructive ideology. In the early years of the reform era, Deng Xiaoping allowed diverse voices to be heard, but he still called the shots—which was arguably necessary during his time of transition. Jiang Zemin sought to build consensus among his peers without falling back on the intimidating measures of the past to do so. During his period of leadership, everyone—leaders and masses—became more aware of events and more confident in voicing independent opinions. "Jiang made the Party 'normal,'" commented Leng Rong; indeed, "part of Jiang's legacy is that China today is a more normal country: virtually no one would return to the Maoist past; the people wouldn't tolerate it."

President Hu Jintao faces a new challenge. In one sense, China's problems of the past, caused by radical political ideology, were self-inflicted and somewhat artificial. Now there is political stability, but issues are more complicated and dynamic: shifts can be sudden; crises erupt without warning. China's problems are real ones.

The situation is further complicated by the fact that, these days, political reform is not solely a question of what China's senior leaders wish to do. Deepening economic reform, and the much freer flow of information which accompanies it, has changed social dynamics. A market economy schools people how to choose. Before reform, people had few choices: you lived where you were born or sent and you worked where you were assigned; there were minimal choices in consumer goods, clothing looked alike, and what little entertainment was available was all the same.

With economic reform, individual ideas and independent decision making are crucial for commercial success; as consumers, ordinary people now routinely decide, choose, and critique. And these same attitudes nurture political democracy. When people grow accustomed to selecting from among great varieties of detergents, foods, fashions, magazines and TV programs, they will, at some point, think it natural to exercise this same kind of choice over their political leaders.

What's more, as China's middle class grows larger and more powerful, its members will want and expect an enlarging repertoire of personal and collective freedoms. There is, therefore, a natural and direct relationship between the economic standard of living of the people, and the political democratization of the government. This relationship may not be linear, but it is, I believe, inexorable. China's leaders recognize this, and hope to manage the process judiciously. With economic growth, China's leaders believe that the more people have, the more they will protect what they have to lose.

Intra-Party democracy is seen as the key mechanism for achieving such stable development. Enabling broad participation in the process of governance—and centralizing transparency—is the essence of political reform and the harbinger of a more democratic China. At the same time, since this new democracy begins within the Party, China currently may be described as a "democracy of the elite" (my term, not China's) incorporating Party members from all sectors of society who are increasingly educated and knowledgeable. This elite—the entire Party constitutes about 5-6% of China's population—contends among itself to determine appointments of leaders and formulation of policy. The underlying theory is that China is run largely by those who are best prepared and most dedicated.

As China's leaders envision today's Communist Party, it is a dynamic, action-oriented vanguard institution, motivated by ideological vision but not bound by ideological dogma. It is a supervisory Party, responsible for the well-being, both material and spiritual, of the Chinese people. It is a leadership Party that, in the Chinese system, seeks the cooperation and political consultation of a united front of diverse sectors of Chinese society, including intellectuals, scientists, business leaders, entrepreneurs, artists, minority groups, religions, very small non-Communist parties, and the like. It is a patriotic Party, the guarantor of the nation's integrity and the holder of the flame of Chinese nationalism. None of this has much to do with the long-in-the-tooth theories of Karl Marx.

* * *

As the Party adapts to a fast-evolving society, and given China's ideological and economic changes, there have been quiet suggestions within China that the Party should consider changing its name, perhaps to something more like the left-of-center liberal democratic parties in Europe. Party theorist Leng Rong acknowledges that the word "Communist" carries negative connotations to many Westerners—imprinted in large part by the authoritarianism and belligerency of the former Soviet Union—and that this may be "a stumbling block" for foreign understanding of China. However, he says, such a change would be impossible.

"The name of the Party has great significance to us," Leng says. "We can't simply change our name to please others...we have our ideals." Thoughtfully, he adds, "Our name is something like a religion—we can't change it. But we're now downplaying its ideological implications."

Leng extends the religious analogy: "There are many Christian countries in the world. If I were anti-Christian, there's nothing I can do about it. I should be realistic and tolerant. Christianity won't bring anti-Christians to misfortune or injury. Similarly, communism won't harm anti-Communists."

According to Leng, the Party's name, and indeed China's entire political system, all bear witness to the CPC's key role in freeing China from foreign domination in the 20th century. To change either of these, name or system, he suggests, would be to negate history. Moreover, Leng argues that CPC one-party rule is "the biggest secret of China's success."

"We know that some foreigners believe that because China has a one-party system we're fragile, because competing social interests could lead to serious social conflicts," Leng says. "We understand our problems, but solutions aren't to copycat Western models. We need solutions that suit China's real conditions."

Emphasizing that "China's stability benefits the world (Deng Xiaoping said that if China was turbulent, it would damage other countries, especially developed ones)," Leng notes that China has become more integrated with the world. This growing connection, he says, has changed China's domestic dynamics. As an example, Leng compared the international response to the Sichuan earthquake (2008) with the reaction to the SARS outbreak (2003).

"With SARS, people all over the world censured the Chinese government as having no respect for human rights, including people's right to life and right to information," he notes. "We were overwhelmed with criticism. Since SARS, we have stressed a people-oriented approach and codified respect for human rights in our constitution."

Still, he believes China has some way to go in making itself fully understood by the international community. "When I visited the U.S.," he says, "I realized that we were far more liberal than many Americans suppose. It's frustrating that China is so much misunderstood," Leng laments. "American understanding of Marxism is very much outdated while ours is very much current. As Deng Xiaoping put it, 'Seeking truth from facts' is the essence of Marxism. It's not that the Chinese are lagging behind the times. It's those people who do not appreciate our fundamental change who are the laggards."

Leng emphasizes that, these days, most people in China "don't care much" about politics and political theories. "Today, people are interested in economics, globalization, specific policies that address specific problems," he says. "Times have changed."

Developing economies require stability, said Wang Weiguang, vice president of the Chinese Academy of Social Sciences. "For example, Brazil and Argentina have good market economies but because their governments were weak and ruling parties kept changing, each party had different policies and ran the economy differently, which made development difficult. Taiwan had its greatest growth during the Kuomintang dictatorship; in Singapore it was during Lee Kuan Yew's authoritarian administration—and some countries enjoyed their greatest growth during military dictatorships." Wang was not suggesting such dictatorships for China but he did stress the advantages of centralized control and pointed to Singapore as a prototype.

"China's three generations of leaders, led by Deng Xiaoping, Jiang Zemin and Hu Jintao, have kept consistent policies," Wang said. "The Party isn't perfect; it has many flaws, but that shouldn't overshadow its great achievements."

★ ★ ★

"I used to be very leftist," said Du Daozheng, the controversial Party intellectual and long-time friend of Zhao Ziyang, the reformist CPC general secretary deposed during the Tiananmen demonstrations in 1989. "I've gone through three major political events: the Anti-Rightist campaign (1958), the Cultural Revolution (1966-76), and June 4th (1989). I'm now retired. I have a large group of old friends. We all reflect on what we've done right or wrong in those bygone days. We must say that we were treated leniently."

"There's no future for China if we should ever retreat from reform," Du continued. "But we cannot take giant steps. Under the Party's leadership, we should move forward 'in slow steps', purposefully, systematically and regularly. We begin by increasing democratic mechanisms within the Party, such as by expanding plurality elections. We continue by allowing more supervision by public opinion and appropriate media criticisms. Here's my guideline: 'When I criticize you, I don't need your permission. When I express my opinion, I will be responsible with respect to the truth.' This would be good enough."

"The more important thing is that China's democracy and legal system are progressing. I'm an optimist. Democratic rule is a global trend that cannot be stopped. There are more than 60 million intellectuals in China with university education or higher. Current leaders do not have the 'political capital' that Mao Zedong and Deng Xiaoping had. Mao was wrong, but he was able to continue in his errors because he had the 'political capital' to do so. Current leaders need to be humble and careful, because they need the people's understanding and support."

★ ★ ★

Single-party political systems have endemic problems: political power can be private, personal, and arbitrarily transferred; as such, they are given to backroom brokering and are vulnerable, when problems arise, to being commandeered by authoritarian strongmen, even madmen. In addition, single parties must control the media to maintain power, and they do not deal well with corruption. All this is patently bad.

Nevertheless, in my opinion, for China in its current condition, with all of its complexities and contradictions, the benefits of one-party rule outweigh its costs. This is especially true as President Hu and his colleagues advance intra-Party democracy. A premature democracy would shift resources to political debate and thereby sacrifice long-term economic and social benefits for short-term political freedoms. A premature democracy would also more rapidly reallocate income among sectors, groups, and classes, which, over time, would not build the economy as potently and therefore not bring the greatest good to the greatest number. Many conclude, however reluctantly, that if China had instituted a multiparty democracy and freedom of the press in 1989, which was what many of the student protesters sought, the Chinese people would not have as high a standard of living as they have today.

At some point, however, these dynamics invert, so that the absence of a true political democracy and a free press would thereafter inhibit, not enhance, China's continued development. For example, corruption is best minimized in a political democracy and by a free press. It is left to China's new leaders to figure out when that point of inflection occurs.

Zheng Bijian, former executive vice president of the Central Party School under Hu Jintao, and a leading theorist, suggests that China's commitment to democratization should not be underestimated—but that it must progress at its own pace. "America had a history of democracy," he notes, by way of explanation. "The first American immigrants, remember, came from England, and the U.S. had relative peace for over 200 years to enable its system to develop. China, on the other hand," he says, "had a poor, largely uneducated population who had experienced nothing but feudalism, civil strife, and foreign invasion and occupation." Thus, Zheng says, "We need time to develop our democracy. Please respect that our practices and trial-and-error steps need to go slow. But," he emphasizes, "just like we've built our economy, we will build our democracy."[10]

So will China have a political system similar to America's? I hope not, and I doubt it, too, because Chinese society has its own characteristics, which will remain distinct for many generations. (It ought not to be counted a source of satisfaction to watch all nations meld into a homogenized global system, although as a very long-term trend it may be inevitable.)

Democracy in China is unlikely to look like the liberal democracies of the U.S., U.K., France, Japan and Korea (which anyway differ considerably among themselves.) Chinese democracy will no doubt take its own form, if only because of the country's huge and diverse population, most of which is still rural, and because of its cultural traditions and historical legacies. But a people with growing economic and social freedoms, and ever greater access to information, will continue to demand a process of growing political freedoms as well. I find it fascinating, thrilling actually, to watch as China moves towards a more democratic future.[11]

Endnotes

1 Author's meeting with Leng Rong, Beijing, January 2009.

2 Gao Zhikai, "Every crisis offers a golden opportunity," *China Daily*, February 7, 2009.

3 Joseph Fewsmith, *China Since Tiananmen: the Politics of Transition* (New York: Cambridge University Press, 2001), 219. Wang Xiaodong writes that without individual [democratic] rights the people "will have no way to stop the [China's] ruling clique from selling out the country for its own self interest."

4 Nicholas D. Kristof, "A Little Leap Forward," *New York Review of Books*, June 24, 2004, 57.

5 Li Fugen, "Chinese Democracy: Progress Finally," *China Today*, 1999; following section.

6 "China Focus: China's grassroots democracy trudges on amid scandals," Xinhua, June 5, 2009.

7 Author's meeting with Li Yuanchao, Beijing, December 2007; Robert Lawrence Kuhn, "Building 'Intra-Party Democracy' in China," BusinessWeek.com, February 20, 2008.

8 Robert Lawrence Kuhn, "China's New Roadmap for Political Reform," BusinessWeek. com, February 27, 2008.

9 Ting Shi, "Party bestows more power on delegates in major reform," *South China Morning Post*. July 19, 2008

10 Author's meeting with Zheng Bijian, Beijing, 2003.

11 Bruce Gilley, *China's Democratic Future: How It Will Happen and Where It Will Lead* (Columbia University Press, 2005).

40

China Threat or China Model?

In 2008, Mark Halprin, a politically conservative commentator, called for a dramatic build-up of the U.S. military: "If we are wise," he wrote, "not with 280 ships but a thousand. Not with eleven [aircraft] carriers, or nine, but 40. Not with 183 F-22s [the then current Pentagon order for Raptor stealth fighters], but a thousand." And he made it clear that such rearmament was necessitated by one factor: the "China threat."

Halprin, like other Western defense analysts, believes that China's armed forces are too large for strictly defensive purposes. China, he said, "understood the relation of economic growth to military potential," and had thus been "able to vault with preternatural speed into the first ranks of the leading nations." He suggested that, unlike America, which tended to govern "reactively and predominantly for the short term, China has plotted a long course in which, with great deliberation, it joins growth to military expansion."[1]

Halprin stressed that he was no "imperialist." "Our object is not to regain the power we and the Europeans had over China in the 19th and early 20th centuries," he wrote, "but, now that things are in flux, to keep China from attaining a similar power over us." He warned that China could soon transition from "David-like asymmetrically planned forces" into "a Goliath-like full-spectrum military, capable of major operations and remote power projection." He added ominously: "To the protest that it is too early to be concerned, the fitting answer is that if anything it is too late."

Though Halprin's rhetoric is perhaps extreme, those who call for an enlarged U.S. military typically invoke the "China threat," a shadowy vision of Beijing's alleged nefarious ambitions and expansionist plans. It envisages China using its increasing economic strength to assert its power beyond its borders, dominating its region and challenging the U.S. as a global super-power with a blue-water navy, offensive intercontinental missiles, space-based weapons and information warfare. Former U.S. Defense Secretary Donald Rumsfeld, for example, asked, "Since no nation threatens China, one must wonder: Why this growing investment? Why these continuing large and expanding arms purchases? Why these continuing robust deployments?"[2]

What, exactly, does the "China threat" entail? Its form mutates, chameleon-like, to match the interests or worries of those who invoke it. In the economic arena, the "China threat" embeds concerns that China dominates international trade, with exports vastly exceeding imports; maintains an undervalued currency which enables predatory pricing; supports a mercantilist system where government subsidies enable unfair competition, and deploys protectionist policies that prevent foreign companies from operating on an even playing field in China's home market.

China maintains a huge trade surplus with almost every country, especially the U.S., and is now the world's manufacturing base in many industries. Its foreign reserves hit $2 trillion, and it leapfrogged Japan as the largest holder of U.S. Treasury debt (approaching $800 billion in 2009), a position China was unlikely to relinquish.

Defective or dangerous products from China also confirm to some that Chinese companies are so set on dominating international markets with lower prices that they will sacrifice quality in order to do so, putting all in jeopardy.

In the resource arena, there are perceptions that China is scouring the world to lock-up oil and raw materials (and claiming oil rights in the South China Sea by bullying its neighbors), and doing business with rogue regimes such as Iran and Sudan, regardless of consequences to others.

In diplomacy, meanwhile, the "China threats" express concern that China is working to supplant the U.S. as a favored nation in Africa, Latin America, and Asia. In early 2009, with the nascent Obama administration mired down in economic crisis, China launched a diplomatic offensive: President Hu visiting Saudi Arabia and Africa, Premier Wen going to Europe, and Vice President Xi Jinping traveling to Latin America.

When briefing the media on these visits, Chinese diplomats and scholars made scant reference to the United States, which some commentators saw as Beijing attempting to take advantage of a perceived geopolitical power vacuum.[3] Apropos, foreign-policy specialist Chen Xiangyang said China would now "seize the high vantage point [in forming] the future world order," adding "we want to send out China's voice, maintain China's image, and extend China's interests."[4]

In support of this long-range strategy, China cancelled $3.6 billion in debt from 49 of the world's poorest countries between 2004 and 2008, and has also provided them with around $30 billion in diverse forms of assistance. Where many see laudatory efforts to reduce world poverty, China's critics find malevolent intent.

Critics are similarly anxious that China now turns out more engineers and science PhDs than any other country—worrying it will come to dominate technology. Some submit the spectacular Beijing Olympics as evidence that China considers its civilization superior to all other's.

Moreover, when foreigners see invigorated and occasionally over-the-top Chinese nationalism, especially among students (as in 2008, following disruptions of the Olympic torch relay), they feel their fears confirmed. And such perceptions—of China threatening Taiwan, occupying Tibet, repressing Uyghurs, seeking to dominate Asia and perhaps the world—are used to support a strategy of "containment" of China.

To many Chinese, the idea of a "China threat" is ludicrous and offensive. China has enough problems at home, they say; its history is one of being invaded by foreign countries, not the other way around. China's concern is to prevent the nation from being fragmented by separatists, rather than to expand beyond its borders.

★ ★ ★

Misunderstandings about China arise easily. Just how easily was exemplified by Professor Wang Luolin, an economist and former vice president of the Chinese Academy of Social Sciences (CASS). Once, while working at CASS, Wang said, he was visited by energy experts from Japan, who asked him about China's energy strategy, and how China conducted energy research. "I didn't know how to respond," he recalled. "At the time China had no energy strategy . . . Of all CASS's many researchers, only one or two of them were studying energy."[5]

Wang gave "some general answers, devoid of specifics because I just didn't know." However, he said, the Japanese visitors "thought I was being secretive, that China had internal plans which I didn't want to reveal!" Such incidents reveal the gulf in perceptions: Japan already had its own energy office in Beijing for a decade, said Wang; it simply never occurred to them that China could be so backward as to have no serious energy research of its own.

Similarly, China's leaders believe that China's desire to develop its economy and raise its technical level shouldn't be seen as in any way sinister. "China is still a backward country," says Minister Leng Rong. "Many new things originate in Europe and America. That's why we stress learning from other countries. We're trying to catch up." In an increasingly globalized world, he adds, it's natural that China should be more outward-looking: "We have much in common with other countries," he says. "We're facing similar challenges. We pay great attention to common security issues, including nuclear proliferation, epidemics, etc. China has fewer and fewer secrets."

Minister Leng cites "two critical issues" that will drive China's future leaders: developing a system of checks and balances in governance, and accelerating the construction of a comprehensive system of social benefits for all citizens (healthcare, pensions, and the like). Assessing how governance works in Europe and America (so that China can adapt what makes sense), Leng enumerates four factors: multiparty politics, media supervision, interest groups (e.g., religions, labor unions), and rule of law. Each, he says, is being studied and evaluated in China. The essence of a multiparty system, Leng contends, is transparency, public supervision and fairness—vital objectives, he says, which China seeks to achieve by, among other mechanisms, empowering local people's congresses. Minister Leng also adds a fifth factor, special to China's system—the mobilization of grassroots Party organizations.[6]

Under Minister Leng Rong, the CPC Party Literature Research Center, which until recently only compiled and edited historical documents (primarily the collected works of Mao Zedong, Deng Xiaoping, and others), now supports China's current senior leaders by analyzing and interpreting key documents and decision making. Their mandate is to learn from the past in order to prepare for the future.[6]

"China's leaders now spend a surprisingly high percentage of their time on international affairs—a significant increase in recent years," Leng Rong says. "Here in our research center, we used to read only *People's Daily* and other Party publications. Now we scrutinize international newspapers and magazines and surf the Internet. Without global knowledge, it's impossible to do our jobs."

★ ★ ★

China's level of development—and capacity—should not be exaggerated, says Cai Wu, minister of Culture. "Foreign countries have too high expectations for China," Cai says. "They hope China can assume international responsibility that's beyond its means and competency." And he adds, "We're still a developing country. Although great achievements have been made, great many problems persist. We have deficiencies, obstacles, contradictions. We're not that strong."[7]

Cai emphasizes that China's development starts from a very low base. "Even if, after years of hard work, we realize our goal of achieving a comprehensive well-off society by 2020 by quadrupling China's 2000 per-capita GDP," he says, "it will still be only about $3,500 (in real terms), which is about half the per-capita GDP of Mexico in 2008." It means, he adds, that "we have no reason to be complacent"—and also that "the idea of a 'China threat' is totally unfounded."

Indeed, Cai argues that the "China opportunity" theory is far more relevant than the "China threat" theory: "President Hu's international strategic thinking is epitomized by his vision of China traveling the 'road of peaceful development' and helping to build a 'Harmonious World'," Cai says. "We hope to bolster world peace through our own development. Confrontation does China no good," he insists. "We have the same objectives as all countries. China has moved from being a stakeholder in the community of nations to being a partner."

Cai condemns what he calls "an astonishing bias or ignorance" in Western criticisms of China, such as "China threat" or "China collapse" theories. "It's ridiculous," he says. "Critics' knowledge and logic deviate stunningly from

China's actual reality." (Interestingly, though "China threat" and "China collapse" seem polar opposites, the negative emotional tone is similar—a foreboding or derogating view of China's ambitions or prospects.)

Politburo member and publicity (Propaganda) head Liu Yunshan likewise laments that, no matter what it does, China will still be criticized by Western media. He gives the example of leadership's decision to broadcast live, in 2005, the launch of the Shenzhou VI manned spacecraft. Noting the risk of a Challenger-like disaster, which could upset the people and embarrass China, Liu explains: "We know that China is criticized for having a controlled media, so we decided to take the risk and open the media for the launch. And what happened?" he asks. "Some foreign media accused China of using the live broadcast to intimidate its neighbors!"[8]

★ ★ ★

Misunderstandings exist on both sides. Some Westerners (particularly Americans) remain suspicious and fearful of China. Many Chinese assume that the problem is not so much that such people are unable to understand China, but rather that they do not want to. In my experience, however, the vast majority of foreigners harbor no hatred of China; they are simply not knowledgeable, and often view China through lenses which admit only certain images—those which conform to media-directed preconditioning. Conversely, Chinese leaders also need a more nuanced understanding of the values of those who seem anti-China but who have genuine concerns, such as, for Americans, trade imbalances and job losses as well as democracy and human rights.

Westerners should be aware that exaggerating China's potential threat may only strengthen the view, popular in Chinese nationalistic circles, that international forces scheme to retard their nation and keep it forever subservient. Such accusations risk triggering backlashes, and engendering policies which could, paradoxically, cause China, in response, to become a threat in reality.

It is therefore vital that foreigners understand China's domestic situation and challenges. Many Chinese people, in fact, perceive something of a "U.S. threat"—based partly on history, partly on current conditions. Chinese people see American armed forces stationed in Korea, and remember the U.S. Army approaching Chinese territory during the Korean War. They see a quasi-military alliance between the U.S. and Japan, China's historic and bitter enemy. They see the U.S. selling advanced armaments and weapon systems to Taiwan, which China fears may one day declare independence. They see U.S. Navy carrier battle groups, each with a dozen or more warships and almost 100 fighter-bomber aircraft, patrolling the seas near China's territorial waters, and U.S. spy planes cruising and listening off China's coasts.

Chinese sensitivities about America were brought home to me when Professor Wang Luolin asked me, in all seriousness: "If China were weak or small, would the U.S. have bombed it over the [2008] riots in Tibet?" It was a reminder of how the U.S. invasion of Iraq and the 1999 NATO intervention in Kosovo have fueled Chinese nervousness over such cross-border interventions.

"Why doesn't America want us to build our own society in our own way?" many Chinese have asked me. "Why shouldn't the Chinese people have the same rights that the American people have to determine what system suits them best?"

★ ★ ★

Asia was once dominated by Japan. Now there's no escaping China, which is using its economic clout to increase its diplomatic influence. For some, this must rankle. Vietnam, for example, which has a long history of conflict as well as friendship with China, has its own desire to be independent and not be dominated by others. China's leaders have sought to reassure such countries, stating constantly that a powerful China will never threaten its neighbors. China knows what it is like to be invaded and oppressed, they say, and will never treat others in the way that others have treated them. (Yet, maneuverings in the South China Sea, where China remains seriously at odds with Vietnam and Philippines on overlapping sovereignties—with conflicting claims and military threats—evince the complexity of translating general principles into specific issues.)

There's no question that there is a new rush of nationalism in China. The issues is whether this is something troubling—or a normal part of a nation regaining its pride. For some, China's economic growth can be alarming. "The Chinese want to absorb our technology and make everything by themselves" is a common complaint. People like Yin Mingshan might confirm these fears: Yin's motorcycle factory in Chongqing, which began by copying foreign vehicles, later applied for more than 700 patents in one year.[9] Its success has been energized by a strong sense of nationalism as well as low wages. "For 100 years we suffered in poverty as Western countries pressured and invaded us. Now there's been an explosion of growth as people use their power and intelligence to build a new strong China," Yin said. And it's not uncommon to hear young people proclaiming their certainty that, one day, China will be the greatest economic power on earth. "We all believe that," confided one.

At the same time, many see China's development as benefitting the world. "If we continue to pursue current reforms we will have a massive middle class, with more accountability and a more open and tolerant civil society," according to Steven Xu, an economic consultant. "If China can succeed in this," he said, "it would be a shining example for other developing countries and a tremendous contribution to mankind."[10]

★ ★ ★

That China and America would increasingly have to work together was highlighted by the financial crisis of 2008. "China and the world are so interdependent," notes Minister Leng Rong. "If the U.S. economy stays strong, China won't have major problems. But if the U.S. economy continues to soften or worse, goes into a deep and prolonged depression, the result would be terrible for China." Such ideas are far removed from the old Chinese view that its geo-strategic relationship with the U.S. was a competition, something of a zero-sum game: if the U.S. gained a point, China lost a point, and vice versa.

And the financial crisis also changed perceptions in the West. Suddenly the focus was not so much on China's trade surpluses or undervalued currency, but its $2 trillion in foreign reserves, and the hope that China's continuing economic growth, though slowed, could help stem the global slide and drive recovery. Suddenly China was no longer being accused of causing the problem but rather being wooed as part of the solution.

Soon after the crisis hit, the leaders of 43 Asian and European nations met, with some historical irony, in Beijing, the capital of socialist China, to address the global capitalist turmoil. In the Great Hall of the People, Mao Zedong's paean to the Communist Revolution, they listened to Premier Wen Jiabao advising how investor confidence will ultimately help the world get through the crisis. "We need even more financial regulation to ensure financial stability," Wen said. "We need to properly handle the relationship between savings and consumption . . . Only in this way can we coordinate economic stability."[11] It was confirmation that China had long moved beyond ideology, and now sought, like almost all nations, simply what worked best for its people in complex and turbulent economic environments.

On her first foreign trip as U.S. secretary of state in early 2009, Hillary Rodham Clinton chose Asia, anchored by her high-profile visit to China, where she emphasized that U.S. priorities were the global financial crisis and global warming.[12] Human rights concerns, she made clear, "can't interfere" with Sino-U.S. cooperation on economics, the environment and North Korea's nuclear weapons. This infuriated human-rights organizations—but the Obama administration's new pragmatism, which included upgrading its regular talks with China to "strategic dialogue," stressed that good relations with China were America's most important bilateral foreign-policy objective. President Hu Jintao told Clinton that he "greatly appreciated" her choosing Pacific Rim Asia for her maiden voyage as chief U.S. diplomat, saying this "shows the new administration attaches great importance to developing relations with Asia and with China."

Such warming of relations coincided with a palpable and increasing assertiveness among Chinese leaders regarding international relations in general. The financial crisis has hurt China, of course, but there is realization that China's relative position in the world has been unexpectedly elevated. As one banker told me privately, "In 2002, U.S. banks came here to lecture us. Now they come here for help. Our bank can buy Citigroup or Bank of America several times over."

In *People's Daily*, columnist Li Hongmei pointed out that in 2003 the U.S. GDP accounted for 32% of the world's total, while the GDP of all emerging economies put together was only 25%; in 2008, however, the figures reversed. "If such a dramatic reversal could take place in just five years," she asked, "how much more will it change in the next five or ten years?"[13] She predicted "a swift reduction of U.S. strength as a unipolar power," stressing that "U.S. strength is declining at a speed so fantastic that it is far beyond anticipation." And she added: "Leading players on the European continent such as Britain, Germany and France are battling their own economic downtrend; and Russia also faces a tough job in reducing its heavy reliance on gas exports and building a modern manufacturing industry of its own."

Thus, she said, "China has grown to be a new heavyweight player and stepped into the limelight on the world stage. Its role in salvaging the plummeting world economy from hitting bottom looms large and active," she suggested, noting Hillary Clinton's remark that "the U.S. appreciates the continued Chinese confidence in the U.S. treasuries." (By recycling its vast net export surplus back to America by purchasing U.S. government debt instruments, China is financing the U.S. deficit, which enables U.S. interest rates to remain low and U.S. consumers to consume more.)

And Li Hongmei added: "If the Cold War was 'a tug of war' between East and West, and a showcase of hard power, what we have today, for the first time in history, is a global, multicivilizational and multipolar competition, and a display of smart power. To be the winner, one has to seek more cooperation than confrontation."

★ ★ ★

Still, the relationship between China and the U.S. is as fragile and fractious as it is vital and volatile, and if it is not proactively set as a mutual priority and ceaselessly watched for fissures, dangers we cannot imagine likely await.

Take the completely predictable and avoidable brouhaha when Timothy Geithner stated in written testimony for his confirmation hearings as secretary of the Treasury in early 2009 that President Obama, "backed by the conclusions of a broad range of economists believes that China is manipulating its currency."

Even the Bush administration had never gone this far, and Geithner's statement was interpreted as an escalation of U.S. complaints. The Obama administration quickly played down the statement's significance, but the damage was done. (Only a few days before, a Chinese leader had asked me what I thought Obama's policies would likely be; I had replied cheerily that Obama's nuanced intelligence and steely pragmatism would lead him to rise above campaign rhetoric and nurture Sino-U.S. relations.) Geithner's words offended China's leaders, particularly given their smoldering conviction that the financial crisis, which was affecting China deeply, was almost entirely U.S.-caused. Statements refuting Geithner's charge came from Chinese bankers, who called it "not only inconsistent with the facts, but also misleading about the reasons for the financial crisis."

Were there political motives in Geithner's move, appealing to certain congressmen, perhaps those with labor constituencies? Either way, to insult America's largest creditor at a financially vulnerable moment was myopic. Western-oriented Chinese reformers, who had methodically advocated that China follow the U.S. model and advice by opening the country's financial markets more rapidly, lost credibility. Internet bloggers hammered them as U.S. patsies and puppets, citing as further evidence the huge paper losses incurred by China's sovereign wealth fund (China Investment Corp.) from its ill-timed investments in Blackstone and Morgan Stanley.

The unhappy result was that even U.S.-friendly Chinese officials became more critical, if only for self-preservation. China's media, meanwhile, was indignant—reflecting the views of China's people, who are almost always more nationalistic than China's leaders. An editorial in the normally mild-mannered English-language *China Daily* fulminated that Washington "should not expect continuous inflow of more cheap foreign capital to fund its one-after-another massive bailouts."[14]

And speaking at the annual World Economic Forum in Davos, Premier Wen Jiabao blamed the U.S. for the economic collapse with phrases denuded of diplomatic niceties: "inappropriate macroeconomic policies," an "unsustainable model of development characterized by prolonged low savings and high consumption," an "excessive expansion of financial institutions in blind pursuit of profit," and "the failure of financial supervision." (Wen did not name the U.S. overtly but any sentient creature knew what he meant.)

Then Wen got personal: "A year ago, American delegates speaking from this rostrum emphasized the U.S. economy's fundamental stability and its cloudless prospects," he said. "Today, investment banks, the pride of Wall Street, have virtually ceased to exist."[15] And he issued a stern warning: "The entire economic growth system, where one regional center prints money without respite and consumes material wealth, while another regional center manufactures inexpensive goods and saves money printed by other governments, has suffered a major setback," he said.[16]

Every Chinese senior leader with whom I spoke felt the same.

A few days later, in their first telephone conversation, President Barack Obama and President Hu Jintao voiced their mutual "intention to build a more positive and constructive U.S.-China relationship."[17] Reportedly, Obama had initiated the call, likely in damage-control mode.

The two presidents discussed the international financial crisis and agreed that close cooperation is essential. Though the "currency manipulation" charge didn't arise, Obama stressed the need to "correct global trade imbalances" and Hu called for both sides to "resist trade protectionism" and to "respect each other's core interests." Chinese scholars said the new U.S. administration appeared inexperienced in foreign affairs and unsure how to handle China. One remarked, "They continued to use campaign language to pressurize Beijing."

A few weeks later, in a shift that reflected the West's eagerness for China's assistance in ameliorating the global financial crisis, Secretary Geithner praised Beijing for "playing a very important stabilizing role in the international financial system today."[18] And a few months later, on his first official trip to Beijing, Geithner, who as a college student had spent two summers at Peking University studying Chinese, said, "We would like to build with China the kind of relationship we built with the G-7 [European economic powers] over the last several decades."[19]

A major step in this direction was the new China-U.S. Strategic and Economic Dialogue, which commenced in 2009 (upgrading the Strategic Economic Dialogue, which had been operating since 2006). Both sides gave these regular communications highest priority, as confirmed by the respective co-chairs: Secretary of State Hillary Clinton and Treasury Secretary Timothy Geithner on the U.S. side and State Councilor Dai Bingguo and Vice Premier Wang Qishan on the China side.

"The financial crisis has shown that China and the United States are just like two sides of one coin," said Yin Zhongli, a senior researcher at the Chinese Academy of Social Sciences. "The two are inseparable from each other. China cares as much about the U.S. economy as the Americans themselves."[20]

★ ★ ★

That America and China, allied with common interests, must work together is not elective. This applies not only with respect to the financial crisis, but also to the incessant wars and threats of war, particularly in the Middle East and South Asia, and the likely proliferation of weapons of mass destruction, which presage an era of unknown vulnerability.

I have told leaders in China that they are no longer immune from crises that might erupt elsewhere: should Iranian theocrats acquire nuclear weapons and long for heaven's reward, cataclysm would wash over every land—and China, with its domestic harmony among imbalanced classes requiring high economic growth, would be devastated. Only collective, responsible action, it seems, can prevent irreparable human catastrophe. For China and America to engage in geopolitical maneuvering, each trying to unbalance the other, is wildly archaic. Unstable nations or those led by irrational rulers, even if they claim to be China's ally and America's adversary, do China no good.

It's also clear that disputes over political systems, which were 19th century arguments that dominated 20th century politics, have become anachronisms, like vestigial organs, in the 21st century. U.S. congressmen who opposed the 2008 financial rescue plan pilloried the bailout bill by branding the policies or programs "socialist." Labels like "socialist" or "capitalist" make no difference; all that counts is whether the policies or programs work. It's a pity Deng Xiaoping can't explain to these U.S. politicians all about black and white cats and why their color is irrelevant when they catch mice.

The financial crisis has realigned world powers and relationships—and China must assume a larger role. To no small degree, world peace and prosperity depends on the bilateral relations between China and America and this relationship depends on realism and respect.

As Beijing's power grows, enhanced ties between America and China, may, ironically, help to reduce the perception in America of a "China threat." I know of no Americans who have not come back from a first trip to China with impressions substantially different from those they had held before their visit.

What's more, despite all the tensions, Chinese people generally seem to like Americans, which makes it all the more perplexing to them that America (as they see it) appears intent on blocking Chinese national interests. Part of the reason for this natural compatibility may be personal similarities—ways of thinking that are practical, flexible, entrepreneurial, and unencumbered by affectation. Many mainland Chinese—particularly those in Beijing—say they feel more comfortable working with Americans than they do with overseas Chinese from, say, Hong Kong. The latter, though they speak the same language, often have an air of superiority toward their mainland cousins—the condescending attitude of supposed expert to supposed acolyte.

★ ★ ★

The long-term trend toward strengthening relations between China and America was symbolized in 2008, when a massive new U.S. embassy opened in Beijing. A 500,000-square-foot compound on 10 acres, costing $434 million, it was the second-largest U.S. embassy in the world (after Baghdad).[21] The eight-story main building, designed using traditional Chinese elements, was wrapped in an outer envelope of a sprawling maze of transparent and opaque glass. With space for 700 staffers and 20 federal agencies, it was already too small—and work began on a 70,000-square-foot annex to house another 230 staffers and ten more agencies.

Not coincidentally, just a few days earlier, the new embassy of the People's Republic of China had opened in Washington. The 250,000-square-foot glass and limestone compound, designed by the two sons of the Chinese-American architect I.M. Pei, was the largest foreign embassy in the U.S. capital. "This is a symbol of the important progress in China-U.S. relations," said Foreign Minster Yang Jiechi, who described the new embassy as "a perfect blend of Chinese and Western cultures."

The broadening of the relationship has more to do with China's emergence as an economic and political force than with U.S. policy, said Randall Schriver, who was deputy U.S. assistant secretary of state for East Asian and Pacific affairs (2003-2005). "A decade ago, the bilateral issues were relatively well-known: Taiwan, human rights, trade. Now, [China's interests] literally span the globe."

★ ★ ★

That the Chinese public now feels growing confidence about their nation's place in the world was highlighted by the 2008 *Pew Global Attitudes Survey*. It found that many Chinese people had an overwhelmingly positive view of China's global standing: 77% of Chinese respondents believed people in other countries had favorable opinions of China—though, in fact, the Pew survey found that in only seven of the 23 other countries surveyed did the majority have a positive opinion of China. Similarly, 83% of Chinese thought their country considered the interests of other nations when making foreign policy decisions—yet in other countries surveyed only 30% thought that China took their interests into consideration.

Most Chinese recognized the growing impact their economy had on others around the world—and believed it was a positive one: only 3% of Chinese thought their economy was hurting other countries. (By contrast, 61% of Americans said the U.S. was negatively affecting other countries.) And nearly six in ten Chinese (58%) thought that China would replace, or already had replaced, America as the world's dominant superpower—though the U.S. was still recognized as the dominant economic power. (Still, 21% of Chinese saw their own country as already the world's top economy.) While most Chinese (77%) agreed that "children need to learn English to succeed in the world today," this was down from 92% in 2002.

The survey also highlighted the potential for continuing international tension: 69% of Chinese had an unfavorable opinion of Japan and 38% considered it an enemy; 34% described the U.S. as an enemy, while just 13% said it is a partner of China.

★ ★ ★

In the eyes of foreigners, both the "China threat" and the "China model" are affected by the perception of how China treats its indigenous minorities. The 2008 disturbances in Tibet, in particular, caught world attention; critical reports in the foreign media left no room for mention of the special support that China has long provided its minorities, which almost never make international news.

Western outrage over Tibet, understandable abroad, is exasperating to most Chinese—common citizens even more than senior leaders. Westerners largely see China suppressing Tibetan people and consider Tibet to be occupied territory, much like Hungary or Poland under the Soviet boot. China insists it has historical grounds for its claims to Tibet, and should be thanked for having freed Tibetans from impoverishment, superstition and servitude. Irrespective of the legitimacy of China's position, the bottom line is that most Chinese—including some not normally supportive of their own government—believe that the West's sympathy for Tibet is just another example of foreign schemes to contain China and thwart its national aspirations.

In the deadly 2009 riots in Urumqi, the capital of Xinjiang Uyghur Autonomous Region, China's severe containment of the marauding mobs of Uyghur Turkic Muslims put China in the uncomfortable position of inflaming international Islamic communities, which China had long been courting. In Turkey, as noted, Premier Recep Tayyip Erdoğan labeled China's actions as "nearly genocide." In Iran, the complex combination of China's alleged suppression of Uyghur Muslims and China's refusal to acknowledge the opposition movement caused some demonstrating chanters to replace "Death to America" with "Death to China." In Algeria, the local branch of Al-Qaida threatened to retaliate with revenge attacks, targeting overseas Chinese workers and interests.[22]

According to Party intellectual Leng Rong, China's policy toward minorities is changing. "Historically, we focused on economic development to help ethnic minority areas," he says (e.g., the GDP of Urumqi, the scene of the bloodshed between Uyghurs and Han Chinese in 2009, grew by a robust 15% in 2008, largely due to preferential infrastructure investment by the government). "But in retrospect, that approach was simplistic. Physical construction was right, of course, but we needed to do more. We should also pay attention to religion, culture, customs, and lifestyle." And he acknowledges that, "as cruel as the old slavery system was, the Tibetan people are reluctant to be governed by others." While the desire for autonomy is a natural desire of all people, Leng suggests that its particular expression in Tibet is shaped by "specific religious reasons."

"There's a delicate balance to be struck," Leng continues. "If we give too much freedom, it can lead to separatism; if we impose too tight controls, we would be accused of disrespect." Leng suggests that the government has to exercise control over Tibetan Lama temples and Uyghur mosques to prevent them becoming "independent kingdoms" which the government cannot enter. "On the one hand, we must respect the temples and mosques, but on the other hand, they need to have effective supervision, without interfering in their strictly religious activities."

Leng sticks to China's official line that "foreign forces" are colluding with Tibetan and Uyghur separatists to destabilize the region—warning that "some foreign elements don't want to see a powerful China; some ultra-right forces intentionally premeditate such disturbances to disrupt China's development."

Nevertheless, he stresses that China's response should be to enhance communications with the world. "As times change, our approach must change," he says. "We must improve the mental or spiritual lives of all the Chinese people, not just cater to their physical needs, and this applies to the Han [majority] Chinese as well as to the Tibetans and Uyghurs. As their quality of life and level of knowledge increase, their spiritual life needs to be respected as well. In history, many riots and insurgencies were caused by religious issues," he adds.

"One thing is sure," Leng Rong summaries, "religious issues are complicated, especially those relating to Tibetan Buddhism and Islam. We should learn from countries that deal well with them."

How such new thinking will affect the situation on the ground remains to be seen.

★ ★ ★

So will China and the West really be able to work together to maintain world stability? Much may depend on the kind of China that emerges—and how well the outside world understands it.

President Hu Jintao's vision may be described as the "China model," a novel and systematic approach to national development that combines the following elements: dynamic economic growth, a powerful (uncontested) central government and strong state sectors (in pillar industries), free markets energized by vigorous private ("non-state") sectors, single-party rule requiring political constraints but promoting democratic reforms, unrelenting media control and enhanced media creativity, personal but not political freedoms, rule of law, scientific and technological excellence, cultural and spiritual enrichment, patriotism and pride in Chinese civilization, protection of the environment, concern for the welfare of all citizens, and a synergistic approach to rectify economic imbalances and assure social fairness—all of which lead, in Hu's vision, to a Harmonious Society. Beijing sees its "China

U.S. President George W. Bush hosts President Hu Jintao during his state visit, with First Lady Laura Bush and Liu Yongqing, President Hu's wife, on second floor of the White House. (April 20, 2006; Xinhua News Agency, Liu Jiansheng).

model" as an alternative to Washington's "democracy model," particularly for developing countries. (This rivalry is sometimes posed as the "Beijing Consensus" versus the "Washington Consensus."[23])

Minister Leng Rong stresses that President Hu's "China model" describes a very different China from that of the recent past. "Our old-time industrialization mentality, just like our old-time political ideology, is no longer suitable," Leng says. "We see things differently than we once did. Prior, we focused largely on material growth. Now we're concerned about all people's needs. That's the power of President Hu's people-oriented policy, and his Scientific Perspective on Development. They were put forward to deal with China's domestic problems that have arisen as a result of reform—but they also reflect the common challenges the whole world faces."

The "China model" was unquestionably boosted by the Beijing Olympics: the flawless flow of the games, with its hypermodern stadiums and high-tech artistry, was a priceless 17-day advertisement of the "Made in China" brand.[24] For a country normally known for its low-cost manufacturing, the Olympics was a re-branding exercise which replaced an image of shoddy, dangerous products with one of cutting-edge technology and world-class organization. Many said they doubted whether any other country could ever produce such an awesome opening ceremony—and when self-assured Chinese athletes won the most gold medals, billions of worldwide television viewers saw China in a new light.

Unfortunately, the subsequent scandal over tainted milk (Chapter 27) reminded China's leaders that reputation can be fragile. Yet, it seemed that the adverse impact of the bad milk was less damaging than that of the slew of earlier scandals over dangerous products. Perhaps the Olympics had enhanced confidence in China's transformation. Perhaps China was increasingly recognized as a sophisticated, innovative, market-oriented society—all of which exemplified the "China model."

★ ★ ★

So, "China threat" or "China model?" China's answer is "Harmony." Harmony seeks to expose the "threat" as empty and enliven the "model" with vitality. In the Olympics' opening ceremony, thousands of performers opened umbrellas displaying the faces of children of every race and ethnicity. It was a symbolic moment—a multicultural, multipolar world radiating "harmony," the theme of the Olympics, the theme of China.

Harmony is the operative word in China. President Hu Jintao has made building a Harmonious Society the overarching goal of his two-term, ten-year administration. He has also made fashioning a Harmonious World the centerpiece of China's foreign policy.

Harmony epitomizes Chinese culture, reaching back to its roots of ancient philosophy and wisdom traditions where harmony was among the greatest of goods. Fast-forward to today: the "harmony model" is the core of the

"China model." China is saying to the world, although not with stentorian voice, that Beijing's "harmony model" is a loftier and more human goal than Washington's "democracy model." (Harmony vs. democracy? Why fight? Neither should lose!)

China's leaders, in their emphasis on harmony, realize that building harmony means improving relations between different peoples, groups, regions and sectors throughout China, and between different races, creeds, cultures and nations throughout the world. It also represents ideal relationships between mankind and nature, an attitude of honor and respect for the environment. Assuming broad-based progress continues to be made, China's "harmony model" theory may become as seriously discussed in the future as the "China threat" theory has been hotly debated in the past.

Endnotes

1   Mark Halprin, "Rich Country, Strong Arms," *Claremont Review of Books*, Summer 2008.
2   Michael T. Klare, "Revving Up the China Threat," *The Nation*, October 6, 2005.
3   Willy Lam, "Beijing Launches Diplomatic Blitz to Steal Obama's Thunder," *China Brief*, Vol. IX, Issue 4; 2.20.2009.
4   Ibid, quoting *Outlook Weekly* (Beijing), February 9, 2009.
5   Author's meeting with Wang Luolin, Beijing, 2008.
6   Author's meeting with Leng Rong, Beijing, August 2009.
7   Author's meeting with Cai Wu, Beijing, 2006.
8   Author's meeting with Liu Yunshan, Beijing, 2006.
9   "China's middle class revolution," BBC NEWS, October 11, 2004.
10 Ibid.
11 Xinhua, October 25, 2008.
12 Glenn Kessler, "Clinton Criticized for Not Trying to Force China's Hand," *Washington Post*, February 21, 2009.
13 Li Hongmei, "U.S. Hegemony Ends, Era of Global Multipolarity Begins," People's Daily Online, February 24, 2009
14 "Keys to the Treasury," *China Daily*, December 17, 2009.
15 Carter Dougherty and Katrin Bennhold, "Russia and China Blame Capitalists," *The New York Times*, January 28, 2009.
16 Jason Dean, James T. Areddy and Serena Ng, "Chinese Premier Blames Recession on U.S. Actions," *Wall Street Journal*, January 29, 2009.
17 Stephen Collinson, "U.S., China pledge to work for more positive relationships," AFP, January 31, 2009, quoting White House spokesman Robert Gibbs.
18 Michael M. Phillips and Stacey Meichtry, "G-7 Softens Criticism of China's Current Policy," *The Wall Street Journal*, February 15, 2009.
19 Rebecca Christie, "Geithner to Reassure China U.S. Will Control Deficits," Bloomberg.com, May 31, 2009.
20 Zhang Ran, "China, US 'like 2 sides of one coin'," *China Daily*, July 20, 2009.
21 Tini Tran, "Huge New US Embassy Reflects Growing US-China Ties," Associated Press, August 4, 2008.
22 Cui Jia and Cui Xiaohuo, Al-Qaida threatens Chinese abroad," *China Daily*, July 15, 2009.
23 Ariana Eunjung Cha, "China Uses Global Crisis to Assert Its Influence," *Washington Post*, April 23, 2009.
24 "'Made in China' brand reaps Olympic dividend," *China Daily*, August 25, 2008.

China Reflections and Visions

A wise Chinese friend offered me advice: "Our achievements are remarkable," he said. "Do not overstate them. Our problems are serious; do not underestimate them. Tell the world what is really going on here," he urged, "what is good and what needs to be better. Give our leaders credit; but give our people more." The momentum for change, he stressed, comes from the bottom up.

My friend praised Deng Xiaoping for having "broken up the old system, repudiated the old ideology, enabled us to think rationally." Jiang Zemin, he continued, "stabilized the situation and pushed forward reform," while Hu Jintao was tackling multiple problems "from a scientific perspective." "What our leaders have done is important," he reiterated, but again said: "what our people have done is more important. Our leaders have excelled to the extent that they have recognized and respected the rights of the people to take the initiative to develop and improve."

Then my wise Chinese friend, who holds an American PhD, advised the world to acknowledge China's progress and refuted Western accusations. "Westerners support human rights and democracy, right? Real human rights give people the freedom to make their lives better. Real democracy means that the government follows the will of the people. Well, what is the will of the Chinese people? They are happier than ever before. Why won't the foreign media acknowledge this?"

The *Pew Global Attitudes Survey* (2008) bears repeating: an astounding 86% of Chinese said they were content with their country's direction, twice the percentage who said they were similarly content in 2002. Only 23% of Americans could say the same.[1]

★ ★ ★

In terms of practical action to advance society, renowned economist Zhou Qiren stresses that China needs to find ways of successfully integrating government action with the views and contributions of ordinary people.[2] "What impresses me most," he wrote, "is that no matter what difficulties they encounter, grassroots people are always able to find solutions." It is such people, he adds, rather than "aloof economists," who are usually the first to take up the challenge of solving their own problems. At the start of the reform era, for example, he notes, everyone knew China's farmers were poor—but no one did anything about it, until the farmers themselves took the initiative to allocate private plots of land, and started growing their own crops. It led, according to Zhou, to "totally different behavior on the farmers' part in the private plots and the collective plots."

Ordinary people, whether working on farms, in companies, or for local governments, are "motivated to better their standard of living," Zhou says, who suggests that reform is simply "the legalization of [people's] solutions to problems." All policymakers have to do, he explains, "is to pay close attention to the grassroots whose spontaneous efforts already contain the solutions."

The challenge, he says, is to find ways "to integrate those dispersed, spontaneous, and piecemeal efforts and turn them into policies or even systems," by obtaining endorsement from the government. Thus the governing apparatus must provide legitimate process for recognition, implementation and improvement. The difficulty, according to Zhou, is that a system will change only if the costs of maintaining it (whether political, social or economic costs) are too high to keep the system working.

Deng Xiaoping's genius, Zhou states, lay in his determination to "face reality and use his political authority to provide support and legitimate recognition for spontaneous reformist practice." Such pragmatism has been instrumental in China's continuing reforms of the past three decades, and Zhou stresses it will be even more necessary in the coming years. "We are facing and will be facing difficulties and challenges, and we may not be able to find the complete right answers in advance," he adds. "So we need to learn from the last 30 years and match grassroots efforts with national authority, to integrate different interests in making the Chinese economy a great power."

★ ★ ★

So, after so many years of rapid transformation, in looking to the future, how do China's leaders think? Speaking after the 2007 National People's Congress, which passed the controversial Property Law protecting private property, Premier Wen Jiabao said, "The speed of a fleet is not determined by the ship which travels the fastest but the one which travels the slowest. If we improve the living conditions of those in difficulty, we improve the well-being of the whole society." It echoed President Hu's Harmonious Society—but also of China's new reality, of a society more disparate than at any time in 60 years.

Wang Weiguang, vice president of the Chinese Academy of Social Sciences, listed the disparity in living standards as one of four critical challenges for

China's future, warning that extreme differences could cause instability—and that chaos in China means trouble for the world. The other key areas he highlighted included natural resources and sustainable development ("competition among countries could lead to conflict, and such fear in the West is detrimental for China"); environmental protection ("industrial pollution threatens quality of life"); and democracy, human rights, and the future of one-party rule.[3]

That China's leaders are prepared to innovate to address these challenges is highlighted by a growing acceptance that non-governmental organizations (NGOs) have a role to play in society, particularly in humanitarian and welfare activities. NGOs complement, and in a sense balance, the role of government. And as these civic organizations achieve their purposes—without contradicting government policy—they will enhance confidence in responsible self-administration and help redistribute social and administrative power.

Traditionally in China's socialist state, the government was entirely responsible for helping the poor and providing relief to the needy. According to Yan Mingfu, a former Party leader fired for supporting CPC General Secretary Zhao Ziyang in 1989—later founder of the China Charity Federation (CCF)—"before reform, private charities were seen as symbolizing a bourgeois class that had suppressed and controlled the proletariat, and were also associated with foreign missionaries—and thus with Western gunboat diplomacy in the 19th and early 20th centuries."

Now however, Yan says, the growing gap between rich and poor has underscored the need for charity, which the government has neither the funds to run nor the resources to manage. Thus, private charities have been allowed to kind of coalesce into a quasi-independent social sector.[4] (To be sure, the government keeps close watch—mindful of what China's leaders consider the subversive role of "charities" in instigating the "color revolutions" in Eastern Europe that undermined those socialist regimes.)

"Back in the days of egalitarianism, it would have been difficult to get anyone to help," Yan says, "but now the disparities are obvious." Furthermore, he adds, "The Cultural Revolution had a withering effect on our national morality. During that terrible decade, people lost sight of ethical standards."

Establishing the CCF (in 1994) was an idea which occurred to Yan when he was vice minister of Civil Affairs (his position of partial reinstatement). "I recognized that many common people have a deep concern for the poor and would like to help them," he says. "We needed a single-purpose organization that would unite these efforts. . .The key is to make people aware of the need. Their love and compassion will do the rest." (Some successful Chinese enterprises are beginning to recognize their responsibilities to fund activities beyond their businesses, such as charity, the arts, education, even sports.)

The CCF has more than 100 branches across China. It helps laid-off workers who have serious ailments by training them with new vocational skills. It helps children who were born with harelips to have them repaired.

"We'll continue until every child in China who needs this surgery has had it," Yan states. "That's hundreds of thousands of operations. We want our children to grow up in the 21st century with smiles on their faces!"

And Yan emphasizes that, with China's demographic changes, there's a growing social need for care of the aged. "More than 10% of the population is now over 60," he notes; as a result, a single working couple may be supporting two sets of parents—and up to four sets of grandparents. Not only this, but today's "young people are more mobile, moving to other cities for jobs. Old people can be stranded without support," Yan adds: the elderly, he says "are running out of relatives to take care of them."

Such issues, he suggests, then "become society's problems." The government has set up housing for old people—such installations can accommodate thousands, but they are not enough to solve the problem. The CCF and other civic organizations have responded by providing community services. "China has learned from Hong Kong and Western countries," says Yan. "We have volunteers who do the shopping, cooking, and laundry and escort old people to doctors. We train social workers who specialize in assisting the elderly."

★ ★ ★

In economics, too, the role of the non-state sector continues to grow in importance. Quan Zhezhu, minister of the All-China Federation of Industry and Commerce, puts it bluntly: "We all know that private business drives China's future," he says. "It already generates more than half of China's GDP and it will continue to increase. The private sector produces roughly 60% of new patents (75% of high-tech), utilizes 60% of investment, and creates 80% of new jobs. All of us support the private sector," he adds, referring to China's leaders. "We've amended rules to remove restrictions; for example, private companies can now do some defense-related business." Moreover, Quan says, "Entrepreneurs—business owners—have become like a virtual party in China, second only to the Communist Party in real power. We listen to entrepreneurs. We're attentive to their needs."

The Party's modern approach is also reflected in its growing focus on science and technology. President Hu calls for creativity and innovation to be hallmarks of the nation's educational and industrial future. There are still challenges and tensions: as one senior leader put it, "We seek balance, optimizing economic growth with environmental protection, but when we must choose between the two, we must still choose growth, because it's just not fair to protect the environment of well-off urban residents while condemning disadvantaged rural residents to more generations of continuing poverty."

But at least these days economic growth is not the only factor the government takes into account. Environmental protection, sustainable development and rebalancing income (i.e., fairness) are taken seriously. When Li Yuanchao was Party secretary of Jiangsu Province, for example, he rejected a proposal to turn Taizhou city into a center for the cement industry. The plan would have generated rapid growth, but would have also created permanent pollution. Instead, Li led a long-term strategic initiative to establish Taizhou as a pharmaceutical and biomedical center. (Taizhou is President Hu's hometown.)

China's leaders are also concerned about the dangers of shoddy products and industrial accidents, both of which, as consequences of uncontrolled growth, remain blights on Chinese society. President Hu has criticized officials for their perfunctory work style, lax management and lack of responsibility, and has pledged to "learn a painful lesson" from accidents such as the mudslide in Shanxi Province which killed nearly 270 people, and the melamine milk contamination scandal (2008).[5]

Another significant change is that spiritual values are playing larger roles in Chinese society. The government's growing encouragement of traditional religion—though not of religious groups deemed threats to stability—is a dramatic break from orthodox Communism's doctrinaire rejection of religion. China now praises its indigenous religion, Daoism, and extols the timeless wisdom of Chinese philosophy—notably Confucianism. Why this historic reversal? There are several reasons: increasing respect for citizen's rights; reducing the appeal of inimical religions; creating a Harmonious Society (in light of income disparities and social tensions); and enhancing China's "soft power" globally as a counterweight to Western culture.

A desire to recraft China's values goes back to the early reform years, when the nation's leaders sought to protect Chinese culture from an influx of Western culture. As foreign films, television shows, and popular music began to return to China in the 1980s, the Party first launched (1983) a "campaign against spiritual pollution" (though it was cut short when its rigidity adversely affected the economy), and then (1986) adopted "building a socialist spiritual civilization" as a fundamental goal.[6] By 1996, after years when China had focused almost entirely on economic development ("material civilization"), President Jiang Zemin again began to emphasize the idea of "spiritual civilization," stressing moral, social, and cultural development. "While we put economic construction as the core task," he said, "this does not mean that other types of work are not important."

The idea of constructing a new "spiritual civilization" was in part an acknowledgment that the old Communist models—selfless workers, peasants and soldiers who sacrificed their individual desires for the collective good— were no longer relevant to a competitive, knowledge-based market economy in which individual initiative was essential, and where personal values, personal opinions, and personal goals were increasingly diverse.

But "spiritual civilization" was also a response to what many saw as the excesses of the market mentality. "China was aggressively developing a market economy with its natural focus on competition—and morality and ethics were suffering," says ideology theorist Leng Rong, also a Party historian.

President Jiang was seeking balance between the material and the moral, Leng explains, at a time when many people "assumed that all China needed to do was dive headlong into commercialism without restraint or reflection." In fact, he adds, "people still need a coherent set of social rules and ethical guidelines to maintain a stable and civil society."

Specifically there was continuing concern that the market would bring with it "an onslaught of Western ideas and values"—some of which Jiang Zemin described as "cultural trash poisoning the people." "We have a saying that expresses how Western culture is more powerful," Leng Rong notes: "'Western culture punches Chinese culture,' almost in the sense of Samuel Huntington's 'clash of civilizations.'" This fear, which Chinese leaders have long shared, was that if traditional Communist values were shattered at a time when China's huge population was experiencing disruptive change, the social fabric of the country could unravel.

At the same time, according to Leng Rong, in an age of globalization, China had a simple choice: "Either close the country back up and keep its culture for a while, or continue its opening-up—which was essential for economic development—and find new ways to protect its cultural integrity." The solution was for China to promote a culture of its own—and not one that was defined solely in negative terms relative to the West. Only a China that was "culturally coherent," Leng Rong suggests, could in the long run "sustain itself as an independent nation."

Thus a new emphasis on "Chinese values and morality" began, reflecting back to traditional Chinese belief systems (much of which had been denigrated by Mao's communism). Previously, the Communist Party used "morality" as a hammer to force people's political beliefs to conform to whatever was the prevailing ideological norm. Jiang Zemin and his successor Hu Jintao, however, framed morality as the purest form of Chinese civilization, embedding a series of high-minded ideals such as honesty, integrity, decency, commitment, dedication, hard work, patriotism, and even etiquette.

In 2006, in the face of a populace predominantly focused on earning money, Hu announced a new socialist code known as the Eight Honors and Eight Shames (or Disgraces). These "new socialist ethical standards" were intended to revitalize Chinese civilization. They consisted of eight pairs of opposing moral values, with a rhyming poetic lilt in Chinese.

- Love the country; do it no harm.
- Serve the people; never betray them.
- Follow science; discard superstition.
- Be diligent; not indolent.
- Be united and help each other; make no gain at other's expense.
- Be honest and trustworthy; do not trade ethics for profits.
- Be disciplined and law-abiding; not chaotic and lawless.
- Live plainly, work hard; do not wallow in luxuries and pleasures.

These admonitions were widely posted in public places, and even turned into songs, which members of China's armed forces, for example, were ordered to learn.

It would be a mistake to say, however, that such concerns about morality imply that money is the only motivation for China's people. While many seek to get rich, and admire entrepreneurs, others have retained a sense of excitement that what they are doing is important for China: Chinese people have a sense of history, and many are thrilled to take part in the nation's recrudescence of pride.

For centuries, while Europe languished through its Dark Ages, China had the planet's premier economy. If China eventually regains first place, which is its current trajectory, the phenomenon will be of historic proportions. As one young Internet businessman told me, "In the past, American entrepreneurs did better than we did; look at Bill Gates. But our generation is different. We'll show the world what Chinese entrepreneurs can do."

★ ★ ★

China still professes allegiance to "communism," yet the term itself, as embedded in the Chinese psyche, stands for something beyond a 19th century system of public ownership, centrally planned production, and authoritarian government—which in economic terms has been everywhere discredited. In China, communism provided the inspiration to restore national dignity; these days CPC theorists concentrate on such historic links to national pride. While leaders and scholars still insist that "pure communism (where everyone is equal and living an abundant life) remains the ideal system, they now describe it as China's "ultimate" goal. To reach this ideal state, they aver, China's economy must pass through a stage that "looks a lot like capitalism"—indeed, some suggest that "capitalism is the early or first stage of communism."

How long does this first stage last? How long, according to Party theorists, will it take for the transitory engine of capitalism to bring about the eventual triumph of communism? The answer seems to be "at least 100 years," comfortably beyond everyone's lifetime. This means that even a good Marxist society, professing equality and classlessness, can embrace with a clear conscience the free-market economics of capitalism, a full-blown private sector, and in all probability a still-growing gap between rich and poor—because in the end the road will lead to the purest form of communism.

When I first heard this rationale, I thought it more comic than clever—a wry caricature of hack propagandists leaked by intellectual cynics. But the 100-year horizon comes from serious political theorists, and I've come to wonder whether there may be more insight here than I originally could see. To envision what may be happening, one needs the eyes of a futurist.

Capitalism, in its current form, has been a working economic model for several hundred years, certainly since the industrial revolution. If we project forward, as futurists do, to the 22nd century, or surely to the fourth millennium, we should not find it unreasonable to suppose a new working model of the global economy.

Although capitalism and liberal democracy seems to be the most efficient system at present, it may not be so a hundred (or a thousand) years from now, given the extraordinary technological forces of change—in computer power, instant communications, artificial intelligence, biotechnology, nanotechnology—all sweeping and shrinking the planet and homogenizing all nations into one world. In a future that will undoubtedly differ from today's world more than today's world differs from that of the first millennium, it is unlikely that global economic systems will have remained static. (Ray Kurzweil, the eminent technology futurist, sees a soon-coming "singularity," when nonbiological intelligence, generated by the exponential growth of computing power, exceeds human intelligence.[7])

The transformation of human life and society will be so astonishing that it is not at all clear what the prevailing economic systems and market mechanisms will be. Who knows what will happen to corporations, capital markets, cash flows, and governments at all levels, when we are all online all the time, when all the work of production is conducted by nonbiological intelligences, when the global network virtually eliminates poverty and brings about worldwide equality, when humans spend their time in creative activities and personal entertainment?

Utopianism? Perhaps we'll never get there. Perhaps we'll destroy ourselves first or face otherwise unbridgeable gulfs. But if the world does become so magically transformed, what will then exist—whether in 100 years or 1,000 years—might well look rather closer to classic communism than to classic capitalism. According to Marx, human societies would develop from primitive to slave to feudal to capitalist to socialist, and finally to communist. Give the old man his due; his day may yet come.

In any event, Chinese entrepreneurs and business leaders have plenty of time to be good capitalists; to pursue their dreams, make their mark, and build their wealth; to pioneer hot new marketable technologies; to leverage China's huge domestic markets; to grow their companies into strong competitors in world markets—while allowing political theorists to proclaim that they are paving the way for the ultimate triumph of communism.

★ ★ ★

The Communist Party's management of society has changed too—and must continue to do so. No longer does it seek to impose ideological strictures on the people, or incite extremism—nor would it be able to do so even if it wanted to. Party leaders today recognize that to maintain legitimacy the Party must deliver substantially greater human rights—personal freedoms, rule of law, political transparency, and public participation in governance—in addition to economic development and improved standards of living. If the Party does not deliver, it will lose legitimacy and then lose power—and Party leaders know it.

As I have said, I believe that, under current conditions and for the time being, one-party rule is China's most suitable system of governance—notwithstanding the trade-offs, particularly limited freedoms, media control and corruption. I also believe that while one-party rule will continue in China, at least in the immediate future, substantial political reform is both essential and inevitable. Because a one-party political system is by definition less democratic than a multiple-party system, those who seek to maintain the former have an affirmative obligation to promote democracy in other, innovative ways. This is why the Party's initiatives of public oversight of officials, intra-Party democracy, governance transparency, local elections, and media reporting of corruption are all vital steps in a long process.

CPC Organization Minister Li Yuanchao, whose views reflect those of President Hu Jintao, has pledged to improve the selection, training and promotion of officials to ensure that their public credibility, as determined by formal surveys, is substantially enhanced.[8] Toward this end, Li is directing the CPC Organization Department in conducting extensive national reforms of the cadre system, which includes the use of reliable public opinion polls.

"Creating credible public feedback mechanisms is now policy," Li says. "These polls will establish benchmarks and enable us to adjust our thinking and strengthen our management; we can set goals for raising public awareness of how officials are selected and for enhancing their administrative credibility. This is our commitment to the people."

To back this up, Li Yuanchao makes a remarkable pledge. "If this target is not met [prior to the 18th Party Congress in 2012], if the public credibility of officials doesn't improve, or if it gets worse, what would I do?" he asks. "I would have only one way to go: I would resign!" For a senior Chinese leader, a young Politburo member and a strong candidate for the next Politburo Standing Committee, to so put himself on the spot is astonishing—and unprecedented in the annals of the People's Republic. "My approach is risky," Li admits, "but as I've said, 'reformers take risks'."

And the Party is taking other steps to achieve its reformist goals. In 2008, the CPC launched an 18-month campaign for Party members and government officials to learn and implement President Hu's Scientific Perspective on Development. Through the campaign, the CPC sought to enhance scientific solutions to multiple problems, and to focus on issues about which people complained most.

Further evidence of the Party's commitment to change came with the announcement of China's first Human Rights Action plan in 2009. According to Information Minister Wang Chen, the plan stipulates "concrete measures, including efforts in poverty reduction, protection of women and children's rights, and economic and social equality."[9] With input from more than 50 departments, public associations and non-governmental organizations, the action plan lays out for the first time specific steps to enhance human rights, which the public can use as a gauge to measure the Party's progress. Wang Chen stressed that the action plan, timed to commemorate the adoption of the Universal Declaration of Human Rights by the United Nations in 1948, would serve as a "strong propeller to push forward China's human rights cause."

In the history of the world, China may be the first country which has determined to secure its system of one-party rule and which, at the same time, has committed itself to bring about democracy, transparency, rule of law and human rights. It is, in a sense, a grand experiment, never before tried, much less done. I would venture to predict that in a thousand years, when the long annals of human political systems are written, China today will be a case study of what happens when a country with a one-party political monopoly seeks to construct a democratic society.

★ ★ ★

Predicting China's future is often likened to reading palms. Foreign pundits offer divergent, polarizing scenarios—from an expansionist world power bullying Asian neighbors, to an internally fragmented country riddled with unemployment, social decay, and ambitious provincial or military chieftains. Just occasionally, the proposed alternatives include a progressively democratic, economically vibrant, internationally responsible nation.

To warn that China might become an aggressor internationally, or implode domestically, may make sense to sell books, but unless there is some kind of economic catastrophe, it does not make sense in the real world. As one Chinese leader told me, such extremes are a reminder that, "Everyone always exaggerates China. When for more than a century the world thought us weak, we weren't really so weak," he said. "And now when the world thinks us strong, we aren't really so strong!"

As for nationalism in China, and the threat of emergent jingoism, some senior leaders dismiss the notion, while others admit concern (especially regarding young people). But most counter the question by asserting that controlling such nationalistic tendencies is another reason why the Party must, for the foreseeable future, continue to rule China and guide the country into responsible statecraft.

A sense of balance is required. China's road ahead seems reasonably straight if not narrow—the destination is clear but there will likely be sway during the journey of getting there. I am cautiously confident that the less sensational scenarios, those of China as a responsible, vibrant and progressive nation, will become the reality. I make my prediction using this one scenario only: excluding untoward events, China's economy will grow, standards of living will rise, the middle class will expand and, with telecommunications, individual freedoms will increase. China will be more democratic as well as more prosperous—and a bulwark of stability in world geopolitics. China's companies will be competitive in world markets and its science and technology will contribute to human knowledge. China's society will be more diverse, its laws more dispositive, and its political leaders more responsive to the will of the people.

China's problems will remain, of course. Income disparity, sustainable development, pollution, corruption, and the like will not disappear, but they will likely go gradually into long-term amelioration. Along the way, there may be crises or inflection points, such as with water resources or imported oil, which could require new kinds of thinking. Political reform, however determined and controlled, could hit some critical-mass threshold where expectations race beyond plan. Some say the decade between 2020 and 2030 will be when to watch.

Yet if the past three decades have proved anything, it's that, despite all its problems, China has been willing to reform and "advance with the times." Deng Xiaoping initiated reform and opening-up by "emancipating the mind" and "seeking truth from facts," thereby unleashing the spirit and energy of the Chinese people. Jiang Zemin modernized the CPC, stressing advanced productive forces, advanced culture, and the interests of all the Chinese people (Three Represents), thus enabling China to consolidate stability and accelerate development. Hu Jintao, through his Scientific Perspective on Development, has integrated multiple objectives—political, social and environmental as well as economic—and provided a mechanism for building a Harmonious Society, which puts people first, embeds the rule of law, and promotes democracy.

There seems little chance that China will simply stand still in the coming years. Many people recognize that while China must continue to innovate and change, it must draw on the progress it has made, and have the fortitude to follow its own path. China's military, fueled by China's growing economy and energized by national pride, will continue to develop and expand, worrying some and highlighting the need for the international community to encourage China toward responsible statecraft and to partner with China in securing a Harmonious World.

Zhang Xiaoshan, chief of the Rural Institute at the Chinese Academy of Social Sciences, emphasizes that it's necessary to take the long view. China has its failings, he says, but he highlights how much has changed in so short a time—"the far greater freedoms of China's young generation these days." Himself a victim of the Cultural Revolution, Zhang says: "I suffered in the past and know better than Western politicians about the darkness of the Chinese system. . . . During the Cultural Revolution, all things were broken down. The darkest parts of humanity were exposed." However, he adds, "maybe if it were not for the Cultural Revolution, we might not have reform. . . . All people suffered from the chaotic political movements. Therefore reform was supported by the overwhelming majority. We've had twists and turns in the past 30 years," he says, "but no such political movements again. It was a lesson drawn from blood and heartbreak that China could never restore the old regime: We must reform, that's the lesson we've learned. That's the strength of the nation."

"I'm optimistic," says Margaret Ren, an investment banker and daughter-in-law of deposed CPC General Secretary Zhao Ziyang, who was kept under virtual house arrest from 1989 until his death in 2005. "For those of us whose families have experienced the highs and lows of China's history, it gives us great satisfaction to witness China's emergence as a strong, decent and responsible nation."

Dr. Song Jian, my mentor in China, recalls Deng Xiaoping's guideline that "we must immerse ourselves in work and bide our time." In determining China's future course of action, Song looks to history for context. "In the past 150 years," he says, "the Chinese people have been humiliated, beaten, starved, and killed; wealth has been stolen—the nation experienced all kinds of suffering. Now," he argues, "we should do what we feel in our hearts to be right—and what fate dictates." Criticism, says Song, is inevitable: he quotes a famous Confucian teaching, which says, "'Feel happy on hearing justified criticism from friends, and kowtow to those who indicate your shortcomings or mistakes.'" China, he acknowledges, "has much room for improvement and a long way to go to build a modernized country. We should listen with care to well-intentioned advice," he stresses, "but we should never rely on anyone but ourselves." As this book was going to press (August 2009), Dr. Song Jian told me that he expected China would reach an inflection point in its industrialization, science and technology, and socio-political development in 20 to 30 years, and that now in his retirement, looking back, he was very proud of what China had accomplished.[10]

Before reform and opening-up, China was isolated and desolate, its people indigent and disconsolate. Three decades on, China is the world's hope to drive the global economy, and an increasingly important and respected participant in international affairs. Overall, the Chinese people are doing far better than could ever have been imagined: never before in human history has the standard of living of so many improved so fast. More important, the Chinese people are happier and freer and more creative than at any other time in their long history. In every sphere of human endeavor, they seek to excel. The Chinese people take great pride in their country as China retakes its long-empty seat at the high table of great nations.

New China's 60th anniversary in October 2009 marked a two-thirds milestone of the Middle Kingdom's epic modern journey. It is likely that the third 30 years will be China's most dynamic but most uncertain period, setting the trajectory for generations to come as the most populous country on earth continues the greatest transformation in history.

Endnotes

1   The Pew survey also found that most Chinese citizens polled rated many aspects of their own personal lives favorably—family life, 81%; job, 64%; household income, 58%—though not as highly as their support for the state of the nation (86%).

2 Zhou Qiren, "Reflections on the Thirty Years of Reform and Opening-up," *Dushu* (Reading) *Magazine*, October 2008.
3 Author's meeting with Wang Weiguang, Beijing, April 2008.
4 All charities must register with the Ministry of Civil Affairs, and must disclose sources of all funds—they are not allowed to accept donations from foreign political groups.
5 "Hu criticizes officials for poor job," Xinhua, *China Daily,* September 20, 2008.
6 "Socialist Spiritual Civilization - China," *Encyclopedia of Modern Asia*, Berkshire Publishing Group.
7 Ray Kurzweil *The Singularity is Near: When Humans Transcend Biology*, and, Viking Adult, 2005.
8 Author's discussion with Li Yuanchao, Beijing, January 2009.
9 "China to issue 1st human rights action plan early next year," Xinhua, December 30, 2008.
10 Author's meeting with Song Jian, Beidaihe, August 2009.

Index